DAWNWARD SPIRE, LONELY HILL

H. P. Lovecraft

DAWNWARD SPIRE, LONELY HILL

THE LETTERS OF H. P. LOVECRAFT AND CLARK ASHTON SMITH
1932–1937

Edited by David E. Schultz and S. T. Joshi

Hippocampus Press

New York

Published by Hippocampus Press
P.O. Box 641, New York, NY 10156.
www.hippocampuspress.com

Hippocampus Press logo by Anastasia Damianakos.
Cover design by Barbara Briggs Silbert.

First Paperback Edition (2020)
ISBN 978-1-61498-175-6 (vol. 1)
ISBN 978-1-61498-299-9 (vol. 2)
ISBN 978-1-61498-305-7 (set)

Contents

vi ❀ *Dawnward Spire, Lonely Hill*

Addenda.. 698
Chronology 699
Glossary of Frequently Mentioned Names... 711
Bibliography 717
Index.. 771

1933

[207]   [ALS]

Shrine of Hyl-Gho on
the Smoking Peak. Hour
of the Nameless Chanting below.
[7 January 1933/RAS]

Dear Klarkash-Ton

I found your welcome letter & the much-appreciated cat-
alogue (which I'll return if you wish it) upon my return from a somewhat unexpected 8-day visit to Long in N.Y. His parents invited me to surprise
him—which I did, besides walking in similarly unannounced upon Loveman,
Kirk, Wandrei, & Talman. I really had a delightful time—visiting most of the
museums & attending a gang meeting of the old-time sort on Dec. 30. I saw
the old year out at Loveman's delightful new apartment—17 Middagh St.,
Brooklyn—& my generous host presented me with a primal Mayan eidolon
of stone, & a very ancient African flint implement with carved ivory handle.
Wandrei's quarters are very neat & pleasant despite their dingy warehouse
neighbourhood, & he seems to be bringing his psychological novel[1] well toward completion. I returned home Jany. 3, & have since been wrestling with
accumulated work & correspondence. Weather favoured me all along—only a
single half-day being really oppressively cold.

I thought you'd find something good in "Visible & Invisible." You are
right about "The Worm Ouroboros", for which I plan to send very shortly.
As I said before, it got so decidedly under the skins of Belknap & myself that
we've been swearing by the great Koshtras ever since. The work is really utterly unique—& unlike anything else even by the same author. It surely deserves a greater fame than it possesses. As for "Zemargad"—I fancy Price
will find it a tough nut to crack. The perfected Lilith-tale does appear to have
a great deal of the Persian in it—which is not remarkable, since the Semites
always borrowed more or less from the Iranians—witness the whole Satan idea.

Glad that the Philistine Lhen-Eighur[2] has chosen a tale as good as "Yoh-
Vombis" for the anthology. Comte d'Erlette's "In the Left Wing" & my "Picture
in the House" seem to be likely co-choices. Now I hope the venture won't pro-
ceed to dissolve in thin air! Just had a note from Satrap Pharnabozus in which he
says that "The Chadbourne Episode" is the last of his Whitehead MSS. Hope he
can get some more from the estate—especially the two later Chadbourne yarns.

What you reveal of "The Dark Eidolon" arouses my acutest anticipa-
tions—& I surely hope that it may find a profitable editorial harbourage. You
certainly excel all competitors—not excepting the professed Orientalist Price—

in the gorgeous presentation of exotic colouring & Beckfordian imagery. Hope the markets won't contract any further—I read the other day of the collapse of a whole pulp group, but none of the items included seemed to be weird or scientifictional media. Bates, Wandrei says, is now out of a job; but if he ever lands another editorship I dare say he will remember those whom he has favoured in the past. Enclosed is an item about Comte d'Erlette which may interest you.[3] (Please return for further lending.) The kid surely is coming on!

Yrs in the ritual of Yashish—E'ch-Pi-El.

Notes

1. *Invisible Sun.*

2. The anthology Price was compiling was not published.

3. The article is unidentified. In a letter to Derleth (written after 25 December 1932) HPL writes: "Congratulations on your waxing fame! That article is highly interesting, & I'm sure the radio address will aid considerably in establishing you as a literary figure" (*ES* 532).

[208]   [ALS]

Memory-Vortex of Zith—
Opening of the Bronze Gate in the
Unscalable Basalt Cliff of Gnaa
[2 February 1933/RAS]

Dear Klarkash-Ton:—

I did indeed get my "Ouroboros"—for which I am devoutly & vociferously thankful. My library is certainly growing—despite its former unusual weakness in the field of the weird. I told you about "Melmoth" & "The World Below." Now a gift from Comte d'Erlette—another set of discards from his library—has still further swelled my list of titles, as witness the following accessions:

Lynch, Bohun	— Best Ghost Stories
M{c}Spadden, J. Walker	— Famous Psychic Stories
(Pub. By Philip Allan, London—a series of anthologies[1] like the 'Not at Nights')	⎰ Creeps ⎱ Shudders

The best thing about this lot is that the Lynch volume contains Blackwood's "Willows". Mine at last! Congratulations on "The Purple Cloud"! Also on the Machen & de la Mare items. No hurry at all about "Visible & Invisible"—if you like it, you might have Dwyer lend you the other volume—"Spook Stories." In one of the anthologies just received there is a tale from Benson's *third* weird collection—"The Room in the Tower"[2]—which I haven't had time to read as yet. I'll surely let you know when I want to avail myself of your bibliothecal generosity—at present I'm simply swamped, with my own new books (plus the last half-year of W.T.) unread!

Hope something about *Zemargad* will turn up in the end. You could use it yourself as a background for many tales. Derleth is developing a tale "The Return of Hastur"—in which he engrafts the Biercian mythology (also used by Robt. W. Chambers) upon the Cthulhu–Yog-Sothoth cycle. In one detail I am having to correct him—for he has (in ignorance of the well-known Arabic etymology of the star-name Betelgeuse—*Ibn al Jauzah*, armpit of the giant) concocted a synthetic word (B'eegls) as an imaginary primal name for Betelgeuse.[3] In inventing the unknown, one must be careful not to contradict the known!

Glad "The Dark Eidolon" landed—but confound Wright for rejecting the Vathek episode! Hope he'll change his mind later on. "King Euvoran" sounds attractive, & I hope it will make either W.T. or *Magic Carpet.* I hope, by the way, that *Astounding* will get on its feet again. There was an item in *Time* the other day which said that the Claytons were again paying on acceptance instead of publication—which would imply that their stock of reserve MSS. is getting near the end. I suppose Gernsback is still withholding 'eckshun' on his debts. One of my clients is about to write an indignant letter to the Authors' League concerning his financial shortcomings—though I imagine its effect will be close to zero. By the way—I've just read your "Dimension of Chance" in the November W.S., & must congratulate you on the tremendously vivid & ingenious way in which you have objectivised the principle of uncertainty. I am saving the tale in my file of Clericashtoniana. Hope you can put the pamphlet across—count on me as subscriber #1.[4] I wish you could include "A Night in Malneant", & other items not likely to find professional berths.

Sorry your local weather has been so forbidding—though anything is better than intense cold. The New England winter continues warm on the whole—a microscopic trace of snow on the lawns last Saturday, but gone the next morning. Even if there is some better weather later it can't be long—for in not so many weeks the vernal equinox will loom nigh. One of the things which compensates for the tragically swift sense of time-passing inherent in advancing years is the proportional brevity which winter acquires!

Before long I hope to get at that Silver Key sequel which Price has tentatively outlined, & which I haven't had time to examine since last August, when he sent it. If I find it too much for me, I'll ship it along for you to try your luck with!

Heard a good poetry reading by Robert Hillyer last Sunday.[5] One by Leonard Bacon next Sunday—& after that one by the celebrated T. S. Eliot.[6]

Yrs. for the Black Heptagon of Yarath—
E'ch-Pi-El

P.S. Belknap has had an influenza attack, & Talman a son (David Fredric), since my visit to N.Y.

Notes

1. Edited by Charles Birkin.

2. *The Room in the Tower* (1912) was in fact Benson's first collection of weird tales; but the U.S. edition (Knopf, 1929) appeared after *Visible and Invisible* (1923) and *Spook Stories* (1928).

3. In a letter to HPL, Derleth cited the name Be'elgs (*Essential Solitude* 538). The name was not cited in the published version of the story.

4. CAS published *The Double Shadow and Other Fantasies* at his own expense in June 1933, in an edition of 1000 copies.

5. Robert Hillyer (1895–1961), American poet, essayist, and translator. He won the Pulitzer Prize for his *Collected Verse* (1933). HPL heard him speak on 29 January.

6. Leonard Bacon (1887–1954), American satirist and poet, winner of the Pulitzer Prize for poetry in 1940 for his book *Sunderland Capture*. His *Lost Buffalo and Other Poems* appeared in 1930. "Although a thorough & ancestral Rhode Islander, he has a wide reputation as an intelligent satirist. I have . . . always liked his stuff, since to me it seems to have something of the 18th century in it" (HPL to Elizabeth Toldridge, 25 March 1933; *Letters to Elizabeth Toldridge* 234). HPL heard him speak on 5 February, and Eliot on 19 February.

[209]   [ALS]

Shores of the Black Lake
T'lai: Time of the Moonless Tide
& the Rising of ＿＿＿＿＿＿ ＿＿＿＿＿.[1]
[c. 10 February 1933]

Dear Klarkash-Ton:—

        I thought Zemargad would be a tough nut! Price is so enamoured of it that he has just retitled his new story "Queen of Zemargad". I know you'll use it effectively. By the way—Price has dug up another cycle of actual folklore involving an allegedly primordial thing called "The Book of Dyzan", [*sic*] which is supposed to contain all sorts of secrets of the Elder World before the sinking of Kusha (Atlantis) and Shâlmali (Lemuria). It is kept at the Holy City of Shamballah, & is regarded as the oldest book in the world—its language being *Senzar* (ancestor of Sanskrit), which was brought to earth 18,000,000 years ago by the Lords of Venus.[2] I don't know where E. Hoffmann got hold of this stuff, but it sounds damn good. I shall ask him to spill particulars to you and me—though you may have met this cycle before. It reminds me of the Scott-Elliot stuff connected with theosophy.

    But your "Infernal Star" sounds about as impressive as anything I've struck lately. As you say, it has the possibilities of a whole series of stories in it. Your plan gives such a vast, elaborate, & convincing background that the events will seem to harbour a bleak realism & significance; & I'm sure that Zemargad will be the tamest & most innocuous of the ingredients.

    Best wishes for "The Secret of the Cairn" & "Star Change". Yes—my Gernsback-mulcted client is Mrs. Heald—whose story was nothing extra, although it surely deserved *some* remuneration.[3] You have my profoundest &

most understanding sympathy regarding "The Dweller in the Gulf", & I hope the copy I read may be a corrected one. W.S. is certainly a tough case. I *had* thought that it was less arbitrary about its contents than *Astounding* & *Amazing*, but evidently it is losing that one virtue. You are certainly right in insisting that matter be published as written or not at all. I made that proviso with W.T. at the outset, & wouldn't contribute to *Strange* because it couldn't guarantee integrity of text.

Too bad Wright rejected "Euvoran"—but I hope to see it sometime in some form or another. That pamphlet or book surely ought to materialise—it seems to me it ought to sell well if advertised in W.T. or some other medium to which you contribute.

Glad the new W.T. is some good. I haven't had a chance to look at a copy for six months, although I still buy it & keep it stacked up awaiting perusal. I must read "The Tower of the Elephant"—Howard has a tremendous amount of undisciplined ability, & sometimes it produces a memorable specimen of elder-world phantasy. I shall certainly look up "The Ice Demon" as soon as I get the next issue.

I certainly felt lucky to get "Ouroboros"—which I am lending to Price. "Visible & Invisible" came back safely. Keep track of my new acquisitions & add them to the catalogue—they're yours to read whenever you wish.

The other day I had a long letter from Harry Bates, who is in Clearwater, Fla. writing a play. Clearwater is between St. Petersburg & Dunedin, & Bates is in touch with Whitehead's father & friends—so that he has learned many details regarding his death. It seems that H S was feeling unusually well up to the Sunday (Nov. 20.) preceding his death. On that day, however, he complained of a "general malaise." That night his small-boy secretary heard a thud in his room (as if a fall had occurred) & upon investigating found H S in a semi-conscious state unable to speak. Doctors & friends were summoned, & word was sent to his father in St. Petersburg. When Mr. Whitehead arrived toward morning, H S recognised him & managed to smile & say "My daddy." Those were his last words. The doctors diagnosed his case as concussion of the brain caused by a fall (the latter of course induced by his general condition) & kept him continuously under opiates. There was no hope, & death came early Wednesday morning—Nov. 23. It was certainly tragic—H S had just got all his books & possessions down from the north, where they had been stored for years, & had finished a new sun-porch on the roof of his house. Old Mr. Whitehead— deaf, 85, & with cataracts forming—is badly affected by the blow. He plans to have H S, himself, & his wife (now interred in the North) ultimately buried side by side in St. Petersburg—where H S is now in a temporary vault. Thus good old Canevin will rest beneath the tropic sky he loved so well, & beside the parents to whom he was so deeply & undeviatingly devoted.

Last week was bitterly cold & followed by the first deep snow of the season—the latter now gradually melting off. Not a bad winter on the whole, but I shall welcome the spring! ¶ Yrs for the Pnakotic Secrets—
E'ch-Pi-El.

[P.S.] Well—here's some odd news! Young d'Erlette borrowed my "Witch House" a week ago—to copy, as he told me—& now comes a letter from Wright saying that the kid has shewn it to him, & that he wants to buy it for $140.00! He can surely have it if he wants it.

Notes

1. HPL's intentional blanks. Both AHT and RAS date the letter to 18 February.

2. H[elena] P[etrovna] Blavatsky (1831–1891), founder of theosophy and author of *The Secret Doctrine* (1888), also wrote *The Stanzas of Dzyan* (1908). HPL included references to some of the elements cited in this letter in his draft of "Through the Gates of the Silver Key" (1932–33), but upon Price's suggestion he removed them.

3. Hazel Heald, "The Man of Stone."

[210]   [ANS; Harry Ransom Humanities Research Center][1]

[Postmarked Providence, R.I.,
21 February 1933]

Hail, Chosen of Tsathoggua! Just a line to pass on a request from The Dark Priest of Ug—Bnādvāī-Aā of Sho-Kan. When you get the circulated story "Flash"[2]—which will come to you from either Howard or Comte d'Erlette (I can't recall the exact list), will you please add to the list E. HOFFMANN PRICE, 1416 JOSEPHINE ST., NEW ORLEANS, LA., & send the tale to him instead of back to Bnādvāī-Aā? I transmit the author's advance thanks. ¶ As you have probably recognised, that mystic primal dope from Price (notes of which I'll send you soon) *was* conventional theosophical stuff (Besant, Leadbeater, &c) after all. Do you know anything about the *real* source of this? Does it have any *real* Oriental source, or is it just a synthetic concoction of the theosophists? I've read almost nothing in that line. ¶ Blessings of Yog-Sothoth—E'ch-Pi-El

[*On front:*] Dweller in the Gulf just recd. from d'Erlette. Will peruse & comment. ¶ Have read it. Great stuff! But the Gernsback ending was *ruinous*. Glad to have seen the real ending.[3] Shall I return this to you? The atmosphere is splendid—that abyss in the midst of desolation produces an unforgettable picture. And the Yarkis—and IT!!

Notes

1. *Front:* Murphy's Hotel and Connecting Annexes, Richmond, VA.

2. A story (nonextant) by Bernard Austin Dwyer.

3. Upon publication of "The Dweller in the Gulf" in *Wonder Stories* (March 1933), CAS discovered that his conclusion for the tale had been severely and inexpertly edited. As a result, he wrote no further tales for *Wonder Stories*. This incident contributed to his withdrawal from fiction writing in the mid- to late 1930s.

[211]   [ANS]¹

[Postmarked Providence, R.I.,
24 February 1933/RAS Catalogue 3]

Congratulations on the printing arrangement! The booklet will certainly be a winner, & I fancy every member of our group will want a copy. It is full of especial favourites of mine, such as "Malneant", "Double Shadow", "Maal Dweb", &c &c. Put me down for a copy—& if I feel flush I may order another for a *lending* copy. ¶ Yes—as my former card has by this time told you, I am letting Bro. Farnsworth have the "Witch House". Probably I never would have gotten around to the crassness of revising it. ¶ Heard an interesting reading by "Waste Land" Eliot last Sunday—he surely is quite a personage! ¶ Springlike weather here yesterday & today. ¶ Best wishes, & blessings of, Narhath-Zin—E'ch-Pi-El

Notes

1. *Front:* Unidentified.

[212]   [TLS, JHL]

Vaults of Chaon Gacca—
Hour of the Weaving in the sepulcher of King Tnepreez.
[1 March 1933]

Dear Éch-Pi-El:

I am glad you are going to let Wright use The Dreams in the Witch House, and I look forward tremendously to the tale's appearance in print. I wish you would write about a hundred more. It is utterly beyond me why you should be dampened in the least by the criticism of time-serving termites, such as Putnams. Personally (such is my confidence, conceit or what you will) I wouldn't permit a thousand rejections to make me think that my own best tales are anything but first-rate. Contemporary judgement, in 49,999 cases out of 50,0000 [*sic*] is almost wholly meaningless. As I told Derleth in a letter to-day, I doubt if any of the popular josses of the present will be heard of at all in fifty years. But I am willing to gamble that you and your work will be known: perhaps not to a very large audience, but certainly to a select and faithful one.

What you tell me (via Bates) about Whitehead's end is very affecting and makes one feel like echoing some of the sentiments about human fate in The City of Dreadful Night. I am sorry indeed to hear of his father's condition. . . . "Our life's a cheat, our death a black abyss."¹ But no doubt, Whitehead died in another faith than that—which is just as well.

I think I wrote about my projected pamphlet of tales. It looks as if there are going to be the usual delays with the Auburn Journal crowd, who are slower than government mules. But I guess it will be ready before next Yulemas.

I am doing some more short tales at present—The Weaver in the Vault and The Flower-Women. The Infernal Star will have to wait, since there is no prospect of landing it as a serial even if completed. Wright is so heavily loaded down with long tales (all of them tripe, I dare say) that he can't even consider anything over 15,000 words till next year.[2]

You can keep *The Dweller in the Gulf.* I have had a letter of apology from David Lasser, managing editor of W.S., saying that he made the alterations only at Gernsback's express order. Gernsback must be loco to have a story spoiled in that fashion. I judge that the idiotic revision has cooked it with readers who might have liked it otherwise. Oh, phooey . . . . . .

The Book of Dyzan [*sic*] is new to me—I haven't read any great amount of theosophical literature. I'll be vastly interested in any dope you or Price can pass on to me. Theosophy, as far as I can gather, is a version of esoteric Yoga prepared for western consumption, so I dare say its legendry must have some sort of basis in ancient Oriental records. One can disregard the theosophy, and make good use of the stuff about elder continents, etc. I got my own ideas about Hyperborea, Poseidonis, etc., from such sources, and then turned my imagination loose.

Too bad about your client. I read her story in W.S., and rather liked it, mainly, perhaps, because I detected your revisory touch. Lasser said he would try to get some action on my arrears from the accounting dept. But I fear that the whole outfit has developed a well-organized system of "passing the buck." I have, by the way, just recently received my check for The Second Interment, which appeared last October in the concluding issue of Strange Tales.[3] And I got it only in response to a polite note to Clayton, asking if the matter had been overlooked. I must say that the depression is "the biggest and best" of its kind—if you'll pardon a lapse into the lingo of American promoters.

I saw the Episodes of Vathek listed at 50¢ in a catalogue (Gotham Book Mart) that came the other day, and am sending for a copy. I am, by the way, submitting The Third Episode to The Golden Book, which has published some mildly fantastic material of late; but of course, I am thoroughly cynical about the chances of acceptance. I know too much about the gutless emmets and pismires who edit magazines—particularly of the "quality(?)" type.

The weather is clear and balmy—first intimation of spring that we've had. If it keeps up, I'll take some of my scribbling out of doors.

Yours, under the sign of the Black Seal, or Sixtystone,[4]

Klarkash-Ton

P.S. Dwyer's tale came, and I am passing it on to Price as per instructions. It is quite good—would be vastly better if the sentiment at the end were left to the reader's inference rather than expressed.

Notes

1. James Thomson, *The City of Dreadful Night* (1874), 16.41–42.
2. In February 1933 CAS composed roughly half of the novelette "The Infernal Star." He never completed it.
3. Cover date of January 1933.
4. An allusion to "The Novel of the Black Seal" by Arthur Machen.

[213]   [AHT]

[early March 1933]¹
Shadow of Ib

[. . .]

What I want to know is the *origin* of this myth-cycle. Some of it is certainly coined by modern theosophists themselves, since the myths exhibit strong signs of 19ᵗʰ century geographical and historical consciousness. The question is whether there is *any* genuine Oriental folklore behind it. And if so, of what race? Hindoo? I must read up in this line if I ever get the time. The only treatise of the sort which I ever saw was Scott-Elliot's "Atlantis & the Lost Lemuria."

Myth-Cycle promulgated by Theosophists

2 Seven prom-ontories emerge whose edges are called Pushkara	LEMURIA or SHALMALI: The Himalayan chain emerged from the sea, and southward of it land slowly appeared, stretching to Ceylon, Australia, Tasmania, and Easter Island; westward till Madagascar and part of Africa emerge, claiming Norway, Sweden, East and West Siberia, and Kamschatka from its predecessors.²
1 First Land, whose highest peak was Mt. Meru, cap of North Pole	HYPERBOREA or PLAKSHA was formed, occupying Northern Asia, joining Greenland and Kamschatka, and bounded on the south by the great sea which rolled where the Gobi desert now stretches its wastes of sand. Spitzbergen, Sweden, and Norway formed a part of it, and it extended southwestward over the British Isles. Baffin's Bay was then land which included the islands now existing there. Climate was tropical, and luxuriant vegetation clothed the sunny plains.³

Yrs for the Sigil of Shamballah
—E'ch-Pi-El

Notes

1. See HPL to E. Hoffmann Price, 2 March 1933 (ms., JHL): "Thanks prodigiously for the loan of the Shamballah dope—which I have copied in condensed form & sent along to Klarkash-Ton for ultimate Barlovian delivery." And also HPL to RHB, 9 April 1933 (*O Fortunate Floridian* 60).

2. This derives from Annie Besant, *Four Lectures Delivered at the Twenty-eighth Anniversary Meetings of the Theosophical Society, at Adyar, December, 1903* (Benares & London: Theosophical Publishing Society, 1904), 74.

3. This appears to derive from Lieut.-Colonel Arthur E. Powell, *The Solar System* (London: Theosophical Publishing House, 1930), 193.

[214]   [ALS, JHL]

> Above the Sunken Citadel
> of Yo. Hour of the Bubbling
> [Postmarked 15 March 1933]

Dear Klarkash-Ton:—

I have one customer already for your book of tales, & believe that most of our gang will want it. I myself am full of expectancy. Hope the Journal will make a good job of it, & keep the misprints down to a minimum.

Yes—I suppose that short fiction is best for commercial purposes. Some time ago Wright accepted a serial from Price—to be run in *1934*.[1] I shall be looking for your new items as they appear. Glad one of the eckshuneers had the grace to apologize for the murder of the "Dweller." That outfit certainly is going to seed.

By this time you'll have received the forwarded matter from Price to be sent to Barlow. I am very curious about this holy city of Shamballah, said to exist unimpaired somewhere in the Gobi; though built by the Lemurians or 3d root race several million years ago. It is here that the Book of Dzyan— parts of which are older than the earth—is kept. Shamballah would make a splendid fictional theme. I wonder if any theosophists or Hindoos pretend to have visited it? As you say, the theosophic myth-cycle is probably based on ancient Indian lore with certain 19th century accessions. Price mentions A. P. Sinnett's "Esoteric Buddhism", Besant's "Pedigree of Man", Leadbeater's "Inner Life", & Blavatsky's "Secret Doctrine" in his bibliography (I've read none of these)—to which might be added Scott-Elliot's "Atlantis & the Lost Lemuria", which I read some years ago. I think I must do some research along this line when I get the time. I found Scott-Elliot quite an imaginative stimulus.

The other day I did 7½ pages of that "Silver Key" sequel, but was forced to pause because of an almost unprecedented rush of bothersome & ill-paid revision jobs. Heaven knows when I can get at it again! I had to discard Price's plan entirely, since it didn't blend at all with the original S. K. In the end, I fear, the Peacock Sultan will complain that I haven't left much of his work in the thing—although I shall very sedulously preserve the cosmic mathematical conceptions he introduces. I fear that collaboration is not my forte. Once I touch a thing at all, I generally have to do it all over in my especial fashion.

Dwyer will be grateful for your verdict on "Flash." What you say of the ending coincides with the view of Wandrei & Derleth.

Glad you were able to find a copy of the "Episodes of Vathek." Hope the *Golden Book* will look favourably on your continuation of #3—although that would be almost too good to be true.

New library accession to report—a gift, which I haven't yet read. "Not in Our Stars" by Michael Maurice. Apparently it is subtly weird, for its benevolent donor[2] describes it as "another swaying of the Curtain." It has no date, but looks fairly recent.

Poor weather around here—when it isn't rainy it's cold. Down to 12° the other morning. But spring is close at hand now! Glad you've had some decent weather—& hope you won't get any of the terrene agitations reported to the south of you. ¶ Yrs for the Sign of Kharazin

—E'ch-Pi-El

P.S. Just heard from Price. He says that according to theosophists, Shamballah keeps itself from invasion through adverse thought-waves which deflect all attempts to reach it—producing bad weather, apparent accidents, &c.

Notes

1. "Satan's Garden."
2. E. A. Edkins.

[215]   [ALS]

Grey Plain before the
Sealed Stone Tower: Hour of
the alien-toned bell stroke within
[24 March 1933/RAS]

Dear Klarkash-Ton:—

Thanks exceedingly for the sidelights on the theosophical cycle. Sinnett must surely be a standard authority, since both you & the Peacock Sultan recommend him. This stuff is certainly worth looking up—the matter of the *invisible planets* being especially promising.[1] As you say, there is probably a good bit of genuine tradition in the lore of theosophy. One thing we can say for the Hindoos is that their mythology shews a better grasp of the earth's transience & insignificance in time & space than any other known to history & anthropology. I wonder how these legends of early things compare with what Col. Churchward claims of the Himalayan priests & their records in the primal Naacal language which tell of sunken Mu?

Obviously, these traditions are very old among the Hindoos; & it would be interesting to discover how they arose. Originally the Aryan creators of Brahmanism had a mythology of personified natural forces homologous to

412 ❖ *Dawnward Spire, Lonely Hill*

those of the Greeks & Romans, & of our Northern ancestors. Could the the-osophical cycle have arisen out of these, or were its germs derived from the non-Aryan subject races of India? Since the Brahmans arrived in India about 2000 B.C., there was plenty of time for the crystallisation of a definite new myth-cycle before the earliest contacts with the Western World. It is not likely that any "Atlantis" ever existed. The evidences of geology & natural history are that no connexion betwixt various Atlantic islands has existed since the appearance of man on the planet. But of course there may well have been important pre-Aryan civilisations & legends in India. Indeed, we know there were pre-Aryan cities on the Indus river.

The notion of the "Akashic" records is indeed an unique one.[2] But I don't think there's much ground for assuming any truth in these tales. To begin with, they assume an antiquity for mankind which is against all the indi-cations of palaeontology & geology. As for the pineal gland—modern endo-crinology has fairly well established its actual function in the human system . . . as a regulator of the chemical & biological changes attending adolescence & maturity. But surely the legends lose nothing in picturesqueness & imagina-tive value through being merely legends.

That book sent by the occultist must have been rather fascinating. Don't you suppose the five-spot dropped out of it? The donor may have enclosed it as a mark of appreciation of the occult significance of your poetry as he in-terpreted it. I wish he'd repeat the process with us all!

From something Price says, I take it that Blavatsky is the best "authority" anent the Book of Dzyan (*not* Dyzan, as I first carelessly transcribed it). Ac-counts of Holy Shamballah would seem to vary—but it's great fictional stuff in any form!

Congratulations on "Vulthoom's" acceptance. "The Weaver in the Vault" promises well, & I hope it may see print. I've done 7½ pages of the Silver Key sequel, but am stalled through pressure of revisory work. Conges-tion grows worse & worse—a novel of 70,000 words, probably needing a thorough overhauling, looms in the offing.[3]

Yrs in the Rite of the Twin Stones—
—E'ch-Pi-El

Notes

1. Cf. *CB* 201: "Planets form'd of invisible matter." The entry dates to the time of this letter.

2. In theosophy, the akashic records (from *akasha*, Sanskrit for sky, space, or aether) are a compendium of mystical knowledge encoded in a nonphysical plane of existence known as the astral plane.

3. This work, which HPL mentions to several correspondents, is unidentified either as to author or as to title. It was probably not published.

[216]   [ALS]
            [THE ELM TREE INN / FARMINGTON, CONN.]
                                        Beyond the Inner Gate:
                                        Hour when the Ancient
                                        Ones Sway on their pillars
                                        [8 April 1933/RAS]

Dear Klarkash-Ton:—
                        Behold my latest attempt to solve the fountain pen
problem—a *29¢* stylographic from a sale at the main Liggett's downtown.
First stylographic I ever used, and it works like a charm so far. Irony—after
all my expensive Watermans & Parkers, is a 29-center to end all my goose-
quill woes? If this keeps up, I'll get another—& stick to stylographics for life!
Some friends of mine swear by them.

Well—I've finished "Through the Gates of the Silver Key." Iä! Shub-
Niggurath! The Goat with a Thousand Young! What a job! I hope Price
won't be offended at my writing a virtually new story. I left a lot of his mathematical concepts in, & hope I didn't raise hell with them. I fear the thing will
disappoint you, for I'm absolutely no good at collaboration. Price's clear-cut,
dominantly *intellectual* mind is so unlike my own dreamy hat-rack that coalescence is really impossible. All I could do was to ride in & hog the whole
works. I doubt if the thing will sell. It comes to 34 pages of my script, which
means that this version is exactly the length of the "Witch House." Carter (at
Price's suggestion) manages to reach the centre of absolute space, & from
there gets sent to a former life 550 years ago—although a bit of forgetfulness
causes the earlier personality to appear *on the earth today*—eventually wandering
into the meeting at which his estate is being settled. I have pepped this up by
having him sent to the transgalactic planet Yaddith *incalculable aeons ago*. He can
return to the *aeon* of the modern earth through the Silver Key, but his oversight prevents his recovering his earthly Carter body—*and his Yaddith body is
that of an utterly alien clawed, snouted thing.* Once on earth, however, he can find a
spell to regain his human form. He constructs a disguise & mask to enable him
to live on earth till he can regain his body. Getting back to earth, & just before
recovering his human form, he learns of the estate meeting & hastens in his
disguise to save his property. He pretends to be an East Indian friend of his
missing self, & tells his story in the 3d person. His cousin—an heir—calls him a
charlatan & detects that his apparent face is only a mask. Tearing off the mask
(at a time when no one else is facing Carter), the cousin sees *what lies beneath* &
drops dead of fright. Before the others in the room can see what the dead man
saw, Carter vanishes mysteriously in a manner previously provided for. I've put
a lot of care into the thing, & tried to develop the terror of cosmic space in an
atmospherically effective fashion. Hope Price will like it & that he won't change
it too badly. I told him to send it to you—making a triangular collaboration—if
he feels dissatisfied yet does not wish to tinker any more himself.

I'm with you in doing most work in summer. I'm really no good at all in winter. Lately I've been utterly swamped, & don't known when I'll ever see daylight again. Added to this is my financial crisis. Much as I hate to leave 10 Barnes, I shall probably have to seek cheaper quarters soon. Fortunately I think I can find a pretty decent bargain on the selfsame ancient hill—in a good neighbourhood, & capable of accomodating my books & possessions. But what an unadulterated hell moving will be! It will render me helpless for a month!

I await sight of the "Weaver" & "Flower Women" with keen interest, & shall try to get sight of the misnamed "Secret of the Cairn" in Hugo the Rat's kosher mekasin. Hope his ekshun on debts won't be delayed beyond all reason—I'd like to set Adolf Hitler on the scoundrel!

Glad your brochure will be ready this month—I shall begin advertising it amongst the gang, & shall shortly order 2 copies myself—one for lending. I won't have my library copy ruined. Morse is a friend of Loveman's whom I met in N.Y. & who has become quite a correspondent of mine—a fine young fellow, assistant librarian at Princeton. He is a great admirer of your work—as indeed who isn't?

What you say of the theosophy cycle & of the special fictionally developable features interests me tremendously. I simply must look up Blavatsky, Besant, Leadbeater, Sinnett, &c. One could, as you say, derive a whole canon of tales from it. It seems to make my Yog-Sothoth stuff pallid by comparison! These *Akashic records* tickle my imagination. It is from them, of course, that the Book of Eibon & the Pnakotic Manuscripts were first devised! By the way—that _____ch incident certainly must have given you a kick! ¶ This pen is too good to be true! It makes my script look even more like hades than usual—but what ease! I feel like getting half a dozen tomorrow!

Yrs. for the Chant of the Plane-Tilting—
E'ch-Pi-El

[217]   [ALS]

Crypt of the Citadel atop
Never-Trodden Yaddith-Gho:
Hour of the Lifting of the Trap
Door from Beneath—————
[Postmarked 3 May 1933]

Dear Klarkash-Ton:—

Stylographic continues very fair, though it does not conduce to aesthetic script. Fountain pens certainly are hell—but I have to have one since I do so much of my writing outdoors.

Price seems to like the S. K. sequel very well, & is typing it in slow stages without any change from my version. Of course, there's no telling how it will go with King Pharnaces—but one can only try.

Glad your "Star Change" is published, even if mistitled.[1] I'll have to look it up. Congratulations on the "Weaver's" acceptance. Sooner or later "The Flower-Women" will also land, I am sure. Price told me about *Astounding's* renaissance, & I'm certainly glad for the sake of those who can produce scientifiction. As for Hugo the Rat—probably he's waiting for the dollar to get as low as the German mark did in the early 1920's. Then—oy, he shood pay it up by his condribudors a'ready! Many appear to be waiting for your booklet with mingled patience & avidity—& I really believe you'll have a very substantial sale for it. Do you intend to advertise it in any of the magazines where you have an admiring "following"?

But what seems to beat all is your new "Death of Malygris"—so appetisingly described in your letter. It would surely appear to contain about all the elements demanded of genuine horror phantasy,—bizarre colour, suggestions of the Outside, suspense, drama, & the stark hideousness which is the soul of weird writing. I surely hope Clayton will take it—though of course it does not come into the "scientifiction" class which forms Astounding's province. Another thing which sounds tremendously promising is your "Aforgomon"[.][2]

Many thanks for the hellish sketches in your letter—they have been duly incorporated into my cherished file of pictorial Clericashtoniana.

Commiserations on the housecleaning ordeal. Moving for me has proved imperative, though there are redeeming features. It seems to be virtually decided that my surviving aunt & I will take the upper half of a trim little Georgian house (built circa 1800 & having a colonial doorway much like that on my bookplate) on the crest of the great hill,[3] adjacent to the library of Brown University. There is space for each to have separate quarters—two rooms apiece—plus a kitchen & 2 splendid attic storage rooms, & the atmosphere of the whole house is extremely mellow & fascinating—old-fashioned fireplaces, mantels, six-panel doors, latches, curving Georgian staircase, wide floor-boards, &c. Despite my lifelong love of old houses, this will be the first I shall ever have lived in. It will be a marvellous bargain—only $40.00 per month (just what I've been paying for this *one* room & alcove), with steam heat & hot water piped from the contiguous college library. But the moving ordeal will be hell's own work. Not only my own room to break up & transport, but my aunt's present flat to be liquidated. However, such a united home at so low a rent— & in a real Georgian house 130 years old—is worth a bit of trouble. I'll let you know when the new address—66 College St.—goes into effect. It probably can't be for more than a month. Thine in Tsathoggua's name—

E'ch-Pi-El.

Notes

1. I.e., as "The Visitors from Mlok."
2. I.e., "The Chain of Aforgomon."
3. In fact, the Samuel B. Mumford House, now at 65 Prospect Street, was built c. 1825.

[218]   [ALS]

From the 66th Vortex of
the new Space-Time Abyss—
Hour of the faint Scratching.
[31 May 1933/RAS]

Dear Klarkash-Ton:—

Well—the upheaval is over, but after settling two
rooms & arranging 2000 books I am certainly in a position to sympathise
with you amidst your own clearing upheaval. Hail, O Brother in boundless
toil! As in your case, things came to light which I had not seen for years. In a
box unopened for a quarter of a century I came across a file of a juvenile astronomical paper which I published from 1903 to 1907, together with some of the
pad sheets on which I hectographed it.[1] This epistle is indited on that archaic
stationery—cast up by the tomb, as it were. Glad you have your books in more
coherent shape. So have I—all the weird items (except such as belong to sets of
standard authors[)] being in one compact group now. I find that the bizarre section of my library (including folklore & mythology) takes up more than 17 feet
of shelfage. I had to get 4 new cases (small, cheap ones) to absorb new material
& make up for the built-in shelves at 10 Barnes. Magazines, papers, & pamphlets also formed a problem. Some could go into the various quaint cupboards
of this delightfully ancient house, but others are on small stands or under the
bed—for my books &c. overflow into the bedroom. For some of my pamphlets I have obtained a tall cabinet with many shelves—& altogether, I have
managed to fix things up at last. But it was a hell of a job while it lasted!

My new quarters are tremendously homelike. I have tried to live up to
the old-fashioned architecture by avoiding crowding & overdecoration—
which I can do because I now have 2 rooms & an attick & kitchen to overflow into. There is a potent charm in coming home through a colonial doorway much like my bookplate, & sitting by an ancient mantel gazing through
small-paned windows over venerable roofs & foliage! On the mantel are old
brass candlesticks, an archaic clock, & some time-mellowed vases—while
over it is a marine view painted by my mother & now re-framed to suit the
Georgian scheme. The whole place is so much like a museum that I keep expecting a guard to appear & kick me out at 5 o'clock closing-time! It surely is
ironic that economy & retrenchment are the motives which brought me to
this ideal relique of the past! My aunt will begin moving in tomorrow—which
means another job for me about as arduous as the one I've been through!

Thanks enormously for the sketches—including the delightful self-
portrait. That coloured Entity's head is a genuine nightmare, whilst the fiend-
ish blossom or tentacle-end keeps one's imagination busy & apprehensive.
Thanks also for the dark, potent, & dizzying lines about the Abyss. I wish I
could see the whole of the poem from which that is an extract!

I shall be on the lookout for the pamphlet, & hope the printers won't hold back much longer. Too bad you didn't patronise the N.Y. firm—though you can try them next time. If this venture even meets expenses, you certainly ought to try another; for there are dozens of things of yours—like "The Epiphany of Death"—which simply cry out to be printed. Glad that Bloch has ordered his brochure. He is a very bright kid of 16, who only recently got hold of me through W.T. He vastly admires your work. The circular is excellent & if you'd like to have me distribute it to my correspondents (many of whom ought to be likely customers), I'll dispose of about 50 for you. One certain customer is the youth who came here from Allentown last year—Harry Brobst. You are a veritable idol of his—in fact, I think he likes your work better than that of any other contributor to the popular magazines.

I certainly hope that the plan for a British edition of your verse will develop well.[2] If so, I want a copy. England is certainly more appreciative of the weird & fantastic than is the U.S., & I feel sure that you would get more intelligent reviews if your poems appeared in the mother land.

Which reminds me—my "Erich Zann' has had another sale—its *fifth!* I wish I could sell some of my other stuff five times over. This sale is to the publishing firm of Denis Archer, London, for a new cheap anthology of weird material. The payment for 5th rights is five guineas, & I suppose I'll get a free copy of the book when it's out. The other four sales were (1) to W. T., (2) to Creeps by Night, (3) to the British ed. of Creeps, & (4) to the London Evening Standard. 3 British to 2 American, including (5) the sale to Archer.

Confound that ass Wright for turning down "Malygris"! I certainly want to see it—but don't bother to re-type it purely on my account. I can very well read the old copy, & will promise to be careful of it if it is in poor condition. So you have a new typewriter? I almost got a portable machine this spring—when I thought I might be moving into smaller quarters where I couldn't have the separate table needed by my ancient & ponderous Remington. When, however, I saw where I was going, I clung to my faithful old boiler-factory—the only typewriter I ever had except juvenile Simplexes & Odells—which I bought in 1906 as a rebuilt machine.

By the way—in my new quarters the Nameless Eikon of pre-human horror has a new function to perform. . . . . . . It is a book-end, situate thus on the top of a broad, glass-doored case in the neighbourhood of an old-fashioned full-mounted terrestrial globe. Slowly, day by day, something sinister appears to be stealing into the books thus supported. New & horrible meanings begin to creep into the text—between the lines, as it were—& one finds hitherto unperceived implications of hideousness in the headings of chapters & the apparently fortui-

tous vertical lines formed by the falling of words beneath one another. A very harmless book on astronomy has begun to suggest the most unutterable cosmic horrors, whilst a textbook of botany hints at monstrous fungi & blasphemous thallophytes more loathsome than the saturnian vegetation of a Klarkash-Tonic drawing! And the text of the book next the Eikon is getting *uneven.* Certain words have commenced to stand out unnaturally from the rest of the text, *&* *what they convey is not to be repeated, or to be perused without apprehension.*

There have been some good spring days, but I have been too closely tied up with moving to take advantage of them. Owing to bad finances, I doubt if I'll be able to take any long southern trip this year—but I may get to N.Y. for the amateur convention early in July, seeing Long, Loveman, Kirk, & the rest.

My "Shunned House" may see the light of day at last. Cook has finally found the unbound edition, & Walter J. Coates—editor of *Driftwind*—plans to bind & market it. I'll see that you get an early copy.

Well—again, let me extend my particularly understanding commiserations anent your drastic housecleaning! Did I mention how much I enjoyed "The Beast of Averoigne"? I read up my back numbers of W T just before moving.

Thine in the forgotten ritual of Mnar—

———E'ch-Pi-El.

P.S. The collaborated sequel to the Silver Key has been put into circulation. You will receive it from Comte d'Erlette.

Notes

1. The *Rhode Island Journal of Astronomy,* 69 issues of which (2 August 1903–February 1909) survive at JHL.
2. Cf. CAS to August Derleth, 23 May 1933: "I have been making a selection of poems from my various volumes at the instigation of an admirer [i.e., George Work] who thinks he can exert some influence with British publishers, and have typed part of the selection, making some minor revisions as I went along" (*SSL* 206). The provisional title was *One Hundred Poems.* As late as June 1937 CAS had hopes that the book might still be published. Heath, Cranton in London published Work's novel *White Man's Harvest* in 1932.

[219]   [ALS, JHL]

Onyx Sea-cliffs of Kho—
Hour when low tide bares that
daemon-carven reef wherefrom men
avert their glance . . . .

[14 June 1933/RAS]

Dear Klarkash-Ton:—

When your letter arrived I was just on the point of dropping a card to congratulate you on the dark fascination of "Genius Loci" & "Malygris"—both of which I perused not long ago. In the former you have succeeded in capturing that vague, geographical horror after which I have so often striven, while the latter is a gorgeous bit of onyx & ebony prose-poetry in which the crawling menace advances as to the sound of evil flutes & crotala. Little Bloch—who seems to be a really brilliant kid—also appreciated "Malygris" intensely. It interested me greatly to hear of the actual folklore background of this lethal phantasy—Montague Summers (of whose work I have read only the Vampire volume) must be full of data rich in fictional suggestions.

Glad to hear that the brochure is at last off the press—& thanks abundantly for the generous idea of sending two complimentary copies. Certainly, there can scarcely be any more appreciative recipient. The proof-sheet gives a piquant foretaste of the enterprise—let us hope that the misprints can be cut down to a minimum. I trust that the venture will at least pay expenses—if not indeed yielding a real profit. Everyone to whom I have mentioned the booklet seems likely to prove a purchaser, & the distribution of the circulars will help. Hope you can reach some of your admirers in the Eyrie—the small-towners ought to prove accessible without a street address. An advertisement in W.T. ought to help—Coates (editor of *Driftwind*, who is issuing my "Shunned House") is thinking of inserting one. Even if "The Double Shadow" only makes expenses I hope you will later issue another collection—perhaps through the other firm you mentioned. If I thought an analogous thing of mine would go across (& perhaps the S. H. will form a trial), I'd like to try issuing my "Innsmouth" & "Mountains of Madness" as a book. By the way—the "Erich Zann" matter illustrates the old distich about the cup & the lip. Only the other day I received a note saying that my permission for publication had arrived too late—although I had answered the agents by return mail. They added that the Archer firm wished to retain my permission in case of a second anthology, & I acquiesced in this design. It is surely a disappointment not to have the five guineas I was expecting!

Thanks exceedingly for the stirring & sonorous "Doom of America", which surely indicates a vividly prophetic mood—it is a remarkable production in every way for the 1913–14 period. Aside from historic interest it is really darned good poetry—full of the colour, fire & thunder of Biblical diction, yet thoroughly original in its imagery. Was it ever in print?[1]

The charm of my new quarters continues to enthrall me. My aunt is now getting fairly well settled, so that the homelike aspect of the place increases. She has set out some familiar flowers in front of the house, & hopes to train up the facade a slip of ivy from the Washington estate at Mt. Vernon. The whole atmosphere is that of the 18th century—my chosen period—& I can scarcely imagine how I ever managed to exist in Victorian houses! Under separate cover I am sending an historic brochure (not without intrinsic interest) whose frontispiece most opportunely illustrates my present environment. Not only does it exhibit the ancient hill & university neighbourhood as a whole—with College St. sweeping up from Market Square—but it plainly shews *this house* at the left-hand margin. I have marked #66 with arrows, & a magnifying glass of moderate power will make it stand out very plainly. You can see the square Georgian design, with smaller rear wing. This is a western view, & the two right-hand windows on the second story (rather obscured by branches in the picture) are those of my study. At the more northern of these—where my working desk stands in the nook formed by the chimney's side—I am now seated. At the bottom of the hill—or rather, climbing up from the bottom— you can see the newly-finished court house, which faithfully follows the ancient Providence-Georgian tradition in its architecture. The whole picture gives a re- markably good idea of my general setting. Note that #66 stands far back from the main line of houses in College St.—being, as I think I said, in a quaint grassy court. It is part of a delightful (& regrettably vanishing) elder world— that world which has most strongly touched my imagination since infancy.

You will receive the Silver Key sequel from Comte d'Erlette, & from you it is to go to our wholesale-slaughter expert R.E.H. I hope it will not disap- point you. Price has not yet submitted it to Satrap Pharnabozus. Yes—the waxwork museum story is mostly my own; entirely so in wording, & also so far as concerns the background of Alaskan archaeology & antique horror. You will find Tsathoggua mentioned.

My aunt & I will be greatly pleased to welcome your friend Miss Sully if she visits Providence, & can undoubtedly display enough historic & antiquar- ian sights to fill a sojourn of any duration. If the East is new to her, she will find in its many evidences of long, continuous settlement a quite unique fas- cination. I wish you could get around this way yourself—if ever you can, I can now save you hotel bills, for I've obtained a camp cot to enable me to lodge occasional guests. Among other things, I'd take you to Arkham (Salem) & Kingsport (Marblehead)!

A delectable warm spell (mercury up to 94°) has just ended. While it lasted, I was unusually active—taking 12-mile walks in the country, &c.—but now I am shivering & lethargic again. I certainly wish that Providence had Charles- ton's or St. Augustine's climate! ¶ Yrs in the ritual of the Unnamed Planet
—E'ch-Pi-El.

P.S. Glancing the other day at the book next the Nameless Eikon, I found myself reading in a highly peculiar fashion—picking out words from odd & unrelated places in the text, as if led to them by some invisible influence. At length a vague hint of some obscure meaning began to develop. The words united to evoke a cloudy, indeterminate vision. A certain *memory* welled up— & shrieking, I dropt the volume *while there was yet time.*

[P.]P.S. [on envelope:] I've just lent young Bloch my collection of your sketches. It ought to prove quite a revelation to the kid!

Notes

1. The poem was not published in CAS's lifetime.

[220]   [ANS, Bancroft Library][1]

[Postmarked Providence, R.I.,
16 June 1933]

Brochures & circulars have just arrived. Thanks abundantly! The pamphlet really presents a very neat & tasteful appearance, & ought to please all its purchasers in every way. I've just read "Euvoran", which I had not seen before, & am impressed with its Dunsanian charm. Those black batlike things remind me of the "night-gaunts" (a name I applied to them at the time) of which I used to dream when I was 6 years old. I shall re-read the other tales soon. Have already sent out 3 of the circulars. ¶ My aunt has just broken an ankle & is at the R. I. Hospital[2]—so that I am again keeping house in solitary state. When she returns, she will have to use crutches for quite a period. Such an accident is certainly damnably provoking! She was answering the doorbell in a hurry, & mistook two steps for one. ¶ Hot spell is over, so that I am shivering & wretched again. However, the house is getting steam heat today. Regards—& thanks and congratulations on the booklet. Thine for the Elder Sign—E'ch-Pi-El.

Notes

1. *Front:* Main Street Looking North from Capitol, Columbia, S. C.
2. Annie Gamwell broke her ankle when she fell down the stairs shortly after moving into 66 College St.

[221]   [ALS]

Field of the Ultra-Spectral Rays
—Hour of the Spiral Wind from Nith
[29 June 1933/RAS]

Dear Klarkash-Ton:—

The hand that indites these words trembles with a decay that is not of years alone, & the haggard face above the page is shrivelled with a thousand lines of horror that were not there two nights ago. For . . . . & may God help me . . . . *I looked with a mirror's aid at a passage in that crumbling tome of elder lore which stands next the Nameless Eikon!* Now—in spite of all of Heaven's vaunted mercy—*I know.* The veil is withdrawn . . . . & I have glimpsed that which has bowed me in convulsive terror for the few days or weeks of life which remain to me. Iä! Shub-Niggurath! Is the Grey Rite of Azathoth no more of avail?

Well—I have read the brochure through now, & can truthfully say that each of the tales retains all its original appeal for me. Indeed—I think "The Devotee of Evil" is even stronger than before, though I cannot quite put my finger on the seat of the change. My favourites, I think, are "The Double Shadow", "The Maze of the Enchanter", & "A Night in Malneant"—though it is indeed hard to assign the other three a lesser status. The whole thing is really magnificent—& a marvellous value for a quarter. I hope the sale will remain steady if not spectacular. I have now distributed quite a number of the circulars, & believe that at least a few of these will result in sales. One sale of "Ebony & Crystal" is also virtually assured. The very reasonable price of the booklet will help its sale—people will fork over a quarter when they wouldn't be so apt to spend a dollar or two. I hope Coates will be wise enough to bind "The Shunned House" cheaply & whittle the price down to a minimum—it would be silly to charge a dollar for one mediocre tale (solely on the strength of typography, paper, & binding) when you are offering *six excellent tales* for *only a fourth* of that sum. Some day I may try "Innsmouth" and "The Mountains" as a booklet, but I can't afford any risks now. As for my earlier rejected tales—I'm beginning to agree with Wright about them, & am not at all sure I wish them to appear. Even my old favourite "The Nameless City" looked pretty naive & shoddy to me the last time I re-read it.

My ancient quarters continue to fascinate me, & one feature of the centuried attic almost arouses me to tenebrous fiction. This is the narrow & hideously nighted space in the attic under the eaves—reached from the attic proper by low doors, & having no windows whatsoever. A man—or an entity not entirely a man—could crawl in there & lurk for years . . . or centuries . . . unsuspected. One can see in only a few inches beyond the squat, black apertures—*& one is not tempted to explore further.* So far as I know, no *living* person has been or looked through the full extent of that black space for 100 or 130 years . . . . . *but is it wholly untenanted?* I am wholly alone in the house now, with my aunt at the hospital & the downstairs neighbour[1] on the high seas bound for Germany—*but what was that creaking above me last night?* Part of that black space is directly over my desk. Perhaps it was only the rats—I hope so—yet I have seen no rats, nor any evidences of them, since coming

here. *Is it right for so ancient a house to have no rats?* Is there anything the rats are afraid of? Hark! . . . what is *that?* Precisely overhead . . . . . . *do rats tramp & pace in measured, sinisterly deliberate steps?* . . . . . . God! . . . . The Elder Sign! . . . .

I hope you've received the historical booklet with a picture of #66, for I'd hate to have it lost. Let me know if you haven't. I fear some copies have gone astray, for several correspondents have not acknowledged them. Possibly the old envelopes I used were not safe. But I'll lend you another copy if the first was lost. Thanks in advance, by the way, for the additional pictures you say you are about to send. Some of those Lurking Fear illustrations were magnificent—especially the unholy wood, & the gryphon gazing down into the gulph.[2]

Thanks prodigiously for the Thibetan article, which I herewith return. I must get hold of that book somehow—it must be a veritable mine of lore. The *rolang* (ugh!) has vast fictional possibilities—I've made a note about it in my hellish book of plot-germs.[3] That Rosicrucian stuff must be highly picturesque. Do you suppose one could get any hints from the literature of the fake organisations which advertise in W.T.?

I think a day will enable Miss Sully to see most of the historic high spots of urban Providence, & I shall be glad to exhibit them when she arrives. Tell her to let me know exact place & date of arrival, & I will be on hand—trusting to ingenuity in establishing identification. When she is in New York she ought without fail to look up the *Longs—230 West 97th St.* They are in a better position to entertain her than any other "gang" family, having a pleasant apartment, a lavish table, a car, & a servant. Sonny Belknap is one of your staunchest admirers, whatever may be his lapses as a correspondent. The Longs' telephone is *RIverside 9-3465.* And by the way—mine is *PLantations 2044*—in the name of my aunt, Mrs. Gamwell. Later on I hope fervently that you can get around here yourself.

Little Bho-Blôk, the Daemon Lama of Nighted Leng, certainly is quite a [boy]. His present efforts are obviously juvenile & extravagant, but he has the genuine atmospheric touch, & will probably develop vastly in the next few years.

The circular you sent is the first I've heard of *The Fantasy Fan,* although several have told me that a new weird magazine (name not given) desiring "modern" weird tales, "not too gruesome", (sounds like Clayton namby-pamby) at ½¢ per word is about to be founded. I must look up the F.F.

My aunt seems to be progressing all right, though the restriction to one position lames her back. She will come home with a nurse next week. Weather is warmer here now, & I've taken several walks of substantial length.

Yrs. for the Exorcism of Iagsat

E'ch-Pi-El

P.S. A new tale by Comte d'Erlette is on its way to you, via one Edward Klein of Cincinnati. Dwyer seems to be holding up the Silver Key sequel, but you'll get it in the end.

[P.]P.S. One misprint in "The Devotee of Evil" was pretty good! Did you notice it? *MACHEN*ism for *mechan*ism! Shades of the White People & the Great God Pan!

Notes

1. Alice Rachel Sheppard (1870–1961).

2. A drawing named "Gryphon Gazing upon the Gulf" appears in *The Eldritch Dark: Collected Prose Poems and Artwork of Clark Ashton Smith* (Centipede Press, 2017).

3. The book is *Magic and Mystery in Tibet* by Alexandra David-Neél. *CB* 192: "Thibetan ROLANG—Sorcerer (or NGAGSPA) reanimates a corpse by holding it in a dark room—lying on it mouth to mouth & repeating a magic formula with all else banished from his mind. Corpse slowly comes to life & stands up. Tries to escape—leaps, bounds, & struggles—but sorcerer holds it. Continues with magic formula. Corpse sticks out tongue & sorcerer bites it off. Corpse then collapses. Tongue become a valuable talisman. If corpse escapes—hideous results & death to sorcerer."

[222]   [ALS]

Nameless Ruins of Iath
Hour of the Lambent Glow
around the Sealed Tower.
[12 July 1933][1]

Dear Klarkash-Ton:—

Your delectably generous envelope duly arrived, & I have since been revelling in the nameless pictured entities & the enthralling pages of "The Colossus of Ylourgne". Iä! Shub-Niggurath! What blasphemous spawn of the pit! Some of these delirious entities almost surpass any I have had before—& are on a scale hitherto unparallelled in my modest collection. Glad to see the originals of the "Lurking Fear" series—you have my profoundest thanks, if not Houtain's cash! And let me add another paean of gratitude for the "Colossus"—which is certainly a magnificent breath from the nether gulphs, with images & atmospheric touches which haunt one persistently. If Satrap Pharnabozus rejected that, I'll . . . . . but then, why should one expect anything sensible from that capricious spawn of Philistia? You must, if possible, get this & other items duplicated & preserved in another booklet like "The Double Shadow".

I duly note the changes adopted in the "Devotee"—all advantageous, I imagine. Everything in the booklet is splendid, & I trust that my especial fondness for D. S., Maal Dweb, & Malneant does not make me appear unappreciative of Euvoran & the rest. It is hard to choose among such brilliants, & any choice represents only a personal mood of the moment. Glad to hear of the increasing sales—both of D. S. & E. & C. W. Paul Cook may order both before long. Glad young Strauch has ordered. He is the home-town bosom friend of Harry Brobst—also an admirer of yours—& a very brilliant youth. A poet, & for some time Asst. Librarian of Muhlenberg College, of which he is a graduate. He visited here last September, & expects to come again this September. His own fiction is embryonic, but he can probably make something of it if he will stick to his own Pennsylvania region, so rich in distinctive spectral folklore. As for addresses—of course Dauber & Pine's is still all right for Loveman. It is only his residence which has changed. I'm asking Long if he received the brochure, but am damned afraid he didn't— since his old address was *823* (not 803) West End Ave., & he hasn't lived on that avenue since late in 1926. His correct present address is *230 W. 97ᵗʰ St.* Incidentally—I've passed on to him, & will pass on to Mrs. Heald, the infor- mation about the bad-debt collector.[2] This certainly sounds promising, & I hope you yourself can ultimately employ her to advantage. Anyone who can extract cash from Hugo the Rat is an expert! Price, too, might use a good [lawyer]. By the way—I'll wager your *Black Book* is quite as interesting in spots as the similarly designated volume of the late unfortunate Friedrich von Junzt! And about the booklet with the picture of #66—damn! I fear 2 or 3 were lost, & imagine that the flap of the second-hand Dauber & Pine envelope I used in all cases was too short to prevent a fatal slipping. Queer, though, that you didn't get the empty envelope, as is usual in such cases. Well—here is *anoth- er* copy, sent first-class, which I *hope* you'll get. The view of the ancient hill is really very representative, & gives an excellent idea of my daily surroundings. You'll see #66 (in a court, back from College St.) quite plainly, marked to pre- vent all error. No hurry about the return of this—though I'd like it back some time—especially on account of the depleted stock due to postal loss. The book- let itself is worth your perusal—having quite a bit of interesting historical data.

Glad you like the "Witch House" in print. The misprints made me see red—especially one on p. 92 (*magical "love"* for *magical LORE*) & another on p. 101 (*"human" element* for *KNOWN element*). I felt honoured to have "Ubbo- Sathla" for a neighbour. Incidentally, those two tales plus the "Museum" thing give our synthetic folklore the biggest simultaneous mass presentation it has yet received. When a reader finishes this issue, he'll be about ready to ask Dauber & Pine to find him a copy of the "Book of Eibon"! I've had three new inquiries about the reality of the Necronomicon, &c. About *The Fantasy Fan*—bless me, yes! If the editor will print any of my rejected stuff for noth- ing he's more than welcome to it! I need extra copies of most of my old junk for lending, & will gladly flood Brother Hornig with as much as he'll use. Probably the thing won't survive long—but there's no harm in getting the good of it as long as it lasts. I'd like to see "Beyond the Wall of Sleep" in type. With your work represented, it will certainly be a venture of which no one need feel ashamed. By all means tell Ye Ed. to write me.

I trust Miss Sully's trip is proving pleasant; & shall, unless contrarily in- structed, be on the lookout July 19 at 6 a.m. at the Colonial Line pier . . . .

which lies right in the lee of the ancient hill's southerly extremity, on a water-front having considerable picturesqueness. The yellow poppy ought to facilitate identification—though it's too bad you couldn't have furnished some of your typical nameless vegetation from Saturn & Antares! A second day in Prov. would enable many picturesque suburbs, (& perhaps ancient Newport) as well as the city proper to be covered; thus affording an extremely [good] picture of R.I. I hope that young Melmoth & Sonny Belknap [take] part in displaying seething Manhattan to the visitor—[& if she is] not already provided with Bostonian guidance, I think that [W. Paul] Cook would be delighted to shew off the Athens of America. I [envy] Miss Sully her coming sight of *Quebec*—to which I fear I can't get this year, since my aunt's accident will probably prevent any long absences on my part. I always envy the Cuban glimpse—you'll recall that I wanted to get to Havana (only 90 miles away) when I was in Key West in 1931, but just lacked the cash.

My aunt, by the way, returned home July 5, with a nurse in constant attendance. She is still largely confined to bed—with the cast still on—though yesterday she was lifted to an easy-chair for the first time, sitting up about 2 hours. Summer, for this household, was certainly pretty well ruined by that casual slip on the stairs! Naturally I have been kept very busy—having to be on duty most afternoons while the nurse goes out. I was unable to attend the amateur convention in N.Y. July 3, 4, 5—from which a tantalising postcard came bearing the signatures of Belknap, Melmoth the Wandrei, Cook, &c.

However—I had a sort of substitute convention right here just prior to my aunt's return, centreing in the long-heralded visit of Malik Taus, the Peacock Sultan . . . . victim of my famous 25½-hour call in New Orleans last year. Shah Malik blew in unexpectedly on June 30 in his 1928 Ford Juggernaut, & during the ensuing 4 days festivities were plentiful. You were a frequent topic of conversation—Price being an especial admirer of your work. I shewed him my collection of nameless likenesses, & he was tremendously jolted by their stark originality & macabre power. They were a complete surprise to him—& I only wish I had had this recent shipment on hand during his stay. I guess I'll have to lend them to him & to little Bho-Blôk some time. Cook stopped in briefly July 1st. on his way to the convention (seeing my present colonial quarters for the first time), & young Harry Brobst was over twice—on one occasion staying all night for a session of triangular literary & philosophical discussion, punctuated by a trip to an ancient churchyard[3] (known to Poe in the 1840's, & completely hidden from all highways by bank walls & centuried houses) on the hill at about 3 a.m. Of what was seen, whispered, & intoned in that hoary & sinister necropolis it were better not to speak. I *hope* that we left the top slab of the archaic & inscriptionless tomb in the northwest corner *exactly* as we found it. Upon our return we made certain obeisances before the pre-human Thing from the Desert of Rock.

On July 2 Price brought his Juggernaut into the service of antiquarian exploration by taking me to a Rhode-Island region which—despite my life-long residence less than 30 miles from it[, & my ⅓ ancestral] connexion with its ancient families—I had never ([through] lack of public transportation facilities) seen before with the [naked] eye. This was the historic "South County" or "Narragansett Country" west of the bay, where before the Revolution there existed a system of large plantations & black slaves comparable to that of the South. The scenery of this territory is ineffably fine, as I had long realised from reading, though none of the choicest areas can be glimpsed from the main trunk highways. On this occasion we began with the marvellously unspoiled colonial seaport of Wickford, & worked southward through the magical land of yesterday. We saw the rambling old snuff-mill where Gilbert Stuart was born in 1755, & the vast Rowland Robinson mansion (1705) amidst its gigantic centuried willows. Nor did we neglect the abandoned "Glebe" or rectory of the Rev. James MacSparran (1727), now spectrally overgrown with a lush profusion of vines & briers. We climbed a hill to the well-known "Hannah Robinson's Rock" (around which revolves a pathetic story)⁴ & enjoyed what is probably the finest landscape vista in Rhode-Island, if not in all New-England—winding blue river far below, green meadows & woodlands, white headland church in the distance, & the remote gleam of the half-glimpsed sea. But the real climax was the wholly unspoiled colonial village of Kingston—ancient seat of King's [now Washington] County, & virtually unchanged since the days when men in small-clothes & periwigs congregated there for the quarterly assizes. The well-kept, centuried houses, enormous shade-trees, venerable court buildings, & quaint 1746 inn, all remain as of yore to fascinate the beholder. And to think I had never seen this gem of antiquity before! Price is now in Irvington, N.Y.—on the edge of the Sleepy Hollow country—visiting with a friend who conducts a school there.

These various neo-Rosicrucian orders must be rather picturesque . . . . surely no tame & commonplace society would be sending its novices to the madhouse! And that lone, forbidding shanty on the sea-cliff, beneath which branch the nighted burrows of the Gnophs & Gnoles! Nrrrgghhh . . . . I surely hope to see your tale based on that horror.⁵ If I ever had any cash to fling around, I think I'd join one of those nut-circles—for they certainly must treat their suckers to an impressive & literarily usable line of bull!

Hope those threatened quakes didn't materialise. Weather has been variable hereabouts. Some days delightful—up to 94°—but others detestably cool. However, I've had my old oil heater of Brooklyn days repaired (no gas connexion here except for the kitchen range), so that I manage to keep alive through the frigid interludes.

And now the vibration from that Outside angle summons me to the nighted Pso-Rho rite. Have I the key-word for tonight? I *hope* so!

Yrs for the Green Incantation—E'ch-Pi-El.

[*Notes on photograph on enclosed brochure: "Providence County Court House. 1933":*] Building with white belfry is original College Edifice (1770). [/] 66 College St. Note Brown Univ. clock tower above, & adjacent John Hay Library.

Notes

1. CAS dated the letter to Summer 1934; RAS to c. July 1933.

2. HPL refers to Ione Weber, an attorney who specifically focused on extracting money owed to authors by magazines edited by Hugo Gernsback.

3. I.e., at St. John's Episcopal Church at 275 North Main Street. The churchyard is mentioned in "The Shunned House" (1924) and "The Messenger" (1929). It was there that HPL wrote "In a Sequester'd Providence Churchyard Where Once Poe Walk'd" (1936).

4. Hannah Robinson (1746–1773) liked to gaze out at Narragansett Bay from a large boulder at Tower Hill Road in South Kingston, RI. She had eloped with her teacher, Peter Simon, whom her father had forbidden her to see, and they reconciled over the matter only after Hannah had become deathly ill.

5. "The House of Haon-Dor."

[223] [ANS; *HK*][1]

[Postmarked Onset, Mass.,
25 July 1933]

Ave, Grand-Seneschal of Averoigne! Spending 2½ days with the young High-Priest of Chaugnar near the sinister sand-eikons of Cape Cod. Back Wednesday. Aunt had half of cast off Friday night, & may be up on crutches by end of week. ¶ Your gifted & agreeable emissary, Hlensu-Li, Priestess of Hyperborea, passed onward to Gloucester Friday morning, after having apparently enjoyed the antiquities of Prov. & Newport. She seems to have created a devastating havock amongst Manhattan's susceptible gallants—I am trying to keep this young rascal Belknap from fighting a duel with Wandrei! ¶ News from the professional front—Wright has just paid Price *half* of what is due him for "The Return of Balkis." ¶ Yrs in the name of the Unutterable Thing—Ech-Pi-El

---

Hail, O Klarkash-Ton! We are having a most enjoyable confab on sea-splendid Cape Cod. I shall write at length when I return to Babylon. I thought Helen Sully utterly charming. The Man from Genoa

---

Belknap is appreciatively reading your Colossus of Ylourgne.

Notes

1. *Front:* Unidentified.

[224]   [ANS]¹

[Postmarked Providence, R.I.
1 August 1933]

Behold a meeting of two Cowled Heads, representing the Covens of N'yog & Leng-Tcho! We have feasted on the Nameless Objects, & are about to invoke That which broods in the Abyss. Incidentally, my learned colleague greatly admires "Euvoran" & the rest of the new brochure. ¶ Thine in the Corpse-Grey Rite—E'ch-Pi-El.

Many thanks for your kind letters. The tales arrived safely and are worth many times over their modest price.

J. F. M.

Notes

1. *Front:* A Shady Walk, Roger Williams Park, Providence, R.I.

[225]   [ANS]

[Postmarked Auburn, Cal.,
10 August 1933]

Dear Éch-Pi-El:

This view of Auburn may interest you. Averaud's mansion¹ is indicated among trees just below vertical arrow in middle background. The slope at extreme upper right is beginning of hill on which I live. House of the fair priestess of Hyperborea is in portion of town (not shown) on extreme left. Yrs/, under the seal of Thasaidon,²

Klarkash-Ton

[*On front:*] Mansion of the Evil Devotee / Old Winery / Hill about the Shrine of Tsathoggua.

Notes

1. The setting for "The Devotee of Evil."

2. Thasaidon is Lord of the Underworld in CAS's Zothique cycle. CAS wrote extracts from "Ludar's Litany to Thasaidon" for "The Death of Ilalotha" and "The Garden of Adompha." Letter 232 contains an extract from "The Song of Xeethra" (untitled there), written four years before as the epigraph to "The Dark Eidolon."

[226]   [ALS]

Cyclopean Ruins of Shog: Hour
of the Lambint Glow around the
Sealed Door
[Postmarked 15 August 1933]

Dear Klarkash-Ton:—

Glad the R.I. booklet came safely the second time, despite the condition of the envelope. I must be more careful about my choice of containers! Now you know exactly the sort of neighbourhood the temple of Yog-Sothoth is in! No hurry about return—indeed, you can keep the thing permanently if you have any use for it. More of those I sent came back than I had hoped for. Hope your mother will find the contents interesting—it does manage to convey a bit of Rhode-Island's distinctive atmosphere.

And now let me thank you most overflowingly for that splendid new set of drawings! Iä! Shub-Niggurath! Ngrrrhh . . . . . . *That face in black* . . . . . *those eyes* . . . . . God! Young Brobst & my aunt both share my admiration for this batch. One of the pictures affords an especially good example of Klarkash-Tonic vegetation—the poisonous flora of Xiccarph & Ksla-Hgor. It certainly delights me to have my collection augmented by these powerful specimens.

Thanks also for "The Flower-Women"—which I'm glad Satrap Pharnabozus has taken at last. It certainly has an outrè charm of its own, & forms a splendid sequel to the "Maze". Glad that "Ylourgne" is about to be published after all. It ought to be a knockout when it appears. I am now looking forward most eagerly to "Haon-Dor", the fragmentary outline of which is tremendously alluring. "Revenant"—for which I am infinitely grateful—is a significant piece of work recalling the midnight magic of "Ebony & Crystal" & "The Star-Treader". It evokes a black, opiate pageantry of inconceivably vast, ancient, & terrible things. I've just lent it to Galpin—whose opinion will certainly not depart far from my own.

By the way—here's some magazine news which may be old stuff to you, but which I pass along just the same in case you haven't heard it before: *Astounding Stories* is to be revived by Street & Smith (79–89 Seventh Ave., N.Y. City) *as a weird magazine* paying 1¢ per word on acceptance. The editor is one Orlin Tremaine—associate editor, Desmond Hall. Another weird magazine, not yet named,[1] is to be issued by Rogers Terrill, Popular Publications, 205 E. 42 St., N.Y. City. Pays 1¢ per word promptly on publication. Still another weird periodical will emanate from the (not very dependable, says Comte d'Erlette) Jay Publishing Co., 125 West 45th St., N.Y. City.[2] This will pay ½¢ per word—tardily, after publication. I suppose friend Hornig has told you about his new appointment as Managing Editor of *Wonder Stories* (query: does Hugo the Rat pay his staff any sooner than he pays his contributors?), & his consequent transformation of *The Fantasy Fan* to an all-weird magazine. As I said on my card, he has taken a lot of my old stuff. He now wants articles on weird fiction, & has suggested using my history of supernatural horror as a serial. The first issue of the venture looks rather amateurish, but it will doubtless pick up later. Hornig asked me what I thought of Forrest J. Ackerman's silly mouthing—& I told him plenty![3] That little simp Ackerman (a boy about 16) wrote me an insolent letter a year or two ago, expressing his utter loathing & detestation of "The Colour out of Space". As for Hugo the Rat—Belknap & Mrs. Heald seem slow in deciding to attempt collection, but I hope they'll make a try before a fresh bankruptcy is pulled! So *Wonder* is now a bi-monthly . . . . . that means so much less work for the new managing editor! By the way—I'm glad your W.T. advertisement is bringing you sales of "The Double Shadow", & that my circularisation is also working.

I am interested to hear your reaction to the "Silver Key" sequel; which Comte d'Erlette thought very poor, & which didn't send Bnādvāī-Aā exactly into ecstacies. To me its limitations illustrate the fact that I can't write decently in collaboration. Unless my own conceptions have free play, I'm relatively crippled. I removed a good deal of didactic abstractness, but perhaps left too much in. The word "facet", alas, is of my own insertion.[4] I also plead guilty to the Swami—which disguise I chose because a turban & beard form a good way of letting a mask get by undetected. Your alternative suggestion is interesting—but the tale has gone already to King Pharnaces . . . . . . acceptance by whom I scarcely expect. Price—who for a moment held out hopes of a second visit here—is still in Irvington, & intends to winter in Florida instead of New Orleans because of the cheaper living. He finds cheques painfully slow in coming in!

Glad to hear that Miss Sully reports favourably anent her eastern reception—her delightful qualities were certainly appreciated wherever she went. In the matter of glowing accounts Little Belknap could equal young Melmoth any day—"divine" & "exquisite" being among the most temperate of adjectives in his epistolary references! By the way—Belknap certainly means to write you before long. He vastly appreciates "The Colossus of Ylourgne", which I lent him.

I envy you your 108° weather—though I trust the epidemic of rattlers will not prove permanent. It gave me a shudder to think of that fellow creeping so close to the High Altar of Tsathoggua! Thank Eblis you were able to invoke the lethal rite of Ub in time! A chicken slain is bad enough . . . . but an Arch-Wizard & High-Priest . . . . It is curious how the serpent-folk seem to be coming back. In New England the gradual abandonment of farming land & consequent [growth?] of the wilderness has abetted their return.

No doubt you received the joint card from Morton & me. His stay was exceedingly pleasant, & was marked by several trips to ancient & picturesque regions. On one rural walk we discovered an antique well-sweep in active use, & paused at a village where the atmosphere of 1820 lingers picturesquely. We also took the sail to ancient Newport—lingering on the cliffs where in 1730 Dean Berkeley wrote his famous "Alciphron; or, The Minute Philosopher". ¶ My aunt's cast is off, but she has not yet tried her crutches to any extent. I am still tied up as nurse's substitute, & will probably have to decline a very tempting invitation [to a farmhouse in New Hampshire].

    Yrs for the Dissolving of the Inner Gate—E'ch-Pi-El

[P.S. on envelope] Your card just recd. I envy you the average of 97°! The nights have been getting devilish cold hereabouts—though for the past 2 days summer has been staging a comeback. However—on the whole, the present year has been very short on warmth in New England. ¶ Congratulations on Malygris! Wright has his lucid moments! ¶ Glad honest old Lumley has ordered a booklet. He is an ineffably quaint character if you get him going! ¶ Hope King Kull will not find Silver Key sequel too tame & civilised. ¶ We shall certainly have to issue a five-foot shelf of horrific source-books—Necronomicon, Eibon, Unaussprechlichen Kulten, Pnakotic MSS., &c. &.—in a uniform binding of ghoul-skin stamped with shoggoth-ichor! ¶ Glad the plague of serpents is abating. Possibly you wove a spell sending them back to the dank fens of Averoigne.

    ¶ Yrs for the alien-angled Eikon

        —E'ch-Pi-El

[P.P.S. on front:] View of Auburn just recd. Infinite thanks! The scene comes out very vividly. What is the attractive domed building. County court-house? The rolling country gives the village a delightful setting. Too bad the Shrine of Tsathoggua could not fall within the radius of the view!

Notes

1. I.e., *Dime Mystery Magazine*.

2. The magazine never appeared.

3. Published in "The Boiling Point"; see Appendix.

4. In "Through the Gates of the Silver Key," HPL refers several times to the "Carter-facet"—"a Randolph Carter of Boston—the fragment or facet of an earthly entity beyond the Ultimate Gate."

[227]   [ANS][1]

                    [Postmarked Auburn, Cal.,

                        17 August 1933]

Dear Éch-Pi-El:

        You should have been here on Monday last—the mercury notched itself at 109°, and the wind was like the breath of a forest fire.

    Hornig writes me that Gernsback has just made him managing editor of *Wonder Stories!!**!!!*

              Klarkash-Ton

Notes

1. *Front:* Unidentified.

[228]   [ANS][1]

[Postmarked Auburn, Cal.,
21 August 1933]

Dear Éch-Pi-El: Yr letter received, and will write soon. This is another view of Auburn, looking east from the grounds of the County courthouse—the domed building in first view that I sent.

The seventh adjuration of Yig seems to [have] taken effect against the serpent people.

Yrs,
Klarkash-Ton

Notes

1. *Front:* Unidentified.

[229]   [ANS; *HK*][1]

[Postmarked Providence, R.I.,
26 August 1933]

Thanks for the additional view of Auburn—it seems to be a delightful place—not only scenically attractive, but neat & well-kept. To reciprocate— here is a view of a scene less than 100 yards from 66 College St.—you'll recognise the clock tower (visible from my aunt's bedroom window, & forming the master reference timepiece of this household) from the frontispiece of that booklet. John Hay, when in college, roomed in the long brick building on the extreme left. The classic pillared building—Manning Hall—was built in 1830. The belfried building fragmentarily seen is the old college edifice of 1770—now called University Hall. ¶ Have finished the new tale—"The Thing on the Doorstep"—but can't decide whether it's any good or not. ¶ Brobst just borrowed my portfolio of Klarkash-Tonic drawings to show to his friends at the hospital. ¶ Re-read your booklet the other day, & was impressed anew by the power & beauty of the contents. "The Willow Landscape" is really one of the most utterly graceful prose-poems I have ever seen! ¶ With nine potent exorcisms of Yig—Yrs for the Goat with a Thousand Young. Ech-Pi-El.

Notes

1. *Front:* [Brown University Campus?].

[230]   [ANS][1]

[Postmarked Auburn, Cal.,
28 August 1933]

Dear Éch-Pi-El:

I shall write soon. I am doing the *IX Chapter of Eibon*[2] at present—a start on that much-requested cycle of occult elder lore! Have also written *The Witchcraft of Ulua* and *The Tomb Spawn*, tales of Zothique. The End joineth the Beginning! Yrs ever,

Klarkash-Ton

Notes

1. *Front:* Unidentified.
2. CAS refers to "The Coming of the White Worm," subtitled "Chapter IX of the Book of Eibon."

[231]   [ANS][1]

[Postmarked Auburn, Cal.,
29 August 1933]

Dear Éch-Pi-El: Thanks for card. Hornig writes me that Gernsback really is in a hole and is anxious to pay authors. Well, I hope the last item is true. Our weather has gone autumnal; a grey sky of smoke and fog, with mercury falling to 54° or 56° at sunrise, and the sun burning dimly at noon.

Will write at length in a day or so.

Yrs,   Klarkash-Ton

Notes

1. *Front:* Unidentified.

[232]   [TLS, JHL]

From that dome in the floating ice-mountain
Yikilth, where the White Worm, Rlim Shaikorth, weeps eternally from his eyeless
orbits those eye-like globules of blood-
coloured matter that form purple stalagmites
as they fall.
[c. 1 September 1933]

Dear Éch-Pi-El:

Thanks for the view of Hope College,[1] which gives a very pleasant idea of your neighbourhood. I wish I could see it all, and know that I would be highly sensitive to the antiquarian atmosphere. You are fortunate to reside in a vicinity so congenial. I trust it will never be desecrated by the inroads of modernism.

Helen, whom I have seen twice since her return, has given me glowing accounts of her trip, and especially of the parts played in it by you and the other members of the "gang." It makes me more anxious than ever—if possible—to come east and meet all of you. I cannot thank you too much or often for your kindness to Helen. She seems to have been overwhelmingly impressed by the superiority of Eastern people in general to the Californians; and I do not doubt that her impression is correct. Out here, we have been afflicted by the riff-raff of America—as well as of several other continents.

I am indeed pleased to know that the pamphlet holds up on re-reading. Quite a number of people have expressed a preference for The Willow Landscape—among them, readers who do not care for the weird.

The title of your new tale, The Thing on the Door-Step, [*sic*] is most alluring, and I hope that you will decide to show it to appreciative readers. I am sure that your doubts concerning the merits of the story are unfounded. I'd like to see you write a number of new tales. Hope that Knopf will have enough sense to recognize a literary classic when he sees it.[2]

By the way, I saw Loveman's well deserved encomium on your work in the last Dauber & Pine catalogue.[3] Incidentally, I blew myself for the Collected Ghost Stories of M. R. James—a bargain if there ever was one. Half of the tales were new to me, and I received bonafide shudders from most of them. J. certainly can devise the most appalling specters—that thing with "cobwebs over its eyes" in The Tractate Middoth, for instance. And The Diary of Mr. Poynter is (pardon my French) one of the damdest things I have ever read. I have promised Hornig to do a brief note on James for TFF.[4] Your monograph on Supernatural Horror will form a great serial for that publication. And I am delighted to know that Hornig will use your unpublished stories. The next number ought to be a marked improvement on the first.

I have not yet completed the IX Chapter of Eibon, but expect to bring it to some sort of conclusion before long. I have renamed it The Coming of the White Worm. The story takes its text from that saying of the prophet Lith, which no man had understood: "There is One that inhabits the place of utter cold, and One that respireth where none may draw breath. In the days to come He shall issue forth among the isles and cities of men, and shall bring with Him as a white doom the wind that slumbereth in His dwelling."

Wright rejected The Witchcraft of Ulua as being too much of "a sex story." Ye gods—when you consider the current cover of the magazine![5] Well, he may be right; but I was aiming mainly at weirdness; and whatever erotic imagery the tale contained was intended to be subordinate to its macabre qualities. Mere bawdiness is a bore, as far as I am concerned.

Wandrei seems to have made a good start with the revived Astounding. He tells me that they want "realistic characters" and a subordinate scientific ground—as well as good writing. This makes it sound a bit unlikely for me; but there is no harm in trying. Anyway, I could probably hit their requirements more easily than those of Dime Mystery, which I suspect is a pretty cheap and lurid affair.

Derleth has sent me the ms. of Evening in Spring. It really makes a very impressive book, with a collective impression of much power and beauty. I am sorry that Helen could not have met Derleth; but Sauk City was too remote from her schedule as planned. She did meet Wright. Also, she saw the Fair at Chicago, and was unfavourably impressed by it.[6]

Thanks for your good opinion of The Flower-Women and the new batch of drawings. Robert Bloch, by the way, has just sent me a rather powerful crayon drawing called Dine and Dance.[7] The diabolism in it is really startling. The boy certainly has promise.

Too bad that Wright turned down the Silver Key sequel. I was pleased to note in the Eyrie that The Dreams in the Witch House had received its proper recognition from readers. Howard certainly leads all comers in the September W. T. Cave's tale is quite good, too. I think that my new version of A Vintage from Atlantis is better written and more poetic than the one you saw.

By the way, did I ever send you the heading I wrote for The Dark Eidolon? I quote it here:

> Thasaidon, lord of seven hells
> Wherein the single serpent dwells
> With volumes drawn from pit to pit
> Through fire and darkness infinite—
> Thasaidon, sun of nether skies,
> Thine ancient evil never dies:
> For aye thy somber fulgours flame
> On sunken worlds that have no name;
> Man's heart enthrones thee, still supreme,
> Though the false sorcerers blaspheme.

With the composition of two more tales, The Madness of Chronomage[8] and Xeethra, I shall have enough stories of Zothique for a volume. Nothing remains except to find a publisher—which, methinks, will be a contract!

Yours for the descent of the Serpent-fire.

Klarkash-Ton

Notes

1. At 71 Waterman Street

2. Allan G. Ullman, an editor at Alfred A. Knopf, had asked for samples of HPL's work. He sent two shipments of his stories to Ullman on 3 August (seven) and 16 August (eighteen).

3. In a blurb for M. R. James's *Collected Ghost Stories* (which CAS purchased from D&P).

4. "The Weird Works of M. R. James."

5. CAS alludes to Margaret Brundage's cover for *WT* (September 1933) illustrating "The Slithering Shadow" by Robert E. Howard.

6. The 1933 World's Fair in Chicago, which opened 27 May, was billed as the Century of Progress Exhibition. HPL parodically referred to it as the "Century of Misdirected Effort" and similar parodic names.

7. Still extant at JHL.

8. See *BB* 9: "A king who beholds a vision not shared by others, and passes into the vision in his hour of need."

[233]   [ANS][1]

[Postmarked Quebec, Canada,
3 September 1933]

Greetings from an Hyperborean Averoigne, O Hierophant of Tsathoggua! My aunt gave me a birthday present of a week's emancipation from nursing responsibilities—by getting others to come in afternoons—& I have hastened to utilise my freedom in snatching at least one real trip from the brief & waning summer! Good old Quebec! There's no place like it! Absolutely a segment of the living past despite all the drawbacks of a slight antiquarian self-consciousness. Delightful hot weather so far—I'm revelling in the glamour of the centuries at its best! Stopped to see Cook briefly in Boston. May try to see Salem & Marblehead on the return trip. Home Thursday. ¶ R. F. Searight of "Brain in the Jar" fame has looked me up & wants me to help in his work. I doubt if I can—he inclines toward scientifiction—but have recommended that he write you on the subject. ¶ I'm now seated on the ancient city ramparts of Quebec—almost light-headed with the mediaeval unreality of the scene! Yrs for the Elder Sign
Ech-Pi-El

Notes

1. *Front:* View from Parliament Buildings, Quebec, Canada.

[234]   [ALS, JHL]

Abandoned Church of St. Toad in
the Crumbling Slums of ancient Yothby.
Hour of the Scratching within the Sealed
Spire.
[Postmarked 11 September 1933]

Dear Klarkash-Ton:—

Well—it was a great trip, as you have doubtless gathered from my postcards. Enclosed are a few more, which may give a slightly better idea of the sights I saw. I had good weather all 4 days in Quebec, & certainly made the most of it. You would certainly appreciate such a place to the limit, for it has all the atmosphere of mediaevalism proper to the Averoigne cycle. It might well be a new-world edition of Vyones or Ylourgne! Priests & nuns everywhere—& even brown-robed barefoot friars now & then visible. Old grey walls—silvered belfries—constant music of chimes, & of hooves clopping over cobblestones—vistas of red roofs, winding ways, broad blue river far below, vivid verdant countryside, & the far-off purple line of the mystical Laurentians . . . . . It is a dream come to life . . . . a picture into which one may walk bodily, as in "The Willow Landscape" . . . . . I'd like to live there from mid-June to mid-September.

And some of the sights en route were by no means to be despised. Cook was free only evenings, so I put in both Massachusetts days exploring. On the outbound trip I visited Winthrop—a maritime suburb of Boston—& went through the ancient Deane Winthrop house, built in 1637 & one of the oldest structures in America. It is ineffably picturesque, & has a secret room in the massive brick chimney. On the inbound trip I "did" Salem & Marblehead (Arkham & Kingsport) for about the millionth time, revelling in familiar scenes and unearthing one or two points new to me. In Salem there is now a marvellous reproduction of the early huts of the 1626–30 settlement—constructed with extreme accuracy, & with an appropriate landscape setting, in one of the city parks.

In Quebec one of the most striking things is the *sky*—the odd cloud formations peculiar to northern latitudes & unknown in R.I. Mist & vapour assume fantastic & portentous forms, & at sunset on Labour Day I saw one of the most impressive phenomena imaginable from my vantage-point on the Citadel overlooking the river & the Lévis cliffs beyond. The evening was predominantly clear; but some strange refractive quality gave the dying solar rays an abnormal redness, while from the zenith to the southeastern horizon stretched an almost black funnel of churning nimbus clouds—the small end meeting the earth at some inland point beyond Lévis. From a place midway in this cloud-funnel, zigzag streaks of lightning would occasionally dart toward the ground, with faint rumbles of thunder following tardily after. Finally—while the blood-red sun still bathed the river & cliffs & housetops—a pallid fragment of rainbow sprang into sight above the distant Isle d'Orleans, its upper end lost in the great funnel of cloud. I have never seen such a phenomenon before, & doubt if it could occur as far south as Providence. Another striking thing is the almost perpetual mist which hovers about the mountains & valleys near Lake Memphramagog, at the Vermont–Quebec line. With such bizarre skies, I do not wonder that the northern races excel those of the south in fantastic imagination.

This will probably be my sole major outing of 1933, since the summer is fast waning; though I may not be as badly tied up this autumn as I had expected. My aunt is recovering very rapidly now—all over the house on crutches & soon to graduate to a cane—& when the nurse leaves (next Thursday) we shall probably install an electrical device for opening the front door from upstairs; a thing which will make my constant availability less necessary than it would otherwise be. In view of this, I shall probably go to Boston with Loveman next month if he is able to make the New England trip he now plans.

Glad the local view proved interesting. Here is a circular of a new local sightseeing service, which shews that I am not the only person to consider Providence's antiquities worth displaying. I certainly wish you could get around here, for I am positive that the omnipresent vestiges of bygone generations & folk ways would give your imagination a prodigious wallop! I could not contentedly dwell in any atmosphere less traditional, & hope fervently that the occasional inroads of vandalism may not reach far during my few remaining years.

Glad the High-Priestess of Commoriom still thinks kindly of the ancient East despite her subsequent glimpses of the Middle West & of (I believe) British Columbia. As for the relative merits of Easterners & Californians—I hardly think, flattering to local patriotism though it be, that a blanket verdict in favour of the former would stand the test of rigorous analysis. So far as I can see, the really cultivated persons of all sections of the Anglo-Saxon world are just about alike—& it is a fact that I have never yet encountered a Californian who proved other than pleasing. As you may be aware, our friend Malik Taus the Peacock Sultan is—despite the rolling-stone nature of his adult years—a native son of the Golden Gate. If any region has a deeper natural courtesy & kindliness than any other—with these qualities extending to the humbler classes as well as to the cultivated—it is probably the old tidewater South represented by the seaward parts of Virginia & the Carolinas. It is just possible that places like Richmond, Fredericksburg, & Charleston possess a profound & pervasive friendliness not parallelled elsewhere. At the same time, the 'coldness & aloofness' of New England is a sheer myth—as Price particularly remarked when we motored through Rhode Island's old South County & paused at various antiquarian shrines. I found the Middle West—as represented by Cleveland—delightfully hospitable—& it must not be forgotten that Young Melmoth, Loveman, & Kirk represent the Middle West so far as innate temperament goes, despite their present residence in the East. Another region that I found admirably genial & hospitable was the lower Mississippi valley—Vicksburg, Natchez, & New Orleans. I never elsewhere saw such spontaneous hospitality from strangers as Natchez affords.

By the way—Price, Little Belknap, & Morton have just had a very pleasant get-together at Morton's museum in Paterson. This was Sultan Malik's first glimpse of Sonny & Morton, & all three seem to be vastly pleased. The Peacock Lord is now southbound—preparing to winter in Florida.

Anent the booklet—every reader who has expressed an opinion to me seems gratifyingly enthusiastic. Brobst, Morse, Bloch, Dwyer, & many others are included in the chorus of commendation. Every now & then I find a new person to whom to send a circular—the latest being one Richard F. Searight of Detroit, whose "Brain in the Jar" (written in collaboration with one Hammerstrom) you may recall in W T back in 1924. Searight has just resumed writing, & is approaching me on the subject of collaboration—although I don't think there is anything I can do for him just now. His trouble seems to be not so much a lack of technical facility as a general commonplaceness & mediocrity of ideas.

I haven't yet typed my new tale, for I continue to be uncertain about its merit. There is a vast lack somewhere in my fiction, & I keep trying to put my finger on it. For one thing, I handle plots & incidents very awkwardly—to correct which I have lately been engaged in an analytical study of the leading weird classics (Poe, James, Machen, Blackwood, your Double Shadow, Dunsany, de la Mare, &c) with a view to isolating their basic elements of power. I make brief synopses of the basic plot essentials & crucial incidents, collating & comparing in order to estimate relative dramatic values.[1] This regimen may or may not help to increase my command of story elements—at any rate, it is worth trying. Concomitantly, I am trying to keep my revisory programme clear enough to give me some continuous & unhampered time for original efforts. We shall see how all this turns out. No further word from the Knopf bunch—they asked for plenty of time in reaching a verdict. I'll tell you when the inevitable polite turndown comes! Fra Samuelus' puff in the new D & P catalogue is, I fear, more amiable than accurate—though I value it none the less on that account. Good old S L! Your purchase of the James item was surely a wise one—I didn't realise that you hadn't read all of M R J. Had I known, I would have insisted on your borrowing my copies of the separate books which virtually cover the same ground as the collection. James is one of the few *really original* weird authors alive, & I have appreciated him more since beginning my present course of analytical study than I ever did before. His light manner had formerly caused me to underestimate him—though I always appreciated things like "Count Magnus" & "The Treasure of Abbot Thomas." Now that I am pulling his & others' stories to pieces, incident by incident, I can see that James has actual substance where others have only atmosphere. Your article on him in the F F will surely be valuable & well-merited.

As I said on my card, the IXth Book of Eibon excites my tensest expectations. God! I dare not think of the actual horror behind those mercifully obscure words of the prophet Lith! I await the hideous revelation in a perspiring palsy of trepidation—& meanwhile hope that it may achieve suitable magazine placement. Damn Satrap Pharnabozus for rejecting "Ulua"! He certainly is a pip for consistency—to howl about excessive eroticism after deliberately adopting a policy of ha'penny satyr-tickling in his damn cover-designs . . . . a policy which amusingly causes his more subservient writers (not excluding the illustrious Quinn &—at times—even the sanguinary Two-Gun Bob) to go miles out of their way to drag in a costumeless wench! But then—consistency & Brother Farny never were very close associates. I certainly think you can make the revived *Astounding*. Enclosed are the letters (which you might return at your convenience) from Editor Hall describing the venture. If all is as he says in the second & personal letter, this thing ought to be ideally suited to you. Of the *Dime Mystery* one cannot say much without an investigation. I've never seen a copy. Have you looked up that Jay Pub. Co. which Comte d'Erlette mentioned?

Yes—"Evening in Spring" is certainly a tremendously powerful thing. Comte d'Erlette has the makings of a real literary figure in him, & it will be interesting to watch his progress year by year. Too bad your fair emissary couldn't have seen him in order to round out a complete inspection of the gang's representative members! I suggested that he get to Chicago at the proper time, but he couldn't arrange it.

Little Bho-Blôk, the Daemon Lama of Leng, is surely quite a boy! He has just sent me two new pseudo-Clericashtoniana—a nameless semi-crustacean Thing called Yogath, & a black, bat-winged Entity taken from a dream I described to him—both of which shew distinct promise. I can well imagine the macabre power of the "Dine & Dance" drawing you mention. I think that his genius is really more pictorial than literary—though one can't tell. He is making a story out of that dream I related to him. Incidentally—he himself never dreams!

As for the new W T—it certainly beats its predecessor for quality. That lousy August issue almost hit the nadir. Your "Vintage from Atlantis" is extremely potent in its new form, & Two-Gun Bob manages to evoke some of his best subterrane suspense & brooding, archaic horror. Even Single-Plot Hamilton achieves more of a suggestion of novelty & substance than he usually does. Comte d'Erlette, though, is below par. I read the whole issue on the train coming back from Quebec.

Your heading for "The Dark Eidolon"—wholly new to me—is really tremendously powerful. The Zothique tales sound admirably alluring, & I wish you could find a publisher for a book of such. Why not try them on Knopf—addressing the chap (Allan G. Ullman) whom Loveman knows?

Alas, autumn draws nigh. However, I'm still able to do quite a bit of writing in the open—on the ancient river-bank or picturesque Prospect Terrace. I trust the chilly spell in your region has now wholly abated . . . . even if you haven't had any more 108's or 109's. And let us hope that the curse of Yig has ceased to operate! ¶ Yrs for the chanting of the Dark Rhythm—

E'ch-Pi-El

[Enclosure: "Seeing Providence," a bus tour brochure.]

Notes

1. This document, "Weird Story Plots," was first published in 2004 (*CE* 2.153–67).

[235]   [ANS enclosure][1]

This is in Montmorency Park—beside the principal glacis (Mountain Hill) betwixt upper & lower towns. The park & street appear in the foreground of the other view. (Chat. Front. & P.O.) A favourite loafing-place of mine. Site of old cemetery, archbishop's palace, & parliament house—made into a park after the burning of the latter.

Notes

1. *Front:* Guns in Park Overlooking Harbour. Quebec, Canada.

[236]   [ANS][1]

[Postmarked Auburn, Cal.,
14 September 1933]

Dear Éch-Pi-El: Thanks for views of Quebec, and congratulations on your trip! It must have been magnificent... Chap. IX of Eibon not yet released. Of course, I have had to suppress the more frightful portions and unbearable implications and have deleted many hideous details anent *The Coming of the White Worm.* ¶ Have written a four p. note on M. R. James for TFF. One William Crawford of Everett, Pa., writes saying that he plans to start a mag of weird and sc. fiction called *Unusual Stories. [remainder cut off in available photocopy]* Yrs under the Yellow Sign,

Klarkash-Ton

Notes

1. *Front:* Unidentified.

[237]   [ANS][1]

[Postmarked Auburn, Cal.,
16 September 1933]

Dear Éch-Pi-El: Letter and views received. Many thanks! Will write ere long and return Hall's letters.[2] A.S. sounds promising under this regime, and I hope it will live up to its promise. ¶ IX Chapter of Eibon now completely rendered from old French ms. of Gaspard du Nord; who, as you recall, figured in *Ylourgne* ... But, as Eibon himself says, this history of the White Worm's advent is told "with such omissions as are needful for the sparing of mortal weakness and sanity." Even at that the slaying of Rlim Shaikorth and the day long streams of blackness that poured from his cloven bulk, is pretty strong. Yrs, Klarkash-Ton

Notes

1. *Front:* Unidentified.
2. I.e., Desmond Hall.

[238]   [ANS; *HK*]¹

Glad to hear that the supreme horrors have been mercifully withheld from your transcript of the 9th Book of Eibon. Good old Bill is all on edge waiting to see it—he claims that our synthetic daemons are *real* ones, & that unseen powers are inspiring us to write of them under the guise of fiction. A rare old bird is Bill—he was overjoyed at hearing from you. ¶ Eager to see your note on M. R. James. ¶ And so still another unremunerative magazine is to appear! Well—I'll be glad to see it, & will doubtless have plenty to dump on it if it materialises. ¶ The Peacock Sultan (as no doubt he's written you) has suddenly changed his mind about Florida & gone back to New Orleans! Same old address—1416 Josephine St. Long & Morton were greatly captivated by him. ¶ I note with interest the view of your local business section. ¶ A 4-day flood ended yesterday. It cleared off hot, & I had a glorious day in the ancient woods & fields north of the town. Hope to get out again today. ¶ Yrs in the Black League. Ech-Pi-El.

Notes

1. *Front:* [Carlsbad Cavern].

[239]   [TLS, JHL]

Obsidian block befor[e]
the hut of Ezdagor on Mt.
Voormithadreth.
[late September 1933]

Dear Éch-Pi-El:
            Thanks for the picture of the Carlsbad subterranea! It certainly looks like an adytum of that Hyperborean underworld through which the Commoriom magistrate and mighty hunter of Voormis, Ralibar Vooz, hero of my latest yarn,¹ was conducted on an extensive tour by a wizard's familiar in the shape of a night-flying archaeopteryx!
        I read with vast enjoyment and envy your account of the Quebec visit. I can well imagine the likeness to Vyones and Ximes, and wouldn't be surprised to meet the bishop Azédérac or the abbot Hilaire in that Place

d'Armes of which you enclosed so inveigling a view.² I am sure that were-wolves might howl at certain times of the moon in the environs of such a city. The sunset that you describe must indeed have been impressive. The on-ly effect of a remotely cognate sort which I ever saw occurred a year or two ago, and I don't remember mentioning it in my letters to you. In this case, the rose and salmon hues of a vivid sunset were reflected in the east, toward the Sierras, on the upper domes and battlements of a huge mass of blue-black thunder-cumulus, which, from time to time, was riven with forked lightning-bolts. It was magnificent and unforgettable; but there was no accompanying rainbow as in the effect that you saw.

Your visits to Winthrop and to Salem and Marblehead must have been a re-saturation in weird centurial atmosphere, too. Even from the coloured cards, I get an impression of something eerie and ghostly that is inherent in these old houses and landscapes.

I return herewith the letters from Desmond Hall, which certainly sound promising. I have submitted three stories, The Tomb-Spawn, The Witchcraft of Ulua and The Demon of the Flower, but have not received a report on any of them as yet. Yesterday I read the October Astounding, and thought it something of an improvement on the magazine as published by Clayton, though inferior to most of the issues of Strange Tales. The best yarns, like Wandrei's,³ were fair; but several items were so trite and flat as to suggest ei-ther a shortage of passable material, or else poor taste or inexperience on the part of the editors. And certain other tales, though good of their kind, were far from weird or "astounding."

William Crawford, of the proposed Unusual Stories, seemed highly ap-preciative of The White Sybil, which I sent him in response to his request for material. I hope that his project will not foozle in the fashion of Swanson's Galaxy; and ventured to suggest that he write to you.

So far I have failed to get a line on the Jay Pub. Co., mentioned by M. le Comte D'Erlette. I bought the current issue of Dime Mystery, which is no less lurid in appearance than the title would intimate. It is certainly going strong for gruesomeness, coupled with melodrama; and our friend Hugh B. Cave is evident-ly a star contributor. Though the general style of the mag is staccato and rapid-fire, it is possible that they might consider something on the lines of Helman Carnby. Certainly they ought not to cavil on the grounds of too much horror, after printing Cave's yarn about the zombi and the vat of hydrochloric acid!⁴

I hope you will decide to give your friends a peep at The Thing on the Doorstep. I am very anxious to see it, or anything else that you may write. I fail to see anything wrong with your handling of plot and incident, which seems al-ways in keeping with the atmosphere and basic substance. It is an interesting feat of analysis, however, to take the work of others apart and note the mechanics of effect. I feel highly honoured that you should include The Double Shadow among those indubitable classics which you are analyzing!⁵ Of those that you mention, I think I care least for Walter de la Mare; but perhaps I have not read enough of his work. My only criticism, however, is that most of his tales are not weird enough, and that the element of character analysis is too obtrusive for artistic balance. James, on the other hand, I should say, has just enough characterization, and does not let it detract from the main effect. But, no doubt, de la Mare is more interested in human idiosyncrasies than in weirdness.

James certainly repays careful study; and I find myself appreciating him even more than I did when you loaned me A Warning to the Curious and Ghost Stories of an Antiquary. Also, I am very much taken with certain of the more inferential tales, such as Mr. Humphreys and his Inheritance, which seem full of unfathomably baleful suggestion. Tour de forces [*sic*] like The Treasure of Abbot Thomas knock one out at the first reading; and, of course, always retain their power; but the less overt yarns certainly grow on the reader. It is an object lesson in what can be done by skilful adumbration and by veiling more or less the main horror.

The enthusiasm roused by The Double Shadow in select readers is certainly encouraging. Two more of your correspondents, R. F. Searight and Lee White Jr., have recently ordered copies. Lumley is certainly a rara avis, and I wish sincerely that there were more like him in this world of servile conformity to twentieth century skepticism and materialism! More power to such glorious heresy as that which he avows. I, for one, would hardly want the task of disproving his beliefs—even if I could disprove them. I must write him again before long.

I sent my appreciation of James (about 1200 words) to Br. Hornig sometime ago. Nothing very novel or startling about the paper; but it may serve to give an idea of James' style, treatment and salient gifts of evocation to those who are still unfamiliar with his books. Later, when I can get the time, I shall do a brief article on The Philosophy of the Weird Tale. This will not touch on the aesthetics of weirdness, which you have covered amply in your monograph, but will deal with the relation of the w.t. to human destiny and evolution, past, present and future, and, in particular, its implicative bearing on man's attitude to the unknown and the infinite. A hell of an ambitious theme! Lumley—but hardly Forrest J. Ackerman—will be pleased by some of the ideas I intend to broach.

Wright has not yet returned The Coming of the White Worm. I'll look over the carbon; and, unless I decide to hold it for revision, will mail it to you for reading before long. You, in turn, might forward it to Lumley, who can return it to me.

I am now midway in The Seven Geases, another of the Hyperborean series. The demon of irony wants to have a hand in this yarn; but I am trying to achieve horror in some of the episodes even if not in the tout ensemble. It brings in the Voormis, those subhuman anthropophagi who figured in Athammaus; and also the mountain Voormithadreth, an extinct four-coned volcano under which is the abode of Tsathoggua and of many other primordial entities. Ralibar Vooz, hunting Voormis (a popular Commorian sport) upon Voormithadreth, intrudes unwittingly on certain private business of the wizard Ezdagor; and Ezdagor, furious at the interruption, puts a geas[6] on Ralibar Vooz; the geas being that he shall go bare-handed into the caves of the Voormis, and fight his way to the subterranean dwelling of Tsathoggua; where, presenting himself before that sleepy and sluggish deity ("Who rises not from his place even in the ravening of hunger") he was to announce himself as "the blood-offering sent by the sorcerer Ezdagor." This geas was duly accomplished; but Tsathoggua, having dined amply a little previous, merely put another geas on the hero and sent him off to the spider-god, Atlach-Nacha, who was weaving his webs across a Cimmerian gulf which had no other bridges . . . And so it went . . . . till he (Ralibar) came to that blind and formless Thing which dwelt in the lowest depths . . . .

I am glad to know that your aunt's improvement is so marked.

Yours for the resurgence of R'lyeh,

Klarkash-Ton

Notes

1. "The Seven Geases."

2. Vyones and Ximes are cities mentioned in CAS's stories set in Averoigne; Azéderac and Hilare are characters in "The Holiness of Azéderac" and "The End of the Story," respectively.

3. "A Race through Time."

4. Hugh B. Cave, "The Corpse-Maker" (*Dime Mystery Magazine*, November 1933). The issue also contained his "The House of Evil," as by Geoffrey Vace. Cave's "The Graveless Dead" appeared in the October issue.

5. It does not appear that HPL made use of any CAS stories in his "List of Certain Basic Underlying Horrors Effectively Used in Weird Fiction" (*CE* 2.171–73).

6. An obligation or prohibition magically imposed on a person.

[240]   [ANS][1]

[Postmarked Auburn, Cal.,
2 October 1933]

[. . .] Donner was no great climb, but afforded a magnificent prospect!! ¶ IX Chapter of Eibon went forward to you some time ago. Wright has not yet returned the ms—but give him time. Nothing yet from A.S.—they must be digesting the weird material that I sent in at leisure. ¶ I look forward to re-reading your monograph with the new additions, and feel highly honoured that you should have mentioned my tales among the standard items. ¶ The Seven Geases is about finished—a hell of an underworld itinerary! Weather here has gone back to mid-summer warmth, reaching the lower nineties yesterday. Of course, I still have my paraphernalia outdoors. Yrs under the seal of sixtystone, Klarkash-Ton

Notes

1. *Front:* Unidentified.

[241]   [ALS, JHL]

> Primal Basalt Bridge
> over the black & oily River Gnar.
> Time of the Bulbous Shape's passage
> up-stream.
> [3 October 1933/RAS]

Dear Klarkash-Ton:—

Well—just to lead off with a bit of melancholy—the enclosed note from Knopf's (which please return) marks the amply expected bursting of the latest book bubble. I knew damn well the whole business was a farce like the Putnam & Vanguard fiascos—yet when Ullman requested the MSS. I hated to leave any stone unturned.[1] Well—my only loss is the postage one way . . . . . . though I feel tempted to address these publishing birds in the words of the proletarian folk-ballad of 15 or so years ago—"Whaddya wanna make them eyes at me for, ef they don' mean wot they say?"[2] As for Desmond Hall—for all the lofty aesthetic tone of his second letter, I fear his revived *Astounding* will prove merely another rubber-stamp mediocrity. I found little of interest in the October number—even Young Melmoth's ingenious opus[3] being (as said Melmoth had indeed forewarned me) quite patently a pot-boiler. Some of the items—such as the opening one—are positively pedicular. Everything follows the thin, atmosphereless, unsatisfying pattern of conventional pulpdom—machine-made & lifeless. I doubt very much if *Astounding* would ever form much of a market for me, though with your adaptability you might gain an entreé—as you did to *Strange Tales*. Hall recently rejected a tale of Belknap's. Incidentally—both Belknap & Melmoth are in personal touch with Hall, whom they depict as a very likeable fellow of about 27. He attended one of the meetings of the gang at Wandrei's a fortnight ago, & produced a very favourable impression. I have not seen *Dime Mystery*, but must look it up—not that I think I could ever sell anything to it. Cave is a thorough pulp-philistine, though he does produce excellent bits (like that nigger story) now & then.[4] He dwells in Pawtucket, R.I.—on Providence's northern border—but I have never met him. Probably my remarks on pulpdom & hack work, made during a brief correspondence last year, convinced him that I am a crabbed, pompous old bigot not worth looking up! Comte d'Erlette is unable to amplify his information regarding the Jay Pub Co.—which he derived from some authors' magazine. He thinks, however, that its product will be more or less like the unlamented Macfadden–Hersey *Ghost Stories* in the nature of its demands—a circumstance which eliminates me! I shall await the outcome of the Crawford venture with interest—& will be glad if it offers a haven, even though unremunerative, for despised & rejected MSS. Let us hope that neither this nor the F F will evaporate in the manner of Swanson's ill-starred venture. I note, by the way, that Hornig is using you & me as drawing cards for his enterprise . . . . in his W.T. advertisement.[5] He says he will begin reprinting my weird fiction history in his October issue—hope his paper lasts long enough to finish it![6] I am very anxious to see your article on James, as well as your future essay on the philosophy of the weird tale. Much could be made of this latter theme—& surely you are the very one to do it maximum justice! If the F F keeps true to its latest-announced policy, it is likely to elicit a vast amount of unique & valuable material.

I welcomed "The White Worm" when it reached me, & will forward it conscientiously in the directions indicated. I've given Lumley Comte d'Erlette's address in case he doesn't know it already. Nggrrrhh . . . what a revelation! Thank God you spared your readers the worst & most paralysing hints—such as the secret of Yilkith's origin, the reason why it bore certain shapes not of this planet, & the history of Rlim Shaikorth before he oozed down to the solar system & the earth through the void from ——————— . . . . but *I* must not utter that name at which you, & Gaspard du Nord, & Eibon himself grew silent! Altogether, this is a stupendous fragment of primal horror & cosmic suggestion; & I shall call down the curses of Azathoth Itself if that ass Pharnabozus does not print it. Good old Lumley will devour it avidly & with real appreciation. He is surely an unique survival from the earth's mystical childhood—a combination of priceless credulity & gorgeous Munchausenism. I think I've told you about his claims of extensive travel in China, Nepal, & all sorts of mysterious & forbidden places, & his air of familiarity with such works as the arcana of Paracelsus, Hermes Trismegistus, Albertus Magnus, Apollonius of Tyana, Eibon, von Junzt, & Abdul Alhazred. He says he has witnessed monstrous rites in deserted cities, has slept in pre-human ruins & awaked 20 years older, has seen strange elemental spirits in all lands (including Buffalo, N.Y.—where he frequently visits a haunted valley & sees a white, misty Presence), has written & collaborated on powerful dramas, has conversed with incredibly wise & monstrously ancient wizards in remote Asiatic fortresses (one of them, referred to as The Oriental Ancient, was in Buffalo last year & had several solemn conclaves with Bill, but has now returned to his own far-off demesne at the edge of the world!), & not long ago had sent him from India for perusal a palaeogean & terrible book in an unknown tongue (unknown & primordial tongues are as easy to Bill as high-school Latin to you & me!) which he could not open without certain ceremonies of purification, including the donning of a white robe! He has, of course, suffered persecution & ridicule, but nothing can swerve him from his devotion to the secret & soul-shattering lore of the nether cosmic gulfs! His own sorceries, I judge, are of a somewhat modest kind; though he has had very strange &

marvellous results from clay images & from certain cryptical incantations. He is firmly convinced that all our gang—you, Two-Gun Bob, Sonny Belknap, Grandpa E'ch-Pi-El, & the rest—are genuine agents of unseen Powers in distributing hints too dark & profound for human conception or comprehension. We may *think* we're writing fiction, & may even (absurd thought!) disbelieve what we write, but at bottom we are telling the truth in spite of ourselves—serving unwittingly as mouthpieces of Tsathoggua, Crom, Cthulhu, & other pleasant Outside gentry. Indeed—Bill tells me that he has fully identified my Cthulhu & Nyarlathotep .... so that he can tell me more about 'em than I know myself! With a little encouragement, good old Bill would unfold limitless chronicles from beyond the border—but I like the old boy so well that I never make fun of him. He is really tremendously likeable—& with a spontaneous gratitude & generosity that are almost pathetic. Whenever I can do him a favour I like to—such as revising his occasional bits of verse. In turn, he has given me two highly welcome books—a Vathek with Mahlon Blaine's illustrations, & Edward Lucas White's "Lukundoo." His reading has really—apart from all romanticised claims—been unusually wide, & his taste in weird literature is emphatically & unmistakably good. Old Bill may be a character, but he's no fool—not by a long shot! You are one of his idols, & "The Double Shadow" will without doubt form a high spot in his library—along with Geber,[7] Pythagoras, & the Pnakotic Manuscripts.

As for my "Thing on the Doorstep"—you shall certainly see it as soon as it is in readable form, but I dread typing the damned mess until I feel sure that it's worth preserving. In its present pencil-scrawled form I fear that no one but myself could decipher it. My analytical-educational reading continues, & I hope the results may shew when I start on another writing streak . . . . . if I ever do. Another thing I'm doing is to send for a patent plot-concocting device (see enclosure)[8]—not that I think it could *directly* give any seriously helpful result, but that I fancy it might indirectly help by implanting certain laws of plot & incident on my subconscious mind. By the way—I've just had a letter from one F. Lee Baldwin of Asotin, Wash., who wants to publish my "Colour Out of Space" as a separate booklet. Nothing could please me more—for that is my favourite among my own tales—but I imagine something will come up to defeat the project. Another new correspondent is one H. Koenig of New York, who says he has been in touch with you & admires your work tremendously. He has a really notable collection of rare weird books—"Malleus Maleficarum" & things like that—& has with surprising generosity offered to lend me any of them. His original inquiry was the now familiar one—as to actuality of the Necronomicon & kindred horrors.

About de la Mare—I agree that *most* of his stuff is too subtle, whimsical, & humanity-riddled to form vital weird literature, & have indeed removed my commendation of his "Out of the Deep" from the new F F version of my historical sketch. However—the fact remains that he *now & then* pulls a

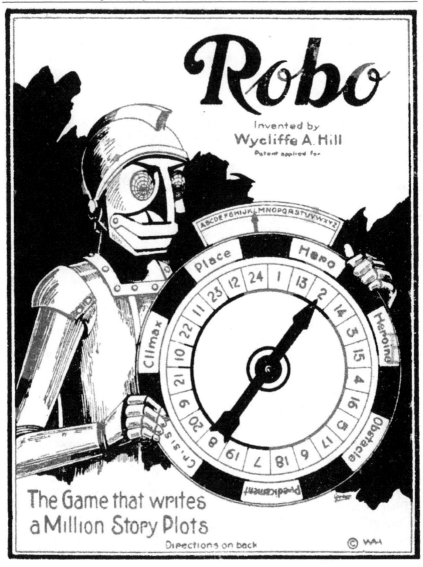

veritable masterpiece in which the subtlety all serves the right end, & which as a whole takes rank with the best of Machen & James. Such triumphs are "Seaton's Aunt", "Mr. Kempe", "All-Hallows", & "A Recluse". He is not, of course, primarily an out & out weirdist—so that I never grouped him with the living "Big Four"—Blackwood, Machen, Dunsany, & James. James undoubtedly grows on one. As you say, some of his less *direct* tales often produce the most potent effects of strangeness in the long run—through their oblique references to monstrous abnormalities about which the reader can imagine what he pleas-

es. "Mr. Humphreys' Inheritance" is certainly packed with this dark sugges-
tiveness—the late uncle's fear of the maze & burning of his ancestor's papers;
the unlabelled book with the sinister Parable which could never be found
again; the alternate ease & difficulty in reaching the maze's centre; the figures
on the metal globe; the globe's thermal properties; the incident of the Irish
yew; the purport of the lettered blocks; the bats (or something else) at the
windows; the bottomless gulf in the paper plan, & that which began to crawl
out of it; the suggestion of ashes in the broken globe . . . . All this calls
up nameless vistas which are the more hideous for their lack of definite outlines. I wish I had added an analysis of this tale to my article—though I fancy
your own appreciation of James may contain some adequate reference.

What you reveal of "The Seven Geases" arouses my most expectant interest—especially the delineation of Tsathoggua's actual lair beneath the hellish
mountain. I hesitate to think of what befel Ralibar Vooz after his encounter
with the blind, amorphous Thing in the lowest depths! By the way—I had a hell
of a dream lately, which so impressed our young friend Bho-Blôk that he's going to write a story about it. I seemed to be clambering over the steep tiled
roofs of ancient gabled houses in a mediaeval town by full moonlight, in company with some 15 or 20 other men under the direction of a young officer in a
silken robe who shouted orders from the ground—where he sat on a great
black horse. We were all in a costume which could not have been later than the
15th century—hose, tight jacket, round-cut hair, & peaked cap with feather. We
were hunting desperately for some Thing of primal evil which was infesting the
town, & against which all exorcisms had proved vain. As weapons we had a
kind of shining metal talisman like an Egyptian ankh—nearly everyone being so
armed. We held our ankhs high up in our right hands, & as far from us as possible. After an endless lapse of time we actually nosed the Thing out & began
closing in on It with our ankhs, of which It was obviously afraid. We, though,
were even more afraid. It was a black, rubbery Thing with bat-wings & a queer
face like an owl's—about the size of a large dog. It began to cheep & titter hell-
ishly when we scrambled closer to encircle It as It crouched against a huge
stack chimney. One man had a great *net* in which he evidently hoped to bag
It. Then suddenly It soared up out of our reach on those evil bat wings which
we had thought merely rudimentary & unusable—& darted dizzyingly toward
the ground. Or rather, toward our leader as he sat on his horse. The officer
gave one great cry—but the Thing was on him. As It touched, It began to *coa-
lesce* hideously with Its victim, so that within a moment there bestrode that
great black horse a nameless hybrid in the robe & cap of our leader, but with
the accursed, owl-like black face of that malign spawn of the pit. At last—as
we paused in a paralysis of fear—It put spurs to Its horse & began galloping
away—turning only once to emit that monstrous titter. Then It was gone—&
I awaked. That was all. Not enough for a story, though I am curious to see
what little Bloch will make of it.[9] By the way—the kid lately shewed me

"Dine & Dance", & I was impressed by its lurking daemoniac quality.

Finished the new W.T. last night, & would say it's about an average is-sue—saved from utter mediocrity of the excellent items of yours & Two-Gun Bob's & Mearle Prout's. This latter is a newcomer, but to me his story seems to have a singularly authentic quality despite certain touches of naivete. It has a certain atmosphere & sense of brooding evil—things which most pulp con-tributions notably lack. Prout will be worth watching if the commercial bug doesn't get him.[10] In "The Pool of the Black One" Two-Gun's manslaughter is a little more varied than usual; while Williamson's interplanetary attempt, though full enough of hokum, escapes many common pitfalls of its genre. Your "Seed from the Sepulchre" is powerful stuff—the punch of the manu-script a year ago is amply upheld by a second reading. Little Belknap's story has great possibilities, but he makes his horror just a bit too scattered & in-volved for maximum power. He admits that this is a thorough pot-boiler. My "Festival" appears for the first time with a correct text, but a reading of it dis-appoints me. It doesn't hold its own with the passage of the years, but today seems crude, awkward, & amateurishly overcoloured. I wrote it just ten years ago—to a month . . . . it being the first tale in which I began to identify "Ark-ham" & "Kingsport" with Salem & Marblehead—which towns, with their sinister huddles of ancient gables, I had seen for the first time in Dec. 1922, & had frequently visited & minutely explored during the intervening months. By the way—the Eyrie contains some interesting misinformation about me from the pen of a youth named Alexander Ostrow, one of amateur journal-ism's latest generation . . . . of whom I've heard, but with whom I've never been in direct touch. Aside from getting my middle name *Philip* instead of *Phillips,* he has me set down as a "Shakespearian authority" . . . . . . which I certainly am not & never was, though I trust I have a proper appreciation of Avon's bard. He furthermore says that he has seen—& possesses—essays of mine on Shakespeare . . . . which is damned interesting in view of the fact that I have never—so far as memory apprises—written a Shakespearian essay in all my long life![11] What the kid is probably doing is getting me mixed up with our gifted & amiable friend *Loveman*—a thing which has been done before in amateurdom. While Samuelus is by no means a Shakespearian specialist, he is (or was up to a decade ago) an arch-Elizabethan, & has written imitations of Shakespeare (you may recall his interpolated Lear & Macbeth scenes) which ring surprisingly true.[12] Ostrow must have come across some of these in old papers, & knowing nothing of S L (whose name has been off the list for years—since long before Ostrow joined), glided over the signature & fastened them on the nearest object with a similar surname. Thus I am saddled with a false reputation in the eyes of Satrap Pharnabozus & his clientele! I shall cor-rect the matter with Sultan Malik, Two-Gun Bob, & all others who count. However, I'm grateful for Master Alexander's flattering opinion of my stuff!

Young Brobst—your especial admirer—is now in Boston, for a year's work at the City Hospital there. I have recommended him to the hospitality of W. Paul Cook—who promises to shew him as much of the ancient town as local vandals have left standing. The devastation of Old Boston in the last two years is positively appalling—whole blocks of ancient brick houses & tangles of ancient alleys ripped ruthlessly down to make way for new streets, parking places, filling stations, factories, & other appurtenances of overspeeded & mechanised modernity. I'll never forget how exasperated I was when I started to shew young Melmoth the sinister "Pickman's Model" region in the North End & found nothing but a sun-drenched desert of gaping foundation-walls!

But at least something is left of old Quebec. That's one place where Bishop Azederac & Abbot Hilaire—& even Gaspard du Nord himself—would find themselves thoroughly at home! As for werewolves—they *are* a leading superstition amongst the Canadian French, hence I doubt not but that their baying has been affrightedly listened for at the massive city gates of the ancient capital. *Loup-garou* is a word calculated to blanch the cheek of any simple *habitant* along the St. Lawrence. As coincidence would have it, I thought quite a bit about werewolves as I sat in the Governors' Gardens in Quebec reading the N.Y. Sunday Times, for the leading picture in the magazine section (really a mere political cartoon attacking the Nazis) was a tremendously malign thing representing a wolf-pack racing down the street of an old European town for all the world like Quebec.[13] I can't resist enclosing it—subject to return at your convenience. The resemblance of the street scene to Quebec—especially the narrow, ancient byways on Ste. Famille Hill—is uncanny, whilst the whole thing makes me think of the climax of my old rhymed "Psychopompos." As for atmospheric effects—you may have phenomena quite as impressive as any in the north, since the proximity of mountains always plays tricks with vapour. That thunderous sunset must have been a memorable sight indeed.

But for the darkly, bleakly sinister, commend me to Salem & Marblehead—Arkham & Kingsport—with their peaked, overhanging 17th century houses! Those old gabled houses certainly carry a spectral imputation nowhere else obtainable—& when we realise that they actually witnessed the witchcraft of 1692, the impression is heightened. I have never found any reason to retreat from my original 1922 enthusiasm for these places. Even a *reproduced* 17th century house has a bit of the macabre quality—at least, if the reproduction is accurate.

Last Saturday a friend took my aunt & me on a motor ride down the east shore of the bay to ancient *Wickford*—the first of the unspoiled colonial [*sic*] towns which Price & I nosed out last July. It was a glorious trip—warm, sunny weather—& formed my aunt's first outing since her accident. She gets out into the garden now, though, & walks across to the adjacent boarding-house for her meals. Sunday we took quite a stroll in the college grounds—the patient using only a cane. Pretty good progress.

Weather still permits a few open-air reading & writing sessions. The leaves will be turning, encouraging woodland trips. Still uncertain about any longer voyages—Boston or N Y—this autumn.

Yrs for the 7th Rune of Eibon———E'ch-Pi-El

P.S. Yesterday Providence had the largest parade in its history—70,000 marching, with bands, floats, & other accessories. In honour of the N R A.[14] The citizenry made quite a carnival of it, but I didn't pause for much of a look. Continuous marching from 2 to 11 p.m.—new divisions assembled as old ones disbanded.

[P.P.S. on postcard enclosure addressed to HPL for "Robo: The Game that writes a Million Story Plots":] I'm going to be sucker enough to send for this, to see if it can help me supply my stuff with the plot element of whose absence so many complain.

Notes

1. Allan G. Ullman of Knopf declined to publish a collection of HPL's stories after *WT* stated that it could not guarantee selling 1000 copies of the book through the magazine.

2. "What Do You Want to Make Those Eyes at Me For (If They Don't Mean What They Say!)" (1916), words and music by Joe McCarthy, Howard Johnson, and Jimmie Monaco.

3. "A Race through Time."

4. Hugh B. Cave, "Dead Man's Belt" (*WT,* May 1933).

5. "CLARK ASHTON SMITH & H. P. LOVECRAFT contribute weird stories to "The Fantasy Fan"—the magazine for readers of weird fiction. Dollar a year—10¢ a copy. Subscribe now! The Fantasy Fan, 137 W. Grand, Elizabeth, N. J." *WT* 22, No. 4 (October 1933): 527.

6. It did not. The magazine folded in February 1935, with the serialization having proceeded only to the middle of Ch. 8 (out of 10).

7. Geber (fl. 14th c.) is the otherwise unknown author of several alchemical works. In *The Case of Charles Dexter Ward* HPL cites a work by Geber entitled *Liber Investigationis.* There does not appear to be a work of this exact title; HPL is probably referring to *De Investigationis Perfecti Magisterii,* one of the books contained in *De Alchimia Libri Tres* (1531).

8. The image is from the postcard HPL had received for the plot robot.

9. In letter 254 HPL notes that Bloch wrote a story based on this dream and published it in his high school paper, but the story has not been located. Decades later J. Vernon Shea wrote another story based on the dream, "The Snouted Thing" (1979); in Shea's *In Search of Lovecraft* (West Warwick, RI: Necronomicon Press, 1991).

10. Prout (1911–1964) published only four stories, all in *WT.* The story in question ("The House of the Worm") borrowed some phrases from HPL's own tales.

11. Alexander Ostrow in *WT,* October 1933: "Your readers might be interested in knowing that not only is Lovecraft a master of weird fiction, but that he is also an authority on Shakespeare" (Joshi, *Weird Writer* 76).

12. "A Scene for *King Lear*" (*Sprite,* August 1917); "A Scene for *Macbeth*" (*United Amateur,* November 1920). Both reprinted in *Out of the Eternal Night.*

13. Actually, the cartoon (reproduced from *Der Gotz,* Vienna) is on the front page of the *New York Times Book Review,* illustrating William MacDonald's "The Germany Hitler Rules" (a review of Calvin B. Hoover's *Germany Enters the Third Reich*).

14. The National Recovery Administration, the primary New Deal agency established by Franklin D. Roosevelt in 1933. Its goal was to bring industry, labor, and government together to create codes of fair practices and to set prices.

[242] [ANS][1]

[Postmarked Auburn, Cal.,
5 October 1933]

Dear Éch-Pi-El: That relay of news from Wright on your last card was certainly encouraging. Knopf ought to know a good thing when he sees it.

Astounding has taken *The Demon of the Flower.* It is certainly encouraging if they will buy work so out-of-the-way as that yarn, which Wright and Clayton thought too recherche.

Of course, Wright sent back the Eibon chapter. Says he will use it, however, if times ever improve—also the Vathek Episode.

Weather continues warm, seldom falling below 70° even at night. I am rewriting an old tale, *The Disinterment of Venus,* but will start some new work pretty soon.

The Witchcraft of Ulua will come to you from Barlow. You may find it instructive to see what is barred from W. T. on grounds of censorship.[2] Yrs,
Klarkash-Ton

Notes

1. *Front:* Unidentified.
2. Wright accepted the story after CAS removed several objectionable passages.

[243] [ANS][1]

[Postmarked Auburn, Cal.,
10 October 1933]

Dear Éch-Pi-El: Your letter and enclosure rec'd. Have called *every* malediction in *Le Livre d' Eibon* on that philistine jackass, Knopf, and am now about to search the Pnakotic Mss. for new curses.**!!** I am glad that my rendering of IXth chapter was not too rotten. Have done a drawing of Tsathoggua which I'll send in my next letter. Maybe it would help Lumley to identify that evil entity! An Indian neighbour recognized the picture as representing what he called "one of the *Old Boys!*" More anon.

Klarkash-Ton

Notes

1. *Front:* Unidentified.

[244]   [ANS][1]

[Postmarked Providence, R.I.,
10 October 1933]

Recent cards recd. Thanks! That river gorge is exceedingly picturesque—&
the arched bridge adds a truly classic note! By the way—I saw Auburn mentioned in a N.Y. Times article yesterday as feeling the results of revived gold-
mining.[2] ¶ By this time you have my epistle telling of the burst Knopf bubble.
Eheu! ¶ Congratulations on making *Astounding*—I feel sure you can become a
steady contributor. Confound W. for rejecting Eibon chapter—but he may
reconsider. Trust Ar-E'ch-Bei will send Ulua along soon. W.T. censorship is a
queer thing—you'll recall that they at first rejected my "In the Vault" as "too
horrible"! ¶ Glad "The Festival" stands up on re-reading—I myself find it
rather crude & overdone after a decade. ¶ Heard from Crawford, but I doubt
he'll care for any of my stuff. He seems to want science fiction only. I've told
him about the Mts. of Madness—which is, in a way, 'scientifiction', although
much longer than he'd probably be able to use. I envy you the warm weather—although for 3 days it has been delightful here. I've been out to the
woods & countryside for 3 days in succession, & am going again this afternoon. Autumn foliage is getting vivid. ¶ Young Morse lately wrote of his keen
appreciation of E & C. He thinks the H-E is a veritable classic. ¶ Have just
taken some pictures of 66 College. Will enclose some in my next. ¶ Yrs for
the Purple Transfiguration—E'ch-Pi-El

Notes

1. *Front:* King's Palace. 750 feet below Surface. Carlsbad Cavern, New Mexico.
2. Duncan Aikman, "Again Bret Harte's Hills Stir to Gold," *New York Times* (8 October
1933): 4, 14.

[245]   [TLS/ALS, JHL]

From the room embossed and paved
with demon faces, in the subterrene palace of Haon-Dor.
[mid-October 1933]

Dear Éch-Pi-El:

I return the Ullman–Knopf communication herewith. Knopf
should remove the Borzoi from his imprint, and substitute either the Golden
Calf or a jackass with brazen posteriors. I wish Herr Hitler had him, along
with Gernsback. If I were a practising wizard, like Namirrha or Malygris or
Nathaire,[1] I'd devise a behemothian Sending and dispatch it to his office. The
Sending would include a brace of penanggalans, and about a dozen rokurokubis with jaws elastic as their necks, and a regiment of poltergeists equipped

with sledge-hammers. Callicantzaris and vrykolakes and barguests and Himalayan Snow-Men and Eskimo tupileks and the more unpleasant Aztec gods would form the main body; and a mass formation of shoggoths would bring up the rearguard. After their passing, the Knopf headquarters would be one with the middens of Nineveh.[2]

In return, here is the epistle from Pharnabozus anent The White Worm.[3] Please do not lose it. Of course, I realize that he has to sell the magazine; and readers who would appreciate Eibon are not to be found in every Methodist chapel, synagogue, packing-house or retail grocery. In fact, I fear that they would form a mathematically insignificant portion of the census-list. I am glad you enjoyed the ms., and trust that Lumley will not be disappointed in its revelations.

That picture of the werewolves—even though a cartoon—is infernally good. Here, by the way, is a recent portrait-sketch of our Lord Tsathoggua, which I made for you the other day. My Indian wood-cutter saw it (as I think I mentioned on a card) and said instantly: "That's one of the Old Boys." He then proceeded to narrate a tribal legend about a young squaw who was carried away by some prehuman entity into a cavern. Nearly a year later, the squaw emerged to the light, bringing with her an infant that was half human and half something else.

The Oct. issue of Astounding was pretty tepid to say the least. I hope that succeeding numbers will be put through more of a delousing process. I guess I told you on the card that they had accepted The Demon of the Flower. The Tomb-Spawn was held by them for over a month, but finally came back, together with The Witchcraft of Ulua.

Dime Mystery seems to be going in for what the British would call "shockers." More action and even less atmosphere than in the other magazines. Cave must be running a regular factory, to judge from the amount that he turns out. Crawford's proposed Unusual Stories will be more pseudo-scientific than weird, to judge from his last letter.

The dream you relate was certainly extraordinary, and it will be interesting to see the story that young Bloch makes of it. With a preliminary notion about the depredations of the rubbery bat-thing, and the *uncommon zeal* shown by the young horseman at all times in trying to hunt it down, the dream really needs no alteration or addition to form the skeleton of a weird short. My own recent dreams have been pretty tame; but in the past I have had some that were memorable. One that comes to mind was fraught with all the supernatural horror of antique myth: I was standing somewhere on a bleak, terrible plain, while past me and over me, with appalling demonic speed and paces and voices of thunder, there swept a vast array of cloudy, titanic Shapes. One of these, as it went by, pealed out the sonorous words "Eiton euclarion," which I somehow took to be the name of the cloudy entity or one of its fellows.[4]

One of my most diabolic dreams, however, was of being somewhere in a high tower room with sloping small-paned windows, above a weird exotic city. At first I was alone in this room—and then, with frightful instantaneousness, it was full of malformed children with bloated and distorted faces, who swam upward around me in the air, beating me over the head with the large, curious brazen pans which they carried. Another dream, repeated many times at one period, was that of being breathed upon by a cold wind which swept me before it with all the irresistible force of a solid body, pressing me down into gulfs of ineffably deranged and confused sensation and entity. Still another, much more recent, was of wandering through a strange city together with other people, under a sense of urgent haste and portentous compulsion. It seemed that we must reach a certain goal before an unnamed doom should overtake us in the open streets. But as I went on, I became aware that the atmosphere was *thickening* slowly but steadily and was taking on the character of a liquid.

The coalescence of the bat-thing with the horseman in your dream makes me think indirectly of my little yarn, The Tomb-Spawn. In this a wizard king is buried in a vault under his throne-room together with a strange ultra-stellar monster that had given him advice, dwelling and dying in the vault. Many centuries later, two travellers, lost in the desert and seeking water, come to the ruined city under which the king and the monster are interred. The pavement of the throne-room has broken through into the vault, and the travellers hear in the gloom below a noise like the regurgitation of a fountain. They descend, and are confronted by an unearthly abnormality with two heads, one of them human, and with human feet amid its elephantine pads. From this horror, root-shaped tentacles reach down into an *empty sarcophagus* carven with royal symbols. The withered hands of an old man stretch out toward the intruders from the abnormality, and they flee toward a ruinous door giving on a second vault. Before reaching this door, they enter a zone of deathly, dissolutional force established by the wizardry of the old king to guard the burial crypt. They dissolve in putrid dust, and the resurrected amalgam of man and star-born monster, forgetful of the ancient spell, follows them and turns to ashes.

No, you hadn't told me about Lumley's travels. Perhaps he is an adept and does it via the fourth dimension. Rocket-ships and stratosphere traffic will never improve on *that* mode for getting you somewhere and back without waste time or motion. Seriously, I am tremendously interested and prepossessed in his favour. I hope he will write me at length when he is through with the Eibon Chapter. The two letters I have had from him certainly contained some fascinating hints. I too would be the last person to make fun of any of his ideas. Anyhow, the bare truth about the nature of things may be more fantastic than anything that any of us have yet cooked up. I, for one, find it as hard to swallow the dogmas of the physicists as it is to down those of the ecclesiasts. Mind, for all that I know, may exist as readily without matter as matter seems to exist without mind; or the two may exist together in a million undetected forms. Five senses and three dimensions hardly scratch the hither surface of infinitude. Which doesn't mean that one should emulate the gullibility of Sir Arthur Conan Doyle.

I hope to peruse The Thing on the Door-Step when you get around to typing it. In spite of your disparagement, The Festival holds it[s] place in my affections, and has an imaginative quality that puts it above the new stories in the current W. T. Howard has some fine romantic fantasy in The Pool of the Black Ones; and Long's tale has the makings of more than a pot-boiler. With more concentration on development and detail, it would have been first-rate. I must re-read the story by Merl [*sic*] Prout. I liked the idea and some of the incidents; but certain crudities rather jarred upon me in the hasty perusal which I gave it. My own tale was chiefly conspicuous for certain scientific horror-touches, carefully accumulated; and if the idea of flesh-eating plants weren't so hackneyed it would deserve a higher place.

Later. This triply blasted Underwood seems to have gone blooey all at once, so I am continuing the letter on the old Reliable Remington.

I hope F. Lee Baldwin will carry out his plan of printing The Colour out of Space as a pamphlet. If he does, put me down for at least four copies. I have, by the way, just received a letter from him asking me the cost per copy of The Double Shadow and the cost of the paper used, etc. He was one of the early purchasers of the pamphlet. The net cost of the D. S. to me was $125.00 for a thousand copies, linotyping being the heaviest item of expense on a small edition. It shouldn't cost nearly so much to print a single story like The Colour out of Space.

Wright has accepted The Tomb-Spawn, and has sprung a genuine surprise on me by suggesting that I do an illustration for The Weaver in the Vault, which is scheduled for the Jan. issue! Well, I can try at any rate. Someone has evidently been extolling my drawings around the W. T. office.

I'll loan you The Seven Geases if both Astounding and W. T. should reject it. I have gone on a little with The Chain of Aforgomon, which I began last spring, and plan to finish this and also The House of Haon-Dor before I attempt any new tales. Haon-Dor, by the way, figures in The Seven Geases, and the description of his subterrene palace, with its entrance guarded by a giant rattlesnake, is one of the weirdest passages in that tale. The thing in the ultimate gulf was Abhoth, "father and mother of all cosmic uncleanness," to whom the Archetypes had sent Ralibar Vooz in the gentle hope that Abhoth would mistake him for one of its own progeny and "devour him according to that custom which it followed." Even Abhoth, however, was suspicious of anything so foreign and outlandish as a surface-dweller; and the doom that finally overtook Ralibar Vooz was more or less accidental.

I agree with you that Seaton's Aunt is a fine weird tale—the best in the one volume (The Riddle) by de la Mare that I have read. I have never seen the others that you mention—All-Hallows' Eve, Mr. Kempe, and A Recluse.

I liked The Tree pretty well as a fantasy, too.

I wondered about that letter from Ostrow in the Eyrie—the Shakespearean portion of it, since I couldn't recall seeing or hearing of anything by you on the immortal William. Of course, he must have confused you with Sam Loveman, who seems to have a remarkable feeling for the Elizabethan. I must confess—probably to my shame—that I haven't looked into any of the old dramatists for ages.

Plus tard. This letter was interrupted the other day by a damnable accident that happened to my mother: the overturning of a pot of hot tea, which scalded her left foot badly. I fear she will be laid up for weeks or months. It is most unfortunate and provoking, though I hope less serious than the effects of your aunt's fall.

Your last card received. Yes, there has been an attempt to revive the old gold-mining industry hereabouts. Any number of amateur placer miners on the local streams; and many old quartz ledges and gravel mines have been re-opened. Also, there has been some hydraulicking in the Sierra foothills above Auburn.

The weather continues phenomenally warm and dry. I am writing this in my shirt-sleeves. Have about finished the drawing for The Weaver in the Vault, and hope that Wright will like it. I'll enclose a rough pencil sketch which gives the idea. The pen-drawing, however, has much more detail, as well as a different arrangement.

Yrs for the exaltation of the gods of Zothique,

Klarkash-Ton

Notes

1. Namirrha appears in CAS's "The Dark Eidolon," Malygris in "The Death of Malygris," and Nathaire in "The Colossus of Ylourgne."

2. The *penanggalan* is a variation of the vampire myth that apparently began in the Malay Peninsula. *Rokurokubis* are yōkai found in Japanese folklore. They look like normal human beings by day but at night gain the ability to stretch their necks to great lengths. They can also change their faces to those of terrifying oni (Japanese ogres) to scare mortals. In folklore, *poltergeists* are troublesome spirits or ghosts that haunt a particular person. *Kallikantzari,* malevolent goblins in Greek folk tradition, dwell underground but come to the surface during the twelve days of Christmas, 25 December to 6 January. The *vrykolakas* is a harmful, undead creature in Greek folklore, generally equated with the vampire of the folklore of the neighboring Slavic countries. The *yeti* or abominable snowman is an ape-like cryptid said to inhabit the Himalayan region of Nepal and Tibet. The *tupilaq* is an avenging monster fabricated by a shaman from animal parts (hair, skin, sinew, bone), and even parts taken from the corpses of children. The vivified creature was placed into the sea to seek and destroy a specific enemy. *Shoggoths* are HPL's invention (see *At the Mountains of Madness*). A *midden* is any kind of archaeological feature containing waste products relating to day-to-day human life.

3. Wright rejected this story on 29 September 1933, stating: "It would occupy 11 or 12 pages in *Weird Tales*, and many of our readers, I fear, would object strongly to reading a prose poem as long as this" (*SSL* 231n3).

4. CAS fictionalized the dream, which he had in childhood (*BB* 78), in "The Clouds," retitled "The Primal City." *Eiton euclarion* is CAS's own coinage.

[246]   [ALS]

Daemon-Curst Wood of Yoth—
Hour that the livid, fungous Boughs
Sway against the muttering Wind
[22 October 1933/RAS]

Dear Klarkash-Ton:—

I am tremendously sorry to hear of your mother's accident, & surely hope that the effects will vanish less tardily than she fears. My aunt joins me in sending most understanding sympathy. Any accident that has a crippling & confining effect is twice as exasperating as any other mishap of equal intrinsic seriousness. Incidentally, my aunt is now much better—getting out to lunch each day (in the boarding-house across the rear garden) & abandoning crutches in favour of a single cane. She also takes brief daily walks in the nearby college grounds, & with my assistance has covered greater distances—last week getting half-way down the hill to the Art Museum, where an exquisite formal garden, with pool, paths, benches, trees, & a glamourous statue of the young Pan in a niche has just been laid out in the inner court. (view enclosed) She has also had several motor rides through the vivid autumn scenery—on two of which I went along.

In my individual programme I have also been enjoying the sunlit autumn weather—some days being delightfully warm. On most afternoons I have taken long rural walks—riding out some main highway on a 'bus, & then cutting across country to some other bus-traversed highway on which I can return. In this way I have come upon some very wild stretches—untouched by modernity, & containing many magnificent vistas & innumerable ancient farmhouses. To me nothing on earth is more fascinating than my ancestral countryside with its rolling hills, valleys, brooks, old mills, stone walls, winding roads, gambrel-roofed farmhouses, rambling barns & byres, gnarled orchards on rocky slopes, farmyards now teeming with the varicoloured fruits of harvest-home, & glimpses of distant white steeples through the towering elms of sleepy villages. Ancient New England! And scenes like this (which can still be found by the careful searcher despite mechanisation, foreignisation, & decay) represent a settled, continuous life of three centuries suggesting the picturesque old world rather than the strident new. So many are the byways of this small state, that I have found several alluring regions never before visited by me. Yesterday I looked up an ancestral shrine I had always heard of but never seen—the Thomas Clemence house beyond the village of

Manton, west of Providence; built in 1654 & having an enormous pilastered chimney of stone. I found it fascinating—in excellent condition & very picturesquely situated—though an Italian suburb is creeping closer & closer to it. This afternoon I am north of the town—in the Quinsnicket or Lincoln Woods region which I have haunted all my life. I am seated at the bend of a road, looking off across the descending country-side toward Scott's Pond & the distant village of Saylesville beyond—a vista so idyllic that I cannot resist trying to convey an idea of it on this sheet. Whenever I see a landscape like this—whose beauty can't possibly be captured in words—I could kick myself or the Fates for my inability to draw & paint. Today is one of the last days I'll be able to do any reading or writing outdoors; for the temperature is falling, & I can't steer my finger muscles when it's much under 70°. I certainly envy you the weather which keeps you in shirtsleeves outdoors at this time of year! By the way—that American River gorge on your card of the 10th is tremendously impressive. Hope you'll get some of the gold in those hills for yourself instead of letting outland prospectors tote it all away.

Thanks tremendously for that vivid & veracious portrait of nighted TSATHOGGUA![1] I have sent it—as a short-term loan—to your young admirer Harry Brobst, who has gone to Boston for a year's general hospital experience. This view, I assume, exhibits It as It appears when Its plastic, viscous matter is in normal equilibrium. At other times It has an aspect which the healthy pencil hesitates to set down. Enormous congratulations on that order for a W. in the V. picture! At last! Since 1923 I have been urging W T to utilise your fantastic genius in pictorial embellishment, & now, after a decade, results begin! Probably, though, others have been rooting—Little Bloch or Brobst or young Shea. The pencil sketch seems to me tremendously powerful; & if the ink original is any better, it must be a triumph indeed! By the way—your aboriginal friend's reaction to Tsathoggua was surely impressive! So, unknown to yourself, you have been delineating a Thing infamous in

American as well as Hyperborean folklore! That bears out old Bill Lumley's contention that our fiction is not really fiction, but profound revelation to which we are unconsciously inspired! Or perhaps the Indians have Hyperborean blood, so that the myths of Eibon descend to them veiledly & indirectly. The tales of the Entity begotten upon the captive squaw surely has a dark thrill—do you suppose it's different enough from the homologous incident in Machen's "Black Seal" to found a story on?

Turning to pictures of a somewhat different nature—here are the views of 66 College St. which I mentioned on my postcard. The perspective of the full view is nothing to brag about, but represents the best I could do from the available vantage-point (courtyard of the adjacent college library) with the two-dollar camera (a Brownie #2 bought in *1907*) employed. I have a vest-pocket kodak, but chose the old Brownie because of the size of the picture. My bedroom window is the one above the door. The next two windows on the left are the south windows of my study—which also has two windows on the west. In another view I've tried to get a more artistic effect by using the high marble library wall as a framework. In taking this view I was ass enough to leave the door shut—thus shewing the modern portal which defaces the fine colonial doorway. The third view shews the doorway above—with my aunt in it. Note the fan carving above. Doesn't this suggest my Talman-drawn bookplate? Certainly, Jonckheer Wilfredus was quite a prophet—the plate having been conceived in 1928 & executed in 1929! If you have any sort of a file you're at perfect liberty to keep these snaps. Betwixt them & the booklet-frontispiece shewing the whole neighbourhood, you surely have quite a visual idea of Grandpa E'ch-Pi-El's present environment!

By the way—apropos of our recent mention of odd atmospheric effects, I enclose a cutting of a recent rainbow which was undoubtedly the most impressive thing of the kind I have ever seen. On the evening in question the whole western sky was a seething lake of mysterious orange light, whilst roofs & windows toward the east blazed with celestial gold. I was going home from downtown, facing the ancient precipice atop which I live & admiring (as I have done for a lifetime) the colonial gables & belfries & spires that picturesquely pierce its dense foliage. Suddenly I noticed a great prismatic bow above the centuried eminence, with the white Baptist steeple (1775) almost at its centre. The unparallelled vividness of the arc itself, the antique loveliness of the vista it framed, the apocalyptic glow on the opposite side of the sky, & the presence of a faint secondary arc outside the main one, all combined to make this the most notable rainbow within my memory. After all, one does not have to go to Quebec for all the meteorological wonders! The next-best specimen I ever saw was nearly 30 years ago at the old home—at sunset on April 30 (the hellish Walpurgis-Eve!) 1904. I hustled home & called my aunt's attention to the phenomenon, so that she got quite a view from an easterly window.

I must see both Haon-Dor & the Seven Geases somehow—in print or out. Wright's epistle regarding the White Worm is certainly a classic of its kind. His occasional citation of learned lore—a sort of foil for his lowbrow policy—has a tendency to make me sigh & chuckle at the same time. And his microscopic pedantry is absolutely priceless. He can print a ream of illiterate crap by half a dozen authors, with grammar, orthography, & everything else all shot to hell—& then behold! A minute question like the use of *both* or the comparison of *unique* becomes an issue of moment! I recall when he picked up my deliberate & intended use of *healthy* for *healthful* in the Whisperer—introduced to give the narrative rural colour. I insisted on its retention. By the way—to pull a piece of counter-pedantry, do you notice that Pharnabozus speaks of the Black Book *and* von Junzt's *Unauss. Kulten*?[2] For shame, Farny! As if any schoolboy didn't know that "Black Book" is a colloquial name for von Junzt's hellish tome itself! I return the document as per request. It is surely worth a place in your cabinet of curiosities! Here are two epistles from Brother Crawford which indicate that *Unusual* may not be as purely scientifictional as first reports would indicate. He has taken "Sarnath" & "Celephaïs"—my early Dunsanian stuff. Can you beat it? If this venture pans out, it ought to beat the F.F. In the first place, it will probably look less amateurish. Secondly, instead of asking us to subscribe & then not paying for stuff, it offers a ten-year subscription (there's N R A optimism & confidence for you!) for matter submitted. It is odd, though, (vide enc.) that Crawford doesn't appreciate good old Canevin. And so F. Lee Baldwin has "The Double Shadow"! Damn! I sent him a perfectly good circular unnecessarily! What you say of the cost of the D. S. is indeed interesting. Baldwin probably wants something less *condensed*, since he means to print only one story. He proposes an edition of 200. I've recommended Walter J. Coates (the chap who means to bind & issue The Shunned House) to him as a printer at once reasonable & conscientious. By the way—W. Paul Cook is now with Coates again indefinitely. About 3 weeks ago he got all fed up on Boston, threw up his perfectly good job, & hit the trail for Vermont (a hell of a time of year to do it!). There's a case of nervous capriciousness! Glad Pharnabozus has taken the Tomb-Spawn. By Crom, what a plot! Nggrrrh! . . . . I wish he'd let you illustrate this as well as the Weaver! I'll send the Doorstep as soon as I get it typed. As for the current magazines—did I mention that I read *Dime Mystery*? Cave's yarn was the only one fit to read. *Astounding* is a bitter disappointment, though Hall seems to be extremely pleasant & cultivated. Belknap & Young Melmoth like him tremendously, & he attended a meeting of the gang not long ago. He is, they tell me, about 27, British, & very cultivated. Belknap thinks he has Jewish blood somewhere, because of his impassioned defence of Israel against the attacks of our old anthological friend T. Everett Harré, who by chance showed up at the meeting. But I guess he's no Gernsback! His decisions are apt to be overruled by his superior Orlin Tremaine—who seems to play the Clayton to his Bates. Belknap says that his tastes, while excellent, seem to be realistic—& that he does not appear to be in sympathy with weird literature at all. He seems to have no sensitiveness to the cosmic. That's the hell of it—they always pick the wrong guys to be editors of the weird magazines! I doubt if I'll ever land anything with this bird. He doesn't sound like the sort to take to Yog-Sothoth & the Necronomicon!

I sent for that "plot Robot", but find it is nothing at all I could use in my own work. All it concerns is the purely conventional hack junk—with hero, heroine, obstacle, crisis, & all that. But it may come in handy in revising commercial tripe for dumb clients—certainly, it gives a very forceful idea of the artificial hokum called "plot" & considered an indispensable factor in pulp fiction.

The de la Mare stories "Mr. Kempe" & "All-Hallows" are in the collection entitled *The Connoisseur & Other Stories*. I own it, & will be delighted to lend it to you if it isn't procurable in your vicinity. "A Recluse" is, I think, in the newest de la M. collection, whose title I can't recall.[3] It is also in "The Ghost Book" (1927), edited by Cynthia Asquith—where I read it. De la Mare has a curious ability to build up a delicately disquieting atmosphere, & I wish he would write more tales like "Seaton's Aunt". By the way—I am now reading some of Rev. Montague Summers' stuff, lent me Koenig. Summers is surely a queer case, with an implicit belief in magic, witchcraft, & vampirism. He claims in sober print to have seen a priest levitated in the air whilst performing some sacerdotal function with the "host" . . . . he & old Bill Lumley would get along delightfully together! As for Lumley—give him a little encouragement & you'll have such a tale of exotic travel as you never before had at first-hand. Or rather, you'll have a series of portentous hints. Bill is too deeply impressed with the peril of speaking lightly about profound things to be explicit or continuous in his Mandevillainy, but is a great boy for vague reminiscent allusions—"when I was in China" . . . . or "an ancient priest in a secret monastery in Nepal told me" . . . . or "when I was in the ruins of a pre-human temple in the East" . . . . . & so on. Biobst, from his letters, thinks he's just a bit wobbly in the belfry—but if so, it only adds to his picturesqueness. He may be crazy, but he ain't no fool! And of course he has nothing in common with nuts like the incomparable Olsen.

As for the Lumleys & Summers's of this world versus the Einsteins, Jeans's, de Sitters, Bohrs, & Heisenbergs—I must confess that I am essentially on the side of prose & science! It is true that we can form no conception of ultimate reality, or of the limitless gulfs of cosmic space beyond a trifling radius, but it is also true that we have a fair working estimate of the phenomena within our own small radius. We may not know what—if anything, as is highly unlikely—the phenomena *mean,* but we do know what to expect within the circle of our experience. No matter what the constitution of the larger cosmos is, certain occurrences come inevitably & regularly, whilst other alleged occurrences—stories of which were invented in primitive times to explain unknown things now conclusively explained otherwise—can never be shewn to happen. Moreover, we now understand the psychological & anthropological laws by which myths arise & flourish, & the curious congeries of self-deceptive qualities whereby plausible & persistent folk-tales are built up out of empty air through accretive diffusion. For example—the famous major tricks of the Hindoo fakirs *have never been performed.* They are pure myths—narrators always having heard them from some one else who in turn heard them from some one else. No person ever saw a fakir throw a rope up in the air, having it held mysteriously aloft till a boy shins up out of sight. No person ever saw a boy put in a wicker box & thrust through with swords, later emerging unhurt. No person ever saw a plant grow many feet out of a pot in 5 minutes. All these things are built-up myths, diffused so speciously & cleverly that even to-day a vast number of people never question their existence—seeking instead to explain them by "mass hypnotism" or some other principle consistent with reality. Today we know pretty well how every type of supernatural belief was born & is maintained, & know likewise that there is no reason whatever to accept any of the improbable & (as now seen) unmotivated assumptions involved. The *really* unknown & unreachable things in the cosmos have nothing to do with the arbitrary & anthropologically accounted-for stories perpetrated from ages of ignorant guesswork & personification through the inertial force of tradition. Incidentally—this recent talk of a new mysticism in science is all damned bunk, as is pointed out in an excellent article in the August *Atlantic*—"Science Has Not Gone Mystical", by Henshaw Ward.[4] Eddington is simply a nice old gentleman brought up as a devout Christian & desperately anxious to twist everything possible into a state of reconciliation with the standby of his infancy. Actually, the quantum theory does not in any way restore free will. Instead, it merely points out that there are certain intra-atomic reactions in which, despite apparent identical antecedents, *we cannot ascertain* which of two courses an electron will take in effecting a given transition. That the particular course is not *cosmically* predetermined, is not asserted or assumed at all! As for "mind"—i.e., consciousness—it seems to me so characteristically a development-product of certain forms of material organisation that the assumption of its non-material existence is a bit gratuitous. At any rate, it is clear that the especial minds of human beings are simply products of cerebral action & wholly dependent on the existence of the brain. But naturally, the imagination doesn't have to recognise these prosaic probabilities!

Your unusual dreams are tremendously interesting, & much fuller of genuine, unhackneyed strangeness than any of mine. *Eiton euclarion!* Of what festering horror in space-time's makeup have you had a veiled intimation? The tower of evil child shapes is surely a tremendous conception—whilst the liquid doom ought to go splendidly in a story. Some months ago I had a dream of an evil clergyman in a garret full of forbidden books, & of how he

changed his personality with a visitor. Fra Bernardus of West Shokan is urging me to make a story of it.[5] Then about a year ago I dreamt I awaked on a
slab of unknown substance in a great vaulted hall, dimly & obscurely lit, &
full of similar slabs bearing sheeted objects whose proportions were obviously *not human*. From every detail I gathered the horrible notion *that I could be nowhere on this planet*. I also felt that my own body was like those of the other
sheeted shapes. But I waked up in very truth at this juncture, so that no *story*
was even begun!

Brrr . . . it's getting too damn cold to write outdoors! Me for town, dinner, & home to steam heat. Getting dark, too—but what a sunset! ¶ Yrs. for
the Epiphany of Abhoth

—E'ch-Pi-El.

P.S. I shall probably visit Belknap next month—thus seeing Loveman, Melmoth, Kirk, & all the rest. His mother has been quite ill—food poisoning—
but is now much better. Possibly I'll see Desmond Hall while in N.Y.

[On envelope:] [P.]P.S. Saw an interesting demonstration of *television* in a local
department store yesterday. Flickers like the biograph pictures of 1898.

Notes

1. Published as an illustration to "The Seven Geases."
2. See Farnsworth Wright to CAS, 29 September 1933 (ms., JHL): "P.S. We frequently
receive queries from our readers wanting to know where they can get copies of the Book
of Eibon, the Necronomicon, the Black Book, and von Junzt's Unaussprechlichen Kulten. I
answer such letters personally, for it would be a shame to destroy the illusion of reality by
broadcasting in the Eyrie."
3. The story is in *On the Edge*.
4. *Atlantic Monthly* 152, No. 2 (August 1933): 186–94.
5. HPL did not write an actual story, but the passage from his letter to Dwyer was published as "The Wicked Clergyman" (later "The Evil Clergyman").

[247]   [ANS, JHL][1]

[Postmarked Auburn, Cal.,
4 November 1933]

Dear Éch-Pi-El: I'll write a letter soon. [I] have been terribly crowded. My
mother's foot is healing slowly _____ tiresome business and she is still in bed.
¶ Hope you secured Ulua from Ar-E'ch-Bei. Have no time to finish any new
tales. ¶ Summer is definitely over—a heavy soaking down here last week
compelled me to move all my writing paraphernalia indoors. The _____
rain is approaching now, and the ground is turning a [new?] green.

Yours for the Dark Evangel, Klarkash-Ton

Notes

1. *Front:* Unidentified.

[248]   [TLS, JHL]

> Tower of black jade in lost Car-
> cosa. Hour when the twin suns are both
> at nadir.
> [c. early November 1933]

Dear Éch-Pi-El:

        This letter would have been written some time ago if it were not for my program of nursing, doctoring, general housework, etc. My mother's burn is healing slowly, and she is still in bed. On the whole, I suspect that the enforced rest will be beneficial to her; but otherwise it is all pretty tedious and exasperating; and with my time so broken up, it is hard to concentrate on story-writing, or even letters.

        I await The Thing on the Doorstep with tremendous eagerness. Hope you received The Witchcraft of Ulua from Ar-Éch-Bei, Phlegethonian Envoy to Phlo-Ri-Dah.[1] Wright, by the way, has finally taken this tale. I submitted a version in which the temptation scene was a little less flamboyant and more subtle.

        I return Crawford's letters herewith. Too bad C. isn't editing the new Astounding—his tastes are really better than those of most editors. He seems to have identified "weirdness" with stock superstition and magazine claptrap, but is evidently appreciative of original fantasy. As to his failure to appreciate Whitehead, I suspect, from something he let drop in one of his letters, that a strong anti-religious bias may have something to do with it.

        Thanks for the fine views of 66 College St. The fan carving certainly does remind me of your bookplate. I'd like to keep these pictures and shall prize them highly. I return the newspaper cuttings. That sunset effect with the rainbow must indeed have been striking. Rainbows are frequent here in the winter and spring, and I have seen immense double arches of the most extraordinary brilliance and perfection. Our weather has been clear again since the storm I mentioned on my card; but stray clouds and fog-banks over the Sacramento valley have given us gorgeous sunsets of gold, orange, crimson and salmon. "The moon-tints of purple and pearl"[2] have been noticeable on several evenings too. The heavy rain (over four inches) was of great benefit; and a velvety green is now visible amid the dry windlestrae of yesteryear. The nights and mornings are pretty sharp, though without frost as yet. I looked for a fine crop of mushrooms after the rain; but none have appeared. Perhaps it is too early—late November and December is their usual time; or perhaps it is an "off" year. They were very plentiful last winter.

Your drawing of the Lincoln woods [*sic*] region conveys a genuine charm, with its leisurely winding road and foreground of trees and background of steepled roofs. Together with your descriptions, it increases and confirms my desire to visit New England at some date not too far in the future.

Glad you liked the portrait of Lord Tsathoggua. Of course, I could only depict an aspect that was renderable in terms of terrestrial form and dimension. Wright hasn't returned my drawing for The Weaver; so I suppose he will use it. Thanks for your advocacy of my pictures. Bloch, I believe, had also mentioned them to Pharnabosus.

Yes, I noticed W's plural mention of The Black Book & Unaussprechlichen Kulten. Shades of Von Junst! [*sic*] ****** In his last letter he apologized for misquoting one of my sonnets several years back in the Eyrie.³ Since I can't remember seeing the quotation I would have remained in ignorance till doomsday if he hadn't told me. I am glad that Crawford took Sarnath and Celephaïs and look forward with pleasure to having printed copies of them. Howard writes me that he has sent Crawford some material. Unusual Stories, at this rate, will be something of a family affair for us, in spite of its avowed scientifictional bent.

What you tell me about the Astounding editors merely confirms my intuitions. Why in hell couldn't the publishers have picked someone who at least knew the ropes and was interested in the game? They fired back The Seven Geases after keeping it for a month; but have not yet returned The White Worm.

I didn't imagine that the plot Robot would be of much use to you. I've never seen the contraption, but have read accounts of it, and judge that it works by a sort of lottery combination and recombination of certain stock elements. Few of my stories, I fear, exhibit what is known in pulpdom as a "plot." Perhaps my current W. T. yarn, The Holiness of Azédarac, comes as near to it as any.

Lumley's hints are certainly inveigling as well as portentous. Apparently he was delighted with the Eibon chapter. The idea of a primeval serpent race seems to be a favourite one with him, since he refers to it in his last letter as well as in one or two previous epistles. Granting that he may be a little mad— well, such madness is infinitely preferable to the sort of thing that commonly passes for sanity. Olsen, as you wisely say, is a totally different matter; megalomania, dementia, mystic delirium and whatnot were all scrambled together in the one interminable screed he wrote me.

Of course, it would seem that the arguments of material science are pretty cogent. Perhaps it is only my innate romanticism that makes me at least hopeful that the Jeans and Einsteins have overlooked something. If ever I have the leisure and opportunity, I intend some first-hand investigation of obscure phenomena. Enough inexplicable things have happened in my own experience to make me wonder. I am pretty sure that I saw apparitions in my childhood; one instance remaining especially vivid in memory. The phantasm was that of a bowed and muffled woman, weeping or at least sorrow-stricken, which appeared one night in a corner of my bedroom in an old house which my parents had rented for several months. It certainly left an eerie impression. Another queer happening, of a totally different kind, occurred four or five years ago. A woman-friend and I were out walking one night in a lane near Auburn, when a dark, lightless and silent object passed over us against the stars with projectile-like speed. The thing was too large and swift for any bird, and gave precisely the effect of a *black* meteor. I have often wondered what it was.[4] Charles Fort, no doubt, would have made a substantial item out of it for one of his volumes.

Montague Summers is certainly a mine of rare erudition; and I will admit that he interests me greatly. Have you seen his The Geography of Witchcraft? I found this book listed at $1.50 in a recent catalogue and have ordered it. Am also ordering (from a firm in Glasgow, Scotland) Lewis Spence's History of Atlantis and a volume on magic by C. J. S. Thompson[5] which sounded very interesting. These volumes were also priced very cheaply. Summer[s]'s translation of the Malleus Maleficarum was listed at one pound five shillings. I coveted this, but did not feel equal to the extravagance.

Re levitation (as allegedly performed by yogis) I have seen it explained as a matter of controlled breathing. A certain rhythmic mode of respiration is supposed to fill the body with *positive* electricity, which temporarily counteracts the negative electric force of gravity. It sounds interesting, even if pseudo-scientific.

The modern explanation of the growth of myths and superstitions is certainly well worked out. Yet, after all, it is possible that brand new psychological theories may in time supersede much that is now regarded as self-evident. Also, there is the fascinating possibility that human beings may in time develop new senses or faculties that will take them a little further into the cosmic penetralia; though, of course, never approaching ultimates or near-ultimates. It may then be suspected that the sources of human thought lie deeper and remoter than has been supposed. We are *not insulated* from the myriad unknown forces of the cosmos that play upon us; and, after all who knows what the *real* effect of these forces may be? Lacking the effect of some unconsidered radiation, the whole trend of human mentation might be totally different from what it is.

I shall be very glad to avail myself of your offer to loan me The Connoisseur. The book is unobtainable locally. In return, let me remind you that any of my books, or all, are at your disposal.

The enclosed clippings may be of interest. I have accumulated a vast mass of oddities by watching the daily papers.

Yours for the resurgence of the Old Ones,
Klarkash-Ton

[P.S.] Hope your aunt has had no set-backs in her recovery. My mother and I appreciate her good wishes.

If Wright returns *The Seven Geases,* I'll lend you my carbon.

Notes

1. At the time, RHB and his family lived in DeLand, Florida.
2. Edgar Allan Poe, "Eulalie" (1845), l. 11.
3. In his editor's prelude to "The Eyrie," Farnsworth Wright extolled the work of both HPL and CAS that appeared in the magazine since its inception:

> It is now more than six years since the first copy of WEIRD TALES appeared on the news stands. The magazine was created to fill a very real demand for something radically different, something that would let the fancy escape from the humdrum everyday life of the world; a magazine whose stories should plumb the depths of occult horror, as Lovecraft has done in so many of his tales; a magazine that should not shrink from the terrible mysteries of madness and wild imagination, but should deal boldly with what Clark Ashton Smith in one of his memorable sonnets calls life's
> > 'dark, malign and monstrous music, spun
> In hell, from some delirious Satan's dream.'" (*WT* 13, No. 5 [May 1929]: 707)

These are lines 10–11 of "Dissonance" (*Ebony and Crystal* 20). Wright had written "some" for "a." He had ordered the book from CAS c. October 1927.
4. One of the stories outlined in *BB* (64) bears the title "The Dark Meteor."
5. Probably *Mysteries and Secrets of Magic.*

[249]   [ALS]

Pit of Yub—
Hour of the Squirmers'
Emergence from the Walls
[13 November 1933/RAS]

Dear Klarkash-Ton:—

"Ulua" arrived from Ar-E'ch-Bei the day following receipt of your card of the Auburnian fane, & I perused it with extreme interest & admiration. Truly, it is a powerful piece—with intimations of horror & loathsomeness which do not soon leave the imagination. The style & atmosphere are admirable—prose-poetry in every line! As I said on my preceding card, I'm delighted to hear of its final acceptance by the Arch-Vacillator. I don't see what he could have originally objected to—unless the present MS. is the later & expurgated version. Ar-E'ch-Bei looked upon it with extreme favour, & I have no doubt that it will be received with the utmost cordiality. Congratulations & thanks for the pre-publication glimpse!

Here is one of the new *Unusual* circulars in case Crawford hasn't yet sent you one. Looks rather promising—though there's no telling how long the venture will last. Most of the gang seem to be contributing one by one.

Sorry to hear that your mother is still confined to bed, & hope she will be up & around before long. This seems to be an unlucky season for the families of our daemon-haunted band—for Long's mother is still laid up with a bad case of food poisoning dating from over a month ago. My aunt is progressing finely—all around the neighbourhood alone now, & once even down town.

Alas for the passing of summer! My outdoor writing came to an end long ago, but I took rural walking trips through the splendid autumn till after All-Souls' day. In my last few walks I came upon a district which I had never before visited despite its location on the city's very (N.W.) rim—Fruit Hill. This place is developing as a fairly high-grade suburb, but some parts are still rustic. At one point on the hill I caught a vista of breath-taking loveliness which included a twilight-bewitched descent of stone-walled pastures, a wooded valley with glimpses of sunset-litten river, dim violet hills against an orange-gold west, a steepled village in a northward vale, & over the rocky eastward ridge a great round Hunters' Moon preparing to flood the plains with spectral light. Now, however, comes the long hibernation. I envy you the new grass—a thing not duplicated hereabouts. After all, you're better off climatically than we are. This morning there's a premature coating of *snow* on the ground—which does not argue well for the mildness of the coming winter! It is a spectacle of bewildering loveliness, however, from this hilltop west window which commands a wide vista of ancient roofs, barren boughs, venerable church-towers, & graceful colonial belfries.

I returned the Koenig books, & he has just sent me 2 more—"Examen of Witches"[1] & a curious "Theory of Apparitions" by one John Ferriar (1813). Before long, Koenig expects to get in touch with Sonny Belknap.

Had an ineffably menacing dream last night which I wish I could weave into a story. About a new circle of friends on which I stumbled—& which turned out to be a coven of hellish daemonolaters. They lived in an ineffably ancient hill street I had never seen before, & all their houses seemed to have bizarre features. Finally, when I called on one of them at an odd hour, I stumbled on something which caused me to flee in horror! ¶ Yrs. for the Litany of the Under Pits

—E'ch-Pi-El

[P.S.] And congratulations again on Ulua!

[P.P.S. on envelope] Suddenly—another warm day! Me for the open! ¶ Wright has asked to see the Silver Key sequel again.

Notes

1. By Henri Boguet.

[250] [ANS][1]

[Postmarked Auburn, Cal.,
16 November 1933?]

[*Salutation missing in available copy*] Weather is still clear and calm, though with fog in the valley below. Mercury fell to 44° last night—too chill for outdoor penmanship. ¶ Sorry about W.'s returned check—it must have been on that rotten Fletcher bank. Mine seems to have gone through all right so far. Yes, the circulars of Unusual are good: I'm afraid the s.f. fans will raise a howl about the pure fantasy element. *Astounding* is now banning the weird because of such protests. ***Just had an order for the D. S. from Trinidad, British West Indies—also one from Mexico. The *Geography of Witchcraft* came. Yrs for the elemental Azoth,

Klarkash-Ton

Notes

1. *Front:* Unidentified.

[251] [ALS, JHL]

Wood of the Gangrenous Fungi
—Hour of the Monstrous Multiplication
[Postmarked 18 November 1933]

Dear Klarkash-Ton:—

By this time you have doubtless received my appreciation of "Ulua". Again, joint congratulations on its intrinsic power & on its final acceptance by the Satrap of Eblis! Before long you will receive "The Thing on the Doorstep" from Bnādvāī-Aā, but I fear you won't find it worth much. Fra Bernardus noticed how inferior the early part is as compared with the ending—& the truth is, the ending is the only really spontaneous part. I had a sort of vision of the final hideous scene, & then laboriously & artificially cooked up a story to account for it. I'll ask you to shoot it along to Two-Gun Bob, & after that it will reach the Peacock Sultan. If all the verdicts up to that point are adverse, I'll take it off the circuit—for the next recipient—Comte d'Erlette—would tear it to pieces anyhow. I haven't inflicted it on Satrap Pharnabozus so far. Incidentally, though—probably through the joint influence of the Peacock Sultan's personal visit & a laudatory epistle from Bnādvāī-Aā—King Pharnaces has asked to see that Silver Key collaboration once more. (I guess I mentioned it on the outside of the Ulua envelope.) Of course that doesn't mean acceptance—but knowing the cuss's eternally vacillating nature, I feel there is at least a chance. Yuggoth knows that both Sultan Malik & I could nobly use our respective ends of the ultimately resultant pazoors![1] Meanwhile I await the Weaver—verbally & pictorially—with the

keenest interest. After 10 years of campaigning, I have certainly earned the
right to see some Klarkashtonic horrors outspread visually on the lethal
parchment of W T! Hope Little Farny keeps up the good work . . . . . . if he
takes the collaboration, I shall pester him for a C A S drawing of some scene
on Yaddith, or of the void beyond the Ultimate Gate.[2] Damn that Hall–
Tremaine team for rejecting the Seven Geases—which I must eventually see.
Hope they'll take the Eibon chapter. I think I mentioned my pleasure at re-
reading "Azedarac" in print—which reminds me, did I make a certain historical criticism when I read the manuscript a year or so ago? I meant to, but may
have become side-tracked. The thing is, that I'm in doubt about the picture of
Roman Gaul in A.D. 475 . . . . especially the idea conjured up by the phrase
"an obsolete variant of the French of Averoigne". I assume you realise that in
475 no such language as *French* existed, the vulgar Latin of Gallia not being
sufficiently differentiated from the parent stock to be any sort of separate
speech. Gaul was the last centre of culture in the declining Empire, (following
Italy, Spain, & North Africa) as such figures as Ausonius, Avienus, Sidonius
Apollinaris, Paulinus, Vigilantius, &c. attest; & towns like Burdigala
(= Bordeaux) were notably erudite. Lutetia Parisiorum, even under occupation by German barbarians, was a great Roman town with baths, temples,
palaces, & a cultivated life. By no stretch of the imagination could the popular
Latin of 475 be called "old French". The Frankish tribes in Gaul (entering
about 350 A D & being nominal allies of Rome) still spoke their German dialect & mixed not at all with the Gallo-Romans. Ditto for the Visigoths &
Burgundians who entered in 406. Only a handful of remote backwoodsmen
could have adhered to the primal Celtic speech of pre-Roman days. The name
Averoigne would undoubtedly have had a pure Latin form *Averonia* or (if derived from a tribe of *Averones,* as the name of *Auvergne* was derived from the
Arverni) *Regio Averonum.* Another thing—I suppose you know that Druidism
was not the dominant religion which Christianity displaced, but that it had
been a proscribed, fugitive faith (like Judaism in Renaissance Spain) since the
edict of Claudius in A.D. 43. Augustus had disfranchised all Druids, & under
& after Claudius Druidic worship became a capital crime. When Christianity
spread into Gaul it was not Druidism but the regular religion of the Roman
Empire—Jove & his congeners—which it displaced. However—I realise that
Druidism was always kept alive secretly in the woodland fastnesses of Lug-
dunensis Tertia (Brittany) & Aquitania Prima (Auvergne . . . . = Averoigne?),
probably lasting till after Charlemagne's time.

I've always been tremendously interested in the melancholy petering out
of the Roman civilisation, & nowhere was the process more vividly illustrated
than in the Gaul of the age of Ambrose's throwback. What an age! Sometimes I fear the present is soon to become a sort of rough parallel. As the
Empire aged, Gaul was split up into more & more provinces (only 6, counting 2 in Rhineland Germany, under the early emperors), until finally there

were *17* (incl. Germany). Then, to get rid of the resultant tangle, all these were bunched into one Praetorian Prefecture of Gallia with its capital at Augusta Trevirorum (= Treves, Germany) . . . . . which in turn soon split up into two divisions—the 10 Provinciae Gallicanae on the north, governed directly by the Praefectus Praetoris at Treves, & the Septem Provinciae on the south, governed by a Vicarius at Arelate (= Arles). The big irruption of Germans was in 406, & after that the regular provincial administration was all shot to hell. Some parts of Gaul were abandoned to the Germans, while the rest were governed by a single official called at first a *patricius* and finally a *comes* (= count). Aëtius, the famous general who defeated Attila's Huns at Chalons, ruled until murdered by the jealous emperor Valentinianus III. Then came the patrician Ægidius, who established his capital at Augusta Suessionum (= Soissons), & upon his death in 465 his son Syagrius—the last of the Roman governors, & in power at the period of Mariamis's sorceries. When the Western Empire fell—the year after Ambrose's backward projection—the *fiction* of Roman rule still persisted—the German usurper Odoacer giving *nominal* allegiance to the Eastern Emperor Zeno at Constantinopolis, whose half of the Roman world was fast becoming Byzantine-Greek in language & spirit. Syagrius offered *real* allegiance to Zeno (in fact, he offered to go to Italy & knock hell out of Odoacer), not recognising any separation of Gaul from the empire, whether its capital were Rome or Constantinople. Zeno, however, did nothing to uphold Roman rule in Gaul, so that after 476 Syagrius was a "governor" without any home government behind him. He held on till 486, when the new Frankish king Clovis defeated him—& finally assassinated him in captivity. This victory made the German Franks paramount in Gaul, & laid the foundations of the modern French nation. However—nothing changed on the surface. Those parts of Gaul which were not thickly populated by the Franks or cognate Germans were left to be administered by Gallo-Roman officials, largely dominated by the political machinery of the now powerful & arrogant Christian church, whose doctrines Clovis had espoused. Clovis's grandsons divided the Frankish domains into two parts Austrasia on the east & Neustria on the west—the latter being essentially Gallo-Roman. From then on the decay of Roman culture in Gaul was very slow. The Saracens came & were repulsed, & Charlemagne flourished & died . . . . yet still the language of the people was more Latin than "French", whilst the educated Gallo-Romans continued to use pure Latin in all formal discourse & written literature. The famous Oath of Strasbourg—A.D. 842—is the last surviving example of the *popular* Gallic language of the Dark Ages. I will cite a bit of it, with Latin & French equivalents, & leave it to you whether it is closer to Latin or to French. And this, of course, is nearly 375 years *after* Ambrose's throwback. This popular speech was, in its day, called *Lingua Romana* as distinguished from *Lingua Latina*. Naturally it could not be called "French" or Lingua Franca, since the language of the Franks was still German. From about this time on, however, more & more of the conquering Franks began speaking the Lingua Romana—so that when the Normans secured a foothold in France (the name *Francia* was always used to designate the area occupied by the solid body of Franks) around 900, it was this tongue, & not Frankish German, which they adopted. Probably we can speak of "French" as a language from around 900 A.D. But to get to the parallel texts—not the devolutionary changes:

[Latina] Pro Dei amore et pro Christiano populo et nostro communi salvamento
[Romana] PRO DEO AMUR ET PRO CHRISTIAN POBLO ET NOSTRO COMMUN SALVAMENT
[Mod. Fr.] Pour l'amour de Dieu, et pour de salut du peuple Chretien et de notre commun salut

[Latina] de isto die in ab-ante in quantum Deus sapere et posse mihi donabit. . . .
[Romana] D'IST DI EN AVANT, IN QUANT DEUS SAVIR ET PODIR ME DUNAT. . . . .
[Mod. Fr.] de ce jour en avant, autant que Dieu me donne savoir et pouvoir . . . . .[3]

All we can say is that *by 842* the popular Latin had begun to display a definite differentiation in the direction of the modern language later called French. No doubt southern specimens, foreshadowing southern dialects, differed somewhat from the northern specimen. To me there is something especially fascinating in this cycle of gradual but ruthless change. I wish some day you would write a tale of somebody who lived down the ages & saw the little details of familiar life crumble around him whilst alien powers & unfamiliar ways engulfed his land & left him an exile from an earlier & forgotten world.[4] A Gallo-Roman in 1175 at the Inn of La Bonne Jouissance . . . . . . But enough of pedantry. Picking up a detail like that in Azèdarac is a sort of Forrest J. Ackerman stunt!

Which reminds me that the new F F blew in yesterday with quite a cargo of interesting material. I see you've spilled the beans anent Eibon & its hellish analogues—which will give poor Pharnabozus quite a jolt! He's been keeping the black secret & answering enquiries personally.[5] Actually, I think it is wise to publish the facts, for a deliberate hoax (so easy to put over) could conceivably cause real embarrassment & expensive enquiry on the part of serious collectors like Koenig. I was glad to see "A Dream of the Abyss"—a magnificent conception. Editor Hornig's learned editorial on the origin of *weird* strikes me as a bit amusing.[6] Of course the noun meaning *fate* comes from the earliest Anglo-Saxon, while the term *weird sisters* applied to the Fates or Norns is also very early. Shakespeare, moreover, used *weird sisters* to signify mere *witches*—

hence after that the transference of *weird* to anything *witchlike* was natural. Probably, however, it was mainly a Scotticism until well into the 19th century. Poe of course had it in mind when concocting the synthetic place-name *Weir*—& he also used it entire, as in the "wild *weird* clime that lies sublime, out of Space, out of Time."[7] Perhaps Hornig is half-right to the extent that Poe did much to popularise the word. Well—all told, the F F certainly fulfils a useful function among weirdists; & I certainly hope it can be kept alive. I haven't dared look through "The Other Gods", for fear of the misprints I'll find. As for my serial article—at the present rate, I predict a conclusion by 1975.

Thanks tremendously for the proboscidian Entity. Ngrrrh .... Your recent larger drawings have elicited ecstatic & admiring shudders from such beholders as little Bho-Blôk & Jehvish-Ei. As for old Bill Lumley—he certainly is a great chap. I wish I could duplicate his state of mind! I'm encouraging him to complete some of his phantasies (such as "The City of Dim Faces") for Hornig or Crawford. The former has taken some of his verse.[8] I've seen several of Olson's [*sic*] inspired epistles—here's one he wrote to me. (Please return) Pretty interesting stuff, if one knows what it's about . . . . . Hugo the Rat or Efjay Akkamin ought to take it & make a scientifictional masterpiece out of it! Being short of cash, I passed up the opportunity to receive a personal call from Savant Olson—though his offer to come & enlighten me for 25 bucks was truly unselfish .... since his round trip from South Dakota would have been away beyond that even on the cheapest 'bus! The true missionary spirit. And to think, I didn't even send the 2 fish for Dr. Conner's "Reflection"! Well—it's not every guy who passes up a chance for "all might & the control of the universe." Fancy! I might, with Olson's aid, have shoved the planets at my will & turned back the hand of time to Ubbo-Sathla itself!!

As for possible deviations from natural law as now understood—of course, one need not be dogmatic; but it still seems as if all the scraps of alleged evidence for such deviations were slight, rare, & highly susceptible of other explanation, as ranged against an overwhelming mass of data in the light of which they appear wildly improbable. The unreliable registration of the human senses, & the effect of imagination or careless attention upon human perception, are among the most salient facts in nature—& we have seen too many marvellous myths & apparent certainties analysed into delusions to feel sure of anything not surviving the test of rigorous investigation. I have often *thought* I witnessed marvels, yet have invariably traced them in the end to natural components & imagination-induced visions. Thus when I was 7 years old I *positively saw* some fauns & dryads in a mystical oaken grove (still unchanged, Yuggoth be thanked!) not far from my house. But they looked *very* like the pictures in the edition of Bulfinch's Age of Fable over which I had been avidly poring! That muffled weeper of your own childhood was certainly a curious impression. As for the Black Meteor—all sorts of theories might be offered. A cloud—a huge kite—a dirigible adrift—Anyhow, I'd go over the list of possible normal causes pretty thoroughly before adopting a Charles Fortian explanation! Which reminds me that I must get hold of Fort's best books (the two earliest I fancy) sooner or later. They are, indubitably, magnificent source material. I've read them.

Speaking of books—I have *not* seen Summers' "Geography of Witchcraft", & would have been strongly tempted had I come across the catalogue item. I may request the loan of it after you've received & thoroughly digested it. I don't believe Koenig has this especial item. Anything by Spence would undoubtedly be piquant—I've read his Atlantis book—& I trust the Thompson item will not prove disappointing. I am now reading Boguet's Discours des Sorciers—translated as "An Examen of Witches" & edited by Summers. It is, as you may know, the work of a French judge who sat on numberless witchcraft cases in the 1590's. All this detailed, first-hand evidence, some of which tallies so significantly with the better-known Salem evidence a century later & 3000 miles away, brings the whole matter of witchcraft practice shudderingly close. There is no question at all that, as demonstrated in Miss Murray's "Witch Cult in Western Europe", a wide & degenerate organisation with fixed rules and ceremonies did exist & conduct hideous rites under a belief of malign supernatural linkage. The Sabbats & incantations were no myths, & it was no phantom foe that the tribunals prosecuted—& that, in Germany, it required that mediaeval Ku Klux Klan called the Holy Vehm to put down. Clearly, whether or not there was any continuous survival from a pre-Aryan Dianic cult, the black & desperate days of mediaevaldom called forth a loathsome concerted revolt against decency & restraint—a revolt which swept in vast numbers of abnormal & degenerate folk, & which probably included widespread poisoning & other forms of encroachment on law-abiding folk. While *burning* was of course barbarous, there is no need to shed any tears over the poor persecuted witches. They had earned plenty! I'd like to see the "Malleus"—which Koenig has. Regarding *levitation*—I think there is little doubt of the fictitiousness or delusiveness of all reported cases. We now realise the weak spots in transmitted report, & know that most alleged yogi marvels never occurred in objective reality. Too much evidence has been accumulated regarding the myth-building process to allow incredible tales to pass muster without verification.

But what you say of *new senses* is certainly worthy of profound reflection. Certainly, our view of nature is purely a subjective & fragmentary one, depending on the meagre sensory equipment called forth by an evolution whose only object is physical survival, not knowledge & perception. That is, the only links we have with the external world are special faculties designed for a very (intellectually) narrow end & having no reference to the process of envisaging or experiencing the cosmos in its totality, or even of forming an approximately full idea of the small section within our conceivable grasp. While nothing in our normal experience is ever likely to call forth any additional senses, it is not impossible that experiments with the ductless glands might open up a fresh sensitivity or two—& then what impressions might not pour in? I doubt, though, if anything new concerning the *sources of thought* would be discovered; since the local cerebral origin of this process, & its unmistakable connexion with simpler forms of nervous excitability down to the crude sensitiveness of the amoebal cell-wall, are so apparent in the light of careful, disinterested research. However, a vast deal might be learnt concerning the *mechanism & operation of thought*—just what modifications of tissue are involved, what transformations of energy occur, whether any wave-motion (rendering telepathy—which is probably an unfounded legend—possible) exists in addition to molecular changes, & whether such a thing as hereditary memory can exist. This last is gorgeous fictional material—as Cline's "Dark Chamber" attests. If you haven't read that volume, I shall insist on lending it to you . . . . . it got young Belknap so excited when he first read it in 1927 that he was reduced to the inarticulate length of sending me a postal covered with nameless pen-&-ink daemons of loathsome amorphousness with only the tremblingly scrawled message *"Read The Dark Chamber!!!!"* Later on our good friend Canevin gave me the copy I now possess. Incidentally—I mailed you "The Connoisseur" last night, & trust you will not find it disappointing. The two stories I recommend are "Mr. Kempe" & "All-Hallows"—especially the latter. I re-read both a couple of months ago, & Mr. Kempe *lost* on a second reading whilst All-Hallows *gained*. This last is certainly a great tale—full of daemoniac suggestion never overdone or obtruded. Speaking of loans— sooner or later I may let you send me "Brood of the Witch Queen" (which I read just a decade ago but wish to reread) & "The Lady Who Came to Stay" (which I've never read, but which Comte d'Erlette & young Jehvish-Ei have extolled to me as something non-omittable).[9] First, however, I'll see whether I can get them at the bibliotheca publica.

Thanks extremely for the interesting cuttings, which I herewith return. I also have kept a file of these things for years—would you care to see some of the choicest items? I'd be glad to lend any number of envelopes full. That fog in Washington[10] surely was a curious 'colour out of space' . . . . . I wonder if the preparations to reprint my story in that state had anything to do with it? The case of the Boer lady—Mevrouw van de Riet—certainly offers dark food for the imagination. She seems to be a sort of female Aleister Crowley[11]—or a striga, lamia, empusa, or something of the sort. An odd—& potentially evil—face. Actually, she probably has the same degenerate psychology found in the old maleficae whom Sprenger & Kramer & Boguet & the other Renaissance prosecutors encountered—no doubt seeking to start cults or groups of loathsome practices wherever she settles. For fictional purposes you could use the South African birth—hinting at a childhood visit to the ruins of Zimbabwe by moonlight, & at whispers overheard there . . . . . . for is that not one of the points visited by the Fishers from Outside? Biegas'[12] art is assuredly tremendous—especially his conception of the four elements. (except the first) He has that unplaceable quality which captures & reproduces an imaginative conception—something which so lamentably few artists really possess, but which certainly tinctures your own products. I'm glad he has secured recognition at last—for my part, I regret to say I never heard of him before. I wish I had the cash to collect specimens of weird art. My young correspondent Richard E. Morse (a friend of Loveman's—& vide current F F)[13] has started something of the sort, but hasn't got very far considering what there is to be collected.

Sorry your mother's burns heal so slowly—but as you say, the rest may do her good. [*marginal note by HPL:* Belknap's mother is just recovering from a bad case of canned-food poisoning.] I think my aunt—who was all worn out with moving last spring—is really the better for her long session of forced inactivity. I can readily understand how tied down you must be—it was the same with me during my aunt's recumbent period. She had a nurse, but I had to be on hand every day while the nurse went out. My aunt is now fully up & about, going outdoors with a single cane & sometimes going around the house without any. The place is getting to look ineffably homelike now that my aunt is actively in charge. Curtains hung, more pictures up, more old family things from storage, &c.—really, it reminds me tremendously (albeit on a miniature scale) of our old home in Angell St.—not 598, but 454, where I was born. The most glamorous thing just at this moment is the view from my desk window—subtly altered & expanded by the vanishing of the leaves. In the foreground, ancient roofs & boughs. In the middle distance twin church towers (now part of the School of Design, but built as a church around 1845) & a Georgian belfry, (of the court house in the frontispiece of that booklet—new, but absolutely in the old tradition) with the space-softened towers of the downtown skyscrapers just beyond. And in the background a narrow strip of far-off purple horizon, with a mystical hilltop steeple silhouetted delicately against the flaming sunset.[14] What a show! It positively keeps my mind off my work! And the kick is emphasised because my room in Barnes St. was a veritable crypt with no view at all—so damn dark I generally kept the curtains down & used (the landlady's!) electric light! Glad the pictures proved interesting. I must try to get some of the interior—at least, of the three fine colonial mantels, one in my study, one in the living-room, & the third in my aunt's bedroom.

What you say of rainbows indicates that Auburn is much more favoured than Providence. I envy you the weather you describe—it has turned cold here, with only occasional days of respite. Another premature snow today—never before have I seen snow so early in November. If this is an augury for the winter, I shall certainly be doubly appreciative of the marvellous *heat* in this joint. Abundant steam 24 hours a day—I never had such a luxury before! I find that the *ultimate* source is not the library next door, but that it all comes from the college engineering building far over the crest of the hill on the middle campus. That plant heats all buildings owned by the university. Some day, I fancy, steam will be a piped municipal utility like gas & electricity.

Glad the N.E. descriptions proved pleasing. You certainly must see this part of the country some day—especially the ancient churchyards & huddled gambrel roofs of Salem (Arkham) & the devious hillside labyrinths of tangled Marblehead (Kingsport). ¶ All good wishes—

Yrs. for the Infra-Red Western Dawn—

E'ch-Pi-El

Notes

1. Monetary unit used in Hyperborea.

2. Despite repeated pleas by HPL, Farnsworth Wright did not commission CAS to illustrate "Through the Gates of the Silver Key" for *WT*. The illustration was done by H. R. Hammond.

3. These lines (varying slightly from one book to the next) appear in numerous histories of the origin of the French language. HPL's specific source has not been identified.

4. See "The Chain of Aforgomon."

5. In an unsigned article by Charles Hornig called "Startling Fact," Hornig quotes CAS as saying ""Necronomicon," "Book of Eibon," etc. I am sorry to say, are all fictitious. Lovecraft invented the first, I the second . . . It is really too bad that they don't exist as objective, bonafide compilations of the elder and darker Lore! I have been trying to remedy this, in some small measure, by cooking up a whole chapter of Eibon. It is still unfinished, and I am now entitling it "The Coming of the White Worm" . . . This worm mentioned in Eibon is Rlim Shaikorth, and comes from beyond the pole on a strange, gigantic iceberg with a temperature of absolute zero.'

"We'll bet that most Smith and Lovecraft fans really believed in the existence of these books (as did the editor). A reader informs us that in the July issue of *Weird Tales*, these books were mentioned in three stories." *FF* 1, No. 3 (November 1933): 38.

6. See an untitled, unsigned note in *FF* 1, No. 3 (November 1933): 46: "The word 'weird' as meaning bizarre probably originated with Edgar Allan Poe, who was one of the greatest coiner[s] of words. In his poem 'Ulalume,' he speaks of the country of 'Weir' from which the word 'weird' was derived to describe anything horrible or unique."

7. "Dreamland" (1844), l. 8.

8. "The Elder Thing" (January 1935) and "The Dweller" (February 1934).

9. Books by Sax Rohmer and R. E. Spencer.

10. I.e., the pogonip; see letter 145n4.

11. Aleister Crowley (1875–1947), an English occultist, ceremonial magician, poet, and mountaineer, known in the press as "the wickedest man in the world."

12. Boleslaw Biegas (1877–1954), Polish surrealist painter and sculptor.

13. Morse contributed a letter to the "Boiling Point" column in November 1933 (p. 40); see Appendix, p. 692. The other item HPL refers to is "Some Modern Book Illustrations," *Californian* 4, No. 4 (Spring 1937): 66–70.

14. St. John's Roman Catholic Church at 352 Atwell's Avenue (since razed), the edifice that became the Free-Will Church of the Starry Wisdom sect in HPL's "The Haunter of the Dark."

[252]   [ANS][1]

[Postmarked Auburn, Cal.,
24 November 1933]

Dear Éch-Pi-El:

Thanks for the *Connoisseur*, which came last night. I'll send you *The Geography of Witchcraft* and *The Lady Who Came to Stay* whenever you want them. *Brood of the Witch Queen* is out at present; but I'll round it up when I have the chance. I was a little vexed by Brother Hornig's "scoop" in utilizing my letter about Eibon, etc. He asked me where and how the books could be obtained; and I didn't think to stipulate that the answer was for his private information! Dumb of me, I'll admit. However, as you say, the hoax might easily go too far. Klarkash-Ton

Notes

1. *Front:* Unidentified.

[253]   [ANS, JHL][1]

[Postmarked Auburn, Cal.,
late November 1933]

This, the local hoosegow and center of legal sculduggery, is a quite impressive edifice. The base is granite, the upper stories are terra-cotta. A fine view of the seven-hilled village is obtainable from the gilded dome.

Notes

1. *Front:* Unidentified.

[254]   [ALS, JHL]

Crest of Unknown Kadath in the Cold
Waste, whence is seen the Insufferable
Perspective. Hour of the Monstrous Looming
from the Unplaceable Direction.
[29 November 1933/RAS]

Dear Klarkash-Ton:—

"Ulua" certainly ought to be well received—with or without emendations. I am looking, too, for the self-illustrated "Weaver in the Vault". Hope the "Demon of the Flower" will bring such a reader-reaction as to make Tremaine & Hall abandon their proposed shift to straight scientifiction. This step is very disappointing to me—I'm not buying the magazine any more—though even under the weird policy I doubt if I could ever have gained a foothold in its pages. Congratulations on the probable cover-design for "The Charnel God"—& still more on the Klarkash-Tonic illustration! My dream of 1923 realised. But damn that ass Pharnabozus for turning down the "Seven Geases". This silly worship of artificial "plot"—an element which I believe to be not only unnecessary but even intrinsically inartistic—certainly gets me seeing red. Hope I can have a look at the 7 Geases—either in MS. or through early F F or *Unusual* publication. I guess I told you that Wright at last gave conclusive acceptance to the Silver Key sequel. Hope a decent reader reaction will prevent his regretting his decision!

I rather like the new F F, & am delighted to see your "Dream of the Abyss" featured. My "Other Gods" is one of the few reliques of my Dunsanian imitative period which doesn't disgust me. "Sarnath", which Crawford is going to use, is much more immature—although our young friend Ar-E'ch-Bei has an anomalous liking for it. It rather embarrassed me to have my *second* set of remarks on Ackerman publicly reproduced,[1] for they make me seem like the leader of an organised campaign to bait the poor little rat—yet I guess no harm is done. The kid had it coming to him after his peculiarly vicious & persistent campaign of irresponsible abuse. His ego needed drastic deflation! It is clear, though, that one must be careful what one writes Hornig. He is a newspaperman first, last, & all the time!

Hope Miss Webber[2] [*sic*] has been able to collect you something from Hugo the Rat—as she has for Mrs. Heald. Hugo still manages to get decent stuff in spite of his delinquencies—I don't buy W S now, but Comte d'Erlette has just sent me a fine story by Carl Jacobi—"The Tomb from Beyond"—clipped from the November issue. If you haven't seen it I'll send it to you.

Koenig certainly has a library & a half. He must be an interesting cuss, & I shall be interested to hear Belknap's report on him if he calls—as he intends—at 230 W 97. I'm now returning Boguet's Discours du Sorciers & Ferriar's Theory of Apparitions—the former of which certainly brings witchcraft close to one. No—Koenig evidently does not possess "The Geography of Witchcraft", hence I shall be eternally your debtor if you will shoot it hither for a brief session after your own first perusal is sufficiently complete. Old Monty Summers assuredly is a case! As erudite as Cotton Mather—& quite as credulous. A sort of Bill Lumley on a more exalted plane. But of course there's no question of the evil reality of witchcraft *practices* as distinguished from their mythical supernatural basis. Evidence such as piled up at all the trials could not come out of thin air. Allowing for delusion in the extreme cases, certain oft-repeated features practically establish the existence of a widespread & persistent organisation of inferior, unbalanced, degenerate characters in the middle ages & later, whose rites & meetings have come down to us in tradition. They probably believed in their own supernatural affiliations, & indulged in every sort of sadistic, murderous, revengeful, & orgiastic excess. I have no sympathy for the "innocent victims" of witchcraft trials, but on the other hand feel quite convinced that these prosecutions—as well as the extra-legal activities of the Holy Vehm in Germany—were valuable agents in preventing a general disintegration of society. The witch-cult was an objective example of that element of reaction against mediaeval piety which appears in certain leering gargoyles & in various sinister undertones in literary & other art. As for its origin—I am wholly against Summers & with Miss Murray. Summers has let his serious acceptance of Christianity bias him. He is blind to dozens of points of resemblance betwixt witch-cult practices (especially festival dates) & primitive-reliques of Nature-worship all over Europe, & makes a very weak argument in his earlier witchcraft book which Koenig lent me. Whether any systematic cult survived from primitive times, we can hardly say; but the old *lore* certainly did survive ready for use when the unsatisfying life & constant doom-dread of mediaevalism stirred up the hysterical psychological epidemics of the Dark Ages. I surely wish you'd write your tale of Hecatean or Mithraic survivals. Classical legend is full of fruitful themes—I have for years been thinking of basing a tale on the celebrated *Oracle of Trophonius*—that yawning cave whose nighted revelations were such that none who had received them ever smiled again.[3] Another thing I hope to see is that just-commenced tale of the cloudy gods.

Speaking of dreams—I think my average of fantastic specimens is now slowly rising after a long minimum. Last week I had a very vivid dream[4] of forming the acquaintance of a group of quiet, well-bred, & apparently wholesome young men, all of whom lived in quasi-bohemian apartments in ancient houses along a hill street in Providence which I had never before discovered (& which doesn't exist except as a wide variant of certain far less ancient streets in the Federal Hill Italian quarter). During the course of the long dream I called on several of these young men, whose point of interest was their knowledge of ancient & mediaeval magic. They were all very finical in one respect—that I call only at appointed times. On one occasion, when I had expressed scepticism about the reality of magic to a group of about 3 or 4 of them, they expressed a credulousnessness almost akin to Lumley's or Summers's—& insisted on giving me a *mild* demonstration of certain things *beyond physics & chemistry*. This they insisted on doing at my home (in the dream, 598 Angell St.)—whither they all trooped (there must have been 12 or 13 of them) one late evening. My mother (then living) had retired, but I admitted them to my room & brought chairs from other rooms so that they might sit in a semicircle. Only then, when they were all together, did I begin to feel anything sinister about them—but under my Welsbach gas-light they seemed too pallid & waxen to be made of flesh—& *they looked too much alike*. Such a resemblance would not have been sinister in twins—but in 12 or 13 men (each about 30) it aroused a vague disquiet. They were in dinner jackets, & looked something like the vampires on the cover of that last *Strange Tales* containing Cave's "Murgunstrumm" & your "Second Interment". They did not lower the light, but suddenly commenced to *sing* in a strange minor key—with tonal intervals not belonging to any terrestrial musical system. All at once I grew dizzy, & began to feel as if the room were whirling in an unknown dimension. Then, although the outlines of the walls remained perfectly clear, my vision began to take in vast vistas of space—represented by aggregates of gigantic cubes scattered along a gulf of violet radiation—whilst my mind began to feel an intolerable consciousness of unrolled aeons . . . . as if all of eternity were about to pour its simultaneous burthen upon me. It is impossible to describe such a mixed sensation—& it lacks absolutely the definiteness & dramatic value needed for fiction. In the dream I was alarmed & repelled—& I seemed to *recognise* some *known & definite evil* which I cannot recall now. I felt obliged to do something toward stopping the rite—& feigned an illness & a wish to retire. The men respected this wish, & withdrew rather mockingly—triumphing, of course, in my admission of an element of validity in the supernatural. (The dream is really *inconsistent*—for despite my initial scepticism, my recognition of a cosmic horror in the rite seems unattended with surprise.) But this was not the end. I was left with a burning curiosity about the thing I had experienced, & at dawn set out for the home of the most learned of this strange group—the man who lived highest up on that unfamiliar hill. When I reached there an unknown evil seemed to brood over the street, & I felt some trepidation in calling *unannounced*—contrary to the custom & wishes of this odd brotherhood. An incident of the walk thither (sight of a single-truck street-car with a certain sign) places the period of the dream around 1907. I entered the ancient house & mounted the creaking stairs—seeming to feel that the whole place had gone far in decay since last I was there. When I knocked at my host's door I felt an unexplained surge of fear. It was promptly opened by the occupant, but I felt sure that this man was not—or *not quite*—my host. He was very provoked & discourteous about my unannounced call, & before long 3 or 4 of the others filtered into the room. Only then did I look beyond a usually-drawn portiere at the farther end—seeing there a laboratory with strange phials & beakers that I had never seen before. In the centre of this laboratory was a table bearing a form in white—that of my host. I felt that he was not dead, but rather that he was somehow more alive—or quasi-living—than any of the precisely duplicated (& still dinner-jacketed) shapes around me. Their talk was very confused. "Now you have seen, you must not come again." . . . "He must not even leave." . . . . . . "You ought to have known" . . . . &c. &c. In the midst of this I suddenly turned & fled. One of the men tried to stop me, but he seemed to have no power of grasping. His hand descended on my arm so that I *saw* it, but I *felt* nothing. It then occurred to me that I had never physically touched any of these queer fellows, the custom of handshaking having been evidently alien to them. Nothing prevented my descent of the stairs, or my passage down the street. At the home of one of the other brotherhood members, that individual was standing on his ancient high steps. He smilingly invited me in, but I hurried on—feeling something ineffably evil & sardonic behind the smile. The dream did not terminate in awakening, but passed off into something trivial—I think the street turned into a modern downtown street, & that I began making purchases in familiar shops. But it was damn vivid while it lasted, & I recalled it at once when I *did* awake. Still, its power resided in some dim lurking element too intangible for any but a master to get on paper. The horror evoked by that incantation in my room, & the night-mare of the ancient house (upon which I *just failed* to stumble), were strange & potent—yet altogether indescribable—things. Only last night I had another dream[5]—of going back to 598 Angell St. after infinite years. The neighbour-hood was deserted & grass-grown, & the houses were half-falling to pieces. The key on my ring fitted the mouldering door of 598, & I stepped in amidst the dust of centuries. Everything was as it was around 1910—pictures, furni-ture, books, &c., all in a state of extreme decay. Even objects which have been with me constantly in all later homes were there in their old positions, sharing in the general dissolution & dust-burial. I felt an extreme terror—& when *footsteps* sounded draggingly from the direction of my room I turned & fled in panic. I would not admit to myself what it was I feared to confront . . . . . . but my fear also had the effect of making me shut my eyes as I raced past the mouldy, nitre-encrusted *mirror* in the hall. Out into the street I ran— & I noted that none of the ruins were of buildings newer than about 1910. I had covered about half a block—of continuous ruins, with nothing but ruins ahead—when I awaked shivering. At the last moment my great fear seemed to be of passing my birthplace & early home—the beloved 454 Angell St.— toward which I was headed. Later in the night I had another dream—about a stretch of lonely seashore & a sense of oppression & fear regarding some-thing the waves might wash up—but this was too slight to be really worthy of record. Young Bloch is using his story based on my mediaeval roof-monster dream as a serial in his high-school paper. I haven't seen it, but will be amused to find out what the kid did with the idea. I hope my increased fantastic dream-ing is a prelude to a new writing spell. All my recent attempts have been so un-satisfactory that I have destroyed them after 3 or 4 pages; & I keep asking myself with increasing frequency whether I am not, after all, unequal to the task of expressing myself in words.

I surveyed the cuttings with intense interest. God! that . . . . . that thing . . . . . in the fathomless, cathedral-like grottoes of Loch Ness . . . . is it in-deed He of whom nightmare's victims have shrieked in the clairvoyant deliri-um preceding waking . . . . . amorphous, cyclopean Tsathoggua? Was not Scotland part of that primal Hyperborea wherein He was worshipped by the beasts & the Ambiguous Folk before the coming of Conan? Who shall say that His lair escaped not the ultimate Doom that ingulphed Commoriom & Uzuldaroum of old? Such speculation, tho' alarming, cannot be dismissed as irrelevant . . . . . nor yet the still darker whispers which call up the very dim &

mercifully unremembered rumours of the *shoggoths* . . . . . but of such things one must not, in defence of one's sanity, speak. Let us *hope* there is nothing—nothing whatever—of truth in that suppressed manuscript of Dr. Fergus MacBain (shudderingly refused in 1763 by the Edinburgh printing house of Kerr, but whispered of by Mark Kerr in his old age, when his mind began to give way) which spoke of a flickering luminescence in the loch—something that waxed & waned *as if in answer to corresponding flashes on the dark part of the moon's disc.* All this is—must be—the merest idle gossip! And of course that tale of the madman at the Inverness asylum—the man found wandering near the loch with a diver's helmet on—is the sheerest lunacy. He was mad before he ever dived in the loch—he *must* have been. Those black depths merely *brought out* a lurking madness that was there before. Any other hypothesis is the *sheerest nonsense.* The doctors do well to dismiss those hints of caverns beneath caverns, litten with some unknown phosphorescence & carven with pictographs full of diabolic revelations concerning the earth's pre-human past. Let me know of any further reports you may receive. And meanwhile I tremble at the thought of this Pacific horror—which has now reached the Eastern press. There have been black legends of nameless messengers sent out from sunken R'lyeh, but none has dared say *what* those messengers are. Has this mystery at last approached an hideous solution? Let us hope not . . . . let us hope devoutly . . . . . I shall very shortly make up an envelope of cuttings for you to see. My best recent specimen—sent by little Ar-E'ch-Bei—seems to be from a Hearst paper, & tells of a linkage betwixt certain *Easter Island* carvings & carvings found in the recently unearthed prehistoric city of Mohenjo Daro in the Indus valley. Have you seen it? If there is anything behind it, it certainly offers the most exciting possibilities for speculation.

Thanks much for the attractive view of Auburn's golden-domed civic palace. What a sumptuous place to lodge the delinquent & the anti-social! Really, one would be tempted to commit a robbery or murder or two in order to secure such quarters! I noticed its impressiveness in the general view of the village, & am glad to see it in greater detail. It surely has admirably classic proportions. In reciprocation I am enclosing a view of Providence's corresponding high spot—the Rhode Island state house on *Smith's* Hill. This rather famous marble edifice, designed by McKim, Mead, & White & completed in 1900, has the only *all-marble dome* in the United States. It is plainly visible from all points near the city's centre, & at night the dome is picturesquely floodlighted. Seen from Prospect Terrace (a small hill-crest park several blocks north of 66 College) it presents an unusually fine appearance—silhouetted against the sunset in conjunction with the Gothic tower of St. Patrick's church, which stands a little northeast of it.

Glad you had a good view of the recent conjunction of Venus & the crescent moon. I saw it from my own west windows, & its natural impressiveness was enhanced by its setting. It was twilight, & the ancient roofs & boughs &

towers & belfries of the hill were silhouetted blackly against a still-orange sky. The windows of the downtown office buildings, just beginning to light up, made the lower town look like a constellation—& the great red beacon atop the 26-story Industrial Trust Bldg. (which dominates the town as the Pharos dominated Alexandria)[6] was blazing portentously. In the southwest the lofty Georgian belfry of the new Court House loomed up darkly save for the lighted clock-face, the floodlights not having been turned on. And just south of this picturesque outline, high in the sky where the orange was turning to violet, floated Astarte's bediamonded crescent with the blazing planet close to its upper horn! It certainly was a sight to gasp at—the black towers & roofs against an orange west, the twinkling turrets of the lower town, & the horned moon with its strangely luminous companion. Assuredly, I shall not soon forget it!

[*Marginal note:*] [♀ will again be in ☽ with Dec. 20. better watch for it.]

The cold hereabouts continues to be punctuated by occasional warm days—my last rural walk (through barren stone-walled fields & bare-bough'd woods not quite unbeautiful even in autumnal desolation) having taken place on Nov. 22—which would have been my maternal grandfather's 100th birthday had he lived to celebrate it. Your mention of still-flaming leaves attests the greater net mildness of your climate—& yet your latitude (39°) is only about 3 degrees south of Providence (42°). Providence on a line with California's northern boundary . . . . . & also with the widely differentiated cities of Chicago & Rome.

Glad your mother's burn is healing, even though slowly. Hope she will be on her feet before long. My aunt continues to improve, though she will probably cling to the cane for some time to come.

I trust "The Connoisseur" arrived safely, & that you did not find "All Hallows" & "Mr. Kempe" disappointing. Aside from these items, the volume is nothing to brag about. Like Blackwood, de la Mare is tremendously uneven; & can be unutterably namby-pamby in a "whimsical", semi-humorous way when the wrong mood is on him. I wouldn't mind getting his new collection—which contains, among other things, that vivid sketch "A Recluse", which I read some years ago in the Asquith "Ghost Book." At his best, de la Mare has a subtlety which scarcely anyone else can approach. I'd give a lot to be able to write something like "Seaton's Aunt."

Well—the night wanes, & a faint gong of horror resounds from a distant tower which I cannot identify. Yrs. for the primal litany of Neph—

E'ch-Pi-El

[P.S. on envelope:] Card just arrived. Thanks for loan offer . . . . I'll be glad to see G. of W. and L who came to Stay at any time. ¶ Hornig is certainly a bit excessive in his journalistic enterprise, but I guess no harm is done. ¶ Just got the final of my pay for the Witch House. ¶ That vista from Donner Pass surely is impressive. ¶ Pleasant & mild today—but not quite warm enough for rural rambles.

Notes

1. "The Boiling Point" for November 1933.
2. I.e., Ione Weber (see letter 222n2). In May 1934 CAS hired Weber to recoup from Gernsback debts totalling $769 in back payments from *Wonder Stories*.
3. *CB* 154: "Trophonius—cave of. Vide Class. Dict. and Atlantic article."
4. August Derleth used this description as the basis of his story "The Dark Brotherhood."
5. CAS based his story "The Treader of the Dust" on this dream.
6. The Industrial Trust Tower at 111 Westminster Street (now the Bank of America Building) is the tallest building in Providence and the 28th tallest in New England.

[255]   [TLS, JHL]

> From the black desert of
> Zoir, beneath the seven
> ultra-spectral suns.
> [Postmarked 4 December 1933]

Dear Éch-Pi-El:

I have just finished reading The Thing on the Doorstep for the second time, and am re-impressed by its power. The theme is carefully developed (needless to say) and the climax comes like a thunderclap. In all frankness, I must disagree with Dwyer or anyone else who criticises any portion of the tale as being below par. I hope you will submit the tale to Pharnabosus. Unless I am grievously mistaken, he will grab it with exceeding promptness. Allah! what a contrast between your handling of this theme and a hunk of melodramatic hooey such as Abd Dhulma, Lord of Fire, in the Dec. W. T.! I instance the Pendarves opus because it deals with a magician who lives on from age to age by absorbing the souls of others: a theme slightly congenerate with yours, but infinitely less impressive and effective in the actual treatment.

Edward Derby's character is well realized. I have one very minor suggestion to make, and this I offer with much doubt and hesitation. I wonder if it would be better to add a hint (perhaps no more than a sentence or phrase) to the effect that Derby's abnormal ability to animate the corpse of Asenath was due to his own far from negligible achievements in dark magic. However, this is perhaps implicit in the tale as it stands.

I trust that Conan and most of the others on the circulation list fully appreciate the treat in store for them. The ms. goes forward to the Cimmerian monarch today.

One of my cards will have informed you of my pleasure in hearing that Through the Gates of the Silver Key has finally received the satrapic approval. Any of the ultramundane scenes in this story would be well adapted to my style of pictorial treatment. I have heard nothing further from Wright about the pictorialization of The Charnel God. Evidently there is no hurry: the tale will not appear till March; and at last hearing W. had not decided whether to favour The C. G. with a cover design or to take the March cover from one of Cave's melodramas.[1]

Speaking of covers, the current W. T. design, though pleasing enough in colour, is curiously suggestive of a Christmas card! I don't wish to be ungallant: but Mrs. Brundage (between you and me and the asymmetric eikon from Crater Ridge) has about as much genuine feeling for the weird as a Jersey cow is likely to possess. The best angles in this picture (the hands of the Chinaman, etc) seem to have been swiped by unconscious cerebration from Utpatel's drawing for The Star-Spawn by Derleth and Schorer.

To touch upon certain points in your last letter: You have certainly shown up my vagueness and ignorance in regard to Gallic history! Of course, if I had stopped to reflect, I ought to have known that the Romans were still strong in Gaul about the time of Moriamis, and that French, as a language was not yet born from the Latin womb. I suppose the fact that I was dealing with a realm no less mythical than Cabell's Poictesme[2] made me doubly careless about correlating its chronology with that of historic Europe. If ever there is any prospect of issuing Azédarac and the other Averoigne tales in book form, I shall certainly correct the anachronistic reference to the "obsolete variant" of French spoken by Moriamis. I think, though, that the Druids can well stand: Averoigne was no doubt even more of a stronghold for the cult than Brittainy [*sic*]; and the Roman occupation (though I have spoken of it in another tale, The Disinterment of Venus) was quite nominal, especially in its religious effect on the Averoignians.

Indeed, the long decadence of the Roman Empire is a fascinating study; and evidently you are thoroughly posted on its details. I agree with you that a fine and poignant story could be drawn from the sensations of a Gallo-Roman who had outlived his own time and had seen about him the gradual crystallization of wholly alien medieval France. The linguistic specimens you quote, showing the transition of Latin into old French, are highly interesting. I wonder if a study (theoretic, at least) could not be made of the obscure racial, mental and palatal peculiarities that led or contributed to this phonetic devolution and clipping of the stately Latin. The study could cover also the development of the other Romance languages.

I have greatly enjoyed the de la Mare volume. Mr. Kempe is a fine tale, and one is not likely to forget either the setting or the central character. However, it seems to me that a stronger suggestive element could easily have been worked in. All Hallows, on the other hand, is beyond improvement and beyond praise. To me, it is even more satisfactory than Seaton's Aunt. The powerfully hinted idea of demoniac *reconstruction* is about as good as anything in weird fiction and is wholly original.

No, I have not read The Dark Chamber, and would be vastly indebted to you for a sight of the volume. The Geography of Witchcraft and The Lady who

Came to Stay are both awaiting your summons. I regret that I cannot altogether share the enthusiasm of Derleth and Shea in regard to the latter. However, it is far from bad, albeit, in the main, a second-rate reminiscence of Henry James. The Geography is a veritable mine of evidence bearing on the witch-cult; and the dark identity of details in numberless cases farscattered in time and place is surely proof of the underlying reality. No doubt the prevalence of the cult in medieval times was partly due to intolerable social misery: this flight into Satanism, supernaturalism and carnal orgy was an avenue of escape for the more neurotic or unfortunate. Also—granting the existence of supernatural powers and their influence on human life—the belief in evil forces and the impulse to propitiate them and form alliances with them was certainly far from irrational. Manichaeism is a practical inference when one considers the world as it is, and tries to explain the world as a creation or playground of superhuman forces.

Other theories than those of Summers and Miss Murray have been advanced anent sorcery. Some time ago, there was a series of articles by one Prof. Rene Thénevin, which appeared in the Sunday supplement of Hearst's Examiner.[3] Possibly you saw a syndication of these articles, in which Thenevin maintained the existence of prehistoric supermen, a little of whose science survived the foundering of former continents and was preserved by ancient priests and medieval witches. From this viewpoint, the witches and warlocks were the only enlightened people in ages of darkness and gross superstition, and their Sabbats were merely secret educational conclaves or class-meetings! If you haven't seen these articles, I'll enclose the ones I have with The Geography. Unluckily, I only procured three or four out of the seven chapters of the series. I know nothing about Thenevin's claims to scholarship; but at any rate his contentions and data are abundantly stimulative to the imagination. In one chapter, he brings forward a theory that the African negroes are a degenerate remnant of the Lemurians, and supports this by instancing the progressive decadence, through historic times, of certain African civilizations. This is pretty much in line with theosophic theories; though, as far as I can gather, Thenevin is not familiar with occultism, or at least has not considered it in forming his own theorem.

Of course, I do not think for a moment that there is any doubt about the true character of the Sabbats and those who participated in them. But Thenevin's ideas anent the survival of the elder lore are not so remote from our own fictional speculations!

I'm glad the newspaper clippings were of interest. Thanks for your suggestion about the Boer witch-woman: she might well have gone to Zimbabwe and imbibed certain vaporous or shadowy outside influences from those unholy ruins. I may yet use her in a story; she certainly looks the part assigned to her.

The pictures by Biegas are certainly powerful. Many years ago, I saw a magazine article giving reproductions of some of his sculptures which, if my memory does not fail me, were even stronger and more striking than this pictorial work. Many of them symbolized music or the work of particular musicians; and the sense of fluent, surging rhythm imparted to the static medium was indeed extraordinary. Some were like sea-billows towering and breaking in a foam of eerie faces. There was one remarkable piece, entitled Beethoven: the to[r]so and head of an austere Titan, with separate faces in the eyeballs! Another, called Chopin, whose details I cannot remember, has left an impression of macabre fury and madness.

Morse sent me a list of his collection of weird literature and art; and it seemed to me that he had a quite respectable beginning. The field of weird art is an immense one however; and no doubt one could spend several fortunes and lifetimes in covering it thoroughly. I imagine some of the most potent examples would come from the Orient, particularly from China and Japan. All peoples and ages would contribute, more or less. By the way, apropos of this subject, did you know that John Barrymore did some quite powerful eerie drawings in his younger days? I have, or did have, an article from the Cosmopolitan (dated somewhere around the early 1900s) in which some specimens were reproduced.[4]

Thanks for that newsphoto of the Ashton house! I knew there were some Ashtons in the South (Virginia, I believe) but had not seen the name before in connection with New England. Most of the family (the old direct line, anyway) were Catholics. One sometimes sees the name spelt Assheton; and there are evidently a lot of Assheton-Smiths or Smithes in England.

Thanks too for the offer to loan me some of your choice clippings. Don't go to any extra trouble in this matter, but you might slip in a few with your letters. I'll read and return them carefully.

My writing is still held up, and I have not finished anything. I hope my mother will be able to get around a little before long.

I enclose a recent letter from Desmond Hall. . . . "Play around with psychoanalysis . . . . suggest that nothing in the universe is inexplicable," etc. Grrrr! I'm afraid I'll have a hard time in suiting the requirements of that crew. Psychoanalysis is not my favorite superstition or form of pseudo-science. However, there is no doubt that some excellent weird or semi-weird tales could be written dealing with obscure physical and mental phenomena, without actual recourse to anything supernatural; and I infer that this is what Hall wants. Anyway, he evidently feels that Astounding needs some variety to raise it out of the ruck; and in this I heartily agree with him. In my own letter, I had expressed polite regret over the narrowing of policy, and had suggested that the magazine could well afford to run at least one tale of non-technical fantasy per issue. Also, I pointed out the glaring inconsistency of science fiction readers, who will swallow any sort of outrageous fairy tale if it is served up with an accompaniment of ray-guns, ether-ships, time-machines, etc.

The Olsen letter, which I return, is most illuminating. Some one, I forget whom, has fathered a book on the sort of cosmogony at which O. is apparently driving. Of course, if you accept the idea that the earth's surface is really the *inside* of a sphere surrounding the negligible remainder of the cosmos, then the space-conceptions implied in your Witchhouse story are most egregiously fallacious. This letter is really a marvel of lucidity compared to the 10 or twelve page monograph on the nobility of ghouls, vampires et al which I received from Olsen in correction of my Nameless Offspring and the errors of Abdul Alhazred. It would seem that the bats in Olsen's belfry—or the spirochetæ in his spinal column—are less gyrationally active than of yore. However, it is plain that he has not relinquished his position of mentor-in-chief to the Weird Tales contributors! His offer to instruct you in person for 25 paltry pazoors is truly magnanimous not to say magnific.

Winter seems to have arrived, and the mercury hugs the freezing-point around sunrise. I envy your steam-heat!

Yours, in the name of Kamog,[5]
Klarkash-Ton

[*Notes on envelope by HPL:*]
Valerius Trevirus ~~De Tribibus Gallicis~~
Simaesis = Ximes
Avionium = Vyones
Flavius Alesius—"Annales" ref. to Averones
as coming from sunken W. continent & bringing
hellish Liber Ivonis

Valerius Trevirus de Noctis Rebus
an hellish necromantic work (circa A.D. 390)

Niger informisque ut ~~deus Sadoqua~~ numen Averonum Sadoqua

Black & unform'd, as pestilent a clod
As dread Sadoqua, Averonia's god.
Theobald's tr. 1711[6]

Eibon tr. Gaspard du Nord 12th cent.

Notes

1. The cover for the March 1934 *WT,* by Margaret Brundage, illustrated "The Black Gargoyle." The illustration referred to below, for the cover of the December 1933 issue, was not for any particular story. Brundage's covers typically were nudes.
2. A fictional country or province that forms the setting of fantasy works of James Branch Cabell, known collectively as *The Biography of Manuel.*
3. René Thévenin (1877–1967), French science fiction writer. He wrote a nine-part series, "A Race of Supermen Who Disappeared 20,000 Years Ago," for the *American Weekly* (the Sunday supplement to the Hearst newspapers) from 15 November 1931 to 10 January 1932.
4. See Hjalmar Hjorth Boyesen, "John Barrymore's Work," *Cosmopolitan* 32, No. 3 (January

1902): 305–8, containing reproductions of four drawings by Barrymore.

5. A nod to "The Thing on the Doorstep."

6. HPL consulted these notes when writing to Fritz Leiber on 25 January 1937 (*Letters to C. L. Moore and Others* 321), which has the dates 390 A.D. and 1711, contrary to his next letter to CAS (see letter 256), which gives the dates 400 and 1727.

[256]   [ALS, Northern Illinois University]

From the Ruined Brick Tower
with the Sealed Door—Hour of the
Black, Beating Wings——
[Postmarked 13 December 1933]

Dear Klarkash-Ton:—

Glad to hear that the "Doorstep" did not impress you as too inadequate—though I still feel a profound dissatisfaction with something about it. In everything I do there is a certain concreteness, extravagance, or general crudeness which defeats the vague but insistent object I have in mind. I start out trying to find symbols expressive of a certain mood induced by a certain visual conception (such as a sunset beyond fantastic towers, a steep, cobblestoned hill street, a great stone vault, a sense of alienage & ineffable antiquity in a house, a stirring of black wings over a black abyss, or a cryptic beam of light from a primordial stone turret in a Asian desert of rock), but when I come to put anything on paper the chosen symbols seem forced, awkward, childish, exaggerated, & essentially inexpressive. I have staged a cheap, melodramatic puppet-show without saying what I wanted to say in the first place. Whether the sensations I strive to utter are actually too nebulous or intangible for concrete utterance, or whether I am simply unequal to the task of uttering them, I have not yet been able to decide; although I tend to incline toward the latter explanation. And—adopting this theory—I am further unable to decide whether my incapacity proceeds from a lack of natural endowments, or whether it is a result of excessive familiarity with pulp fiction & its puerile crudities. But be all this as it may, the fact remains that whatever I write lacks the subtlety & maturity needed to give really effective expression to the mood behind the picture. For example—at present I am haunted by the cloudy notion of brooding, elder forces surrounding or pervading an ancient house & seeking to achieve some sort of bodily formulation. Well & good. A real artist could make something of the idea. But when I sit down & try to think up the suitable elements—the nature of the elder forces, the reason for their concentration in this spot, the precise manner of their manifestation, their motive in seeking embodiment, & their procedure when embodied—I find that every idea occurring to me is hackneyed & commonplace. What I get is a mere catalogue of stock paraphernalia too crude & derivative to have any convincingness or adult significance. What I wanted to say remains unsaid—& the mystery of an old, shadowy house's suggestions remains unexplained. Thus I feel poignantly the truth of that observation in W. Compton Leith's "Sirenica"—"but woe to those who are made to dream the creator's dream without his finer understanding or his skill of capture."[1] During the past week—& largely under the imaginative stimulus resulting from my trip to Plymouth's archaic lanes & bordering hills—I have been constantly attempting tales; though each one has been destroyed after a few pages because of the imaginative barrenness & cheap, concrete mechanicality revealed. After all, it may be that my relation to phantasy is that of the appreciative reader & spectator rather than that of the utterer or creator. At any rate, I shall not finish any more tales unless they are better than my previous attempts. Meanwhile the experimenting goes on . . . . . the quest for even half-way adequate images & incidents. I'll think over that possible change in the ending of the "Doorstep" tale. If there were any objection, it would be merely that the use of magic on Derby's part is *unnecessary*. The principle of *exchange* is so fully outlined before, that the existence of consciousness in the transferred victim is provided for without an additional element. However, it might be more effective—because less outrageously improbable in atmosphere—to go back & start the matter afresh by having the survival of consciousness in the corpse something resulting from a special & immediate sorcery rather than from the general mental mastery established by Ephraim–Asenath. In that case Asenath (as Edward would come to realise when the pull from the grave began to be apparent) would have had time during a death struggle to formulate a spell holding her consciousness to her soon-to-be-dead body. This would have to be indicated in Edward's final communication. *Then* it might be that Edward, when realising that his mind was being crowded out, could be represented as weaving a spell to preserve a trace of consciousness in the buried body after his mind-vibrations were transferred to that horrible vehicle. However—it is doubtful whether he could be willing to do this *voluntarily*, even to save the world from Ephraim, since the experience of being in a rotting body, with consciousness, would be so necessarily hideous. The transfer of *personality* to the corpse must of course be *automatic*, since *exchange* is the basic principle of the whole story. The dead Asenath could not take over Edward's body without sending his personality somehow into her own remains. It is this *inevitability* which creates the whole story. Also, it is unnecessary to invoke magic in the matter of the corpse's escape from its shallow grave. Asenath could have escaped had she wished to, but she did not so wish. There was no need of securing liberty for a dead & anyhow unwanted corpse when a good living body in the outside world was about to be seized. Indeed, Ephraim–Asenath probably took a grim pleasure in the idea of thrusting Edward's consciousness down into that corpse-pit of horror. She never thought the poor sap would have the stamina to escape, even though he had nerved himself up to the killing. And so it goes. There might be an

increase in plausibility to have Asenath & Edward unable to survive consciously in a dead body without additional special spells—& yet this idea
would involve an extra element easily capable of cumbrousness, besides sub-
tracting measurably from the air of *inevitability* pervading & motivating the
whole tale. There would be a sort of decrease in atmospheric *unity*—& a very
sharp contradiction of the aura of *essential passivity* (except in simple, desperate
lunges under direct & irresistible stimuli) surrounding Edward's character. In
a word, I can see reasons both for & against the change; & will reflect carefully upon the matter. We'll see what Two-Gun Bob & the Peacock Sultan have
to say about it. I'm still undecided whether I'll let young Comte d'Erlette tear
it to shreds. After two or three more verdicts I may consider a trial on Satrap
Pharnabozus—though I don't want to overload him after his belated acceptance of the collaborated piece. And I don't like the psychological effect
on myself of repeated rejections. L'affaire Knopf is still too damned recent.

In my last letter to King Pharnaces I most emphatically & persuasively (I
hope) suggested that a Klarkash-Tonic design be appended to the Malik–
Abdul collaboration; but what will come of the matter I cannot say. I shall
certainly repeat the suggestion in future epistles, & there will probably be
plenty of time for His Majesty to decide—since he usually postpones the
publication of accepted material as long as he can, damn his soul! You could
give those cosmic abysses a pervasive awesomeness which no other artist
could approach. I most certainly hope you will have the "Charnel God"
job—& that this tale will have the cover-design too. The allocation of cover-
designs is a curious business. I've never had one, & Belknap has had only
one—of his "Death Waters" late in 1924. Price, on the other hand, has been
repeatedly favoured—& Munn had one for his very first contribution. But it's
hardly sour grapes which makes one remark that the honour is nothing much
to lose. The present perpetratress of chromatic vacuities is about on a par
with the unlamented Senf in point of cheerful non-weirdness, besides being
amusingly unoriginal. Utpatel ought to feel flattered—for besides the imitation in the current design, Derleth tells me that last month's woman-&-skull
motif was a direct adaptation of an Utpatel end-piece which Pharnabozus
bought & never used.[2] The only really good regular artist that W T ever had
was Rankin. He really had something of the feel of the bizarre. I note a drawing
of his in the current issue, but fear it's a left-over & no indication of renewed
service on his part. Incidentally—this issue is below par. Young Melmoth's
"Lady in Grey" is the best tale—a remarkable atmospheric achievement—with
Two-Gun's "Old Garfield's Heart" as a good second. Apart from these two,
there's nothing worth reading in the whole damned issue.

Regarding Roman Gaul—of course, the people were largely of the Gallic
race, but they had the culture of Rome & employed Roman names. Local
municipal officials were native Gallo-Romans, but provincial governors (of
gawd knows what race-stock in that age of imperial mongrelism) & the army

were sent out from Italy. The matter of Druids is really quite all right; for although they were outlawed & officially obsolete, they really had tremendous influence in their remote backwaters. Even to the Romans in Italy they represented something fascinating & forbidden, & furtive consultations of them (as modern dupes consult clairvoyants & other representatives of unofficial supernaturalism today) were by no means infrequent among those supposed to hold them in abhorrence. For example—if we are to believe the account of Vopiscus in the Augustan History, at least two Emperors—Aurelianus & Diocletianus—consulted Druid priestesses in Gaul despite the outlawry of the sect. In the Regio Averonum, of course, Druidism was stronger than anywhere else—a circumstance perhaps connected with the doubtful & possibly very strange origin of the old tribe of Averones themselves. You of course recall that famous passage in Flavius Alesius, where it is suggested that the Averones (a dark race like the Aquitani) came from a great land in the western ocean which had sunk beneath the waves. Alesius has some fascinating references to a terrifying set of tablets—the *Liber Ivonis*—in the possession of the Averones, which was said to have been brought by them from the lost ancient land whence they came. Whether this could be identical with that infamous *Livre d'Eibon* which in the 12ᵗʰ century the wizard Gaspard du Nord translated from some (so far) unascertained language into the French of Averoigne, is a problem with which scholarship must sooner or later wrestle. But of the dark & curious reputation of the Averones there can of course be no doubt. All scholars recall the reference to this tribe & its hellish pre-Druidic deity in Valerius Trevirus' famous & rather sinister poem (circa A.D. 400) "De Noctis Rebus":

NIGER.INFORMISQVE.VT.NVMEN.AVERONVM.SADOQVA.[3]

Thus rendered in Theobald's translation (London, 1727):

> Black & unſhap'd, as peſtilent a Clod
> As dread SADOQUA, Averonia's God.

Rome is a subject which has fascinated me uncannily ever since I first heard much of it around the age of six. From the moment I picked up any idea of its nature, history, & characteristics, & held in my own hands the actual Roman coins (about 2 dozen—now in my possession) of my grandfather's collection, I have had the most persistent sensation (out of which an occultist would make a case of metempsychosis, & a pseudo-scientist one of hereditary memory) of some ineluctable connexion with the ancient Respublica—of complete identification with the world of M. Porcius Cato, P. Cornelius Scipio, C. Laelius, M. Tullius Cicero & T. Lucretius Carus. It is at times almost as strong as my feeling of membership in the more recent eighteenth century—an actual Roman coin, statue, stela, sarcophagus, household utensil, or weapon moves me with the oddest sort of *pseudo-memory;* whilst pictures of Roman scenes prompt a kindred

feeling mixed with certain unexplainable objections as if to *anachronisms* I cannot
consciously place. It is utterly impossible, too, for me to regard Rome in a *de-
tached* way. As soon as I get behind the age of the Saxons in England, say 450
A.D., my sense of personal connexion with my own blood-ancestors of the
north utterly vanishes—giving place to a natural & unshakable feeling of *being a
Roman*. Thus I cannot discuss Rome with an anti-Roman (cf. his "Worms of the
Earth" &c) like Two-Gun Bob without a sense of *personal anger* which I can re-
press only with difficulty. The idea of the republic of the consuls & empire of
the Caesars being other than *my country* is simply impossible for me to entertain.
I recognise Rome's defects, but always have to excuse them as I would England's & America's. I cannot envisage antiquity except as a Roman. Anterior to
the Saxon-England period, my own forbears become to me nothing more
than "*those* Germani who harass *our* Roman frontiers along the Fluvii Rhenus
et Danubius." Conan's identification of himself with the barbarous tribes
who fought Rome is a feat of imagination I cannot possibly envisage—nor
can I understand the feelings of those pious Puritans of early New England
who viewed antiquity from a Biblical & Hebraic angle. To me, the idea of being anything but a Roman in ancient times is as grotesque as the idea of being
anything but an Englishman is in modern times. Rome—to my subconscious
mind—is the *norm* of antiquity. The northern races are simply opponents
across the Rhine & Danube, or border people lately made Roman; whilst the
"Holy Land" of the Sunday schools is simply a remote Syrian region which
our general Cn. Pompeius took from a bunch of squabbling princelets in the
consulship of M. Cicero & C. Antonius, whilst cleaning up the empire of the
Seleucidae after the victory over Mithridates. Greece, too, has not for me the
direct kinship it has for Loveman. I respect its superior culture, but I feel toward it the slight hostility of one who recalls the insults of the Tarentines, the
plottings of Macedonia with Hannibal, & the haughty rebuffs of Diaeus & the
Achaean League—all of which forced us to subjugate the Hellenic world &
form out of it the ROMAN provinces of Achaia, Epirus, Illyricum, & so on. I
think of Greeks as cultivated but somewhat sycophantic aliens—good tutors
of rhetoric & philosophy, but a little servile, unctuous, ratlike, sharp, & ef-
feminate—in a word, not quite as much *men* as real ROMANS. I can understand the tinge of patronage in the contemptuous diminutive expression
Graeculus. In a word, I have to think of the whole Grecian world from a *Roman* angle—something connected with eastern wars & proconsuls & foreign
travel & academic studies. In the ancient world, home means the temple-
crowned hills & crowded lanes of ROMA, or the semi-wooded slopes &
hilled fields & sprawling villas of the Sabine countryside. I even have a curi-

ous & anomalous sense of kinship with the hawk-nosed, broad-templed Roman *physiognomy,** aberrant as it is from the Nordic standpoint of my own blood. All *other* non-Nordic physiognomies repel me violently—but the *Roman* features (which of course have no living representatives today), as displayed in the realistic portrait statuary of the republican age, produce in me a profound feeling of *stirred memories* & *quasi-identity.* I have the curious subconscious feeling not only that *people around me once looked like that,* but that *I once looked like that.* Which is rather amusing in view of the fact that I am actually the *utter reverse* of Roman in appearance—tall, chalk-white, & of a characteristic & unmistakable Nordic English physiognomy. In school I took to Latin as a duck to water, but found all other languages alien & repellent. French seemed to me a pitiful decadence-product; German a hateful tongue from across the Rhine-Danube frontier. Greek I liked & respected—but I found it difficult, & tended to translate it mentally into Latin. Nor have I ever quite ceased to have Roman *dreams* of the most puzzling vividness & detail. You probably recall the one I had in October 1927,[4] in which I was a provincial quaestor named L. Caelius Rufus serving in Hispania Citerior & accompanying the proconsul P. Scribonius Libo & a cohort of infantry into the mountains behind Pompelo—where a nightmare doom overtook us all. I told that dream in full to Belknap, & he incorporated it without any linguistic change in his "Chaugnar" story.[5] The vivid reality of that dream is impossible to describe. I lived *for days* as a Roman in Spain—rising, reading, talking, travelling—even after six years the memory is *disconcertingly* vivid. In view of phenomena like that I can well understand the supernatural beliefs of ages when psychological science—with its knowledge of early unconscious impressions & the associations, selective perceptions, & disproportionate image-retentions resulting from such—was unborn. Actually, I suppose my Roman "memories" come from a peculiar chain of associations. I love *anything* in the *past,* & from infancy had a feeling of living in the bygone age represented by Providence's ancient hill streets & the old books in the attic at home—i.e., the 18th century. *Real* antiquity— 2000 years instead of a mere 150 years ago—represented an *intensification* of this time-defying feeling; & of all antiquity, only that of *Rome* was *realistically close* because *only the Romans used our alphabet* & had architectural forms (I doted on pictures) like the arches & columns & pediments of our familiar Georgian architecture. Also, my grandfather's Roman coins were (except for an Egyptian ushabti & a bit of mummy linen) the only *actual objects of the ancient world* which we had at home & accessible to my actual touch. I cannot begin to

---

*The blood composition of the Roman people is still highly obscure. A large Nordic element probably did exist, but it was mixed (largely through the Etruscans) with much brachycephalic Alpine & possibly Semitic stock.

suggest the feeling of *awe* & *anomalous familiarity* which those coins—the actual products of Roman engravers & mints, & actually passed from Roman hand to Roman hand twenty centuries ago—awaked in me. The half-effaced designs of imperial heads of symbolic figures—the almost illegible lettering— S. C.... COS. III .... CONSTANTINVS ..... COMMODVS .... AEQVITAS .... Even today as I take them out & look at them the old feeling of uncanny Roman linkage returns. And in the front parlour downstairs (a really hauntingly beautiful room, furnished in an old-gold motif with ebony-&-gilt woodwork & a great pier glass) was a *life-size* marble reproduction of the *Roman* portrait-bust popularly (& erroneously) known today as "Clytië"[6]—the only *life-size* piece of statuary in the house, & highly impressive on its gilded pedestal. (We still have it—& have resurrected it from storage to adorn a niche in the Georgian living-room at 66 College) Well—anyhow—of all these incidents, plus some timely allusions to Rome in a childish reading-book & some pictures of Roman ruins which my grandfather had brought back from Italian travels, was compounded my strange feeling of kinship & identification, with all its peculiar intensity. Despite a multiplicity of other interests it has never left me—so that one of my most poignant experiences was a first sight of the splendid Pantheon model in the Metropolitan Museum in 1922. To this day I have a touchy *Roman patriotism* which resents any slight toward the ancient Mistress of the World, & which exults in all the visible symbols of Roman dominion—the fasces, the glistening eagles, the she-wolf, the triumphal arch, the sonorous Latin speech ...... & all this despite the absence in my veins of any drop of non-British blood or any hereditary tradition apart from England & New England. I have *Welsh* lines on the paternal side which might let my fancy form links with Machen's Britanno-Roman world of Isca Silurum & the Second Augustan Legion—but (because of my father's early death & my rearing amidst my mother's family) I did not know this till long after the beginning of my Roman predilections—in the later years when I studied the genealogical charts & notes which were either uninteresting or largely unintelligible to me in early childhood. [My father's maternal grandmother was a Morris of Clasemont, Glamorganshire—an Anglo-Welsh line of Norman origin, but including native Cymric lines (Rhys, Jenkins, Parry, &c) some of which profess descent (probably fabulous) from Owen Gwynedd & other Welsh princes. When I first learned of this, I liked to imagine an extension back to the Roman occupation, & a strain of real Roman blood proceeding from some centurio or legatus in the legions of A. Plautius, T. Flavius Vespasianus, P. Ostorius Scapula, L. Suetonius Paullinus, Cn. Julius Agricola, or some other conqueror.] Anyhow, I acquired a tremendous instinctive sense of Roman linkage, & ransacked libraries with almost morbid avidity for anything & everything pertaining to Rome. Especially was I on the lookout for *anything which would bring the period of Roman culture toward the present*—hence my disproportionate interest in the late Empire (which I always recognised as decadent &

mongrelised, & inferior to the Ciceronian age) & in the last survivals of Roman culture in Italy, France, & Spain. Half the stories I wrote during that research period (when I was 14, 15, & 16) had to do with strange survivals of Roman civilisation in Africa, Asia, the Antarctic, the Amazon Valley, & even pre-Columbian North America. They are all destroyed now, but I wish I had kept the one (based on an actual dream of 1904) about *Roman Providence*, with its familiar hills crowned with many-columned temples & its forum near the site of the Great Bridge (I had a marble bridge there—the Pons Æbutii, named from L. Æbutius, the founder of the colony of B.C. 45, which was tragically cut off from the mother respublica whence the colonising fleet of six quin-quiremes had sailed). I had Roman wars with the Narragansetts, Wampanoags, & Pequots, a gradual blood mixture which gave the whole mass of Eastern Indians their still-unexplained (in view of the known Mongoloid basis of the whole race) aquiline features, & a final destruction of MOTIATICVM (Ind. *Moshassuck*) by an earthquake. I had the story begin with the exhumation of a Roman column on the ancient hill during the digging of a sewer-main—the universal perplexity it aroused, & the dreams it inspired in one lone student. My native highway Angell Street (*actually* the Wampanoag Trail, older than English colonisation, & *naturally* determined as the shortest line between the ford at the head of the bay & the narrow ferrying-place in the Seekonk River) was a Roman road, lined with tombs as it stretched beyond the marble temples & brick-&-plaster houses of urban Motiaticum. All very childish—but illustrative of a tendency from which I am not even now free. Regarding the formation of the Romance languages—the scarcity of records of the Dark Ages, the lack of data concerning the extent of *aboriginal* speech-survivals (Etruscan, Gallic, Iberian, &c) amongst the rural peasantry of the various regions in question, the fragmentary knowledge of vulgar as distinguished from educated Latin idioms in each of these regions, & the unsolved problem of the exact dialectic affiliations of the various Teutonic invaders—Visigoths, Heruli, Langobardi, Ostrogoths, Vandals, Franks, Burgundians, & so on—all combine to make the precise causes & steps of the parallel mutation-processes highly obscure. However, many significant inferences can be made. There were of course two distinct kinds of change at work—a general internal weakening of Latin common to all the Roman world & manifest in the lapse of inflections, the outcroppings of typical solecisms, &c., & a set of specific local aberrations due to distinct regional causes (usually barbarian invasions.) In Italy, despite a good deal of Teutonic invasion, the internal weakening was the principal cause of de-cay. Vulgar forms long existing (in some cases Etruscan, Oscan, & Umbrian *archaisms* surviving from prehistoric times) began to come uppermost, though without any specifically *alien* influences. To this day, the Italian vocabulary is singularly free (save for new coinages to express new objects) from words of non-Latin derivation. In France & Spain most of the local influences toward change were Teutonic—very little buried aboriginal influence surviving. Spain's

case, of course, was complicated by the *Arabic* influence—a much stronger
thing than is commonly realised. Few seem to recall that in the Dark Ages
many Aryan Spaniards lived almost like Arabs in the towns—speaking Arabic
though retaining a neo-Latin personal nomenclature & the Christian religion
(for which they had an Arabic version of the Bible).* Modern Spanish has a distinctly Oriental cast. The details of Romance-language study—including Portugese, Catalan, Gallician, Provençal, Roumanian, & all the radically different
peasant dialects of Italy—could keep a whole university foundation busy for
generations, as I quickly realised in the days of my intensive inquiries. Such
work is not for me—whose linguistic aptitude is notoriously bad. But the subject certainly is fascinating & hard to let alone.

I'm glad you found the de la Mare book interesting, & am almost ready
to agree that "All-Hallows" at least equals the more famous "Seaton's Aunt".
I think I felt its profound suggestive potency more thoroughly upon re-reading
it this autumn, than upon reading it originally in 1926. There is an unforgettable
horror about that lonely seacoast church, the minute, subtle influences seeming
to pervade it, & the black suggestions of malign reconstructions here & there
visible. As for Cline's "Dark Chamber"—it goes forward under separate cover, & if you don't find it one of the most evilly menacing books you ever
read, I miss my guess. Good old Canevin doted on it, whilst Sonny Belknap
became ecstatic to the point of inarticulateness over its shadows & overtones.
For years after he & I read it we used to point to spots on the Palisades
across the Hudson & fancy we saw the dim walls of a ghostly Mordance Hall
. . . . . especially at twilight, when strange shapes stood out darkly against the
fading west. God, but I'd give three-fourths of my soul to be able to write a
book like that—with all sorts of shades of macabre mood poignantly crystal-
lised without the least trace of extravagance or slopping-over! Keep it as long
as you like—& that goes for "The Connoisseur", too. I'll be tremendously
grateful for the "Geography" whenever you find a convenient time to shoot it
along. Possibly you'd better not bother about "The Lady Who Came to
Stay"—for I fancy your opinion of it would be closer to mine than either
Comte d'Erlette's or little Jehvish-Êi's. I can imagine what tenebrously moving stuff there is in the Summers book. When I read that & the "Malleus Maleficarum" (which I guess I'll ask Koenig to lend me), I shall feel that I've
begun to know something about witchcraft! This sort of documentary evidence certainly brings the old practices damnably close to the stream of daily
life. As I have said, there can be no doubt of the former existence of a widespread orgiastic & ceremonial cult of anti-social degenerates—& to me Miss

---

*the real Moors called them *Mozarabes* or mock-Arabs, & tended to look down
upon them as inferior pretenders, as we look down on imitative immigrants.

Murray's theory seems the closest to truth of any yet advanced. All this belief in a cosmic background of what average human beings call "evil" is a natural result of mediaevalism's ignorance of the fortuitous, momentary, & utterly negligible position of terrestrial mankind in the infinite & eternal cosmos. The Thevenin hypothesis is essentially imaginative pseudo-science—like Lewis Spence's Atlantean dreamings, Col. Churchward's "Mu" stuff, & the theosophists' elaborate history and cosmogony. There is no evidence of any civilisation anterior to that which gradually developed somewhere within striking distance of the Nile & Tigris-Euphrates valleys, & which gradually became diffused as far as China, Easter Island, Peru, & Mexico. The negroes are not by any stretch of the imagination a *degenerated* race, but are very obviously *rudimentary* & *primitive*—an early offshoot from the main stem of *homo sapiens*. The declining African cultures so often cited—of which that of Zimbabwe is the best known—are too clearly a case of *Caucasian origin & negroid replacement* to form any argument for a decaying negro stock. Anthropology & ethnology bear this out—for the East African tribes (those which had cultures) all have tremendous mixtures of non-negro blood, whereas the always-apelike West Africans represent the flat-nosed, thick-lipped inferior stock in full purity. There is no doubt at all that great Semitic colonies—Phoenicians, Sabaean, Arabian, &c.—once existed all the way down the East African coast. Not "supermen", but simply *white* men. Your recent cutting is of extreme interest in this connexion. It is pretty easy to see that whatever civilisation prehistoric Africa had, came from the normally recognised superior races—who dwelt amongst the blacks as the English, French, Arabs, Dutch, Germans, & Portugese have done in historic times. Ebony Sambo never had any more cultural capacity than he has today! But Thevenin is damned interesting, just the same, & I'd be intensely grateful if you could lend me the *two* articles in his series of *nine* (*not seven*, as you have thought) which I do not possess & have not seen. These missing articles are for *Nov. 22* & *Nov. 29, 1931*—being the *second* & *third* of the series. Reciprocally, I can lend you any of the other articles of the series, & urge you to let me know which of the following dates you lack: *Nov. 15, 1931, Dec. 6, Dec. 13, Dec. 20, Dec. 27, Jany. 3, 1932, Jany 10.* Of these, I have duplicates of the first & last, & will be glad to let you have them permanently if you lack them. For the articles I possess I am indebted, variously, to Two-Gun Bob, Little Belknap, & Ar-E'ch-Bei. By the way—I enclose something about the new Henseling theory of Mayan antiquity which may interest you.[7] This seems to be seriously intended—however unfounded it may turn out to be. And speaking of cuttings—I've included quite a bunch of gems from my morgue in the bundle with "The Dark Chamber." You may not think the selections very brilliant—but they are simply what has appealed to my particular imagination for one reason or another, setting up chains of associative imagery. I may never develop any of them as stories—but I thought them worth saving just the same. No hurry at all about their return.

About weird art—young Morse sent me his list a year ago. One notable lack at that time was any specimen of Long's favourite *Segrelles*,[8] who figures in one of the cuttings coming to you. This bird is certainly a titan of malign phantasy. The Mayans—as illustrated by your cutting—certainly were weird artists par excellence. I'd like to shew you some of the huge Mayan sculptures (mostly *casts*, but titanically impressive for all that) in the American Museum in N.Y. & the Peabody Museum of Harvard College in Cambridge. Biegas' sculptures must be tremendous—I never heard of them before. Nor did I know that John Barrymore was ever a weird artist—though his brother Lionel's early career as an etcher of the ordinary sort is common history.

Yes—Olsen is certainly less picturesque than he used to be. His early harangues to Whitehead on "C-space" & "the vortexes", & his discourses to Conan the Cimmerian on Christ as a Vampire, exhibit a pyrotechnic ebullience scarcely parallelled in this recent emanation. I recall how he told Canevin that abstinence from food would give one immortality. Blood is death; food makes blood; therefore, no food, no death! How simple—yet the world is too dense & callous to accept this great truth & win eternal life! Your Olseniana would seem to be of the really vigorous & colourful sort! I wonder if anybody has ever *answered* one of the fellow's epistles![9]

By the way—this business about special lunar radiations is highly interesting. If Prof. Stetson is right about the matter, then my chief objection to the original "Moon Pool" (as an *All-Story* novelette, June 22, 1918) falls flat. I panned Merritt in the readers' column for having *moonlight* open the strange door in the primal Ponapean masonry when *sunlight* (chemically identical) had no such effect.[10] Other readers must have done the same, since the point was removed in the book edition. And yet if this idea of electric distinctiveness is correct, then Merritt was *more correct than he himself knew*. But this remains to be seen. One must use caution in accepting novel data. Thanks vastly for sight of the item.

Marquis d'Esmond's letter is certainly explicit enough. He has many excellent & high-sounding intentions, but they don't always work out right! I can understand his aversion for the *conventionally* weird, but fear he desires something too prosaically clear-cut & too laden with technical atmosphere to be really artistic. I think a good part of your work could be made to meet his demands, though I doubt if any of mine could. I hereby return the document with much appreciation. My own dissatisfaction with the bulk of published weird material may or may not spring from a source basically like Frére d'Esmond's. What I object to is crudity, conventionality, & puerile concreteness in the symbols & incidents used to embody the given mood. I don't like a supernaturalism which childishly *contradicts* (rather than vaguely *extends*) the laws of the cosmos, or capriciously departs from any coherent conception of complex natural entity. Common legends with their arbitrary extravagances & unconvincing vestiges of primitive naivete & ignorance, seem to me especially poor material unless handled with tremendous adroitness & atmospheric power. Really potent suggestions of the supernormal can come only through subtle and highly atmospheric *hinting*—momentary *glimpses* of something *not too well defined,* just beyond the scope of full or dependable visibility. But I despair of ever being able to write anything of this description myself.

Regarding the surname *Ashton,* I imagine it is originally of geographical derivation, connecting the possessors with estates in the region of Ashton-under-Lyne, in Lancashire. Incidentally—there is a village of Ashton in Rhode Island, named for the Lancashire original (a great cotton centre since 1769) because of its textile industries. The Ashton family is of great antiquity in Providence, James Ashton having been on the military rolls in 1654. In 1700 or shortly after the family owned wharves & warehouses along the waterfront, indicating participation in the town's pioneer sea-trade. At present our quasi-landlord (the superintendent of Brown University's real estate, from whom our *direct* landlord rents the house of which we occupy the upper half), to whom we complain about all leaks, bad ceilings, & the like, is a Mr. Ashton—& the presence of his son in college as a thriving sophomore indicates a vigorous & creditable local continuation of the line. This line is of course Protestant, like all ancient New England lines. Anyhow, I fancy you will find your remote kin creditably upholding the traditions of the house whether in Old England, New England, or Virginia!

Thanks for the interesting view of Auburn's outspread roofs—the town certainly must be extremely pleasant, despite the occasional visitations of the frost-daemon. It's cold as hell in Providence right now—mercury going down to 18° or so some nights. I haven't been out of the house in two days—thank Cthulhu, Tsathoggua, & Mr. Ashton for the steam which saves an old man's life! And to think of that hot Plymouth Thanksgiving only a week & a half ago!

By this time you will have received my card expressing the pleasure & admiration with which I read "The Seven Geases". Congratulations on Satrap Pharnabozus' reconsideration—I feel sure that he will decide favourably this time. That bird's caprice & vacillation are something to marvel at!

Crawford tells me that *Unusual* will soon be out—albeit in a humbler format than at first proposed. Pulp paper, 44 pp. 6 × 9, 10 pt. type, price 10 cents. He has asked for a biography & picture of me for his third issue. I've cooked up something—but in accordance with orders must cut it down to 900 words.[11] I'll let you see it presently. Koenig has high hopes for the magazine, but I am inclined to fear that it will be hard to float—though at last accounts Crawford spoke of the possibility of getting the Am. News Co. to handle it. Baldwin still professes his intention of publishing "The Colour Out of Space"—he is now borrowing my old stories, of which he has read only a few.

My aunt & I both hope your mother will be up & around shortly. Confinement to bed is certainly an exasperating process, as my aunt can well testify from recent experience!

Again let me thank you for the proffered bibliothecal loan. I'll mail "The Dark Chamber" as soon as the weather lets me get out to the P.O.

Yrs. for the Black Catechism of Primal Averonia—

E'ch-Pi-El

Notes

1. P. 64 (of 1916 ed.).

2. The cover art for both issues does not illustrate a story.

3. *De Noctis Rebus* translates to "On the Things of the Night" (by analogy with Lucretius' *De Rerum Natura* [On the Nature of Things]). A literal translation of the line (a good iambic hexameter) would be: 'Black and shapeless, Sadoqua [is] the god of the Averones."

4. If HPL did describe his dream in a letter to CAS, it has not been found.

5. I.e., *The Horror from the Hills*.

6. HPL refers to the original marble portrait bust (c. 40–50 CE, Naples?) in the British Museum of a woman, possibly the younger Antonia; long identified as the nymph Clytie.

7. Robert Henseling (1883–1964) was a German astronomer and writer, author of "The Scope and Antiquity of Mayan Astronomy," *Research and Progress* Vol. 4 (1938): 121–28.

8. Josep Segrelles Albert (1885–1969), painter and Valencian illustrator.

9. August Derleth informed CAS in a letter of 20 May 1932 (ms., JHL) that he wrote a letter to Olsen, "and couldn't resist having a little fun with him."

10. HPL's letter on the subject has not been found. He refers to Harlan True Stetson (1885–1964), American astronomer and physicist, for whom a lunar crater is named. The following text was omitted from the book version: "'There is a powerful quality in moonlight, as both science and legends can attest. We know of its effect upon the mentality, the nervous system, even upon certain diseases. [¶] 'The moon slab is of some material that reacts to moonlight. . . .'"

11. HPL's first version of the autobiographical "Some Notes on a Nonentity" (written 22 November 1933; published in 1943) ran to about 3000 words. The abridged, 900-word version (which Crawford did not publish) was long thought to be lost, but the typescript recently surfaced. See "Notes on a Nonentity," *Lovecraft Annual* No. 4 (2010): 163–65.

[257]   [ANS][1]

[Postmarked Providence, R.I.,
14 December 1933]

Well—no sooner had my epistle gone out of the house than the expressman brought your welcome packet—the "Geography" & the "Lady". Have thumbed through the pages of the former, & it looks as though it promises an even rarer feast than the kindred volumes I have recently read. Old Monty's scholarship certainly is profound to the very last degree. I shall be interested to see how far the "Lady" comes toward justifying the intemperate admiration of Comte d'Erlette & Jehvish-Êi. ¶ "Dark Chamber" & cuttings will go on the road as soon as I get down town. The weather has slightly moderated, so that I may make it today or tomorrow. ¶ This card shews a finely panelled room taken from an old house at the foot of the hill not so very far from here. I never saw it in its original site, but have visited it in its present Brooklyn habitat. Another room from the same house is in a museum in Minneapolis, Minn.—young Melmoth's home territory.[2] The old brick house, stripped of its fine wood-work, still stands—in a neighbourhood of slowly decaying commercialism.

Yrs with the blessings of Nefren-Ka—
E'ch-Pi-El

[P.S.] Glad to see the item about Crowley. What a queer duck! He is the orig-inal of Clinton in Wakefield's "They Return at Evening."[3]

Notes

1. *Front:* Parlor, Joseph Russell House, Providence, R. I., 1773. The Brooklyn Museum.

2. The John and William Russell House (1772) at 118 North Main Street, one of the first large, grand houses built in Providence during the mercantile era. By the early 20th century it was a rooming house, and it was stripped of its interiors, now found in museums across the country. The room HPL refers to is at The Minneapolis Institute of Art.

3. HPL refers to the story "'He Cometh and He Passeth By'" in *They Return at Evening.*

[258]   [ANS][1]

[Postmarked Auburn, Cal.,
16 December 1933]

Picture on back shows the uptown section of Auburn as seen from courtyard of local high school. ¶ Yr last received. Thanks for impressive view of Provi-dence State House. *Geog. Witchcraft* and *Lady who Came to Stay* will go forward to you very shortly. Hope you have received *The Seven Geases.* Wright says he wants another look at the ms., so am instructing Ar-Ech-Bei to forward it di-rectly to the Chicago Satrap after his perusal. Weather in this section of the citrus belt is fit for Dante's frozen circle. Yrs in the name of Michael Scott,
Klarkash-Ton

Notes

1. *Front:* Unidentified.

[259]   [ANS; RAS 1/Supplement]

[late December 1933]

[Printed card]
—In Tsathoggua's name, for the Nighted Solstitial Sabbat—E'ch-Pi-El.
MDCCCXXXIII.

"CAS and Marion Sully
For Éch-Pi-El, from Klarkash-Ton—Jan. 18th, 1934."

1934

[260]   [ALS]

Dear Klarkash-Ton:—

I am inexcusably remiss in acknowledging the safe receipt & interested perusal of the Summers book & "The Lady Who Came to Stay", but you will perhaps pardon me upon learning of the hectic round in which I have been ingulph'd. Briefly—the past fortnight has marked my long-postponed visit to our young friend Belknap; a period so crammed & choked with activities that I have scarcely had time to breathe. I am still in teeming Manhattan as I begin these lines, though only Yuggoth knows whenever I'll have time to finish them before my now imminent return to civilisation.

I left Providence by night coach immediately after a festive home Christmas—enjoying a duplicate Yule at the Long mansion. Since then I have seen a good deal of all the gang—especially Loveman & Wandrei. Samuelus never changes or grows old, & on this occasion has been as generous as usual—presenting me with no less than three museum pieces for my collection; an Egyptian *ushabti* (about 10″ high—of bitumen-covered wood), a small Mayan idol, & a small Balinese carving of a monkey with covered eyes (evidently one of the famous Japanese triad). He has also given Belknap a fascinating little Egyptian piece—a terra-cotta sphinx-scarabeus. My *ushabti* is ineffably fascinating, & will form the central point in my collection from now on. I saw the old year out at the Loveman flat—amidst a small gathering which included the mother of the late poet Hart Crane.[1] Wandrei, too, is as delightful as usual. He introduced me to Desmond Hall of *Astounding Stories*—a very pleasing and cultivated chap, though obviously not much interested in my work. Another literary contact was with T. Everett Harré, the fellow who edited the anthology "Beware After Dark". He is a tremendously genial person—who now has a room at an hotel only a block from Belknap's. One of the most interesting things about him is his *cat*—a superb white-&-black creature named William, betwixt whom & himself a deep & sincere mutual attachment exists. But the most interesting contact of all is still to come—in the form of a dinner engagement tonight, unless something intervenes to prevent it. For behold . . . . whom is Grandpa Cthulhu about to meet but A. MERRITT himself—immortal creator of "The Moon-Pool", "The Snake-Mother", "The Dwellers in the Mirage", & a dozen other exotic thrillers! It seems that he knows about me & my stuff, & likes the latter considerably.

Hearing through a friend of Harré's that I was in town, he got in touch with me, & the aforementioned appointment is the result. He seems to be a damned successful business man—associate editor of the Hearst Sunday supplements with their Theveninic & other sensational messages. I'll tell you what he's like after I see him. Incidentally—I've seen two of the boys behind the semi-pro weird-scientifiction game . . . . Julius Schwartz & Conrad Ruppert of the erstwhile *Science Fiction Digest,* now called *Fantasy.* Ruppert, a pleasant little German-American, is the printer of the venture, & also prints *The Fantasy Fan.* Schwartz is a not unprepossessing young Jew attending the College of the City of N.Y. They called on Belknap & me a week ago, & seemed to regard us with the deference due to great literary lights! Needless to say, you are one of the most effulgent divinities in their pantheon. I haven't had time to look up Hornig in Elizabeth (which isn't far from N.Y.), but imagine he is a likable kid of the same general type. And by the way—Harré likes your work tremendously.

Another interesting person is Howard Wandrei, younger brother of our Melmoth. I was utterly astonished by the length to which he has carried his weird art—a thing whose earlier stages were indicated by the drawings for "Dark Odyssey". His skill & prowess are now absolutely marvellous—positively breath-taking. He is right in your class, & a glance at his work suggests such craftsmen as Sime, Beardsley, Harry Clarke, & other fantastic notables. You yourself probably set him going—he revels in nameless entities, blasphemous Sabbats, & everything of that nature. Some of his work is done in batik—a specimen of this being now on display at the Decorators' Club here, & written up (with illustration) in the decoration column of the N.Y. Times magazine last Sunday.[2] Such is his amazing proficiency, that he may be the first to put the name of Wandrei on the map—although he is not even nearly as personably likeable as Donald. He also writes fiction—as the current W T attests.

Another thing I've done in N Y is to get my fountain pen tinkered with. At last I have a point which feeds almost too freely—filling the looped letters, especially when nearly empty. I may let well enough alone & not try to have it regulated further—for I know damn well that any constriction of the feed will overshoot the mark & merely reopen my age-old problem of insufficient flow. This point is delectably smooth—though my wretched script does not do it justice.

I bought the new W T as soon as it came out, & was delighted with your drawing for "The Weaver in the Vault". So far as I can see, the fine strokes did not interfere in the least with good reproduction—the cut is splendid, although of course the original may have had additional merits not to be deduced from it. The thing has a haunting atmosphere, & makes one long to read the tale—which I haven't been able to do yet, since Sonny Belknap borrowed my magazine as soon as I got it, & seems now (the young rascal!) to have mislaid it. I must get another copy before the edition is sold out. Meanwhile I am anxious to see your sketch for "The Charnel God." I hope Wright will let you do the Silver Key design—the story is scheduled for July. During my brief glance at the current issue I saw a *Rankin* sketch—but fear that it was merely a belated left-over. Vita brevis, ars longa![3] And they're still using that camel heading of Belknap's "Desert Lich" (1924) as an impersonal tail piece!

But before I leave the topic of my present visit, let me mention the very interesting glimpse of our friend *Koenig*—he of the Cyclopean library—which I had the other night. I called him on the telephone & he came over to Belknap's—bearing with him a tremendous typed catalogue of his bibliothecal treasures; carbons of which he presented to my host & myself, with cordial invitations to borrow whatever we like whenever we like! Koenig is just as genial & likeable in person as on paper—a blond, blue-eyed German-American whose aspect of boyish youth is oddly at variance with what must be his actual age. (He holds important positions, & is a World War veteran.) He is highly cultivated & intelligent, but extremely modest. Conservative in his views & bearing—refreshingly free from the Bohemian pose. His admiration of your work is profound & sincere. The size & quality of his library is virtually staggering—yet it developed in conversation that *he has not read "The Dark Chamber"*! I instantly offered to supply that deficiency—hence let me suggest that, when you are finally through with the volume, you send it not to me but to him . . . *H. C. Koenig, 540 E. 80ᵗʰ St., N.Y. City.* And by the way—he pronounces his name as if it were spelled *Kay'nig.* I hope "The Dark Chamber" didn't disappoint you—indeed, I feel quite sure it couldn't have done so.

So far I've had only one glimpse of Kirk—at his shop (now moved 2 doors eastward) in 8ᵗʰ St. We invited him to a meeting of the gang at Sonny's, but he didn't shew up. He doesn't look a jot different from when I first saw him in 1922.

Belknap has a new fad now—tropical fish. They are like me—tending to languish when the temperature is under 80°! Their variety & liveliness make them rather more interesting than goldfish.

Thanks enormously for the two nameless sketches. The barb-haired entity is truly a frightful anomaly, whose habitat can surely be no closer to this prosaic world than Yaddith or G'lini. Thanks, too, for the loan of the sea-serpent & Loch Ness cuttings. I enclose something from the *Times* anent our Caledonian friend—which you can retain if you wish. As soon as I get home I'll send you as many of the unread Thevenin articles as I possess. Which reminds me—all of us here were vastly interested in the Egypto-American relique & letter of your Palo Alto correspondent. The seal certainly looks Egyptian enough from the photograph—but one pauses regarding the locale of discovery. Such portentous patness argues something too good to be true, & I fancy a close investigation would reveal one or another of the myriad forms of clever fakery. Thanks vastly for the loan. There certainly is a provocative element in some of the Egypto-Mayan resemblances (my new Mayan idol looks very much like a late-Egyptian figure in the Metropolitan Museum), though I doubt if Yucatan & the Nile had any closer link than the general diffusive process which carried certain cultural forms across Southern Asia & the Pacific. Which reminds me—Belknap has Churchward's "nut" classic "The Children of Mu" out of the library, & I hope to skim through it before going home. Old Churchward certainly is a second Lumley! He thinks he can read the undecipherable hieroglyphs of the Mayas, & has no difficulty at all with "Naacal—the original primal language of all mankind." The state of mind of a person like that must be highly blissful!

Home again
—Jany. 11, 1934.

Well—I couldn't finish this in New York after all! Every moment crowded to the last—& at that, I had to skip some of the museums I had planned to see. That little imp Belknap didn't return my W T, so that I shall have to buy another copy. I'll comment in my next epistle on the "Weaver" & on Howard Wandrei's story.[4] My final day in N.Y. was marked by the gaining—with Loveman's aid—of a phenomenal book bargain: the late Arthur Weigall's "Wanderings in Roman Britain"—which I have wanted for years—for only a half-dollar. Knowing my odd sense of Roman identification, you can well picture my degree of interest in *Roman Britain,* the sole point of convergence of Rome with the locale of my blood stream. Weigall's is the best of all popular volumes on the subject, & I have long been on the lookout for it. As you probably know, Weigall was an ardent disciple of Sir Arthur Keith's theory that we have vast amounts of Britanno-Roman blood in our veins, owing to the merely cultural rather than physical nature of the Saxon replacement. By a melancholy coincidence, Weigall died only a few days before my acquisition of his long-sought volume.[5]

Another book-bargain was a life of the poet Thomas Lovell Beddoes,[6] remaindered at a ridiculous figure on the counters of the Liggett drug stores. Knowing of your long-time interest in Beddoes, Loveman suggested that we get you a copy—which was accordingly done. I've brought it home along with my own copy, & will send it to you when I return the volumes so generously lent to me. Hope you'll like it—it looks damned interesting, though I've not yet had a chance to read it. Young Melmoth has also laid in a copy—making the book very well represented amongst the gang!

But about "Moon-Pool" Merritt. He turned out to be absolutely delightful—a stout, sandy, genial chap of about 45 or 50, with a ready smile & twinkling grey eyes. He took me to dinner at the Players' Club (occupying Edwin Booth's[7] old home in Gramercy Park) & discoursed incessantly on weird, cosmic, & literary subjects. Most of his views are very sound & sensible, though he is a trifle inclined to believe in pseudo-scientific extravagances like the Thevenin stuff. His authority in the offices of the American Weekly would seem to be very great—& I imagine he is instrumental in inclining it toward the field of scientific sensations. He agrees with me that the original Moon Pool novelette is his best work, though he himself has no copy of it. All his work seems to be very zestful & spontaneous, & I doubt if he fully realises the extent to which the popular conventional tradition has tainted him. He has travelled a good deal, knows Mayan ruins at first-hand, & is a close personal friend of old Nick Roerich—whose paintings fascinate me so ineffably. His generosity is extreme, & he has promised to give me the two works of his which I have not read—"The Metal Monsters" [*sic*] (in *Argosy* instalments) & "Burn, Witch, Burn" (as a book). He is now at work on a sequel to the latter volume—a tale centreing in the fabulous city of *Ys* (supposed to be sunk off the coast of Brittany) & involving the little-known legendry of *shadow magic*. From what he says, it ought to be a winner—though there will obviously be many concessions to the standards of popular romance. Incidentally—he is tremendously impressed with your Averoigne tales, especially "The Holiness of Azederac." I've told him about your booklet & am now sending him a circular . . . . . hope he'll act on my suggestion! I shewed Merritt the letter & photograph from your Palo Alto correspondent, but he agreed with Wandrei, Belknap, Morton, myself, & the rest that there is a conscious fake somewhere. This despite his firm opinion that the Mayan culture had distinct influences *from the east* (instead of from the west, as I believe). By the way, I am herewith enclosing the three Thevenin articles which you have not seen. #1—Nov. 15, 1931—is to keep, since I have a duplicate. The other two I'd like returned—though absolutely at your leisure. Some day I hope we can get hold of the missing numbers—2 & 3. Possibly little Ar-E'ch-Bei might have them—I'll have to ask him.

My first week in New York coincided with the spell of hellish cold of which the press doubtless informed you. Fortunately the all-extensive subway system enabled me to get virtually everywhere without being exposed more than two blocks continuously to the arctic outer air. Such short distances can be endured after a fashion—much as a hot stove can be *momentarily* touched by one's finger without harm to the latter. The worst temperature through which I dashed (with handkerchief over nose & mouth) was 3 above—& I was none the worse permanently for a 2-minute exposure, though for the moment my heart action was whipped up rather alarmingly. Luckily the last half of the visit was a warm-weather affair—the mild spell still persisting.

I didn't change the fountain pen flow—for this delectable ease of writing is something too precious to be sacrificed. I don't care if some of the loops are filled up—probably they wouldn't be if I used common ink instead of this Shaeffer product. At last I have two really workable pens—an old ideal of mine—which ensures me decent writing conditions even when one gives out. By the time the second one goes haywire, I'll have time to get the first patched up & adjusted to suit me.

I appreciate profoundly all that you say concerning the uncertainty & inadequacy of creative attempts—& am greatly encouraged by your remarks and citations. Regarding "The Thing on the Doorstep"—here is a card from Sultan Malik indicating that Dwyer is not alone in finding flaws in the tale.

514 ❦ *Dawnward Spire, Lonely Hill*

Two-Gun Bob hasn't yet reported—it being likely that he will incorporate his opinions in his next long letter. Comte d'Erlette's verdict will probably be a savage one—though it will doubtless contain useful points.[8]

I shall look forward to your tale of Regio Averonum in the Age of the Antonines, & trust that you can successfully borrow a copy of Valerius Trevirus from the library of Miskatonic University. The hints of the Bactrian Carnamagos[9] (who retained surprising amounts of primal Persian lore, & who wrote in Greek despite his existence under the rule of the Parthians [he is said to have survived into the period of Sassanid Persian dominion]) are assuredly of the greatest importance—as are also (if indeed applicable to the Averones, a matter disputed by some) the terrible adumbrations of the Alexandrian Neo-Platonist Kranaos (fl. circa 350 A.D.).

As for my Roman pseudo-memories—I doubt if there is anything really organic in them. If hereditary recollection were indeed a fact, it would be of too generalised a type to account for anything as specific as my linkage with the Tiber's banks. The actual cause must be connected somehow with my early impressions—perhaps with the fact that of all the ancients only the Romans used the *alphabet* we use. In infancy I attached tremendous importance to *letters*—knowing the common (Roman) alphabet at the age of two, though I did not learn the Greek alphabet till I was six. This is a very probable *main* cause for my Romeward bias. However—if Weigall is right (his book is ineffably fascinating) we must all have a fair trace of the mixture which passed as Roman in the days of the Empire—a mixture no doubt containing at least a trace of the real old Latin-Sabine-Oscan-Umbrian-Samnite-Etruscan blood of the Respublica. He says:

> "These Roman-Britons are our ancestors, &, even if we allow as many as 3 generations to the century, they are only separated from us by about 45 generations, & in many cases we must be much nearer to them than that. In other words, the blood of the Romans has only passed through 45 persons in reaching our veins, & so short a sequence is not sufficient to have produced much change in the nature of that blood."[10]

S.P.Q.R. . . . . . Alala! Perhaps after all I have a lineal forbear or two with names like L. Caelius Rufus or P. Scribonius Libo!

Your own mediaeval & Oriental linkages are certainly quite as singular as my Roman & 18th century ones—& I can well imagine how the local Hindoos must have impressed you. I'd like to see some of those early Orientales of yours—I'll wager you came near to beating our friend the Peacock Sultan at his own game! This reminds me—young Schwartz of *Fantasy Magazine* has an old *Black Cat* with a tale of yours.[11] He wouldn't part with it for any amount (for you are a revered idol of all the young scientifictionists), but Wandrei intends to borrow & copy it. I shall probably see it as a sub-loan from Melmoth.

Regarding dreams—your vision of the dark & craggy journey was certainly a winner, as was likewise that used in Sadastor. Recently I have had several dreams of *utter & desolate outsideness*—presence in a bleak, alien landscape which I gradually come to feel was *not on the earth*—but none of them form in any sense a genuine story.

And now I must thank you prodigiously for the books so kindly loaned—both of which I digested & appreciated before my departure for Manhattan's shores. The Summers volume produced the same sense of witchcraft's tangible reality & noxious proximity as the author's other work on the subject. Of course old Monty lets his fanatical Christian-Catholic orthodoxy bias him amusingly—yet his perfect honesty as a scholar makes him always present the other side of a disputed question, even if only as an abhorred thing to be (attemptedly) knocked over at once. He is undoubtedly absurd in trying to connect such ecclesiastical seceders as the Waldenses & the Albigenses with the subterranean witch-cult (most of the real Christian heretics were ascetics rather than daemoniac orgiasts); the only possible resemblance betwixt the two kinds of groups being a common opposition to the established faith. But to Summers any non-Catholic is a devil—be he a pious saint like Jonathan Edwards or a degenerate Satanist like Gilles de Rais.

Congratulations on your Petronius & Apuleius. I paid more than you did for very mediocre & non-illustrated editions! I, too, wish I could see more of Segrelles. Too bad recent Dunsany material is so flat—but in sober truth not only he but Machen, James, & Blackwood seem to have petered out completely. All of the Big Four are still living—yet they no longer truly enrich weird literature. Wakefield is pretty good—I'll enclose "They Return at Evening" as a loan in the coming shipment. You'll probably find at least four of the tales especially absorbing—"The Red Lodge", "He Cometh & He Passeth By" (based on Aleister Crowley), "And He Shall Sing", & "The Seventeenth Hole at Duncaster." In other tales, Wakefield's brisk sophistication is too apparent.

I liked "The Lady Who Came to Stay" very much, despite its restriction of the supernatural element to the common *larva domestica*. Of course it hasn't, for me, the kick it has for Comte d'Erlette—for the *cosmic* element is almost wholly lacking. Yet for all that it's great stuff. It has a tremendous atmospheric power—& the characterisation of the repressed & sinister old spinsters is superbly portrayed. This is precisely the sort of thing Little Augie revels in—hence I don't wonder at his bias. Phoebe is a tremendous figure—a malignantly authentic type frequently found in a declining aristocracy. In a play—"The Double Door"—which I saw a fortnight ago as Loveman's guest, something very similar was delineated.[12] My mention of the book has interested my aunt, hence I am holding it for her to read after she gets through with a pile of library items. I'll have it on its way home within a fortnight—together with the Summers volume, the Beddoes biography, & the copy of "They Return at Evening." Again let me thank you most profoundly for the dual loan. And meanwhile, as before suggested, you might (but not till you're finally through with it) send "The Dark Chamber" to Koenig instead of directly to me.

As for E. T. A. Hoffmann—if you're like me, you'll find him distinctly disappointing. I read a several-volumed translation in 1925–6,[13] & could not at any point become really enthralled. He is *grotesque* rather than terrible, & his constant snickering & comicality make one think of Poe's weakest side—the side (undoubtedly engendered by Hoffmannic influence) which produced such awkward extravagances as "The Devil in the Belfry", "The Angel of the Odd", "The Spectacles", "The Man Who Was Used Up", "Never Bet the Devil Your Head", &c. One or two items weren't so bad, but for the most part Ernst Theodor Wilhelm struck me as pretty much of a false alarm. It may be merely my crudity of taste—but I simply couldn't get excited over the famous fantaisiste.

Recent advices from Crawford indicate a long delay in the issuance of *Unusual.* First he said Christmas, then New-Year's, & now he thinks that *March* will be the fateful date. I surely hope the venture won't peter out altogether. The *Fantasy* boys—Schwartz & Ruppert—were rather dubious about its success, because of the heavy expenses incident to the rather ambitious format. Crawford is still worrying about the matter of marketing—acceptance by the Am. News Co. being very doubtful. He wants me to try to place *U S* with some local agency in Providence—which I'll gladly do, although I doubt if it will be accepted. I'm no salesman—& I recall my notable non-success in placing Houtain's wretched rag of 12 years ago.

By the way—congratulations on the birth of Michael Weir, in whose veins flows the blood of such hellish forebears! He makes a good companion for my Ward Phillips & Lewis Theobald, Jun. But if my recollection of "A Good Embalmer" be correct, there was really no need for his creation.[14] Hornig as a literary critic has very obvious limitations, & I'd hardly take his verdict on matter emphatically beyond his reach. Which reminds me—*Fantasy Magazine* (erstwhile S. F. Digest) is now looking for weird fiction, & would undoubtedly be ecstatically grateful if you would let them have something.

Had an interesting shipment of loaned books from Koenig during my absence—before he learned I was in his town. Baring-Gould's werewolf volume (which I've always wanted to see), the second & latest Asquith anthology "When Churchyards Yawn", & a small book of short tales by Francis C. Prevot entitled "Ghosties & Ghoulies". Hope I can get at reading them before long—though at present I am utterly submerged in the mass of accumulated work & correspondence which I found on my return. The Asquith book contains Machen & Blackwood tales which I've never read—though they may be old.

And so it goes. I'll have to pause now and get at a revision job which has been on hand a week—but which didn't get forwarded to me in N Y. Hope I haven't forgotten any intended enclosures—if I have, I'll chuck 'em in another envelope & send it in the wake of this one.

I duly received & appreciated your Yuletide greeting. Did you notice young Ar-E'ch-Bei's personally printed card, in which he drew upon our synthetic pantheon for background?[15] Derleth's was rather clever—combining business with fraternalism, as is doubtless the custom with super-energized young hustlers.

Sunset … & my west window holds me spellbound. Towers stand out darkly against an orange sky, & the downtown windows are beginning to be lit up. Soon the great red beacon atop the 26-story Industrial Trust Bldg. will flame into life—dominating the town and the harbour like the Alexandrian Pharos.

Which reminds me—I don't believe I mentioned the genuine Greek head (of a maiden, somewhat less than life size) which Loveman now has—in a niche designed & electrically lighted by his roommate McGrath. It is really an exquisite thing—of delicate, almost translucent Parian marble, & with a technique indicating original work of the Praxitelean period. It certainly seems not to be a Roman copy. This item—together with the Egyptian statuette obtained a couple of years ago, form the high spot of the "Loveman Museum."

I trust that California escaped the worst rigours through which the East has passed, & that your entire winter will prove a mild one. Today New England is having a respite from cold—bright sun, & thermometer almost up to 50°. The trouble is that this sort of thing doesn't last. Reports from Cook indicate temperatures of *50 below* in Vermont! ¶ Yrs for the Formless Shadow
—E'ch-Pi-El.

Notes

1. Grace Edna Hart Crane (1878–1947).

2. Walter Rendell Storey, "Hand-Weavers Show Their New Fabrics," *New York Times* (31 December 1933): 12: "Discerning decorators appreciate the new handwoven fabrics and the attention the makers give to original textures. The design often arises from the process of weaving. A robust appearance is now favored, and the rugged individualistic hand-woven fabrics present a pleasing foil to the smoother, machine-made textiles which may be used with them. [. . .] batik technique, originally adapted from the Javanese, is indicated in several hangings. Especially successful is one by Howard Wandrei picturing a mermaid and an octopus."

3. "Life is short, art is long [i.e., long-lasting]."

4. "The Weaver in the Vault" and "In the Triangle."

5. On 3 January.

6. By Royall H. Snow.

7. Edwin Thomas Booth (1833–1893), famous 19th-century American actor who toured America and Europe, performing Shakespearean plays, and brother of John Wilkes Booth. He founded Booth's Theatre in New York in 1869.

8. For Robert E. Howard's brief comment on the story, see *A Means to Freedom* 719. For Derleth, see his letter to CAS, 24 February 1934 (ms., WHS): "I have just recently finished THE THING ON THE DOORSTEP, which I enjoyed. I am dispatching it to Robert Bloch shortly. H. P. didn't do so well by it, to my disappointment. His inferiority complex is undermining his ability. To wit: the story isn't really finished, for the entity is still alive. He does not explain how the suspect, the narrator, is still at large. Why did he not have the Thing go to the sanitarium or asylum and burn the body, then come to narrator with signed statement as he did, narrator being out on bail. A good close, I should think, rather than hanging in the air. But the story otherwise was up to snuff."

9. Mentioned in "The Infernal Star," "Xeethra," and "The Treader of the Dust"; see *BB* 12.

10. Arthur Weigall, *Wanderings in Roman Britain* (London: Thornton Butterworth, 1926), 20.

11. Either "The Mahout" or "The Raja and the Tiger."

12. *Double Door: A Play in Three Acts* by Elizabeth Apthorp McFadden. HPL described it as "based on the fortunes of the strange Wendel family & their gloomy, shuttered mansion in 5th Ave." (HPL to Annie Gamwell, 25–26 December 1933; ms., JHL).

13. Probably *Weird Tales* (1885).

14. See *FF* 1, No. 6 (February 1934): 92, 96: "Stories to Come . . . In response to requests, we are publishing this list of stories which we have on hand: [. . .] *The Embalmere* [*sic*] *of Ramsville* by Michael Weir." CAS's story was published posthumously as "A Good Embalmer."

15. RHB's card read "By the nine Saturnian satellites or the scales of great Cthulhu or something similar I wish you the usual Merry Christmas MCMXXXIII" [all caps, with each word on a separate line].

[261]   [ANS, JHL][1]

> [Postmarked Providence, R.I.,
> 24 January 1934]

Yrs. just arrived. Thanks abundantly for the delightful picture, which goes into my choicest archives. You certainly seem to have a pull with Father Time—for I'd never take you to be only 3 years my junior, which is chronologically the case. The setting is splendid, & gives an added idea of the beauty of the region. I am fond of town-overlooking hills like that. The younger Miss Sully is certainly of very pleasing aspect. ¶ Thanks also for the other enclosures. That page of cats is delectable—& I shall preserve it in my feline files & shew it to my many furry visitors! Exceedingly glad to see the Carthaginian views—I followed the Prorok[2] excavations with interest, but never before saw pictures of them. Roman objects, of course, dominate—for the old Punic stuff was pretty well sunk after the last Punic war. The article on the age of the earth, & of life, is highly absorbing. ¶ All books—Summers, Lady, Wakefield, & Beddoes—are on their way to you in 2 post bundles. Glad "Dark Chamber" is headed for Koenig. ¶ Another letter about the use of Erich Zann in a London anthology. ¶ Glad you've had mild weather. No cold spell here so far. The misty greyness & abnormally sprouting fungi you mention sound tremendously fascinating. ¶ Young Shea has an idea for a time story which he doesn't feel equal to developing—so I think I'll quote it to you in my next letter & see whether you'd care to do anything with it. ¶ And again let me express my gratitude for the picture! Yrs for Third Shadows—E'ch-Pi-El

[On photo side:] A good view of my impressive next-door neighbour. [With arrow:] Entrance to #66.

Have at last read "The Weaver in the Vault." Great stuff! The atmosphere of that unhallowedly ancient crypt is tremendously vivid!

Notes

1. *Front:* John Hay Memorial Library, Brown University, Providence, R. I.

2. "Count" Byron Khun de Prorok (1896–1954), Hungarian-American amateur ar-chaeologist, anthropologist, and author of four heroic travelogues. In the late 1920s and early 1930s, he undertook expeditions in Africa pursuing ancient legends and eventually claimed to have found evidence that Atlantis lay in North Africa and the location of the Biblical land of Ophir.

[262]   [TLS, JHL]

> Hour of the dawning lum-
> inosity in the sunless gulf
> of Aforgomon.
>   [c. late January 1934]

Dear Éch-Pi-El:

Your New York visit seems to have been signalized by a number and variety of "contacts!" I was vastly interested by your account of the divers notables, A. Merritt, Hall, Koenig, Howard Wandrei, Harré, and the editors of SFD. Merritt's new projected story about the city of Ys certainly sounds like a humdinger. I had surmised that he was largely responsible for the moiety of outré and scientific articles in the Hearst supplements. Harré must have been interesting—I like very much his anthology, Beware after Dark, with its enthusiastic preface. This collection, to my way of thinking, is much better than the Hammett volume, Creeps by Night, which I have recently acquired. Your Erich Zann was almost the only genuinely atmospheric tale in Hammett's selection, most of the others being pretty mundane and sophisticated.

I'd certainly like to see H. Wandrei's batiks and drawings, and hope that Donald will send me the photograp[h]s which he has taken or intends to take. By the way, Melmoth gave me some interesting mementoes of your visit, in the shape of snapshots including Long, you and himself. These seemed very life-like indeed.

Returning to Merritt, if you will give me his address, I'll be very glad to send him a copy of The Double Shadow gratis. I am glad to know that the Averoigne stories appealed to him. Harré's expressed admiration of my work is very gratifying, since I think that H. has shown remarkably sound taste in his anthology, and therefore his opinion would be significant.

The Loveman museum must indeed be a choice and rare collection! The ushebti, [*sic*] Mayan idol and Balinese monkey-carving sound ineffably fascinating, and such generosity was truly apropos, if you know what I mean. I'd like to see these—and also the Greek maiden's head that you describe.

Congratulations on the improved ductility of flow in your fountain-pen! It would certainly make an immense difference, particularly to one who does a large amount of writing. Personally, I've almost given up the use of pens, and employ a common steel dip on the occasions when one is really requisite.

I am glad the drawing for the Weaver appealed to you. The reproduction was not at all bad, to judge from the copies on local news-stands. Wright seems to have been pleased with my design for The Charnel God, and has now ordered one for The Death of Malygris (April.) The Witchcraft of Ulua, for which I *could* have done something especially good, will appear as a filler, sans illustration, in the Feb. W. T. I hope W. will give me a chance at the Silver Key sequel—probably he won't want a drawing for it till two months before the publication date.

Howard Wandrei's tale in the last W. T. was quite good and original, I thought. Conan, as usual, put on a very entertaining and imaginative show. Merritt's Woman of the Wood, though excellent, impresses me as being somewhat overrated. the [*sic*] other tales in the issue were hardly noteworthy.

I imagine Koenig's library must be very much the same sort that I myself would accumulate with ample money and facilities. I envy him with all my heart, since volumes of outre and fantastic literature are among the few desiderata of my existence; and my own collection is painfully limited.

I forwarded The Dark Chamber to Koenig several days ago, as per instructions. As you will have gathered from a former letter, I enjoyed the book greatly. The theme of mnemonic delving is a tremendous one, and the story certainly suggests a lot. From the standpoint of pure weirdness, it seems to me that the story would have been better with a minimizing of the erotic element, which, for my taste, does not add to the atmosphere. But no doubt the author was not trying for pure weirdness. Re the treatment of music in this tale, I think that it is inferior to your mode of treatment in Erich Zann. Cline, it seems to me, tries to be too definite; and one cannot be definite about music. Thanks again for the loan of The Dark Chamber. I am certainly glad to have read it; though you will perhaps infer that my estimate of the book is not quite so high as yours and Long's. I believe—coming down to comparisons—that you and Long have both done sounder work than the D.C.

Later. Yr. card and the books came, and I hasten to thank you for the Wakefield loan and the gift, jointly with Es-El, of the book on Beddoes. I read one of the Wakefield stories last night—"He Cometh and he passeth by—" and found it excellent, especially in the suggestion of the diabolic Shadow. Crowley is surely a picturesque character, to have inspired anything like Clinton! I know little about Crowley myself, but wouldn't be surprised if many of the more baleful elements in his reputation were akin to those in the Baudelaire legend . . . that is to say, largely self-manufactured or foisted upon him by the credulous bourgeoisie.

Beddoes is indeed an old favourite, and I consider Death's Jest Book as good as anything in Elizabethan literature, with a superadded subtlety and atmosphere which none of the old dramatists seem to have had. I shall read this book by Royall Snow with immense avidity.

Glad you liked the snapshot of Marion[1] and myself. It is considered very good. Thanks for the card showing the impressive next-door edifice!

Re the scarab discovery, I too doubt if it ever came f
me this does not necessarily mean that it is a fake. After all, then
why one of the prehistoric American peoples shouldn't have used an
symbol. The Egyptians surely had no copyright on beetles. Coincidental and
development seems the likely explanation of the matter.

I hope you have found time and inclination for some new work. Surely
you need feel no uncertainty about The Thing on the Doorstep. Malik's card,
which I return, sounds pretty enthusiastic to me, and I do not imagine that
his criticisms involved anything very radical.

I finished, after a fashion, the long-deferred Chain of Aforgomon, and
have already had it turned down by Pharnabosus, on the plea that "it sagged
as a tale toward the end," whatever that means. Pharnabosus ordered a drawing for The Death of Malygris. This I have just finished, and am inclined to
think it is the best of my W. T. illustrations so far. A recent poem, In Slumber, was accepted by the satrap and I have suggested that he let me do a design to accompany it. Here is the poem:

IN SLUMBER

The stench of stagnant waters broke my dream,
Wherethrough had run, with living murmur and gleam,
The Rivers four of the Earthly Paradise:
From the azured flame of those effulgent skies,
And valleys lifting censers of vast bloom,
I saw drawn down into a deathlier gloom
Than lies on Styx's fountain. By such light
As shows the newly damned their dolorous plight,
I trod the shuddering soil of that demesne,
Whence larvæ swarmed, malignant and obscene,
Like writhen mists from some Maremma reeking:
Through the gross air, fell incubi went seeking
Their prey that slumbered helpless; at my knee
There clung the python-bodied succubi;
I heard the wail of them that walked apart,
Each with a sucking vampire at his heart;
And, as I stumbled loathly on, the ground
Was rent with noiseless thunder all around
To pits that teemed with direr prodigies:
Grey, headless coils, and worm-shaped in
Unmeasured, rose above the moon that
Black as a corpse in heavens thick and
The rusty clang and shaken soot of
Deafened and stifled me; from p
Slime-mantled horrors boiled with

To pour in frothing fury down the abyss.
Then, from an outmost circle of that hell,
The tumbling harpies came, detestable,
With beaks that in long tatters tore my breast—
And wove from these their crimson, wattled nest!

Congratulations on the Weigall purchase. I certainly like the theory about the Britanno-Roman blood in modern English veins. Forty-five generations isn't such a great remove after all; and it sounds credible enough. I rather think that my own inheritance is predominantly Celtic; but it wouldn't be so surprising if there were a drop of Roman blood somewhere in the line.

If you have not before seen pictures of Prorok's excavations, you might be interested in his book, Digging for Lost African Gods, which I possess. This I'd gladly send you for a long-term loan. Lewis Spence's The History of Atlantis, which came not long ago, also might interest you, if you have not already seen it.

I fear that the chances are none too good for Unusual Stories, particularly in view of the recently announced deficit of The Fantasy Fan. This tallies with my own experience in printing a one-shot like The Double Shadow. I am discontinuing my ad in W. T., since returns are not enough to justify the expense. And I still owe the printer a sizable sum.

Science Fiction Digest wants only weird tales with a rationalistic explanation, I understand. I don't think I have anything that would quite fill the bill at present. I have, however, sent them a recently revised copy of my translation of Baudelaire's Rêve Parisien—a poem which might be of interest to scienti-fictionists as well as fantasists.

The new shipment of books from Koenig certainly sounds like rare meat! I've never seen any of the items you list. I have, by the way, ordered a new Machen book, The Green Round, which Derleth recommended; also, the Edith Thomson[2] anthology, Keep on the Light, which contains my yarn, The Isle of the Torturers. These have not yet arrived. I hope Machen's volume won't be too much of a disillusionment.

As to Hoffmann, I guess my reaction would be similar to yours. The three or four tales of his that I have seen were distinctly disappointing.

Yes, I shall assuredly endeavour to collate the texts of Valerius Trevisus [*sic*] and Carnamagos when I write that tale of Regio Averonum.[3] Regarding Kranaos of Alexandria, there are those who maintain, if I mistake not, that his somewhat ambiguous though terrible suggestions referred to the inhabitants of primal Thule rather than to the Averones; but since the Averones were tainted with a dark strain Hyperborean ancestry, it is possible that he included them by implication his black shadowings of the unmentionable. . . .

I'll return T noisseur and your miscallaneous [*sic*] clippings before long. The The articles [*sic*] were certainly stimulating, whatever their scientific . I shall comment specifically on some of the other clippings in my next letter. Needless to say, I found them all of grea

Have you heard from Lumley of late? I wrote him around N
and received a letter later in the month, expressing apprehension as to the
possible non-delivery of a letter from me, through the blundering of a mail-
carrier. It seems he has had considerable trouble with his mail. I wrote again
promptly, but have heard nothing since.

I thought you would like that page of felines! All of them were beauties! I
don't think I have ever mentioned my two cats—the black and sinister witch-cat,
Simaetha, and the roistering Maltese, General Tabasco. Simaetha, in her wanderings, must have lapped up an alchemist's elixir—I have really lost track of her
age. Her somewhat baleful aspect is heightened by a permanent oblique list of
head and neck, acquired many years ago in a most heroic and protracted vigil at
the mouth of a rat-hole. The devoted animal stayed there for days without moving!

The weather continues mild, though with fog once more in the offing. I
believe you would enjoy it thoroughly. // Malik Taus has sent me a card, announcing that his safari has reached the wilds of Oklahoma without mishap
or ambuscade; so it seems likely that he will appear in Auburn during the not
far distant future.

Keep the enclosures. You might, however, send the lizard article to Lumley—I think he would prize it. The implications of that steady rapid growth
of iguanas, etc[.], through recent generations are simply terrific!

Yrs for the pilgrimage to Chorazin,[4]
Klarkash-Ton.

Notes

1. Marion Sully (1911–1994), younger sister of Helen V. Sully and daughter of Genevieve
K. Sully.
2. Actually Christine Campbell Thomson.
3. Possibly "The Oracle of Sadoqua"; see *BB* 48.
4. Khorazin (or Chorazin) is a village cursed by Jesus (Matthew 11:20–24; Luke 10:13–15)
for rejecting his work. Early medieval writers believed the Antichrist would be born there.
Chorazin is cited in M. R. James's "Count Magnus."

[263]   [ALS]

At the Monolith on the Mound
—Hour that the Dogs Howl
[Postmarked 11 February 1934]

Dear Klarkash-Ton:—

My recent visit surely did include a pleasing plethora
of high spots. Merritt's address is % *American Weekly, 235 East 45th St., N.Y.
City*—& I'm sure he'd feel vastly complimented were you to send him the
D. S. . . . of which he knows, both from my oral panegyric & from the circu-

lar I later despatched. Glad Young Melmoth has sent you pictorial records of the gathering at his place—even though they do make Grandpa E'ch-Pi-El look rather blank.[1] In that seated portrait I was caught with my mouth slightly open—talking, as usual—before I knew my host was pulling the trigger, hence the view looks even more stupid than I ordinarily do. Little Belknap came out darkly sardonic enough to suit even his Baudelairian ideals! I surely hope that Melmoth can get some half-decent photographs of his brother's drawings; for truly, the best specimens are incredibly powerful things. He has promised me some. Harré is quite a character—& I agree with you that his anthology is much superior to Hammett's. This latter was a vast disappointment to me. And by the way—let me congratulate you on the inclusion of "The Isle of the Torturers" in the latest "Not at Night."

I haven't yet had time to place the *ushabti* & the Mayan image in my collection, since the arrangement will require considerable thought—but meanwhile they glower provisionally from an odd-&-end shelf in my bedroom. Sometimes, in the night, I fancy I hear whispers . . . . first in one cryptic speech & then in another . . . . & there arise in the dark vague visions of monstrous pylons & waving papyrus-reeds, curiously mixed with glimpses of stone pyramids & hideous sacrificial processions. Thousands of years ago—thousands of miles apart . . . . . the stately Nile, & the steaming Guatemalan jungle. Did either know of the other? And then, from the bookcase-top in the library, comes a thin, obscure vibration more ancient & more terrible than aught which nighted Khem or the realm of Chac-Mool could send. It . . . . the Nameless Eikon . . . . with its message of forgotten horrors from abysses of time older than man, older than the planet . . . Iä! Shub-Niggurath!

I shall be on the alert for the Charnel God & Malygris illustrations, & hope fervently that you will be assigned the S. K. job. I've mentioned it twice to Wright, & wish you'd suggest tactfully that the task would not be unacceptable to you. It surely does please me to witness the fulfilment of something I've been rooting for since 1923! Another hopeful art note is supplied by the presence of two certainly new *Rankin* drawings in the Feb. issue. Betwixt you & Hugues le Sorcier there ought to be considerable relief from the prevailing pall of mediocrity—& if Howard Wandrei could be dragged in, what a triad it would make! Enormous thanks, by the way, for the two recent heads—the semi-insect King & the beak-snouted entity!

Yes—H W's recent tale had a very distinctive power & originality, though its construction was visibly amateurish. Storytelling is obviously a secondary art with him. Two-Gun Bob did well with his "Rogues in the House", though primary honours are really to be divided betwixt the "Weaver" & the Merritt reprint. Your tale has a profound, chilling menace, & "The Woman in the Wood" actually struck me as more powerful than it did in 1926. A matter of atmosphere—curious how opinions differ! I was glad to see "Ulua" in the February issue, & don't think the revision did any real harm. The tale by Sultan Malik,[2] however, has been spoilt by Wright-prompted changes. I saw that tale in New Orleans when it was half done, & later read the completed original MS. It was splendid—but Satrap Pharnabozus has taken all the subtlety out of it. As a whole, this issue is far from notable—the Dyalhis & Pope tales are utterly & dispiritingly wretched.

Koenig's library certainly has some splendid & unusual items, though it is rather hampered by his insistence on *first editions*. That is something I can't understand. What I want is the *text*—& it can be a 1st or an 101st for all I care, so long as the wording is authentic & legible. I've now read up the loaned books. Baring-Gould's werewolf book had many anecdotes & allusions new to me, & the brief Prevot sketches could be made into splendid tales. The Asquith anthology was fair—Blackwood's contribution being the best.[3] Hope Koenig will like "The Dark Chamber". Belknap, Canevin, & I certainly found it a knock-out. Of course the erotic element was more or less padding, though it contributed to the general air of foul morbidity about Mordance Hall. Cline certainly did rub in his musical knowledge rather baldly, as if he wished to let the reader know about it—but I can forgive him anything in view of his picture of Richard Pride & the mad groping backward through time. I'm afraid it's stretching group-loyalty a bit to assume that Belknap or I have achieved—or could achieve—anything to beat that! Glad Beddoes & Wakefield came through safely. If you like the latter—who tends to suggest M R James—I'll send you his second collection, "Others Who Returned". I don't know Beddoes as well as I ought, but the Snow volume will tend to renew my interest. And speaking of books—Bnādvāī-Aā has just lent me (not by request, but evidently because the latter parts hit my antiquarian side by touching old New Orleans) the prodigious & widely exploited "Anthony Adverse"[4]—which will probably keep me busy for an indefinite period when I'm able to get at it.

As for Aleister Crowley—I rather thought at first that his evil reputation was exaggerated, but Belknap says that Harré has met him & has found him indescribably loathsome in mind, emotions, & conduct. This from Harré is quite a damning indictment, for Belknap tells me that T. Everett himself is far from squeamish or fastidious in his language & anecdotes when amidst the sort of company that dissolves inhibitions. But Crowley was too much for him. He didn't relate particulars—but said that the evil Magus made him so nauseated that he left abruptly. I guess Crowley is about as callous, unclean-minded, & degenerate a bounder as one can often find at large—though he undoubtedly has talents & scholarship of a very high order. It seems to me I heard that he is in New York now—London won't stand for him any longer. And this reminds me that I forgot to return that old cutting of yours which mentions him—permit me to repair the omission now.

About that scarab—there are three possible theories excluding actual presence in the western world since Egyptian times. It could be really Egyptian but planted as a hoax, it could be faked & planted, or it could be of Indian workmanship with accidental Egyptian resemblances. I'm not enough of

526 ❋ *Dawnward Spire, Lonely Hill*

an archaeologist to venture an opinion. While without doubt the Mayans retained some memory of a heritage in common with certain old-world races, it seems absolutely certain that no contact with other cultures occurred after settlement in America. No old-world artifact has ever been found in Central America, & vice versa. Thanks for the item about the Nova Scotian treasure buried by 'a tribe known as Incas, from Peru or Mexico'. It surely would be piquant if something of that kind ever came to light—I'll have to go up & investigate! I've wanted to see Nova Scotia for ages.

Congratulations on the acceptance of "In Slumber"—which is really magnificent. I profoundly hope that King Pharnaces will give you the illustration job. But damn that grandson of a dog for his rejection of "Aforgomon"! He may take it later, though. As for *Unusual Stories*—I presume you've received the rather pathetic "Advance Issue". Here are 2 letters which shed more light on the predicament. Assuredly, the future doesn't look any too bright. On the other hand, Hornig says that things look a bit better for the F F. Evidently his appeal was not altogether fruitless. About the erstwhile *Science Fiction Digest*—now *Fantasy Magazine*—it has broadened its policy to include the weird. Young Schwartz was so anxious for material that he has taken the worst & tamest of my left-overs—"The Tree", & the verses "The Nightmare Lake" & "The Outpost."[5] He'd certainly be grateful for anything you might send.

That Weigall book—to the thorough reading of which I couldn't get around till a couple of weeks ago—was a veritable treasure-house of data anent a Britain whose life & splendours most have forgotten. As fascinated as I have always been by Roman Britain (one of my great controversies of 20 years ago was with a chap[6] who claimed that Roman civilisation & the Latin language never had any foothold in Britain outside the camps & large towns—gad, but I wish I'd had Weigall to quote then!), I never before realised how utterly & stably Roman a province it was, & how many tangible reliques still survive from the past. Think of arches & walls & towers still surviving, *which were a thousand years old when William the Conqueror landed!* Of course such things are scattered, & in some cases only lately exhumed—or distinguished from mediaeval masonry—but they are there! The description of the Arthur Machen country—Caerleon-on-Usk—is fascinating. That amphitheatre described in the Roman dream chapter of "The Hill of Dreams" has been dug out of its covering mound during the last decade, & now stands almost as it was when built by the Second Augustan Legion under Sextus Julius Frontinus in A.D. 78—before the destruction of Pompeii in the home land. Its condition is so perfect that it probably forms the finest Roman amphitheatre now existing—in better shape than the Colosseum, though of course not even comparable in size. Weigall makes it clear that virtually all of Britain south of our much-discussed Loch Ness was as solidly Roman in culture as Italy itself—that everybody outside the wild border tribes spoke Latin, called himself a Roman, & (like all the inhabitants of the non-Greek or western parts of the Empire) bore a

Roman name. Typical names of British citizens of the period are T. Valerius Pudens, Aurelius Senecio, C. Julius Galenus, C. Fabius Sanfeius, C. Valerius Maecicus, Cassius Secundus, M. Aurelius Nepos, C. Mannius Secundus, M. Petronius, Aurelius Ambrosius, M. Julius Maximus, Felicius Simplex, Flavius Bellator, Verecundus Diogenes, L. Valerius Taucinus, Julius Vitalis, Sex. Valerius Genialis, &c. &c.* Some of these people were native Celts; others were legionaries of the army—from all over the Empire—& their descendants; a very few were *real* Romans of the hawk-nosed, broad-browed Tiber breed. Most of the legionaries stayed in Britain when discharged, & married native (but Roman-named) Celtic wives. They represented recruits from all over the Empire—Gaul, Germany, Spain, Greece, Thrace, Hungary, Dalmatia, & even North-Africa, Syria, & Mesopotamia. Some pretty bad non-Aryan elements, from Herr Hitler's point-of-view, mixed in! However—the Nordic enthusiast may be consoled by the fact that a very marked majority were Northern Gauls & Germans—regular guys according to the severest Nazi standard! The Second Augustan Legion (which Machen brings so close to us) was from the German Rhineland originally, though its members married Welsh wives & recruited their sons to the same old Eagles. Thus the old town of Isca Silurum which Avellaunius saw in his dreams was one in which tall blond or red-haired people, with a few darker types, strode in Roman attire & with Latin on their lips—building temples to Fortuna, Diana, Minerva, & the popular Persian Mithras (who gave Christus a run for his money as head of the new religion in the 4th century A.D.), patronising the baths & amphitheatre, & erecting funeral stelae in no way differing from those along the Via Appia. Rural villas were often of the highest magnificence—with splendid mosaic pavements—& no house in town or country lacked its running water & central furnace heat. There is no indication that the quality of British-Roman architecture was in the least below that of Rome's best. Indeed, it is clear that Britannia was one of the leading parts of the later Roman world . . . . . as we may well imagine from the very large number of later Emperors who were either crowned there or spent a great deal of their time there. Eboracum (York) was plainly as prominent an

---

*The writing-out of these Roman names reminds me of the strange, persistent mania which I had as a small boy for writing long lists of Roman names. The practice stirred in me a queer, uncanny sensation half of pomp & grandeur, & half of pseudo-memory. I even used to scrawl them on the woodwork of the cellar & attic—CAELIVS. RVFVS—M. COCCEIVS.—L. VARGVNTEIVS—Q. HERENNIVS. SENECIO—TIB. ANNIVS—CORNELIVS. LENTVLVS. CRVS—D. ATEIVS. CAPITO—&c. &c. Only a few years ago (so small is the world!) a Providence physician who had lived since 1924 at 598 Angell St.[6] was talking with Loveman at Dauber & Pine, & spoke of the queer Roman scrawls in the attic of his house! He thought a pretty queer duck must have lived there!

imperial seat as any town in Italy or Gaul. Londinium was slow in becoming the metropolis, but it got there at last. As a pre-Roman Celtic village it was very obscure—so obscure that Caesar paid no attention to it when, on his second expedition, he marched from Durovernum (Canterbury) to Verulamium (St Albans), crossing the Tamesis at what is now Chelsea—then far west of London. However, it began to grow soon after it was rebuilt following Boadicea's revolt (A.D. 61), & later on it was highly important & finally supreme. In the middle of the 4th century it became a real official centre—Londinia Augusta—& the residence of the governor of Britannia Prima (i.e., south of Thames) It then occupied both sides of the river, with a London Bridge bearing bronze statuary. Part of the garrison was a detachment of our favourite Second Legion—gravestones to certain of its members, such as Valerius Celsus & Vivino Marcianus, being found at several points. The later Roman walls were the same which lasted through the Middle Ages to modern times (1766), & which today mark the legal boundaries of "The City." We even have a *picture* of a bit of Roman London's waterfront (vide sketch)—occurring on a pottery lamp dug up near St. Paul's Cathedral. The houses look curiously modern—making it clear that the modern gabled or slant roof (not needed in the almost snowless Mediterranean world) was developed by the Romans to suit the harsh climate of their northern

colonies. But the most striking part of Weigall's work is his original research on the last melancholy phase of Roman Britain—the abandonment by the army & the final Saxon Conquest. It was in the course of this research that he so thoroughly exploded the idea that the Britanno-Romans were all killed off or driven into Wales & across to Brittany. Instead, he proves, they were for the most part first enslaved & then absorbed by the Saxon conquerors. They lost their language & institutions, it is true—but they lived to transmit their blood to posterity, & are perhaps an even larger factor in our ancestry than the Saxons & Normans. However little of the real hawk-faced Latin-Sabine-Oscan-Umbrian-Samnite-Etruscan blood of old Italy we have in our veins, we **certainly** have had *hundreds if not thousands of lineal blood progenitors who spoke Latin, wore togas, & bore names like Aulus Aufidius, Januarius Martinus, P. Proculinus, S. Valerius Amandus, & L. Julius Juvenis.* This is now established quite beyond conjecture—we don't have to rely on the stray Welsh or Cornish strains in our ancestry to link us with the old world of Avellaunius. Any of the most Saxon-looking lines on our charts may go back to some Britanno-Roman woman married to a Saxon chief, or some Britanno-Roman prisoner or serf whose son became a "Saxon" freeman. Weigall upsets a good many of our common notions about the fall of Roman Britain. It was no sudden thing—Latin was spoken everywhere except along the conquered coast until almost the dawn of the 7th century. "King Arthur" was *not* a Celtic-speaking chief who fought Roman & Saxon alike, but a typical Latin-speaking Britanno-Roman named Artorius who wore a Roman helmet & was kept busy enough fighting Saxons alone! The Saxon conquest was a slow & painful process. As early as 300 A.D. the southeast coast began to be menaced by Saxon pirates, & not long afterward a great chain of fortresses was erected there—at Branodunum (Brancaster), Gariannonum (Burgh—near Yarmouth), Felixstowe, Othona (Bradwell), Ythan-ceaster in Essex, Regulbium (Reculver), Rutupiae (Richborough), Dubrae (Dover), Portus Lemanis (Lympne), Anderida (Pevensey), & Portus Adurni (Porchester). This whole region was formed into a military district called Litus Saxonicum—or the Saxon Shore—& put in charge of an important general styled "Comes Litoris Saxonici". In 368 the Saxons made such alarming incursions that the Emperor—Valentinianus—sent the Spanish general Theodosius (father of the subsequent Theodosius the Great) to protect the province. He took up headquarters at Rutupiae (parts of the Roman fortress still exist) & did a pretty successful job of temporary cleaning up. At that period all possible troops were transferred to the east coast—among them our Second Augustan Legion, which left Caerleon for ever & took up its station at Rutupiae. Meanwhile the wild & unromanised Celts of the North, aided by tribes from Ireland, were creating general hell along the upper border. The famous Stilicho gave them a setback, but in 401 he had to return to the continent to protect Rome itself from the Goths—& he took the 6th Legion with him. In 410 the Emperor Honorius announced that he could send *no more* troops to Britain— but he did not *withdraw* any, as is commonly stated. Most had trickled out before. There was a return of a few troops a little later on, but in 423 more were withdrawn; while by 440 there were no *imperial* legions left. But Britain was *not,* as often stated, "out of the Empire". It considered itself a Roman province, & was stoutly defended by its native "auxiliary" troops—what we would call the "militia" or "national guard." In 442 the Saxons began to seize permanent strips on the south & east coasts, but they did not at once get inland. (How instinctively I still say *they*—associating myself with *Roman* Britain even though it is a Saxon-grammar'd language that I write!) The chief defenders were now the famous Vortigern (a Welshman who spoke Latin) & the Roman Aurelius Ambrosius. Now come (452) Hengist & Horsa, & the seizure of land in Kent & Sussex by the Saxons. Later in the 5th century we see the whole east coast up to Yorkshire conquered by the invaders—& many of the Roman garrisons massacred. Meanwhile Rome itself passed into Teutonic hands, while in Gaul (vide my earlier epistle) Syagrius was conquered by the Franks. But still parts of Roman Britain held out! Aurelius Ambrosius led the Romans till about 490, & then comes Artorius—"King Arthur". Around 500 Artorius drove the Saxons back to the very coast, & came near to freeing the island of them. He did more than poor old Syagrius could do across the Channel—& gave Roman Britain (or the bulk of it) a good 50 years of respite. The next Roman leader was Aurelius Caninus, & after him came his son Aurelius Candidanus—the last of all. The Saxons were now vastly reinforced, & the Angli were swooping in just north of them to bequeath a permanent name to our homeland, our race, & our language. *582* is the last sad date. At that time the Germanic hordes defeated the bulk of the Romans at Dirham—10 miles east of Bristol & 10 north of Bath—& killed Aurelius Candidanus & two other British generals. The earthworks of the Roman camp at this place are still visible. After this Bath, Cirencester, & Gloucester fell to the Germans, & Teutonic invaders everywhere became the overlords & gentry, pushing down the Romans to subordinate social positions. Latin must have been spoken by the conquered stock for a century or more—but it was no longer the tongue of the rulers. Not all the towns were destroyed. Many had been deserted for years, & fell to ruin gradually—through neglect. Others were peaceably occupied by the Saxons, so that their Roman buildings suffered only a gradual replacement. Often the Saxons would build a town to suit themselves *beside* a conquered or deserted Roman city, so that the Roman ruins lie somewhat apart from the later English city. Thus at Chester (Roman *Deva*) & Worcester (Uriconium)—which latter place a correspondent of mine in Wales[8] has only just visited. Anyhow, the fact remains that *there was a Roman Britain until 582 A.D.—over a century after the technical overthrow of the Western Roman Empire.* We are just 1352 years away from ancestors of ours who spoke Latin & called themselves Romans. The signing of the Magna Charta, which we associate so closely with ourselves, *was nearer to the Roman last stand of 582 than it is to us in 1934.* As for the *length* of the Roman period in our ancestral history—counting from the real conquest by Aulus Plautius in A.D. 43 (though many coastal towns were Romanised long before that—Caesar having opened up the country in B.C. 54) to the last stand of Aurelius Candidanus in 582, we may set down *539 years*—a longer time than that separating the death of Chaucer from ourselves, & a century longer than the whole period since the discovery of America! Surely we had quite an opportunity to get a Roman impress, as one generation after another of our actual forefathers bore such names as Julius, Aurelius, Valerius, Flavius, & Cassius, & gave their sons such praenomina as Aulus, Marcus, Caius, Sextus, Tiberius, Decimus, Publius, & Titus! S.P.Q.R.! ROMA! It may be added that no modern scholars shew any tendency to dispute the dicta of Weigall regarding the later history of Britain & the survival in ourselves of the bulk of the Roman-British population. We may enjoy the sensations of being Romans without the least fear that we are kidding ourselves or seizing too hastily upon flimsy data. By the way—if you'd care to see the Weigall book, consider it wholly at your disposal!

Which reminds me—thanks vastly for the offer of a Prorok loan, which I hereby snap up at once! I've read one of the two Spence Atlantis books, but I'm damned if I remember *which* one! Possibly I'll let this wait a while—at least, till I find out. Glad you're getting the new Machen item—I'll have to get it myself if it's as truly typical of good old Artorius Macenus as Comte d'Erlette would have us believe. Glad you liked the Thevenins—no hurry about them or any of the others which I sent. Enclosed are a few things anent Loch Ness & its cryptic denizen—& also a couple of others which, also, you needn't return) of more or less fantastic & scientifictional provocativeness. Prof. Alter's[9] theory would restore our old idea that a vast number of the stars may have attendant planets, whilst the tale of the Lizard People makes me think of Two-Gun Bob's Valusia, & also of my own old "Nameless City." It likewise reminds me of that cutting of yours about the slow, insidious progress of the saurian generations toward their former mesozoic magnitude. Ædepol, what possibilities! I saw three of the great East Indian lizards alive at the Bronx zoo in 1926—possibly I mentioned it to you at the time. They died not long afterward, & can now be found stuffed at the American Museum. As per request, I'll pass this item along to good old Bill Lumley. Incidentally—the post office must have done you dirt in the matter of reaching old Bill, for (vide enclosed) he has been complaining of not hearing from you. He has spoken before about trouble with his mail—one of my letters having been delayed inordinately.

The collation of VALERIVS. TREVIRVS (don't get that name wrong! As you know he was one of the Germanic TREVIRI—a native of AUGUS-TA TREVIRORVM [modern *Treves* or *Trier*] on the right bank of the Mosella, which Ausonius called the second metropolis of the Empire & which still has a magnificent Roman gate surviving) with Carnamagos will certainly constitute a highly important piece of scholarship, & add vastly to the authoritativeness of your history of Regio Averonum. The allusion of Kranaos of course needs a vast amount of elucidation & interpretation, but there certainly is much to be said for a connexion of the Averonas with the Hyperboreans. In no other way can the exclusive presence of the *Liber Ivonis* among them be easily accounted for—a point which, when combined with what Kranaos hints, makes a case of tremendous significance.

Yes—the Peacock Sultan is on the move, a card from the Osage country having reached me not long ago. I wish I could participate in the conference soon to take place at the Villa Ashtonia! Meanwhile I think the whirling dervish intends to get a personal glimpse of Two-Gun Bob, the Terror of the Plains,[10] if he can manage it. That's another session I wish I could be in on! Incidentally—I hope he hasn't lost my copy of "The Worm Ouroboros" which I lent him damn near a year ago—as soon as I got it & before I had a chance to re-read it! May he be marooned atop Koshtra Pivrarcha if he has!

I was extremely fascinated by your description of your feline colleagues, & wish that I might see pictures of the nighted & saturnine Simaetha & the bluff & bellicose Genl. Tabasco. Simaetha would surely seem to be a true heir to the most sorcerous traditions of Hyperborea & Regio Averonum—not unlike those reputedly immortal felines who guarded the shrine of Sadoqua, & whose regular disappearances at New Moon figure so largely in the folklore of mediaeval Averoigne. One recalls the disquieting suggestions in Jehan d'Artois' *Roman des Sorciers* concerning the huge black cats captured at those very singular Sabbats on the rocky hill behind Vyones—the cats which could not be burned, but which escaped unhurt from the flames, uttering cries which, though not like any known human speech, were damnably close to the unknown syllables forming part of the Tsath-ritual in the *Livre d'Eibon*. Here on the ancient hill, as I may have mentioned, I am in close touch with the secret & portentous Kappa Alpha Tau (Κομψῶν Αἰλουρῶν Τάξις) fraternity[11] which meets on the roof of a shed across the garden beneath my west window. The president, Peter Randall, is an elderly black & white gentleman of aristocratic & sacerdotal descent, who inherits the darkest arcana of Bubastis & Meroë. Like me, he is no lover of cold weather, but appears at the club only when climatic conditions are favourable. His aloofness from ordinary mortals both human & feline is proverbial, but he has at last permitted me to break through his reserve, so that he now even rolls over in an undignified & kittenish fashion when he sees Grandpa E'ch-Pi-El approaching. The Vice-President, Count Magnus Osterberg (belonging to a Scandinavian household in Waterman St.), is a huge & handsome tiger with a white face & gloves & boots, whose aristocratic reserve is quite equal to Pres Randall's. He & Peter are very close friends, but neither ever pays the slightest attention to any other feline. When one is out alone, he always looks about for the other; & when they have found each other they generally take up permanent stations about two feet apart—dozing, surveying the semi-rural scenery of their back-garden oasis, or exchanging courteous & affable glances. Casual approaches of other cats are unheeded, but when any outside Grimalkin becomes actually obtrusive & overbearing (no cat of K.A.T. calibre *would* become so!), Count Magnus displays the hardier side of his nature. (Pres. Randall has outlived his combative years, hence repels foes only with chilling glances.) Magnus never *picks* a fight, & often goes to considerable lengths of tact to avert a vulgar brawl—but when the other guy becomes insistent, so that a gentleman must either fight or bear the imputation of tarnished honour, then just watch the scion of the ancient Osterberg line! All the hardy blood of generations of Norrland jarls, & all the cryptic lore learnt from the Lapp & Finnish warlocks, then come to the fore—& the fur that flies during the ensuing moments is not often the tiger-&-white miniver of Count Magnus Osterberg! Just as I have never seen Count Magnus provoke or incite a combat, so have I never seen him retreat. A true gentleman & Nordic nobleman, by God! Both Pres. Randall & Vice Pres. Osterberg have their favourite spots for taking the air—the President favouring the clubhouse roof (which is in his yard) & Count Magnus his own back fence, slightly to the north. Each, however, is very courteous about transferring the seat of a colloquy to the other's chosen territory. As for the others—the secretary is a large Maltese, recently elected to replace a grey part Angora who has withdrawn from the fraternity. The Treasurer—Stephen Randall, who looks enough like Peter to be his son, though he has no white spot on the end of his tail—is also newly chosen, supplanting a small tiger who resigned. Other members are a titanic coal-black warrior with a stentorian voice, a pale yellow gentleman of fairly martial tastes, an exceedingly handsome double-pawed tortoise-shell, & a large, pale tiger—tolerated more or less on probation. When four or five are assembled on the clubhouse roof beneath my window, the effect is the most companionable kind of thing imaginable. Count Magnus, moreover, sometimes honours this household with a visit. Of other local felidae—non-members of the Kappa Alpha Tau—one may mention the white & black huntress at the boarding-house across the back garden, who is my aunt's especial favourite. Last summer, after some of her own kittens were eliminated by the local Nazi committee which decided they didn't come up to the best Aryan standard, she adopted two exquisite little tigers with unopened eyes from some unknown source & proceeded to rear them with scientific solicitude. One was later given to appreciative owners, but the other (an utterly fascinating & incredibly companionable little rascal) became my most frequent visitor & constant playmate. Because of his sprightly, insolent precocity I called him *Alfred Galpin* after our iconoclastic young friend . . . . & how he did climb over my desk & chair & shoulders & all the surrounding points of vantage . . . . . threading his way over tables & among ornaments without ever breaking a thing! But alas! One sad day in mid-December he failed to appear in his wonted haunts, & he has never since been seen. All mourn his absence—& try to picture him as the recipient of some kindly rather than tragic fate. Perhaps he skipped & sidled toward one of our glorious hillside sunsets & passed into the fourth dimension, there to remain as an acolyte of the panther-god Hra in the City of Never, always as young as on the day he came. But it was a blow to the K.A.T. to lose so promising a future member. Count Magnus has vowed vengeance upon any Entity responsible for the disappearance!

I envy you your weather—God, if you could see the spell that Providence has just been through! The worst cold wave in the history of the city's weather bureau—*17° below zero* one day, which has never been even approached before. The next thing to it was the terrible winter of 1917–18. Narragansett Bay almost frozen over—for the second time since the appalling winter of 1778–79, when the Royal troops in Newport nearly perished of cold, notwithstanding that many were Hessians & used to the bitter winters of inland Germany. Naturally I stayed indoors—where, thanks to the marvellous heat piped in from the college engineering building, the mercury was comfortably up in the 80's all 24 hours of the day. I hope like the dickens that I can manage to get down to the Florida & pay young Ar-E'ch-Bei a visit in a couple of months . . . . though financial prospects are against it.

Yrs. for Sylvanus Cocidius & the Secret Altar of Mona—
—E'ch-Pi-El

P.S. And let me reiterate my thanks for the picture, which holds a place of honour in my gallery. ¶ Also—notify me if you'd like to borrow Artorius Vigalis' Wanderings in Roman Britain. ¶ I wish we could find good old Bill

Lumley a picturesque-looking elephant image to replace his lost Bengal specimen! (Vide his epistle) I shall be on the lookout.

Notes

1. See *SL* 2, facing p. 328.
2. "Tarbis of the Lake." HPL had helped Price with the story.
3. "A Threefold Cord."
4. A best-selling novel by Hervey Allen.
5. Of these, Schwartz published only "The Outpost."
6. I.e., Edward H. Cole. See HPL to Cole, 14 December 1914 (ms., JHL).
7. I.e., Dr. F. J. Farnell, who treated HPL's mother.
8. I.e., Arthur Harris; cf. HPL to Harris, 13 April 1934 (ms., JHL).
9. Dinsmore Alter (1888–1968), American astronomer and meteorologist, and director of the Griffith Observatory in Los Angeles.
10. HPL refer to Robert E. Howard by this epithet in the satire "The Battle That Ended the Century."
11. Because 66 College Street was on Brown University's fraternity row, HPL devised the mock K.A.T. fraternity (standing for *Kompson Ailuron Taxis*, or band of elegant or well-dressed cats) for the cats from the adjacent boarding house.

[264]   [TLS, JHL]

> In deep Dendo—hour
> of the spiral dawning.
> [early March 1934]

Dear Éch-Pi-El:

Your last would have had an answer ere this; but I managed to catch a severe cold—the first of the season, and, I hope, the last—which has disinclined me even toward letter-writing, for the past week.

The card came today—thanks for the imposing picture of the John Hay Memorial Library. Hope that Prorok and the returned volumes will arrive safely. I am awaiting A. Vigalis and Others Who Return with immense expectations. My advance thanks for the much appreciated loan.

I am glad you liked my note on James—the title given it was Hornig's. It was at least a clear summing up of James' special and salient qualities. Lumley's The Dweller is a fine thing, and I was pleased to see it in print.[1] I wrote again to Lumley the other day, having received a line from him. Evidently some of his previous letters, or mine, must have been sunk without trace in the mails. I return herewith the letter from him enclosed in your last.

Before I forget it, let me thank you for Merritt's address. I mailed him an inscribed copy of The Double Shadow some time ago, and hope he will enjoy the contents.[2]

Koenig wrote, acknowledging The Dark Chamber, and offering to loan me a catalogue of his library. Needless to say, I accepted the offer, and shall be vastly interested to look it over. Like you, I fail to comprehend the mania for first editions—any correctly printed edition with good clear type will fill the bill as far as I am concerned.

Your reaction to The Weaver in the Vault is gratifying. I rather like this tale myself. I must re-read The Woman in the Wood: I went over it rather hastily, and may like it much better on a second perusal. I admired the idea tremendously, but received the impression of choppiness in some of the writing. Merritt, it seems to me, sometimes sounds like a gifted and imaginative newspaper man who has set out to do some fine writing. If he could transcend his journalistic and pulp magazine experience, he would be a world-beater.

Dunsany's The Curse of the Wise Woman sounds rather inviting. I have, by the way, received the new Machen book, The Green Round, and have read it with mixed reactions. It is well written, and the mystery and suggestion are well handled. It does not, however, have the powerful climax of his earlier horror tales; and conventional poltergeist phenomena, smashing of windows, crockery, etc., by an unknown force, are repeated overmuch in the latter part. I received also the new Not at Night anthology, Keep on the Light, and was struck by the immense superiority of the items taken from Weird Tales, over others which, I presume, are by British authors. Howard's Worms of the Earth and Whitehead's The Chadbourne Episode were the leaders.

Wright found my drawing for The Death of Malygris satisfactory, and has ordered one for The Colossus of Ylourgne (June issue.) In my last epistle to Pharnabosus, I conveyed an intimation that I should regard it as an honour if he were to delegate to me the illustrating of The Silver Key sequel. If it does not fall to me, I fervently hope that Rankin will be the artist selected for the job. Howard Wandrei would be a great addition to the W. T. pictorial staff, to judge from the photographs of some of his pictures which Donald has recently sent me. I was particularly impressed by a thing called The Sorcerer's Workshop—a mélange of ingenious and provocative abominations.

Truly, matters don't look very hopeful for Crawford's venture. He seems to be having worse luck with the printing than I did with my disastrous and ill-omened one-shot, The Double Shadow. I still owe the printer fifty pazoors, and have been stalling him off because of the continued delay in magazine payments. I am, by the way, giving the Gernsback outfit a broad hint that some legal action will be forthcoming unless they pay up a good installment of their arrears at an early date. Wandrei recommends Nat Schachner,[3] one of the star scientifictionists, as a capable lawyer for such collections. Schachner must have had some experience with old Hugo, since he contributed a number of stories to W.S. some time back. I must admit that the idea of setting a Jew to catch a Jew is one that appeals to me. But, on the whole, I'd prefer to collect something without legal bother and expense, if I can.

So Sultan Malik has gone into the garage business! Shades of the Silver

Peacock and the Hashishins! Well, perhaps he is displaying a modicum of wisdom at that. No matter how serious the depression becomes, the U.S. population will go on running its chariots till the last tire blows out and the ultimate half-pint of gas is exhausted.

However, I am sorry that the Malik's Occidental progress will be delayed. I hope he can hit Auburn either in the late spring or early autumn—the best seasons here. The winters are too wet and the summers are not only hot but arid. We continue to have heavy, soaking showers; and the Sierran snowfall has deepened considerably during the past week. Spring flowers are appearing in quantity, the season being a good two weeks earlier than usual. So far, we have not had any snow in Auburn this year. I certainly commiserate you on the run of blizzards that have afflicted New England. Truly, you are fortunate to have such comfortable housing-conditions, to offset the outdoor rigours.

Judging from Harré's reactions, it would appear that Aleister Crowley is a pretty hard specimen. I had discounted the legends on general principles, knowing nothing whatever about the mysterious magus.

I am fascinated by your account of Roman Britain. The period has been passed over so briefly by most historians, that I hadn't realized the length and thoroughness of Roman tenure. Indeed, I am most eager to read the Weigall book. I'd certainly like to think that I have a little of the old Latin blood. Certainly some of my forbears, on the paternal side, must have been in Lancashire at the time of the occupation, when Lancaster, Ribchester and other places were Roman camps. My father remembers the Roman roads, and the walls at Chester in Cheshire; but either he had not seen, or did not recall, a tower built in the time of Hadrian which forms part of the castle at Lancaster. I believe I'd get a tremendous thrill out of visiting the English and Welsh counties and seeing such antiquities.

When one comes to realize it, the power and shadow of Rome survives in myriad ways; and there are many trains of association which, if one follows them, connect us with the Latin past. For instance, the California sherry that I drink (my favourite kind of wine) is a legitimate descendant of the wines of Xeres that were imported to Rome in the days when Andalusia was part of Hispania Ulterior. I imagine that the process of making is similar, apart from the modern practice of fortifying the wine with more or less distilled grape-spirit. Distillation, which seems to have originated with the Chinese, was brought into Europe by the Arabs and was little known before the 13th century. At least, this is my impression.

I enjoyed your account of the K.A.T. fraternity in Providence. Simaetha and Tabasco are certainly full of feline originality and character. Simaetha, I notice, still keeps her Maltese offspring in order by an occasional razor-keen and lightning-swift slash of her ivory claws. She has all the look of an enraged witch's familiar on such occasions; and her slitted yellow eyes are demoniacal enough at times. However, she will purr amiably, like any harmless house-cat, if stroked. Tabasco, in spite of his burliness, is really very good-natured, though he has a habit of querulous and persistent miauling acquired in his somewhat puny kittenhood. Unluckily, I have no pictures of my companions; but I shall make some drawings of them at the first suitable opportunity, and will send you these if they are successful. I really think that Simaetha must be connected with the guardian felines of the fane of Sadoqua: her incredible age and undiminished vigour are more than suggestive of such lineage. Count Magnus and Peter Randall certainly sound like aristocrats capable of maintaining the highest traditions of noblesse oblige. And I can easily picture that rascal of an Alfred Galpin.

I hope you can find a suitable elephant image to replace the one lost by Lumley. *One should make sure, however, that the selected eikon has nothing to do with Chaugnar Faugn.* Many lost secrets must be exchanged in the night by your Mayan image and *ushabti* . . . and those uttered by the Nameless Entity are, it is to be hoped, *forever lost* in the black oubliettes of bygone cycles.

Thanks for the clippings and for your kind permission to keep them. I am particularly taken by that account of the lost city of the lizard people. The theory that planets are formed by accretions of cosmic atoms is certainly plausible, and would multiply the likelihood of alien systems similar to ours throughout the universe.

The Loch Monster, it would seem, is beginning to shrink from the glare of publicity; at least, there have been fewer accounts of it in recent papers. Apart from the creature reported in Sweden, I have seen a rumour of one in an Irish Lough; also, of one in a Nevada lake! I'll return the Thenevin articles in my next. Your mixed assortment of clippings went back with the books. Among these, I was especially taken with the drawings of the London artist, Spare. The man certainly must have had a vision of paganry and demonry! His drawings made me think of Machen's The Great God Pan. He'd certainly be an ideal illustrator for that story, and also for The White People. There is grand literary material in those ruins. I think too that you will find much that is provocative in Prorok's account of the antiquities of North Africa. The number and magnitude of Phoenician, Roman and prehistoric remnants is simply staggering. Note that picture of the rutted pavement at Timgad—at least, I think it was at Timgad (I have an inaccurate memory for names, dates, etc.)

I hope to finish my new Zothique story, Xeethra, before long. This infernal cold has knocked me out lately. I believe I must have caught it by a three days' abstinence from anything vinous. (This isn't altogether a joke, since I believe that wine has a distinct prophylactic value.)

Yours for the Cauldron of Abundance,

Klarkash-Ton

P.S. I can loan you *The Green Round* and the new *Not at Night*, if you have not yet seen them.

A few clippings and drawings enclosed. All are to be kept.

Notes

1. "The Dweller," *FF* 1, No. 6 (February 1934): 88.

2. Merritt was writing *Creep, Shadow!* when he received *The Double Shadow* and found that the title story anticipated certain elements in his novel, necessitating rewriting. See Sam Moskowitz, ed., *A. Merritt: Reflections in the Moon Pool* (Philadelphia: Oswald Train, 1985), 112.

3. The science fiction writer Nat[han] Schachner (1895–1955) was trained as a lawyer.

[265]   [ANS][1]

[Postmarked Auburn, Cal.,
7 March 1934]

Dear Éch-Pi-El:

The book arrived yesterday—many thanks! A. Vigalis is full of treasures, and I am enjoying the Wakefield stories. The Cairn strikes me as being perhaps the best.[2]

Spring is apparently full-blown in these parts—mercury went up to 70° yesterday. Hope there won't be a return to brumal rigours.

Hazel Heald's story in the current W. T. is very good.

Yrs., Klarkash-Ton

Notes

1. *Front:* Unidentified.

2. "The Cairn" is in *Others Who Returned.*

[266]   [ALS, Northern Illinois University]

At the Edge of the Voor—Hour
When the Aklo Colours coruscate
[Postmarked 9 March 1934]

Dear Klarkash-Ton:—

Commiserations on the cold! By this time I trust its force is wholly spent, leaving your energies unimpaired. Abundant thanks for Comte de Prorok—who safely arrived in conjunction with the returned material. Haven't had time to read him yet—but the pictures are ineffably alluring. My Roman soul expands so quasi-reminiscently to the imposing vestiges of imperial Carthago, that the older Punic city recedes almost to second place. I'll have this perused & on its return trip before too long—& meanwhile I trust you have safely received Artorius Vigalis & Alteri qui Reveniunt.[1] Glad you've secured "The Green Round"—I think I'll gratefully accept your loan offer of that, since I'd like to see what it's like before sinking $1.50 in the Argus. The new Not at Night sounds good, although "The Chadbourne Episode" is by no means good Canevin's best. I don't believe I'll bother you to

The Letters of H. P. Lovecraft and Clark Ashton Smith ❋ 539

lend that, since I've probably read everything in it that's any good. Your "Isle of the Torturers" & two-Gun Bob's "Worms of the Earth" are undoubtedly the headliners. Koenig has now returned "The Dark Chamber", & like you he is inclined to rave about it a bit less than Sonny Belknap & I do. You'll find Koenig's catalogue a tantalising thing—& a fruitful source of valuable loans. Sooner or later I trust he'll make his library still more effective by letting down the bars against non-first editions. I'm sure Merritt will appreciate "The Double Shadow", & hope he'll send you an acknowledgment. By the way— I've just read his "Metal Monster" after all these years, & am literally on my hind legs cheering! Ædepol, what a picture of *utter, alien non-humanness!* I've never seen anything like it before, & can understand why Merritt calls this his "best & worst" tale.[2] The human characters are wooden puppets—artificial pulp stock figures—but the descriptions of *regions & phenomena*—oh, boy! The scene (or perhaps you know all this) is among the mountains of Turkestan— that same mysterious Asiatic upland which old Nick Roerich (Merritt's close friend) has so imperishably exploited in his strange paintings. I tried to catch the Roerich aura in my "Mountains of Madness", but Abe has me licked from the start. He is certainly the supreme master of *non-human suggestion*—& I wish to gawd he could be pried loose for ever from the fringe of the pulp under- world & its moods, values, & methods. Glad you like Lumley's verses—I've helped him put quite a number of these items into shape. Yes—in getting him an elephant I shall be very careful not to let it approach the perilous like- ness of Chaugnar Faugn! What the ushabti & the Mayan image & *It* mutter to themselves & to one another in the night is *bad enough.*

Thanks tremendously for the four nameless horrors—the two sent directly, & those transmitted by Herr von Koenig. That hirsute fellow looks like some- thing from the pages of Monty James—while that tentacled, half-vegetable enti- ty is certainly the product of no terrestrial or solar-system or galactic spawning! As I said on the card, that "Weaver" drawing was splendid. But what shall I say of the design for "The Charnel God"? Iä! Shub-Niggurath! That cyclopean, columned, hieroglyphed hall, & those two doubtfully-gliding corpse-bearers! Something to get under the skin & haunt the imagination subtly & pervasively! Truly a triumph. I am now tremendously anxious to see the Malygris sketch— & vastly glad to learn of the acceptance of a "Colossus of Ylourgne" design. Your art work is certainly landing big at last—a fulfilment of my decade-long prayers! I hope Pharnabozus will assign you the "Gates of the Silver Key" sketch. That would make the thing a thorough product of our group! And so Melmoth has at last sent you pictures of his brother's sketches! I haven't been so favoured as yet—tho' of course I saw the real sketches themselves last De- cember. Yes—that "Sorcerer's Workshop" is certainly a marvel.

Crawford is indeed having a hard time. He has just sent me a sheet ex- emplifying his first efforts at printing, & I cannot but reflect that he still has much to learn. His shortage of type is another grave handicap—but hope &

determination still seem to fire his mind! I'm sorry to hear that "The Double Shadow" has involved such a loss, & hope that gradual sales later on may help to mend the deficit. I continue to boost it at all possible opportunities—both to new acquaintances & to others who have not yet secured it. Let us hope you can eventually arrange to get something out of Hugo the Rat. Eh deedn't know it Meestah Schechner vass ah smart lawyer a'ready. Oy! He shood make Hugo pay det money ef he hass to boin his shop to get it! Meanwhile the Peacock Sultan is having a great time mending cars among the Osages. He'll probably write you about it. Most of his clients are of the noble aboriginal strain—government wards blowing in their oil-land money in fantastic ways. What they can do to the stoutest metal chariots would require the scientifictional imagination of an Edmond Hamilton or Nyctzin Dyalhis to explain! The latest case is of a car with the bottom of the petrol tank punctured—an old squaw had been driving it across the hills & meadows (roads are ignored) chasing rabbits, & a sharp rock refused to move out of the way . . . . perhaps heeding the Dunsanian dictum "rock should not walk in the evening".[3] Just how stationary Malik will remain, one can scarcely predict. Even with his new job, I doubt if his deathless wanderlust can quite be curbed—hence you & Two-Gun may see him yet. When he does hit Auburn, I trust it may be at an auspicious season.

Congratulations, by the way, on the spring flowers! Providence, as usual, has suffered extremes. On Feby. 26 there was an almost record-breaking snowfall (vide enc.), yet precisely a week later the hydrargyral column[4] rose to almost 70°—giving a marvellous foretaste of spring. Upon this latter occasion I broke hibernation, & for the first time in 1934 fared forth to the wild domed hills & hanging woods—overcoatless, but with caoutchouc[5]-clad lower extremities. What a day! I sloshed over familiar slopes & forest vales white & brown with an alternation of melting snow & fragrant, awakening earth. A magic of vague expectancy flickered in the air & in the vernal sunlight, whilst on every hand there resounded the gurgling music of a thousand transient rivulets & swollen brooks. I never saw the streams & ponds so high before—& when I crossed the wide Blackstone I found all its lower banks overflowed . . . . with great trees & cottage roofs rising from an aqueous expanse like reliques of sunken Lemuria. I surely hope that the disastrous floods of 1927 will not be repeated! Since Monday the weather has been less genial, & a moderate snowfall last night emphasised the fact that (in the language of New England folklore) "March hill is still to be climbed." But even so, I guess the extremes of hyemal horror are done for.

If you found my scattered remarks on Britannia Romana of interest, it is needless to say that you will find Artorius Vigalis' ampler exposition still more so. As you say, other historians have dismissed the period briefly—this being due, of course, to the traditional fallacy that our ancestry has nothing to do with the Britanno-Romans. John Richard Green, in his famous History of the

English People, swallows this fallacy whole, & adds to it the widespread error that Britain was never Romanised except in the towns. Of course both of these misconceptions were challenged from time to time. Huxley, from careful ethnological, historical, & archaeological research, insisted that the Saxons did not accomplish any total racial replacement except perhaps in East Anglia, & that the ancestry of the West-English stock (including most emphatically the Devonshire lines forming the bulk of my paternal heritage) is unquestionably mainly pre-Saxon British.[6] That (plus my Welsh lines) joined me on to the Celts, but left the question of Roman stock still open. However, even in the matter of Romanisation there was much divided opinion. Against Green's position many vital objections have always been raised—based on certain allusions in old chronicles, on the extent of rural Roman reliques in England, & on certain subtler bits of evidence—as, for instance, that of the very name of the *Welsh* . . . . this word being unmistakably a variant of the common Teutonic word for a *Roman provincial* (never applied to non-Latin-speaking tribes), and analogous to such easterly continental variants as *Vlach* & *Wallach* (cf. Roumania). The Saxons *did not* use this word in connexion with the warlike tribal Scots & the coast-ravaging Irish—whom they would inevitably have confused with other British-Islanders had all been tribal & Celtic-speaking. On the contrary, they restricted it to the Britons of the old Roman province which now became England—the element whose un-Saxonised remnants were pushed into that westerly region thenceforward called Wales. This is the strongest possible evidence that the bulk of the Britons whom the Saxons conquered were Latin-speaking Roman provincials. The fact that the *modern* Welsh speak Cymric, & that it was Cymric which the fleeing islanders carried into Brittany in Gaul, is entirely irrelevant in this connexion. It is well known that the Celtic tribes of the *extreme west* of Britain were never Romanised, but that a virtual frontier existed betwixt them & the civilised Silures & Ordovices of the Britannia Secunda. (cf. "Worms of the Earth") Naturally, when the Roman (= Wallach-Welsh) refugees began to filter amongst them, they held a position of entrenched superiority & gave their language to the newcomers rather than adopting Latin speech. And of course the relatively few Roman refugees could hardly keep their Latin long amidst a Cymric majority. The Celts who went to Brittany were not civilised Britons at all, but merely tribesmen of the west who *secondarily* felt the impact of the Saxons. (cf. corrupt forms of the Arthur legend) That the Cymric Welsh as a whole are not typical Britons is proved by their dominantly Mediterranean or melanochroic racial cast. The Britons as a whole were much more Nordic than Mediterranean, & the Gallic & Germanic legions increased the tall blond element. True, the southwestern Britons were *originally* Mediterranean; but if the modern Welsh were refugees from *all over Britain,* as the anti-Romans used to claim, they *wouldn't* be short & dark like the old Silures & Ordovices. The fact that the present population is exactly like the old unromanised local tribes proves that it is descended from them, & that it does not represent the wholesale sweepings of all the pre-Saxon islanders. Therefore its Celtic speech does not indicate that the whole of non-urban Britain spoke Celtic under the Romans. Oddly, the word meaning a Roman provincial—applied because many fleeing provincials settled in the given region—has become connected with a population which was never Roman! Of such paradoxes is history composed—no wonder there are confusions & controversies! Now all this—largely under the influence of Huxley—was pretty well demonstrated before Weigall's time. Ever since the 1880's histories have been more & more conceding the thorough Latinisation of Roman Britain—these concessions being constantly backed up by the results of archaeological excavation. Indeed, it was before Weigall had published anything that I had my own memorable controversy on the subject with the genial & scholarly "amateur journalist" Edward H. Cole—an orthodox devotee of the old Green view. That was in 1914—just 20 years ago—& even without Artorius Vigalis' support I found enough authorities to give Cole a thorough licking & make him admit it. (I mentioned the fact to him recently in connexion with my new Vigalis book!) Thus, in relation to the two questions of (a) whether the pre-Saxon British population survives in us, & (b) whether it was a thoroughly Romanised population, Weigall's real task was simply to confirm an affirmative view already well-grounded. What will probably be remembered as his *distinctive* contribution, is his thorough demonstration—backed up by the evidence of hundreds of grave stelae excavated in every part of Britain & recording family alliances betwixt the Roman legionaries & the native populations— that we are largely descended not only from the Romanised Celts (which Huxley &c. had indeed shewed before), *but from the actual Roman troops sent into Britain from outside.* It is Weigall, most emphatically, who has added to our known heritage the actual physical blood of the eagle-bearing ranks of A. Plautius, P. Ostorius Scapula, A. Didius Gallus, Q. Veranius, L. Suetonius Paullinus, Petronius Turpilianus, Trebellius Maximus, Vettius Bolanus, Petilius Cerealis, M. Julius Frontinus, Cn. Julius Agricola, Sallusticus Lucullus, & all the rest. S.P.Q.R. ROMA! Personally, I suppose I am about 50-50 Teutonic & Britanno-Roman. My paternal lines, involving Devon, Cornwall, & Wales, are probably preponderantly pre-Saxon despite certain known Saxon lines (like Carew of Haccombe) & considerable Norman blood. My father's maternal line of Allgood is Northumbrian, & perhaps includes Danish strains—though its ancestral seats of Nunwick & Brandon White House are near the Roman station of Hexham in the region of Hadrian's Wall . . . . . anciently *Axelodunum.* Maternally, because of the East Anglian preponderance in New England stock, I suppose I am considerably Saxon—Phillips & Whipple come from Norfolk, & so on. And yet even of the maternal strain a good many lines are from farther west—Perkins from Newent, Gloucestershire, & so on. I guess it's pretty fair to assume that I have as good a chance as any other average

Englishman to be at least one-half Britanno-Roman. I envy your father his memories of the old land, & hope ardently that I can some day find a way to see its limitless wealth of ancestral landmarks. My correspondent Edkins (the chap whose letter against weird fiction I shewed you last year) is going over this coming summer, and & I envy him bitterly. He was born there, but was brought to America as a memoryless infant & has never been back. I may possibly—later—ask you to send Vigalis on to him instead of returning it directly; for he's getting rather interested in my descriptions. But of course it can't be denied that the Saxon sweep completely broke our Roman cultural heritage. What we inherit of the Roman tradition—fortunately a vast amount, giving us a national character of colonisers, administrators, & upholders of a temperate civil order—is what came in with the Normans. Nothing more fortunate than the Norman Conquest ever occurred in modern history—for it brought us back into the classical western world which has Greece & Rome behind it, & saved us from the childish, mystical pure-Teutonism which even to this day gives Germany an extravagant, ill-proportioned national psychology. Yes—I know that California has other links with the old Roman fabric which we lack in New England . . . . . the link of Hispanic culture. Sherry— from Xeres to Auburn—an unbroken chain! In these latter years New England is getting floods of neo-Latins—French-Canadians, Italians, & Portugese—but the circumstances of the immigration are not such as to bring us any very important legacy from the republic of the Scipiones!

You must not fail to draw me at least sketchy likenesses of Dame Simaetha and Genl. Tabasco—for the more you say of them, the more interested I become! Dwyer has just sent me some fascinating snaps of his black imp—a veritable fragment of the eternal Night! I mentioned them to Count Magnus the other day as he crouched on his beloved back-fence, & his answering purrs & rubbings were eloquent of curiosity. But behold! There is news from Ulthar! Not many days ago Mrs. Spotty, the white & black lady at the boarding-house across the back garden (Alfred Galpin's foster-mother of last summer) was delivered of the liveliest & most fascinating set of triplets ever beheld on this side of the River Skai.[7] Eyes just open. Two—both Maltese—are promised to discriminating ailurophiles elsewhere; but the third—white & black like mamma—will be retained & reared. It is needless to say that I shall do considerable friendly borrowing in the weeks to come, when little Belknap (as I shall call him) is less dependent on immediate maternal vicinage! I hope he will not follow little Alfred Galpin into the baffling abyss of invisibility! There's a fine black & white feline—Oswald—at Sultan Malik's new habitat!

Glad the cuttings proved of interest. Here are a few more—largely about our Loch Ness friend & his kinsfolk elsewhere. Hope you can base some sort of a yarn on the lizard people. Zimbabwe, too, offers possibilities . . . . . station of The Fishers from Outside . . . . . Whether the Alter planetary theory can hold water remains to be seen, but it is at least a boon to scientifictionists

to know that a multiplanetary cosmos has some basis in contemporary speculation. I am enclosing herewith a cutting about a new microscopic-telescopic
principle which ought to be capable of very vivid fictional use. You might return this, though there is not the least hurry about it. This new Zworykin idea
would seem to remove (in theory, at least) virtually all limits from the extent
of microscopic & telescopic magnification[8]—thus putting a sound basis behind things like O'Brien's "Diamond Lens" & that French story of images
projected from Venus (can't recall name, but Cook lent it to me years ago.
Rather mediocre handling of a splendid idea.).[9] Thanks exceedingly for the
cuttings enclosed. That man with the telescopic eye is surely a bit of walking
scientifiction—while the pyga sounds much like one of your pictorial entities
come to life! The sunken Roman city in Morocco appeals especially to my
imagination . . . . . . what would a diver find if he were to lift the trap-door in
the floor of the temple of the *Magnum Innominandum* & go down those lightless steps? . . . . By the way—I hope that "Xeethra" may achieve a favourable reception in the palace of King Pharnaces.

"The Charnel God" easily dominates the current W. T. Keller's serial is
simply lousy, like most of the continued stories in the magazine. And yet Doc
can turn out a great yarn when he feels like it—as attested by "The Thing in the
Cellar", & the older tale of the sorcerer & the country which rested on a living
monster. "Winged Death" is pretty much a ghost-written Ech-Pi-El-ism.[10] All
that honest Mrs. Heald had to start with was a cloudy idea about somebody
killing somebody with bugs. Then she got a medical friend to shed some light
on poisonous African insects, & decided to give the tale an African cast. That
was all I had to go on. The plot—with the idea of transferred personality &
the returning & ceiling-writing death-envoy—is entirely my own. But it
doesn't pay to do this sort of work—when one could have just as good
chances of *full* pay with a piece nominally as well as actually one's own. I've
cut it out now—though the last two reliques of my collaboration (one more
Heald opus & the collaboration with Sultan Malik) are yet to be printed.[11]

Ar-E'ch-Bei wants me to get down to De Land May 1st., & I surely pray
all the Dark Gods that I may be able to swing it financially! I pine for the
sight of live-oaks & Spanish moss! Of course I'd try to stop in Charleston &
St. Augustine—& if possible get to Williamsburg, where the colonial restora-
tion has progressed enormously (Capitol & Governor's Palace now up) since
I was last there in 1931. If I can make it, I shall probably meet our weird colleagues Single-Plot Hamilton & Jack Williamson, who are wintering in Key
West & will stop in De Land as they return northward. They have informed
Ar-E'ch-Bei that they wouldn't mind encountering Grandpa. I think I could
manage to be tactful with Hamilton—for damn it, the boy *could* write if he'd
only forget the cursed pulp ideal! His "Monster God of Mamurth" was magnificent! Williamson is a very promising kid, although I'm afraid pulpdom will
'get' him before he has a chance to form a real literary personality.

Belknap has just sent me Young Melmoth's new tale "Colossus" from *Astounding*. The conception is splendid, & some of the descriptive passages are vivid, but the whole effect suffers from concessions to the pulp ideal. There is a good deal of dubious astronomy, & the quasi-human nature, instruments, & pursuits of the macrocosmic beings is a trifle unimaginative & unconvincing. Certainly, interplanetary tales are the hardest of all things to develop in a really powerful & artistic way. I don't believe I'll ever have the temerity to attempt one, though I lately drew up a sort of code or set of rules governing interplanetary writing which I shall follow if I ever do make the attempt.[12]

Well—the day is warming up. Guess I'll go down & get a few errands done, though the temperature does not beckon one to the woods & fields. Hope your cold is now a thing of the past. Will report later on Prorok.

Thine in The Bond of Pnath—E'ch-Pi-El

Notes

1. I.e., H. R. Wakefield's *Others Who Returned*.

2. So said Merritt in *FF* 2, No. 1 (September 1934): 7.

3. The words appear in the speech of the Man in Act III of *The Gods of the Mountain*, in *Five Plays* (1914).

4. *Hydrargyrum* is an obsolete word for mercury; thus HPL writes of a thermometer.

5. Unvulcanized rubber.

6. See Thomas Henry Huxley (1825–1895), "On Some Fixed Points in British Ethnology," in *Man's Place in Nature and Other Anthropological Essays* (New York: D. Appleton & Co., 1894), 253–70.

7. From HPL's "The Cats of Ulthar."

8. Vladimir Kosmich Zworykin (1888–1982), Russian-American inventor and pioneer of television technology. He invented a television transmitting and receiving system employing cathode ray tubes. He played a role in the practical development of the electron microscope.

9. Maurice Leblanc (1864–1941), *The Three Eyes*, tr. Alexander Teixeira de Mattos (New York: Macaulay, 1921).

10. Keller's "The Thing in the Cellar" appeared in *WT* (March 1932). The serial is "The Solitary Hunters." The other tale HPL refers to appears to be "The Hidden Monster" (*Oriental Stories*, Summer 1932). HPL had revised "Winged Death" for Hazel Heald.

11. Heald's "Out of the Aeons" appeared in *WT* (April 1935).

12. I.e., "Some Notes on Interplanetary Fiction."

[267]   [ANS; *HK*][1]

[Postmarked Providence, R.I.,
19 March 1934]

Glad Vigalis & Wakefield duly arrived. I agree with you about the superiority of "The Cairn". Meanwhile I've finished Prorok & will return presently. I find it tremendously fascinating—not only regarding the prodigious wealth of

Roman material (more than I ever suspected, though I knew N. Africa was the richest part of the Empire in the age of the Antonines & shortly afterward), but regarding the suggestions of thousands of years of prehistoric life. It renews the belief which I have had for years, that archaeology is one of the richest fields for imaginative impressions. I feel like writing half a dozen tales of millennial crypts, sunken galleys, & mountainous basalt desert tombs with sarcophagi *not quite* of human shape! I have always wondered how far down into Africa the Phoenicians & Romans ever penetrated. Did any of them ever encounter the outposts of the Fishers from Outside? Thanks again for the glimpse of this fascinating volume. ¶ The view on your card is vastly interesting. Does this part of Auburn still look the same? And is the picture really an old one, or a modern posed affair? It certainly carries all the aura of the early days. ¶ I envy you the good weather. More snow here. Sunday the hill was so slippery that college students were lined up to watch & spoof the skidding motorists—some of whom were completely turned around. My aunt telephoned to the police station & had barriers put across the head of the street till it could be sanded. I slipped down 3 times when I went out! Warmer weather since then—but I suppose there'll be a fresh snow storm soon! ¶ Yrs for the Daemon of the Cyclopean Crypt—Ech-Pi-El

Notes

1. *Front:* Unidentified.

[268]   [ANS][1]

[Postmarked Providence, R.I.,
22 March 1934]

"Green Round" & Wakefield duly recd. Th[anks!] Please send Arturius Vigalis (but not till you['re] fully through with him yourself) to

> ERNEST A. EDKINS,
> 925 LINCOLN AVE.,
> HIGHLAND PARK, ILLINOIS.

That's the lucky cuss I told you about, who's about to spend a summer in England. Prorok started back home yesterday. Great stuff! ¶ I'll return "The Green Round" shortly. It is really extremely interesting—with some very potent reflections of that persistent sense of unreal worlds impinging on the real world which so many imaginative people have. In the casualness & unexplainedness of the phenomena it recalls some of Machen's queer prefaces—such as that to "The Three Impostors". Its faults are—mainly—a certain rambling diffuseness, tameness, [&] over-use of typical stylistic mannerisms. Not one of Machen's greatest—but typically Mach[enian] for all that. I'm

vastly glad to have read it. ¶ Your admirer Harry Brobst (back in to[wn] for a tonsil operation) dragged me to a cine[ma] called "The Ghoul" yesterday afternoon.[2] So[me] of the scenes not at all bad in their visual effect & imaginative implications. ¶ Again thanks for the glimpse of the Green Round. I [must] buy a copy later. ¶ Yrs for the Sign of Nodens—
    Ech-Pi-El

Notes

1. *Front:* American Falls from Goat Isle, Niagara Falls. [Top edge cut off in photocopy.]
2. *The Ghoul* (Gaumont British Picture Corp., 1933), directed by T. Hayes Hunter; starring Boris Karloff, Cedric Hardwicke, and Ernest Thesiger.

[269]   [ANS][1]

[Postmarked Auburn, Cal.,
23 March 1934]

Dear Éch-Pi-El:

          Thanks for card. Will write soon. Hope you will have rec'd *The Green Round* and *Others Who Returned* ere now. Glad you are enjoying Prorok—no hurry at all about returning the book. You are dead right—archaeology is a vast and little-tilled field of imaginative possibilities. Hope that Prorok will suggest some stories to you. That card of lower Auburn represents the town all right; but the coach, etc., was placed for the occasion. Weather here is fast turning into summer—no rain, and the grass already beginning to turn yellow. Hope your monsoons are over. Yrs for the brazen tower of Tsathoggua,
          Klarkash-Ton

Notes

1 *Front:* Unidentified.

[270]   [ANS enclosure with returned story; RAS 8.123]

[written on letter by Farnsworth Wright
to CAS dated 23 March 1934]

      The nameless spawn of Yub & Yoth! No wonder his damn'd magazine never prints anything worth reading except by accident! ¶ "The Clouds" is *magnificent*—one of the most potent and moving things I've read in recent years.[1] A breathless menace hangs over the scene from the first, & the doom—when it comes—is *really adequate*.

      I surely hope this will get into print somehow. Hold it a while for possible shifts of Satrap Pharnabozus' capricious alleged mind; & if he doesn't come around, let the F F have it. You surely have material for another brochure, if such could be managed.

Yrs for the Rhythm of the Gulf—E'ch-Pi-El

Notes

1. "The Primal City" (titled "The Cloud-Things" and "The Clouds" in early drafts).

[271]   [ALS]

> Arkham: the Nameless Graveyard on
> Hangman's Hill: Hour when the vast sinister
> Willow with twisted roots shakes against the wind
> [Postmarked 13 April 1934]

Dear Klarkash-Ton:—
                        Your extremely welcome envelope of treasures arrived
just as I am about to hop off on the long-anticipated journey. Tomorrow
night at midnight I board the Manhattan coach, & the ensuing morn will find
me at the cyclopean Temple of Chaugnar for a week's blasphemous worship
under the guidance of the young high-priest Bel-Nha-Plong. Naturally I shall
likewise behold Es-El at the teeming mart of Dhian-Pi,[1] Melmoth in his
haunted & shadowy backwater, to say nothing of such lesser lights as adorn
the metropolitan zone. At another sinister midnight—April 22–3—I shall
board another dark & doubtful space-ship for the haunted realms of the
South . . . . darting down without a pause to antique Charleston, where (in an
hellish grove of live-oaks which knew the fearsome footfall of Poe in 1828—
when he was serving at Ft. Moultrie) I shall perform the nameless Sabbat-
rites on monstrous May-Eve after a week amidst the crumbling Georgian gables & walled gardens of the country's most fascinating city. Then—unless I
shall have received contrary word from little Ar-E'ch-Bei (whose father is in
somewhat uncertain health)—I shall plunge deeper into the austral zone,
where the Spanish moss hangs thicker, & the palmettos are fallen & proceeding to De Land via Jacksonville. I've been through De Land—a rather pretty
place in a modern way, though without interesting antiquities—before, but
believe Barlow lives on the outskirts of the town in a region largely rural. I
imagine I shall have a rather good time, for Ar-E'ch-Bei is a very bright & interesting kid. Before quitting Florida I must see ancient St. Augustine once
more—but I have no hope of getting to Key West or Havana. Besides seeing
Hamilton & Williamson, I may possibly meet Ray Cummings (famed for his
"Golden Atom"), who is now at Ft. Lauderdale—somewhat north of Miami—& may pause in De Land. He once praised my work in the Eyrie.[2] His
early stuff had cleverness, but his latest serials . . . . . !!! Well, I trust that tact
will find me something pleasant to say! Don't know how long my stay will be.
On the return trip, I'll have to cut out most incidental stops, for I never before attempted to travel so far on so little cash.

Glad Prorok returned intact, & hope Brobst will be prompt & careful with Artorius Macaenas. If anything evil befalls it, I shall consider that I owe you a copy. No hurry about sending Vigalis to Edkins. Trust you let Miss Sully read it—as per my card—as at great length as she chose. She expressed great interest in your outdoor oral extracts. Edkins is in no hurry—his trip won't begin till well into summer. I thought you would find Vigalis of marked interest—he was a genuine eye-opener to me. I shall probably have Edkins pass him on to Bnādvai-Aā after taking notes. Don't know how many of the ancient sights E A E will be able to take in, but I envy him every one. Wonder whether this newly unearthed theatre at Verulamium will rival the one Vigalis describes at Isca Silurum? Britanno-Roman archaeology is certainly having a spurt of late to match the epoch-making excavations elsewhere.

Thanks tremendously for all the cuttings—many of which are the very thing for my files. The Etruscan article interested me vastly after my recent sight of the huge terra-cotta warriors in the Metropolitan, & of the reproduced tomb-paintings lent to the R.I. School of Design. No people is more mysterious & inexplicable than this seemingly alien stock in the midst of the Italic tribes—a stock to whom so many of the familiar Roman forms & institutions are due. If this Pironti discovery[3] turns out to be true (it is still disputed, not withstanding the assertion of the article), a vast step will have been made toward solving the riddle . . . . although new riddles are at the same time created. Assuming that the language was indeed a variant of archaic Greek, then how did this obviously southern & perhaps eastern race come to possess an Aryan language? Of course their adoption of Greek art forms was the result of a later contact with the Greeks—within historic times. I give it up. The nearest previous approach to the deciphering of the Etruscan was made by the late Prof. Trombetti of Milan,[4] who considered himself on the verge of victory at the time of his sudden death a few years ago. Whether his notes & researches form the basis of the present study I don't know. I am retaining this article in my archives with enormous gratitude. Nor is my gratitude less for the splendid sheet of Roman mosaics in colour—which likewise goes into my archives. I have no other reproductions of such things on a similar scale or in colour. Pavements like these are what archaeologists find all over England—for wherever the Roman culture went, the typical architectural forms & decorations appear. This Corinthian villa must have been the home of a Roman, for the Greeks did not tend to adopt Roman forms. One may see at a glance the plainly Italic and non-Hellenic nature of the technique despite the Grecian subjects & setting. By the way—that snow-clad Acropolis view is extremely interesting. Glad that the old rock is still safe—it would be ignominious if such a survivor of noble centuries should come to grief in this degenerate age. The case of the Parthenon itself is bad enough—a perfect vestige of the glory of old Hellas . . . . . . & assuming its present ruined form only in modern times . . . . . . 1687 . . . . . . the eve of the expulsion of King

James, the period of Sir Edmund Andros in New England, the 52nd year of Providence's existence . . . . . to think that the Parthenon was standing in full glory when King Philip's War raged over Rhode Island, when Roger Williams died, & when Pardon Tillinghast built his wharf for West-India vessels (above which, on the hill, he still lies buried) on Providence's curving Town Street! The Greenland marble deposits make one think of Olathoë in the land of Lomar . . . . . . the Pnakotic Manuscripts tell what was carved from them immemorial aeons ago![5] As for Lemuria—you have by this time seen the similar cutting which crossed yours in the mail. That ought to be good story-material—to have the explorers find water-worn traces of the cyclopean architecture of the Third Root Race—reputedly the denizens of Shalmali! And speaking of the deep—that carnivorous ocean lily would form another splendid theme . . . . & how you could *illustrate* it! The artificial summer caused by burning gas wells excites my envy—I wish we could find some wells to burn over here! Suppose such a thing happened *on the Antarctic continent* near the Mts. of Madness—fancy the primal secrets revealed by the melting of the aeon-old ice!

The vampire-bat item was indeed unusual. I had an idea these fellows didn't go for human beings very much. And I was very glad to read of the extent of archaeological work in Peru. The feline bits were abundantly welcome—especially the picture of stalwart Pop Eye, of whose exploits I read some time ago in a news item. That boy certainly looks able to take care of himself . . . . & I shall certainly urge his election as a corresponding member of the Kappa Alpha Tau! The piano-playing Mickey also looks like good younger material! Lord Haggis's exploit is typical of many similar feats of which I have read. There is genuine mystery in this feline sense of direction—& it is obviously linked with that sense of strong local attachment so notable in cats . . . . & in myself as well.

Speaking of Ulthar & its colonies—I am infinitely your debtor for that haunting & subtly disquieting likeness of the daemon-link'd Simaetha! Verily, I can glimpse the latent nightmare in those slitlike, widely-spaced eyes! It is clear that those eyes have look'd upon things whose very mention would blast a common mortal. When you can corner the belligerent & elusive General I'd appreciate a sketch of him as well—for I feel that there must be a vast amount of hearty likeability in the bluff old veteran. By the way—a friend of mine named John Quincy Adams, who lives at Adams' Market farther north on the ancient hill & spends most of his time at the Art Club next door, has just suffered a severe mauling & tearing . . . . . the result of an argument with a moving motor. He's recovering, though—despite a limp. Mr. Adams is generally to be found curled up on an ancient chest in the main gallery of the Art Club; & he knows Grandpa E'ch-Pi-El so well that he comes over and jumps in the Old Gentleman's lap when the latter sits down. He is a huge tiger with a touch of Persian or Angora, & retains the playful & affectionate disposition of a kitten despite his undeniable middle age. With suitable encouragement, he even rolls over on his back & kicks! Spring weather is swelling the attendance at the K.A.T. meetings, & Pres. Randall is now to be found regularly on his favourite shed roof . . . . . . usually with Count Magnus just two feet away. The grey twins across the garden, alas, left for their new home last Monday . . . . I hope they'll like it. When I get home from my wanderings their little white & black brother here will be a very big boy!

Glad you are availing yourself to the bibliothecal generosity of Freiherr von Koenig. I read "Shapes in the Fire" around 1925—*after* having read the revised "House of Hounds"—& the H of S prototype⁶ sounded abominably affected to me. Is it possible that I haven't read the finished product? God! if I only had a copy! I endeavoured to get Harré to slip it into his anthology, but the publishers vetoed it because of length. The prototype is splendid, but redolent of Yellow-Book 1890ism. The superiority of the 1908 version is incalculable. "Xelucha" is great stuff—probably the next best thing in the book. Shiel is a queer cuss—& bewilderingly uneven. His cardinal fault is a certain florid, fleshy quality of extravagance & wilful eccentricity—but how he can write when he wants to! The first half of "The Purple Cloud" nearly rivals "The House of Sounds".

I guess "The Metal Emperor" isn't so much inferior to the original version as Barlow believes. The non-humanness surely is titanic! As to the human puppets—the trouble with them is their obvious conventionality. Same old romance—same old heroism—just pulp stuff. If only Merritt could *completely* break away from this kind of thing!

Thanks prodigiously for the weird sketches accompanying Simaetha. That beaked entity is a wicked customer—while the heavy-lipped citizen of Averoigne looks as if he might be the Black Man of a witch coven in his spare moments. I was glad to see the Malygris design, which has a peculiar kind of impressiveness—& I await the others with eagerness. I fear though, that as you say, Satrap Pharnabozus has not heeded my suggestion anent the Silver Key. However—if he has Rankin, there's a chance of something good.

Well—Crawford has been stirring at last. Just recd. sheets of my "Celephaïs" with a sketch by Huey⁷ which could be a lot worse. The press work is a home job, but I fancy it will pass muster. Several annoying misprints, though. The whole issue is finished except for the cover, & I fancy we'll be seeing it soon. After all, little Bill was no faker! It surely is too bad that a wider public can't be found for "The Double Shadow." But I'm damn'd if I'd *give* away such a splendid thing except to persons who can't pay—or to those who would normally receive complimentary copies.

As my card apprised you, Sultan Malik is on the move again—& I guess you'll see him before long. By this time he must be down at Cross Plains confabulating with Two-Gun Bob—of whose painful motor accident Dec. 29ᵗʰ I guess I've spoken before. Then a dip into old Mexico, & then—I believe—a pilgrimage to the Tsathogguan shrine before settling (as much as a wandering Wahabi can ever settle!) in San Francisco . . . . which I think is his native town. Better take him out on Crater Ridge toward the pillars of the Singing Flame, where the fragments of pre-human eidola will help to de-Osagise his driving habits!

Damn Wright for his Xeethra reception—& let me hope he'll be more sensible concerning "The Last Hieroglyph". . . . . whose plot sounds magnificent. You already know what I think of "The Clouds"—& of that ass's verdict. Possibly he'll change his mind! The spell of that shadowy masterpiece clings about me yet. It must be printed some day—somehow! Old Bill Lumley was vastly taken with it.

I guess we about agree on Young Melmoth's "Colossus". "Black Thirst" had a lot of the conventional stuff, but the atmosphere of utterly unknown evil & menace is extremely distinctive. By the way—the story by Eando Binder in the new F F isn't at all bad despite its occasional dragging & its obvious derivativeness from Arnold's old "Night Wire".[8] There's a real sense of brooding terror, & some quite effective verisimilitude.

I envy you the 77° weather, no trace of which Providence has had as yet. I've tried to write outdoors—on Prospect Terrace—two or three times, but falling mercury has soon driven me in. Believe me, I shall welcome the sight of palmettos & live-oaks . . . . . indeed, I wish I were going straight south instead of stopping in N Y. But I'll be glad to see the gang, anyhow, whatever the thermometer may read! ¶ Cards will apprise you of the course of my wanderings, & indicate how soon De Land will form temporary address. God, but I wish I could get down to Havana!

Yrs. for the Purple Rune of Ulthar—
E'ch-Pi-El

P.S. At last young Melmoth has sent those photographs of his brother's fantastic drawings. Very effective—& I've an excellent idea of the originals, though of course the real drawings have certain qualities which the camera cannot catch. I'm now lending the prints to various members of the gang.

[P.P.S. on envelope] Just got a joint postal from Sultan Malik & 2-Gun Bob. They appear to be painting Cross Plains red! Malik will next head toward El Paso—& Mexico. He'll doubtless keep you posted on his motions—& on his coming advent to Averoigne.

[P.P.]P.S. Just discovered that I *didn't* send you the Lemurian cutting I thought I did. But you have the essentials.

Notes

1. Meaning Dauber & Pine (D & P), where Loveman worked.
2. See Cummings's letter in praise of HPL in *WT*, June 1926; rpt. in Joshi, *Weird Writer* 66.
3. Francesco Pironti, author of *Il deciframento della lingua etrusca* (1933).
4. Alfredo Trombetti (1866–1929), an Italian linguist active in the early 20th century. His

La lingua etrusca was published in 1928.

5. All references to HPL's "Polaris."

6. *Shapes in the Fire* contains "Xélucha" and "Vaila," an early version of "The House of Sounds" (the latter included in *The Pale Ape and Other Pulses*).

7. Guy L. Huey. HPL parodies him in "The Battle That Ended the Century" as "Mr. Goofy Hooey."

8. Eando Binder (pseudonym of Earl and Otto Binder), "The Ancient Voice," *FF* 1, No. 8 (April 1934): 117–23. HPL refers to H. F. Arnold, "The Night Wire" (*WT*, September 1926).

[272]   [ANS; Grill 506][1]

[Postmarked Charleston, S.C.,
25 April 1934]

Hail, Chosen of Tsathoggua! Had a pleasant week in N Y with Sonny Belknap, Young Melmoth, Es-El, & the others. Left there Sunday midnight & spent Monday morning in Washington—exploring the ancient Georgetown section. Richmond in the p.m. & Raleigh, N.C. in the evening. Hit Charleston Tuesday at dawn. Stopping at the Y & doing the venerable town as usual. No other place quite equals it, I think—not even Quebec. Nothing changed since my last visit—'31. Full summer here—rich green vegetation, hot days, straw hats, & all. In Wash'n & Richm. it is merely springlike—with delicate young foliage. And in N Y winter still persists—chill winds & bare boughs. There is a real kick in passing from winter to summer in a few hours. Am feeling great—with twice the energy I had up north. On to Savannah May 1—& in De Land to meet Ar-Ech-Bei May 2, unless plans change. Had a joint card from Two-Gun Bob & Sultan Malik in Cross Plains, & later one from Malik in Juarez, Mexico. He ought to be getting out your way before long. Trust all flourishes in Averoigne. This heat is magnificent—I'm sitting in the Battery, sans hat, coat, & vest . . . picking up tan & looking out across the sunswept harbour to the low line of historic Fort Sumter. Surely hate to move on. Charleston is the place for me! Yrs under the nighted Seal of Kthun—
E'ch-Pi-El

Notes

1. *Front:* [The Old Exchange, Charleston, S.C.]

[273]   [ANS]

[Postmarked Charleston, S.C.,
27 April 1934]

[Souvenir Folder of Magnolia Gardens and Middleton Gardens, S.C.]
    E'ch-Pi-El

[274]   [ANS; Grill 505][1]

[Postmarked Charleston, S.C.,
30 April 1934]

Yr. card of [. . .] [found me in] Charleston. [Trust that the books came] back safely. [. . .] By this time Edkins [will be starting on his journey.] He sends from Montreal [a note from the ocean] liner Duchess of Atholl—[. . .]. Trust young Ar-Ech-Bei is [keeping "Xeethra"] for my perusal. ¶ So you don't [like "Bells] of Oceana"? Of course, it has its er[rors,] but the pervasive *tension* [betwixt] [. . .] natural menace give me a big kic[k. I] am told that Burks founded this on an [actual] incident—that at one time, when em[ployed on] the ships in the navy transport, he act[ually] had the impression of hearing tiny bells [out] at sea ¶ I understand that Crawford's [new] magazine is out at last—called [*Marvel*] *Tales*. Hope he'll be able to keep it up. ¶ The other day I sent you a folder of a famous Charleston garden which [might] appeal to your [sense] of _____[. In] Charleston I always go to [this place & have been there on three afternoons.] [. . .]
Ech-Pi-El

Notes

1. *Front:* Unidentified.

[275]   [ANS, JHL][1]

[Postmarked Auburn, Cal.,
4 May 1934]

Dear Ech-Pi-El: Recd. card and gorgeous folder from Charleston. Hope this will reach you in care of Ar-Ech-Bei. Am expecting to hear the trumpets of the Peacock Sultan at any time. We'll do what we can toward the encarnalising of Auburn and its environs. Regards from Averonia to yourself and Ar-Ech-Bei.

By the secret name of Yog-Sothoth,
Klarkash-Ton

Notes

1. *Front:* Blind Digger Indian age 108 Copr. Oct 3, 1912 Banbrock Photo, Auburn Cal.

[276]   [ANS; RAS 2.77][1]

[Postmarked De Land, Fla.,
1 May 1934]

"86° here yesterday, grandpa is in his element" [nine lines typed, signed] Ar-Ech-Bei "Explored Savannah 8½ hrs on my trip down, grand place." [Eleven handwritten lines, signed] Ech-Pi-El

Notes

1. *Front:* A Beautiful Southern Sunset Scene

[277]   [ALS, appended to letter to CAS by RHB, Bancroft Library]
[10 May 1934/RAS]

Hail, Great Vergama! I'll add a line to the epistle of my young host, with his permission. Having a great time down here, and feeling 20 years younger! You ought to see the bas-relief plaque of Cthulhu that Barlow has just made—a marvellous thing, which precisely embodies my conception of Wilcox's dream-plaque in the story. He is also doing a splendid clay statuette of the elephant-god Ganesa (prototype of Sonny Belknap's Chaugnar) for good old Bill Lumley. It ought to send the old boy into ecstasies. I never realised what a sculptor Ar-E'ch-Bei is till I saw him at work on these specimens ¶ Edition of the Shunned House recently came from Cook,—you'll see a bound copy in the course of time. ¶ Had some trips to interesting antiquities— old Spanish sugar mill antedating 1763, old Franciscan mission (picturesque arched ruins) of 1696, site of old Turnbull plantation of 1768, &c. ¶ Have had some interesting rows on the lake—which we have named The Moon Pool. ¶ Ar-E'ch-Bei is enclosing his latest picture, which you can keep. Later we'll send you snaps—including one with a great coach-whip snake. This is Yig's favourite stamping-ground, & R H B has shot many of his children to use in binding books. Some of the local ophidians have magnificent skins. ¶ Duly recd. your card. Thanks! That old Indian surpasses even me for venerable years!

Well—now to get this in the mail! Yrs in Iog-Sôtot's name—
E'ch-Pi-El

[P.S.] Iä! Shub-Niggurath! The Goat With a Thousand Young! Just got card from you & Sultan Malik at P.O.! Diabolic greetings to you both! Would that we might be present to swell the chorus of Eblis' praise!——E'ch-Pi-El

Just to be sociable I shall add a line of greeting.
RB

[P.P.S.] Your new story is magnificent.[1] Take Ar-E'ch-Bei's advice, & don't cut anything out. ¶ Xeethra hasn't come yet. ¶ Have seen *Marvel Tales* at last. Not so bad for an amateur venture.

Notes

1. Probably "The Last Hieroglyph."

[278]   [TNS, JHL][1]

May 19th, 1934.

Dear Éch-Pi-El:—

Thanks for cards and clipping. Will write letter shortly. Florida must be your element, and I wish that I too could emigrate there for awhile! Price went back to Oakland, after several sessions under the mystic oak, and initiations into the technique of gold mining. Hope he will be up this way again presently. Our bousing was more of the Sufi order than you may have inferred from our joint card. ✱ Glad that Vergama was up to sample—I have now extended the tale, as I told Ar-Ech-Bei. Am meditating a gruesome yarn on modern necrophagy—either as inherited blood-taint or successive demoniac possession. Yrs for the Sabbat of St. John's eve.[2]

Klarkash-Ton

Notes

1. *Front:* Blank.
2. Saint John's Eve, 23 June, is the eve of the feast day of Saint John the Baptist.

[279]   [ALS, JHL]

Jungle of Kled—Hour that
the Monolith turns on its
Carven onyx Pedestal.
[c. late May/early June 1934][1]

Dear Klarkash-Ton:—

Your welcome pair of epistles arrived just as I had finished my half of a joint postcard—which I enclose as it stands. As you see, I continue to linger in the shadow of Krang's tropic temple—beguiled by the unparalleled hospitality of the young High-Priest. I must be moving along soon, though.[2] Hopes of Havana are well-nigh extinct, but I shall get a week in ancient St. Augustine if it kills or breaks me! Incidentally—here are some snaps of the Barlovian scene which may interest you, & which you can add to your files if you like. They will shew up better if you magnify them as strongly as possible. In one of them you will see Grandpa (eyes closed inadvertently from sun-glare) holding a very nice distant cousin of Simaetha & Genl. Tabasco; & if you will study the background closely with a glass, you'll see good old Doodle-bug gravely trotting into view. Another batch of views has gone forward to the Hyperborean High-Priestess E'ch-Vi-Es, with a request that they be brought before your eyes. Today the household is lamenting the vanishment of Jack, the largest of the younger Kappa Alpha Tau members, who has not been seen since yesterday morning, when he displayed signs of indisposition. I surely hope he'll turn up safely somehow! My particular friend, though, is the dark tiger "High"—who is on hand & in his customary lively health.

The bas-relief of Cthulhu continues to fascinate me. What an artist little Ar-E'ch-Bei would be if he only had the full use of his eyes! Ganesa—or Chaugnar—has now received a coat of impressive green paint, & looks as though he had been excavated from amidst the ruins of a primal Hindoo temple. I really hate to let him go—though I haven't the heart to deprive good old Lumley of a thing he wants so ardently. I hope to get photographs of both clay masterpieces at a 4-for-a-dime gallery in De Land . . . & incidentally, when I'm there I think I'll let 'em snap Grandpa's faded phiz, so that you can get an idea of how the Old Gentleman looks in his last days. Another thing—Ar-E'ch-Bei & I will probably be able to get phonograph records made soon, thus giving you an inkling of how we sound. My voice is a devilish rasp—the most unpleasant I have ever heard.

I've read *Marvel Tales* at last, though without finding anything of startling merit in it. The next issue—with something of yours, & Sonny's splendid "Dark Beasts"—will undoubtedly be better.[3] I hope the enterprise will manage to survive somehow, even if the typography & format remain crude. In particular, I hope that Crawford can issue the 9th Chapter of Eibon, as suggested. A cheaply printed & reasonably small edition ought to prove considerably less of a white elephant than The Double Shadow. As for price—the D. S. did give a tremendous lot for astonishingly little!

Extra! Later! Rejoicing in the Kappa Alpha Tau! *Jack has returned!* He shewed up at night, but with a curious weakness & lack of muscular coördination. He *staggers* oddly. It is possible that a snake bit him (damn Yig & all his spawn!), but I think the poison will work out & allow him to recover. He eats very sparingly & languidly, but purrs appealingly. If he doesn't recover, I'll have Two-Gun Bob come over here & eat all the local snakes alive!

At last I've read the May W T—& find it distinctly above the average, though not quite up to the April standard. This has 3 good stories, which its predecessor had 4. "The Tomb-Spawn" is splendid—with a magnificent twist at the end. I recall your own mentioning the plot. "Scarlet Dream" is also the real stuff—full of the tension & mystery needed by a weird tale. And Two-Gun's "Queen of the Black Coast" is veritably a prose poem. Of the minor stuff, Jacobi's thing is probably the leader. I suppose the June issue ought to be out by this time—I must look for it in the village.

I shall peruse Xeethra with interest whenever it arrives. Don't, however, take all of Sultan Malik's suggestions too seriously. Remember that nowadays he is all saturated with pulp ideals inculcated by Otis Adelbert Kline, August Lenniger, & other art-despising business men. On the other hand, some of his suggestions might be ingenious & acceptable. Let me see Vergama again if it takes any radically different form. As for Wright's possible acceptance of this tale—who can predict anything about that bird?

I'll wager you had a splendid visit with the Peacock Sultan—his bulletins indicate that the event was a high spot for him. He is certainly lucky to have

met both of the distant demigods of the circle—you & Two-Gun Conan!!
The picturesque old mines of Averoigne—especially the polychromatic mineral
spring one owned by your uncle—fascinated Malik immensely; & he is resolved
to incorporate them into a tale. They certainly sound fascinating in the extreme—& the idea of a buried river channel is tremendously picturesque. Wish
you could get hold of one of these & make a rich strike some day!

Your more recent expedition with the House of Soo-Lhi also sounds extremely impressive. That road through haunted ravines, past waterfalls, & between Cyclopean ramparts must be a veritable highway to realms of phantasy;
& the view from your maximum elevation would seem to tax one's powers of
description to the utmost. I wish you could capture some of this beauty &
grandeur pictorially—the postcards which I've seen from time to time doubtless do not more than suggest the whole complex actuality. What you say of the
flowers suggests a region about as gorgeous as that shewn in "Beyond Cathay."

Incidentally—as I noted on the card—young Ar-E'ch-Bei is utterly
transported by the beauty & strangeness of his new pictorial acquisition. He
means to ask for more in the future, as his exchequer permits—his taste running to non-terrestrial landscapes with divergences from earthly scenery &
vegetation especially well-marked. I seem to recall certain items in your loan
of 1926 which ought to fill the bill if you still have them. Weren't there some
Martian or Saturnian views with strange hills in the background?

Thanks prodigiously for the hellish heads. Ngrrrhrr!!! My collection of
Clericashtoniana gradually grows. It is now going the rounds of new correspondents & is due down here (from Baldwin & Rimel) before long. Ar-E'ch-
Bei hasn't seen the newer items, including that daemoniac head which impressed Brobst so much .... the eldritch black thing that stares & stares &
stares . . . . . .

Thanks also for the sheet from friend Merritt's American Weekly. These
hints of primal civilisations in lower Africa .... Zimbabwe . . . Ophir . . . The
Fishers from Outside .... are monstrously fascinating, & arouse all sorts of
picturesque speculations regarding lost worlds. Perhaps the negro is a newcomer in a region once splendid with the bizarre cities & temples of white
races whose name, date, aspect, & deeds are alike forgotten.

I continue to flourish in my present subtropical milieu, & dread to get
back to the devitalising chill of the north. Well—the return will be by gradual
stages anyhow. I shall pause in Richmond & Washington—seeing young
Morse in the later place. In N Y I shall confabulate as usual with Sonny Belknap, & if not broke may go up the river to see Dwyer.

Yrs for the Onyx Arcana of Kny'an—E'ch-Pi-El.

P.S. Little Ar-E'ch-Bei is simply throwing fits over "The Colossus of
Ylourgne". I'm certainly glad to see it in print at last. Those nameless *Things*
in the drawing are stupendous!

[P.P.S. on envelope] Ar-E'ch-Bei wishes you would tell him as much as possible about HZUILQUOIQMNZHAH, [*sic*]⁴ the paternal uncle of Tsathoggua—cf. "Door to Saturn."

Notes

1. An envelope that may have been used to mail this letter is postmarked 9 June 1934. The letter itself was, however, almost certainly written days if not weeks earlier, as internal evidence and missives to other correspondents indicate.
2. HPL stayed with RHB from 2 May until 21 June.
3. *Marvel Tales* published nothing by CAS.
4. In a letter to RHB (16 June 1934; TLS, JHL), CAS spells the name Hzioulquoigmnzha and Hzioulquoigmnzhah.

[280]   [ANS, enclosure to previous letter?]¹

> [No postmark; enclosed with a letter
> c. late May or early June 1934]

All hail! Ar-E'ch-Bei duly recd. "Beyond Cathay," & is in ecstasies over it. I don't blame him—someday I'll take a plunge in the same direction. I well recall this marvellous creation from the batch of 1926. ¶ Glad you & Malik had such congenial sessions. He spoke of his interest in that mine which once belonged to your uncle. The speed which he has lately achieved in old Juggernaut makes one dizzy to contemplate! ¶ Shall be eager to see the extension of the Vergama tale. Also the tale of modern necrophagy. Hope this latter can get past the censorious eye of Satrap Pharnabazus. ¶ Still having a great time here. Ar-E'ch-Bei is making a check list of all your published tales. Can you give any data on the early Black Cat ones? ¶ Yours for the Infra-Red Rune of Dagoth, E'ch-Pi-El

Notes

1. *Front:* [A coconut tree in Florida.]

[281]   [ANS]¹

> [Postmarked Auburn, Cal.,
> 15 June 1934]

Dear Éch-Pi-El: Letters and enclosures rec'd and will answer shortly. Thanks for snapshots—these show you very well under a *large* reading-glass. Am anticipating the records—also *The Shunned House*. Not much news here—the weather has gone screwy with fog, cloudiness, thunderstorms, and what not. Wright plans to use one of my drawings of Tsathoggua with *The Seven Geases*. Yrs,
                    Klarkash-Ton

Notes

1. *Front:* Unidentified.

[282]   [TLS, JHL]

> Salt-pale desert of Dhir,
> at the hour of the
> multisonous beating of
> invisible drums.
> [c. 16 June 1934]

Dear Éch-Pi-El:

I hope that this will find you still domiciled at the Barlovian manor. Your prolonged visit there is certainly enviable from all angles. The pictures of yourself that you sent, under a strong reading-glass, appear to prove the salubriousness of the Florida climate. Incidentally, I am glad to note that Ulthar is well represented, and have studied with interest the picture showing the kitten and Doodlebug.

I wish I could see that famous bas-relief of Cthulhu! I have done what I could toward elucidating the genealogy of Tsathoggua, and am sending Ar-Éch-Bei the result of my delvings into the Parchments of Pnom, the chief Hyperborean authority on such matters. Pnom has much more to say about Tsathoggua than about Cthulhu, Yog-Sothoth and Azathoth; but no doubt you have access to other records, mainly concerning these entities; and I'd be glad of more specific information about them. As I am pointing out to Ar-E'ch-Bei, Pnom's account of Ts. can be reconciled with the legendry told to Zamarcona [*sic*] in The Mound. The myth, through aeons, was varied in the usual mythopoeic fashion by the cavern-dwellers, who came at last to believe that merely the images of Tsathoggua, and *not* the god himself, had emerged in former cycles from the inner gulf. Ts., travelling fourthdimensionally from Saturn, *first entered the Earth* through the lightless abyss of N'kai; and, not unnaturally, the Yothians regarded N'kai as his place of origin. Undoubtedly the god *now* resides in N'kai, to which he returned when the ice overwhelmed Hyperborea.[1]

I was glad to know that Beyond Cathay proved satisfactory to Ar-Éch-Bei, and am now loaning him a large consignment of my more exotic pictures. Glad to hear also that "The Colossus" was up to sample. My drawing for it was pretty lousy, apart from the demons. Wright, by the way, is planning to use a pen-drawing of Tsathoggua (which I gave him some time ago) as an illustration for The Seven Geases. I may or may not have told you that he accepted my new version of The Last Hieroglyph. No, I am not taking Malik's suggestions too literally. But in this case, I really saw a chance to improve the story. I couldn't adopt his suggestions about Xeethra; and my revision of this tale (which I'll send you if Wright still rejects it) is merely a slight abridgement of the first version.

By all means don't forget me, if you have photographs taken of the two clay deities! I can imagine Lumley's rapture when he receives the Ganesha–Chaugnar. I look forward also to those phonograph records.

Glad to hear that the missing Jack had returned. I certainly hope that his weakness and lack of coordination were not due to snake-bite. If they were, the local reptilia are certainly due for a cleaning-out. So far, I have not encountered any rattlers this summer, but have already killed three of the deadly Black Widow spiders, which seem to have established themselves quite numerously in this neighbourhood. The females (who carry the venom) are small, shiny, and marked on the thorax with orange red.

Yes, Auburn is quite in the center of the old mining district. I am glad that you and Ar-Ech-Bei found the pamphlet of interest. Thanks exceedingly for the postcards and alluring folder!

I'd write at greater length, but want to mail this as soon as possible. Will enclose a few clippings from Ulthar which I have saved for you.

Yrs;, [*sic*] under the civic seal of Yoth,

Klarkash-Ton

Notes

1. The "genealogy" CAS sent RHB was published as "The Family Tree of the Gods" in the Summer 1944 issue of the *Acolyte;* rpt. in *PD*. It was meant to reconcile certain statements HPL made about Tsathoggua in "The Mound."

[283]   [ALS]

Tower of the Gibbelins[1]
—Hour of the Shrieking
[25 June 1934/RAS]

Dear Klarkash-Ton:

As my card of recent date has apprised you, the 7-week Barlovian sojourn is over at last. I never saw people as super-hospitable as the Barlovii, & I can only hope I did not impose upon them! I am now, as of yore, wallowing in the midst of my beloved antiquity—sitting on the terraplain of ancient Fort San Marcos, against whose solid coquina walls the cannonades of a dozen foes have thundered in vain. It gives me an enormous kick to be back amidst the visible symbols of the past. Each day I wander through lanes & past structures that were there when Elizabeth was queen, & in everything am treated to a pageant of the ages. There is no other place just like St. Augustine—as I suppose I said with equal emphasis in 1931. The old wood-&-coquina houses, the small balconies, the ancient circular walls, & the magical walled gardens, all recall a bygone colonial Spain which the rest of the world has well-nigh forgotten. I've explored many houses & gardens which were not formerly open to the public, & have taken renewed pleasure in those I knew before. Among other things, I have seen the skeletons (still lying in place) recently exhumed on the site of the bygone Indian village of Seloy just north of the town. They are of Christianised natives, & probably date from the later 1500's. I really believe I'm enjoying venerable San Agustin even more than I did the first time, & bitterly regret that shortage of cash cuts me down to a single week. As it is, I'm steering a perilous enough course—my food quota being cut down to 20¢ per day. [dinner—1 can beans or spaghetti 0.10; ½ pkg. ginger wafers 2½¢. Total 12½¢. Supper, ½ pkg ginger wafers 2½¢; 1 cup ice cream 0.05. Total 7½¢. Grand diurnal total, 20¢ . . . Total per wk, $1.40] But even with this economy I can't outstay the week, as it would interfere with later stops. The Dwyer visit is probably doomed as it is.

Glad you found the De Land views of interest. Enclosed is a photograph of Ar-Ech-Bei's Cthulhu bas-relief—which I'll ask you to return at your leisure. It shews the effect of the thing pretty well. I shipped the original to myself in a cigar-box stuffed with Spanish moss, & hope to Tsathoggua it arrived in decent shape. I'll send you a photograph of the Chaugnar statuette as soon as I get an envelope big enough to mail it in—it's a 4 × 5. The original reached old Bill Lumley in safety, & he appears to be quite childishly delighted with it. He's just sent Ar-Ech-Bei a book as a mark of his appreciation. Chaugnar was painted green, but Cthulhu was left the colour of the original clay.

Thanks tremendously for the feline cuttings! I can see that the Atlantic coast has no monopoly on notable kinsfolk of the jungle's lords . . . . as indeed was made apparent before through descriptions of the felidae of Woods' Dry Diggings.[2] Lord Catspaw & the Messrs Johnson are all obviously gentlemen of quality, & I trust the matter of social procedure amongst them may soon be settled with honour & satisfaction to all. Slushfoot's snow-white progeny are certainly remarkable indeed—& would appear to have a link of common ancestry with Doodlebug. By the way—Barlow manor expects an increase in its furry population through the agency of the little tigress "Low", & the probabilities are that at least one or two of the newcomers will possess something of old Doodlebug's snowiness. Jack, I am pleased to say (he will be "Uncle Jack" when the new generation arrives!), is now as well as ever, though he still carries his head slightly on one side as a reminder of his painful experience. I guess I told you how he mewingly led the family down to a clump of palmettoes near the lake, where reposed a dead snake with chewed-up head. Undoubtedly he tried to eat something that wasn't good for him! One more rattler was killed (by Charles Johnston)[3] before I left De Land, & his hide is now in the final stages of drying. Glad the brood of Yig haven't been numerous around Woods' Dry Diggings of late—& hope the spiders won't wax & overwhelm you as in Munn's old story. Two-Gun Bob reports a sort of plague of small scorpions at Cross Plains—& incidentally, he has sent me a huge spider in alcohol which I'll see when I get home. ¶ Did I tell you that Henry, the last of the Barlow infant opossums, departed this life on June 10th? It was a severe disappointment for he seemed quite strong & likely to survive. ¶ Those infant bobcats are fascinating, & I'll wager their owner will hate to turn them over to the zoo. I'd try to keep them—didn't the Romans have pet leopards?

Ar-E'ch-Bei, with his mania for systematisation, will be infinitely grateful to you for your transcripts from the Parchments of Pnom. I am mostly interested to know that Pnom's account can be reconciled with the rambling lore gathered in subterrene K'nyan by Panfilo de Zamacona, & am especially impressed by the knowledge of Tsathoggua's present whereabouts. Suppose an expedition were to be sent to unearth It? What would ensue?

Ar-E'ch-Bei will also be ecstatically thankful for the loan of the pictures—which he will try to photograph, & some of which he will probably try to buy. He really deserves to see a good assortment of your best things, as the gang did in 1926. He has just now photographed some of my own smaller Clericastoniana, which I have lent him. We are both eager to see the picture of Tsathoggua which Satrap Pharnabozus has accepted for the 7 Geases. Congratulations on the Last Hieroglyph! If Farny doesn't take Xeethra, I must see

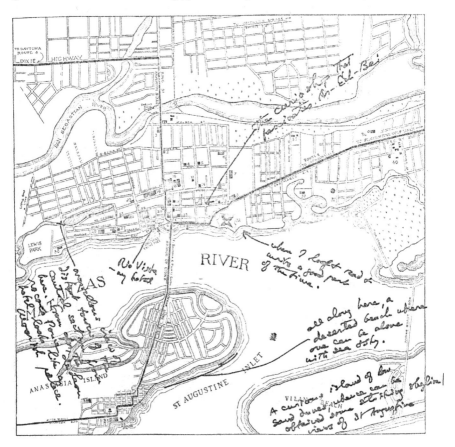

it in MS. Glad you're not letting the Peacock Sultan make a hack of you!

Well—only 3 more days in ancient San Agustin! I hate like hell to move on, but financial arguments admit of no comeback. I'll stop off a day in ancient Charleston if it kills me! Next stop will be Richmond, but I'll have to abort Williamsburg. Then a few hours in Fredericksburg—& goodbye to the Old South. Washington next, where I may pause a night or two. Then a day—or part of a day—in old Philadelphia. Then a few days at Sonny's in decadent Manhattan—& then home at last. My aunt will hardly know me—I actually am greyer than when I started, for every hair cut seems to clip off brown & leave white! Yrs for the Rite of the Elders—

E'ch Pi-El

P.S. I enclose a view of myself which Ar-E'ch-Bei took with his new 5 × 7 camera. It really is rather good—giving you a pretty good idea of what the old man looks like today. Too bad the phonograph project fell through.

Notes

1. Alluding to "The Hoard of the Gibbelins" (in *The Book of Wonder*) by Lord Dunsany.

2. The original name of Auburn before the town was renamed in the 1849 gold rush.

3. The Barlows' hired hand. A few postcards from HPL to him survive (see *O Fortunate Floridian* 417–18).

[284]   [ANS][1]

[Postmarked Auburn, Cal.,
23 July 1934]

Dear Éch-Pi-El: I've been intending to write for weeks and will answer yr letter soon. Recently enjoyed a 2nd visit from the Peacock Sultan. Little news otherwise, except that Wright has taken *Xeethra* and Gernsback has remitted 50 pazoors on account! Will send on shortly some books by W. Hope Hodgson, which H. Koenig loaned me and said to forward to you. Under the Black Seal, Klarkash-Ton

Notes

1. *Front:* Unidentified.

[285]   [ANS; Grill 507][1]

[Postmarked Providence, R.I.,
28 July 1934]

Congratulation on the remittance from Hugo the Rat! [. . .] Two-Gun Bob visited the Carlsbad Caverns last month and gives a tremendously powerful

description of them [rivaling that in one of the booklets?]. Little Bloch has placed a story in W.T. at last—The Secret in the Tomb." [. . .]
E'ch-Pi-El

Notes

1. *Front:* Unidentified.

[286]   [ANS, RAS 7.20]

[Postmarked Nantucket, Mass.,
29 August 1934]

[["Souvenir Folder of Nantucket, Mass." containing nine postcards: [1] [Map of] Nantucket Mass.; [2] Sankaty Head Lighthouse, Nantucket, Mass.; [3] White Elephant, Nantucket, Mass.; [4] [Old Mill, Nantucket Island, Mass.; [5] Ash Lane, Nantucket Island, Mass.; [6] Stone Alley, Showing South Tower [Unitarian Church] and Town Clock / Nantucket Mass.]; [7] Quince Street, Nantucket, Mass.; [8] The [Jethro] Coffin House, Oldest on the Island, built 1686, Nantucket, Mass.; [9] Main Street Business Section, Nantucket, Mass.; [envelope verso] Harbor View, Nantucket, Mass. Other images show Atheneum Public Library; Bathing Scene and Jetty; Waterfront; The Old Ivy Cottage on Liberty Street; Dover Street; Ocean House; Cliff Beach Bath House; Steamer Martha's Vineyard; Stone Alley; The Lone South Shore, The Chopping Bowl Tea Garden; Martin's Lane; Brant Point Light; Sunset in the Harbor; Monument Square; St. Mary's Church (Catholic).]]
Yours for the Ebon Tide
—E'ch-Pi-El

[287]   [ALS]

Cave of Zhod—Hour of the
Tapping beyond the Inner Wall
[8 September 1934/RAS]

Dear Klarkash-Ton:—

All Hail! And how fare the sorcerers & daemons of Averoigne? Am enclosing a bulletin from Searight about Hugo the Rat's recent doings which he wants me to relay to you. Possibly all this is an old story—but there's no harm in shooting it along anyhow. Other things in Searight's letter may be of interest—especially the tragic fate of his old-time collaborator Hammerstrom.

As I said, I duly received the Hodgson books—& when I came to read them I was veritably knocked cold! Ædopol, what splendid stuff! Suggestions of unknown presences & conditions . . . . sieges by hellish things from the abyss . . . . . & the magnificently expansive cosmic vistas in "The House on the Borderland"! This bird knows how to evoke atmosphere of the most authentic sort—just what to say & what not to say. It is hard to realise that he is the same chap who wrote the essentially mediocre "Carnacki, the Ghost-Finder." I've made a note on Hodgson for my article, & have sent it to Hornig for publication at the proper time.[1] This stuff certainly requires major mention in my history of weird literature. Curious I didn't ever strike Hodgson before—but it's a pleasure to discover totally new things late in life. If Koenig speaks truly in the new F F, we have another discovery—Charles Williams—coming to us.[2] I'll be interested to learn whether you share my enthusiasm for Hodgson. Amusingly enough, it wasn't till day before yesterday—as I was resurrecting the carton to send the books on to Comte d'Erlette—that I stumbled on the small paper-bound "Stories After Dark" by Barry Pain. I don't recall any mention of this—but I assume that it's Koenig's rather than yours. Anyhow, I'd send it on to M. le Comte. I had read one or two of these sketches in reprint form, but the real high spot—"The Undying Thing"—was new to me. Gad, what a yarn! It suggests all sorts of things, & the absence of any concrete description of It is a genuine asset. I ought to mention this in my article, though I haven't so far done so.[3]

Well—I presume you've received messages relating to my wanderings. Morton & I had a good time early last month—visiting all sorts of suburban places including ancient Newport. Then toward the end of the month I embarked on my final outing of 1934. I began by visiting one of the old amateur crowd—Edward H. Cole—near Boston; & incidentally seeing W. Paul Cook, who came down from Vermont. We did various ancient places—Salem, Marblehead, Haverhill, &c.—but Cook had a sort of nervous collapse & had to return prematurely to Vermont. The second half of my outing, though, was the real climax—since this was nothing more or less than a trip to ancient *Nantucket,* which I had never seen before, though it lies only 90 miles (6 hrs. by coach & boat) from my own doorstep.

The folder I sent has probably given you some idea of the place. And *what* a place! Nowhere else—Charleston, Quebec, Salem, or Newport—has the past survived so *perfectly.* The old town is *exactly* as it was a century ago—cobblestoned streets with colonial houses, windmill, hitching-posts, horse-blocks, & silver doorplates, picturesque lanes & wharves—everything pertaining to the bygone days of whaling prosperity. The island was settled in 1660, & formed part of New York till 1692, since when it has belonged to Massachusetts. Whaling made it great, & the decline of that industry caused its decline. Summer vacationists have preserved & restored it. I explored all the old streets, museums, windmill, &c. minutely, & saw Saturn & his ring [*sic*] through the glass of the Maria Mitchell observatory. A bus trip around the island took me to the quaint former fishing village of Siasconset. In covering the suburbs of the town I used a hired *bicycle*—the first time I'd ridden a wheel in 20 years. It quite rejuvenated me! I had a 3d floor room during my week's stay—with a fine view of town, harbour, & sea.

I may have a visit from one or more Wandreis this month. Donald & his mother are now driving East, & after some sightseeing expect to take Howard home to St. Paul. Their Eastern itinerary may include Providence. ¶ Barlow is now in Washington—as he's doubtless told you. ¶ I'm now in solitary state—my aunt being in Maine for a fortnight. ¶ You ought to see little black Sam Perkins, my new feline visitor, who's just initiated into the K.A.T.! ¶ Rumours of new weird magazines multiply, but I don't take much stock in them. ¶ Yrs for the Black Goat

—E'ch Pi-El

P.S. Ar-Ech-Bei says he's sent you a carbon of his typescript of my Fungi. There are several errors—hence I'm enclosing an errata list which I hope you'll use in making corrections on the MS. I'm sending the unpublished Fungi to Hornig to see if he wants them.

Notes

1. The *FF* serialization of "Supernatural Horror in Literature" did not reach Ch. 9, where the insert about Hodgson would have gone. It first appeared separately as "The Weird Work of William Hope Hodgson" and was later incorporated into the final version of the essay.

2. H. C. Koenig, "The Intellectual Shocker," *FF* 2, No. 1 (September 1934): 10, 15.

3. He did not do so.

[288]   [ALS, JHL]

Gateway of the Zhirns—
Hour of the Chanting Within
[Postmarked 30 September 1934]

Dear Klarkash-Ton:—

I welcomed all the recent bulletins, & am grateful for the piquant enclosures therein. The account of El Medinine recalls the Prorok volume, while the Honduran discoveries open up all sorts of imaginative vistas. Returned material—Thevenin &c—all safely re-filed.

Nantucket certainly was a revelation. I am still thinking about it, & surely hope I can get there again next summer. It is hard to realise that so perfect a fragment of the elder world can exist so close to the prosaic scenes one knows—though for that matter, Providence's ancient hill still retains a vast amount of the colour & quietude of yesterday. Nantucket—or any unspoiled & traditional part of New England—would surely welcome you as a valued acquisition if you were ever to settle here; & I hope you'll be able to do it some time. Anyhow, I trust you can get around here on a not-too-hurried visit before long. At the same time I don't think that California is, as a whole, so relatively on the toboggan as you may imagine from surface indications. In the first place, all the world is in more or less chaos today. Secondly, it seems to me (judging purely by reports, at a vast distance) that most of the freakish phenomena are largely concentrated in *southern* California—a region which, in view of the size of your state, has no more to do with your habitat than the backwardness of Tennessee has to do with Rhode Island. I never think of the Los Angeles region as really *California*—the name signifying to me the historic north-central part of the state with its traditions of 1849 & gold & redwoods & the Sierras & Ambrose Bierce & Bret Harte & San Francisco & Golden Gate shipping & everything of that sort. This, it would seem to me, forms a sort of separate world poles apart from the tawdry huddle of real-estate booms & Rosicrucian temples & cinema centres & crazy evangelists & proletarian prophets whose tom-toms resound faintly & distantly, leagues toward the south. Nor do I think that anybody need worry about Upton Sinclair & his probable rise to power. I used to be a hide-bound reactionary before surrounding events forced me to think—actually *think*—of the political-industrial-economic order & its inevitable trend; but nowadays I realise that the wholesale application of machinery to industry has totally destroyed the old relationships between individuals & the total amount of work to be done—so that laissez-faire capitalism has actually come to the end of its rope. There is absolutely no way in which, under the old order, more than a small fraction of the idle population can ever (even amidst the greatest commercial prosperity) be employed again—since with labour-saving machinery all the possible work of the world (including supplying of *new* demands such as the blind reactionaries rave about) can be performed by a relatively few persons. As long as the old laissez-faire order lasts, it will never again be possible for any person to be sure of a chance to earn a livelihood, no matter how industrious and willing he may be. There will always be millions (literally not less than that) of capable men, willing & law-abiding, for whom no industrial places can be found, and whose sole alternatives under the present system will be charity or starvation. There is no getting around this. It isn't merely the alien radicals who recognise the state of things, but all the best & soberest American thinkers from John Dewey, Stuart Chase, Glenn Frank, Gifford Pinchot, Pres. Roosevelt, &c. down. It may be said almost dogmatically that *something must be done*. The old system—& even the old kind of business "prosperity" (for a select few while others starve)—leads absolutely nowhere except to a suffering bound to breed violent & disastrous revolution . . . . so that today the worst possible incendiaries are those greedy old-time Republicans who fight the New Deal with meaningless catchwords & seek to promote starvation in the interest of increased profits & more yachts for the shrewd & lucky. Only the blind grabbers & hangers-on of irresponsible private commerce are today sufficiently self-deluded to fancy that the old order will work any more. The real question is not *whether anything is to be done*—but *what is to be done*.

And here, of course, personal opinions differ. Sonny Belknap & other dupes of European ideas want a general upheaval & a new "ideology"—a whole new set of cultural values. This, to my mind, is wasteful & disastrous; since all the real values of life flow from *cultural continuity*. My belief is that the future ought to form a sane & gradual outgrowth of the past—with no *cultural* overturn at all, & with only such economic changes as will restore to the ordinary man the certainty of being able to exchange his services for the necessaries of life. I am, therefore, diametrically opposed to communism & everything else derived from the deceptive pseudo-science of Marx & Lenin. On the other hand, I realise that analysis has revealed our need for adopting many courses which, in our complacent ignorance of yesterday, we once ridiculed & opposed as *socialistic*. We know today that laissez-faire economics will not serve to feed all the population under a regime of mechanised industry; that work for every man no longer *naturally* exists, so that some system of artificial spreading (at the expense of private industry's profits) must be adopted to avert wholesale pauperdom & revolution. This means the strict governmental regulation of all large-scale industry & commerce; the fixing of working hours & wages; the introduction of old-age pensions & unemployment insurance—& other measures which make the old-time business pirate howl. We must have these things or blow up altogether; & it is simply frivolous & irrelevant to complain (as the dupes of the old order do) that this *purely economic* oversight forms a denial of "individual freedom" analogous to the effects of Nazism or bolshevism. Such complaints are merely the fruit of ignorance or of unpatriotic self-interest. Naturally, we do not know precisely what our unprecedented dilemma calls for. There must be infinite experimentation before we can adapt ourselves to the ultra-mechanised regime which has rushed on us unawares. It may be that private industry cannot stand the profit-reductions needed to float the nation as a whole—& in that case public ownership will have to come . . . . though of course this does not have to mean the inverted cultural values & silly exaltation of manual over cerebral work which the bolsheviks preach. If achieved through peaceful & gradual evolution it will involve no social overturn at all. Skilled brain work will continue to be rewarded more amply than brute stevedoring—& it will mean nothing to the general culture that the recipients of these rationally graded wages will be working for the nation instead of merely swelling the unnecessary private fortunes of a few lucky individuals. There is absolutely nothing in this probably necessary *socialism* (not *communism*) which need alarm the most socially & aesthetically conservative individual. Indeed, it argues a grotesque & un-aristocratic exaltation of mere money matters when anyone shrieks that a *purely economic* change means a change in our civilisation & traditions! The great problem is *how to start* the sort of evolution we need. It is easy to plan, but abysmally difficult to get any rational measure *actually in motion*. That is why we must go slowly & cautiously, lending our support to *anything headed in the right direction which has a real chance of adoption*, even if it does not suit us exactly as some other plan which has less chance of adoption. The public is slow & stupid, & would never consider a plan of real boldness & intelligence all at once. They must be led away from the present impossible order by slow degrees—becoming used to contraventions of laissez-faire capitalism one at a time. The New Deal, in spite of its present internal inconsistencies & frankly experimental phases, probably represents as great a step in the right direction as could *now* command any chance of support—hence it is the one & only course now deserving endorsement by intelligent friends of America's future. As the limitations of its measures appear, one by one, the public will probably be ready to remedy them through further departures from the old order; though such departures could never be 'put over' without the intermediate step as an emotional solvent. Therefore I may be counted as a friend of the present administration & a welcomer of any such rational socialism as may be needed to keep all the people employed & set the nation once more in a state of decent equilibrium.

Well—so far as I can see, Upton Sinclair is out for much the same thing. It is true that he has held some doubtful political ideas in the past—but are these ideas any more absurd, or even *as* absurd, as the suicidal opposite fallacies harboured by Mr. Hoover & the 'respectable' business world? Moreover, he has modified many of these ideas under the impact of existing realities. Nor was he *ever* a communist or disciple of extreme European radicalism. He always had his own sort of socialistic thought, stemming from our normal hereditary sources. One need not agree with all his details of belief, or ask too much of his temperament as a legislator, to concede that he probably forms an infinitely lesser evil in comparison with an Old Guard Grab-Our-Profit[1] candidate. A reactionary could work vast harm amidst the conditions of today—& of course Sinclair, if elected, will always be subject to enough legislative pressure to curb any extreme personal idiosyncrasies which he might otherwise display. Therefore, I believe I'd vote for Sinclair (diametrically as I disagree with his theories of aesthetics, & little as I think of his novels) if I were a Californian. I can't see anything Russian in this 100% Anglo-Saxon descendant of Virginia gentlemen—& I believe that he has moved toward middle-course reality from *his* direction as decidedly as I have moved toward it from *my* opposite direction. A decade ago I thought he ought to be chloroformed—today I probably hold largely the same general views that he holds. Such are the mutations & ironies of time & growth!

As for the Rhode Island riots—they were very brief & local, & might have been in Vienna so far as any general effect on the state is concerned. Most of the participants seem to have been restless French-Canadians—emotionally addled by strike activities which were none of their business, & additionally prodded by some of the professional outside communists who flock to scenes of industrial strife as flies flock to diseased meat. The governor—a cultivated aristocrat of the old Providence stock, & a devoted upholder of the New Deal—dealt with the situation in an admirably moderate & impartial way . . . . as is proved by the equal volleys of curses hurled at him by greedy mill-owners (he closed some mills for a day or two in the interest of public quiet) & rapacious labour agitators. His job is surely a delicate & unenviable one!

News from #66 is neither interesting nor cheerful. In the first place, I'm just pulling out of a hellish siege of indigestion which had me in bed—or dragging betwixt there & the kitchen & bathroom—a week, & good for nothing a week more. And in the second place the Kappa Alpha Tau & I are mourning the loss of our brightest & sprightliest scion—none other than little Sam Perkins himself! He was found lifeless in the ancient garden on September 10th, & now sleeps beneath the grasses amidst which he loved to play in life. And as late as Sept. 7 he was over here climbing around Grandpa's shoulders & chewing the papers on the desk! He had had a spell of illness early in August, & this must have been some obscure & aggravated recurrence. Blessed little Piece of the Night—Tsathoggua's youngest & tiniest son! In his momentary flash of existence—June to September—he never learned the horrors of winter or the seething vortex of modernity beyond the confines of his own garden oasis. And who shall say the gods found him less important than the longest-lived & worldliest philosopher? During his last weeks he became fully initiated into the Kappa Alpha Tau, so that his little black presence was often seen on the clubhouse roof beside the ampler bulk of black-&-white Pres. Randall & tiger Vice-Pres. Osterberg. But all things pass—& today Mrs. Spotty Perkins hunts mice & chases grasshoppers childless & alone! I am sure that mother Simaetha & Genl. Tabasco will share the grief of their eastern kin. Pray give them my regards—& let us hope that their effectiveness in guarding Indian Hill against the Things from Outside may never wane!

Glad to hear that the Spawn of Yig have been less abundant in Averoigne this year—though the nighted & sinister arachnidae can scarcely be called pleasant successors! Hope the ankle-bite proved wholly transient. Your king snake friend has relatives in De Land, as I may have mentioned. As natural foes of rattlers, they are tolerated & protected there. Speaking of De Land—at last reports Jack was quite well, & had become the uncle of a sprightly & attractive brindled brood—the first progeny of his sister Low.

Ar-E'ch-Bei will undoubtedly welcome the added & clarifying Tsathogguan data. I agree that the dark Entity must still lurk in lightless gulfs below, & that an expedition toward It would scarcely be judicious. Perhaps some records of such expeditions & their disagreeably sudden conclusions may eventually be discovered & brought before the public. Glad to hear that you are to illustrate two more tales—I look forward to both with keen expectancy. It will interest me to see what Ernst (a writer at times by no means bad) & Miss Moore will do in the illustrating line. Ar E'ch Bei shewed me the "Shambleau" sketch, which certainly displays vast cleverness even if it lacks the indefinable menace & cosmic remoteness that you or Howard Wandrei would put into it. As a writer, Miss Moore is certainly *the* discovery of the last few years. No other newcomer is even in the running. Yes—I like the recent F F, & believe that Hornig is probably learning from experience. He told me of his dedicatory plan—we ought to feel complimented at our grouping with Poe! I shall be glad to see "Aphrodite" & "The Clouds" in print. Koenig's article interested me vastly—& he has now sent me the first two Charles Williams books with instructions to pass on to you. As later recipients, Rimel & Dwyer wish to be on the list. I have not as yet had a chance to read the volumes, but will report on them when I do. Glad "The Plutonian Drug" has appeared, & that the immortal Effjay has deigned to look tolerantly upon it. Effjay's kind condescension in the matter of my "From Beyond" has quite paralysed me with astonishment & gratitude![2] I saw #1 of *Terror Tales*, & that was quite enough. Rumours of new weird magazines persist—of a rival to W T issued by the Winford Pub. Co. (whereof I never before heard), & of the bare possibility of a revival of *Strange Tales* by Street & Smith under the editorship of Desmond Hall. Time will tell. The Winford thing, I am led to believe, will be of very low grade—like T T or the late unlamented *Ghost Stories*. Glad you've seen "The Metal Monster" & "The Blind Spot".[3] I fancy that the former succeeds more *in spite of* its wooden human characters than *because* of them—for anything obviously artificial & cheap cannot but detract from the net impression. Baldwin says he is going to lend me a sequel to "The Blind Spot".[4] Merritt's new serial is now running in *The Argosy*,[5] but I missed the opening & didn't bother to get the rest. I shall borrow the sections from Rimel after it is complete. The future book version, I am informed, will differ considerably from the magazine text. Merritt will have a short story—"The Drone"—in the Sept. *Fantasy*—which will also contain Young Melmoth's "The Chuckler"—a sequel to my "Randolph Carter". Schwartz says he intends to dedicate each coming issue of F M to some weird magazine—an interesting variant of Hornig's idea.

Poor Bill Crawford seems all balled up as usual—& is talking (at a time when he can't get *anything* printed) of trying to issue *two* magazines—M T & *Unusual!!* He is also trying to argue with me about weird literature—& thereby revealing appalling depths of hill-billy ignorance, together with a curious egotism & incapacity for simple reasoning. He started a similar argument with Comte d'Erlette, but because so grotesquely abusive (with or without provocation from the not always gentle Comte) that the Sieur dropped him in disgust. Little Belknap has had some marvellously successful sales lately—having dropped all literary aspirations for the nonce, & turned to the grinding-out of pulp formula-products under the tutelage & agency of Otis Adelbert Kline. Glad the "Fungi" still please you on long-distance re-reading—& hope you'll write my corrections into the text.[6] I think I'll let Hornig reprint, if he wishes, those which appeared merely in the *Prov. Journal* & the amateur press.

I note with interest your stage of progress in dealing with Hugo the Rat, & will relieve Brother Searight's mind regarding the possibility of your being caught in some fresh trap of the wily near-Stavisky![7] Oy, soch ah man iss Hugo for ah new beezness heh shood mak a'ready! Under the circumstances I fancy your best course is to let present methods continue to work. Miss Weber is surely a wonder in her ability to extract anything at all from the eel-like culprit! The idea of pooling lawsuits might be good for some of the smaller victims—each sharing in the initial cost. I wish Sonny had the guts to go after the 25-odd fish owed him for that tale published in the quarterly back in 1930.[8] The damned sewer-rats simply *ignored* every enquiry the kid made!

Well—as you see, I surely have become a premier Hodgson fan! Do you know anything about W H H & his career? Koenig tells me he was killed in the war. All told, I believe that nobody but Blackwood can equal or surpass him in capturing the exact shades of the cosmic horror mood in all their actual details. But he was uneven—again like Blackwood. "Carnacki" is very weak, artificial, & stereotyped as a whole despite the strong points which you justly point out—& the "Glen Carrig" certainly suffered a letdown half way through. As soon as the castaways have dwelt on the island long enough to become familiar with it, & as soon as the sea-things become tangible realities employing obvious siege strategy, something of the story's original tension & sense of malign expectancy is lost. Also—the attempt to use 18th century English rings absurdly false to any sincere devotee of the 18th century. I agree about "The Ghost Pirates"—& what a wealth of technical sea lore it contains! I wonder if Hodgson was ever a sailor? But the masterpiece, so far as I can see, is "The House on the Borderland". Boy—that dim, brooding air of menace! And that stupefying cosmic sweep! I am all on edge to read "The Night Land". If it equals the other major three I'll have to send for that note I gave Hornig for the article & insert some reference. Meanwhile I have the Williams books, & will send them Averoigneward as soon as I've had a chance to go through them. Something warns me that they won't quite equal Hodgson. Incidentally, I'm anxious to learn what Comte Auguste-Guillaume thinks of the latter.

Leaves are beginning to turn hereabouts, though the landscape still holds a predominantly aestival aspect. There have been some decently warm days, so that on several occasions I have done reading & writing outdoors. Day before yesterday I spent the afternoon in my favourite countryside north of Providence—doing my writing partly on a stone wall overlooking a magnificent sweep of valley & distant steepled slopes, & partly on a rocky cliff overlooking a silent tarn in the midst of deep woods. There won't be many more times that I can sit around like that in the open—though I hope I can indulge in less sedentary rural expeditions throughout October. Wish there'd be a warm late autumn like 1920, '28, & '31. Well—at that, I've had quite a summer, with De Land & Nantucket as high spots!

Every good wish—

Yrs. for the sunken monolith of Gnoph—

E'ch-Pi-El

574 ❈ *Dawnward Spire, Lonely Hill*

P. S. Old De Castro (Danziger) has turned up again—destitute, going blind (he says), & with his wife an advanced consumptive. He wants Belknap and me to help him with some fiction, but I doubt if we can do very much. Poor old boy—he is a born charlatan, but after all there's something clever & likable about him. I hope he can manage to pull along somehow!

Notes

1. HPL parodies the designation of the Republican party as the GOP.
2. Under "Our Readers Say": "This story is really good, the one by H. P. Lovecraft. Science in a weird atmosphere, 'From Beyond;' interesting, and the story worked out completely satisfactorily. This will probably horrify a number of readers, but as far as I know, this is the first story I have ever liked by Lovecraft; but I like it very well." *FF* 1, No. 11 (July 1934): 161.
3. By Austin Hall and Homer Eon Flint.
4. *The Spot of Life* by Hall alone.
5. *Creep, Shadow.*
6. RHB had made a typescript of the poem (thirty-three sonnets only, at the time), but with errors that had gone uncorrected. HPL sent CAS a list of the errors.
7. Serge Alexandre Stavisky (1888–1934) sold worthless bonds and financed his pawnshops on the surety of "the emeralds of the late Empress of Germany," which proved to be glass.
8. See letter 118n1.

[289]   [ANS; *HK*][1]

[Postmarked Providence, R.I.,
17 October 1934]

Hail, Klarkash-Ton! Under separate cover I'm forwarding Koenig's two Williams books, & I'll be anxious to know what you think of 'em. Essentially, they are not horror literature but philosophic allegory. Direct reproduction of the texture of life & the substance of moods is not the author's object. He is trying to illustrate human nature through symbols & turns of idea which possess significance for those taking a traditional or orthodox view of man's cosmic bearings. It isn't our kind of stuff—for Williams isn't seeking to express the *indefinable feelings* experienced by man in confronting the unknown. His characters react to the symbolic & patterned marvels according to certain traditional philosophic concepts—not in the natural, irregular fashion of actual life. To get a full-sized kick from this stuff one must take seriously the orthodox view of cosmic organisation. However—I enjoyed the tales objectively, & fancy you will. Send 'em on to Comte d'Erlette when you're through with them. I doubt if Rimel or Dwyer would care for them. What do you think? ¶ Dwyer, by the way, has just got into a C.C.C. Camp.[2] At 38, that's quite a feat! ¶ Autumn chill is curtailing my outdoor sessions, but the scenery is exquisite. ¶ Yrs for the Stone of Suleiman—Ech-Pi-El.

[P.S.] Thanks for the Sinclair book³ which just came—I'll read & comment on it later. Of the two Williams books, I prefer "War in Heaven."⁴

Notes

1. *Front:* Unidentified.

2. The Civilian Conservation Corps, a New Deal program (1933–42) designed to employ unmarried men in a variety of functions, from planting trees to firefighting. Membership was generally restricted to men from the ages of eighteen to twenty-eight.

3. Apparently Upton Sinclair's *I, Governor of California, and How I Ended Poverty.*

4. The other book HPL forwarded must have been must have been *Many Dimensions*, sequel to *War in Heaven,* in which the Stone of Suleiman appears. He said he had received two books that Koenig mentioned in his article, but Koenig mentions five books in toto. In February 1936, HPL received on loan from C. L. Moore *The Greater Trumps* and *The Place of the Lion,* so possibly the other book he forwarded was *Many Dimensions* or *Shadows of Ecstasy.*

[290]   [ALS, JHL]

> Bottomless Chasm of Zhun—
> Hour of the Green Shining Below.
> [Postmarked 28 October 1934]

Dear Klarkash-Ton:—

Both of your recent epistles—with their absorbing plenitude of enclosures—were safely received & keenly appreciated. My digestion is now back to normal, though in general strength I remain rather below par—& am bothered by a devilish sort of writer's cramp in my right hand. I shall, if it keeps up, have to take to a pencil or the typewriter—notwithstanding my hatred of the latter device & its clatter.

Coincidence regarding feline disasters has surely reached a malign maximum—for lo! Sad advices from Charles Johnston in De Land tell of the vanishment of the venerable white Doodlebug whose photographic likeness you have beheld! He disappeared three weeks ago; & in view of the ophidian population of the district, very little hope is now entertained. This will be a bad blow for little Ar-E'ch-Bei when the news reaches him in Washington! Now I suppose High & Jack will be candidates for the presidency of the De Land chapter of the Kappa Alpha Tau! But the existence of others' woes does not lighten one's own—hence I extend the fullest measure of sympathy regarding the swallowing up of General Tabasco by the vast void! Good old warrior! And just as I was hoping to see a likeness of him! One is still tempted to hope that some miracle may bring him back. If not, may he have met his end as a true fighter should, with a high ring of the slain around his dying form. What Entities he may have faced on his last field of action, none may tell—but I feel sure they must have been far more formidable than any mere spawn of earth. Perhaps the Nameless Eikon hints a clue—now that I turn to view it, it seems to harbour an unwonted leer. I marvel not that Mother Simaetha mourns in desolation. Tell her to use her darkest arts in divining & withering the curst hidden power whereby the hero fell. Outside my window the elders of the K.A.T. shake their heads in sympathy. I shall consult with them—especially with the valiant Count Magnus—on possible measures of divination & reprisal!

By this time you doubtless have the Williams books. Rimel & Dwyer seem to want to see them, & I guess Comte d'Erlette will despite his vast rush. He has not yet read all the Hodgsons. Dwyer, by the way, has a new address for the nonce—*C.C.C. Camp 25, Peekskill, N.Y.* He succeeded in entering the C.C.C. despite his 38 years, & seems to be having a marvellous time. He's just been made editor of the camp paper,[1] & expects to win a leader's chevrons before long. It will be a good experience for him—& will help to whittle down his excess weight. About Williams—from his books I could well imagine him a priest, though Koenig's article does not mention any sacerdotal dignity. Koenig, by the way, does not know much about Hodgson, but understands that he was killed in the war. I am still awaiting "The Night Land" from Comte Auguste-Guillaume.

Well—I've read the Sinclair opus with keen interest, & have likewise gone over the wealth of cuttings you so thoughtfully sent. Thanks a thousand times for this enlargement of my perspective! Sinclair certainly does want to move things quickly, & it is perhaps unfortunate that he has chosen the present time—when the milder experiments of the existing administration should commend the support of all truly far-sighted citizens—to make a bid for power. Still—considering everything in its fullest historical perspective (which the hard-boiled "business" economist never does)—I must say that I honestly believe him to be a lesser evil than blind Hooverism. He has his weak spots & extravagances, yet his general orientation is in the direction toward which all western civilisation is inevitably moving. On the other hand, the Republicans who hate & fear him represent a thoroughly exploded order of things, based on long-vanished modes of industry, which can never hope to keep more than a fraction of the population fed & clothed, & which leads directly to a desperate revolution. The *Chronicle* (speaking frankly, of course, for capitalism) presents many interesting arguments, but in many ways shews that its concern is for *economic institutions* rather than *people*. Some of the parallels it draws are open to question, & Prof. Kreps[2] reveal his limitations when he naively says that

> "Plans to be successful must not only be based upon facts, but should be capable of execution without disrupting established institutions."

Now this is merely a plea for a static worship of dead words, mouldy documents, & vanished dreams. Certainly we do not wish to disrupt any really vital *social & cultural institutions;* but none of these is involved in the sort of disruption demanded by reasonable economic change. Established *economic* institutions must constantly be disrupted as modes of industry & distribution change, & it is both asinine & suicidal to fancy that a set made to fit a bygone agricultural age can be preserved in a mechanised age like that of the present & future. The whole relation of the individual to industry has been altered—& the whole relation of resources to the community is equally revolutionised. All this is excellently treated in Stuart Chase's recent "Economy of Abundance".[3] The empty catchwords of "initiative", "opportunity", "individualism", "enterprise", "stamina", "American spirit", "self-sufficiency", &c., &c., currently slobbered by Republican politicians have no more bearing on anything in today's machine world than have the meaningless taboos of eoanthropi or the hieratic precepts of Egyptian priests. Every condition on which they were founded is absent from the interrelated welter around us. We *must* disrupt existing institutions *so far as they pertain to the control & distribution of resources*. But only a disingenuous pleader for plutocracy would try to confuse *this* kind of "disruption"—or economic rearrangement—with the total *cultural* disruption attendant upon violent upheavals like the Russian revolution.

The more I reflect on the present economic crisis in relation to all the forces involved, the more I am forced to repudiate the whole fund of economic & political folklore on which the reactionaries base their plea. It is dead material—words—attitudes—illusions—prejudices—without any bearing on existing things & existing needs. I never fully appreciated all this before, because I never really *thought* about economics prior to 1930, when world events began to compel thought in this field. Formerly I was an arch-conservative; all for a royalist, aristocratic order. My conversion has by no means been hasty; but has come step by step, as facts have driven me. For of course you realise that no reputable thinker today (you can't call people limited to business thinking, with the profit motive held paramount, such) endorses unsupervised capitalism. Virtually *all* the *disinterested* world of philosophers & historians recognises the absolute need & inevitability of change. John Dewey—Bertrand Russell—H. G. Wells—Stuart Chase—the late Thorstein Veblen—indeed, the list is too long to complete. Laissez-faire capitalism is as dead as feudalism or trial by ordeal of iron or water. It no longer offers more than *part* of the people *any chance* or earning food & shelter—& any attempt to restore its full provisions in the United States would be the signal for a really justified uprising of the starving & the desperate. Change of some sort is not a theory but an arrived & inescapable condition. The question is merely one of *what* change, and *how rapid* a change, we shall have.

I don't doubt but that Sinclair wants to move too fast—yet I really think that is better, just now, than trying to sit on the safety-valve. Some of his extreme plans will doubtless become modified as he sees the obstacles which stand in their way—this being indeed already apparent, as you yourself point out. Others may not be as bad as they sound. There is, for example, no need of preserving private banking if the people's funds are generally transferred to state banks before any lapse occurs—& the same is true of those private utilities (light, power, transportation, &c) which some have hitherto used as in-

578 ❦ *Dawnward Spire, Lonely Hill*

vestments. These investments were anti-social to start with, for no one has any right to expect private profit from widespread services whose only object should be to perform certain functions for the community. It is only according to a false & obsolete system of values that the destruction of large-scale private industry is to be deplored. It must come some day anyhow—& the only question is how fast it shall come. I would prefer a fairly gradual evolution, but it may well be that the New Deal as a whole is too slow for immediate needs. There are millions to be fed, & some way must be found to deliver to them the unused wealth hoarded uselessly by the graspers of private profit. If it can't be managed legally, it will be managed by violence. The world is going to see a period of continuous upheaval until some fresh condition of fairly stable equilibrium can be worked out—some fresh balance between human needs & available forces, whereby the average individual may again have a chance to obtain food & shelter in exchange for his services. Naturally we can't go through such a period of readjustment without much discomfort on the part of many—but all that has to be reckoned with & borne. It won't do any good for the few beneficiaries of the dying order to try to hang on to their yachts & extra cars by throwing monkey-wrenches into the wheels of inevitable change. They might well just as well shut up, face facts, & help to make the inevitable changes less uncomfortable through the use of their technical skill. But of course they won't! Instead they'll join Jim Beck & Bainbridge Colby & Al Smith & Reed[4] & all the rest of the archaic yappers in sabotaging any intelligent attempt at necessary experimentation. That's human nature! If the people turn from the moderate New Deal to the extremes of Sinclair, Huey Long, Bilbo,[5] & their congeners, it will be largely because the reactionaries have hampered moderate measures in every possible way. And so it goes. Schools of thought as moderate as that of the *New Republic* consider Sinclair a lesser evil in spite of his obvious drawbacks, & I doubt if I could conscientiously be on the other side considering what the only real other side is. So many of the current objections are based purely on *words* & popular prejudices. Suppose, for example, Sinclair *does* advocate many measures practiced in Soviet Russia? Is that necessarily against him? As a matter of fact dozens of *individual features* of the Soviet programme are well worthy of emulation & adaptation by the nations of the western world. That would not mean a full reproduction of the Russian upheaval. It would merely mean a sensible recognition of certain intrinsically wise & useful measures, considered without prejudice & irrespective of their source. Naturally, each one would be tremendously altered in its adaptation to a highly industrialised Anglo-Saxon milieu. But to exclude & condemn some sensible idea merely because the Soviets happened to think of it first, is positively childish. There's plenty in Russia that we *don't* want—but what has this to do with what we *do* perhaps want? Sinclair is far enough from the alien New York communists who yearn for another Moscow! Probably the least desirable feature of the

Sinclair programme is that involving an influx of indigents—but even this may perhaps be exaggerated. If the plan in any way succeeds, its duplication in other states would probably serve to keep such a migration within bounds. Of course I can see how alarming the whole thing looks to anyone on the spot—but the fact is that all change must begin somewhere some time . . . . & the need of legal change, if we are to avert a revolution, is pretty manifest today! We were pretty close to a revolution just before Hoover was kicked out.

Well—that's the way I look at things. Of course I'm the rankest of laymen, & wholly unable to estimate the effects of given causes; but just now even a layman can appreciate the lack of any future in laissez-faire capitalism. *That* can almost be counted out of any argument. The question is one of a suitable substitute or modification—& here we are all at sea. It seems to me that the first thing is to break up the existing deadlock & start *something* . . . . *anything*. Until capitalism is really shaken, it will make no concessions, but will simply wait till a revolution blows the whole civilisation up. It is our job, then, to shake it—to shake it until its upholders are willing to think & plan for some alternative order yielding them less profit. They won't start thinking & planning until they're booted in the behind—hence it is now necessary to boot 'em! Undermine their foundations, & then they'll *have* to use their practical ability for some purpose other than personal purse-stuffing!

In some ways I differ sharply with the conventional philosophy to which you still profess allegiance—these differences arising partly from my strong sense of a tremendously & permanently altered balance of forces & resources in the modern machine world, & partly from my lifelong & directly anti-Marxian conception of *cultural* values as distinct from *economic* values.

For example—even before I gave thought to these matters I always despised the bourgeois use of *acquisitive power* as a measure of human character. I have never believed that the securing of material resources ought to form the central interest of human life—but have instead maintained that *personality* is an independent flowering of the intellect & emotions wholly apart from the struggle for existence. Formerly I accepted the archaic dictum that only a few can be relieved of the engulfing waste of the material struggle in its bitterest form—a dictum which is, of course, true in an agricultural age having scanty resources. Therefore I adopted an aristocratic attitude; regretfully arguing that *life,* in any degree of fulness, is only for the fortunate few whose ancestors' prowess has given them economic security & leisure. But I did not take the bourgeois position of praising struggle for its own sake. While recognising certain worthy qualities brought out by it, I was too much impressed by its stultifying attributes to regard it as other than a necessary evil. In my opinions, only the leisured aristocrat really had a chance at *adequate life*—nor did I despise him because he was not forced to struggle. Instead, I was sorry that so few could share his good fortune. *Too much human energy was wasted in the mere scramble for food & shelter.* The condition was *tolerable only because inevitable in yesterday's world of scanty resources.* Millions of men must go to waste in order that a few might really live. Still—if those few were not upheld, no high culture would ever be built up. I never had any use for the American pioneer's worship of *work & self-reliance for their own sakes.* These things are necessary in their place, but not ends in themselves—& any attempt to make them ends in themselves is essentially uncivilised. Thus I have no fundamental meeting-ground with the rugged Yankee individualist. I represent rather the mood of the agrarian feudalism which preceded the pioneering & capitalistic phases. My ideal of life is *nothing material or quantitative,* but simply *the security & leisure necessary for the maximum flowering of the human spirit.* To my mind no other supreme ideal is sound—& if this is "un-American", then so much the worse for what the politicians call "American". Actually, I believe that my ideal has flourished naturally in many parts of America—Virginia, South Carolina, & even my own New England before the cursed revolution of 1775–83. It is by no means a supine or decadent one—for it involves points of honour, inviolateness, responsibility, & courage fully as arduous (& in many cases more so) as any brought out by the fight for worldly resources. It is that of the gentleman as distinguished from that of the tradesman—& is to my mind especially worthy of upholding because of its repudiation of that *calculativeness* & *ulterior motivation* inseparable from the acquisitive character. That everyone could not feasibly pursue it in the agricultural age of scarcity was a source of genuine regret to me.

Well—so much for the past. Now we live in an age of easy abundance which makes possible the fulfilment of all moderate human wants through a relatively slight amount of labour. What shall be the result? Shall we still make resources *prohibitively hard to get* when there is really a plethora of them? Shall we allow antique notions of allocation—"property", &c—to interfere with the rational distribution of this abundant stock of resources among all who require them? Shall we *value hardship & anxiety & uncertainty* so fatuously as to *impose these evils artificially* on people who do not need to bear them, through the perpetuation of a set of now irrelevant & inapplicable rules of allocation? What *reasonable* objection is there to an intelligent centralised control of resources whose primary object shall be the elimination of want in every quarter—a thing possible without removing comfortable living from any one now enjoying it? To call the allocation of resources something "uncontrollable" by man—& in an age when virtually *all* natural forces are harnessed and & utilised—is simply infantile. It is simply that those who now have the lion's share don't want any fresh or rational allocation. It is needless to say that no sober thinker envisages a workless equalitarian paradise. Much work remains, & human capacities differ. High-grade service must still receive greater rewards than low-grade service. But amidst the present abundance of goods & minimisation of possible work, there must be *a fair & all-inclusive allocation of the chances to perform work & secure rewards.* When society *can't* give a man work, it must keep him comfortable without it; but it must give him work if it can,

& must compel him to perform it when it is needed. This does not involve interference with *personal* life & habits (contrary to what some reactionaries say), *nor is the absence of insecurity anything to deplore*. If "stamina" and "Americanism" demand a state of constant anxiety & threatened starvation on the part of every ordinary citizen, then they're not worth having! Better far to be "decadent" than to tolerate such a brutish waste of human energy! All this feverish complaint about the "dependence" of the modern citizen is simply a savage echo of the old petty-bourgeois concept of *acquisitive power* as the only ultimate measure of human quality. I spit upon this concept today from the standpoint of a rational socialist, as I spat upon it yesterday from the standpoint of an agrarian feudalist. I regard it as something fundamentally hostile to all that is best in mankind & the human spirit.

But of course the real need of change comes not from the mere fact of abundant resources, but from the growth of conditions making it impossible for millions to have any chance of getting *any* resources under the present outworn set of artificial rules. This development is no myth. Machines had displaced 900,000 men in the U.S. **before** the crash of '29, & no conceivable regime of "prosperity" (whereby a *few* people will have abundant & flexible resources & successfully exchange them among one another) will ever make it possible to avoid the permanent presence of *millions* of unemployed, so long as old-fashioned laissez-faire capitalism is adhered to. The feeble argument that new machines create new jobs has no serious standing. The ratio is wrong. For every 10 men employed in some *new* industry, 100 or more are displaced in *all* industries. Every day sees the development of some new device which makes every sort of work performable by fewer & fewer men. Even if the *proper* supplying of the *entire* population *would* keep everybody naturally busy (which is unlikely in view of the ease of duplication. The technocrats of 1932 brought out some profoundly significant truths!), laissez-faire capitalism offers no way for the entire population to get purchasing-power enough to demand proper supplying. The whole dying system is self-defeating. Really, it is not the Sinclairs, but its own dead weight & unworkableness, that are killing it!

Without wishing to boast, I must remark that I recognised this matter of technological unemployment long before the depression, though I then (in the depths of my thoughtlessness) advocated a wholly different solution. Being then a convinced feudalist, I believed that the great industries would eventually come out into the open and *visibly* instead of secretly control the government. I advocated *letting them do it*—believing that they would have the sense to handle the growing problem of human displacement themselves. I thought they would recognise the revolutionary peril of the unemployed millions of the future, & would *voluntarily* curtail profits enough to spread work among more men, & provide old-age pensions & unemployment insurance. I assumed that the *funded proprietor* of the future would come to feel the same basic responsibilities as those felt by the *landed proprietor* of the past—& that eventually the great accumulations of wealth would once more breed a *real gentry* with non-acquisitive interests & a true ability to use cultivated leisure to advantage. I now see how tragically I overestimated the rationality of the plutocrat. Instead of the benign aristocrat I had looked for, we had only the 'let-'em-starve' profit-Shylock of the Hoover era!

And so I have readjusted my ideas. I fancy you can see that, with me, the process has not been any wild emotional jump like Sonny Belknap's plunge into Russian bolshevism. I have gone almost reluctantly—step by step, as pressed by facts too insistent to deny—& am still quite as remote from Belknap's naive Marxism as I am from the equally naive Republican orthodoxy I have left behind. I am as set as ever against any *cultural* upheaval—& believe that nothing of the kind is necessary in order to achieve a new & feasible *economic* equilibrium. The best of culture *has always been non-economic.* Hitherto it has grown out of the *secure, non-struggling* life of the aristocrat. In future it may be expected to grow out of the secure & not-so-struggling life of whatever citizens are personally able to develop it. There need be no attempt to drag culture down to the level of crude minds. That, indeed, *would* be something to fight tooth & nail! With *economic opportunities* artificially regulated, we may well let *other* interests follow a natural course. Inherent differences in people & in tastes will create different social-cultural classes as in the past—although the relation of these classes to the holding of material resources will be less fixed than in the capitalistic age now closing. All this, of course, is directly contrary to Belknap's rampant Stalinism—but I'm telling you I'm no bolshevik! I am for the preservation of all values worth preserving—& for the maintenance of complete cultural continuity with the Western-European main stream. Don't fancy that the dethronement of certain purely economic concepts means an abrupt break in that stream. Rather does it mean a return to art impulses typically aristocratic (i.e., disinterested, leisurely, non-ulterior) rather than bourgeois. There is nothing in *bourgeois* culture which need be mourned. It was cheap & contemptible from the start. I can sympathise with the anti-commercial attitude of the classical Greek as distinguished from the essentially bourgeois Phoenician.

As for the quality of the present unemployed—while of course they *include* the permanently shiftless, it would be folly to suppose that they *consist wholly* of such elements. Millions of the unwillingly idle are just as efficient as those still at work—pure accident having determined which shall be on which side of the employment line. However, the anomalous present position of the unemployed certainly tends to lower their morale . . . . especially in the case of young fellows maturing during the depression & thus wholly without the experience of working. But this is the fault of the system, not of the men. *They* didn't & don't want to be unemployed. It's up to the moulders of society to dope out a new system obviating such wholesale unemployment. We never had it on so vast a scale before, & it can't last indefinitely without evil consequences. Something in our economic organisation has long been changing, &

the results of the change are now manifest for the first time—suddenly thrust on our notice as the culminating arch-depression has emphasised their cumulative magnitude. Nor will it do a bit of good to play the ostrich & deny that any change *has* occurred. Facts are facts, & denials don't change them!

Whether any real decadence has indeed overtaken the Aryan race is another matter demanding separate consideration. It so happens that the last few generations have witnessed profound changes of thought & custom through the progress of human knowledge & mechanical technology; & some of these changes have undeniably tended toward the breakdown of traditional inhibitions. Absence of religious restraints has operated adversely on those lacking aesthetic standards & practical sense, while the multiplication of material luxuries* has certainly promoted a trace of softness & effeminacy in the race. On the other hand, I do not regard the rise of woman as a bad sign. Rather do I fancy that her traditional subordination was itself an artificial & undesirable condition based on Oriental influences. Our virile Teutonic ancestors did not think their wives unworthy to follow them into battle, or scorn to dream of winged Valkyries bearing them to Valhalla. The feminine mind does not cover the same territory as the masculine, but is probably little if any inferior in total quality. To expect it to remain perpetually in the background in a realistic state of society is futile—despite the most feverish efforts of Nazis and Fascisti. However—it will be some time before women are sufficiently freed from past influences to form an active factor in national life. By the time they do gain influence, they will have lost many of the emotional characteristics which now impair their powers of judgment. Many qualities commonly regarded as innate—in races, classes, & sexes alike—are in reality results of habitual & imperceptible conditioning. When Western civilisation again attains something like an economic equilibrium, I believe it would pay to conduct a scientific enquiry into any possible decadence of the culture or race-stock, & to plan whatever remedial steps may be judged necessary. This would not mean any such drastic blundering & book-burning as the Nazis are now staging, but would involve a more systematised ethical instruction, & the encouragement of certain tendencies at the expense of others. But first to get a sound economic foundation . . . . . . & what a hell of a job that is going to be!

Well—even now, in spite of all these ponderous pages, I can see that I haven't put over the real foundation of my attitude. Accordingly I'm asking young Shea to shoot you a typed summary of my beliefs which I prepared about a year ago when anti-New-Dealers began to stir me into action. Hope the young imp hasn't lost it—I haven't had a real letter from him in ages, & he has moved

---

*we must not confuse this growth of *luxury* with the possible future growth of *security*. It does not hurt a man to know that his old age is provided for, but it *may* soften him to ride on cushions where he used to walk—& so on.

from Pittsburgh to Salisbury, Md.—on the Eastern Shore. Another thing I'll send you . . . . when my amiable opponent Edkins (the bird to whom you sent the Weigall book) returns it . . . . . is a reply to some *Providence Journal* editorials which I prepared last April just before going south.[6] In this reply I deal specifically with the current cant about "Americanism", "self-reliance", & so on. The introduction—with its American Revolutionary parallel—may seem odd in view of my own bitter & well-known hostility to the separation from our rightful Sovereign & Mother Land; but I must explain that I have always recognised a basis for colonial dissatisfaction in pre-1775 conditions. Emphatically, a new deal was called for; & I would have sympathised (as did Burke & Pitt)[7] with the colonists until the treasonable idea of secession from the Empire came up. *Then* I would have cast my lot with King & Parliament; since the *larger* issue of racial & cultural solidarity overshadowed the previous *local* issue. A real friend of justice would have striven for better colonial conditions *within the Empire*. Hence my parallel. In 1775 we had a largely unworkable system, & it had to go (albeit at an excessive & all too tragic cost). In 1934 we have another (conditions having outstripped forms)—& that, too, will have to go . . . . at a lesser cost, let us hope. In 1775 pamphleteers claimed that any changes from the old system involved *a loss of real freedom*—& in 1934 we hear much the same nonsense from Republicans & plutocrats. This parallelism I have sought to point out in replying to the *Journal's* frantic anti-Roosevelt editorials. Of course they didn't print my letter—but I had the satisfaction of writing it, & am having the added satisfaction of shewing it to a few correspondents. But enough of economics & sociology for the present. What an old bore Grandpa is getting to be!

Thanks for spotting the two additional errors in Ar-E'ch-Bei's "Fungi" text! I've corrected them in my copy, & shall advise the youthful acolyte of Krang to do likewise in his. Some day, when I feel able to formulate fiction again, I may work up some of the ideas contained in these jingles. Hope "The Chain of Aforgomon" will please Satrap Pharnabozus in its new form. I was glad to see "The Seven Geases" in print, & shall welcome "Xeethra" & other self-illustrated features. Any news of the new weird magazine promised by "Winford Publications"? Probably it'll be a low-grade thing like *Terror Tales*. The bizarre cuttings all proved of interest—especially the one about the felidae & the hellish Sabbat. Which reminds me that the monstrous day approaches . . . . & is heralded by many a cryptic whisper amongst the elders of the Kappa Alpha Tau. Alas that little Sam Perkins is not on hand to genuflect before the carven monolith in the nighted wood! He never saw either a May-Eve or an All-Hallows!

Hope Young Melmoth can get out to Averoigne next month. My last word from him was a card from Montreal postmarked Oct. 3, in which he said he was going to hit Providence sooner or later. He hasn't appeared yet, hence I have about given up hope. At least, I'm not staying home & watching the driveway every day!

I envy you the pleasant autumn with its mild daytimes—though apparently (for such are nature's paradoxes) you haven't had as summery an October as Asotin, Wash.—far north of you. Rhi-Mhel reports temperatures of 85°, cherry-trees blooming, & an apple-tree half-blossoming & half-bearing a crop of autumnal fruit! Rhode Island's October has not been notable for warm or pleasant days, though a few have appeared. However—favouring Fate gave me a series of motor trips whereby I saw more gorgeous foliage in the course of a single week-end than I ever saw before in my life!

These occurred in connexion with a visit to Edward H. Cole (my host of last August) in the Boston zone. On Oct. 20th we explored a section of north central Mass. which I had never before visited, & in which I saw some of the finest autumnal leafage & landscape vistas that I have ever beheld. The focus of the trip was West Townsend, where we lunched at a rambling tavern built in 1774, & patronised the quaintest old general store that I've seen in 30 years. Nearby is the Wallis Brook State Forest, where we revelled in wooded hills, rock waterfalls, & leafy gorges of indescribable picturesqueness. From nearly every point the distant bulk of Mt. Wachusett loomed up, & once we had a splendid view of a steepled village in a valley. On the 21st Cole & his wife brought us back to Providence—picking up my aunt at #66 & setting out for the ancient Narragansett Country which Price & I explored last year. We visited venerable Wickford with its drowsing wharves & elm-shaded Main Street, & later struck inland to the gorgeously lovely spot where Gilbert Stuart's birthplace—a snuff-mill built in 1750—broods beside the Pettaquamscutt or Narrow River. As I told you in '33, this ancient structure has been fully restored—wheel & all—so that it can grind tobacco into snuff as well as it did when Stuart's father ran it 180 years ago. The surrounding landscape is doubly beautiful in autumn, & Cole insisted on some adventurous explorations which resulted in our getting partly lost. A heated Chevrolet is a very useful aid to explorations in late October!

Current news is not abundant. Young Bloch has just placed his second story ("The Feast in the Abbey") with W T . . . & little Ar-E'ch-Bei is taking an art course at the Corcoran Gallery in Washington. Young Morse is also in Washington—so that he & the Priest of Krang ought to have some congenial discussions. Old Bill Lumley is still poetising, & says he is getting a prose phantasy into shape . . . which he'll probably want us to revise! ¶ Black & white Pres. Randall & tiger Vice-Pres. Osterberg are on the clubhouse roof outside my window, & both send sympathy to Mother Simaetha regarding the General's last retreat! ¶ Yrs for the Horned Guardian—E'ch-Pi-El

Notes

1. The camp paper of the Peekskill Civilian Conservation Corps camp was the Blue Mountain Survey. Dwyer's story "The Old Dark House" appeared in it.

2. Theodore John Kreps (1897–1981), professor of business economics at Stanford (1930–62).

3. Stuart Chase (1888–1985), author of such volumes as *The Tragedy of Waste* (1925), *Men and Machines* (1929), *The Nemesis of American Business and Other Essays* (1931), and *A New Deal* (1932). Chase was a strong critic of unscrupulous corporate practices and a pioneering proponent of consumer protection.

4. James M. Beck (1861–1936), U.S. representative (Republican) from Pennsylvania (1927–34) who gave up his seat because of his opposition to the New Deal. Bainbridge Colby (1869–1950), co-founder of the United States Progressive Party and secretary of state under Woodrow Wilson (1920–21). Alfred E. Smith (1873–1944), governor of New York (1919–21, 1923–29) and Democratic candidate for president in 1928. James A. Reed (1861–1944), U.S. senator (Democrat) from Missouri (1911–29).

5. Theodore G. Bilbo (1877–1947), governor (1916–20, 1928–32) and senator from Missouri (1935–47) who advocated populism and expressed hostility to bankers. Huey Pierce Long, Jr. (1893–1935), radical governor of Louisiana (1928–32) and advocate of a wealth redistribution scheme titled "Share Our Wealth."

6. "The *Journal* and the New Deal."

7. Edmund Burke (1729–1797), British political theorist, and William Pitt the Elder (1708–1778), prime minister of Great Britain (1766–68), both of whom expressed guarded sympathy with the cause of American independence.

[291] [ANS enclosure, JHL][1]

[In envelope postmarked 3 November 1934]

Hail, Hierophant of Tsathoggua! Here's the article I told you about, just returned by Edkins. Hope the handwriting won't be a bar to perusal. This is not the most thorough & analytical of the two articles, but is the one which deals with most of the common Republican hokum & delusion. The other ought to be coming from young Shea before long unless the little rascal has lost it. In that, I endeavour to trace the rise of certain concepts & the development of certain needs in an historical way.[2] ¶ Just recd. the new F F dedicated to you.[3] Congratulations! I was delighted to see "The Primal City" in print—that, as you know, is one of my favourites. Fancy Wright rejecting a thing like that! Also glad to see "Medusa", "On Fantasy", &c. ¶ I notice mention of a new **high-grade** weird magazine in England—*Tales of the Uncanny*—with contributions by Blackwood, &c.[4] This would seem to be what we have all been longing for for years! Wish I knew the address—I must get hold of a copy somehow! ¶ No hurry about returning either the enclosed or the article which Shea will send—so long as they get back some day. ¶ Yrs for the Onyx Altar
—E'ch-Pi-El

Notes

1. *Front:* The Carrie Tower, Hope, Manning and University Halls at Left. Brown University, Providence, R. I.

2. "The *Journal* and the New Deal" and "A Layman Looks at the Government."

3. The issue for November 1934. HPL was the dedicatee of the October issue, Poe that of the December.

4. *Tales of the Uncanny* (1934–38), published by the World's Work and edited by H. Norman Evans. Only three issues are known to have been published; they consisted of a mix of reprints and original stories.

[292]   [ANS; *HK*][1]

[Postmarked Providence, R.I.,
10 November 1934]

Glad the Williams stuff didn't bore you. I doubt if Rhi-Mhel would care much about it, & Comte d'Erlette has said specifically that he won't have time to wrestle with it—so probably (unless a veto intervenes) you'd better shoot it to Fra Bernardus at his new address—C.C.C. Camp 25, Peekskill, N.Y. ¶ I received "The Night Land" from M. le Comte—who confessed that he couldn't wade through it. It is truly atrociously verbose & dragged out—& the pseudo-archaic style (which resembles no English ever spoken or written from Chaucer onward . . . . merciful god, those quasi-Latin *infinitives!!!*) is at once pitiful & ridiculous. So, too, is the naive sentimentality. But for all that it has some *magnificent* pictures & suggestions of unknown horrors of the night—I'm tremendously glad to have read it despite all its faults. ¶ M. d'Erlette also sent me his new detective book—"The Man on All Fours"—& I guessed the solution as early as page 32. Damn clever story, though. ¶ Glad you still like my "Wall of Sleep"—the first tale of mine you ever saw, I believe. I was tremendously pleased to see your "Primal City" in type. ¶ Relieved to hear that the Night-Gaunt didn't get in, & trust that old Simaetha survived the Sabbat unharmed. Yrs for The Watcher of The Northwest. Ech-Pi-El.

Notes

1. *Front:* Unidentified.

[293]   [ANS, by CAS and Donald Wandrei][1]

[Postmarked Auburn, Cal.,
21 November 1934]

Dear Éch-Pi-El:

Melmoth and I are holding a session among my wizard towers! Wish you were here to utter the third incantation!

Klarkash-Ton

Written from the heart of the cryptical dwelling-place the Elder God Klark-Ash [*sic*] Ton: Greetings! I would that you were here in abysmal & hyper-cosmic conclave roaming with us the enigmatic regions beyond time, & after [?] space.

Melmoth II

Notes

1. *Front:* Unidentified.

[294]   [ANS][1]

[Postmarked Boston, Mass.,
25 November 1934]

Greetings, O Klarkash-Ton & Young Melmoth, who I understand are—or recently have been—assembled in joint convention! If the young visitor is still there, I hereby authorise his host to chastise him for not including Providence in his late Eastern itinerary! ¶ Culinarius is down in ancient Bostonium for a week, & will later spend some time with his sister in Sunapee, N.H. He has a lot of old family papers with him, including letters from a soldier at the front in the war of 1812, Civil War letters, & some from forty-niners—including a rare, rich, & racy specimen (written in 1853) in which *Auburn* is mentioned. We're going to lend this to Klarkash-Ton very shortly. ¶ Visited the old Royall mansion in Medford yesterday—built in 1737. Splendid specimen of early Georgian. ¶ Warm spell ended yesterday—it is now as cold as hell. Grandpa's outdoor season is just about over! ¶ Last night we called where there are three fine cats—they send greetings to Mother Simaetha, & pray that Genl. Tabasco may yet turn up somewhere. ¶ Shall be home again tonight. ¶ Patriarchal blessings to all. ¶ Yrs for the Crescent of Black Stars—E'ch-Pi-El.

This Wanderer is certainly having one of the spells that give him his nickname. Lucky devil. Of course you won't be able to read this, so it doesn't matter what I say.
W. P. Cook

[*Note on front:*] Built 1676 on the site of the Rev. Increase Mather's parsonage, where Cotton Mather was born. In the "Pickman's Model" district—as Young Melmoth may remember.

Notes

1. *Front:* Paul Revere Home, Boston, Mass.

1935

[295]   [ANS, JHL][1]

[c. 10 January 1935]

Dear Éch-Pi-El: The round-robbin [*sic*] from the gang came several days ago. Would that I could have attended those memorable conclaves to deliver in person such oracles of Tsathoggua as may not be committed to writing.

A letter will follow this ere long. Correspondence, for numerous reasons, has been [exceeding?]ly difficult of late. Yrs for the dark Eidola.

Klarkash-Ton

Notes

1. *Front:* Unidentified.

[296]   [ALS, JHL]

House of the Gnoles—[1]
Hour of the Thin Pittering
[16 January 1935/CAS]

Dear Klarkash-Ton:—

Glad to hear that the round robin duly arrived. We had a delightful session in N.Y., & the main meeting at Belknap's was the best within my memory—with every invited guest present. You'll note 15 different signatures on the message.[2] Ar-E'ch-Bei blew in on Christmas morning, & Belknap found him quarters at an hotel 6 blocks north of the Long abode. Meanwhile Young Melmoth had landed fresh from Averoigne—while his gifted artist-brother arrived directly from St. Paul. I myself joined the crowd on the morning of Dec. 31st. This was Ar-E'ch-Bei's first Manhattan visit since infancy, so Sonny Belknap took him in charge & introduced him to all the museums, galleries, bookstalls, &c. It was hard work to keep the kid from spending everything he had, including his return fare to Washington! He picked up many bargains in books & pictures—including a copy of George W. M. Reynolds' "Wagner the Wehr-Wolf" for 15¢ . . . the lucky little cuss! I landed an excellent modern edition of Lewis's "Monk" for a dollar. The big gathering at Belknap's Jan. 2 was a high spot—as you may judge from the attendance. Scarcely less notable was the meeting at Loveman's two nights later, when our host got out his magnificent collection of Clericashtoniana. I hadn't seen this material since 1922, since Loveman only recently brought it from Cleveland. Belknap, Ar-E'ch-Bei, & Young Melmoth had *never* seen it before. I fancy it's the best collection of the sort outside Averoigne itself—there must be 300 or 400 items. I vividly recog-

589

nised most of the drawings, & they gave me the same kick as in 1922. Little Ar-E'ch-Bei went virtually delirious over them—from now on he'll be pressing Es-El for loans for photographic purposes. On still another occasion Koenig shewed us all over his Electrical Testing Laboratories—a weird place full of bizarre devices for testing the durability of every conceivable sort of household electric appliance by duplicating the conditions of ordinary wear & tear. Naturally we did the museums—mostly the Egyptian & classical sections of the Metropolitan. We also had sessions at the new Wandrei flat in Greenwich Village—at 155 W. 10th St., over a somewhat well-known 'bohemian' restaurant called "Julius's". Ar-E'ch-Bei seems to have had a good time, despite occasional attacks of faintness & digestive trouble. He left on the morning of Jany. 7th, arriving in Washington late that night. I left the following midnight, & reached my native shores at dawn. Since then I've been weltering in accumulated work, with no daylight yet in sight!

All the returned material safely arrived. Glad young Jêhvish-Ei sent on the political harangue—it's so long since the little rascal has written me that I didn't know but he might neglect it! Thanks immensely for the generous array of cuttings. Gibson's portrait interests me vastly; since I had heard of the gentleman before, yet had seen no view of him. What a boy! Smut, too, is no slouch at scale-tipping! Recent cold weather has kept the Kappa Alpha Tau largely indoors, so that I haven't seen my furry neighbours of late as much as I'd like too. That new reckoning of the senses has a good deal to recommend it. I've often wondered at the *time*-perception of some people, since I have absolutely no sense of duration. On the other hand, I have a pretty fair instinctive sense of *direction* . . . I don't get lost or turned around easily. Possibly this might form a special sense. But the most striking thing is this account of a 'blasted heath' in Maine. I never heard of such a desert before, & am inclined to suspect exaggeration & overcolouring . . . . especially in view of its source. Abie Merritt's *American Weekly* is damned interesting, but it does love to go in for a sort of modified Charles Fort-ism! I certainly would like to learn more of this Novanglian wonder. Which reminds me—I hear that the famous "Moodus noises" are active again in central Connecticut. These rumblings in the ground, which occur periodically or occasionally, were a basis for all sorts of superstitions & sermons in colonial times—I think I referred to them in one of my tales.[3] They are probably caused by shifting strata around some geological "fault".

Thanks for the view of the bridge at Woods' Dry Diggings. Don't let your correspondence weigh on you—it pays to take things as easily as you can. Trust you had a pleasant Yuletide—my own was especially festive, with the first *tree* I've had since boyhood. December was quite packed with lectures & other art events—as I may have mentioned previously.

I guess I told you in the round robin how keenly I enjoyed "Xeethra." Great stuff! And now I must virtually invent new superlatives to describe "The Dark Eidolon"—which I didn't get a chance to read till last night. I was on the point of dropping you a card of congratulation—for verily, that story's gorgeous opulence & cosmic suggestion surpass all previous standards. For the second consecutive month you absolutely dominate W. T.¶ Yrs for the Vinum Sabbati[4]—E'ch-Pi-El

P. S. I suppose the Peacock Sultan has told you all about his plans to acquire houses & lands in San Carlos or Redwood City & become a feudal fixture! He certainly has made a go of the pulp racket—spawning yarns faster than he can write & calling in the dictaphone's aid!

Notes

1. Alluding to "How Nuth Would Have Practised His Art upon the Gnoles" (in *The Book of Wonder*) by Lord Dunsany.
2. In other letters, HPL notes that attendees at the annual gathering included HPL, RHB, Frank Belknap Long, Jr., James F. Morton, Samuel Loveman, Rheinhart Kleiner, George Kirk, Herman C. Koenig, Donald and Howard Wandrei, Arthur Leeds, Wilfred B. Talman, and Dean P. Phillips and his unnamed friend. The fifteenth person is unknown.
3. HPL does not specifically mention the Moodus noises in "The Dunwich Horror" but something similar in the area of his fictional Dunwich, MA: "Noises in the hills continued to be reported from year to year, and still form a puzzle to geologists and physiographers."
4. The wine of the Sabbath. Cited in Machen's "Novel of the White Powder" (a segment of *The Three Impostors*).

[297]   [ALS]

Ruins of the primal Citadel
—Hour of the Sentient Wind
[30 January 1935/RAS]

Dear Klarkash-Ton:—

Glad to hear that the political harangues didn't prove wholly beyond perusal. It is only in late years that I have paid the least attention to political or economic matters—my former position being a mere instinctive & irrational acceptance of monarchical conservatism in its most extreme form. The discussions incident to the depression first awaked me to realities in the domain of society & government, & caused me to examine this field with the same impartially analytical attitude which I had previously reserved for natural science. As a result, I first took the *liberal* side of a debate in the spring of 1931—in St. Augustine, where I visited with an old-school Republican of the sort I used to represent.[1] Since then I have had plenty of debates in both directions—with blind Hooverites on the one hand, & radical sprigs of the "intelligentsia" on the other hand. I have yet to see why a rational readjustment of subsistence opportunities need involve any such cultural chaos as young Belknap & his precious Marxists are so eager to precipitate!

The recent metropolitan sessions surely were enjoyable—&, as I have mentioned, extremely Klarkash-Tonic in atmosphere & subject-matter! Too bad you couldn't have duplicated or rivalled them during Melmoth's visit by getting Sultan Malik up from Oakland. By the way—I presume he has notified you of his transfer to his new Djinn-built palace on the crest of Mount Kaf—otherwise Redwood City. A very good move for him. I can imagine the congeniality of the sessions at the Palatium Sullianum from a snapshot I received not long ago—with yourself at the extreme left & a very prepossessing grey gentleman called "Son" at the extreme right. You are surely fortunate to have such neighbours—& they, in turn, undoubtedly appreciate having Tsathoggua's high-priest within reach. I have heard several times from Mrs. Sully, who is—most emphatically—as brilliant & appreciative a person as one could well encounter. Yes—the gradual sending of items has obviously built up the Clericashtonic section of the Loveman Museum far beyond your recollection. The H-E illustrations are magnificent—though not all are there, if one may judge by the numbers on the back. "Fear" is a titanic thing in conception, though small in size. And what a golconda of entities, eidola, & fragmentary vistas! I hope Barlow can get me some good photographs of the high spots!

"The Dark Eidolon" is gaining a clamorous & unanimous panegyric among all my correspondents—& it certainly deserves it. Ædopol, what a yarn! It comes close to the best W T has ever printed. Confound that ass Pharnabozus for rejecting "Aforgomon"—but let us hope he'll change his mind in typical Wrightian fashion! I wait to see all the new items—& I hope you won't sacrifice anything in "Naat" to the tyrant's puerile demands. I'm stuck near the end of my own current attempt—"The Shadow Out of Time"—since I can't get the unharassed leisure I need. Nor am I satisfied with the parts already written. I simply *can't* write a *short story* any more—this has grown into a young novel in spite of my most violent efforts. When this & one other plot are out of my system, shall endeavour to experiment with fantastic dream-fragments of another sort.

A combination of Maine's blasted heath & Connecticut's Moodus noises would certainly form a splendid testimonial to Tsathoggua's lordship in the lightless depths of N'Kai! Thanks vastly for the vivid page anent Salvador Dali—who certainly goes his eminent compatriot of 'Los Caprichios' [*sic*][2] one better in the grotesque line! ¡Madre de Dios—que loco! Years ago I read "Maldoror"—or parts of it[3]—& this pictorial stuff certainly plays up to it! I wish I could have seen that exhibit in N Y—wonder if it was on when I was there! The cutting—with much appreciation—goes into my files. Thanks, too, for the appealing view of Don Miguel & Señor Madera—some pair! So far, however, the Kappa Alpha Tau hasn't admitted any rodents—not even the squirrel who calls regularly at the boarding-house across the garden. I mourn the continued loss of Gen. Tabasco (as of Doodlebug down in De Land), but am glad to hear that Mother Simaetha flourishes.

Speaking of files—as I was a while back—I've just acquired an incredible device for keeping some of mine .... nothing less than *two* dark walnut chests of drawers which I found at a fire sale & have piled up into a single tall cabinet. It fits in my study admirably, & has a mellow colonial look harmonising with the atmosphere. With 10 new drawers at my disposal, I can get a vast stack of loose cuttings & MSS. & pamphlets nearly out of the way & ready for consultation. I've wanted an outfit like this for years. Belknap had a single chest of drawers (of a pale green finish which I wouldn't care for) for Christmas, & I guess envy set me to intensive bargain-hunting!

Your weather report fills me with a fresh burst of envy—& of a deeper green than Sonny's cabinet! For look (vide enc.) at the dose we're getting here! 13″ of snow—worst since 1920. Traffic crippled—temperatures from +16° to -5° day after day . . . . I haven't been out for a week! ¶ Am enclosing a letter of 1853 from the neighbourhood of Woods' Dry Diggings. Please return some time, but absolutely no hurry. ¶ Gradually absorbing "Malleus Malleficarum", lent me by Koenig. ¶ All good wishes—& don't work too hard. ¶ Yrs for the Nameless Transmutation of Gnaran-Hofash—E'ch-Pi-El.

Notes

1. Dudley C. Newton (1864–1954).

2. *Los Caprichos* is a set of 80 aquatint prints made by the Spanish artist Francisco Goya in 1797 and 1798, published as an album in 1799.

3. Comte de Lautréamont (pseudonym of Isidore Lucien Ducasse, 1846–1870), *Les Chants de Maldoror* (1868). HPL may have read from the edition published by the Casanova Society (1924).

[298]   [ANS enclosure to previous; AHT]

Here's something darned interesting, which I've been meaning to lend you for ages—ever since it came into my custody last November. It is a letter from a Massachusetts 49-er (of Wilbraham or "Dunwich"), written in 1853 & starting out with a reference to good old Averoigne! I'll wager you don't come across local references as early as this every day! This chap Tupper (great-uncle of the late amateur journalist Mrs. Miniter, among whose papers it was found by W. Paul Cook) seems to have been rather a rough diamond, with a peculiarly robust & sportive imagination! He returned east & lived to a ripe old age. I couldn't find any mention of *Weaver Creek* in the gold show programme you sent me. Do you know where it was? The stationery, I understand, was quite characteristic. Cook has had me take charge of a lot of Mrs. M.'s ancestral papers (including letters from a soldier in the year 1812) until a suitably appreciative blood heir can be found. Later—if you're interested—I'll send you a letter from another Tupper brother written at Rio de Janeiro as he was bound around the Horn for California.

E'ch-Pi-El

[299]   [ALS]

Megalithic Ruins beneath the Desert
—Hour of the Chill Wind from the Black
Trap-door.
[Postmarked 26 March 1935]

Dear Klarkash-Ton:—

        Glad to hear of the new fictional productivity, & hope to behold the fruits thereof in due course of time. Hope they all land with Satrap Pharnabozus sooner or later—& in forms reasonably like the original. Zothique surely is fertile soil![1] The future titles have an alluring sound, & I trust the "Offspring" may somehow get past Little Farny's timid glance. A recent experience of little Bobby Bloch does not form an encouraging omen—for Pharnabozus turned down a yarn of his (about a chap who found that his bedfellow in an hotel was a badly decomposed cadaver) on the ground of excessive horror, bringing up the now-classic case of 1924 . . . . . C. M. Eddy's "Loved Dead" (the latter half of which *I* re-wrote!) & the Indiana Parent–Teacher's Association. Poor Farny—he's like a dog which has received a nerve-breaking scare, & cringes every time anything reminds him of it! "The Dark Eidolon" was surely a memorable tale—& if it didn't lead all rivals by a big margin at the closing of the polls, so much the worse for the electorate! Regarding the scheduled "Out of the Æons"—I should say I *did* have a hand in it . . . . . I *wrote* the damn thing! The original museum-mummy story submitted for revision was so utterly lousy (some crap about a Peruvian miner trapped underground) that I had to discard it altogether & prepare a fresh tale. But it's really foolish to attempt jobs so extensive, when with the same amount of work one could write an acknowledged story of one's own. This is the last collaboration of the sort I shall ever attempt—indeed, I've turned a deaf ear to all further suggestions from Sultan Malik, Mrs. Heald, kid Bloch, & others. Which reminds me that I've finished "The Shadow Out of Time"—65 pages of pencil script. I am woefully dissatisfied with it, & may destroy this version as I did the first last autumn. In my present state of doubt I am reluctant to type the thing—so Comte d'Erlette has generously agreed to attempt a deciphering of the original text, & to render a tentative verdict. If he says it's worth saving, I shall get a typed copy somehow & send it on the rounds—starting with Averoigne. If not—the waste basket & a fresh start. Incidentally—M. le Comte has hectored his publishers—Loring & Mussey—into writing me & asking to see some of my junk with a view to possible book publication. Ho, hum! Since this is the *5ᵗʰ* time I've been approached with a kindred request—without visible results so far—I'm not so childishly steamed up about the matter as I might have been years ago. However—I've shot along a few reams of bull just for the technical sake of leaving no stone unturned. It'll come back soon enough! Anyhow, I appreciate Little Augie's solicitude in bothering about the matter. Regarding W T issues—February was pitifully mediocre except for the Canevin reprint . . . an old favourite of mine. March is an improvement—with Searight & Stoker leading, as you point out. Too bad Farny cut out a finely mystical motto from Searight's tale—a dark paragraph from the avoided & pre-human Eltdown Shards . . . . those hideous clay tablets dug up in an archaic rock stratum, whose monstrous interpretation only certain adepts in elder lore & pre-Naacal palaeography have ever attempted. "Julhi" is pretty much a formula yarn, despite Miss Moore's undeniable power to [evoke utter] strangeness, & to suggest monstrous _____[. However,] Wright's propaganda in favour of popular action stuff, plus the author's own weakness for 1900-esque romantic slush, are combining with deadly effect—so that perhaps another single-plotter is to be added to the ranks already adorned by Messrs. Hamilton, Ward, Morgan, et al. Little Ar-E'ch-Bei—the premier Moore fan—is quite concerned about the slipping of the new luminary; & is urging the gang to find some excuse to shoot her tactful words of advice counteracting the tradesmanlike recommendations of Satrap Pharnabozus . . . . . & the philistinic suggestions of Prince Effjay of Akkamin, who has been volunteering collaboration! Haven't read the Kline & Ernst serials, & doubt if I shall. The older I get, the more I become exasperated with the sterilities of the cheap, ancient pulp formulae. By the way—you doubtless know ere this of the F F's lamentable & untimely death. Too damn bad! It filled a place all its own as a forum for weird enthusiasts, & nothing else is likely to supply the vacancy. Leedle Shoolie's *Fantasy Mekasin* will take over some of the features, but its devotion to scientifiction will prevent it from helping much. Lean times for ghoul-grubbers—Hill Billy Crawford's *Marvel Tales* is also having a hard time, though not yet extinct. Poor Bill smashed some fingers in his press—& now his pardner Eshbach[2] has walked out on him! But incidentally—I must not fail to report that that the weird-science-fiction-fan population of Providence has just been swelled by a very energetic new electron . . . . as I had quite forcibly impressed on me last week. I was reading the paper one evening when my aunt entered my study to announce a caller . . . . a "Mr. Sterling" . . . no relative, as you will soon perceive, of your late eminent friend & fellow-Californian. Close on her heels the important visitor appeared . . . . in the person of a little Jew boy about as high as my waist, with unchanged childish treble & swarthy cheeks innocent of the Gillette's harsh strokes. He *did* have long trousers—which somehow looked grotesque upon so tender an infant. It appears that he is one of the endless kid fans clustering around the weird-science pulps & the fantasy sheets, who had read my stuff & learned my address from someone in the fantasy world. He's a typical N.Y. Yid—but his papa has just been made assistant manager of the local fur emporium of considerable Novanglian reputation—, so he's a Providentian now—in the Classical High School. And oy, vhat ah shild . . . vhat a shild! If they all come as precocious as this, I don't wonder that Der Schön Adolf is afraid they'll juggle the shirts off the German people's backs! Damme if the little imp didn't talk like a man of 30—correcting all the mistakes in the current science yarns, reeling off facts & figures a mile a minute, & displaying the taste & judgment of a veteran. He has already sold stories to *Wonder* . . . .& **collected from Hugo the Rat** (it takes a Yid to catch a Yid!) . . . . & is bubbling over with ideas. A red-hot Klarkash-Ton fan, too. Others in his family have reviewed books for the N.Y. *Herald Tribune* & written for various "slicks". And now— being fully weaned from Mellin's Food & encased in lungk pents—he is pre- pared to conquer ancient Providence! He vants he shood organise it ah brench by der Science Fiction League here, &c. &c. &c. Vell, vell! I gave him some duplicate F F's & other items, & he says he's going to call again. Hope he won't become a nuisance—I don't want to discourage him in any way, for he really does seem like an astonishingly promising brat. What a compact miniature world these kids have among themselves—Little Charlie Hornig, Julius Schwartz, Conrad Ruppert, Mortimer Weisinger, &c. &c. &c.! It is

---

Glad to learn—from your letter & previous appreciated postcard—that the quaint humours of Mr. G. Washington Tupper[3] brought renewed merri- ment to the b'ar-infested gulches of Woods' Dry Diggings after all these years—82 of them! He surely must have been quite a boy! I'll be interested to know anything you may find concerning *Weaver Creek*—which would appear to have been very close to Averoigne. Herewith I am enclosing the one other 49-er item contained in the Miniter papers—a letter written at Rio *to* the spor- tive George before he left Wilbraham. This is by his elder brother William—a less buoyant & ebullient soul, as you will see, but the first of the Tuppers to follow the aureate lure to far-off & half-fabulous Cal-ee-for-nye-ay´. Note the fancy stationery—which in those days evidently discharged the function of our contemporary picture postcards. By the way—in the spring a party of old-time amateur journalists including myself will have the melancholy- sentimental task of returning to the ancient soil of Wilbraham the last mortal ashes of one of these selfsame Tuppers—the niece of George & William, born in 1843 [*sic*] & mother of Edith Miniter.[4] She died & was cremated in 1919, & had always expressed a wish that her ashes be scattered under the rose bushes at Maplehurst, back home. For some reason her daughter neglected to fulfil her request—though herself living at Maplehurst. But now that the daughter is dead, the Boston amateurs have secured the cinerary urn from a local colum- bariun, & mean to mingle Jane Tupper Dowe at last with her ancestral earth. Mrs. Miniter (who, incidentally, once turned down a chance to revise the un- published manuscript of "Dracula" in 1893!) is buried in Wilbraham's spectral "Dell"—not far from the grave of her robustious great-uncle George.

Sultan Malik certainly seems to be revelling in Redwood—has he told you of Nimrod, the huge white hunting-leopard who calmly walked in on him & decided to become a permanent fixture? The Kappa Alpha Tau has a natural leader at last! Maybe it's the lost Doodlebug strayed across the continent from De Land—but if so, his appetite (3 saucers of milk & 2 bowls of spaghetti & dried meat are just a light lunch to this gent!) & hunting prowess have grown! What a boy! Last month he dug a gopher out of its hole & brought it for his new master to see before devouring it. Another time the Peacock Sultan had to intervene—for the dog's sake—in an attack he made on a huge collie who had been eyeing his bowl of beans too narrowly. He also enjoys riding in Juggernaut . . . . . look out for Mother Simaetha's safety if the Sultan brings him along on his next visit! Or perhaps, though, so venerable a witch can curb him with Tsathogguan incantations. Am interested to hear of your new office—which certainly ought to prove a great boon for master & visitors alike. Sorry that illness has harassed Indian Hill, & that you could not participate in the Feather River trip. The spring, though, will bring numberless opportunities. Your description of the local flora causes me to gnash my teeth with envy amidst the barren boughs & bleak brown meads of Novanglia's March. Averoigne certainly has it all over ancient Rhodinsula so far as climate is concerned! However—in the mater of felidae, we're holding up our end! My late little friend Sam Perkins has a successor in the person of his tiny brother John, born [February 1935] _____ & a spirited little devil—hissing manfully at any fingers intrusively poked at him. He was one of a litter of four, the other three of which are now distributed elsewhere. I expect to borrow John very frequently during the weeks & months to come, & hope he will be careful of his health & avoid his brother's untimely end. He ought to make a fine Kappa Alpha Tau recruit by next autumn. Which reminds me that the prefatory rustlings of spring are bringing the elder K.A.T. officials back to their clubhouse roof. I had a long talk with the tiger vice-president yesterday.

Yes—that double chest of drawers is certainly a noble asset. Wish you could find a place for such—I had difficulty in doing so, but finally tucked it beside a full bookcase near a south window. Perhaps I mentioned that I piled one chest atop the other in order to have a single tall cabinet . . . . single floor-space, double capacity!

Thanks immensely for the cuttings. That sheet with prehistoric thumbprints on one side & invading ant hordes on the other is quite a dual item! And petrified falls—& giant mummies—& more sea-serpents . . . . Speaking of Halifax—as one of the cuttings does—note one of the enclosed items. Aside from the miraculous carving, the idea of an island near a populous city *which has never felt the tread of human foot* has certain undeniable possibilities.[5] Those Roman archaeological cuttings deserve a special word of thanks. Ædepol, what treasures the consul Mussolinus is exhuming from the past! I had no idea so much of the Golden House still existed![6] And that officers' club & house are fascinating—while the notion of an aeon-hidden Sibylline grotto surely spurs the imagination!

When I last wrote, Providence was groaning beneath a record-breaking blanket of snow, whilst I was marooned indoors because of the cold. The winter has not, however, averaged even nearly as bad as its predecessor. I managed to get out to several lectures—poetry readings by Susanna Valentine Mitchell[7] & the famed Archibald MacLeish—author of "Conquistador"—& an excellent discourse on Hokusai at the local museum, in connexion with a notable exhibition of his prints. Japanese art certainly appeals to me as few other aesthetic forms succeed in doing. Another lecture was on contemporary Russian Soviet art—with lantern-slides. Very interesting—& I was astonished to see how relatively well the bolshies are doing despite the incubus of the Marxian fallacy of "social purpose." Some of them take their dogma lightly, & produce very passable work in the historic Byzantine tradition. Others, of course, follow the freakish "ideology" of Lenin & produce nothing but cheap poster propaganda. Paradoxically, none of this art is as radical in an aesthetic way as the decadent work of western artists—the cubist, surrealist, &c. stuff. But even the best of it is merely a fraction as good as Russia could have had if she had only avoided a violent revolution. Still another interesting lecture was on the recently uncovered 9th & 10th century mosaics in the great church of Hagia Sophia in Constantinople—by Thomas Whittemore, who had charge of the uncovering.[8] Now that the building has been wisely transformed to a museum, the modern trappings are being cleared away—leaving it as it was in its prime. This edifice has always fascinated me—a product of Rome's final decay (A.D. 532–8), yet embodying the majesty of Roman design in one titanic swansong. It has, of course, the subtle Oriental touches which had begun to develop as a separate Byzantine architecture—& these mosaics, installed 300 to 400 years later, are utterly Byzantine in their technique. The building is one of the best preserved of all the large structures which have come down from the fringe of classical antiquity. When it was erected, Latin was still the language of Western Europe & North Africa, & the Roman people had not yet begun to realise that the occidental half of their empire had irrevocably fallen. Justinianus brought the Eastern Empire to its apex of power—even reconquering Italy for the time being. People in that age must have felt somewhat like people today—with impending change in the air—yet nothing really radical happened. It was over a century before the Moslem wave swept the Mediterranean littoral, & 400 years before the lowest ebb of the Dark Ages was reached. The latest lecture I have heard was at the college last Monday night—on the cosmic rays, by Prof. W. F. G. Swann of the Franklin Institute.[9] Aided by lantern-slides & apparatus, the speaker succeeded in making me understand a good many recent points about these mysterious radiations which I had not previously appreciated.

Wintry conditions began to let down during February's third quarter, & there is reason to hope that the spring will be a fairly early one. The break in my hibernation came rather early this year—precipitated by a visit from a very interesting young man—Robert Ellis Moe, a son of my old amateur journalistic friend Maurice W. Moe of Milwaukee—March 2–3. This youth, who graduated from the University of Wisconsin in 1933 with high honours in electrical engineering, at once stepped into an excellent position with the General Electric Co. He was lately transferred to Bridgeport, Conn.—which puts him within a cruising radius of Providence (130 m) & N.Y. (60 m). I had not seen him since he was a little towhead of eleven—& he certainly has grown! 22 now. He came in "Skippy"—his faithful chariot of a source & vintage precisely like those of Sultan Malik's famed Juggernaut—& I shewed him all the colonial sights of ancient Providentium & of the quaint little seaports down both sides of Narragansett Bay—Warren & Bristol on the east shore, & East Greenwich & Wickford on the west shore. The weather was very favourable—about 50°—& I certainly welcomed the sight of the countryside after so long an urban incarceration. My guest seemed highly appreciative, & expects to come again. I'm suggesting that he get in touch with Sonny Belknap & Loveman & others of the gang (many of whom know his father) in N.Y. Koenig—himself an electrical engineer—ought to prove especially congenial. Young Moe took some pictures with his camera, but not many of them turned out well. As you will see by the enclosed, he is an astonishingly bad *aimer* for so scientific & mechanical a lad! The view of the Wickford building shews a Rhode Island house of the sort most typical around 1750 to 1770. Of the same basic pattern—though spoiled by the excrescent porch & modern door & windows—is the Sarah Whitman house in Providence, where Poe called so often in the 40's. In snapping this literary shrine, young Moe boldly sliced off the whole second story!

But the real season-opening came with the first *pedestrian* outing—which occurred March 6, when the thermometer rose to 65°. On this occasion I took a 12-mile walk through the northern suburbs (including Pawtucket, home of the glib & ghoulish Mr. Hugh B. Cave!) to my favourite Quinsnicket countryside—which I enjoyed despite leaflessness overhead & slush underfoot. Something vernal seemed somehow in the air—& when sunset came, the spectacle of glowing Venus & the young Moon (an infinitely thin crescent) in the west was altogether irresistible. A later excursion—March 9, when a relative took my aunt & me to ride—extended through the terrain east of Providence, just across the line in the ancient Province of the Massachusetts Bay. We had some excellent vistas of woods, fields, & white village spires, & could feel on every hand the subtle magic of returning spring. However—there's undoubtedly a lot of cold and dismal weather ahead, & I wish fervently that I could get down to Charleston & meet summer early! Such is not very likely this year.

Have been too abominably busy for much reading beyond current periodicals—but went through the recent Dunsany volume, "Jorkens Remembers Africa", not long ago. Occasionally clever & amusing, but—alas—not the old Dunsany of "A Dreamer's Tales". The Asotin boys—Baldwin & Rimel—lately sent me a copy of the collected instalments of Merritt's "Creep, Shadow", which they very skilfully bound themselves . . . in heavy leather. So far I have had no chance to peruse it—but I look forward eagerly to that pleasure, since everyone tells me it is considerably above the recent Merritt average. Speaking of books—little Shea recently sent me the enclosed account of a new anthology which sounds extremely promising.[10] So far as I can recall, I have not read any of the stories mentioned. By the way—did I mention in my last epistle the splendid edition of Poe with Harry Clarke illustrations which Ar-E'ch-Bei sent me? Those pictures are truly marvellous! I thought I had seen them all before—in copies casually thumbed through—but it appears that I had missed many. Tsathoggua, what an artist! Do you know all the drawings? Those which especially "get" me are the illustrations to "MS. found in a Bottle" (in colour), "Silence—A Fable" (Klarkash-Tonic vegetation), "Marie Roget" (dragging the corpse to the river), "Landor's Cottage" (Sime-like otherworldness), "M. Valdemar" (nggghhrr!!), & "The Premature Burial" (ngghyaaa!!!). Oddly, the printed text seems to vary a trifle from the standard versions—so that "Valdemar" ends with the words "detestable *putridity*" instead of "detestable *putrescence*"—a very bad change from the standpoint of rhythm.[11] But God! those pictures! Incidentally—kid Ar-E'ch-Bei seems to be a particular favourite of the gods. After picking up "Wagner the Wehr-Wolf" for 15¢ in N.Y., the little rascal has now found a paper-bound copy of its companion-novel, "Faust & the Demon", in Washington for a *dime!* Some time before his N.Y. trip he acquired a copy of Gustav Meyrink's "The Golem"—very hard to obtain—which he is going to lend me. My own one recent purchase is of an infinitely useful volume of more general character—the new 1-volume Modern Encyclopaedia, now issued by Grosset & Dunlap for $1.95, & full of contemporary items not to be found elsewhere. I really needed this badly—my latest other encyclopaedia being a 1914 one. I was sorely tempted in 1933, then the original $3.50 edition came out, but now I'm glad I waited. It chronicles some events as recent as last November. Fancy finding neutrons, N.R.A., Nazis, &c. in an encyclopaedia!

Old Adolphe de Castro's wife died Jany. 23, & I sent him a note of sympathy. I cannot, however, attempt any revision of his book—some of whose absurdities I believe I described to you last December. I shall merely touch up awkward passages gratis, give the kindliest general opinion I can, & return the volume with the suggestion that others be approached.

You may have a visit from some youthful fans before long—Fred Anger of Berkeley, who has called on the Peacock Sultan several times, having mentioned a design of organising a pilgrimage to the Abbey of Vyones, which would include quite a number of San Francisco enthusiasts. With the steady growth of your fame, you may yet have to retire to some hidden fastness in the hills to avoid the increasing throngs of lionisers!

And so it goes. Of the enclosed, only the specifically labelled items need [be returned].

Yrs in the fellowship of Thasaidon—E'ch-Pi-El

P.S. New *Marvel Tales* just came. Not so bad in appearance, & none of the contents is conspicuously crude. I think the best tale is the unambitious bit by John Benyon [*sic*] Harris—"The Cathedral Crypt."[12]

[P.P.S.] Extra: Just added *6* new units to my filing equipment—cardboard cabinets with 4 drawers each—wooden front & frame, imitation wood finish. These 24 new drawers will do wonders for my filing system.

[Enclosures; upper:]
Sarah Helen Whitman house—
Benefit St., Providence, R.I.
Visited by Edgar Allan Poe, 1847–8.

Photograph by Robert Ellis Moe
    March 2, 1935.

H. P. Lovecraft in foreground.
    Please return to HPL

[Lower]

Photograph by Robert Ellis Moe

Typical 18th century Rhode Island house.

[notes by R. E. Moe:] Main Street of Wickford / Mar. 3, 1935

Notes

1. CAS had recently completed "Necromancy in Naat" and "The Black Abbot of Puthuum."

2. Lloyd Arthur Eshbach (1910–2003), science fiction writer and publisher. He later edited the *Galleon* and published a poem and a story by HPL in the magazine.

3. George Washington Tupper (1830–1908), a prospector in the days of the Gold Rush.

4. Jennie E. T. Dowe (1840–1919), an amateur journalist. Upon her death, HPL wrote a poem, "In Memoriam: J. E. T. D." (*Tryout*, March 1919) as well as a brief prose tribute; both items were published in *In Memoriam: Jennie E. T. Dowe*, ed. Michael White (Dorchester, MA: [W. Paul Cook], 1921).

5. *CB* 209 is a transcription of the newspaper article, dateline of Halifax, 3 March 1935. The cutting HPL sent CAS exists among CAS's papers at JHL.

6. The Domus Aurea, an immense landscaped villa built on the Palatine Hill in Rome for the Emperor Nero after the fire of 64 C.E.

7. Susanna Valentine Mitchell (1896–1979), a local poet.

8. Thomas Whittemore (1871–1950), American archaeologist who devoted himself chiefly to Byzantine and Coptic art.

9. William Francis Gray Swann (1884–1962), British physicist and director of the Franklin Institute (1927–59) in Philadelphia.

10. *The Grim Thirteen*, ed. Frederick Stuart Greene.

11. The reading "putridity" is found in Sarah Helen Whitman's copy of the *Broadway Journal* (20 December 1845), in which Poe himself made the revision from "putrescence" found in all other appearances. It is now regarded as the most authoritative text of the story.

12. "The Cathedral Crypt," *Marvel Tales* 1, No. 4 (March–April 1935). John Beynon Harris wrote more commonly under the pseudonym John Wyndham.

[300]   [ANS][1]

[Postmarked Auburn, Cal.,
5 April 1935]

Dear Éch-Pi-El:

Thanks for loan of highly interesting Rio de Janeiro epistle. . . . will write soon—am running a hospital single-handedly at present with both parents laid up. Sold *The Chain of Aforgomon*, *The Treader of the Dust*, *The Black Abbot*, and *Necromancy in Naat* to the capricious satrap of weirddom!!! *Out of the Eons* is damn good! Ngghh! Those eyes!

Klarkash-Ton

Notes

1. *Front:* Unidentified.

[301]   [ALS]

Summit of Mt. Ngranek[1]
—Hour of the Fog with the Eyes
[11 April 1935/RAS]

Dear Klarkash-Ton:—

Tremendously sorry to hear of the simultaneous illness of your parents, & hope the coming (if not already arrived) mildness of spring will aid in restoring both to health. I presume the accident of last year—the scalding with hot water—formed quite a tax on your mother's constitution. With two parents on your hands, your own programme must be an exhaustingly arduous one!

Abundant congratulations on your quadruple sale to Satrap Pharnabozus! That will keep his poor old rag from going entirely to seed. "The Last Hieroglyph" (which I greatly enjoyed in MS. last year) easily leads the April issue, with Howard Wandrei's "Hand of the O'Mecca" as a good second. This latter becomes extremely convincing through its convincing local colour. Quite a few Finns have settled in western Rhode Island—& some day it might be possible to devise some yarn linking their immemorial background of dark wizardry with the rocky, brooding hills of ancient New England. The Bernal story—about the duplicated man—uses an idea which I've long been entertaining. "Shadows of Blood" is a bewildering mass of historical error. *Huns* in *Caligula's* time . . . . Ædopol! I don't believe the tribe even *existed* then as a separate unit in the Tartar-Scythian welter of Central Asia! At any rate, the Romans never heard the name till over 300 years after Caligula—when the Huns, after pestering the Far East for a hell of a while, were turned back by the building of China's great wall & began to bother the west. They first appear in Roman history in A.D. 376, when—after licking the Goths & Alani—they settled in Thrace with the "permission" of the Eastern imperator Valens. Glad you like "Out of the Æons"—which is, as I may have mentioned, virtually an original story of mine. All that survives from the initial Heald outline (worthy Mme. H. never bothered to write out any actual text for it!) is the basic idea of a living brain discovered in an ancient mummy. I was certainly glad to see it get a Rankin drawing—the only one in the issue, if I mistake not.

Glad you found the Rio article of interest. Here is an article (which, like the various weird cuttings, you need not return) on *modern* Rio, by a Providence traveller & author—Marc T. Greene[2]—whose aunt is a lifelong friend of my mother & aunts. I surely wish I could get a sight of this fascinating town—so famous alike in its own right, & in the annals of Yankee seamanship.

The early spring which I mentioned seems to have been a sort of false start—since recent days have averaged rather chilly. Rains, gales, & even snowflakes yesterday. No further outings, therefore, to report. Plan to visit Edward H. Cole in Boston May 3–4–5—with side trips to ancient Marblehead, &c.—& surely hope the weather will be decent by then. The funeral cortege to Wilbraham has been postponed till May or June on account of Cook's uncertain programme.

Spent 48 solid hours transferring material to my new filing cabinets (both the 2 bought in January & 6 little fellows picked up last month), & as a result my miscellaneous junk is in better shape than at any other time within a quarter of a century. But even so, a hell of a lot still remains in cardboard boxes or piled on open shelves.

Galpin plans to visit New England for the first time next July. I shall certainly be glad to see the young rascal (now *33*—how time flies!)—my only first-hand glimpse having been during the memorable Cleveland conclave of 1922. He expects to come in a car with his wife & an academic colleague.

I lately read Gustav Meyrink's "The Golem"—lent me by little Ar-E'ch-Bei. The most magnificent weird thing I've come across in aeons! The cinema of the same title which I saw in 1921 was a mere substitute using the name—with nothing of the novel in it.[3] What a study in subtle fear, brooding hints of elder magic, & vague driftings to & fro across the borderline betwixt dream & waking! There are no *overt* monsters or miracles—just symbols & suggestions. As a study in lurking, insidious *regional* horror it has scarcely a peer. It does for the ancient, crumbling Prague ghetto what I vainly sought to do for rotting Newburyport in "The Shadow over Innsmouth." I had never seen the novel before, but mentioned it in my article as a result of having seen the cinema.

Now I perceive that I ought to have given it an even higher rating. If you haven't read it, you ought to get on Barlow's lending list. I've also read Merritt's "Creep Shadow"—which is pretty cheap beside "The Golem". Essentially popular pulp romance—though there are some vivid hints of cosmic *outsideness* & a splendid series of climactic tableaux.

Of the four little niggers at the neighbouring hostel, one—a delectable duplicate of his late brother Sam—remains. Mr. John Perkins . . . . all black except for a tiny white shirt-stud, playful & belligerent, & just beginning to purr! Some boy! He is a frequent guest at 66, & sends his regards to Simaetha. ¶ Hope to hear soon of improved health at Indian Hill. ¶ Yrs for the Black Sign—H P L

P.S. Did I mention reading Comte d'Erlette's new detective novel "3 Who Died"? Better than its predecessor. I didn't guess the outcome till p. 145 (out of 252). ¶ Also read Hugh Walpole's "Portrait of a Man With Red Hair." Sinister atmosphere, but no open supernaturalism. ¶ Old de Castro has just given me a copy of Baudelaire's letters—in French.

Notes

1. Alluding to "The Other Gods." The mountain was also cited in *The Dream-Quest of Unknown Kadath*, but CAS had not seen that work.

2. Marc T. Greene (1879–1966), son of Albert Rowland Greene and Anna Susan (Bissell) Greene.

3. *The Golem* (Deutsche Bioscop, 1915), directed by Paul Wegener; starring Paul Wegener, Henrik Galeen, and Lydia Salmonova.

[302]   [ALS, on stationery (and envelope) designed by R. H. Barlow]

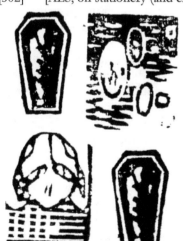

Tropic Jungle of Kham
—Hour that the Moon strikes
the Leprous Crystal
[Postmarked Daytona Beach, Florida
16 June 1935]

Hail, Klarkash-Ton, 1001st Tentacle of Tsathoggua!

▲   As I greet thee, I could call attention to the present happy duplication of last spring's temporary address . . . whereby the Patriarch E'ch-Pi-El is to be found in the Temple of Krang in the tropic jungle, & to be reached, as before, with the following formula: ℅ R. H. BARLOW, BOX 88, DE LAND, FLORIDA. ▲ Hope all is well on Indian Hill, & that the advent of milder weather is benefiting your parents. Sultan Malik has recently replaced good old Juggernaut with a new (or rather, rebuilt) Terraplane, & he & young Fred Anger may be invading your quarters before long if not headed off. ▲ Do you want to read a copy of Meyrink's tremendously powerful & subtle weird novel, "The Golem"—which Ar-E'ch-Bei is circulating along a select list? If so, drop a card to the present custodian . . . young Rimel, of Asotin, Wash. ▲ Enclosed is something Searight wanted me to send you . . . also some other odds & ends, including a view which includes 66 College St. ▲ This sadly reminds me that an ancient row of buildings on lower College Hill is now doomed—to make room for a new building of the R.I. School of Design. There are, however, mitigating features—since the bottom edifice of the row will be preserved, restored, & incorporated into the new edifice, whilst the latter will be of the purest Providence-Georgian design. Amongst the material preserved will be one of those ancient inn-yard archways, for which Providence is so famous. No other perfect specimen (there's a bricked-up one in Richmond & a boarded-up one in Philadelphia) exists in the U.S. ▲ More bad news for K.A.T. Rimel's snow-white Crom—after being exiled across the river because of alleged poultry depredations—has joined that mysterious company of the vanish'd to which Gen. Tabasco & Doodlebug already belong. Possibly the Peacock Sultan has told you of valiant Nimrod's 6-day disappearance. Down here in the jungle there are rumours that old Dood is still alive—gone native & roaming the steaming swamps in savage & uninhibited splendour. In Providence Mr. John Perkins is getting to be a peppy black devil—so martial in habits as to form a problem among the local felidae. He was a visitor of mine most days until my departure on the present visit. ▲ By the way—I think I've got you 3 Double Shadow customers recently. My last circular went to one of these—so if you have any more, I'm in line for a fresh supply.

▲ As for recent events—young Moe paid me another visit in his car April 27–8, & we put in quite a busy 2 days of exploration. On the 27th we visited ancient Newport—seeing 2 old windmills, a flock of sheep, the house of Bishop Berkeley (1729), the lofty cliffs, the strange rock cliff called "Purgatory", & the venerable town itself . . . with 1698 Quaker Meeting House, 1726 Anglican church, 1739 colony-house, 1749 library, 1760 market-house, 1763 Jews' synagogue, & private dwellings as old as 1675. The next day we went to the ancient whaling port of New Bedford, & thence to the Round Hills estate of Col. E. H. R. Green (son of the old miser Hetty Green) in S. Dartmouth, where the old whaling barque *Charles W. Morgan* (built 1841) is preserved at a wharf—solidly embedded in concrete as a permanent memorial exhibit. We went all over the vessel—which is tremendously fascinating. We then explored a region—S.E. R.I. & S. Mass—which I had never seen before in my life. Splendid unspoiled countryside with idyllic white-steepled villages of the old New England type. Later we returned to Providence, & I reluctantly saw my guest off toward Bridgeport. ▲ On May 3-4-5 I visited E. H. Cole in the

Boston zone, but was harassed by cold weather. I did, though, get some glimpses of Marblehead. ▲ Leedle Meestah Stoilingk—the Providence sojourner I told you of—is shortly to return to his beloved N'Yuk. He is a great admirer of yours, & recently took some photographs of the Thing that Stares & Stares & Stares! ▲ Which reminds me—on May 25 young Hornig (W.S. editor & late F F publisher) paid me a full day's visit. Nice chap—faintly suggesting young Melmoth, though of vaguely Semitic features. Bright as a dollar, & seems to appreciate Old Providence. Little Sterling was on hand—making quite a convention of the event.

▲ And now the big trip . . . invitation to visit R H B upon his return to De Land . . . & here I am! Started June 5, & stopped only at Fredericksburg & CHARLESTON. Feeling great—subtropical environment peps me up astonishingly! Don't know how long I'll stay—R H B urges 2 months! Bigger household this time—R H B's father & brother being home. Local felidae include High & Jack of last year, a few others, & a couple of patrician yellow Persians! Yrs by the Lethal seal. E'ch-Pi-El

[Enclosures]

[Postcard by R. H. Barlow, 15 June 1935; 3 clippings: "A Mysterious Island" (about Gillis Land), "Runes in Rhode Island" (about Norsemen in America), and a printed photograph of College Hill, Rhode Island, with HPL's note:] The house outlined in the ink circle is 66 College St. Large white building is John Hay Library.

[303]   [AHT]

For Klarkash-Ton, 7th Incarnation of Eibon the Unfathomable
Motto to be prefix'd to "The Seal'd Casket", by R. F. Searight, Esq., *Weird Tales,* March, 1935.

 . . . And it is recorded that in the Elder Times, Om Oris, mightiest of the Wizards, laid crafty snare for the demon Avaloth, & pitted dark magic against him; for Avaloth plagued the earth with a strange growth of ice & snow that crept as if alive, ever southward, & swallowed up the forests & the mountains. And the outcome of the contest with the demon is not known; but wizards of that day maintained that Avaloth, who was not easily discernible, could not be destroyed save by a great heat, the means whereof was not then known, although certain of the wizards foresaw that one day it should be. Yet, at this time the ice fields began to shrink & dwindle & finally vanished; & the earth bloomed forth afresh.
                    —Fragment from the Eltdown Shards.[1]

Notes

1. HPL's transcript of this epigraph to Searight's story does not mean that he wrote it. In a letter to Searight (15 January 1934) HPL states: "I like the fragment from the Eltdown Shards, too. . . . The only change I have made in the quotation is the substitution of a dissylable for a trisyllable in one place in the interest of good prose rhythm." *Letters to Richard F. Searight* 16–17. HPL presumably copied out the passage for CAS because he had mentioned that the *WT* appearance had omitted it.

[304]   [Envelope, JHL]

[June 1935]

P.S. Having held this letter to allow Barlow to enclose one of his own,[*] I've just learned from Sultan Malik of a relapse on your father's part. Please accept my sympathy—& the hope that the patient may soon be better. Hope you'll be ready for a visit from the Peacock Sultan & his young Vizier An-ghah before long.

[305]   [TLS, JHL]

Hour of the ninefold sounding of
the green brazen gong in Mho-Lhun,
citadel of the primal gods of doom.
[late June 1935]

Dear Éch-Pi-El:

I was doubly rejoiced to receive your letter and to learn that you are again domiciled in the temple of Krang, amid the subequatorial flora.

I should have written you several cycles ago, but, apart from the time-consuming domestic conditions, a sort of slump or doldrums appears to have overtaken me, and I've lacked the energy for letters even when I could have found the time. It's a damnable condition, no doubt partly due to the prolonged monotony, with small recreational escape or relief. You are certainly fortunate to be able to get away on trips and visits.

Thanks for the enclosures. Searight's quotation from the Eltdown Shards is a valuable contribution to the somewhat limited list of renderings of prehistoric lore. However, it is to be discreetly hoped that not *too much* of that lore will find translation into living languages. The clippings are interesting too. I must confess that I had never heard of the elusive Gillis Land,[1] which could afford a very fertile theme for imaginative fiction.

Sorry to learn the bad news from Ulthar, anent Crom. Let's hope that there are no vengeful poulterers in his hunting-grounds beyond the black River. As to Tabasco, it's plainly a case of exeunt in mysterium,[2] and no faintest rumor of his fate has ever reached me. Simaetha still flourishes, as does the redoubtable Son. I did some caretaking for the latter personage, while his mistresses were away recently in the Yosemite; and I can testify that his appe-

---

*which he hasn't finished yet! I give him up!

tite, though sufficiently robust, is not equal to the capacity of Dame Simaetha. Some day, if I ever come into a fortune, I'm going to find out just how much liver she would consume at a sitting! No, I hadn't heard about Nimrod's six day absence. He must have been out for big game!

A recent card from the White Peacock hints that his trip Auburnward will have to be postponed. I'm sorry, since I had looked forward to seeing him as well as the Berkeley "fan," Fred Anger. Maybe they'll make it later in the season.

Thanks for Ar-Ech-Bei's offer of The Golem. However, I read the book several years ago, when it was loaned to me, by a young friend in the Bay region. I agree with you that it is a most consummate and eerily haunting study in strange atmosphere; probably one of the best things of the kind ever written.

My parents are a little better, and I am trying to settle down to some writing. My mother's condition, however, is one of settled feebleness, with seriously impaired eyesight; and no great or permanent improvement can be hoped for. My father, too, has a condition of high-blood pressure and "pipestem" arteries, and has to guard against much exertion. It all puts me "in a spot," since there is no one to whom I can delegate the job of housekeeping, etc. There are no near neighbors, and none at all whom I'd care to ask for any favors.

By the way, I have taken up carving as a spare-time diversion; though of course the spare time is none too abundant. The materials used so far, are a sort of talc or steatite from the Kilaga mine where Price got some specimens for Morton; and bits of mineralized dinosaur bone (of which I once sent you some exemplars) from Clifford Gap. Also I've used a yellowish claylike material which I rather suspect was originally dinosaur steak, since it occurs in combination with the aforesaid bone. Under separate cover I am sending you a little carving of Cthulhu in d.b., also, a cameo depicting one of the hyperborean wizards (Om Omris [*sic*], perhaps) in d.b. The latter is for Ar-Ech-Bei. The top shelf of my bookcase of weird fiction is now guarded by sundry teraphim, including The Archetype (pale grey rhyolite) The Blue Goddess (pale blue talc) The Ghoul (light purplish talc) St. Anthony, Eumolpas, The Satyr, The One-Eyed Simulachre (mottled reddish-brown and red and white talc) and The Hippocentaur (dinosaur bone) Also, there is a tiny head of Eibon in d.b., and a mask of Tsathoggua in cherry-gum, and several still unnamed entities, two of which I have painted in gold and black. The mottled talc, in especial, lends itself to grotesquery. Some day if I ever have the time and the tools, I'd like to try working some of the local igneous rocks, which are very hard and close-grained, and would probably take a high polish, like porphyry. The rhyolite pebble with which I experimented was partly decomposed, and not so difficult to work; but the center was hard as hell, and I had to do the finishing touches with a file! Granite would be easy compared to some of this stuff on Indian Hill; but any sculpture wrought from it certainly should be permanent, relatively speaking. I've no ambition to make life-size sculptures;

and, I think, will always confine myself to small heads and statuettes. Large sculpture, in my opinion, has no proper place except as an architectural adjunct.

I'm enclosing a line for Ar-E'ch-Bei.

Yours, by the Shemhamphoresh,[3] the ineffable Name,

Klarkash-Ton

[P.S.] I find, to my consternation, that I've not returned the W. H. Tupper letter, and inclose it herewith, with apologies for the untoward delay. Keep the enclosures of clippings and poems, or give them to Ar-Ech-Bei.

Notes

1. A mysterious Arctic island, sighted and named in 1707 by the Dutch captain Cornelius Gillis.
2. I.e., *Omnia exeunt in mysterium* ("All things resolve into a mystery"), a medieval expression.
3. A Tannaitic term describing a hidden name of God in Kabbalah. Cf. CAS, "Cycles," l. 14: "He calls upon Shem-hamphorash, the nameless Name."

[306]   [ANS; Grill 508][1]

[Postmarked De Land, Fla.,
1 July 1935]

[. . .]: Thanks effusively & overwhelmingly for the two nameless 'eikons' which arrived this afternoon. Iä! Shub-Niggurath! The Goat with a thousand young! […] if one is for A_____ [. . .] with a sigh. ¶ [Still having a great time &] feeling like a prize fig[hter. Some time] ago we explored a strange [tropical river—]Black Water Creek—where [canopies of] cypresses _____ amidst [festoons of moss &] palms with twisted, writhing [roots lean] over the edge of the glassy stream [in] a scene like the Congo or Amazon[, with] pallid flowers & fungi in the [floor of] the twilight forest aisles, & lush [creepers] interhung with ghoulish ___. [Almost] like that river at Silver Springs which I [described] last year . . . but I enjoyed it more [because] we had a slow rowboat instead of [a fast] launch. ¶ All hands [went to ____] last Friday. ¶ Hope all [flourishes in] Averoigne. Thanks again for [the two] eidola from the Caves of Ng[ranek]. ¶ Yrs for the ___ Image of T[hebes?],
Ech-Pi-El

Notes

1. *Front:* Unidentified.

[307]   [ALS, JHL]

Jungle Temple of Krang—
Hour of the Stirring in the Lake
[25 July 1935][1]

Dear Klarkash-Ton

Your welcome epistle arrived soon after the sending of my card—& I immediately (as I feared I'd have to!) turned over the Om Oris bas-relief to my gifted young host. Meanwhile I am exulting in your truly splendid interpretation of Cthulhu, & appreciating with utmost keenness the genius you display in your new aesthetic field. Bless my soul, but is there *any* limit to your accomplishments? The dinosaurian medium adds to the exotic charm of your achievement—& I reflect with tantalisation upon those teraphim in varied media which you describe so alluringly. I hope you'll eventually be able to secure photographs of these things & circulate them amongst the gang—for it would be a pity if no idea of the recent triumphs could be generally diffused. The titles sound alluring in the extreme—& the medium in each case seems delightfully appropriate. Those ebony-&-gold effects must be fascinating—& I wish you luck in your experiments with harder rock materials. Miniature sculpture certainly has infinite possibilities, though I am not quite as severe on life-size effects as you are. However—I agree that for *fantastic* subjects a smaller size is distinctly preferable . . . except in the case of sphinxes, &c. . . . & I suppose they do fall, as you suggest, largely within the architectural field. It is interesting to compare your sculptural work with that of my multi-gifted host . . . . . photographs of whose elephant-god & Cthulhu bas-relief I shewed you (or he shewed you—I forget which) last year. He *models from clay*, working in a plastic medium, whilst you *carve* from solid substances. The two methods, despite a superficial similarity of results, are really vastly different in method & technique—& produce differences in effect which the discriminating can recognise. Yours is really the more classic & traditional art. Since doing the pieces known to you, Ar-E'ch-Bei has modelled a curious monster—suggested by the prehistoric saurians—which he calls "Groonta". Sooner or late he'll have to get it photographed & send around prints—it's really great stuff. Well—again, thanks for the dinosaurian Cthulhu . . . . & pray accept Ar-E'ch-Bei's unstinted gratitude for the sinister Om Oris.

You certainly have been undergoing a trying & exhausting experience, & I am glad to hear that your parents shew some signs of improvement. I wish that their recovery might be more complete—& indeed hope that summer may give them added strength & comfort—but any amelioration is welcome enough. Too bad something can't be done about the excess of work which falls on you. Would it be possible to get some sort of helper who would piece out in exchange for his board & meals? Certainly, the weight of the whole establishment must be a tremendous burden—a burden so heavy that I wonder how you can carry it & continue your aesthetic activities at the same time! I would be simply helpless under such a load. What a shame that you can't manage a rest or vacation trip of some sort!

Hope Sultan Malik & his young vizier An-Ghah will get around to Averoigne before long. Nimrod's absences have been fewer since the 6-day jaunt, but the other morning he returned from an all-night session completely covered with tar & so full of some unknown nourishment that he omitted one of his usual Gargantuan meals . . . an almost unprecedented thing for him! No word from Crom . . . he & Tabasco & Doodlebug must be absent on some pilgrimage beyond the reach or dreams of man. Glad that Mother Simaetha remains hale & hearty, & that good grey Son has such kindly & sympathetic care during the absence of his home folks. The Barlovian felidae send their profoundest compliments to their brethren of Averoigne. Jack—he of the snake-bite experience of last year—is Doodlebug's successor as president of the local Kappa Alpha Tau chapter, though the luxurious indoor Persians Cyrus & Darius probably claim a greater share of human attention.

California seems to be getting quite dominant in weird-dom. Did I tell you of the plan of Anger & L. C. Smith to issue certain weird items on a mimeograph? They say they have a complete index of W.T.—from the beginning to June '35—half finished, & their second scheduled item is my "Fungi from Yuggoth."[2] Whether they ever get to the point of issuing the latter remains to be seen.

I liked Searight's extracts from the Eltdown Shards very much—but agree that too liberal quotations from such cryptic volumes might decrease the mystical reputation of the latter. Also—the indefinite multiplication of such books is not wholly to be encouraged. Young Bloch (whose steady placements in W.T. bespeak a budding pulpist success) has been especially prolific in creating monstrous hypothetical tomes . . . such as Ludvig Prinn's *De Vermis Mysteriis*, Comte d'Erlette's *Cultes des Goules*, &c. &c. &c. His latest—if I recall aright—is the Seven Somethings-or-other of Elipus the Learned . . . or words to that effect.

Glad you are familiar with "The Golem"—if ever you care to re-read it, Ar-Ech-Bei's copy is at your disposal. It surely is one of the finest & subtlest atmospheric studies I have ever seen. By the way—Ar-Ech-Bei intends to write you soon (if he doesn't enclose something in this envelope) & thank you at first-hand for Om Oris. Another ambition in his young head is to publish your next volume of collected poems . . . . "Incantations", I believe you mean to call it.

There was no need to worry about the W. H. Tupper letter—nobody else was waiting to see it. It was not as colourful a document as Brother George's hearty specimen, but its time & place & stationery give it a certain antiquarian charm & importance. I have placed it amongst the material which I shall send home to myself ere I quit these subtropical shades.

Thanks tremendously for the two new poems, which R H B & I perused with equal pleasure & appreciation. They hold all the ebon magic customarily associated with your pen, & weave an atmosphere that enchants as it engulfs. I surely hope that another collection of your verse can appear before long—

whether under Ar-Ech-Bei's auspices or otherwise.

I am grateful, too, for the cuttings—which I am saving, & which I will return on request if they chance to be loans rather than gifts. All are interesting—& the one on Malta is tremendously fascinating to me because of my previous interest in the prehistoric subterranean temples which honeycomb the rocky bulk of that ancient & cryptical island. As you may recall, an article in the Geographic on the rock temples of Malta[3] was *half* the source of my old yarn "The Nameless City" . . . . the other half being Thomas Moore's "Epicurean."[4] While articles in the *American Weekly* are seldom to be taken literally, it is obvious that much has been unearthed in Maltese archaeology since 1920. Proof of a really evolved civilisation in the Mediterranean region as early as 7000 B.C. would certainly upset many settled nations of cultural distribution—though it probably would not alter the dominant idea that the *first* seal of civilisation was in upland Asia—with opposite lines of advance which reached India, China, Polynesia, & prehistoric America on the one hand, & Babylonia, Egypt, & the Mediterranean on the other hand. The worship of *fat women* was certainly comic—as seen in retrospect. Personally, I think I prefer ibis-headed monstrosities to the types suggested in the Maltese carvings! The Hedges article on Atlantis[5] forms a fairly typical summary of the arguments of certain enthusiasts, but does not seriously challenge the accepted conclusions of geology & anthropology. "Atlantis" remains a myth—the real probability being that cultural elements from the old world reached the new by way of India & Polynesia.

The articles on serums & gland extracts have all sorts of fictional possibilities—some of which have been cleverly used already, while others await the hand of the capable expert. The dinosaur track article is full of alluring mystery. I surely hope the monster in question can be found—even though you won't be likely to get hold of his bones for sculptural purposes!

Well—my visit continues to be a thoroughly delightful event, & threatens to drag itself out to unprecedented lengths. I never saw another family as stupendously—awesomely—hospitable as the Barlows. I was supposed to go north & meet a friend (M. W. Moe of Milwaukee) who is coming east this month, but this proposition was vetoed so vociferously by both Bob & the colonel that I find myself staying indefinitely on. The crowd has lost one congenial member in the person of Bob's brother Wayne—a 2nd Lieut. at Ft. Sam Houston, Texas—whose furlough expired & who therefore had to return to the scene of his martial labours. I guess I mentioned that Ar-Ech-Bei was building a cabin across the lake to house his varied activities. He chose a spot shadowed by giant oaks (the regular northern & British kind—*not* the live-oak of the South), & hence tentatively called Druid Grove. The edifice is now virtually complete, & printing operations (results whereof you will see in time) are going on within. Last week I cleared a road through the scrub palmetto wilderness from the landing to the road leading to the grove—an exploit to which a pair of badly blistered hands affords eloquent testimony. We also read, write, revise, classify books, &c &c. Ar-E'ch-Bei has just read Huysmans' "A Rebours" for the first time—a gift from W. Paul Cook. On June 17 we visited a fascinating place—*Black Water Creek,* a tropical river whose lush scenery suggests the Congo, Amazon, & other exotic streams found in history & legend. I guess I told you about this on my recent card. It winds through a steaming jungle of tall, moss-draped cypresses, whose grotesque, twisted roots writhe curiously at the water's edge. Palms lean precariously over the bank, & vines & creepers strow the black dank earth of the bordering forest aisles. Sinister sunken logs loom up at various points, & in the forest pallid flowers & leprous fungi gleam whitely through a perpetual twilight. It is much like the river at Silver Springs of which I wrote you last year—though I enjoyed it even more because of the more leisurely observing conditions. At Silver Springs I was whizzed ahead in a launch; this time we (Ar-Ech-Bei, Wayne, & I) went along slowly in a rowboat. Each bend of the tortuous stream brought to light some unexpected vista of tropical luxuriance, & we absorbed the spectacle to the full. Serpents & alligators were somewhat in evidence—though none came near our boat. I hope for more trips of this kind, since I find myself especially sensitive to the beauty of subtropical scenery. All this, though, would doubtless be tame to your father—who I think you said has travelled in equatorial South America.

Before I forget it—have you any more of those Prose Pastels which you let Hornig use in the F F? Young Donald Wol[l]heim, 801 West End Ave., N.Y. City, is now editor of *The Phantagraph,* official organ of the Terrestrial Fantascience Guild, & is eager to duplicate the exploits of the F F.[6] Anything from you would delight him inexpressibly. ¶ Yrs for the Chant of Bal Sagoth—[7]
E'ch-Pi-El

P.S. It would delight old Bill Lumley if you were some day to carve an elephant head for him.

[P.P.S.] Just got new *Marvel Tales.* Not so hot! Anger & Price speak of visit as imminent.

Notes

1. RAS had written a postmark date of 24 January 1936

2. The "index" did not contain alphabetical listings of authors and titles; it was merely a running list of the tables of contents. The planned edition of *Fungi from Yuggoth* did not appear.

3. William Arthur Griffiths, "Malta: The Halting Place of Nations," *National Geographic* 37, No. 5 (May 1920): 445–78.

4. The novel *The Epicurean* (1827) relates the story of Alciphron, leader of the Epicurean sect in Athens in the 3rd century BCE, on his journey to Egypt to learn the secret of immortality.

5. F. A. Mitchell-Hedges (1882–1959), known as "Mike Hedges," had sought the "lost city of Atlantis" in the area of modern Belize.

6. CAS wrote ten "prose pastels," perhaps a nod to Stuart Merrill's *Pastels in Prose.* Only the

first five appeared in *FF* under the heading "Prose Pastels." All ten appeared so designated in the *Acolyte*. None appeared in *Phantagraph*.

7. Alluding to Robert E. Howard's "The Gods of Bal-Sagoth."

[308] [Enclosure: Proof page of "In Mayan Splendour," from *The Goblin Tower*]
[RAS 2.79/7.26]

Sample of what we're doing for Sonny Belknap

[309] [ANS][1]

[Postmarked Charleston, S.C.,
26 August 1935]

Hail, Chosen of Tsathoggua!

In ancient Charleston at last—was so anxious to get here that I cut out Savannah! It surely is great to be among familiar English colonial antiquities again—white steeples, fanlighted doorways, railed double flights of steps, &c.—after such a session with Old Spain. But Charleston looks *northern* after Florida—less moss on the oaks, fewer and smaller palmettos, no jungle effects, no rainy season, &c. Having a good time wandering among the tombs & other reliquiae of the past. Staying at the Y—Aug. 26–7–8–9 . . . too broke to hold out any longer. Only momentary stops afterward—then 66!

Ar-E'ch-Bei paid me a surprise visit in St. Augustine Friday—coming up by 'bus from Dayton to say a second adieu. I shewed him most of the San Agustinian sights.

Hope things are getting along at least tolerably on Indian Hill. Old Bill Lumley immensely appreciates the carved sorcerer you sent him. Hope you'll photograph your local teraphim & give the gang a look at the prints.

Well—in less than a week I'll be up north! I dread the thought of plunging into cold weather!

Yours for the Outer Shadow—
E'ch-Pi-El

Notes

1. *Front:* Unidentified.

[310] [ANS by Donald Wandrei, HPL, and Frank Belknap Long, JHL][1]
[Postmarked New York, N.Y.,
7 September 1935]

Clark—Will write you letter soon. Hope ill-health in your family has now turned to a brighter picture. HPL visiting me, a perfect guest, and the essence of phenomenal health after his long sojourn in Florida. Needless to say, he did *not* accompany me to this bar, where I am sipping a beer! . . . . . . As ever . . . . Donald

---

I'm glad young Melmoth exculpates Grandpa from the suspicion of having patronised the bar above which he sleeps. Having a delightful time seeing all the gang—though the north seems anomalously chilling & barren after the tropics. Visited all the Poe shrines in Richmond, & had a day in Washington & a morning in Philadelphia. Hope all is improving in Averoigne! ¶ Yrs for the Black Pillar—Ech Pi El

---

I am not ashamed to confess that I think it an excellent bar.
Greetings
    F B L Jr.

Notes

1. *Front:* Julius'—New York's oldest bar.

[311]   [ANS][1]

[Postmarked Auburn, Cal.,
7 September 1935]

Dear Éch-Pi-El: This view will give you some idea of the older and more atmospheric part of Auburn.

    I'll write soon—have been more or less under the weather, with domestic conditions little if at all improved. Have managed to execute a few more eidola, and should have some of the best ones photographed ere long. I'll be glad to hear from Ar-E'ch-Bei, and am hoping that his plan for printing my verses will materialize. Yrs in the faith of the Old Ones,
    Klarkash-Ton

Notes

1. *Front:* Unidentified.

[312]   [TNS, on four postcards][1]

Meridian of the black plenilune
[c. mid-October 1935]

Dear Éch-Pi-El:
    I had meant to acknowledge your card of condolence before

this, but seem to have fallen into a deplorable habit of general procrastination. Letters, even the most necessary ones, seem to remain unwritten.

The blow of my mother's passing has been a heavy one for us;[2] but it is some consolation that she went with little or brief suffering. She was able to walk about and talk within a few minutes of the final stroke. My father has borne up pretty well, all things considered; and I have been compelled to take a little care of myself, and have now gained back some of the weight and energy which I lost during the summer.

Writing has been in abeyance; but I have managed to do a few more carvings. It is surprising what one can do, by the utilization of odd moments that would otherwise go to waste. I really think that these little sculptures have about saved my life, since they have given me a new interest and preoccupation at a time when I needed it most. Some of the results obtained are so unusual (I have worked out various modes and tricks of treatment, including a hardening process for the finished carvings) that I believe the sculptures would puzzle many professed experts. I'll have the promised pictures taken soon and will send you copies. Later, I'll loan you a few actual specimens by express, if you'd care to see them. It occurs to me that we might have a little fun with Morton by submitting some of the most ancient and mysterious-looking ones for his appraisal, with an appeal for information as to the problematic art-age and civilization to which they belong! However, it probably wouldn't do to let him think that *I* have any connection with the carvings!

Two pieces, Dagon and The Outsider, were inspired by your stories. I think I shall have to be unselfish and make you a gift, presently, of The Outsider. Other pieces, done during the past summer and fall, are entitled: The Goblin, Saber-Toothed Nightmare, Devil-Chick, Atlantean Warrior, Lemurian Ghost, Swamp-Feeder, The Sorcerer Transformed (a Goya subject), Asmodeus, the Black Pan, the Great Head, the Gargoyle, Temple Guardian, Young Elemental, Ouroboros, Hyperborean Snake-Eater, Chinese Magistellus; The Blemmye, Maiden Blemmye,[3] The Inquisitor Morghi, The Terminus, Thibetan Demon (a Janus-faced horror) and The Death-God of Poseidonis.

Ar-Ech-Bei sent me The Shunned House. He has certainly done a creditable job on the binding! The story itself holds up superbly on re-reading. The disciple of Krang seems determined to put out my Incantations, and I certainly hope that his plan will materialize.

Yours for the eating of the black lotos,
            Klarkash-Ton

Notes

1. *Front:* Unidentified.

2. Mary Frances Gaylord Smith died on 9 September 1935.

3. The Blemmyes were a nomadic Nubian tribal kingdom that existed from at least

600 BCE to the 8th Century CE. They became fictionalized as a legendary race of aceph-
alous monsters who had eyes and mouths on their chests.

[313]   [ANS; RAS 7, p. 10]¹

[Postmarked Boston, Mass.,
c. 17 October 1935]

[HPL's portion as reproduced is illegible.]

Sympathy and affectionate regards from your old friend
Sam Loveman

Notes

1. *Front:* Unidentified.

[314]   [ALS, University of Kansas]

Slope of Inaccessible Ngranek
—Hour of the Night-Gaunts' Flight
[23 October 1935]

Dear Klarkash-Ton—
                    Delighted to receive your recent pictorial communica-
tions, which still further augments my visual knowledge of brooding Averoigne.
You have meanwhile, no doubt, received the joint card from Es-El & myself,
despatched from the ancient lanes of Boston. Es-El's all-too-brief visit to New
England was a very welcome event, & I hope a half-promised repetition may
occur next month. He is now conducting an independent book business, & has
occasion to look over the stock of sundry bookstalls in these parts.
    I am glad to hear that your mother's final illness was unattended with
grave suffering, or with any long period of prostration. The blow to you &
your father can well be imagined, & you surely need the rest & recuperation
you are now getting. It is really quite providential that your sculptural avoca-
tion developed when it did—being finally under way when the need for just
such an occupation became greatest. With time & philosophic readjustment
your energies will increase—so that before many weeks I trust I shall be hearing of new stories from the crest of Indian Hill.
    I shall certainly be most tremendously grateful for the loan of a repre-
sentative array of Tsathogguan teraphim! It wouldn't be a bad idea to send
such a collection on the rounds of the gang, as you did with the crate of
paintings back in 1926. Certainly, devotees like Ar-E'ch-Bei & Melmoth &
old Bill Lumley ought to have a chance to see this recent & striking phase of
Averoignian genius! And meanwhile, as I've said before, I'll be infinitely glad
to see some photographs of the mysterious eikons. From your remarks on

the various pieces—& the processes you have devised in connexion with them—I feel certain that they have a strange & disturbing imaginative glamour. The idea of putting over a hoax on Morton is surely an alluring one—which might well be carried out with a little coöperation from Sonny Belknap or some other denizen of the Noveboracense[1] area. Or perhaps young Ar-E'ch-Bei could send some cryptic & aeon-worn specimen to James Ferdinand by mail—with glib tales of its having been found at the bottom of a shallow Florida lake, or in a reef long submerged by the boundless Atlantic . . . . . Ar-E'ch-Bei is quite a boy for hoaxes . . . . as is also little Kenneth Sterling, the Child-Wonder of Israel. And I'll wager that certain of your eidola would make even a seasoned archaeologist do a little puzzling & guessing before settling down to hard-boiled scepticism! I feel honoured that two of the images should have drawn their names from my fictional attempts—& would certainly form a classic example of Cthulhueal gratitude if, as you suggest, "The Outsider" were to come my way as a gift! Your "Cthulhu" already occupies a place of honour among similar tri-dimensional bizarreries on the top of a cabinet, with an old-fashioned bell glass over it. The names of some of the recent teraphim seize the eye & the imagination in a most tenacious way . . . & I surely hope that such gentry as The Swamp-Feeder, the Blemmye, & the Sabre-Toothed Nightmare may be included in the travelling loan exhibit.

Glad to hear that Ar-E'ch-Bei has sent you "The Shunned House". His skill in binding is steadily on the increase; & when he has all the apparatus he needs, he will be able to produce some notable work. No doubt I told you of the fine leather copy he bound for me in Washington—surprising me with it when I struck De Land last June.[2] I'm strongly hoping that "Incantations" will get under way soon. Select your poems with care—& be sure to demand proofreading privileges. Despite the marks of inexperience in Ar-E'ch-Bei's earlier typography, I feel confident that he can give you a better-looking volume than the *Auburn Journal* could. When it is printed & bound, Es-El can probably utilise his bookselling facilities to get it actively on the market—cataloguing it in his typical & inimitable way.

Meanwhile I trust that Krang's acolyte has duly sent you his amateur paper, *The Dragon-Fly*, containing among other things some selected aphorisms of yours. To my mind this is the best amateur paper of the season—being altogether without crude matter. It is just what we need for the qualitative renaissance now under way—& I hope the Lord Garoth will carry out his intention of making it a regular quarterly. Amateurdom is slow in getting started this year. The September *National Amateur* has not yet appeared, & the critical bureau (under the veteran Truman J. Spencer) was so tardy that I stepped in & rustled up a set of reports from the various reviewers—including myself.[3]

No doubt cards &c. have kept you in touch with the major events of the weird circle. Price is off for Mexico, with visits to Two-Gun Bob & to New Orleans as subsidiary features. Petaja is entering the U. of Montana at Missoula, & Cook has gone to E. St. Louis, Ill. to coöperate in a neighbourhood newspaper venture. *The Phantagraph*—would-be successor to the late F F—is out, & contains some commendable things despite general crudity. Young Brobst is married, & is taking a course at Brown in addition to his nursing work at the Chapin Hospital. Rumours darkly hint at the coming demise of *Fantasy Magazine*—or its merger with Hill-Billy's spasmodic *Marvel Tales*. Searight has an infant son, & Howard Wandrei has succumbed to the hymeneal yoke. Old Bill Lumley is turning to prose fiction—I've just fixed up a yarn for him, in exchange for which he has given me a delightful translation of the Book of the Dead—by Sir E. Wallis Budge. [I meant to make Ar-Ech-Bei do the typing; but found that the MS. could be read by no one but myself, so had to do the job myself. By a singular stroke of irony, Old Bill's title is "The Diary of Alonzo *Typer*"!!!] M. le Comte d'Erlette's new detective novel—"Sign of Fear"—is out, & he has sent me a copy. I suppose I must read it & express my pleasure & approbation to the author.

Recent W T issues average only about 2 good yarns per issue. In Sept., "Vulthoom" & the Bloch attempt; in Oct. "Cold Grey God" & the Flanders piece. The poor old rag certainly is going down hill . . . . . not that it had very far to go in the first place!

My "Shadow Out of Time" is going the rounds, & will reach you sooner or later. Hope it won't prove a bore—I can't like it very well.

New England has enjoyed an unusually warm autumn, so that my season of activity has been somewhat protracted. I think I wrote you of my sessions with Cole Sept. 20–23—during which we visited the spectral "Dunwich" country, & had an enjoyable day in the maritime realm of Cape Cod. Oct. 8 my aunt & I had a ride to *New Haven*, which gave me my first opportunity to study that ancient city in detail. In the 7½ hrs. at my disposal I covered most of the high spots—old buildings, museums, botanic gardens, & general landscape & architectural effects. It is a spacious, sleepy city grouped around an enormous green whereon stand three ancient churches in a row. Not as many colonial houses as in Providence, but a great deal of centuried traditionalism in the atmosphere. Elm-shaded streets, mansions of the 1830 period, & the omnipresent shadow of Yale University . . . . whose oldest surviving building dates from 1752. The *new* Yale quadrangles have a peculiar fascination—being utterly perfect fac-similes of Gothic & Georgian architecture. Shutting out the external modern world, they form neat, self-sufficient little oases of the past—so that a stroll through them is like walking bodily into a dream. I spent hours just circling about in them & absorbing imaginative colour.

Then—just a week ago—Es-El blew in on the N.Y. boat at 6 a.m. . . . . pausing for a brief session at #66 before we both departed for ancient Boston. Much of our time at the Hub was taken up with bookstall-combing, but we also worked in a good deal of sightseeing & museum-visiting. Enclosed is just a glimpse of what we saw at the Mus. of Fine Arts. Returning to Providence Friday noon, we made the rounds of local bookstalls—bringing to light several fine ones about which I had not known before. It seems that a new sort of booksellers' row is growing up in the western part of town . . . . I must take Morton there next summer.

All this vacationing has certainly played hell with my programme! It was weeks before I got all my accumulated newspapers read up, & even now a whole stack of borrowed books (including the Wells–Huxley "Science of Life") patiently awaits my perusal. Meanwhile the Kappa Alpha Tau is doing well. At this moment a drowsy, overgrown (but still playful) mass of black fur in the adjacent easy-chair purrs his regards to the ancient Simaetha . . . a mass which has expanded from the tiny fistful of last February: little Johnny Perkins! Johnny spends most of his time over here—& I always treat him with catnip. So far he has not formally joined the fraternity—indeed, he shews an embarrassing lack of respect for old black & white Pres. Randall . . . offering to fight rather than fraternise with that amiable patriarch!

With every good wish, & thanks in advance for any glimpses of the teraphim which I may get—

Yrs by the Unspoken Name of the Chasm—E'ch-Pi-El

Notes

1. Adjectival form of Novum Eboracum (New York).

2. RHB inscribed the book "For HPL—who only wrote it—with the compliments of the binder. R. H. B. June 9, 1935. On the occasion of his second visit" (Squires, *H. P. Lovecraft and the Lovecraft Circle,* 4). Kenneth W. Faig, Jr. points out (in *Lovecraftian Voyages* 58) that "This copy was discovered among HPL's effects by Mrs. Gamwell in 1938 or so and returned by her to Barlow."

3. "Some Current Amateur Verse."

[315]   [ANS; *HK*][1]

[Postmarked Providence, R.I.,
28 October 1935]

Iä! Shub-Niggurath! What a galaxy of brooding malevolence! Thanks endlessly for the dream-stirring sketches—which are splendid in themselves, beside making one eager to behold their carven originals. I think the star of the bunch is the Poseidonian Death-God—which haunts the imagination in a way not easy to describe. But all are so fascinating that the decision is a close one. Later I hope to see more of these views—as well as some photographs & originals. The crypts of Pnath are surely yielding forth a fresh exhumation of primal horror! ¶ Young Schwartz, who has set up as a literary agent, & to whom—at his eloquent solicitation—I last month entrusted the "Mts. of Madness" MS. as a mere detail of unhoping routine, has just staggered me by announcing that

Astounding Stories has *accepted* the damn'd thing! At last . . . after 4 years & a half! If his information is correct, I shall be the gainer by some 315 bucks after the deduction of his 10% commission. I shall be glad to see this item (so contemptuously rejected by Wright) in print at last, & hope Street & Smith won't mess it up too badly. It represents the most serious work I have ever done, & its prior rejection was a very discouraging influence. ¶ Glad you've received *The Dragon-Fly*—which is certainly good work for a beginner. Now for "Incantations"! ¶ Warm weather continues—I was out for a walk both yesterday & the day before, & may go today! And in 3 days comes the hellish Sabbat! ¶ Yrs. by The Seventh Sign of Yogh—Ech-Pi-El.

Notes

1. *Front:* Unidentified.

[316]   [ALS]

Cave of the Shining Trapezohedron[1]
—Hour of the Purple Glow
[10 November 1935][2]

Dear Klarkash-Ton:—

I am starting this before receipt of the cryptic eidola, & will report on the latter in a postscript ere the envelope be sealed. Count on an old man's honesty to ensure Ar-E'ch-Bei's safe receipt of the Snake-Eater—sight of which I shall vastly appreciate. Needless to say, the youthful recipient will be as delighted as I shall be with the Outsider! Your later edition of the eater—with his ample & toothsome morsel—sounds doubly fascinating!

Additional drawings—& photographs when the latter are ready—will surely be gratefully received. And the still subsequent loan-exhibit of *originals* will certainly form an event! It would surely be fun to give good old James Ferdinand a bit of puzzlement with the Black Dog & the Nameless Entity. W. Paul Cook ought send them from East St. Louis, whither he has migrated on a newspaper venture . . . . he dwells in sight of the prehistoric Cahokia Mounds!

Hope "Incantations" material will soon be ready for the young publisher. I don't think the small size of the volume will worry him—indeed, with his small hand-press he is hardly equipped for large-scale work. He can print only one good-sized page at a time. Have you seen "The Goblin Tower" as yet? I set up a good deal of that myself last summer. The typography is nothing to brag about, but Bob learns by experience & you'll find better work in "Incantations". I'll try to make him send me the proofs. Slower work, but worth it for the sake of accuracy. Belknap was astonished & delighted when the complete & elaborately bound "Goblin Tower" burst on his sight—though it came at a rather tragic time for the Long household, Sonny's aunt having been instantly killed in a motor accident near Miami Oct. 20.[3]

Thanks abundantly for the addition to my Auburn gallery. Bless my soul, but you really have a delightfully quaint old town—for after all, 1849 reaches back to a world in which the 18th century tradition was scarcely extinct in many phases. The New Orleans Hotel has any admirable air of quaintness—as indeed have many of the other buildings in Averoigne's older sections. By mentally piecing some of the cards together, one can get an excellent idea of the Woods' Dry Diggings of George Tupper's time. For instance—a previous card had shewn that N.O. Hotel from the *other* direction, while there are diverse views of Commercial St. & the Round Corner. I feel that it would be easy to step back 85 years or so & meet George at the Post Office where the stage draws up! Incidentally, did I mention that I saw George's grave at Wilbraham when I was there with Cole last September? He has the finest stone of any of the Tuppers!

Well—I certainly was glad to see the "Mountains" accepted at last. But listen to this: *Astounding* has *also* taken my *new* story "The Shadow Out of Time"!! Can you beat it? Young Melmoth had submitted it without my knowledge. This brought $280.00. The dual incident is certainly one of the most encouraging experiences I've lately had—though I realise it amounts to no more than a pair of luck-shots, not at all likely to be repeated.

However, it doesn't take much to encourage an old man—so the other day I found myself writing a new story! "The Haunter of the Dark" is its present title, & I finished it yesterday. Don't know whether it's worth typing— but I'll read it over again. 24 pages of MS.—may come near 30 of double-spaced typing. Acting on the suggestion of somebody in the Eyrie, I dedicated it to young Bloch.[4] I'm killing him off in return for his delightful disposal of Grandpa in "The Shambler from the Stars." He left me spattered all over the room, but I leave him in neater shape—as a body sitting rigidly at a desk & gazing out a west window, with an expression of unutterable fear on the twisted features. The scene is in Providence, & the abode of the victim is #66—indeed, I've described the place a bit. This tale wouldn't be placeable anywhere save in W T—perhaps I'll let Wright see it after he's had a chance to reflect on the fate of the "Mountains."

Hope *The Dragon-Fly* with the Epigrams of Alastor duly reached you. I like the venture immensely, & hope Ar-Ech-Bei will keep it up. It is just what amateurdom needs at the present moment to assist in its qualitative renaissance. The typography shews an improvement over that of the Goblin Tower, representing substantial progress as a printer on the youthful editor's part.

Nov. W T could be worse—3 stories worth reading. I liked "The Way Home", by Paul Frederick Stern, very much. Never heard of the author before,[5] but he's certainly a good guy to keep one's eye on. Two-Gun & Sultan Malik also seen to advantage. Indeed, I like Malik's "Hand of Wrath" better than any other recent product of his.

Another *Unusual Stories* from Hill-Billy—& this issue has some very fair matter. Bloch's & Petaja's stories excellent, & Dilbeck's not so bad.[6] You'll note Petaja's Anglicised pseudonym of E. Theodore Pine. It's really a translation, for *Petaja* is the Finnish for pine-tree.

Incidentally, the proposed Rimel–Petaja successor to the F F seems to be reluctantly shelved. But the Shepherd–Wollheim *Phantagraph* will be worth watching. Many improvements are planned, & there will be an article by Two-Gun (probably serialised) on the prehistoric background of his Conan tales.[7]

Sultan Malik must be back from Mexico by this time. He revelled in Aztec temples & pyramids, & was held up 3 days by a landslide. Once on a rocky detour he had his gasoline tank ripped open, so that he had to mend it temporarily with chewing gum!

Warm weather hereabouts persisted all through October—vastly postponing my hibernation season. I was out nearly every afternoon—in the woods & fields with writing materials.

My black friend John Perkins of the Kappa Alpha Tau's younger generation is drowsing in a neighboring chair, & sends his regards to the venerable Simaetha. He is a very big boy now, but in many ways recalls the infinitesimal inky atom of last spring. Grandpa gives him catnip every time he comes to call, & he has developed a keen sense of gratitude—& anticipation. He now has 3 little brothers at the boarding-house, for all of whom good homes have been found. One coal-black, two black & white. I shall enjoy watching the furry mites until their age permits them to leave the maternal breast & migrate to their new abodes.

Later

After all, I've typed the new story, & here's a copy of it to set in circulation. Hope you won't think it's too trite & altogether impossible. Nor hurry at all about reading it—but when you're completely through with it you might send it along to Sultan Malik—who will surely be back in Redwood City by that time.

Still Later

Iä! Shub-Niggurath! The Goat With a Thousand Young! *They* have come!! Nggïh . . . nngh . . . . Thanks a thousand times—& infinite congratulations on the veritable masterpieces you have achieved! Both look as if they might have been exhumed from aeon-forgotten ruins in Mu or Cimmeria or Commoriom, & I'll wager I could give good old Mortonius a jolt with either of them! They catch a certain elusive spirit which no other modern grotesques I know of have caught. "The Outsider" reeks of the tomb & the nameless burrowers of night, while "The Snake-Eater" suggests whole cycles of hellish pre-human life. If Ar-Ech-Bei doesn't veritably gurgle over the latter, I'll resign from the priesthood of Azathoth! I'll forward the S.E. to its youthful recipient as soon as I've had a few days to admire it.

¶ Card from the Peacock Sultan in today's mail. He's still visiting Mashburn at Houston, & working on the deathless Pawang Ali.[8]

¶ Mr. Perkins isn't here today, but on the shed roof outside both the President & Vice-President of the Kappa Alpha Tau are sprawling. Warm weather continues, though it's foggy at present.

¶ Well—again, superabundant thanks & congratulations anent *Them!* "The Outsider" is going to have a prominent place in my decorative scheme. I ought to lend him to Ar-Ech-Bei, but don't want to spare him! Guess I'll make a photograph. ¶ Yrs for the Wood of Shaggai⁹—

—Ech-Pi-El

Notes

1. Alluding to "The Haunter of the Dark," which HPL had just completed.

2. RAS had dated the letter simply August 1935.

3. Mrs. William B. (Cassie) Symmes (1872–1935), for whom HPL ghostwrote the preface to *Old World Footprints* (1928). See David Goudsward, "Cassie Symmes: Inadvertent Lovecraftian," *Lovecraft Annual* No. 9 (2015): 130–35.

4. See B. M. Reynolds in "The Eyrie," *WT* 36, No. 5 (November 1935): 652: "Contrary to previous criticism, Robert Bloch deserves plenty of praise for *The Shambler from the Stars*. Now why doesn't Mr. Lovecraft return the compliment, and dedicate a story to the author?"

5. Not a new writer to *WT* at all; "Stern" was a pseudonym of Paul [Frederick] Ernst (1899–1985), a regular contributor. See letter 317.

6. *Unusual Stories* 1, No. 2 (Winter 1935): Robert Bloch, "The Black Lotus"; E. Theodore Pine (Emil Petaja), "The Two Doors"; Lionel Dilbeck, "The River Dwellers."

7. I.e., "The Hyborian Age," first published in the *Phantagraph* (February, August, October–November 1936) and then as a booklet (1938).

8. E. Hoffmann Price wrote several stories about the detective Pawang Ali for *Clues* and other mystery magazines.

9. Introduced in "The Haunter of Dark"—apparently a planet even more distant than Yuggoth.

[317]   [ALS]

Desert of Nizab-Yun—
Hour of the Black Mirage
[2 December 1935/RAS]

Dear Klarkash-Ton:—

Glad to hear that the "Haunter" didn't seem too impossible, & hope that others along the circuit may be equally lenient in their judgment. It does not satisfy me—indeed, I don't think that any *short* story can express in what I have to say nowadays. Every time I try to develop an idea it stretches out to novelette length unless forcibly restrained. Don't hurry about passing the MS. along—& by the way, if it is still with you, you might add to the circulation list (at the bottom) the name & address of honest Hill-Billy— *William Crawford, 122 Water St., Everett, Pa.* I have not yet tried this effusion on Wright, but would be willing to wager that he'll reject it when I do. I hope to get one or two more written before I do any submitting in this quarter. Meanwhile, however, I have let Hill-Billy try "Innsmouth" on *Astounding*—though without any expectation that it will be taken. This [text lost in crease] definitely removed from the science fiction field to be really eligible in the Tremaine sanctum. Still—the dual acceptance of "Mts." & "Shadow" has vastly encouraged me, so that I shall probably make further attempts in the same direction. The incident shews that *Astounding* is not as rigidly limited to purely scientific formula-yarns as I had feared. I hope you will try your luck with A S as soon as you have anything new to send, for the prompt payment on acceptance forms a delightful contrast to Wright's increasingly Gernsbackian tactics. Incidentally—I hope an up-turn in your health will speed the day of your next productive period, so that there will be no long gap between the stories now appearing & the new crop. I am looking forward to "Aforgomon" in the new W T—of which I haven't yet obtained a copy.

Thanks endlessly for the sketches of "Asmodeus" & "Chaugnar's Cousin". E'ch-Si-Kheh has spoken gratefully & enthusiastically of the former, & I shall insist on his shewing it to me when next I invade his metropolis. I shall on that occasion take along "Cthulhu" & "The Outsider" to shew the gang. I meant to shew them the former last summer, but made a mistake & sent it home from De Land. Which reminds me that I must send Ar-E'ch-Bei his Hyperborean Serpent-Devourer before many days! It is interesting to know that this latter gentleman's archaeological aspect is not intentional! However, the result may be even more effective than as if it were premeditated. The more recent examples of this deft reconstruction sound fascinating indeed, & ought to set James Ferdinand Morton scratching his curly white mane in a very ecstasy of puzzlement! "The Venerian" must be a winner in its class—& the Cat-Goddess (for which, no doubt, ancient Simaetha obligingly posed) surely suggests something which reached the Mound-Builders only through a long process of descent down the aeons. Images of this sort, no doubt, filtered from Hyperborea into Olathoë, & thence southward to Hsu-Qui & even into subterranean K'nyan in the years before the _____rs came. The odd striations & pittings of the [Hyperborean] Snake-Eater & other specimens certainly seem like something beyond the classification of any merely terrestrial archaeologist. When I see some of the elusive items I'll give opinions as to their relative exoticism of aspect. Hope you'll have good luck with the photographs. I'll surely send you the first prints I get of "The Outsider"—whose fascination grows upon me as I view it day by day. It ought to be photographed from different angles—as close up as possible, with the aid of a portrait lens. Regarding the loan of originals—it might be wise to check with the mail, & _____ routes are less _____, though an advance _____ be appreciated. In the interim you might think out the route which you'd like to have the exhibition traverse. Since distance is a factor in shipment rates, you would want to arrange a route involving as short gaps as possible. You could start with Sultan Malik, thence to Two-Gun, thence to Ar-Ech-Bei, & so on—although I'll confess that the number of logical recipients ahead of Providence puts a strain on my patience! On the return trip I think Petaja & Rimel ought to be favoured. But you can make up your own list, & I'll suggest any others whom I consider appreciative. Possibly you won't want the list very large because of the time consumed in wide circulation. In time I wish you could derive some adequate revenue from your sculptural skill—a not inconceivable development, though the limited munificence of Averoigne's local connoisseurs scarcely constitutes what one might call a big beginning! Still—many a tale & poem of Poe drew no more in a material way, & every dinar counts! Good luck with Pegasus—may he fly high! It seems to me that a really fascinating subject would be one of the great Easter Island images in miniature. While not giving you much scope for original imagination, it would form an invitation to your skill to duplicate the brooding mystery characteristic of the cyclopean megaliths themselves. That future project—a literal materialisation of the Cthulhu-image—certainly sounds impressive & alluring! When the time comes I'll send you a crude diagram of Ol' Cloolie as I originally imagined him—the fixed image being in some respects (arrangement of feet &c) different from Ar-E'ch-Bei's bas-relief. But possibly all that is explained in the story—which I haven't re-read in years.

That illustration in the de Givry volume[1] sounds fascinating indeed, & I'd be delighted to have a sketch of the daemon flute-player some time. I've never seen the volume, nor do I recall any Teniers picture corresponding to the one you describe. Some of those works on magic & witchcraft surely do contain curious plates—I recall many in the Summers books & translations Koenig has lent me, & have a few in my own library. In Spence's Encyclopaedia of Occultism there are one or two striking specimens—a Sabbat after the elder Breughel, Antichrist by Michael Volgemuth,[2] &c. &c. And speaking of weird art—young Morse has just sent me a rather interesting thing which proves what some of the pulp hacks could do if they only had the chance. You doubtless know the routine work of one *Eliot Dold* in *Astounding Stories*—better than the worst, but essentially just the usual junk. Well, in 1923 he illustrated a book of bum vers libre by the cheap publisher Harold Hersey—& hang me if he didn't achieve some magnificent Beardsleyan effects in his macabre designs! The volume is called "Night". I was truly astonished to see such fine work from a confirmed junk-peddler—yet who can say what many of the hacks might not do if they only had the chance? I can, for example, picture passable things of extreme distinction from Rankin. I'll lend you "Night" if you'd care to see it. Perhaps you already know it—but if not, it would give you a new respect for Dold.

Glad you've seen both *Dragon-Fly* & "Goblin Tower". Ar-E'ch-Bei is certainly learning the bookmaking craft very rapidly, so that "Incantations" is likely to outshine either of these earlier specimens. *The Dragon-Fly* is easily the best amateur paper of the season. Edkins is a great old boy—it's a pity he didn't follow a literary instead of a commercial career. Regarding "Incantations"—I hope you won't be too hyper-critical in choosing specimens for inclusion, for many pieces which you might consider minor are nevertheless too graceful to be lost. They certainly ought to be printed in book form at some time or other. Look at the "Goblin Tower"—many of whose items are admittedly not Belknap's best. I'd certainly include some Baudelaire translations—those in "Sandalwood" have been repeatedly praised. Some day I hope your literal *prose* Baudelaire can see the light of print .... as it may through Ar-E'ch-Bei or otherwise. A few of the French verses, too, should be there. I shall insist that I be given proofreading privileges—& in the end you'll probably get the most accurate text since "Odes & Sonnets". I would suggest that you give the matter of *arrangement* careful thought—don't leave it all to your publisher.

Just recd. the belated September *Fantasy* with the composite story.[3] Misprints play havock with the latter's text, but on the whole the thing is no worse than one might have expected. The differences between authors are amusing—see how quickly Two-Gun makes a sort of sanguinary Conan of the mild professor of geology! The biography of Sultan Malik is interesting, though the portrait didn't come out any too well—in my copies, at least. The news column has one interesting bit—viz., the information that the author of "The Way Home" is really *Paul Ernst*—"Stern" being an anagram for the true surname. Well—once again we see what good things some of these hacks *could* do if they *would*. The present revelation does not amaze me unduly, since I've seen some good older things of Ernst's—written before he became such facile pulpist. One thing in F M makes me see red, & that is the attempt at *grading* the current magazine output. In most cases values are *completely inverted*. Thus in the Nov. W T the only things of merit were "The Way Home", "Hand of Wrath", & "Zamboula"—yet none of these received more than a "d", while the mediocre "Flame-Flowers" thing drew a "c". Hope *The Phantagraph* will have a higher standard.

Kappa Alpha Tau sends regards to Simaetha. One of Johnny's little brothers lingers on here—I wish they'd keep him permanently! His upper half is black, & his lower white—a quaint effect. Johnny cuffs him around, but he seems to like it! Possibly the Peacock Sultan has told you of valiant Nimrod's disappearance & return after 5 weeks. Old Nim certainly deserves to be the national K.A.T. president! ¶ 5″ snowfall here Nov. 23, but it didn't last long on the ground. ¶ Some pretty fair lectures at the college recently—Prof W. B. Savery on recent Am. philosophers. Sir Norman Angell on the international mesa, &c.[4] ¶ Yrs for the Avatar of Shaggai—

E'ch-Pi-El

P.S. Did I tell you that Pharnabazus took the story I fixed up for old Bill Lumley? 70 bucks—& I'm insisting that good old Bill keep it all. The canny Satrap asked him how it happened that the style looked so much like Grand-pa's—& he replied with the unvarnished facts.

Notes

1. Grillot de Givry (1870–1929), *Witchcraft, Magic & Alchemy*, tr. J. Courtenay Locke; with 10 plates in colour and 366 illustrations in the text (London: G. G. Harrap, [1931]). The book contained an engraving of a painting by David Teniers the Younger (1610–1690).

2. Michael Wolgemut (1434–1519), German painter and printmaker.

3. I.e., "The Challenge from Beyond."

4. William Briggs Savery (1875–1945), professor of philosophy at the University of Washington (1902–45) and a follower of George Santayana, William James, and John Dewey. Sir Ralph Norman Angell (1872–1967), British lecturer, journalist, author, and Member of Parliament for the Labour Party. He served on the Council of the Royal Institute of International Affairs, was knighted in 1931, and awarded the Nobel Peace Prize in 1933.

[318]   [ANS; RAS 2.78]

[mid-December 1935]

[Printed Christmas card.]

Yrs by the Shadow of Yuggoth—Ech-Pi-El. 1935.

1936

[319]   [ALS]

Beyond the Tunnel of Silence—
—Hour of the Boiling in the Gulf
[24 January 1936/AHT][1]

Dear Klarkash-Ton:—

I was extremely glad to receive both recent bulletins
from Averoigne, & am grateful for all the varied contents. The pictorial items
are fascinating, & I long to see the originals of those which represent carvings. The coloured entity with horns is really quite a major triumph—the kind
of thing which Ar-Ech-Bei photographs with reverence, or borrows on long-
term loans! That figure from Teniers surely makes quite a Nyarlathotep—
though N. is supposed to be rather more anthropomorphic. Sooner or later I
believe I'll gratefully take advantage of your offer to lend the De Givry volume—though at the moment I am so driven to the wall with insistent matters
that I couldn't promise a very quick return. I envy you these acquisitions! I've
read the Vampire book, and certainly must borrow Spence's "Mysteries of
Britain". Meanwhile I'm sending under separate cover the little volume with
the Dold illustrations. I hardly think it will disappoint you—& you will wonder afresh that a Street & Smith hack could do such splendid work. No hurry
whatever about return.

Your sculptural activities are surely developing into something big, & I
rejoice to hear of the increasing professional demand for carvings. The rising
prices are heartening indeed—& who knows but that you have struck a bo-
nanza which will really yield a tolerable income? It would be a curious and
dramatic twist of fate if, after a long career of writing & painting, your most
spectacular fame were to come suddenly from an activity entirely new to you!
One thing that pleases me is that some of the sales have been of serious fantastic efforts as distinguished from conventional things done to order. The
names of your latest products are alluring in the extreme, & make one eager
to see either the carvings themselves or representations of them. As for the
much-anticipated loan exhibit—I fancy Es-El is about the best person to start
the circuit. His home address is unchanged—*17 Middagh St., Brooklyn, N.Y.*—
although he has moved into a smaller apartment in the same house. His business address is Room 1705, *104 Fifth Ave., New York City*—the *Bodley Book
Shop*. This latter is a large room divided into two by a makeshift partition—on
the 17th floor of an office building. It is filled with treasures well calculated to
awake the envy of the litterateur, the antiquary, & the bibliophile. The exhibit,
I presume, had better go to the home address—though you might ask Samu-

elus in advance which destination he'd prefer. By the way—his book is out at last, & makes a splendid appearance. Enclosed is a circular including a description of it. I surely hope it will draw kindly treatment from reviewers. Well—Es-El ought to be able to give all the Manhattanites their views of the exhibit, & from him it can come to me. I—after a sufficient period of admiration—will send it down to Ar-E'ch-Bei; & by the time he's ready to send it on you can have mapped out a future itinerary. Two-Gun, Malik, Rhi-Mhel, & Æmilius Petaia would surely be sorry not to have a glance at these magical wares from the wizard of Vyones!

Meanwhile I rejoice at the despatch of "Incantations" to the Temple of Krang. The contents would seem to me admirably selected, & I am impatient for the task of printing to get under way. I shall insist that Ar-E'ch-Bei send me proofs—& with three persons reading them, we ought to put the Averoigne Journal office to shame! Lord Garoth's printing is improving by degrees, & there's no question but that you'll get a better book than "The Goblin Tower". Glad you received the "limited edition" of Ulthar.[2] This Yuletide enterprise took me completely by surprise, & pleased me infinitely.

Sorry you've evolved nothing new in the fictional line, & hope the spring will bring several new specimens. No—Tremaine didn't take "Innsmouth", but Hill-Billy Crawford is about to print it both as a book & in his magazine. By the way—ere this you've doubtless seen the new issue of F M, in reduced size, proceeding from Hill-Billy's press. A better job than I expected him to turn out. You've also probably seen the Feb. issue of *Astounding*, with the start of the "Mts. of Madness". The illustrator of the tale did well—indeed, he must have read the text closely in order to reproduce the archaean Things so well. The pictures correspond in every detail to my original visual image—as is strikingly seen by comparing them with the guide-sketch which I made when writing the story five years ago.[3] In the text you will notice my change regarding the unity of the Antarctic continent—occasioned by Byrd's positive evidence of a year ago.[4] I fixed that up—altering all references throughout the story—last spring. Haven't yet read the Jan. W T—for during recent weeks the congestion of my programme has been appalling. Nor have I read *Astounding*—though it contains a tale of Belknap's of which he thinks rather highly.[5] Indeed, I am surrounded by mountains of unread material of every kind!

Old Bill Lumley will be effusively grateful for any Easter Island material you may have. Which reminds me to thank you for the cutting about those curiously carved rocks in the Folsom region. This business sounds tremendously interesting, & I surely hope the discoverer can interest the archaeologists of the U. of Cal. Who knows but these things are reliques of the same pre-human Horrors who left behind the Crater Ridge eikon now reposing on my bookcase top? I surely wish you could get around to Folsom & conduct some first-hand investigations! By the way—is the cutting to be returned? If so, let me know—it is still safe.

About that Cthulhu drawing—I've searched everywhere, but can't find a trace of it! But I feel sure that Ar-E'ch-Bei has a duplicate which he'd be happy to lend you when the time comes. Also, I recall having made a copy for one or the other of the Asotin boys—Eph-Li or Rhi-Mhel—a year or so ago.[6] If worst comes to worst I could reread the story, ransack my memory, & try my luck with another diagram. Meanwhile I trust that a block of the right sort of material may turn up. What you say of the ¾ bust of the Cthulhuan relative interests me greatly—though perhaps the supreme achievement will be the 5 × 3 Tsathoggua. Nggrrrhh!!! But I must see some pictorial representation of this when it is done!

Commiserations on the bad weather—tho' the absence of biting cold is something to be thankful for! Although today is viciously cold here—probably the worst of the year—the R.I. winter in general has averaged rather mild so far. Up to Poe's birthday[7] snows were few & quick-melting—but now we have a heavy coat of the niveous element. This vicious cold dates only from the preceding midnight, & I certainly hope it will prove short-lived.

Around New Year's I paid Sonny Belknap a week's visit, seeing most of the gang, though missing both the Igs—Koenig & Hornig. We had several gatherings, & I attended a dinner of the Am. Fiction Guild—during the course of all of which I met several science-fiction idols (those I can recall are Arthur J. Burks, Otto [of "Eando"] Binder, & Maurice J. Kaplan [Jacques Bartel]), plus the "fan" Donald Wollheim, for the first time. Also saw good old Seabury Quinn for the first time since 1931. Visited Es-El at both home & bookshop, & likewise foregathered with Young Melmoth, Young Albrecht Dürer, Kirk, Talman, Leeds, Little Mr. Sterling (who was in Prov. around Christmas & expects to be again next week), Kleiner, Morton, & the rest of the group.

On two occasions I visited the new Hayden Planetarium of the Am. Museum, & found it a highly impressive device. It consists of a round, domed building of 2 storeys. On the lower floor is a circular hall whose ceiling is a gigantic orrery—shewing the planets revolving around the sun at their proper relative speeds. Above it is another circular hall whose roof is the great dome, & whose edge is made to represent the horizon of N.Y. as seen from Central Park. In the middle of this upper hall is a projector (that looks like a "space ship" or like one of the armoured Martians in "The War of the Worlds") which casts on the concave dome a perfect image of the sky—capable of duplicating the natural apparent motions of the celestial vault, & of depicting the heavens as seen at any hour, in any season, from any latitude, & at any period of history. Other parts of the projector can cast suitably moveable images of the sun, moon, & planets, & diagrammatic arrows & circles for explanatory purposes. The effect is infinitely lifelike—as if one were outdoors beneath the sky. Lectures—different each month (I heard both Dec. & Jan. ones)—are given in connexion with this apparatus. In the annular corridors on each floor are niches containing typical astronomical instruments of all ages—telescopes, transects, celestial globes, armillary spheres, &c.—& cases to display books, meteorites, & other miscellany. Astronomical pictures line the walls, & at the desk may be obtained useful pamphlets, books, planispheres, &c. The 25¢ planispheres are the cheapest I ever saw—& good, too. I bought one apiece for Sonny & young Melmoth, so that the little rascals won't get the constellations wrong in their future stories, as they have in past ones! The institution holds classes in elementary astronomy, & sponsors clubs of amateur observers. Altogether, it is the most complete & active popular astronomical centre imaginable. It seems to be crowded at all hours— attesting a public interest in astronomy which certainly did not exist when I was young. Enclosed is a postcard (the scene, as it were, of "The Dweller in the Gulf") reproducing one of the paintings in the upper corridor.

Amateur journalism—best represented today by the National Amateur Press Association—has been picking up of late, & one paper as large as 107 pages, 6 × 9, has appeared . . . . . in your own state, by the way. I'm asking the editor to send you this, since it contains an article of mine—"Some Notes on Interplanetary Fiction"—which may interest you.[8]

Glad to hear that Simaetha still flourishes. I feel very much bereft though the moving-away of the venerable black & white president & tiger vice-president of the local Kappa Alpha Tau chapter—these gentlemen having accompanied their human family to another neighbourhood. I look wistfully at the deserted clubhouse roof! But Mr. John Perkins still flourishes & often visits his old Grandpa Ech-Pi-El—& his smaller brother, Gilbert John Murray Kynymond Elliot, Earl of Minto, likewise adorns the local scene. Lord Minto is black & white, & promises to become a very distinguished K.A.T. member. ¶ Yuggoth, but it's cold today! ¶ Yrs by the Talisman of Gna—E'ch-Pi-El

Notes

1. RAS dated the letter simply late January 1936.

2. I.e., RHB's 42-copy edition of *The Cats of Ulthar*.

3. The illustrator was Howard V. Brown. HPL's story not only received interior illustrations but the cover design for the February 1936 issue. For HPL's own drawing of one of the Elder Things, see "[Notes to *At the Mountains of Madness*]" (*CE* 5.245).

4. See *CF*$_L$ 3.22 and other passages revised from the original version.

5. "Cones."

6. See *Letters to F. Lee Baldwin* 91. HPL sent Baldwin a copy of his drawing of Cthulhu, dated 3 June 1934.

7. 19 January.

8. The *Californian*, edited by Hyman Bradofsky. HPL speaks of the large Spring 1935 issue.

[320]   [ANS]¹

February 5, 1936

Dear Éch-Pi-El: This is to acknowledge your letter and the loan of the Hersey–Dold production. Many of the drawings are surprisingly good and compare favorably with those of Alastair² and other post-Beardsley artists. Will write before many days—also start the carvings on their travels. Yrs.,
                    Klarkash-Ton

Notes

1. *Front:* Unidentified.

2. Pseudonym of Hans Henning Otto Harry Baron von Voigt (1887–1969), author of *Fifty Drawings* (New York: Knopf, 1925).

[321]   [ALS, JHL]

Moonless Moor of Shaggai—
At the Tolling of the Cracked Bell in the
Dark Tower
[23 March 1936/RAS]

Dear Klarkash-Ton:—

Well—I *did* survive the arctic winter (+4° was the lowest here, & there were long spells of days when it did not exceed +20°), but only in a fragmentary way! 1936 is certainly proving one of my bad years so far. All in with grippe in late January, & before I had shaken it off my aunt came down with a still worse attack—which developed complications & which has now necessitated her sojourn at an hospital for a period that will probably vary between a fortnight & a month.¹ Amidst all this upheaval my usual programme has gone completely to pieces. Revision jobs have had to be refused, & letters have gone not only unanswered but in some cases (*not* that of the runes from Zothique!) even unopened. Everything has had to slide whilst I devoted myself to the mingled duties of nurse, secretary, market-man, butler, & errand-boy. Now that my aunt is in the hospital, I have a bit more time—but the accumulation of correspondence & other obligations is hopeless. If I get by without a nervous breakdown I'll be doing damn well—though after all, the situation is a lot worse for my aunt than it is for me! The weather has now become quite vernal, temperatures above 60° being fairly frequent. But I see we are behind Averoigne in that respect. The flood situation has affected some parts of the state—even Pawtucket (on our northern border) to some extent—but Providence is still dry land so far. (Seaports are generally safe. This city has not been under water since 1815, & then it was an oceanic storm & tidal wave rather than a river flood. Only the downtown district could be flooded. This ancient hill could be inundated only by a world-destroying cataclysm.) Hartford—only 65 or 70 miles from here—is in very bad shape, with electric power gone & under martial law. Its papers have to be printed in neighbouring cities, & the homeless have created an acute problem.

Meanwhile I am awaiting with keen interest the loan exhibit of Hyperborean sculpture which I presume Es-El, Bel-Nha-Plong, E'ch-Si-Kheh, Young Melmoth, & other megalopolitan sorcerers are at present enjoying. The list of titles whets my appetite beyond measure—& I shall group them closely, as you suggest, when preparing to enjoy their malign & alien fascination. I hope I shan't delay sending them to Ar-E'ch-Bei as long as I delayed sending the Hyperborean Snake-Eater (I could hardly bear to let it go!)—but anyhow, he'll get them safely in the end. Needless to say, he will be second to none in his avid appreciation. It seems as though some others ought to see this galaxy of grotesque masterpieces—young Morse, Sultan Malik, Miss Moore, Old Bill Lumley, Rhī-Mhel, &c.—so that you might be thinking out a return route between now & the time Young Krang sends the assortment on. But I leave that to you. Morse may possibly see it during Es-El's tenure, since he occasionally makes brief trips to N.Y. Glad Ar-E'ch-Bei sent you the Cthulhu sketch—& later I'll take great interest & pride in seeing the materialised image from the story. Meanwhile the new titles capture my imagination—especially "Renascence", as described. These things surely will be a find for the archaeologists of the future—& I wish them luck in guessing at the civilisation which evolved them. But I surely am sorry that the market for eikons did not prove permanent. It certainly looks as if the weaver of pure fantasy—be it in literature, painting, sculpture, or what-not—were fated to ply his art on a dominantly non-remunerative basis . . . . unless, as you suggest, he happen to get the right kind of publicity & "super-salesmanship".

Glad you've seen the new Herm volume—which is certainly the most welcome event in a long time! The format in general does the poems justice, & most will agree that the edition was well worth waiting for. I've tried to boost the sale by enclosing one of those circulars to each of my almost innumerable correspondents.

I thought you'd find those Dold drawings worth seeing. What a pity the artist has to waste his talents in grinding out routine illustrations for the pulps! By the way—if you haven't started the volume back to #66 (& there's not the least hurry), you might change the route & send it to *Koenig* instead. E'ch-Si-Kheh has never seen it, but would like to very much. Speaking of drawings—that Mayan bat-god is fascinating, & goes with much gratitude & appreciation into my select album of Clericashtoniana.

I appreciated that postcard of the old bank at Coloma—which surely looks like some jungle-grown shrine in deserted Commoriom! According to the map in the *Journal's* Gold Show issue, Coloma is only a short distance S.E. of Auburn. Is it still inhabited, or does it form a "ghost town" housing only the beasts of the wild & the spectres of other days?

Glad you've seen the printed version of the Mts. of Madness. I'm certainly pleased with the illustrations—so much so that I can forgive occasional misprints such as *palaeocene* for *palaeogean*. I now have the final instalment, & shall dismantle two sets of copies (I have 3) in order to extract & assemble the story . . . of which I have no typed copy. I shall correct the misprints from the rough draught—which I shall then give to Ar-Ech-Bei. Meanwhile Hill-Billy Crawford is a-figgerin' on printing "Innsmouth" as a booklet—as well as using it in *Marvel Tales*. I've read one set of proofs & am expecting another. Hill-Billy hopes to get some illustrations by Derleth's gifted friend Utpatel—whose occasional work in W T you have possibly seen. Whether the thing will ever really materialise remains to be seen. I'm sceptical of Hill-Billy's bungling projects—though the fellow is undoubtedly the epitome of well-meaningness. Oh, yes—& I've learned that "The Shadow out of Time" will appear complete in the June *Astounding*.

Speaking of the pulps—here's something which may be old news, but which ought to be potentially good news for you. Hugo the Rat has sold *Wonder Stories* to the Margulies group (Standard Publications, 22 W. 48th St., N.Y. City), which is just as reliable financially as the Rat is unreliable. Pay is 1¢ a word on acceptance, & Belknap is loud in his praise of the treatment accorded him by other magazines of this group. Apparently this revives a market which had become—in any financial sense—dead. I hope you'll try some stories on Margulies[2]—who has just asked me to submit stuff, although I have nothing suitable on hand. He claimed that he wants really good material—not necessarily of the formula pattern—& any length up to 10,000 words will be considered. My advice is, go to it! Which reminds me that I'm glad to hear of your fictional plans—especially concerning *De Sadoquae Oraculo*. I have long been curious about the doings in Averonia (or Regio Averonum) in Roman times; for it is well known that the Averones were a tribe apart, feared by the rest of the Gauls, who bequeathed to their Gallo-Roman descendants a dark & dubious heritage. Have we not the disturbing lines of Valerius Trevirus to make us ponder . . . & tremble? There are buried ruins in Averoigne which it would be well not to disturb. Let us pray to the mild, small gods of Pegāna that no spade will ever uncover them!

Possibly Ar-E'ch-Bei has mentioned the call he had last month from the gifted author of "Shambleau". It is unfortunate that the visit had to have so melancholy a background—for, as you may be aware, the Florida tour of Miss Moore & her mother was to lessen the shock caused by the accidental death of Miss M's fiance on Feby. 13. The Young Right Arm of Krang liked the Moores very much, & hopes they will repeat their trip under less immediately sad circumstances next summer—as they have some intention of doing.

Glad *The Californian* duly reached you, & that you liked the article on interplanetary fiction. Hope you'll soon be turning out some space-yarns free from the characteristic defects noted! Here (under separate cover) is another current amateur journal of lesser size but vastly higher average quality . . . the *Causerie* of our anti-weird friend Edkins. In his review of "The Goblin Tower"[3] he points out some genuine weak spots, but is obviously callous toward the *massed effect* of some of the weird poems . . . such as "Night Trees" & "The White People". These two papers—as well as *The Dragon Fly*—surely indicate that amateurdom is on the up-grade—a circumstance which impels me to enclose an application blank in the hope that you may wish to jump into the N.A.P.A. arena. Bringing Edkins back was quite a triumph—of which I feel distinctly proud!

The depleted K.A.T. is heartened by the advent of a new jet-black & battle-scarred veteran who seems to be running for the presidency. Meanwhile Mr. Perkins & Lord Minto are fast growing up into eligible adulthood. Johnny has already had a fight with the newcomer. Glad to hear of Simeatha's immutability. The worst news comes from the slope of Mt. Kaf—where Nimrod's absence from the Peacock Palace seems likely to become permanent. Weeks have fled without word of the warlike wanderer! I appreciated the picture of Ching, & wish I might meet the gentleman in person!

Thanks extremely for that page of fantastic social cartoons. Most of them surely contain some powerful strokes of imagination—& that "Bad Conscience" really displays macabre genius; a genius doubly remarkable because of the artist's youth. This drawing has, as you point out, a distinctly golem-like atmosphere.

Got the March W T, but have so far read only the "Black Abbot". This is tremendously fascinating—full of a malign sense of hidden horror & aeon-old charnel secrets. I doubt if anything else in the issue can approach it. Well—now I await the eidola with impatient expectancy. Hope the gang in N Y are duly appreciating them!

Yours by the Green Flame—E'ch-Pi-El

P.S. I'll surely let you know—with much appreciation—when I'm ready to borrow De Givry. Yuggoth! the unread volumes piled before me!

Notes

1. In fact, Annie Gamwell had breast cancer and underwent a mastectomy.

2. Leo Margulies (1900–1975) edited numerous pulp magazines, including *Startling Stories* and *Thrilling Wonder Stories*.

3. [Ernest A. Edkins], *"The Goblin Tower,"* *Causerie* (February 1936): 2–4.

[322]   [ALS, JHL]

Central Unlighted Space
—Hour that the Darkness Moves
[Postmarked 23 April 1936]

Dear Klarkash-Ton:—

Your card of the 2nd & epistle of the 17th duly arrived—but no word as yet from Es-El about the sculptures. I dropped him a card of enquiry yesterday, & hope it will produce some result. Knowing his lax habits of correspondence, I am not inclined to fear the non-arrival of the shipment. Indeed, in the few letters I have been able to get off to N.Y. correspondents I have urged them to get in touch with Es-El—assuming the sculptures to be there & on display. I am surely anxious to see them myself, & Ar-Ech-Bei is equally avid. You really ought not to have been so generous about the De Land–ward expressage, since the privilege of inspecting the collection is well worth the expense. Thanks, though, a thousand times for your thoughtfulness. I'll tell the Right Hand of Krang to ship them directly to Averoigne when he is through with admiring & photographing them. Your local devotee Harry Brobst is tremendously impatient for the things to arrive. And oddly enough, one of the luminaries to see them in Providence may be your own comparative neighbour Sultan Malik! The Peacock Lord, as he may have written you, is planning an eastern trip—& if it materialises he intends to include Providentium's ancient hill in his itinerary.

Since my last letter my aunt's recovery has been steady. She left the hospital for a convalescent home on April 7th, & on the 21st returned to 66. She now takes brief outdoor walks, & ought to be very well back to normal in another month. As yet my programme is not much lightened, & is complicated by my own wretched health—a kind of general exhaustion which prevents my concentration on any task without frequent rest, plus uncertain eyesight, plus (at the moment) a hell of a cold. Correspondence, revision, & reading are still in chaos—indeed, I fancy that only the ruthless practice of neglect & repudiation will ever clean up my schedule!

But even so, I don't believe my present burdens are even nearly as bad as yours—& my hat is off to you for the amount you can accomplish under such adverse circumstances. I couldn't even begin to compete! I don't wonder at your fatigue—indeed, the wonder is that you can get around at all—but I think the discouragement ought to be lightened just a bit by pardonable pride in your own stamina. I hope most profoundly that you can eventually work out some less exhausting arrangement—perhaps securing some able-bodied helper who would take over some of the heavier manual tasks in exchange for his food & lodging. Meanwhile one's sentiments must be divided among sympathy, admiration, & sheer wonder at what you manage to do. Such burdens would flatten me out into sheer unconsciousness! Well—anyhow, let us hope that part of your efforts can be transmuted into useful cash through the medium of *Astounding, Weird,* the new & de-ratted *Wonder,* & other publications more or less in your line! Congratulations on your final receipts from the Arch-Rodent!

Thanks immensely for the cuttings, & for the pleasingly sinister sketch of Tsathoggua's progeny. From the young daemon's colouring I infer that his mother does not share his father's hellish blackness! That mediaeval print is typical & fascinating, & I shall preserve it in my collection. Eventually I shall take advantage of your offer to lend the de Givry volume—with this & others like it. Those dark Esquimau carvings are provocative indeed. I've seen the originals of something very like them—life-size wooden Esquimau figures in the Museum of the Am. Indian in N.Y. Some are jet black & infinitely horrible—one being an almost indescribable god of nightmare. I wish there were available pictures of these things. But those lunarians of Cheuvau certainly take the prize. Nggrrhh . . . what entities! The good doctor certainly knows how to capture the essentials of grotesque horror! Still—coming down to cold facts, I don't see that he excels you in the least, or that he even shews a comparable imaginative variety & artistic sense—judging, of course, from these few pictures only. I wish you could connect with his market while the fashion for such things lasts. I wonder if Galpin could tell you anything about Paris art dealers & their ways? I return the cutting herewith as per request. The "Phantom Light of Ringold"[1] makes me think of a similar Rhode Island mystery of a century ago—the so-called "Palatine Light" which glimmered mysteriously at sea off Block Island. Local superstition called it the ghost of a ship—the *Palatine*—reputed (though unjustly) to have been looted & burned by wreckers in the 18th century, & its real nature has never been settled.[2] It has not been reported in 50 years. Probably it was some auroral phenomenon—exaggerated & distorted in the island folklore. I saw that item about Shepley's fear of a collision in the local paper. Very possibly such things have occurred in the past—so that fragments of other worlds may indeed lie embedded in ours. The idea has been used more than once in science fiction, but is still good for re-use. No one has yet done it full justice. That item about the possible Pleistocene skull in California is highly interesting. Only a decade ago the idea of immensely ancient man in America was ridiculed, but now all at once a whole flood of contrary reports appear. Did I ever lend you, by the way, the cutting of a German scientist's theory (based on an interpretation of Mayan chronology) that the civilisations of Middle America extend back to 8000 B.C.? Needless to say, such a theory is not to any extent accepted today. I heard an excellent illustrated lecture on Mayan ruins the other night, & the speaker claimed that nothing behind A.D. 68 can be traced.

Glad the Dold–Hersey volume has gone to Ech-Si-Kheh. He recently sent me some excellent mimeograph copies of the long guide-letter which I wrote him when he was about to visit Charleston.[3] Glad *Causerie* arrived. A second number will review Es-El's Herm—with, I hope, a reasonable degree of sympathy. Young Morse, by the way, may possibly prepare a review of "The Goblin Tower" for the "fan" press. I wish I could effect at least a loose coalition between the weird-science "fan" & amateur worlds. Possibly the recent recruiting of young Wollheim (of *The Phantagraph*) to the N.A.P.A. may help.

Hope some time you can present good old Lumley with a statuette or two. He is vastly disappointed at not hearing from you lately. The loan of any Easter Island cuttings you have would also delight the good old boy. I hope to sub-lend him a copy of the Am. Museum's magazine with an excellent Easter Island article—lent me by Koenig. Old Bill is now recovering from a sprained arm—sustained, so he says, during some mystical investigations in Ghost Valley. I presume he has told you all about Ghost Valley!

Speaking of indisposition—another admirer of yours, little Kenneth Sterling the scientifiction fan, has been through a tremendous siege. Operation for abscess of lower colon—blood transfusion—intra-venous nourishment—but he's pulling around again all right now. A month ago he had only about a 50-50 chance to survive. Now he's about to embark on a programme of extensive tutoring to see if he can make up lost scholastic time & enter Harvard in the autumn, as previously planned—at the age of 16.

The account of your new sculptures is indeed tantalising—& the Outsider on my desk leers ghoulishly at the mention of his new 5½″ brother. I am also fascinated by the idea of your Illustrations for Untold Tales . . . . . especially the hellish Night Scene in No-Man's Land. Some time I hope these drawings can get circulated among the appreciative. Also—when the drawings are done, you ought to write the stories to go with them!

Crawford plods along with "The Shadow Over Innsmouth", though less than half is in print. Some of the mistakes are so bad that a table of errata will be necessary.[4] The four Utpatel illustrations are pretty good—although one of them shews the *bushy-bearded* nonagenarian Zadok Allen as *smooth-faced*.

The last two W T's aren't quite as bad as usual; indeed, the March issue (with your Black Abbot, the unusual Binder story, Hamilton's departure from his formula, & the promising Kuttner attempt) is distinctly remarkable as judged by recent standards. April is redeemed by Jacobi's really atmospheric tale, Comte d'Erlette's old-timer (which I read in MS. years ago), & Bloch's rather vivid "Druidic Doom". I haven't read any recent *Astounding*. Next month my "Shadow Out of Time" will appear.

I surely hope you'll be able to stage one of your prolific writing periods before long. Ordinarily I'd say that no story of merit could be written in odd moments—but you are such a wizard for triumphing over obstacles that I'll wager you can do it—& brilliantly, too! I don't know when in the devil I can ever write anything more. Indeed, I've about come to the conclusion that I'm not a natural writer. If I were, I wouldn't be so dependent upon favourable conditions for production.

April hereabouts—after a deceptively warm March—has been depressingly cold. I wish to Yuggoth I could get to Charleston or south of there—but the prospects of travel this year are slim indeed. Doubtless you've read of the floods which paralysed the East. Providence escaped, though streets were under water 4 miles south of it—while Hartford, 60 or so miles to the west, suffered a major calamity. The view from my window is just beginning to take on vernal aspects—a few shrubs leafing out, forsythias & a few other early blooms in evidence, & grass a vivid green. In a month more there ought to be some decent warmth—which will tend to set me on my feet physically. I see Mr. John Perkins disporting in the garden below, & think I'll see if I can secure him as a guest. He is at present engaged in an attempt to capture some entomological specimen not discernible to my aged vision. The big black devil was a year old in February.

Well—again I extend commingled sympathy & best wishes, plus renewed thanks for all the enclosures.

Yrs by the Carven Key—E'ch-Pi-El

Notes

1. "PASCO, Wash., Feb. 18.—(INS)—'The phantom light of Ringold' has been seen again, according to word reaching here from that section. Being an unsolved mystery in the Ringold district, the phantom light has been noticed in barren hills as well as on populated highways. Citizens of high repute have sworn to its authenticity. It appears, according to tales related here, only in foggy or rainy weather. The light assertedly gives the impression of an automobile with only one headlight. Innumerable motorists have reported running in a ditch to avoid being struck by an oncoming car—only to have a beam of light flash past them and continue on down the highway. Motorists driving high-powered automobiles allegedly have pursued the phantom light, only to have it disappear when they approached it. A search for tracks or some plausible solution of the mystery always has resulted in failure, according to reports." [International News Service]

2. An apparition reported near Block Island, RI, said to be the ghost ship of a lost 18th-century vessel named the *Palatine*. The legend is based on the historical wreck of the *Princess Augusta* in 1738, which became known as the *Palatine* in 19th-century accounts, including John Greenleaf Whittier's "The Palatine."

3. I.e., *Charleston*.

4. An errata sheet was printed, but, as HPL predicted, it, too, contained errors.

[323]   [ANS]¹

[Postmarked Auburn, Cal.,
22 May 1936]

Dear Éch-Pi-El:

I've just read *The Shadow out of Time* with prodigious pleasure, and must congratulate you on a magnificent piece of work. Will write soon at length. Trust the carvings will reach you presently and will not prove a disappointment. Yrs, in the faith of Nyarlathotep,

Klarkash-Ton

Notes

1. *Front:* Unidentified.

[324]   [ALS]

Bottomless Well of Yeguggon—
Hour that the Snout Appears
[20 June 1936]

Dear Klarkash-Ton:—

I was surely delighted to receive your favourable opinion of the "Shadow"—since it helped to counteract the devastating effect of a scorching criticism from young Shea—a diatribe which left the story very little excuse for existence. I am not very well satisfied with the tale myself, & believe that the time may have come when I ought to take a long—if not permanent—vacation from fiction-writing. The A.S. text was marked by many misprints—& made annoying by the wretched capitalisation & punctuation. Fancy "Moon" & "Moonlight" in caps! A.S. also has annoying little tricks like changing "Great God" to "Great Heavens", & altering names of primal fauna & flora from their simple English form to the cumbrous scientific form (thus *dinosaurs* becomes *Dinosauria*). In some cases good spelling is altered to bad (as *subterrene* to *subterrAne* . . . which has no existence as an adjective), while there are unjustified verbal changes (as *demoniac* to *demonic*). In places the sentence-structure also suffers. But the worst mangling was done to the "Mts. of Madness"—whose printed form fills me with despair. All the normal paragraphs are chopped into small bits in imitation of the juvenile pulp "action" style—the original rhythm, emotional modulations, & minor climactic effects being thereby destroyed. Nor is this the worst. Important passages are left out—especially toward the end—thus decreasing the vitality & colour, & making the action mechanical. So many vital details & impressions are missing from the concluding parts that the effect is that of a flat ending. After all the detail & description *before* the encounter with the shoggoth in the abyss, the characters are shot up to the surface without any of the gradual experiences & emotions which make the reader *feel* their return to the world of man from the nighted, aeon-dead world of the Others. All sense of the *duration & difficulty* of the exhausted climb is lost when it is discussed objectively in only a few words, with no adequate hint of the fugitives' reactions to the scenes through which they pass. Among actual *plot* points omitted is one where the explorers notice (through a dropped battery) that the revived Old Ones have been pausing perplexedly before that ominous & grotesquely crude *palimpsest carving* in the passage to the sunken sea. I had a hell of a time correcting 3 copies of the text—knitting up shredded paragraphs & reinserting deleted passages in fine pencil printing on the margins. I shall never submit anything more to A S without some sort of preliminary understanding!

This text-correcting formed part of my present feverish struggle to get my affairs whipped into some sort of shape again after the recent chaos. The whole business has me just about on the edge of a nervous breakdown. One thing I had to do was to get my files cleaned up after years of neglect—an ordeal which (including the correcting) took 4 days . . . including 2 nights of sacrificed sleep. But at least I know where to find things once more.

General conditions are somewhat on the mend. My aunt's health improves, & the coming of warm weather has been of benefit to me. There was no really decent weather till April 28, but since then warm days have not been rare. I have taken my work out to Prospect Terrace a good deal, & have had one or two rural walks. The landscape is now rich with the luxuriant verdure & blossoms of summer, & I hope to arrange for some ampler rambles ere long. I have scant hope, however, of being able to accept Ar-Ech-Bei's De Land invitation.

On May 4 the R.I. Tercentenary observances began with a costumed parade which started at the college gate—just a stone's throw from here. Later there was a mock-session of the rebel legislature of May 4, 1776—held in costume in the selfsame room of the ancient colony-house (1761) where the original session was held. In this, each old-time deputy was impersonated by a lineal descendant—Gov. Green representing his ancestor Col. Arnold, who offered the original set of treasonable resolutions severing Rhode Island from the lawful authority of the Crown. The acting & pageantry were so excellent that one might easily have fancied the bygone period returned—with the intervening 160 years merely a bad dream. I was one of the relatively few spectators lucky enough to get into the Colony-House & witness the proceedings. In the afternoon—in a ceremony at the State House which I did not attend— Gov. Curley of Mass. presented to Gov. Green a copy of the recent resolutions of the Mass. General Court, rescinding the banishment imposed by that august body upon Roger Williams in Oct. 1635. After 300½ years, Mr. Williams no doubt highly appreciates this delicate mark of consideration!

To pile on the historic atmosphere—the longest walk I've taken so far was to the westward country just beyond the village of Manton (on the city's sunset rim) to see a house now reported to be the oldest still standing in Rhode-Island. I had seen it before, but wished another look in the light of its lately-acknowledged seniority. Of added interest to me was the fact that I am directly descended—in the 8th generation—from the man who built & first inhabited it. I found it still in good condition. Thomas Clemence—a friend of Roger Williams—built it in 1654, after making a trade with a young Indian named Wissawyamake for 8 acres of land, & its architecture—including the prodigious stone chimney—is typical of that early period. It has not been radically changed, though the old diamond-paned windows are gone, whilst a dormer window, an eastward extension, a northward "lean-to", & an ugly little porch have been added. In the yard is an ancient well & well-sweep—

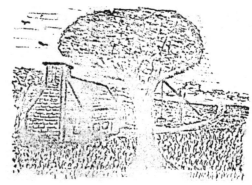

one of the few examples of the latter remaining in Rhode Island. The present owner & occupant is an aged gentlewoman in quite destitute circumstances, descended from Thomas Clemence in another line. The accompanying crude sketch is an attempt to shew the place not as it is today, but as it was in the builder's own period—without the porch & wings & dormer. It forms a pretty good example of a very old Rhode Island house—a house of the period *preceding* the age which produced the graceful, familiar types of "colonial" architecture. There are quite a number of these old houses left in New England—& in Mass. there are reliques of still earlier types of construction—the patriarch of them all being the Fairbanks house in Dedham (betwixt Providence & Boston), erected just 300 years ago in 1636. Possibly you recall my mentioning my trip to the Fairbanks House in 1929.[1]

By the way—before I get off the subject of antiquities (which, I fear, I seldom do for long!)—I must mention the very interesting & gratifying genealogical discovery on which I stumbled last month—when I learned for the first time that I am a great-great-great-great-great-great-great-great-great-grandson of the Elizabethan astronomer who introduced the Copernican theory into England! For one who has always been a keen amateur devotee of celestial science, this was indeed a stimulating find. Ordinarily I am a very sluggish genealogist, being content to take what existing charts tell me & let it go at that. Last month I ran into a caller of my aunt's—an old lady related to us in the Field & Wilcox lines—& she mentioned how proud I ought to be of our common forbear, *the astronomer John Field or Felde.* That rather floored me, since our charts carried the Field line back only to the original Providence settler John Field, who died in 1686, & I knew *he* was no moon-starer![2] Well—it soon turned out that the ancestry of this settler has been known for ages among genealogists, though I had no inkling of it. The 16th century astronomer (whose 1557 Ephemeris contained the first English account of the Copernican system, & who has been called "The Proto-Copernican of England") was the Providence colonist's *own grandfather*—hence *my* 9-times-great-grandfather. It certainly gave me a kick to get a real man of science in my pedigree—which as a general thing is lousy with clergymen but short on straight thinkers. [But I'll be hanged if this new discovery hasn't added *one more* damn divine to the bunch—for it seems that the Prov. colonist's maternal grandfather was the Rev. John Sotwell, Vicar of Peniston in Yorkshire!] Later I looked up the standard Field genealogy (by F. C. Pierce) and found out all about the line. It comes from one Sir Hubertus de la Feld [of the family of Counts de la Feld, seated near Colmar in Alsace], a follower of William the Conqueror who took lands in Lancashire in 1069; the Providence stock springing from the Yorkshire branch centreing around Sowerby, Ardsley, & Thurnscoe. I have copied an abundance of notes & now have my Field lineage straight back—in exactly 20 generations—to Roger de la Feld of Sowerby, born in 1240. But it's the *astronomer* who chiefly interests me, & about whom I am anxious to learn more. I have a triple allotment of Field blood, being descended from no less than 3 of the Providence settler's grandchildren. [children of John Field's daughter Hannah, who died in 1703.]

Thanks exceedingly for the new card of Woods' Dry Diggings, which considerably sharpens my mental picture of that undoubtedly quaint & fascinating town. I see you even have historic *ruins!* No doubt much of the present layout would evoke familiar memories in the sprightly George Tupper of Wilbraham, were he able to upheave the substantial granite marker in Maple Dell Cemetery & take ship once more for the rollicking scenes of '53!

Among the recent items in my attempted conquest of chaos was a reading-up of the contemporary W T issues. Two-Gun's serial is really splendid despite the "monotonous manslaughter" & confusing nomenclature . . . . Yuggoth! how that bird can surround ancient meglithic cities with an aura of aeon-old fear & necromancy! His "Black Canaan" is likewise magnificent in a more realistic way—reflecting a genuine regional background & giving a clutchingly powerful picture of the horror that stalks through the moss-hung, shadow-cursed, serpent-ridden swamps of the far south. Bloch is doing well—following up his "Druidic Doom" with the "Faceless God" & "Grinning Ghoul". Comte d'Erlette's "Telephone in the Library" could be a lot worse, & Single-Plot Hamilton at least belies his title in "Child of the Winds". Burks spoils his "Room of Shadows" with a certain hack treatment. M. J. Bardine's "Harbour of Ghosts" has promise—& atmosphere. So has Harold G. Shane's "Lethe". I was glad to see "Ennui" in the May issue, & am on the lookout for next month's "Necromancy in Naat."

1936 is certainly a bad-luck year for the gang! To the sundry misfortunes chronicled in my preceding epistle must be added the serious kidney operation just undergone by good old Edkins—who seems, however, to be pulling around pretty well for a chap of 68.

But the worst blow for me pertains to my furry rather than bipedal friends—a blow which has laid low the Providence chapter of the Kappa Alpha Tau. It is still too recent for me to discuss temperately—but alas, it is all too true. For my two best-beloved neighbours are no more. This week both John Perkins & little Lord Minto succumbed to some malady which is afflicting all the felidae of the neighbourhood—a thing which may be an obscure epidemic, yet which may be the malign activities of some contemptible poisoner. The sad end of the brothers seemed connected with some digestive disorder, & recalled the equally sad fate of their bygone brother—little Sam Perkins—in 1934. If this *is* the work of some wretched neo-Borgia, I hope to hell somebody feeds him a poison a thousandfold more painful than that which he has subtly applied his innocent furry victims! I am sure that Simaetha extends her sympathy—& I trust she will invoke the blackest curses upon the poisoner (if such there was) at the next midnight Sabbat on Crater Ridge. Perhaps one expansive evil will has struck at both the vanished General Tabasco & his Providence kinsfolk.

Turning to less tragic themes—your state has received a new accession from among the personnel of the weird group ... none other than young Hornig of the lamented F F, who is in San Francisco on a newspaper job secured him by good old Abe Merritt. You may possibly see him in the course of time. He is a very likeable fellow—in whom a Semitic strain produces not the least resemblance to his quondam boss Hugo the Rat. When passing through Indianapolis he stopped off to see Miss Moore, who liked him very much.

¶ Since beginning this epistle I've had a most depressing & staggering message—a postcard with the report that good old Two-Gun Bob has committed suicide.[3] It seems incredible—I had a long normal letter from him dated May 13. He was worried about his mother's health, but otherwise seemed perfectly all right. If the news is indeed true, it forms weird fiction's worst loss since the passing of Whitehead in 1932. Few others of the gang had quite the zest & spontaneity of good old R.E.H. I certainly wish I could get a bulletin saying the report is a mistake! '36 certainly is a hellish year!

Turning to less melancholy news—Galpin has just written a detective novel (his *only* piece of fiction save for a weird tale in 1919—"Marsh-Mad")[4] & expects to dispose of it promptly and remuneratively. There's youthful optimism for you! It is called "Death in D Minor",[5] & is based on his experiences at the Schola Cantorum in Paris back in 1925.

Am still eagerly awaiting the loan exhibit, which is doubtless delayed in N.Y. so that all the gang there can see it. Just got *Causerie* with its Herm. review.[6] If I can't get you a copy I'll lend you mine. ¶ Yrs by the Sign of Yoth
—E'ch-Pi-El

Notes

1. There is no mention of the Fairbanks house in any of the letters compiled in this volume. See "An Account of a Trip to the Antient Fairbanks House . . ."

2. See Kenneth W. Faig, Jr. "Quae Amamus Tuemur: Ancestors in Lovecraft's Life and Fiction" *The Unknown Lovecraft* (New York: Hippocampus Press, 2009): 45–46n42.

3. Howard shot himself on June 11. The postcard HPL received was from C. L. Moore.

4. Alfred Galpin, "Marsh-Mad: A Nightmare," *Philosopher* 1, No. 1 (December 1920): 7–8. Rpt. in *Letters to Alfred Galpin* 236–38.

5. Galpin later renamed his novel *Murder in Montparnasse*. It was never published. See HPL to Galpin (20 June 1936), in *Letters to Alfred Galpin* 223–24.

6. Edkins had reviewed Loveman's *Hermaphrodite and Other Poems* in *Causerie* (June 1936): 2–4.

[325]   [ANS][1]

[Postmarked Providence, R.I.,
19 September 1936]

Greetings from a convention of those who admire the galaxy of nameless eikons! Too bad Ar-E'ch-Bei, who was here last month,[2] couldn't stay over & participate. Have an epistle to Averoigne started & will be returning the unholy shipment before long.[3] Trust things have been going well in Zothique & Hyperborea.

> Yrs by the Unutter'd Yellow Sign
> —E'ch-Pi-El.

Cordial greetings from the passer through.—J. F. M.

We fear the presence of Tsathoggua. Morton is now exorcising him. SSS. H. Brobst

Notes

1. *Front:* Betsy Williams Cottage, Roger Williams Park, Providence, R. I.

2. RHB was in Providence from 28 July to 1 September.

3. HPL had the assortment of CAS's sculptures on loan from 1 August to 29 September.

[326]   [ALS, JHL]

Crypt of Thoggon
—Hour of the Slimy Trail
[Postmarked 29 September 1936]

Dear Klarkash-Ton:—

Early in August the travelling loan exhibit arrived on the ancient hill, & became the cynosure of more than one pair of admiring eyes. My own delight and appreciation were unbounded, & it is with rage & tooth-gnashing that I survey the empty purse which forbids me to emulate Es-El & young Melmoth in their annexation of a horror apiece! The longer I survey the array, the more I hate to send them along. Each item has its individual & peculiar charm, & picking favourites is a hard & variable business. Just at the moment my fancy lingers over Nos. 13, 8, 1, & ⋋A—but it might easily switch to any of the others. What a museum might be formed of shapes such as these! In exhibiting them I have added my own "Outsider" &

"Cthulhu" to the group. Melmoth says he has made snapshots of the pieces—including those purchased by him & Loveman.

My chief fellow-admirer was, as coincidence would have it, none other than the young archimage to whom I was directed to forward the collection—the mighty Ar-E'ch-Bei, Right Arm of Krang! Little Bobby blew in suddenly & unexpectedly for a long-term stay on July 28, & in the course of a month became quite a Providentian. The household at De Land has been dissolved, & it is very doubtful whether the youthful heir will ever return thither. Instead, he is headed for Leavenworth, Kan., where his mother & maternal relatives are. The long enforced absence from his books, printing-press, binding materials, &c. &c. &c. forms a severe blow, & he doesn't know when he can get settled with them again. The resultant delay of "Incantations" certainly is hell! Meanwhile he is busy planning a *mimeographed* magazine to be called *Leaves*—in which he wants to include your ending of the 3d Episode of Vathek. Even unsettledness can't keep the kid idle!

Ar-E'ch-Bei has grown a formidable set of moustachios & side-whiskers which contrast oddly with his still-juvenile appearance. He stopped at the boarding-house across the garden. I shew'd him most of the local sights, & we have taken trips to such ancient places as Newport, Salem, & Marblehead—the Salem–Marblehead trip being made in the company of Leedle Meestah Stoiling, who has been in Lynn (on the shore) recuperating from his last spring's operation & preparing to enter Harvard in September. Bob also made a visit to New Bedford, where cousins of his reside. His constant raids on the local bookstalls were limited only by his finances, & he also dug up considerable genealogical data at the libraries. It develops that he is my *sixth cousin* according to the following lines of descent from a common forbear:

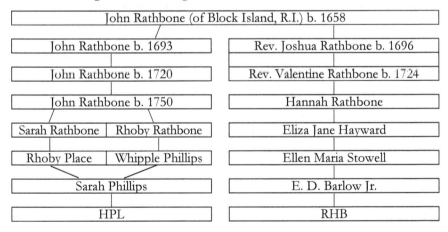

John Rathbone (of Block Island, R.I.) b. 1658	
John Rathbone b. 1693	Rev. Joshua Rathbone b. 1696
John Rathbone b. 1720	Rev. Valentine Rathbone b. 1724
John Rathbone b. 1750	Hannah Rathbone
Sarah Rathbone / Rhoby Rathbone	Eliza Jane Hayward
Rhoby Place / Whipple Phillips	Ellen Maria Stowell
Sarah Phillips	E. D. Barlow Jr.
HPL	RHB

It is curious that, although Ar-E'ch-Bei is young enough to be my son, he & I are both descended from old John of 1658 in exactly 7 generations. Bob surely made himself very useful hereabouts—repairing several of my disintegrating books, mending a busted Aztec calendar-stone & a newly-shatter'd Kien Lung vase,[1] &c. &c. His next long trip may lie in a westward direction, so that it is not impossible to imagine him as invading Averoigne & climbing Indian Hill!

But Krang's acolyte & the Old Gent were not the only ones to gloat over your Tsathogguan grotesqueries. On Aug. 6th there arrived amidst these Plantations no less a figure than the venerable Adolphe Danziger de Castro, veteran Biercian & one-time revision client of mine. He paused in Providence (at an hotel) for 5 days—en route from Boston, where he had been to perform the melancholy rite of scattering his late wife's ashes on the sea in accordance with her final wish. Old 'Dolph, now 77, is the same amiable charlatan as ever. I had not seen him in person since 1928, but the years have aged him less than they have me. He tried to wish some insanely unprofitable revision jobs on me, but I managed to stand him off without offending him. Meanwhile Bob & I shew'd him around the town, & derived considerable enjoyment from his pompous reminiscences of the great. He told of how Swinburne admired his poetry, how he made William H. Taft president, how he saved the Mexican states of Sonora & Chihuahua from bankruptcy by drafting sets of divorce laws which attracted American trade, &c. &c. &c. On one occasion we all sat on a tomb in the hidden hillside churchyard & wrote rhymed acrostics (at Ar-E'ch-Bei's suggestion) on the name of *Edgar Allan Poe*—who ninety years ago wander'd through that selfsame necropolis whilst on visits to Providence. Old 'Dolph was vastly taken by the cryptic eidola, & regretted his inability to add one or more to his modest collection of exotiques. Incidentally—it turned out that he used to know the family of that young California chap Kuttner, who is making such a promising start in W T. Still another admirer of the eikons was young Brobst, who came over with his wife during Ar-Ech-Bei's visit . . . while Morton added to the list. So all in all, your sculpture has had quite an exhibition in antient Providentium!

Hope all is tolerable on Indian Hill. I know how rushed & oppressed you are, so don't try to write until you can do it without crowding things. I've felt like hell most of the summer. Cold weather had me down & out till mid-July—with nerves & digestion all shot to pieces. Then a brief respite—but now the goddam autumn is closing in, & Grandpa is due for more lassitude & hibernation. Yuggoth, what a climate! Took a Newport trip July 11, & on July 18–19 my good old amateur friend Moe & his son were here. On July 22 I saw Peltier's comet at the Ladd Observatory (a place I used to haunt in youth)—just a haze-circled disclet in the 12″ telescope. Around the same date I had a marvellous windfall of books—items left behind by the old lady downstairs,[2] who was moving away. A ten-vol Chambers' Encyclopaedia, a 5-volume biblical commentary, a *good* Liddell & Scott to replace my disintegrating one, &c. &c.[3]

Ar-E'ch-Bei shew'd me the MS. of "Incantations", & I noticed several poems I had not seen before. Splendid stuff! I'm not sure but that this will form your best book! ¶ Schwartz has some vague plan for trying to get my junk reprinted in England [a plan which will almost certainly come to nothing], & in connexion with it I sent Wright my two last tales—"Doorstep" & "Haunter"—in order to make sure I had exhausted all cisatlantic possibilities. Imagine my surprise when he *accepted* both of them! ¶ New "fan" magazines are getting to be thicker than flies—but the best of them is probably that which young Willis Conover of Cambridge, Md. is to start in conjunction with one Corwin Stickney of New Jersey—*The Science-Fantasy Correspondent.*

Edkins has been having a devil of a time—second operation of incredible painfulness which nearly killed him. But he is now steadily recovering, & will leave for Florida next month. A great old boy!

By this time you have doubtless heard full details of poor old Two-Gun's suicide—how he shot himself upon hearing that his mother was dying. What a blow for his father! R E H's library has been given to his alma mater—Howard Payne College at Brownwood—as the nucleus of a Robert E. Howard Memorial Collection. All sorts of plans (mostly unfeasible) are afoot for posthumous collections of his tales, & such items as his "Hyborian Age" (an outline of his prehistoric world) & P. Schuyler Miller's bibliography & history of Conan the Cimmerian take on a melancholy timelessness. The blow to weird fiction is an irreparable one—& obituaries will be numerous. Quite a sizeable one from me will appear in *Fantasy Magazine.* Ar-E'ch-Bei has prepared a fine elegiac sonnet which Wright has accepted for W T. This is Bob's first professional acceptance, & it is unfortunate that the event has such a melancholy background! By this time, of course, you'll have seen the sonnet—which I'm sure you'll like. I suppose you've also seen *The Phantagraph* with R E H obituary notes.[4]

Ar-Ech-Bei left here Septr. 1, & paused a week or so in New York—seeing Sterling, Belknap, Koenig, Howard Wandrei [Young Melmoth is home in St Paul], &c. He then headed westward, losing a ten-spot en route & having to telegraph his mother from Chillicothe, Ohio for emergency funds. In Indianapolis he called on Miss Moore, who was very glad to see him & thought he looked better than he did last winter. He is now safe in Leavenworth, once more under the maternal eye.

Other notes on the weird-fan younger generation—Leedle Meestah Stoiling, avoiding for the nonce a second operation, is now returning from N.Y. to Cambridge, & will have as an address Room A-11, Lionel Hall, Harvard University. And little Maggie Sylvester of Denver is in New York for an art course or something—to be addressed at 157 E. 37th St.[5] The new young weird-&-science-fiction editors, Willis Conover & Corwin Stickney of the *Science-Fantasy Correspondent,* recently made a trip to N.Y. & saw most of the weirdists & pulpists there—although they missed Belknap, who was away at Ocean Grove, N.J. These kids, by the way, seem to be planning quite an ambitious magazine. *Still another* fan magazine about to make its bow is *Supramundane Stories,* edited by one Nils H. Frome,[6] Box 3, Fraser Mills, British Columbia. These things really grow too numerous to catalogue—& will kill one another off if they ever get to the point of appearing. *Fanciful Tales* (Shepherd–Wollheim) is still in the press, & I suppose Hill-Billy Crawford expects to issue his revived *Marvel* sometime. The Blish–Miller *Planeteer* still remains only a name—at least, so far as I am concerned.[7] Hornig, failing to find a job in California, is back in ancient Elizabethtown—but is not, alas, resuming the good old F F.

I trust you duly received the triangular card from Morton, Brobst, & me. We had some very congenial sessions Sept. 11–12–13. Did I mention that Morton had just won the crossword-puzzle championship of the U.S. at the Boston convention of the Puzzlers League? He will receive a silver loving-cup in commemoration of this achievement.

By the way—that churchyard acrostic business . . . originally merely a half-hour's idle pastime . . . has had some amusing echoes—with more perhaps to come. Although it would never have occurred to Ar-Ech-Bei & me to submit our results for publication, old Dolph *did*—& secured an acceptance from Brother Farny! After that, Bob & I did send our results in—but they were turned down because Satrap Pharnabozus had already taken one. Now that the ball has been started rolling, we're giving the "fan mags" a chance to print our specimens. Meanwhile correspondents have begun to emulate us—young Kuttner being the latest. My old friend M. W. Moe of Milwaukee—who was here in July & saw the hidden hillside churchyard—prepared a very clever variant & is about to incorporate *all* the acrostics into a hectographed booklet for use in his English classes. Nor is that all. The youthful Comte d'Erlette is editing a Wisconsin Poetry Anthology for the [sometimes straight & sometimes racketeering] publisher Henry Harrison, & having seen Moe's acrostic decided to include it in the volume.[8] All this from little Bobby's idle notion of writing an acrostic (his original idea was to have each of us contribute parts to a single poem, but this soon proved impracticable), while seated on a tombstone on a summer's afternoon. If I can find a carbon of the various texts I'll send it along . . . . to be returned at your complete leisure.

Have been having a hell of a rush—almost as bad as last spring because of the time perforce lost during Ar-Ech-Bei's long visit. Reading & correspondence in chaos—& the other week I was up 60 hours without sleep finishing a damnable piece of revision which had become overdue. (It involved the compilation of a complete reading guide covering the whole of literature, the sciences, & the arts!)[9] Weather getting cold—yet I still managed to totter out to the pastoral meads & darkling groves now & then, as well as to do occasional reading & writing in the sun on Prospect Terrace. Haven't read the Oct. W T, but its predecessor was uniformly lousy—except, probably, for the instalment of Two-gun's serial, which I haven't yet read.

Well—I shall probably be getting the cryptic eidola off this afternoon. Hate to see them go, & wish I weren't too damn broke to detain one or two!

Hope they arrive in good shape. Two were broken in transit from Young Melmoth, but Ar-E'ch-Bei repaired them masterfully. ¶ Hope all is reasonably well in Averoigne. ¶ Yrs by the 7th Avatar of Zhin-Kalath
—E'ch-Pi-El

[P.S.] Had a very pleasant letter from Virgil Finlay the W T illustrator—who certainly is a brilliant chap.

[P.P.S.] Ar-Ech Bei's new address will be % GEORGE H. GEIGER, 104 THIRD AVE., LEAVENWORTH, KANSAS.

[enclosed card]
Just mailed the eidola & found that the postage doesn't come anywhere near what you sent. Furthermore, *you* oughn't to be paying for *my* enjoyment of the eikons anyhow! So here's a modest refund which conscience & a sense of justice impel me to make!

¶ Am reading Hamlin Garland's book of occult dope—lent me by Comte d'Erlette. Some swell source material for macabre fiction—though the "manifestations" recorded tend to be trivial. Usual stuff, for the most part. ¶ Yrs by The Onyx Stela
———E'ch-Pi-El

[P.P.P.S. on envelope:] Last moment—note change of Ar-E'ch-Bei's address from that given within. He's just transferred to another uncle's household, & is to be reached:

% H. M. Langworthy
810 W. 57th ST. TERRACE,
KANSAS CITY, MO.

Notes

1. Qianlong (Ch'ien-Lung) (1711–1799), sixth emperor of the Manchu-led Qing dynasty.

2. See letter 221n1. It is not certain what HPL means, for Ms. Sheppard is listed at 66 College in Providence directories through 1942.

3. Probably William Jenks, *The Comprehensive Commentary on the Holy Bible.*

4. *Phantagraph* for August 1936 contained HPL's "Robert Ervin Howard: 1906–1936" (an abridgment of "In Memoriam: Robert Ervin Howard") and other memorials to Howard.

5. Margaret Sylvester [Ronan] (1918–2010), correspondent of HPL (1934–37). As Margaret Ronan she wrote the preface to a school edition of HPL's *The Shadow over Innsmouth and Other Stories of Horror* (New York: Scholastic Books, 1971).

6. Nils H. Frome (1918–1962), a Canadian fan and correspondent of HPL (October 1936–1937), editor of *Supramundane Stories.*

7. James Blish (1921–1975) and William Miller, Jr., (1921–1979?) published several issues of a mimeographed fanzine entitled the *Planeteer.* HPL's poem "The Wood" was scheduled

to appear in the *Planeteer* 2, No. 1 (September 1936): 5–6; pages containing the poem were printed, but the issue was not completed or published.

8. Adolphe de Castro, "Edgar Allan Poe" (*WT,* May 1937); RHB, "St. John's Churchyard," and HPL, "In a Sequester'd Providence Churchyard Where Once Poe Walk'd" (*Science-Fantasy Correspondent,* March–April 1937). HPL's poem was reprinted in *WT* (May 1938) as "Where Poe Once Walked: An Acrostic Sonnet." Maurice W. Moe wrote a poem of his own and published it, along with HPL's, RHB's, and de Castro's, in a mimeographed booklet, *Four Acrostic Sonnets on Poe* (1936). Moe's poem was published in *Poetry out of Wisconsin,* ed. August Derleth and Raymond E. F. Larsson (New York: Henry Harrison, 1937). Henry Kuttner's Kuttner's "Where He Walked" was not published. The five acrostic poems were published in David E. Schultz, "In a Sequester'd Churchyard," *Crypt of Cthulhu* No. 57 (St. John's Eve 1988): 26–29.

9. The "reading guide" was written for Anne Tillery Renshaw's *Well Bred Speech.* HPL's work on the book was for naught, since most of his revisions and additions (including the essay now called "Suggestions for a Reading Guide") were omitted from the final version.

[327]　　[ANS]¹

[Postmarked Auburn, Cal.,
13 October 1936]

Dear Éch-Pi-El:

Carvings and your letter arrived some days ago. Glad that you and Krang's acolyte were so much taken with the primal and diabolic teraphim. Will write anon. Have recently done a definitive representation of Tsathoggua in serpentine. Yrs., Klarkash-Ton

Notes

1. *Front:* Unidentified.

[328]　　[ANS]¹

[Postmarked Auburn, Cal.,
13 November 1936]

Dear Éch-Pi-El:

Letter will follow this in a day or two. Hope all is well in witch-ridden Arkham. You would enjoy the clear, warmish autumn days on this Druidic hill of mine in outermost Averoigne.

I send you the Sign of the Elder Entities.
Klarkash-Ton

Notes

1. *Front:* Unidentified.

[329]   [TLS, JHL]

> Palace of the Mithridates, at the serving
> of the strychnine-seasoned supper.
>   [27 November 1936]

Dear Éch-Pi-El:

I might have written before this, but have been stayed by the realization that your press of correspondence is no doubt far heavier than mine. Anyway, you should have had a couple of cards from me; the first one acknowledging the return of the sculptures.

I am pleased that you and Ar-Ech-Bei found the collection of teraphim so much to your liking. I infer, though, that my list of titles, which corresponded to the numbers on the bases, was not passed along. The names were really a good part of the fun. No. 1, the little cameo that you mentioned, was The Black Dog of Commoriom; no. 13, the unicornous female monster with claws and carapace, was The Harpy; no. 8, the slim black thing with rows of ciphers on its body, was The Reptile-Man. And the one you referred to as ᚼA must have been The Entity from Algol. The number (9) was erased from its base. ᚼA is merely a signature—my first two initials in old Etruscan.[1]

Dagon, which Donald bought, was really the masterpiece of the whole lot.[2] He sent me some excellent photos of it and the others. If you haven't seen copies of these photos, I'll ship them along to you presently. Don't worry about not feeling able to buy anything: you will, in time, become the recipient of more than one gift. At present I am experimenting with the making of moulds for five pieces and hope to make some more accurate casts in the hardest plaster obtainable. These, I believe, might sell as "novelties," if offered at prices running from 50¢ upward. Certainly this seems the best way to make money from the stuff, if any is to be made. Few people, especially in this neck of the woods, will pay more for an original sculpture than they would for a cast of some cheap abomination from the 5 & 10. That being the case, I see no reason why I should waste any more of my originals upon them. Incidentally, I can have an exhibition of sculptures at the Crocker Art Gallery in Sacramento after the first of the year. According to the director, who came to see my stuff some time ago, prices should range from $5.00 for the smallest originals up to $50.00 for my largest piece, an eleven-inch statuette. The last-named would please you, since it represents a monster somewhat akin to Cthulhu—in fact, so much so that I have christened it Cthulhu's Child.

I hope that your routine is less overburdened now and that weather and health conditions are at least tolerable. Here, things are pretty much the same, though my father seems slightly improved for the present. We have had a long dry fall, with only the veriest sprinkling of rain; and at present indications such weather may continue indefinitely. The nights, though, are getting colder, and have sometimes been little above the freezing-point. As for my own condition—well, I pretty nearly succumbed to various worries, griefs and bedevilments a little while back. But a round scolding from Mrs. S.,[3] in addition to even more self-beratement and ridicule, is getting me out of it. I think I shall soon become like that old Persian king who thrived upon upas and aconite.

I re-read The Haunter of the Dark with immense pleasure, and look forward to a like experience with The Thing on the Doorstep. It would have surprised me prodigiously if Wright had *not* accepted these tales. I believe he would accept anything of yours that didn't violate his cast-iron prejudices about length and "plot." As to the proposed English collection of your tales, I must say that it sounds like a damn good idea. For some reason, British publishers seem more receptive to weird collections than their American congeners. Our old friend Doc. Keller, I notice, has had some of his stuff published in France.[4]

I have written to Ar-Ech-Bei, and feel more concerned over his general hard luck than over such trivial details as the delay of Incantations. As I told him, there's no hurry in presenting the book to a world that has not yet exhausted the edition of E. & C. printed 14 years ago.

Thanks for clippings and acrostics. I return the latter, as per request. Yours and Barlow's strike me as being much the best ones. Such things must be damnably hard to write, and I have never attempted them. But if I could have joined that group in the old churchyard, I am sure that I should have felt a similar inspiration and impulse toward emulation.

The crop of Fan magazines is even more amazing and astounding and weird and wondrous[5] than most of the stuff to which they devote their attention, enthusiasm and criticism. Surely two or three of such things, with interests divided between pure fantasy and its more or less scientific coeval, would be enough. I rather agree with your estimate of Science-Fantasy Correspondent. Science Fiction Critic, issued by Claire P. Beck[6] of Lakeport, Cal., is refreshingly sound and genuinely critical, from what I have seen of it. Young Beck came to visit me some months ago and impressed me by his intelligence. But I confess I don't see how these magazines can survive: they are getting thicker than wood-mushrooms after a warm rain.

Howard's death startled and shocked me as it must have shocked everyone else. It is understandable but infinitely tragic and regrettable . . . Sometimes, though, the anticipation of an event is more unbearable than the event itself; and I wonder if Howard might not have pulled through if the nurse had been less frank.

I admired Barlow's memorial sonnet greatly. Your prose tribute, and that of Price, were fine.[7]

I enclose a recent poem. Wright accepted it and will no doubt print it before long.[8]

Yours for the resurgence of R'lyeh and the melting of the ice-cap from utmost Lomar.

Klarkash-Ton

Notes

1. See Rickard 12: "Most of the carvings are signed on the bottom in a rather unusual manner. It consists of the letters K and A, with the K facing backwards. According to Smith, the turned about K stood for both C and K in our alphabet. The inscription, then, stands either for the initials of Clark Ashton, or for the nickname given him by Lovecraft, 'Klarkash-Ton'."

2. The statue is shown on the spine of CAS's *The Abominations of Yondo*.

3. Genevieve K. Sully.

4. Probably the French translation of David H. Keller's novel *The Eternal Conflict* (1949), *La Guerre du lierre* (Issy-les-Moulineaux: La Fenêtre ouverte, 1936).

5. The adjectives describing fan magazines correspond to the titles of actual pulp magazines.

6. Beck later printed an edition of CAS's *Nero and Other Poems*.

7. "The Eyrie" (*WT* October 1936; with RHB's "R.E.H.") contains a quotation from Price (following HPL's letter excerpt): "To which E. Hoffmann Price, the only WEIRD TALES author who knew Howard personally, adds: 'I know of few people whose sudden death would be such a savage kick on the chin. Lovecraft says it is the saddest blow to writers since the death of Henry S. Whitehead—and I answer, saying, 'Be damned to writing—it's a lot worse blow to anyone who knew Bob and his parents.' Bob Howard was as complex and likable a character as one would meet in many a long day's march. There is going to be much wailing among the fantasy fans, and just as much among those who read only Howard's vivid action stories in other books—but the heaviest of it is coming from those who met him in his native territory'" (378–79). But see EHP's comments following HPL's "In Memoriam" in *Fantasy Magazine* (September 1936): "I won't add to Lovecraft's critique of Howard—except this true bit: I got a copy of a Cross Plains paper, reprinting one of Howard's last stories, a western. And though feeling pretty damn much kicked in the solar plexus, I turned to read the story. Listen, brother—in a couple of lines I began to grin, and then laughed right out. It's kind of insulting your intelligence, my explaining that, but who cares, you're too far on to kick back, so here goes—as I read that yarn, Howard himself popped up in every line of it, so vividly and humanly, it was like talking to him again, and I couldn't believe he was dead—I mean, the illusion of reality was so intense. That means, dear sir and fellow sufferer, that Robert Ervin Howard could write, and that his much vaunted fantasy yarns were just childish and immature growing pains to what the man could do when he was writing with both hands! By God, getting a hearty laugh out of me the day I heard he had croaked took genius and nothing else. And with all due respect to HPL's tribute, I offer this as a tribute to end all tributes—I nearly busted a gut laughing through that story, in spite of feeling about as low as I ever remember feeling about anyone's curtain lines. You either get this one hundred percent or you miss it and think I've got a hell of a sense of humor" (32).

8. "Song of the Necromancer."

1937

[330]   [ALS]

Pinnacle of Zith
—Hour of the Upward Lightning
[Postmarked 5 February 1937]

Dear Klarkash-Ton:—

Your cards of Oct. 13 & Nov. 13, with the interesting glimpses of Regio Averonum, formed gratifying evidences of your continued tri-dimensional sojourn pending the arrival of an ampler bulletin. I was glad to learn that the eidola safely reached you, & trust they were undamaged. Two of the pieces were broken when they arrived here, but Krang's acolyte mended them most ingeniously with cement—as he did my long-broken Aztec calendar-stone & a Kien Lung vase which I broke during his visit. I envy the young rascal his dexterity!

My last report, I believe, was dated around the first of October—no inclement period in vampire-haunted Averoigne, but the end of outdoor reading & writing beneath the polar auroras of the Land of Lomar. However, I arranged to take occasional trips to the woods & fields till well over the line in November. The unique feature of my autumnal explorations was that I succeeded in discovering several splendid rural regions within a three-mile radius of here *which I had never seen before.* One is a wooded hill—Neutaconkanut—on the western rim of the town, whence a series of marvellous views of the outspread city & adjacent countryside may be obtained. I had often ascended it before, but the exquisitely mystical sylvan scenery beyond the crest—curious mounds, hummocked pastures, & hushed, hidden valleys—was wholly new to me. Late in October—the 28th, to be precise—I explored this region still further—including the country west of Neutaconkanut & the western slopes of that eminence itself. At certain stages of this ramble I penetrated a terrain which took me half a mile from any spot I had ever trod before in the course of a long life. I followed a road which branches north & west from the Plainfield Pike, ascending a low rise which skirts Neutaconkanut's western foot & which commands an utterly idyllic vista of rolling meadows, ancient stone walls, hoary groves, & distant cottage roofs to the west & south. Only 2 or 3 miles from the city's heart, & yet in the primal rural New England of the first colonists! Just before sunset I ascended the hill by a precipitous cart-path bordering an ancient wood, & from the dizzy crest obtained an almost stupefying prospect of unfolded leagues of farmsteads & champaigns, gleaming rivulets & far-off forests, & mystical orange sky with a great solar disc sinking redly amidst bars of stratus clouds. Entering the wood, I saw the actual sunset through the trees, & then turned east to cross the hill to that more familiar cityward slope which I have always known. Never before had I realised the great extent of Neutaconkanut's surface. It is really a miniature plateau or table-land, with valleys, ridges, & summits of its own, rather than a single hill. From some of its hidden interior meadows—remote from every sign of nearby human life—I secured truly marvellous glimpses of the remote urban skyline—a dream of enchanted pinnacles & domes half-floating in air, & with an obscure aura of mystery around them. The upper windows of some of the taller towers held the fire of the sun after I had lost it, affording a spectacle of cryptic & curious glamour. Then I saw the great yellow disc of the Hunter's Moon (2 days before full) floating above the belfries & minarets, while in the orange-glowing west Venus & Jupiter commenced to twinkle. My route across the plateau was varied—sometimes through the interior, but now & then getting toward the wooded edge where dark valleys slope down to the plain below, & huge balanced boulders on rocky heights impart a spectral, druidic effect as they stand out against the twilight. I did not begin to cover the full extent of the plateau, & can see that I have a field for several voyages of discovery in the spring. Finally I came to more familiar ground—where the grassy ridge of an old buried aqueduct gives the illusion of one of those vestigial Roman roads in Arthur Machen's Caermaen country—& stood once more on the well-known eastward crest which I have gazed at since infancy. The outspread city was rapidly lighting up, & lay like a constellation in the deepening dusk. The moon poured down increasing floods of pale gold, & the glow of Venus & Jupiter in the fading west grew intense. Then down the steep hillside to the car line (too cold for enjoyable walking when there was no scenery to compensate for shivers!) & back to the prosaic haunts of man.

Oct. 20 & 21 were phenomenally warm, & I utilised them in exploring a hitherto untapped region down the east shore of Narragansett Bay where the Barrington Parkway winds along the lofty bluff above the water. I found a highly fascinating forest called the Squantum Woods—where there are great oaks & birches, steep slopes & rock ledges, & breath-taking westward vistas beyond the trees. On both occasions there was a fine sunset—then glimpses of the crescent moon, Venus, & Jupiter . . . . & the lights of far-off Providence from high places along the parkway. On my expedition of the 20th a particularly congenial bodyguard or retinue attended me through the sunlit arcades of the grove—in the persons of *two tiny representatives of the Kappa Alpha Tau,* one grey & one tortoise-shell, who appeared out of nowhere in the midst of the sylvan solitudes. Blithe spirits of the ancient wood—furry faunlets of the shadowy vale! I wonder where their mother was? Judging by their diminutiveness, they could scarce have been fully graduated from her as a source of nourishment. Probably they appertained to an hospital whose grounds are contiguous with the mystical forest. Both were at first very timid, & reluctant to let Grandpa catch them; but eventually the little grey fellow became very purr-ful & amicable—climbing over the Old Gentleman, playing with twigs & with Grandpa's watch-charm, & eventually curling up & going to sleep in the grandpaternal lap. But little brother remained suspicious & aloof—clawing & spitting with surprising vehemence on the one occasion when Grandpa caught him. He hung around, however, because he didn't want to lose his brother! Not wishing to wake my new friend, I carried him about when I continued my ramble—little tortoise-shell brother tagging along reluctantly & dubiously at a discreet distance in the rear. When the grey faunlet awaked, he requested to be set down; but proceeded to trot companionably after Grandpa—sometimes getting under the old gentleman's feet & considerably retarding progress. Thus I roamed the venerable forest aisles for an hour & a half—till the ruddy disc of the sun vanished behind the farther hills & treetops. As I emerged from the wood, I feared that my faithful retinue might follow me on to the parkway & incur the perils of motor traffic—& was considering expedients for discouraging their further attendance—but discovered that they were not without native caution. Or perhaps they were wholly genii loci, without real existence apart from their dim nemorense habitat. At any rate, Little Grey Boy paused at the edge of the grove with a mewed farewell (& a wish to be respectfully remembered to Dame Simaetha)—& naturally little Tortoise-Shell had no great eagerness to follow. I bade them a regretful & ceremonious adieu—& on the next day looked for them in vain.

On the whole, though, our autumn was notably lacking in visual splendour. Not as prematurely cold as I had feared, but with the dullest October foliage within my memory. Half the trees were swept bare by heavy rains as soon as they began to turn, whilst the other half remained green for an anomalous length of time—the leaves then falling almost as soon as they did turn. *Red* hues were especially rare. The result was a tremendous loss of glamour—although we heard of gorgeous woodlands at points not many miles away, while the Vermont & New-Hampshire leafage is said to have been of unparalleled magnificence. Comte d'Erlette also told of riotous & record-breaking autumnal colours in Wisconsin. We had quite a snowfall Nov. 24—phenomenally early for Rhode Island—but it did not remain long on the ground.

Meanwhile the season of lectures & kindred indoor sports is upon us. Not so long ago I attended a meeting of the local organisation of amateur astronomers—"The Skyscrapers"—which functions more or less under the auspices of Brown University—& was astonished at its degree of development. Some of the members are really serious scientific observers, & the society has just purchased a well-known private observatory whose presiding genius recently died.[1] It has separate meteor, variable star, planet &c. sections, which hold meetings of their own & report as units, & enjoy the use of the college observatory. At the recent meeting there was an address on early R.I. astronomy, & the reflecting telescope of Joseph Brown—used to observe the transit of Venus on June 3, 1769 & owned by the college since 1780—was exhibited.

Recent W T issues sustain the accustomed discouraging average. November had a tale by the late Two-Gun Bob with powerful touches, plus unexpectedly good stuff by McClusky, Bloch, & Whipple. Two-Gun also shines posthumously in December—his description of the ancient ruins holding a very striking quality. Bloch's Haitian tale has good touches, & Kuttner's story is excellent—with a real punch for a climax. "Portrait of a Murderer" is poor, & "The Theatre Upstairs" does not live up to its atmospheric possibilities. Comte d'Erlette's offering is just another pot-boiler, & Sultan Malik's collaborated venture is standard "eckshun" stuff with just a touch of redeeming mystery & suspense. "Out of the Sun" is incredibly bad—almost touching W T's low-water mark. I didn't care very much for "The Album" (despite a certain atmospheric effectiveness) because of the anachronisms—the tacit assumption that successful photography existed in the 18th century (actually, nothing like a permanent photograph existed before Niepce's achievement of 1814), & the absurd gibberish supposed (judging from the date the book began to work, as indicated by its captures) to represent the English of the late 18th century. Tsathoggua! but what sort of insanity gets hold of these birds (W. H. Hodgson is the classic & memorable offender, & Seabury Quinn has also pulled some choice boners in this line) when they try to represent the diction of an age which after all is, historically speaking, essentially modern? Haven't they ever read Goldsmith & Fielding & Johnson & Gibbon & Smollett & the dozens of other prose writers of that fairly recent yesterday? What in Yuggoth's name causes them to drag down from the remoter reaches of antiquity a cobwebbed jargon more Chaucerian or Elizabethan than anything else, & serve it up as contemporary with Burke's speeches & the Declaration of Independence? Actually—assuming a date around 1780—the message in the book would have run something like this:

> *To Whomſoever May Open This Book:*
> This is ſet down as a Warning to you, Sir or Madam, that you are not to open this Book beyond the Place mark'd by a red Riband. It wou'd be better for you to throw the whole Book unopen'd into the Fire; but being unable to do ſo myſelf, I cannot hope that you will. I do neverthelefs adjure you to look nowhere in it beyond the Riband, left you loſe yourſelf to this World, Body & Soul; for truly, it is a Tomb for the Living.

I haven't had time yet to read the Jany. issue, but am immensely pleased with Finlay's drawing for my "Thing on the Doorstep." It is infinitely superior to his design for the "Haunter."

Meanwhile the "fan magazines" pile up—there must be 25 or 30 of them now, making a little world of amateur journalism like the N.A.P.A. or the good old U.A.P.A. You doubtless saw the large anniversary *Fantasy*, with my badly misprinted obituary of Two-Gun Bob. *The Phantagraph* appears regularly, & the other day I received the first issue of *Fanciful Tales*—with 59 misprints in the text of my "Nameless City." I haven't seen *The Science-Fiction Critic,* whose youthful editor called on you,[2] but have been asked for contributions by publishers in British Columbia, San Francisco, East Orange, N.J., & various other points on the way. The first issue of the Conover–Stickney *Correspondent* lives up to expectations, & Stickney's typographical accuracy ought to be cited widely & loudly as a model for all young publishers. This journal is going to carry on the reprinting of my "Supernatural Horror in Literature" from where Hornig left off.[3] A revived *Marvel Tales* from Crawford is still promised—but heaven only knows when that bird will do anything! Glad "Innsmouth" reached you safely. The typography, format, & binding [could] hardly be worse—but the Utpatel drawings [redeem] it. I corrected all the errors I had [found] before sending the volume, but more have [since] revealed themselves—hence the enclosed list. [You c]ould incorporate the changes in the text as I did with penknife & pencil. Well—it's a book, anyhow!

I trust you safely received the autumn *Californian* containing the correct text of that Morse sonnet to you which *The Phantagraph* badly misprinted. In the same issue you'll find some interesting prose & verse by Rheinhart Kleiner concerning our old gang in New York a decade ago.[4]

Two-Gun's death continues to evoke melancholy echoes. Undoubtedly it was a peculiar *piling-on* of strains which brought about the rash finale. A difference of even one small factor might have averted the tragedy. *If* he had not worn himself out with sleepless vigils for more than a year . . . *if* (as you suggest) the nurse had not given him the bad news so early . . . . But alas, it is too late now! There will be no successor to fill his peculiarly distinctive place. Price may try to parallel some of his work—but the difference will be easy to perceive. Ar-E'ch-Bei spoke all too truly when he wrote:

"Conan, the Warrior-King, lies stricken dead".[5]

Ar-E'ch-Bei, incidentally, seems to be acquiring a certain measure of content in Kansas City—taking a quite exacting course at the Art Institute there. It's a toss-up whether he'll turn to literature or pictorial art as a primary medium of expression. In the interim he mourns his separation from press, type, binding apparatus, & the cherished volumes in his "Vaults of Yoh-Vombis". Here's hoping a volume of "Incantations" will mark a glorious reunion next year!

Edkins is coming along finely (though set back a bit by a bronchial cold)—responding to the blessed warmth of Florida, whither he migrated early in November. Even the last ill-effects of his terrible August operation have now vanished. In the Winter *Californian* he will have a story called "The Affair of the Centaurs"—representing his own closest approach to the fantasy field which he views with so little sympathy.[6] I'll see that you receive a copy of this. Another good recoverer is little Kenneth Sterling—now avidly mopping up the difficult first-year curriculum at Harvard, & troubled but little by his health. He has chosen *Poe* as the subject of the year's primary research-&-theme project.[7]

Glad the acrostics proved amusing. I haven't much use for artificial stunts of this sort, since no aesthetic end is served by the imposition of a puerile & irrelevant mechanical handicap in versification. You could easily have beaten all hands in our idle contest of last August. Old 'Dolph's effusion impressed me not all profoundly—& even less profoundly was I impressed by his attempt last month to furnish a "revised" version of mine! A couple of weeks ago I was again egged into numbers by a remark of Finlay's—who was lamenting the decline of the old-time custom of writing verses on current works of art & literature. Just to prove that I am in truth a survivor of the 18th Century, I felt impelled to produce the following:

To Mr. Finlay, Upon his Drawing for Mr. Bloch's
Tale, "The Faceless God".

In dim abysses pulse the shapes of night,
Hungry & hideous, with strange mitres crown'd;
Black pinions beating in fantastic flight
From orb to orb thro' sunless voids profound.
None dares to name the cosmos whence they course,
Or guess the look on each amorphous face,
Or speak the words that with resistless force
Would draw them from the hells of outer space.

Yet here upon a page our frighten'd glance
Finds monstrous forms no human eye should see;
Hints of those blasphemies whose countenance
Spreads death & madness thro' infinity.
What limner he who braves black gulfs alone
And lives to make their alien horrors known?

Well—one thing leads to another, & before I knew it I had this specimen on paper too:

To Clark Ashton Smith, Esq., Upon his Phantastck
Tales, Verses, Pictures, & Sculptures.

A time-black tower against dim banks of cloud;
Around its base the pathless, pressing wood.
Shadow & silence, moss & mould, enshroud
Grey, age-fell'd slabs that once as cromlechs stood.
No fall of foot, no song of bird awakes
The lethal aisles of sempiternal night,
Tho' oft with stir of wings the dense air shakes,
As in the tower there glows a pallid light.

For here, apart, dwells one whose hands have wrought
Strange eidola that chill the world with fear;
Whose graven runes in tones of dread have taught
What things beyond the star-gulfs lurk & leer.
Dark Lord of Averoigne—whose windows stare
On pits of dream no other gaze could bear!

These things seem to be more or less in my Fungi from Yuggoth tradition of 7 years ago—maybe I'll try them on the "fan mags". No use bothering Old Farny with 'em—he turned both of Morse's similar sonnets down.

Ascending from doggerel to poetry—many thanks for the advance glimpse of "Song of the Necromancer". It has a peculiarly effective dreamlike pageantry which makes me hope for its eventual incorporation in "Incantations". I'm certainly glad Satrap Pharnabazus had the good sense to accept it!

Glad the "Haunter" stood up well under a second reading, & hope the "Doorstep" did the same. As for that British collection Leedle Shoolie Schvartz has in mind—I don't think anything will come of it. And I doubt if any of my immortal works will ever be translated into French like Doc Keller's—or into Swedish like some of Sultan Malik's! One small item to the good (the modest extent of precisely £1 sterling) is the prospective reprinting of "Pickman's Model" in British "Not at Night Omnibus" to be issued next spring. I hope they use the real text, & not the emasculated one with the "Oh, gracious me!" ending which Wright put over on me in the recent reprint.[8] I'm giving Old Farny hell for that!

Thanks extremely for the cuttings—weird & feline alike. 24-toed Thomas seems to be just the right sort of Kappa Alpha Tau material! The spectral items are all fancy-stirring—& those anent witch-doctors, African & Australian, arouse the usual psychological & anthropological speculations.

I'm glad to hear that your father is somewhat better, & hope that your worries & burdens may be kept at as low an ebb as possible. Certainly, you ought never to succumb to discouragement; for with your driving energy & fund of unique & versatile genius the prospects must always be brighter than momentary depression-spells might sometimes seem to suggest. You ought, even in the midst of the most seemingly intolerable conditions, to thank Tsathoggua & the shade of Eibon for the inexhaustible fund of creative zeal & ability with which nature has endowed you—a fund which keeps you turning out splendid artistic material in half a dozen fields in spite of handicaps which would reduce the average aesthetic creator to nervous chaos & exhausted silence. I'm surely glad that Mrs. Sully—whose household, I trust, rounded out a uniformly pleasant sojourn in Seattle—helped to jolt you out of the state of incipient pessimism lately besetting you.

Yes—the travelling exhibit surely met with thorough & enthusiastic appreciation in these parts, as it likewise did in Manhattan. The list of titles was indeed missing, much to my regret—& malign coincidence aggravated the matter by making me unable to find the letter in which you had referred to some of them by name. However, I did identify "The Harpy" from a combination of memory & inference—& enjoyed then all even in their incognito state. I'm accursedly sorry that I missed "Dagon", & would surely appreciate the loan of the photographs you mention—which I have *not* seen up to now. Some time I hope I can invest in some of these carven horrors—in a suitable way, & not through 'bumming 'em offen you'! This year my fiscal state is as perilous as the Vesuvian slopes in A.D. 79! Your idea of moulds & casts interests me vastly—for it really is a crime that some of your sculptural triumphs are not widely distributable. If some of the world's greatest statues— the bronzes—are made in moulds, why can't some of yours be? With proper apparatus, perfect casts can be made from any piece of statuary without harming the original in the least—indeed, the Metropolitan Museum will make a cast of any of its statues for an appropriate price. Thus Loveman, for $7.50, got a splendid cast of that Greek athlete's head which is such a post-card-featured show piece. Some day, through a similar deal, I want to get hold of a stern old Roman's head—a portrait-bust of the republican period— which has always taken my fancy.

[*Marginal note:*] Old Bill Lumley is ecstatically eloquent about the Winged Daemon you sent him!

Congratulations, by the way, on your prospective exhibit at the Crocker Art Gallery. That ought to be a great step on the way to recognition—& perhaps to profitable sales as well. I feel flattered that your piece de resistance bears a name derived from my own synthetic myth-cycle. Blessings on Cthulhu's Child! Incidentally, Finlay tells me that he has done quite a bit of "sculpting"—sometimes (for lack of friable stone in his region) from large hardened lumps of plaster. You & he ought to compare notes. Ar-E'ch-Bei's art school products are, I judge, increasingly clever . . . at least, I so judge from the tiny image of a sleeping feline (black as Mater Simaetha) which he sent me at Yuletide.

I trust, by the way, that your Yule was duly festive. Ours here was commendably cheerful—including a turkey dinner at the boarding-house across the garden, with a congenial Kappa Alpha Tau member meandering among the tables & finally jumping up on the window-seat for a nap. We had a tree in front of the hearth in my aunt's living-room—its verdant boughs thickly festooned with a tinsel imitation of Florida's best Spanish moss, & its outlines emphasised by a not ungraceful lighting system. Around its base were ranged the modest Saturnalian gifts—which included (on my side) a hassock tall enough to let me reach the top shelves of my bookcases, & (on my aunt's side) a cabinet of drawers for odds & ends, not unlike my own filing cabinets, but of more ladylike arrangement & aspect. Of outside gifts the most distinctive was perhaps that which came quite unexpectedly from young Conover, the editor of the new "fan mag" (which is, by the way, about to absorb Schwartz's *Fantasy*) in Cambridge, Maryland . . . daown awn de Eastern Sho'. For lo! when I had removed numberless layers of corrugated paper & excelsior, what should I find before me but the yellowed & crumbling fragments of *a long-interred human skull!* Verily, a fitting gift from a youthful ghoul to one of the hoary elders of the necropolitan clan! This sightlessly staring monument of mortality came from an Indian mound not far from the sender's home—a place distinguished by many archaeological exploits on the part of the enterprising editor & his young friends. Its condition is such as to make its reassembly a somewhat ticklish task—so that I may reserve it for the ministrations of some expert mender like Ar-E'ch-Bei upon the occasion of a future visit. Viewing this shattered yield of the ossuary, the reflective fancy strives to evoke the image of him to whom it once belonged. Was it some feathered chieftain who in his day oft ululated in triumph as he counted the tufted scalps sliced from coppery or colonist foes? Or some crafty shaman who with masque & drum called forth from the Great Abyss those shadowy Things which were better left uncalled? This we may never know—unless perchance some incantation droned out of the Book of Eibon will have power to draw strange emanations from the lifeless & centuried clay, & raise up amidst the cobwebs of my ancient study a shimmering mist not without power to speak. In such a case, the revelation might be such that no man hearing it could any longer live save as one of those hapless entities 'who laugh, but smile no more'!⁹

By the way—Sultan Malik is lavish in his appreciation of the hellish carven entity lately received from you. So moved with admiration was he, that he wrote me a long & enthusiastic description of the alien horror immediately upon receipt. I can well imagine its sinister power—& judge from the Sultan's description that it is *not* one of those which went the rounds last summer. Malik has, I presume, told you of the sorrow reigning at many-pillar'd Irem—over the total vanishment in the evil & mysterious hills of Khi-Khi, Conquering Lion of Judah & pupil of the likewise-vanish'd Nimrod of yesteryear. Positively, the Kappa Alpha Tau must take definite action against the hellish forces which are engulfing some of its finest members from General Tabasco down! I trust you will instruct Dame Simaetha to prepare her most potent & revengeful magic, & to bring the matter up at the very next Estbat on Crater Ridge!

Heard a good lecture recently on the early coastal civilisations of Peru—some of which are as ancient as the mountain civilisation. I was astonished to learn of the size of the some of the cities recently excavated. Being built of perishable adobe, they have to be protected as soon as exposed. The mural designs bespeak a high order of artistic development, & resemble the patterns on the textiles unearthed with mummies. The earlier of the two civilisations—Nazca, which preceded Chimu—goes back to the early centuries A.D. One may only speculate upon its origin & degree of autochthonousness. The present lecture was well supplemented by lantern slides & by specimens of textiles, pottery, & other artifacts.

Commiserations on the cold weather in Averoigne—a cold which I see has extended as far south as Los Angeles. Our Eastern winter has so far been very warm—temperatures of 60° & over extending well into January. However, I've been feeling rather on the bum—an early exposure to cold having started my old-time winter foot-swelling, & a combination of indigestion & general weakness (perhaps a touch of grippe) being superadded to that. ¶ Yrs by the Twined Trident—E'ch-Pi-El

P.S. Old De Castro has gone to California & is staying with young Kuttner. You may see the cuss eventually, for I suppose he'll want to get north to visit his old stamping-grounds.

[P.P.S.] Belated congratulations on the enclosed review, which Ar-Ech-Bei forwarded with instructions to return to you.

[P.P.P.S. on envelope:] Have you seen the winter *Californian* with R H B's "Night Ocean"?

Notes

1. The private observatory of Frank Evans Seagrave (1859–1934) was located at 119 Benefit Street; it is now at 47 Peeptoad Road, North Scituate, RI. Seagrave's executor, Wayne F. Angell, died on 7 July 1936.
2. The *Science Fiction Critic* was edited by Claire P. Beck (1919–1999). The Beck brothers published CAS's *Nero and Other Poems* (1937) and RHB's edition of HPL's commonplace book (1938).
3. It did not. HPL had prepared a synopsis of the chapters published in *FF*, to bring readers of *Science-Fantasy Correspondent* up to speed, but it was not published until 1974.
4. See Kleiner's "After a Decade and the Kalem Club," *Californian* 4, No. 2 (Fall 1936): 45–47, and his poem "After a Decade" (p. 44 of the same issue).
5. RHB, "R. E. H.," l. 1.
6. *Californian* 4, No. 3 (Winter 1936): 15–26.
7. Published as "The Horror Element in Poe." *Californian*, 5, No. 3 (Winter 1937): 33–45.
8. HPL seems to refer to the change of "But by God, Eliot," in the final sentence to "But by heaven, Eliot."
9. Poe, "The Haunted Palace" (l. 48).

Appendix

Annie E. P. Gamwell

Postcard to Clark Ashton Smith

[Postmarked Providence, R.I.,
30 November 1938]

Nov. 30, 1938

My dear Mr. Smith—

   I am still in the midst of my sad memories & the many things which my nephew loved. His loss becomes more serious continually. I found these cards & hope you will care for them. This card is a new excellent old library very near our house, the Providence Athen[a]eum.

Sincerely, A. E. P. Gamwell

H. P. Lovecraft

[Review of *Ebony and Crystal*]

EBONY AND CRYSTAL by CLARK ASHTON SMITH. (4to 152 pp. The Auburn Journal, Auburn, Calif., 1923.*)

Between the urbane sterilities of our bearded Brahmins and the psycho-analytical clinics of our younger intellectuals, American poetry fares badly indeed; a condition expressed with melancholy force by George Sterling[†] in his introduction to the third book of verse from Clark Ashton Smith. More truly sensitive to the wilder dreams of men, and more sublimely cosmic in his imaginative sweep of fancy's chartless chaos than any native versifier since Poe, Mr. Smith has remained in relative obscurity outside his Californian domain because of a public trained to distrust beauty and the adventure of the spirit.

  "Ebony and Crystal" is an artist's intrepid repudiation of the world of trolleys and cash-registers, Freudian complexes and Binet-Simon tests, for realms of exalted and iridescent strangeness beyond space and time yet real as any real-

---

*Actually 1922.—Ed.

†Sterling (1869–1926), a leading Californian poet of the period, had been CAS's mentor since 1911. He also wrote a preface to CAS's second book, *Odes and Sonnets* (1918).—Ed.

ity because dreams have made them so. Mr. Smith has escaped the fetish of life and the world, and glimpsed the perverse, titanic beauty of death and the universe; taking infinity as his canvas and recording in awe the vagaries of suns and planets, gods and daemons, and blind amorphous horrors that haunt gardens of polychrome fungi more remote than Algol and Achernar. It is a cosmos of vivid flame and glacial abysses that he celebrates, and the colourful luxuriance with which he peoples it could be born from nothing less than sheer genius.

The summation of Mr. Smith's exotic vision is perhaps attained in the long phantasmal procession of blank verse pentameters entitled "The Hashish-Eater; or, The Apocalypse of Evil". In this frenzied plunge through nameless gulfs of interstellar terror the Californian presents a narcotic pageant of poisonous vermilion and paralysing shadows whose content is equalled only by its verbal medium; a medium involving one of the most opulent and fastidiously choice vocabularies ever commanded by a writer of English.

Mr. Smith, born in 1893, was the author of an amazing volume at nineteen.* He has kept faithful to the splendour that knows no shackles, and whether in his cosmic orgies or his simpler love-poems has always fulfilled the Cabellian aspiration—"to write perfectly of beautiful happenings".†

From "Supernatural Horror in Literature"

Of younger Americans, none strikes the note of cosmic terror so well as the California poet, artist, and fictionist Clark Ashton Smith, whose bizarre writings, drawings, paintings, and stories are the delight of a sensitive few. Mr. Smith has for his background a universe of remote and paralysing fright— jungles of poisonous and iridescent blossoms on the moons of Saturn, evil and grotesque temples in Atlantis, Lemuria, and forgotten elder worlds, and dank morasses of spotted death-fungi in spectral countries beyond earth's rim. His longest and most ambitious poem, *The Hashish-Eater,* is in pentameter blank verse; and opens up chaotic and incredible vistas of kaleidoscopic nightmare in the spaces between the stars. In sheer daemonic strangeness and fertility of conception, Mr. Smith is perhaps unexcelled by any other writer dead or living. Who else has seen such gorgeous, luxuriant, and feverishly distorted visions of infinite spheres and multiple dimensions and lived to tell the tale? [His short stories deal powerfully with other galaxies, worlds, and dimensions, as well as with strange regions and aeons on the earth. He tells of

---

The Star-Treader and Other Poems (San Francisco: A. M. Robertson, 1912).—Ed.

†James Branch Cabell (1879–1958), American novelist and essayist. The quotation—"at what cost now, in this fleet hour of my vigor, may one write perfectly of beautiful happenings?"—derives from the "Auctorial Induction" of Cabell's *The Certain Hour* (New York: Robert M. McBride, 1916), 17.—Ed.

primal Hyperborea and its black amorphous god Tsathoggua; of the lost continent Zothique, and of the fabulous, vampire-curst land of Averoigne in mediaeval France. Some of Mr. Smith's best work can be found in the brochure entitled *The Double Shadow and Other Fantasies* (1933).]*

Clark Ashton Smith

[Fantasy and Human Experience]†

I should like to point out a few considerations which, apparently, have been overlooked by Mr. Julian Gray in his thoughtful and well-written criticism of science fiction in the letter columns of the June *Amazing Stories*.

To begin with, it seems to me that his definition of literature as being exclusively a study of human reactions and character-development is rather narrow and limited. Literature can be, and does, many things; and one of its most glorious prerogatives is the exercise of imagination on things that lie *beyond* human experience—the adventuring of fantasy into the awful, sublime and infinite cosmos *outside* the human aquarium. In this genre, of which science fiction is one branch, the main interest lies in other elements than mere character-reaction and development, such as would properly be emphasized in a tale of ordinary events and conditions.

Of course, science fiction can, has been, and will be written with a close attention to verisimilitude in such matters. But for the initiate in this type of fiction, and highly imaginative and fantastic fiction in general, the real thrill comes from the description of the *ultrahuman* events, forces and scenes, which properly dwarf the terrene actors to comparative insignificance. For many people—probably more than Mr. Gray realizes—imaginative stories offer a welcome and salutary release from the somewhat oppressive tyranny of the homocentric, and help to correct the deeply introverted, ingrowing values that are fostered by present-day "humanism" and realistic literature with its unhealthy materialism and earth-bound trend. Science fiction, at its best, is akin to sublime and exalted poetry, in its evocation of tremendous, non-anthropomorphic imageries. To demand in such tales the intensive earthly observation of a Hardy is idle and beside the point; and one who approaches them from this angle will miss the true value and beauty.

---

*The portion in brackets was added when HPL revised the text for the *FF* serialization (although this portion did not appear in *FF*).—Ed.

†The letter was published under the title "An Answer to Mr. Julian Gray's Recent Criticism in Our Discussions Columns." The present title was supplied by Charles K. Wolfe, editor of *PD*.—Ed.

It seems to me, too, that Mr. Gray makes a pretty sweeping statement in his remarks about science fiction authors. Doubtless there are hacks in this branch of writing, as in all others; but, on the other hand, there are sincere imaginative artists. One only has to name A. Merritt (at least in his earlier work, such as the original novelette version of "The Moon Pool"), Stanton Coblentz, who has written some gorgeous fantastic satires, John Taine, a master of authentic science, and H. P. Lovecraft, whose "The Color Out of Space" goes infinitely beyond anything of H. G. Wells in its sheer imaginative scope and creation of atmosphere. To say that science fiction writers are "men of doubtful education and still more doubtful intelligence" because they prefer imaginative happenings, cosmic forces, atmosphere, etc., to psychological analysis, is an utterly pointless and senseless statement. But, since there is a fixed gulf, wider and deeper than Erebus, between imaginative people and those who lack imagination, it is no doubt equally senseless to argue this question.

Certainly, however, one must admit that there is vast room for improvement in the general body of science-fiction. This improvement, it seems to me, could lie in the direction of more skilful and finished writing, the exclusion of the trite and overworked, and the elimination of many stories which, on close analysis, are revealed as mere gangster tales or ordinary adventure stories with a futuristic or ultra-planetary setting. A few editorial measures of this sort would go far to remove the reproach which can justly be brought against science-fiction magazines. As a well-wisher, a reader—and also a writer of this genre—I sincerely hope that such an improvement will in time be brought about.

There is one other matter that I should like to touch upon: Mr. Gray's preliminary remarks about the general development of literature. To judge from these, one would think that the world's literature is marked off in perfectly distinct, geological strata! and that all the former, more primitive layers are now hermetically sealed beneath a deep and solid stratum of realism. This, however, is not the case. Romanticism, both in novels and short magazine stories, is still the most popular and widely read genre; and as for the supernatural, which Mr. Gray puts at the archean bottom—well, even that despised branch of literary endeavor is having its innings, both with writers and readers. Apart from folk-lore, the literature of the supernatural is almost a modern invention anyway; and some of the best work in that genre is being done at the present time. Realism, even though it is the only form favored by the alleged "quality magazines" and the self-appointed critical pontiffs, certainly doesn't have the field all to itself. And I think one can safely predict that it never will. The intolerable conditions of modern life and mechanistic civilization, will, one thinks, be more and more conducive to the development of a literature of imaginative "escape."

There is still another angle which occurs to me, *apropos* of Mr. Gray's letter. After all, why shouldn't literature, or at least one literary genre, emphasize

what he calls the "inhuman," which, more properly, is the non-human or extra-human? Isn't it only the damnable, preposterous and pernicious egomania
of the race, which refuses to admit anything but man's own feelings, desires,
aims and actions as worthy of consideration?

This egomania, alas! is manifested in other ways than through literature,
and lies at the bottom of that ruthless aggrandization, that maltreatment of
weaker life-forms, that presumptuous meddling with the delicate balance of
planetary forces, which may sweep our present-day civilization into the limbo
of the dinosaurs. I fear that many super-scientific tales, which depict a world-
wide catastrophe as the result of human meddling with nature, may prove to
be all too prophetic. Any type of writing that would serve even in the smallest
degree as a brake on the madly careening wheels of this racial egomania, is, it
seems to me, more than praiseworthy from a moral standpoint if from none
other.

Clark Ashton Smith
Auburn, California

P. S. On re-reading Mr. Gray's letter, I find that I have forgotten to mention the matter of H. G. Wells, which he brings up. Doubtless it is the particular trend of Wells' mental development that has led him, in latter years, to
abandon the writing of science fiction for that of sociological novels. Wells,
when he wrote the marvelous "Time Machine," "The War of the Worlds,"
and other fine fantasies, had in him much of the artist, perhaps even a little of
the poet. These, however, have been progressively smothered and drowned
out by the growth of the pedagogue, the utilitarian "humanist."

As to Aldous Huxley, I have not read his "Brave New World," which, I
should judge from reviews, is marked by the same congenital pornography as
Huxley's ordinary novels. Satire, of course, is a well-recognized function of
much science fiction, and perhaps some of it has been a little too subtle for
Mr. Gray's apprehension. He seems to have missed Stanton Coblentz, of
whom I have already spoken. If I cared to, I could name others in whom the
satire is even more subtle and implicit.

If Mr. Gray should find my language somewhat violently polemical in
places, he must realize that I have merely availed myself of that parliamentary
privilege which he, in his own letter, has already avowedly pre-empted.

In conclusion, let me recommend to Mr. Gray, and to others who are
similarly minded, the perusal of imaginative fiction for what it really is rather
than for what it isn't. Also, he should realize that there are intelligent (and not
necessarily immature) people who have the courage to dissent from the limited and grossly materialistic definition of literature which he has laid down,
and who, moreover, are not overawed by the burden of present-day authority.

[On "Garbage-Mongering"]

I should like to say a few words anent one or two points which P. Schuyler Miller raises in his interesting letter in the June *Wonder Stories*.

Personally, I cannot see that science fiction is, as he puts it, "unfortunately limited" in its range of expression. At least, I do not think that a type of literature so avowedly imaginative would benefit materially by invading, as so much modern fiction has done, the field of clinical analysis and sex-physiology. That sort of thing has been done *ad infinitum* and *ad nauseum* by non-imaginative writers, such as are favored by the professional "intelligentsia" of our sex-demented republic; and one of the most refreshing things about science fiction, and fantastic fiction in general, is the avoidance of such tritenesses.

To me, the best, if not the only function of imaginative writing, is to lead the human imagination *outward,* to take it into the vast external cosmos, and *away* from all that introversion and introspection, that morbidly exaggerated prying into one's own vitals—and the vitals of others—which Robinson Jeffers has so aptly symbolized as "incest." What we need is less "human interest," in the narrow sense of the term—not more. Physiological—and even psychological analysis—can be largely left to the writers of scientific monographs on such themes. Fiction, as I see it, is not the place for that sort of grubbing.

Certainly I do not think that H. G. Wells, in the tedious analytic novels of his later phase, would be a good model for an imaginative writer. Wells, in his earlier years, wrote some marvelous fantasies. But afterwards, he was more and more seduced into sociology, psychoanalysis, etc., etc., till his stories became a truly awful example of everything that fiction should not be. No doubt they are excellent treatises, but as tales they are simply unreadable.

What science fiction chiefly needs, I should say, is a rigorous raising of literary standards, an insistence on good English as opposed to the jargon of magazine hackwriting. Form and finish are all too often lacking in stories otherwise excellent.

As to gaining the recognition of the "highbrows"—well, I hope that science fiction will never gain it, if the winning of this guerdon must involve an emulation of the squalors and tediosities, the highbrow pornography and general garbage-mongering of the current school of realistic novelists.

Re the celebrated strictures of one Mr. Schwartz, it appears to me that they hardly need refuting, since they are patently ridiculous. "Slack-mouthed" youths and mental subnormals in general are not likely to be interested in either science or imagination, such as is purveyed by *Wonder Stories* and other magazines of the same type.

[Realism and Fantasy]*

Mr. Miller's very able and urbane letter in the December issue makes me feel that my own recent letter on the problem of realism versus fantasy might be supplemented and qualified by a few remarks.

First of all, it should not be inferred that I have the least desire to prescribe limits for the development of science fiction or any form of fiction. On the contrary, I believe that all possibilities should be sounded and explored. When I decried realism in my letter, I was inveighing mainly against what I see as the limiting and sterilizing influence of a too slavish, uninspired literalism in modern writing. It did not, and does not, seem to me that science fiction would benefit by the adopting of such fetters—or, to vary the image, a clipping of the eagle's wings to a conformity with those of the barnyard fowl. Such literalism, as in the case of Zola, is the most quickly outmoded of literary forms. On the other hand, I do not think that the genuine, imaginative realism of Hardy, including an ever-present apprehension of the cosmic mysteries and fatalities that environ life, will ever be outmoded.

Also, in my letter, as Mr. Miller implies, I was considering ultimate artistic values, and not the question of expediency. Undoubtedly the realistic wave is entering science fiction, and the trend will have to work itself out. Like all other trends, it has both good and evil possibilities. I have merely tried to warn against the evil ones. The best possibilities lie in the correlation of observed data about life and human problems with inspired speculation as to the unknown forces of cosmic cause and effect that undoubtedly surround and play upon life. The evil lies in a meaningless Dreiserism, an inartistic heaping of superficial facts or alleged facts, which, after all, through our perceptional limitations, may be erroneous, or, at least, too incomplete to permit the safe drawing of dogmatic inference.

Tomorrow, the accepted theories of science and human psychology may be superseded by a brand-new lot; and it is partly because of this shifting, unstable ground on which the thing called realism stands, that I regard pure, frank fantasy as a more valid and lasting art-expression of the human mind.

In one sense, fantasy of one kind or another is about all that is possible for us, handicapped as we are by a partial and lopsided sense-equipment, and occupying a highly precarious position amid infinities and eternities whose concerns are perhaps wholly alien to our welfare or comprehension. Any true realism, it seems to me, must include a facing of this position, and not a treatment of life as if it were an air-tight compartment shut off from the unknown cosmos, and complete and independent in itself.

Mr. Miller's definition of the three main stages in literary evolution is

---

*The letter was published under the title "Mr. Smith to Mr. Miller." The present title was supplied by Charles K. Wolfe, editor of *PD*.—Ed.

well-drawn, I think. It may interest him, and others, to know that my own final preference for fantasy was reached through a varied course of reading that followed pretty much the outlines he has indicated. I began with children's fairy tales, went on through Haggard, Kipling, Balzac, Flaubert, France, etc. But through it all I have kept a profound admiration for Poe. My present enthusiasms include Blackwood, Lovecraft, John Taine, Machen, etc.—and, of course, Dunsany. I have also succumbed to the pervasive charm of Merritt.

To go back to the matter of realism, as an expedient for the furthering of science fiction, I must admit that I will not quarrel with Mr. Miller's viewpoint. And most assuredly I will not fling any stones or bouquets of asparagus at fellow-scribes who can win the attention of the main-guard of criticism. More power to them, if they can. I reserve the right to join the fray myself.

I am going to make a suggestion, which is, that the treatment of human "realities" through imaginative satire could well play an extensive part, as a corollary of this development. Perhaps, just at the present time, it would be more valuable than stuff done in the Hemingway vein. I[t] could conceivably reach, I am sure, a large and receptive audience. We are badly in need of a new Swift, who could write the Gulliver's Travels of current folly, corruption, dullness and madness. Stanton Coblentz has done some fine things of this type; but there are vast, unsounded possibilities.

I feel like a Time Traveler, after reading Mr. Miller's quite flattering classification of my own work as being ahead of the age! Howbeit, perhaps I am merely one of those unfortunate and perverse individuals who are constitutionally "agin the Government." When fantasy is acclaimed by Irving Babbitt, and is published regularly in *Harpers* and *The American Mercury,* I may take refuge in the writing of case-histories! That is to say, if I have not emigrated to the Abbey of Thelème or gone to Mohammed's paradise in the meanwhile. Literature is a grand old merry-go-round; and like the serpent of eternity, it always has its tail in its mouth. Also, as Mr. Miller hints, there may be some additional hoops in the ringsnake.

My apologies for pied metaphors; also for the Einsteinian liberties I have taken with Mr. Miller's curve.

[On the Forbidden Books]*

"Necronomicon," "Book of Eibon," etc., I am sorry to say, are all fictitious. Lovecraft invented the first, I the second. Howard, I believe, fathered the German work on the Nameless Cults. It is really too bad that they don't exist as objective, bonafide compilations of the elder and darker Lore! I have been trying to remedy this, in some small measure, by cooking up a whole chapter of Eibon. It is still unfinished, and I am now entitling it "The Coming of the White Worm."

*The letter was published in Charles D. Hornig's article "Startling Fact." The present title was supplied by Charles K. Wolfe, editor of *PD.*—Ed.

. . . This worm mentioned in Eibon is Rlim Shaikorth, and comes from beyond the pole on a strange, gigantic iceberg with a temperature of absolute zero.

[The Tale of Macrocosmic Horror]

Dear Editor:

I have read with much interest the fine letter from A. Lewis in the "Cauldron."

Mr. Lewis, in laying down rules for the development of the weird tale, has presented a viewpoint which will no doubt seem impregnable to the average intelligent person, in whom exclusively humanistic values of thought have been inculcated.

At the same time, however, I should like to indicate certain weaknesses and limitations which I see in this viewpoint, especially in regard to the tale of macrocosmic horror and fantasy. This type of story, because of its very character and purpose, should not, it seems to me, be bound strictly by "the practical requisites of literature in general." In a tale of the highest imaginative horror, the main object is the creation of a supernatural, extra-human atmosphere; the real actors are the terrible arcanic forces, the esoteric cosmic malignities; and the elements of human character, if one is to achieve the highest, most objective artistry, is properly somewhat subordinated, as it cannot be subordinated in a tale of ordinary and natural happenings. One is depicting things, powers and conditions that are beyond humanity; therefore, artistically speaking, the main accent is on these things, powers and conditions.

A sense of the superhuman is to be conveyed; therefore one does not want the human—at least, not to the extent that would impair and detract from the proper focus of interest. For this reason, I fear that the weird tale, if written mainly as psychological analysis, would tend to forfeit some of its highest and rarest values. Modern literature has become so thoroughly subjective, so introverted in its tendencies, so preoccupied with the anthropocentric, that it seems desirable for one genre, at least, to maintain what one might call a centrifugal impetus, to make "a gesture toward the infinite" rather than toward the human intestines.

This is not saying that Weird Fiction would not gain by more verisimilitude in the presentation of its terrene actors. But their reactions can be indicated more succinctly, with more stress on events, outward forces and atmosphere, than in fiction dealing with the natural and the normal.

For instance, let us take some concrete examples from modern Weird Fiction. In authors such as Algernon Blackwood and Walter de la Mare, it seems to me that the accent is primarily on human character. But in their work (at least, in any of it that I have read) one fails to find the highest imaginative horror, the overwhelming sweep of black, gulf-arisen wings, such as is conveyed in the best tales of Ambrose Bierce, Poe and H. P. Lovecraft, where human character is treated more briefly and subversively.—Clark Ashton Smith

[Crossword Puzzles]

Horizontal

1. Fabulous monster (pl.)
11. Arabian hero
12. Kind of demon
14. High-flavoured
15. Chinese dynasty
17. Biblical king
19. Name of Buddha
20. Egyptian god
25. Another Chinese dynasty
26. Measured (obs.)
27. Deserted city in India
30. Gold (Sp.)
31. Hebrew month
32. One of the names of Ashtoreth
33. Two hundred
34. Cloth with a corded surface
36. Groups of large islands
37. Ejaculation of reproach
38. Fantastic grimace (obs.)
39. To plow
40. Notre Seigneur (ab.)
45. Indian
46. Kind of fairy
48. Oriental river
51. Dynasty of eastern emperors
52. Ancient kingdom of Africa
54. Well-known circus animal (pl.)

Vertical

1. Exclamation
2. Low-lying meadow (obs.)
3. Egyptian god
4. Name of a certain card
5. Horse-tailed antelope
6. Early
7. Obstacles
8. Glass in the making
9. One of a European people
10. Strait (ab.)

13. Fabulous sea-monster
16. Another sea-monster
18. Oriental sect
19. Ridiculous
21. Musical note
22. Another name of Ashtoreth
23. Await
24. Lively (obs.)
25. Exclamation
28. Well-known island
29. Common suffix
35. Grammatical term (ab.)
37. Iron (chem. sym.)
41. Machine used in medieval pageants
42. Old-time weapon
43. To drive in or down
44. To speak hoarsely
46. Genus of grasses
47. Plant
49. Latin pronoun
50. Shepherd's crook
51. Eleven hundred
53. Ells geotch (ab.)

¹H	²I	³P	⁴P	⁵O	G	⁶R	I	⁸F	⁹F	¹⁰S
¹¹A	N	T	A	R	■	¹²A	F	R	I	T
¹³R	■	¹⁴G	A	M	Y	■	¹⁵T	S	I	N	¹⁶M
¹⁷O	¹⁸G	■	H	■	X	■	H	■	T	■	¹⁹F	O
²⁰S	H	²¹U	■	²²T	■	²³A	■	²⁴F	■	²⁵H	A	N
²⁶M	E	T	■	²⁷A	²⁸M	B	²⁸E	R	■	³⁰O	R	O
³¹A	B	■	³²A	N	A	I	T	I	S	■	³³C	C
³⁴R	E	³⁵P	■	³⁶I	N	D	E	S	■	³⁷F	I	E
³⁸I	R	P	■	T	■	E	■	K	■	³⁹F	A	R
⁴⁰N	S	■	⁴¹P	■	⁴²B	■	⁴³T	■	⁴⁴B	■	⁴⁵L	O
E	■	⁴⁶P	E	⁴⁷R	I	■	⁴⁸A	⁴⁹M	U	⁵⁰R	■	S
■	⁵¹M	O	G	U	L	■	⁵²M	E	R	O	⁵³E
⁵⁴C	A	M	E	L	O	P	A	R	D	S

HORIZONTAL

1. One of the names of Ashtoreth.
7. Greek demon.
13. Incestuous wife of Time.
14. Goddess of the seasons.
16. Norse god.
17. Three-fours of Sion.
18. A countryman or clown.
20. Akin.
21. English river.
22. Linden.
23. Bible name.
25. Slowly (mus.)
26. Lake.
31. Consonantal digraph.
32. Fabulous Oriental bird.
33. Common digraph.
34. Changeling. (obs.)
36. Genus of American plants (pl.)
37. Oriental basilisk.
38. Interjection expressing sorrow.
39. Private path (Eng. dialect.)
40. Volcano.
41. Note in Guido's system.
42. Biblical city.
43. French article.
44. Turkish arrow.
45. Kingdom in Genesis.
48. Hawk's leash.
50. Southern state (abbr.)
52. Tree.
53. Man's name.
55. Bird.
57. Pronoun.
58. Obsolete astronomical term (Pl.)
61. Prefix.
63. Sorcerer (pl.)
65. Constellation.
68. Polynesian girl's name (used in poem by Rupert Brooke).
71. Aeolian city.
72. Lizard.
75. Kind of East Indian cloth.
78. One of an Oriental people.
79. Fairy. (obs.)
80. Pigment (variant spelling).
81. Aborigine of Rajputana.
83. Hole through which metal runs into a mold in castings.
84. Dutch coin.
85. Cap of state worn by the English kings. (pl.)

VERTICAL

1. Mediterranean thirst-provoker.
2. Egyptian god.
3. Fabulous python in Flaubert's "Temptation of St. Anthony."
4. Consonantal digraph.
5. Shout of triumph (pl.)
6. Hindu goddess.
7. Exclamation (pl.)
8. Scandinavian demon.
9. City in Deuteronomy.
10. Chinese dynasty.
11. Anoint. (obs.)
12. Honey mixed with rose-juice.
15. Month of the Jewish year.
16. Latin pronoun.
19. Digraph.
22. French article.
24. Roumanian coin (pl.)
25. One hundred thousand (Hindustanee).
26. Province of India mentioned by Marco Polo.
27. Heraldic device.
28. Man's name (Italian).
29. Butter (Hindustanee).
30. Second person singular of common verb (solemn).
31½. Enclosed garden or yard.
33. Island in a river (obs. variant).
35. Chinese name of Buddha.

37. Sunday (abbr.)
39. Indestructible bone.
39½. Gold.
40⅓. English river.
40⅔. Goddess of revenge.
44. Prophecy (obs.)
44½. Consonantal digraph.
46. Genus of plants to which taro belongs.
47. Worthless (Hebrew).
48. Solitary.
49. English plural of Hindu word meaning camel (used by Kipling).
50. Odin's brother.
51. Friend (Fr.)
52. European bison.

54. Prefix meaning great.
56. Phonetic marking (pl.)
59. Pool below a waterfall.
60. Low caste East Indian.
62. Region bordering on hell.
64. Friend (Sp.)
66. Hindu cultivator.
67. Digraph.
69. Digraph.
70. Gold coin of the reign of James the First.
72. Also.
73. Suffix meaning to bear.
74. Transpose (abbr.)
75. Tuberculosis.
76. Exclamation.

¹B	²A	³A	L	⁴T	⁵I	⁶S			⁷A	⁸L	⁹A	S	¹⁰T	¹¹O	¹²R
¹³O	P	S		¹⁴H	O	R	A		¹⁶T	H	O	R	¹⁷S	I	O
¹⁸T	I	K	¹⁹E		²⁰S	I	B		²¹U	S	K		²²L	I	N	D
²³A	S	A	E	²⁴L							²⁵L	E	N	T	O
R		R		E		²⁶L	²⁷O	²⁸U	²⁹G	³⁰H		A		S		M
³¹G	³¹½H		³²S	I	M	O	R	G	H	A	N	K	A		³³E	E
³⁴O	A	³⁵F			³⁶A	L	O	E	S				³⁷S	Y	L
	³⁸W	O		³⁹L	³⁹½O	K	E		⁴⁰E	T	⁴⁰½N	⁴⁰⅔A	⁴¹U	T
			⁴²U	R				⁴³E	T				
	⁴⁴O	⁴⁴½C	⁴⁵Z	O	⁴⁶A	⁴⁷R		⁴⁸L	⁴⁹U	N	E		⁵⁰V	⁵¹A
⁵²A	S	H			⁵³R	A	⁵⁴M	O	N				⁵⁵E	M	⁵⁶U
⁵⁷U	S		⁵⁸A	⁵⁹L	M	U	C	A	N	T	A	⁶⁰R	S		⁶¹I	M
R		⁶²L		I		⁶³M	A	G	E	S		O		⁶⁴A		L
⁶⁵O	⁶⁶R	I	⁶⁷O	N							⁶⁸M	⁶⁹A	M	⁷⁰U	A
⁷¹C	Y	M	E		⁷²E	⁷³F	⁷⁴T		⁷⁵T	⁷⁶A	⁷⁷T		⁷⁸A	I	N	U
⁷⁹H	O	B		⁸⁰O	K	E	R		⁸¹B	H	I	⁸²L		⁸³G	I	T
⁸⁴S	T	O	O	T	E	R				⁸⁵A	B	A	C	O	T	S

77. Harlot (Shakespe[a]rean).
80. Old Testament (abbr.)
82. Exclamation.

———————

HORIZONTAL

1. Prince of the east, in medieval demonology.
7. Pagan festival observed in Christian countries.
14. Embroidered scarf worn by Catholic priests.
16. One of the Signs in astrology.
17. Carousal.
18. Seized and tore, as a hawk does.
19. Colouring used in Hindu pottery.
20. Son of Caleb. (I. Chr. 4: 15.)
22. Article (Arabic).
23. Devil.
26. Egyptian principle of the universe.
29. One of the planets.
30. Siamese demon.
32. Runis (abbr.)
33. Invisible superman in story by De Maupassant.
35. Digraph.
36. Isis.
37. Murderer famous in poetry.
38. Victim of fratricide.
40. More (obs.)
41. Infernal goddess.
42. Affirmative.
44. Rabbinical seed of resurrection.
45. Greek letter.
48. Exclamation of grief.
50. Digraph.
52. Son of Ra.
54. Witch.
55. Biblical giants.
58. Quadruped (pl.)
59. Master of Horrors (abbr.)
60. Patagonian deity.
61. Latin prefix meaning descent or decline.

VERTICAL

1. Firkin of ale (abbr.)
2. Demon who tempted Buddha.
3. Donkey (Fr.)
4. To kill or injure by piercing a wax image with pins.
5. Guerdon.
6. Palm leaf prepared for writing on with a stylus (pl.)
8. Giant (obs.)
9. Couch of a wild beast.
10. One-eyed and one-footed star-god of the Australians.
11. Measure of land.
12. Scandalous condition of antique statues.
13. Plural suffix.
15. Goddess of the Babylonians.
21. Medieval demon.
22. To stray from the strait [*sic*] and narrow path.
24. Violation of law (obs.)
25. Fabulous giant.
27. Mexican tree.
28. Devil who has charge of gambling-houses.
33. Exclamation.
34. Month of the Jewish year.
37½. Right excellent (abbr.)
39. Phoenician name of the Creator.
43. To summon from the vasty deep.
46. Dutch wine-measure.
47. Exclamation of disgust.
48. Belonging to the past.
49. Single in kind.
50. Latin verb to love.
51. Omen (obs.)
52. Dark-coloured.
53. To depart in haste (followed by hence).
56. Preposition.
57. Ibidem (abbr.)

¹A	²M	³A	⁴I	⁵M	⁶O	N	█	⁷B	⁸E	⁹L	¹⁰T	¹¹A	¹²N	¹³E
¹⁴F	A	N	N	E	L	█	¹⁵I	█	¹⁶S	A	U	R	U	S
█	¹⁷R	E	V	E	L	█	S	█	¹⁸T	I	R	E	D	█
█	A	█	¹⁹U	D	A	█	H	█	²⁰I	R	U	█	E	█
²¹B	█	²²E	L	█	²³S	²⁴A	T	²⁵A	N	█	²⁶N	²⁷U	█	²⁸A
²⁹E	A	R	T	H	█	³⁰N	A	T	█	³¹E	B	L	I	S
L	█	³²R	U	█	³³H	O	R	L	³⁴A	█	³⁵U	E	█	M
³⁶I	O	█	³⁷A	³⁷½R	A	M	█	³⁸A	B	³⁹E	L	█	⁴⁰M	O
M	█	⁴¹A	T	E	█	⁴²Y	⁴³E	S	█	⁴⁴L	U	Z	█	D
O	█	E	█	█	█	V	█	█	█	█	N	█	█	E
⁴⁵T	⁴⁶A	⁴⁷U	⁴⁸W	⁴⁹O	█	O	█	⁵⁰A	⁵¹O	█	⁵²S	⁵³H	U	█
⁵⁴H	A	G	⁵⁵A	N	⁵⁶A	K	⁵⁷I	M	S	█	⁵⁸A	I	S	█
█	⁵⁹M	H	⁶⁰S	E	T	E	B	O	S	█	⁶¹D	E		

Things Near and Far

¹B	²R	³A	⁴L	⁵E	⁶Y	█	⁷M	⁸E	⁹R	¹⁰I	¹¹N	¹²O
¹³R	O	T	A	T	E	█	¹⁴D	R	A	M	A	S
¹⁵A	U	L	I	C	█	¹⁶G	█	¹⁷R	I	A	N	T
¹⁸K	N	A	R	█	²³C	A	²⁰P	█	²¹D	U	D	E
²²E	D	S	█	¹⁹V	O	L	E	²⁴E	█	²⁵M	O	N
²⁶S	S	█	²⁷R	A	T	L	I	N	²⁸E	█	²⁹W	T
█	³⁰G	A	P	█	█	█	█	³¹A	L	A	█	█
³²R	³³S	█	³⁴P	O	³⁵T	³⁶L	³⁷U	C	K	█	³⁸R	³⁹T
⁴⁰O	L	⁴¹E	█	⁴²R	O	O	S	T	█	⁴³L	E	E
⁴⁴H	E	A	⁴⁵P	█	⁴⁶O	D	S	█	⁴⁷G	I	S	E
⁴⁸M	E	S	A	⁴⁹S	█	E	█	⁵⁰S	U	N	U	P
⁵¹E	V	I	N	I	⁵²N	█	⁵³B	E	A	G	L	E
⁵⁴R	E	S	E	N	T	█	⁵⁵R	E	M	O	T	E

Horizontal

1. Western poet.
7. Breed of sheep.
13. Revolve.
14. Plays.
15. Pertaining to a royal court.
17. Mirthful.
18. Gnurl or knot in wood.
19. Officer (colloquial).
21. Dandy.
22. Belonging to Ed.
23. Rapid flight of notes in music.
25. Human being (Scotch).
26. Scilicet, or namely (abb.).
27. Part of a ship's rigging.
29. Weight (abb.).
31. In a certain mode or fashion.
32. Royal Society (abb.).
34. Unpremeditated hospitality.
38. Right (abb.).

40. Man's name.
42. Parch.
43. Nautical term.
44. Pile.
46. Shakespe[a]rean oath.
47. To graze, or pasture. (rare)
48. Cliffs of the plain.
50. Dawn.
51. Evening (colloquial)
53. Hunting-dog.
54. To show anger or irritation.
55. Foreign.

Vertical

1. Important part of a vehicle.
2. Perambulation; also, a discharge of firearms. (pl)
3. Mountain in Africa.
4. Den or hiding-place.
5. Et cetera (abbr.)
6. Pronoun.
7. Doctor of Medicine (abb.)
8. Go astray.
9. Loot.
10. Mohammedan priest.

11. American ostrich.
13. Manifestation.
16. Effrontery (slang).
19. Small bed.
20. Prince Edward Island (abb.)
23. Fog or smoke.
24. Establish by law.
27. Strike sharply.
28. Animal.
32. Author of "Gray Face".
33. Portion of a garment.
35. Also.
36. Vein of metal.
37. United States Ship. (abb.)
38. Outcome.
39. Tent of the aborigines.
41. Believes.
43. Language.
45. Part of a window.
47. American dependency.
49. Wrong-doing.
50. To perceive or comprehend.
52. Nevada Territory (abb.)
53. Brother (abb.)

Clark Ashton Smith by
Walter Blythe,
Wonder Stories
(October 1930).

[Miscellaneous Puzzles]

```
    M Y R M E C O L E S
  S H E O L     H A S P S
  Y O N I   C A   P T A H
Y E W     H O L M     T O W
  N A N   E S T O   B E G
  I   E L S   N Y X   U
E T A   O P H I T E   A N A
S E B   N E R E I D   E S T
A   A C E R   C O I R   O
R A C A   I D O L   M O L L
S H U     S A D E   L I L
  A L C O   Y O   C H I C
  S U A V E   S C A T H
  S M A R A G D I T E
```

```
S E P T E N T R I O N A T E
  F E E   U R A L   O B I
  T R A D   I O   K I B E
O   D E       A R       A
U R N   O A F S   G A R
R U   H A G T A P E R   L C
A T E   R   L L   S   A C H
N I L   E N A C T S   C H I
A L L A   E N O W   S H E M
B A S T   E T N A   D E M I
A N   Z   E E   M   I M
D T   A A   S T   O H   C E
S   E N N A   W O O D   S
  A T Y G I A R T E S
```

First puzzle (solution grid):

```
■ H E R A T ■ A G L E T ■
B A L ■ G O E T Y ■ T U P
E N ■ G N U ■ O R T ■ T U
Z ■ A ■ I R E N E ■ A ■ N
A B A S ■ S O Y ■ A M O K
N O M E S ■ S ■ C H I O S
■ H ■ W A N ■ H I E ■ R
N E B E L ■ H ■ D A F F Y
Y A U L ■ O A R ■ P R A U
S ■ R ■ E P H O D ■ A ■ L
S I ■ D A H ■ L E X ■ Y A
A D O ■ S I M L A ■ D U N
■ A S P E R ■ A L M U G ■
```

Second puzzle (solution grid):

```
■ S E M P I T E R N A L ■
W ■ L E O ■ ■ A E R ■ G
R S ■ W A N ■ A B B ■ O R
O H M ■ ■ A ■ ■ I R A
T O I ■ L A T H E ■ N I M
H O T ■ A M O U R ■ L O E
■ N E C R O P H A G A N ■
M ■ R O F ■ ■ T A W ■ Z
O M ■ O S E ■ H O Y ■ L I
L A C ■ ■ N ■ ■ S I R
O P H ■ G E O D E ■ A N C
C L I ■ A G U A S ■ U G O
H E C A T O N S T Y L O N
```

V	I	L	L	O	N	■	B	A	L	Z	A	C
A	L	I	A	S	■	■	C	A	I	R	O	
T	I	N	Y	■	H	A	P	■	C	O	I	N
H	O	E	■	C	I	■	O	G	■	N	E	T
E	N	■	S	H	E	L	L	E	Y	■	L	E
K	■	B	O	A	■	O	■	N	U	N	■	S
■	■	O	■	N	I	G	H	T	■	U	■	
A	■	W	O	T	■	O	■	L	O	T	■	D
R	M	■	W	E	B	S	T	E	R	■	F	A
M	E	W	■	D	E	■	U	R	■	S	O	U
I	R	A	S	■	N	O	G	■	B	A	R	D
D	O	R	I	C	■	■	S	E	D	G	E	
A	U	D	R	E	Y	■	J	U	L	I	E	T

R	O	M	A	N	Y	■	F	R	A	N	C	E
A	P	E	L	L	E	S	■	O	G	I	E	R
S	H	A	G	■	S	A	C	■	O	L	L	A
P	E	D	A	L	■	G	A	R	N	E	T	S
E	L	■	E	O	N	■	R	O	I	■	S	E
D	I	E	■	T	E	M	P	E	S	T	■	R
■	A	L	P	■	S	E	E	■	T	U	B	■
L	■	D	A	S	T	A	R	D	■	T	A	M
I	M	■	S	O	L	■	S	U	H	■	L	A
G	A	U	T	I	E	R	■	N	O	M	A	D
E	R	N	E	■	S	E	P	■	R	A	N	D
I	L	I	U	M	■	C	H	A	L	I	C	E
A	S	T	R	A	L	■	T	H	A	L	E	R

```
        M  A  N  D  O  R  A
    E  R  O  S     U     O  B  O  E
    P  E  A  T     L     A  B  E  L
 O  H  O     I  B  S  E  N     R  E  X
 R  A     N     E  E  L     U     M  A
 A  S  S  O  I  L     M  A  R  T  I  N
 N     O     N        L     R        T
 G  O  U  R  D  S     C  A  L  I  P  H
 E  R     E     A  H  A     O     A  I
 S  A  C     C  L  E  F  S     A  R  C
    T  A  R  A     I     A  L  U  M
    E  N  I  D     N     D  A  T  A
          B  E  N  Z  O  I  C
```

```
    L  E  S  B  O  S     W  E  I  M  A  R
 P     L  A  Y     A  R  E     N  O  G     C
 I  T     N  G     L  O  D     A  R     O  O
 L  A  N  D  O  R     D     G  N  O  M  E  N
 A  R  C  A  N  I  C     C  R  I  S  P  E  R
 T        L  E  G        O  T  E        A
 E  L  D     S     I  N  A     E     C  U  D
    O  A  T     L  O  B        D  A  N
 D  U  G     M     E  M  B     P     P  A  M
 U        M  A  C        I  R  P        A
 N  E  M  O  R  A  L     G  R  E  A  T  E  N
 C  L  E  R  I  C     B     U  M  L  A  U  T
 A  O     A  N     M  U  T     I  I     R  R
 N     A  L  E     U  D  A     E  N  T     A
    B  I  E  R  C  E     J  U  R  G  E  N
```

Grid 1

```
C A R I B ■ L A M I A
U R ■ O R L E T ■ A B
M E A ■ O R C ■ A M Y
I S L A M ■ C O R B S
N ■ L I O N E L S ■ S
■ V I S ■ O ■ E C C ■
A ■ A L U M I S H ■ A
N O N E S ■ S A I N S
N I T ■ U N I ■ N A T
U N ■ U R I A H ■ D U
S T O P E ■ C O P A N
```

Grid 2

```
L O T O P H A G I ■ M A G N I F I C O
A M U ■ O N U S ■ T R I ■ L A B
M O R T ■ M O L E ■ B E E N ■ Y O N I ■ I
P O M E ■ O M A R ■ U L N A ■ U S E D
R ■ O U ■ L I A ■ I
E ■ O ■ P E N F I L E D ■ A ■ M ■ C
Y U G A S ■ A D O ■ S R I ■ R ■ A B C
S T E L A ■ N ■ E ■ C A R A T
■ E E ■ M Y S T E R I A R C H ■ A D ■
M O ■ L A C ■ L I
B A V I N S ■ A N E ■ R I V A G E
E Y O T ■ P A L ■ A M O R
B L A R E ■ S ■ H ■ A ■ M ■ L I E G E
A T H ■ K A L I ■ N Y E S ■ T O B
L A S ■ Z I M R I ■ D U R E S ■ Y T U
I N ■ A N A ■ C I I ■ R
Z E D ■ I O R ■ Z A L ■ E L L ■ H A N
E ■ A ■ R O I ■ H I D ■ R A E ■ E
■ H I E R A C O S P H Y N X E S ■
```

S	A	T	A	N	O	P	H	A	N	Y
E	V	A	D	E	■	R	A	N	E	E
T	A	R	O	T	■	E	N	D	O	W
■	R	E	N	■	T	■	T	E	N	■
M	■	S	■	A	U	F	■	S	■	T
Y	S	■	E	B	L	I	S	■	Z	A
L	O	K	■	R	U	G	■	M	E	R
I	L	■	U	■	U	■	A	■	T	A
T	E	■	R	A	M	P	S	■	A	N
T	■	D	I	S	■	I	T	U	■	L
A	R	I	M	A	S	P	I	A	N	S

Clifford Gessler

Treader of Obscure Stars

Nearly everyone has his special enthusiasm for some otherwise obscure writer. One of our preferences of this kind is for the ringing, swinging, sometimes sonorous and sometimes slyly humorous balladry of Frank Belknap Long, author of "The Man From Genoa" and other poems, reviewed last year. Long's pet literary enthusiasm, in turn, is for the verse of Clark Ashton Smith, a California writer whose "Ebony and Crystal" and "The Star-Treader" Long showed us over numerous cups of very powerful coffee at his home in New York. Smith is a newspaperman, with the Journal at Auburn, Cal., who escapes from the grind of reality in somber and sometimes powerful "odes and sonnets," deriving much of their color and atmosphere from the rich associations of the ancient world, which the author is able to turn to uses of often highly effective imagery. Despite his sometimes stiff and antiquated diction, and a tendency to spin them out to too great length, Smith's poems pack considerable punch.

Various

In re exhibitions of Smith's artwork

A number of new canvases are on display in the Claremont hotel gallery. These include two huge paintings by M. [*sic*] Hibi, talented Japanese artist. Both are of blossoming fruit trees, rendered in a manner typically Japanese.

Of McLeod Batten's decorative paintings recently hung, Harry Noyes Pratt, director of the gallery, says: "The average patron of the galleries has been in the habit of passing by Mrs. Batten's work with little more than an uncomprehending glance, oblivious to the splendid beauty of her canvases. Abstract they are, it is true, if one attempts to penetrate to the meaning of them, but they, can be viewed with regard merely to the loveliness of their pattern and real enjoyment found, just as one might find it in a stained glass window. Come to think of it, what lovely windows some of these things of hers would make, rendered in terms of colored glass!"

In the small gallery are shown a group of paintings by Clark Ashton Smith, the California poet. Smith is untaught in art. His paintings are purely of his own expression. To quote Mr. Pratt again:

"Nevertheless there is in these, water colors, these paintings on silk and other fabrics, a certain primitive beauty which commands attention in spite of their manner of expression. Without in the least being imitative, they remind one of the work of the early Italians. They possess undoubted elements of primitive artistic expression, a fantasy of beauty such as one might expect from the imagination of a poet."

Florence Wieben Lehre, "Artists and Their Work."
Oakland Tribune (3 July 1927): sec. B, p. 4.

It will be a relief to many to know that, if they will just visit the Claremont hotel art gallery, they may see a collection of paintings that can please without requiring a previous education in the "isms" of art. The exhibition is decidedly conservative. But happily so. For it balances some of the other shows of this part of California that are more extreme in their modernism than the Claremont show could possibly be in its conservatism.

H. Hibi attains distinction of color in a quiet way. His [*sic*] "Early Spring," showing a rugged pear tree in bloom, is much stronger than his "Midspring," which, though pleasing, is slightly turgid in its harmonies. Both imposing works.

Traces of a naive expression are in Clarke [*sic*] Ashton Smith's paintings on fabrics. His is not great art, nor "arrived." But some day Smith may surprise himself and the world by stepping out of his timidity and doing something truly big with what he apparently summons from the sub-conscious.

Florence Wieben Lehre, "Artists and Their Work."
Oakland Tribune (17 July 1927): Sunday sec., p. 5.

George Sterling recognized him as a poetic genius. He is also an artist with the brush. Other Fellows will be interested to learn that Clarke [*sic*] Ashton Smith is in town, with an exhibition of his paintings, to be shown at 1631 La Vereda road, Berkeley. Incidentally, his translation of Baudelaire is almost completed.

Oakland Tribune (28 September 1928): sec. B, p. 28.

The Boiling Point

[September 1933]

Only the hottest of controversies will be printed in this column—radical arguments that will bring your blood to 'The Boiling Point.' We start this department off by presenting one of the most blasphemous articles it has been our pleasure to read. It is by Forrest J. Ackerman, and he calls it

'A Quarrel With Clark Ashton Smith'

No doubt this will be the commencement of a lively discussion between the readers. It is the editor's intention to print the most interesting arguments on both sides of the case. I have this to say: it seems to me that Wonder Stories is going far afield when it takes such a horror story as Mr. Smith's "Dweller in Martian Depths" and, because it is laid on the Red Planet, prints it in a magazine of scientific fiction. Frankly, I could not find one redeeming feature about the story. Of course, everything doesn't have to have a moral. The thrilling scientifilm, "King Kong," for instance, has no moral to it—except, perhaps, to be careful of Fay Wray, if you are a great prehistoric ape—but it has a point, at least: to interest. And 'Dweller in Martian Depths' didn't interest me. I don't know, maybe it did others. But it disappointed me very greatly to find it in a stf publication. In Weird Tales, all right. I don't like that type of story, I wouldn't read it there. I fail to find anything worth-while in an endless procession of ethereal lites, [*sic*] phantastic visions, ultra-mundane life, exotic paradises, airy vegetation, whispering flutes, ghastly plants, and dirge-like horrors. May the ink dry up in the pen from which they flow! Or, at least, Mr. Smith, direct those tales elsewhere—NOT to a stf publication, because I do like your science fiction like "Master of the Asteroid" and "Flight into Super Time." But 'stuff' like "The Light From Beyond" . . .

Well, let's hear from someone in favor.

(Make "The Boiling Point" boil you indignant fans. Don't let this guy Ackerman get away with it. Your replies will be published in this department. We would especially appreciate a reply from Mr. Smith himself in defense of his stories.)*

[October 1933]

You will remember the terrific outburst Forrest J. Ackerman made upon Clark Ashton Smith's stories and weird tales in general in last month's column. Shortly

---

*"Our Readers Say," *FF* 1, No. 2 (October 1933): 14: "'The Boiling Point' is going to be a great department. I was interested by the article on 'Science Fiction in English Magazines' by Bob Tucker. I predict that 'The Fantasy Fan' will be a success. With all best wishes"—Clark Ashton Smith

after the issue went to press, we received the following postscript to his article which he requested to have printed at the beginning of this month's column.

"I could as well pick on John Taine—a favorite author, mind you—for 'The Time Stream' in Wonder Stories, another story considered doubtful science fiction. My only interest is to keep stf. in the stf. publications, and let fantasies and weird tales appear in the magazines featuring that type.

"It is to be hoped that Mr. Smith will discover many of his admirers thru the writings of readers caring to present arguments."

It is only fair that Mr. Smith himself should have the first blow against Mr. Ackerman's argument, in defense of his own stories. He calls his defense "Horror, Fantasy and Science."

"Mr. Ackerman's fervent and ebullient denunciation of my stories, followed by Editor Hornig's invitation to join the melee, is not to he resisted.

"I infer that Forrest J. Ackerman considers horror, weirdness and unearthliness beyond the bounds of science or science fiction. Since horror and weirdness are integral elements of life (as is well known to those who have delved beneath the surface) and since, in all likelihood, the major portion of the universe is quite unearthly, I fail to understand the process of logic or syllogism by which he has arrived at this truly amazing proscription.

"Let me recommend to Mr. Ackerman, and to others like him, a more scientifically open and receptive attitude of imagination. If Mr. Ackerman were transported to some alien world, I fear that he would find the reality far more incredible, bizarre, grotesque, fantastic, horrific, and impossible than any of my stories.

"In regard to 'The Light From Beyond,' I cannot see that this tale is any more fantastic and unreal than others dealing with unknown dimensions or planes of hyper-space. Physical entry into such planes is improbable, but form an alluring theme for fictional speculation.

"It is curious that Mr. Ackerman should profess to like 'Flight Into Super-Time,' a story which is wilder, if anything, than, than the ones he has denounced. I might also add that it was written as a satire on time-travelling, and should not have been read too seriously.

"Of course, it is Forrest Ackerman's privilege to dislike my stories, and to express his dislike whenever he chooses. I have merely tried to point out that he is in error when he condemns them as being inherently unsuitable for a scientifiction magazine."

H. P. Lovecraft also defends the weird tale:

"As for Ackerman's ebullition, I fear he can hardly be taken seriously in matters involving the criticism of imaginative fiction. Smith's story was really splendid, except for the cheap ending on which the Editor [of] Wonder Stories insisted. Ackerman once wrote me a letter with a very childish attack on my work—he evidently enjoys verbal pyrotechnics for their own sake and seems so callous to imaginative impressions."

August W. Derleth liked everything in "The Fantasy Fan" except the letter in this department from Forrest J. Ackerman "Who," he says, "while usually quite interesting, nevertheless has the unpleasant habit of trying to make everything over into his own image."

R. H. Barlow gives an open reply to Mr. Ackerman in defense of Clark Ashton Smith.

"To my mind you are deplorably lacking in imagination to so condemn some of the finest work of the greatest living fantasy writer. Must you be so literal, physical, in your interpretation of imaginative literature? Clark Ashton Smith, whom I have the honor of knowing, is primarily and foremost a poet, his work having received the highest commendation of such persons as Edwin Markham, George Sterling, etc. Truly, his colourfully nightmarish visions are far superior to the conventional type of—forgive me—trash—printed in the average mercenary scientifiction magazine. The mere fact that a few helpless ray-projectors, heroine consisting mainly of lipstick and legs, and a dastardly villain, are not dragged in by the nape of their respective necks certainly does nothing to impair the excellence of his dulcet prose, but rather is an agreeable relief."

Come on, now, everybody join in the battle!

[November 1933]

Herewith we continue the Ackerman–Smith debate, which is waxing hot.

"The Ackerman–Smith controversy assumes all the aspects of a mad comedy. To assail and reprehend the writings of Clark Ashton Smith is as preposterous and futile as a dwarf transporting a huge mountain peak upon the tip of his tiny finger. Either Forrest J. Ackerman is daft or an imbecile or a notoriety-seeking clown and knave. Clark Ashton Smith stands alone in the realm of present-day weird and fantastic literature, and, therefore, above all his contemporaries. He is still King: and has yet to be dethroned."—Robert Nelson.

"Personally, I thought that 'The Light From Beyond' was very good, and I saw nothing weird about it. It was fantasy and not stf., but some of the greatest classics of so-called science fiction have been almost pure fantasy. Witness: Merritt's 'Snake Mother' and 'Moon Pool,' and Taine's 'Time Stream.' Ackerman's objections to this were particularly obnoxious to me, as I thought it one of the best stories ever written. Certainly, there should be something more to science fiction than rays, machines, villains, heroines (composed of lipstick and leg, as Mr. Barlow rather bitterly expresses it), as has been stressed so greatly of late. There should be an element of fantasy, strong characters, and a well-developed plot in addition. The lack of those is why so many weird story lovers (like Mr. Barlow) can find so much fault with stf, I do not blame him. I, myself, as a reader, will stop reading stf. when the fantasy element is dropped completely."—William Crawford.

"Not so much in rebuttal to Mr. Ackerman as to toss another stick onto the fire, let me confess that the scientific fiction type of literature seems to me among the dullest written. I avoid whenever possible, except in such cases where it passes the boundaries into the weird and horrible. Of course, the work of Wells is an exception. This may be blasphemy to most of your readers, but there it is. To return to Mr. Ackerman's complaint; I fail to see why it is any more deplorable for Wonder Stories to publish Clark Ashton Smith's horror story than for Weird Tales to publish Edmond Hamilton's pseudo-scientific effusions. And it was Amazing Stories that had the honor to publish "The Colour Out of Space" by America's master of the weird, Lovecraft."—Richard E. Morse

[December 1933]

The Smith–Ackerman debate is still going strong, with Smith in the lead. However, the Ackerman side is taking a big leap with the following defenses. The first comes from Allen Glasser, who says:

"I am surprised at the vicious remarks being made about Forrest Ackerman. He really doesn't deserve any such abuse. Perhaps his writings are a bit flamboyant and over-enthusiastic; but surely that's no great fault. To those who know him well, Forrest is a fine fellow; and his zeal for science-fiction merits praise rather than censure."

Donald Alexander is all for Ackerman and wishes to make no secret of it:

"I've been watching the controversy in 'The Boiling Point.' It seems to me that young Forrest J. Ackerman is by far the most sensible of the lot. Instead of intelligently answering his arguments, Messrs. Smith, Lovecraft, Barlow, etc., have made fools of themselves descending to personalities. Ackerman is a most interesting type of 'crank.' (Everyone who writes in to a magazine is a 'crank.' So'm I). At least, F. J. A. shows signs of a rudimentary intelligence, which most cranks don't. I agree with him. 'The Light from Beyond' and several other Smith yarns, had no place in *Wonder Stories*. WS calls itself a science fiction magazine. Smith's story under discussion isn't science fiction, so, it had no place in such a magazine. F. J. A. is right there. I see no reason why Lovecraft should condemn Ackerman for not liking Smith. After all, we each have our own tastes. Smith, in my own opinion, is a poor writer. His stories are all like the ravings of some fearfully diseased mind. Lovecraft, on the other hand, is a fairly good writer. But I'm wasting good typewriter ink; your readers haven't enough intelligence to grasp such a common sense argument as the one presented by Ackerman, so they call him a nitwit, while he actually has more sense than the lot of them thrown together. If there were a hundred-million Forrest J. Ackermans in the world, it'd be a better place to live in, at least we'd have a little common sense used occasionally."

Now, while we are very glad to find defenses on the Ackerman side, we must disagree with Mr. Alexander when he calls our readers too ignorant to grasp an argument put forth by Mr. Ackerman. Their eager disapproval with logical objections contradicts this theory. And then again, the mere fact that they are science fiction and weird fans puts them above the average, for such readers must be broadminded and open minded, and not the "What's-good-enough-for-father-is-good-enough-for-me" or "There-ain't-no-such-animal" types. We believe that this letter leaves cause for rebuttal on the part of Messrs. Smith and Lovecraft.

Forrest J. Ackerman, of course, does not like the way he has been treated, and has this to say about it:

"Pardon me, do; but why did you run 'The Boiling Point' in a foreign language? What a vocalberry on those Weird Men Smith and Lovecraft! And I think I'll have to change my tag from 'Forrest J. Ackerman, Scientifictionist' to 'Forrest J. Ackerman, Ebullitionist'. The two got the word in within the first line of comments. Now Mr. Smith will be calling Mr. Lovecraft 'Plagiarist', and then maybe Mr. Smith (the 'Skylark') will burst in and say that HE owns the original. Let's have a contest . . . Just thought of it—the original Paul illustration that I treasure *would* be from *Smith's* story, 'The City of the Singing Flame.' I don't get the connection: the Lovecraft says in print 'a very childish attack', and in his personal reply to me 'your bright and candid letter.'!?"

It can be seen by the above letter that Ackerman really holds no hard feeling toward the Weird Men; just a bit of mockery and rare Ackerman wit.

Just to show that we are always open to both sides, following are a couple of fans who still choose to 'lay it on thick.'

"Personally, I thought that 'The Light From Beyond' was very good, and I certainly could see nothing weird about it. It was fantasy, yes, and not stf, but some of the greatest classics of so-called science fiction have been almost pure fantasy. Witness: 'The Snake Mother,' 'The Moon Pool,' 'The Time Stream' (Ackerman's objection to this was particularly obnoxious to me, as I thought it was one of the best stories ever written. Certainly it offered the most food for thought), 'The Skylark of Space' (partly fantasy), 'The Princess of Mars,' and other greats. Certainly, there should be something more to science fiction than rays, machines, villains, heroines, (composed of lipstick and legs, as Mr. Barlow rather bitterly expresses it) as has been stressed so greatly of late. There should be an element of fantasy, strong character, and a well-developed plot in addition. The lack of those is why so many weird story lovers (like Mr. Barlow) can find so much fault with stf. I do not blame him. I, myself, as a reader, will stop reading stf when the fantasy element is dropped completely."—William Crawford (Editor of *Unusual Stories*)

"What does this Ackerman guy know about weird and fantastic fiction? From the way he writes, he must be an unimaginative person unable to stretch his mind away from space-ships and foreign star-clusters. I get that he is an egotistical radical and one who doesn't like something that is not even intended for him. So far, in telling about his collection, he has described a sort of madhouse. However, I certainly would like to see this madhouse, as I can appreciate a thing or two that is connected with stf. At heart, I am truly a

...d and fantastic fiction fan."—F. Lee Baldwin

There seems to be enough controversy in this month's discussion to bring in enough letters to fill next month's. Write in and give us your opinions on the subject. Are Smith's tales fit for *Wonder Stories?* Does Ackerman know what he's talking about, and are the Weird Men justified in their criticisms of him? Here's hoping to hear from you.

[January 1934]

After five months, the Smith–Ackerman debate is still waxing hot. We open this month's column with another rebuttal from Ackerman:

"Since the pros and cons on my Boiling Point article have changed around to discussions of character, I wish to state that I do not like H. P. Lovecraft's attitude. I was interested in his closing sentence in the second issue, and also in Mr. Derleth's. They were both interesting to analyze. But I resent Mr. Lovecraft's further uncalled for remarks. If I am not qualified to judge any weird tales, he is not qualified to call names. It seems to me of late that his palsy-walsy Clark Ashton Smith has been turning out an overabundant amount of literature—but goodness! I don't think the man egotistic and attempting to draw attention to himself! The man likes to write, and so do I. Yet Mr. Lovecraft says of me 'peculiarly ridiculous', because I make absurd comments to focus people's eyes on me; and write voluminously for the same reason, I take it. But I don't keep a scrap-book. That's not very consistent with the nature described, is it? And ask Mr. Hornig what my answer was when he proposed a 'Forrest J. Ackerman' issue of *The Fantasy Fan*. What a puffing up I should have gotten had I been *that* sort of person. You tell 'em Charles—what I said: 'No!' Not that I see what difference it makes who writes articles and how many of them there are in one issue, as long as they're good—which I hope mine are. But people *will* talk. And so I am not obliging with an autobiography of myself for the 'Famous Fantasy Fans' feature either.

"Furthermore, Mr. Lovecraft, you seem to have forgotten something. I keep my letters from famous writers. You say I once wrote you a very childish attack on your work. But your answer to that letter was: 'I was very pleased to get your bright and candid letter this morning.' That is a different story.

"I write these paragraphs in my behalf, because, being more of a weird fans' magazine, I can't expect many voices on my side from *The Fantasy Fan* readers. If you will see the third paragraph in the letter of C. Ferry and B. Rogers in the December Wonder *Stories,* however, you will find that the gentlemen are three times over as vehement and acidic as I. You might call them unknowing supporters.

"To Robert Nelson, who says I must be daft or an imbecile or a notoriety-seeking clown and knave (and does it in one breath), I can only answer that I thought it was a foregone conclusion that fantasy fans were 'daft' anyway, and that examination of the ratings of the members of my alma mater graduating class might prove differently about the second statement, and that I think I have cleared of the third already.

"Richard E. Morse's letter has impressed me as the one that really 'says something.' His thought had not occurred to me before, and it is worthwhile considering. *Weird Tales* allows science fiction; why not *Wonder Stories* weird tales? As the science fiction fan I am always eager to see stf in *Weird Tales* and any other magazine. I see that the process can easily be reversed. So Mr. Morse 'has' me. The argument is settled.

"Numerous Eyrie letters knock stf in *Weird*; I only did the same, but from the other side of the fence."

H. P. Lovecraft also retaliates:

"Glad you are giving the vociferous Master Ackerman a hearing—it's always well to let both sides of a debate have an equal chance. But I fear that Effjay the Terrible and his allies don't make out a very strong case. The tirade to which exception was taken was not merely an assertion that Smith's 'Dweller in Martian Depths' is unsuited for a science fiction magazine. It was a wholly gratuitous and intemperate attack on the story itself, written with a slap-dash extravagance and obviously sadistic gusto which plainly showed either a complete lack of analytical understanding and imaginative sensitiveness, or (as it was probable) a mere boyish desire to show off and attract notice. However, Ackerman is young, as proved by his tendency to regard ordinary civilized language as alien and incomprehensible. Now that he's had a good barrage from the general public, it would be just as well to leave him in peace. Five years from now he'll go beyond any of us in laughing at his explosions of today."

William H. Dellenback also has something to say:

"I am not a Weird Man; indeed, I have read *very* few weird stories that I have considered really good. Therefore, this is not so much a defense of Smith (who, I believe, is absolutely wrong in trying to link weird fiction with science fiction), as a rebuttal to Ackerman. However, first let me say that I think you are making a mistake, Editor, in publishing, and readers, in writing, letters which make too personal remarks. Aside from the fact that they are not true, the Boiling Point is for arguing about principles and not for calling antagonists names.

"But on with the dance—Forrest says that 'Dweller in Martian Depths' and 'The Light From Beyond' should not have been published in *Wonder Stories*. He also calls 'The Time Stream' doubtful material for a stf. publication.

"Point 1—In regard to Forrest's dislike of Smith's excessive vocabulary, I will say this is purely a matter of personal opinion. And I respect his opinion (which is more than do Messrs. Lovecraft, Barlow, and Nelson.) even though I don't agree with him. As a change from the average run of stf stories, I enjoy Smith's wonderful language; I believe I have read very few stories as beautifully told as 'The Light From Beyond'. And though I don't like his weird stories, nevertheless, his manner of telling seems to me admirably fitted to weird fiction.

"Point 2—I agree heartily with Mr. Crawford; science fiction would indeed be dull, if it consisted of nothing but the ideas Mr. Barlow lists. Fantasy is an integral part of stf; and while the three above mentioned stories were, for a large part, fantasy, they also contained the elements of strict stf.

"Point 3—Finally, if no other explaining will suffice, I can only offer this last fact: Such stories provide variety, and there many who will like them. So, if you don't, Forrest, just forget about it. Stf can not be composed of all inter-planetary yarns, or all medical, or all of any other type."

We hereby give notice that the Smith–Ackerman debate will be concluded in the February issue. It has just about run its course. If you have anything to say, you'd better say it now. It's your last chance. In next month's column, Clark Ashton Smith presents a rebuttal to the vociferous letter of D. Alexander's in our December issue. Mr. Smith is glad to know that Ackerman is being given an even break. We hope that this friendly argument has been well-taken by all concerned and will cause no hard feelings.

[February 1934]

"Donald Alexander's letter caused me to reread carefully my own answer to Forrest Ackerman's epistolatory critique. Since my one concern was to meet Mr. Ackerman's arguments on their own ground, I am puzzled by the assertion of Mr. Alexander that I had made a fool of myself by descending to personalities. Off-hand, I should have said that my letter was about as free of that sort of thing as it could conceivably have been. Perhaps there were a few mildly ironic touches; but certainly nothing of an invidious nature was implied or even intended. I do not think that any good purpose is ever served by abusive personalities. If my letter was derogatively personal, I really wonder how Mr. Alexander's should be classified."

—Clark Ashton Smith

H. Koenig suggests that we missed a golden opportunity by not supplying the debaters with gloves and entering them in the Golden Glove Contests in Madison Square Garden!

"When you shout, pertaining to Smith stories, 'May the ink dry up in the pen from which they flow!' you affect the refined and sensitive minds of the admirers of beautiful things, and cause them to exclaim, 'Here, indeed, is one who endeavors to do something in words as terrible as in actuality: cleave the head of a genius in twain!' Hence our fitting denunciation of you, Mr. Ackerman, for attempting to backbite one of the greatest writers America has ever produced."

—Robert Nelson

"When some well-meaning person says that Ackerman has more sense than Smith and Lovecraft combined, he is just being ridiculous. If Clark Ashton Smith has a diseased mind, as Mr. Alexander states, I would for one like to be exposed to the germ."

—Duane W. Rimel

"I have been following with interest the Ackerman adventures in your pages. I am wondering if he ever wrote any stories, besides criticizing them?"
—Natalie H. Wooley

"The Ackerman–Smith debate amuses me. Of course, I am squarely on Smith's side, and don't understand why you publish the more puerile of the letters on the matter, such as the one by Lloyd Fowler."*
—August W. Derleth

"The whole argument was caused by Ackerman claiming that Smith's 'Dweller in Martian Depths' should not have appeared in *Wonder Stories.* Smith should have sent the story to *Weird Tales,* thus avoiding a clash with Ackerman, who, I take it, has no use for weird literature. Or the editor of *Wonder Stories* should have foreseen some catastrophe and promptly returned it to C. A. Smith, who I esteem very highly, by the way."
—F. Lee Baldwin

We stated last month that the Smith–Ackerman debate would end in this issue—and so it has. Many of our readers have started to get bored with it—and more than that, some ill-feeling has been aroused. We go further to state that there will be no more department known as "The Boiling Point." The name implies that everything contained therein should be boiling hot—and these boiling hot arguments, as we have found out, create an unpleasant atmosphere for many concerned. THE FANTASY FAN is attempting to bind the lovers of science and weird fiction tighter together with friendship, and not to separate them thru dislike of each other's ideas. However, to take the place of "The Boiling Point" we are starting a new department next month entitled "Your Views." This will not contain any debates, but the opinions of you, the readers, on various subjects which we will nominate. So, write in to us immediately answering the following questions: "What is there in the 'horror' story as associated with weird and fantastic fiction? Is there any virtue to them? How can they be defended when people will read them and say that they are distasteful to the well and normal mind? Why does a person wish to read a sinister tale of evil or monstrosities? Is it healthy reading? Is it not morbid?" Forrest J. Ackerman has suggested this subject. Let's see what you think about it.

---

*Lloyd Fowler, "Our Readers Say," *FF* 1, No. 4 (December 1933): 51–52: "Please keep on using the same kind of paper and add more pages. Was sorry to hear that TFF is leaning toward weird fiction. Why do you encourage superstition with all the pronouncements of science against it? I like the magazine fine, all except the weird part. I never have read a good weird tale. Why do they print the science fiction and interplanetary stories of Kline, Hamilton, and Williamson in *Weird Tales,* for weird tales, interplanetary stories are not weird."

Addenda

[170a]   [ANS][1]

[Postmarked Providence, R.I.,
7 January 1932]

Thanks for the view. A mild New Year's permitted me to spend a mild New Year's in Boston with W. Paul Cook, & here is one of the Georgian vistas we observed. We did five museums—Germanic, Semitic, Peabody, (anthropology) Agassiz, (nat. hist.) & Fogg (art).

¶ Congratulations on Avoosl—you are surely a fixture in the magazine world! Have just looked through the new W.T., & think Wandrei's story is about the best item, with Robert E. Howard's as second. Derleth dislikes Howard's tale—& perhaps it is rather synthetic.[2] The background of dark lore is probably what makes me fall for it. I must sometime use von Junzt & the Black Book, & take mottos from the mad bard Justin Geoffrey.[3] ¶ Yrs for the Voorish Gate—E'ch-Pi-El

---

1. *Front:* Leverett House (Lowell House Tower at Left) Harvard University Cambridge, Mass.

2. *WT,* February 1932: Donald Wandrei, "The Tree-Men of M'Bwa"; Robert E. Howard, "The Thing on the Roof."

3. HPL did cite von Junzt (and even came up with his first name, Friedrich, which Howard had neglected to supply) in several stories beginning with "The Dreams in the Witch House," written in February 1932. That story also cited the *Black Book.* Justin Geoffrey was mentioned in "The Thing on the Doorstep" (1933).

[189a]   [ANS][1]

[Postmarked Providence, R.I.,
9 May 1932]

Thanks enormously for the impressive view of California's scenery. I must get around your way some day—for here we have nothing as bold & rugged as this. Congratulations on Ubbo-Sathla! Now if Wright will only take The Double Shadow, I'll feel that I have some influence in his sanctions! We have good outdoor weather here. Still in doubt about travel potentialities, but will be getting started on whatever trip I do take in about a week.
Yrs in the Nighted Brotherhood of the Andean Monolith—
E'ch-Pi-El

---

1. *Front:* University Hall and Manning Hall, Brown University.

Chronology

No.*	Sender(s)	Date
1	HPL	12 August 1922
	CAS	late August/early September 1922
2	HPL	27 September 1922
	CAS	c. 1 October 1922
3	HPL	5 October 1922
	CAS	17 October 1922
4	HPL	12 November 1922
	CAS	late November 1922
5	HPL	2 December 1922
	CAS	5 December 1922
6	HPL	5 December 1922
	CAS	23 December 1922
7	HPL	11 January 1923
8	HPL	21 January 1923
	CAS	late January 1923
	HPL	9 February 1923
9	HPL	25 March 1923
	CAS	c. April 1923
10	HPL	11 June 1923
	CAS	20 July 1923
11	HPL	30 July 1923
	CAS	c. early October 1923
12	HPL	17 October 1923
	CAS	2 November 1923
13	HPL	4 December 1923
	CAS	mid-January 1924 (two items)
14	HPL	25 January 1924
	CAS	c. February 1924
15	HPL	c. 3 March 1924
	CAS	c. March 1924
16	HPL	24 July 1924
	CAS	early March 1925
17	HPL	14 March 1925
18	CAS	20 March 1925

*Unnumbered items are conjectural based on content in the other letters.

No.*	Sender(s)	Date
	CAS	13 August 1925
19	HPL	18 August 1925
	CAS	c. 23 August 1925
20	HPL	28 August 1925
	CAS	mid-September 1925
21	HPL	20 September 1925
	CAS	early October 1925
22	HPL	9 October 1925
	CAS	late October 1925
23	HPL	4 November 1925
	CAS	c. mid-November 1925
24	HPL	24 November 1925
25	CAS	8 December 1925
26	HPL	12 December 1925
	CAS	late December 1925
27	HPL	27 December 1925
	CAS	mid-January 1926
28	HPL	18 January 1926
29	HPL	20 January 1926
	CAS	early February 1926
30	HPL	9 February 1926
	CAS	mid-February 1926
31	HPL	26 February 1926
	CAS	March 1926
32	HPL	26 March 1926
33	CAS	14 Aril 1926
34	HPL	16 April 1926
	HPL	late April 1926
35	CAS	9 May 1926
36	HPL	14 May 1926
	CAS	c. early June 1926
37	HPL	17 June 1926
	CAS	4 July 1926
38	HPL	15 July 1926
	CAS	c. early August 1926
39	HPL	9 August 1926
	CAS	early October 1926
40	HPL	12 October 1926
	CAS	late October 1926
41	HPL	29 October 1926
	CAS	early November 1926
42	HPL	16 November 1926

No.*	Sender(s)	Date
	CAS	early December 1926
43	HPL	11 December 1926
	CAS	late December 1926
44	HPL	2 January 1927
45	HPL	17 January 1927
	CAS	c. 18 January 1927
46	HPL	21 January 1927
	CAS	early February 1927
47	HPL	18 February 1927
48	HPL	8 March 1927
49	CAS	early to mid-March 1927
50	HPL	15 March 1927
	CAS	late March 1927
51	HPL	24 March 1927
52	HPL	4 April 1927
	CAS	early April 1927
53	HPL	16 April 1927
	CAS	early May 1927
54	HPL	12 May 1927
	CAS	late May 1927
55	HPL	3 June 1927
	CAS	18 June 1927
56	HPL	24 June 1927
	CAS	c. 11 July 1927
57	HPL, D. Wandrei	14 July 1927
58	HPL, D. Wandrei	15 July 1927
59	HPL et al.	21 July 1927
	CAS	late July 1927
60	HPL et al.	1 August 1927
61	HPL	2 August 1927
62	HPL, Munn, Cook	14 August 1927
63	HPL	30 August 1927
	CAS	c. late August 1927
64	HPL	1 September 1927
65	HPL	5 September 1927
	CAS	c. late September 1927
66	HPL	1 October 1927
	CAS	early October 1927
67	HPL	15 October 1927
	CAS	c. mid-November 1927
68	HPL	27 November 1927
	CAS	late December 1927

No.*	Sender(s)	Date
69	HPL	28 December 1927
	CAS	c. late January 1928
70	HPL	31 January 1928
	CAS	mid-February 1928
71	HPL	18 February 1928
	CAS	early March 1928
72	HPL	13 March 1928
73	CAS	mid-March 1928
74	CAS	20 March 1928
	HPL	late March 1928
75	HPL	2 April 1928
	CAS	mid-April 1928
76	HPL	19 April 1928
77	CAS	27 May 1928
78	HPL	7 June 1928
79	HPL, D. Wandrei, Long	18 July 1928
	CAS	August 1928
80	HPL	31 August 1928
	CAS	c. mid-October 1928
81	HPL	27 October 1928
	CAS	6 November 1928
82	HPL	15 November 1928
	CAS	24 November 1928
83	HPL	8 December 1928
84	HPL	late December 1928
85	HPL, Loveman	5 January 1929
	CAS	5 February 1929
86	HPL	13 February 1929
	CAS	10 March 1929
87	HPL	22 March 1929
	CAS	early April 1929
	HPL, Loveman	8 April 1929
88	HPL	14 April 1929
89	HPL et al.	26 April 1929
90	HPL	2 May 1929
91	HPL, Dwyer	15 May 1929
	CAS	26 May 1929
92	HPL	5 June 1929
	HPL, Morton	18 June 1929
93	HPL	3 July 1929
	CAS	July 1929
94	HPL	29 July 1929

No.*	Sender(s)	Date
	CAS	c. mid-September 1929
95	HPL	20 September 1929
	CAS	30 September 1929
96	HPL	3 October 1929
	CAS	c. late October 1929
97	HPL	29 October 1929
	CAS	c. mid-November 1929
98	HPL	19 November 1929
99	CAS	26 November 1929
100	HPL	3 December 1929
101	CAS	10 December 1929
	HPL	mid-December 1929
102	HPL	19 December 1929
103	CAS	9 January 1930
104	HPL	17 January 1930
105	CAS	27 January 1930
106	HPL	2 February 1930
107	CAS	17 February 1930
108	HPL	27 February 1930
109	CAS	11 March 1930
110	HPL	c. 19 March 1930
111	CAS	2 April 1930
112	HPL	10 April 1930
113	CAS	23 April 1930
114	HPL	10 May 1930
115	HPL	29 May 1930
116	HPL, Dwyer	4 June 1930
	CAS	early to mid-June 1930
117	HPL	23 June 1930
118	CAS	29 June 1930
119	HPL	18 July 1930
120	CAS	30 July 1930
121	HPL	6 August 1930
122	CAS	22 August 1930
123	HPL	28 August 1930
124	HPL	1 September 1930
125	HPL	10 September 1930
126	CAS	begun early September 1930
	HPL	before 25 September 1930
127	HPL	c. 25 September 1930
128	CAS	c. early October 1930
129	HPL	October 1930

No.*	Sender(s)	Date
130	HPL	14 October 1930
131	HPL	17 October 1930
132	CAS	c. 21 October 1930
133	HPL	29 October 1930
134	CAS	c. 24–30 October 1930
135	HPL	7 November 1930
136	CAS	10 November 1930
137	HPL	mid-November 1930
138	CAS	17–23 November 1930
139	HPL	29? November 1930
140	CAS	mid-December 1930
141	HPL	25 December 1930
142	CAS	c. early January 1931
143	CAS	10 January 1931
144	HPL	c. 18 January 1931
145	CAS	c. 27 January 1931
146	HPL	8 February 1931
147	CAS	c. 15–23 February 1931
148	HPL	26 March 1931
	CAS	c. early April 1931
149	HPL	15 April 1931
150	HPL	12 May 1931
151	HPL	15 May 1931
	HPL	c. 11 June 1931
	CAS	c. mid-June 1931
152	HPL	25 June 1931
	CAS	July 1931
153	HPL	1 August 1931
154	CAS	c. early August 1931
	HPL	9 August 1931
155	HPL	14 August 1931
156	CAS	mid-August 1931
157	HPL	23 August 1931
	CAS	c. early September 1931
158	HPL	11 September 1931
	CAS	mid-September 1931
159	HPL	23 September 1931
160	HPL	5 October 1931
	CAS	early October 1931
161	HPL	13 October 1931
162	CAS	c. 23 October 1931
163	HPL	30 October 1931

No.*	Sender(s)	Date
	HPL	1 November 1931
164	HPL	c. 6 November 1931
165	CAS	c. 12 November 1931
166	HPL	20 November 1931
	CAS	late November 1931
	HPL	c. late November 1931
167	HPL	early December 1931
168	HPL	mid-December 1931
	CAS	c. late December 1931
169	HPL	27 December 1931
170	CAS	early January 1932
170a	HPL	7 January 1932
171	HPL	16 January 1932
172	HPL	January 1932 (enclosure)
	CAS	c. late January 1932
173	HPL	28 January 1932
	CAS	early February 1932
174	HPL	8 February 1932
	CAS	mid-February 1932
175	HPL	18 February 1932
	CAS	mid-February 1932
	CAS	late February 1932
176	HPL	26 February 1932
177	HPL	2 March 1932
178	CAS	c. early March 1932
	HPL	c. 4 March 1932
179	HPL	11 March 1932
180	CAS	c. 15 March 1932
181	CAS	mid-March 1932
182	HPL	21 March 1932
183	HPL	26 March 1932
	CAS	late March 1932
184	HPL	4 April 1932
185	CAS	c. 5 April 1932
186	HPL	15 April 1932
187	CAS	c. 15 April 1932
188	HPL	20 April 1932
	CAS	c. late April 1932
189	HPL	6 May 1932
	CAS	early May 1932
189a	HPL	9 May 1932
190	HPL	13 May 1932

No.*	Sender(s)	Date
191	CAS	14 May 1932
192	CAS	24 May 1932
	CAS	c. early June 1932
193	HPL	11 June 1932
194	HPL, Price	15 June 1932
195	HPL	10 July 1932
	CAS	mid-July 1932
	HPL, Morton	c. 25 July 1932
196	HPL	c. 26 July 1932
	CAS	early August 1932
197	HPL	early August 1932
	CAS	mid-August 1932
198	HPL	27 August 1932
	HPL, Cook (?)	31 August 1932
	HPL	c. 2 September 1932
	CAS	early September 1932
	HPL, D. Wandrei	c. 13 September 1932
199	HPL	17 September 1932
200	CAS	c. 19 September 1932
201	HPL	23 September 1932
	CAS	29 September 1932
202	HPL	8 October 1932
	CAS	mid-October 1932
203	HPL	28 October 1932
	CAS	early November 1932
204	HPL	18 November 1932
	CAS	late November 1932
205	HPL	5 December 1932
	CAS	mid-December 1932
206	HPL	21 December 1932
	CAS	late December 1932
207	HPL	7 January 1933
	CAS	late January 1933
208	HPL	2 February 1933
	CAS	c. 8 February 1933
209	HPL	c. 10 February 1933
	CAS	c. 19 February 1933
210	HPL	21 February 1933
211	HPL	24 February 1933
212	CAS	1 March 1933
213	HPL	early March 1933
214	HPL	15 March 1933

No.*	Sender(s)	Date
	CAS	c. 19 March 1933
215	HPL	24 March 1933
	CAS	c. early April 1933
216	HPL	8 April 1933
	CAS	April 1933
217	HPL	3 May 1933
	CAS	May 1933
218	HPL	31 May 1933
	CAS	c. 7 June 1933
219	HPL	14 June 1933
220	HPL	16 June 1933
	CAS	late June 1933
221	HPL	29 June 1933
	CAS	early July 1933
222	HPL	12 July 1933
223	HPL	25 July 1933
224	HPL, Morton	1 August 1933
	CAS	early August 1933
	CAS	c. 9 August 1933
225	CAS	10 August 1933
226	HPL	15 August 1933
227	CAS	17 August 1933
228	CAS	21 August 1933
229	HPL	26 August 1933
230	CAS	28 August 1933
231	CAS	29 August 1933
232	CAS	c. 1 September 1933
233	HPL	3 September 1933
	HPL	c. early September 1933
234	HPL	11 September 1933
235	HPL	enclosure to above letter
236	CAS	14 September 1933
237	CAS	16 September 1933
238	HPL	20 September 1933
239	CAS	late September 1933
	HPL	c. 1 October 1933
240	CAS	2 October 1933
241	HPL	3 October 1933
242	CAS	5 October 1933
243	CAS	10 October 1933
244	HPL	10 October 1933
245	CAS	mid-October 1933

No.*	Sender(s)	Date
246	HPL	22 October 1933
247	CAS	4 November 1933
248	CAS	c. early November 1933
	HPL	early November 1933
249	HPL	13 November 1933
250	CAS	16 November 1933
251	HPL	18 November 1933
	CAS	c. 22 November 1933
252	CAS	24 November 1933
253	CAS	late November 1933
254	HPL	29 November 1933
	CAS	c. late November 1933
255	CAS	4 December 1933
256	HPL	13 December 1933
257	HPL	14 December 1933
258	CAS	16 December 1933
	CAS	c. late December 1933
259	HPL	late December 1933
260	HPL	c. 8–11 January 1934
	CAS	c. 20 January 1934
261	HPL	24 January 1934
262	CAS	c. late January 1934
263	HPL	11 February 1934
	CAS	c. late February 1934
	HPL	c. early March 1934
264	CAS	early March 1934
265	CAS	7 March 1934
266	HPL	9 March 1934
267	HPL	19 March 1934
268	HPL	22 March 1934
269	CAS	23 March 1934
	CAS	c. late March 1934
270	HPL	c. early April 1934 (enclosure)
	HPL	early April 1934
	CAS	c. 9 April 1934
271	HPL	13 April 1934
272	HPL	25 April 1934
	CAS	c. 26 April 1934
273	HPL	27 April 1934
274	HPL	30 April 1934
275	CAS	4 May 1934
276	HPL, RHB	1 May 1934

No.*	Sender(s)	Date
	CAS, Price	c. 7 May 1934
277	HPL, RHB	10 May 1934
278	CAS	19 May 1934
	CAS	c. 21 May 1934
279	HPL	c. late May/early June 1934
280	HPL	enclosure to above letter?
281	CAS	15 June 1934
282	CAS	c. 16 June 1934
	HPL	c. 21 June 1934
283	HPL	25 June 1934
284	CAS	23 July 1934
285	HPL	28 July 1934
286	HPL	29 August 1934
287	HPL	8 September 1934
	CAS	September 1934 (several items)
288	HPL	30 September 1934
289	HPL	17 October 1934
	CAS	c. mid-October 1934
	CAS	c. late October 1934
290	HPL	28 October 1934
291	HPL	3 November 1934
	CAS	early November 1934
292	HPL	10 November 1934
293	CAS, D. Wandrei	21 November 1934
294	HPL	25 November 1934
	HPL et al.	2 January 1935
295	CAS	c. 10 January 1935
	CAS	c. 12 January 1935
296	HPL	16 January 1935
	CAS	late January 1935
297	HPL	30 January 1935
298	HPL	enclosure to above letter
	CAS	February? 1935
	CAS	early March 1935
299	HPL	26 March 1935
300	CAS	5 April 1935
301	HPL	11 April 1935
302	HPL	16 June 1935
303	HPL	enclosure to above letter?
304	HPL	June 1935 (envelope)
305	CAS	late June 1935
306	HPL	1 July 1935

No.*	Sender(s)	Date
307	HPL	25 July 1935
308	HPL	enclosure to above letter?
309	HPL	26 August 1935
310	HPL, D. Wandrei, Long	7 September 1935
311	CAS	7 September 1935
	CAS	after 9 September 1935
	HPL	after 11 September 1935
312	CAS	c. mid-October 1935
313	HPL, Loveman	c. 17 October 1935
314	HPL	23 October 1935
	CAS	c. 24 October 1935
315	HPL	28 October 1935
	CAS	early November 1935
316	HPL	10 November 1935
	CAS	c. late November 1935
317	HPL	2 December 1935
318	HPL	mid-December 1935
	CAS	January 1936
	CAS	January 1936
319	HPL	24 January 1936
320	CAS	5 February 1936
	CAS	March 1936?
321	HPL	23 March 1936
	CAS	2 April 1936
	CAS	17 April 1936
322	HPL	23 April 1936
323	CAS	22 May 1936
324	HPL	20 June 1936
325	HPL, Morton, Brobst	19 September 1936
326	HPL	29 September 1936
327	CAS	13 October 1936
328	CAS	13 November 1936
329	CAS	27 November 1936
330	HPL	5 February 1937
	CAS	late February 1937

Glossary of Frequently Mentioned Names

Ackerman, Forrest J (1916–2008), American agent, author, editor. Ackerman had been a science fiction fan since the late 1920s; he corresponded sporadically with HPL from around 1931 onward. He was the instigator of the feud chronicled in "The Boiling Point" (q.v.).

Baird, Edwin (1886–1954), first editor of *WT* (March 1923–April 1924), who accepted HPL's first submissions to the magazine. Also editor of *Real Detective Stories*.

Barlow, R[obert] H[ayward] (1918–1951), author and collector. As a teenager he corresponded with HPL and acted as his host during two long visits in the summers of 1934 and 1935. In the 1930s he wrote several works of weird and fantasy fiction, some in collaboration with HPL. HPL appointed him his literary executor. He assisted August Derleth and Donald Wandrei in preparing the early HPL volumes for Arkham House. In the 1940s he went to Mexico and became a distinguished anthropologist. He died by suicide.

Bates, Harry (1900–1981), editor of *Strange Tales* and *Astounding Stories*.

Bierce, Ambrose (1842–1914?), journalist and writer of tales of supernatural and psychological horror that were much admired by HPL.

Blackwood, Algernon (1869–1951), prolific British author of weird and fantasy tales whose work HPL greatly admired when he read it in 1924.

Bloch, Robert (1917–1994), author of weird and suspense fiction who came into correspondence with HPL in 1933. HPL tutored him in the craft of writing during their four-year association.

Brobst, Harry K[ern] (1909–2010), late associate of HPL who moved to Providence in 1932 and saw HPL regularly thereafter.

Cave, Hugh B[arnett] (1910–2004), prolific pulp writer who lived in the Providence metropolitan area and sporadically corresponded with HPL.

Clark, Lillian D[elora] (1856–1932), HPL's maternal aunt. She married Dr. Franklin Chase Clark in 1902. From 1926 to her death, she shared quarters with HPL at 10 Barnes Street.

Cole, Edward H[arold] (1892–1966), longtime amateur associate of HPL, living in the Boston area. Editor of the *Olympian*.

Conover, Willis (1920–1996), weird fiction fan who edited the *Science-Fantasy Correspondent* (1936–37) and was a late correspondent of HPL.

Cook, W. Paul (1881–1948), publisher of the *Monadnock Monthly*, the *Vagrant*, and other amateur journals; a longtime amateur journalist, printer, and life-long friend of HPL. He first visited HPL in 1917, and it was he who urged HPL to resume writing fiction after a hiatus of nine years. In 1927 Cook published the *Recluse*, containing HPL's "Supernatural Horror in Literature."

Crawford, William L[evy] (1911–1984), editor of *Marvel Tales* and *Unusual Stories* and publisher of the Visionary Publishing Company, which issued HPL's *The Shadow Over Innsmouth* (1936).

De Casseres, Benjamin (1873–1945). Poet, critic, and friend of Smith; he contributed the introduction to *SP*.

de Castro, Adolphe (Danziger) (1859–1959), author, co-translator with Ambrose Bierce of Richard Voss's *The Monk and the Hangman's Daughter*, and correspondent of HPL. HPL revised his "The Last Test" and "The Electric Executioner."

de la Mare, Walter (1873–1956), British author and poet who wrote occasional weird tales much admired by HPL for their subtlety and allusiveness.

Derleth, August W[illiam] (1909–1971), author of weird tales and also a long series of regional and historical works set in his native Wisconsin. After HPL's death, he and Donald Wandrei founded the publishing firm of Arkham House to preserve HPL's work in book form. For the joint correspondence of HPL and Derleth, see *Essential Solitude*.

Dunsany, Lord (Edward John Moreton Drax Plunkett) (1878–1957), Irish writer of fantasy tales whose work notably influenced HPL after HPL read it in 1919.

Dwyer, Bernard Austin (1897–1943), weird fiction fan and would-be writer and artist, living in West Shokan, NY; correspondent of HPL.

Edkins, Ernest A[rthur] (1867–1946), amateur journalist associated with the "halcyon days" of the National Amateur Press Association (1885–95). He came in touch with HPL in 1932.

Eddy, C[lifford] M[artin] (1896–1967), pulp fiction writer living in the Providence area for whom HPL revised several stories in 1923–24 and who also worked with HPL on ghostwriting work for Harry Houdini in 1926.

Finlay, Virgil (1914–1971), one of the great weird artists of his time and a prolific contributor of artwork to the pulps; late correspondent of HPL.

Flagg, Francis. *See* Weiss, Henry George.

Galpin, Alfred (1901–1983), amateur journalist and correspondent of HPL. He studied music in Paris and was also a scholar in French literature.

Gamwell, Annie E[meline] P[hillips] (1866–1941), HPL's younger aunt, living with him at 66 College Street (1933–37).

Gernsback, Hugo (1884–1967), editor of *Amazing Stories, Wonder Stories,* and other pioneering science fiction pulps.

Hall, Desmond W[inter] (1911–1992) associate editor of *Astounding Stories.*

Hamilton, Edmond (1904–1977), popular and prolific author of "weird-scientific" stories for *WT.*

Heald, Hazel (1896–1961), of Somerville, MA; client of HPL, for whom he ghostwrote five stories.

Hersey, Harold (1893–1956), pulp editor who edited the *Thrill Book* (Street & Smith) and later worked as editor for Clayton Publications and Bernarr Macfadden.

Henneberger, J[acob] C[lark] (1890–1969), founder of *College Humor* (1922) and the original publisher of *WT.*

Hodgson, William Hope (1877–1918), British author of weird fiction whose work had fallen into obscurity until it was rediscovered in the 1930s, largely through the efforts of H. C. Koenig.

Hornig, Charles D[erwin] (1916–1999), editor of the *Fantasy Fan* (1933–35) and associate editor of *Wonder Stories.*

Houtain, George Julian (1884–1945), amateur journalist who established the semi-professional humor magazine *Home Brew,* for which he commissioned HPL to write "Herbert West—Reanimator" (1921–22) and "The Lurking Fear" (1922) and CAS to illustrate the latter.

Howard, Robert E[rvin] (1906–1936), prolific Texas author of weird and adventure tales for *Weird Tales* and other pulp magazines; creator of the adventure hero Conan the Barbarian. He and HPL corresponded voluminously from 1930 to 1936. He committed suicide when he heard of his mother's impending death.

Keller, David H[enry] (1880–1966), physician, psychiatrist, and popular science fiction writer.

Kirk, George [Willard] (1898–1962), member of the Kalem Club. He published *Twenty-one Letters of Ambrose Bierce* (1922) and ran the Chelsea Bookshop in New York.

Kleiner, Rheinhart (1893–1949), amateur poet and longtime friend of HPL. He visited HPL in Providence in 1918, 1919, and 1920, and met him frequently during the heyday of the Kalem Club (1924–26).

Kline, Otis Adlebert (1891–1946), prolific writer for *WT* and other pulp magazines; also a literary agent for Robert E. Howard and others.

Koenig, H[erman] C[harles] (1893–1959), late associate of HPL who spearheaded the rediscovery of the work of William Hope Hodgson; editor of *Reader and Collector.*

Kuttner, Henry (1915–1958), prolific author of science fiction and horror tales for the pulp magazines, and a late correspondent of HPL (1936–37). HPL introduced him to C. L. Moore (1911–1987), whom he would later marry.

Long, Frank Belknap (1901–1994), fiction writer and poet and one of HPL's closest friends and correspondents. Late in life he wrote the memoir, *Howard Phillips Lovecraft: Dreamer on the Nightside* (1975).

Loveman, Samuel (1887–1976), poet and longtime friend of HPL and Donald Wandrei as well as of Ambrose Bierce, Hart Crane, George Sterling, and Clark Ashton Smith. He wrote *The Hermaphrodite* (1926) and other works.

Lumley, William (1880–1960), eccentric late associate of HPL for whom HPL ghostwrote "The Diary of Alonzo Typer" (1935).

Machen, Arthur (1863–1947), Welsh author of weird fiction. He corresponded sporadically with August Derleth.

Merritt, A[braham] (1884–1943), writer of fantasy and horror tales for the pulps. His work was much admired by HPL in spite of its concessions to pulp formulae. His late novel, *Dwellers in the Mirage* (1932), may have been influenced by HPL.

Moe, Maurice W[inter] (1882–1940), amateur journalist, English teacher, and longtime friend and correspondent of HPL. He lived successively in Appleton and Milwaukee, WI.

Morse, Richard Ely (1909–1986), poet, librarian, and late correspondent of HPL.

Morton, James Ferdinand (1870–1941), amateur journalist, author of many tracts on race prejudice, free thought, and taxation, and longtime friend of HPL.

Munn, H[arold] Warner (1903–1981), prolific contributor to the pulp magazines, living near W. Paul Cook in Athol, MA.

Orton, Vrest (1897–1986), a correspondent of Lovecraft living in New York. He designed the cover for W. Paul Cook's *Recluse*, wrote *Dreiserana, a Book about His Books* (1929), founded the Stephen Daye Press in Brattleboro, VT, and in 1946 started the Vermont Country Store.

Price, E[dgar] Hoffmann (1898–1989), prolific pulp writer of weird and adventure tales. HPL met him in New Orleans in 1932 and corresponded extensively with him thereafter.

Quinn, Seabury (1889–1969), prolific author of weird and detective tales to the pulps, notably a series of tales involving the psychic detective Jules de Grandin.

Schwartz, Julius (1915–2004), editor of *Fantasy Magazine* who acted as HPL's agent in marketing *At the Mountains of Madness* to *Astounding Stories.*

Searight, Richard F[ranklyn] sporadic contributor of weird and science fiction tales to the pulp magazines. He corresponded with HPL from 1933 to 1937.

Shea, J[oseph] Vernon (1912–1981), young weird fiction fan from Pittsburgh who began corresponding with HPL in 1931.

Sommer, William (1867–1949), American Modernist painter from Ohio. Friend of Samuel Loveman.

Sterling, George (1869–1926), California poet and early mentor of Smith.

Sterling, Kenneth (1920–1995), young science fiction fan who came into contact with HPL in 1934. He later became a distinguished physician.

Stickney, Corwin F. (1921–1998), copublisher with Willis Conover of *Science-Fantasy Correspondent* (1936–37), later titled *Amateur Correspondent* (1937f.), edited by Stickney alone.

Strauch, Carl Ferdinand (1908–1989), friend of Harry Brobst and correspondent of HPL. He later became a distinguished professor and critic.

Sully, Helen V. (1904–1997), friend of CAS who visited HPL in Providence in 1933, then saw Donald Wandrei and others in New York.

Talman, Wilfred Blanch (1904–1986), correspondent of HPL and late member of the Kalem Club. HPL assisted Talman on his story "Two Black Bottles" (1926) and wrote "Some Dutch Footprints in New England" for Talman to publish in *De Halve Maen,* the journal of the Holland Society of New York. Late in life he wrote the memoir *The Normal Lovecraft* (1973).

Wandrei, Donald (1908–1987), poet and author of weird fiction, science fiction, and detective tales. He corresponded with HPL from 1926 to 1937, visited HPL in Providence in 1927 and 1932, and met HPL occasionally in New York during the 1930s. He helped finance CAS's *Sandalwood* and helped HPL get "The Shadow out of Time" published in *Astounding Stories.* After HPL's death, he and August Derleth founded the publishing firm Arkham House to preserve HPL's work and CAS's *Selected Poems.* For their joint correspondence, see *Mysteries of Time and Spirit.*

Wandrei, Howard (1909–1956), younger brother of Donald Wandrei, premier weird artist and prolific author of weird fiction, science fiction, and detective stories; correspondent of HPL.

Weiss, Henry George (1898–1946), American poet, writer and novelist. His science fiction stories and poetry appeared under the pseudonym "Francis Flagg" in *Amazing Stories, Astounding, Tales of Wonder, Weird Tales,* and others.

Whitehead, Henry S[t. Clair] (1882–1932), author of weird and adventure tales, many of them set in the Virgin Islands. HPL corresponded with him and visited him in Florida in 1931. HPL wrote a brief eulogy of Whitehead for *WT*.

Wollheim, Donald A[llen] (1914–1990), editor of the *Phantagraph* and *Fanciful Tales* and prolific author and editor in the science fiction field.

Wright, Farnsworth (1888–1940), editor of *Weird Tales* (1924–40). He rejected some of HPL's best work of the 1930s, only to publish it after HPL's death upon submittal by August Derleth. Referred to as Satrap Pharnabozus, Pharnabeezer, etc., by Smith and Lovecraft. Satrap signifies a petty or secondary ruler.

Bibliography

A. Works by H. P. Lovecraft

Books

The Ancient Track: Complete Poetical Works. 2nd ed. Edited by S. T. Joshi. New York: Hippocampus Press, 2013.

The Annotated Supernatural Horror in Literature. 2nd ed. Edited by S. T. Joshi. New York: Hippocampus Press, 2012.

The Cats of Ulthar. Cassia, FL: Dragon-Fly Press, Christmas 1935. Text in *CF*$_L$ 1.

Charleston. [New York: H. C. Koenig, 1936.] Text in *CE* 4.

Collected Essays. Edited by S. T. Joshi. New York: Hippocampus Press, 2004–06. 5 vols. [*CE*]

Collected Fiction. Edited by S. T. Joshi. New York: Hippocampus Press, 2015, 2017. 4 vols. [*CF*$_L$]

Commonplace Book. Edited by David E. Schultz. West Warwick, RI: Necronomicon Press, 1987; text in *CE* 5. [*CB*]

Dreams and Fancies. [Edited by August Derleth.] Sauk City, WI: Arkham House, 1962.

Essential Solitude: The Letters of H. P. Lovecraft and August Derleth. Edited by David E. Schultz and S. T. Joshi. New York: Hippocampus Press, 2008. 2 vols. [*ES*]

Fritz Leiber and H. P. Lovecraft: Writers of the Dark. Edited by Ben J. S. Szumskyj and S. T. Joshi. Holicong, PA: Wildside Press, 2003.

Fungi from Yuggoth: An Annotated Edition. Edited by David E. Schultz. New York: Hippocampus Press, 2017.

Further Criticism of Poetry. Louisville, KY: George G. Fetter, 1932. Text in *CE* 1.

Hail, Klarkash-Ton! Being Nine Missives Inscribed upon Postcards. [Glendale, CA: Roy A. Squires, 1971.] *Contents:* Nine postcards from HPL to CAS. [*HK*]

A History of the "Necronomicon." Oakman, AL: Wilson H. Shepherd (The Rebel Press), [November 1937]. Text in *CF*$_L$ 2.

Letters to Alfred Galpin. Edited by S. T. Joshi and David E. Schultz. New York: Hippocampus Press, 2003.

Letters to C. L. Moore and Others. Edited by David E. Schultz and S. T. Joshi. New York: Hippocampus Press, 2017.

Letters to Elizabeth Toldridge and Anne Tillery Renshaw. Edited by David E. Schultz and S. T. Joshi. New York: Hippocampus Press, 2014.

Letters to F. Lee Baldwin, Duane W. Rimel, and Nils Frome. Edited by David E. Schultz and S. T. Joshi. New York: Hippocampus Press, 2016.

Letters to James F. Morton. Edited by David E. Schultz and S. T. Joshi. New York: Hippocampus Press, 2011.

Letters to Rheinhart Kleiner. Edited by S. T. Joshi and David E. Schultz. New York: Hippocampus Press, 2005. [*RK*]

Letters to Robert Bloch and Others. Edited by David E. Schultz and S. T. Joshi. New York: Hippocampus Press, 2015.

Letters to Wilfred B. Talman and Helen V. Sully. Edited by David E. Schultz and S. T. Joshi. New York: Hippocampus Press, 2019.

A Means to Freedom: The Letters of H. P. Lovecraft and Robert E. Howard. Edited by S. T. Joshi, David E. Schultz, and Rusty Burke. New York: Hippocampus Press, 2009. 2 vols.

Mysteries of Time and Spirit: The Letters of H. P. Lovecraft and Donald Wandrei. Edited by S. T. Joshi and David E. Schultz. San Francisco: Night Shade, 2002. [*MTS*]

O Fortunate Floridian: H. P. Lovecraft's Letters to R. H. Barlow. Edited by S. T. Joshi and David E. Schultz. Tampa: University of Tampa Press, 2007.

Selected Letters. Edited by August Derleth, Donald Wandrei, and James Turner. Sauk City, WI: Arkham House, 1965–76. 5 vols. [*SL*]

The Shadow over Innsmouth. Everett, PA: Visionary Publishing Co., 1936. Text in CF_L 3.

The Shunned House. Athol, MA: Recluse Press, 1928 (printed but not bound or distributed until 1959–61). Text in CF_L 1.

Supernatural Horror in Literature as Revised in 1936. Arlington, VA: Carrollton-Clark, 1974. Text in *CE* 2.

Stories

"The Alchemist." *United Amateur* 16, No. 4 (November 1916): 53–57. In CF_L 1.

"Arthur Jermyn." See "Facts concerning the Late Arthur Jermyn and His Family."

At the Mountains of Madness. Astounding Stories 16, No. 6 (February 1936): 8–32; 17, No. 1 (March 1936): 125–55; 17, No. 2 (April 1936): 132–50. In CF_L 3.

"The Beast in the Cave." *Vagrant* No. 7 (June 1918): 113–20. In CF_L 1.

"Beyond the Wall of Sleep." *Pine Cones* 1, No. 6 (October 1919): 2–10. *FF,* 2, No. 2 (October 1934): 25–32. In CF_L 1.

"The Call of Cthulhu." *WT* 11, No. 2 (February 1928): 159–78, 287. In *Beware After Dark! The World's Most Stupendous Tales of Mystery, Horror, Thrills and Terror,* ed. T. Everett Harré. New York: Macaulay, 1929. 223–59. In CF_L 2.

The Case of Charles Dexter Ward. In CF_L 2.

"The Cats of Ulthar." *Tryout* 6, No. 11 (November 1920): [3–9]. *WT* 7, No. 2 (February 1926): 252–54. *WT* 21, No. 2 (February 1933): 259–61. In CF_L 1.

"Celephaïs." *Rainbow* No. 2 (May 1922): 10–12. *Marvel Tales* 1, No. 1 (May 1934): 26, 28–32. In CF_L 1.

"The Colour out of Space." *Amazing Stories* 2, No. 6 (September 1927): 557–67. In CF_L 2.

"Cool Air." *Tales of Magic and Mystery* 1, No. 4 (March 1928): 29–34. In CF_L 2.

"Dagon." *Vagrant* No. 11 (November 1919): 23–29. *WT* 2, No. 3 (October 1923): 23–25. In *CF*$_L$ 1.

"The Doom That Came to Sarnath." *Scot* No. 44 (June 1920): 90–98. *Marvel Tales of Science and Fantasy* 1, No. 4 (March–April 1935): 157–63. In *CF*$_L$ 1.

The Dream-Quest of Unknown Kadath. In *CF*$_L$ 2.

"The Dreams in the Witch House." *WT* 22, No. 1 (July 1933): 86–111. In *CF*$_L$ 3.

"The Dunwich Horror." *WT* 13, No. 4 (April 1929): 481–508. In *CF*$_L$ 2.

"The Evil Clergyman." *WT* 33, No. 4 (April 1939): 135–37 (as "The Wicked Clergyman"). In *CF*$_L$ 3.

"Ex Oblivione." *United Amateur* 20, No. 4 (March 1921): 59–60 (as by "Ward Phillips"). *Phantagraph* 6, No. 3 (July 1937): 2–4. In *CF*$_L$ 1.

"Facts concerning the Late Arthur Jermyn and His Family." *Wolverine* No. 9 (March 1921): 3–11; No. 10 (June 1921): 6–11. *WT* 3, No. 4 (April 1924): 15–18 (as "The White Ape"). *WT* 25, No. 5 (May 1935): 642–48 (as "Arthur Jermyn"). In *CF*$_L$ 1.

"The Festival." *WT* 5, No. 1 (January 1925): 169–74. *WT* 22, No. 4 (October 1933): 519–20, 522–28. In *CF*$_L$ 1.

"From Beyond." *FF* 1, No. 10 (June 1934): 147–51, 160. In *CF*$_L$ 1.

"The Haunter of the Dark." *WT* 28, No. 5 (December 1936): 538–53. In *CF*$_L$ 3.

"He." *WT* 8, No. 3 (September 1926): 373–80. In *CF*$_L$ 1.

"Herbert West—Reanimator" (as "Grewsome Tales"). *Home Brew* 1, No. 1 (February 1922): 84–88 ("From the Dark"); 1, No. 2 (March 1922): 45–50 ("The Plague Demon"); 1, No. 3 (April 1922): 21–26 ("Six Shots by Moonlight"); 1, No. 4 (May 1922): 53–58 ("The Scream of the Dead"); 1, No. 5 (June 1922): 45–50 ("The Horror from the Shadows,"); 1, No. 6 (July 1922): 57–62 ("The Tomb-Legions"). In *CF*$_L$ 1.

"The Horror at Red Hook." *WT* 9, No. 1 (January 1927): 59–73. In *You'll Need a Night Light,* ed. Christine Campbell Thomson. London: Selwyn & Blount, 1927. 228–54. In *Not at Night!,* ed. Herbert Asbury. New York: Macy-Masius (The Vanguard Press), November 1928. 27–52. In *CF*$_L$ 1.

"The Hound." *WT* 3, No. 2 (February 1924): 50–52, 78. *WT* 14, No. 3 (September 1929): 421–25, 432. In *CF*$_L$ 1.

"Hypnos." *National Amateur* 45, No. 5 (May 1923): 1–3. *WT* 4, No. 2 (May–June–July 1924): 33–35. In *CF*$_L$ 1.

"In the Vault." *Tryout* 10, No. 6 (November 1925): [3–17]. *WT* 19, No. 4 (April 1932): 459–65. In *CF*$_L$ 1.

"The Lurking Fear." *Home Brew* 2, No. 6 (January 1923): 4–10; 3, No. 1 (February 1923): 18–23; 3, No. 2 (March 1923): 31–37, 44, 48; 3, No. 3 (April 1923): 35–42. *WT* 11, No. 6 (June 1928): 791–804. In *CF*$_L$ 1.

"Memory." *United Co-operative* 1, No. 2 (June 1919): 8. In *CF*$_L$ 1.

"The Moon-Bog." *WT* 7, No. 6 (June 1926): 805–10. In *CF*$_L$ 1.

"The Music of Erich Zann." *National Amateur* 44, No. 4 (March 1922): 38–40. *WT* 5, No. 5 (May 1925): 219–34. In *Creeps by Night: Chills and Thrills,* ed.

Dashiell Hammett. New York: John Day Co., 1931. 347–63. In *Modern Tales of Horror,* ed. Dashiell Hammett. London: Victor Gollancz, 1932. 301–17. *Evening Standard* (London) (24 October 1932): 20–21. *WT* 24, No. 5 (November 1934): 644–48, 655–56. In *CF*$_L$ 1.

"The Nameless City." *Wolverine* No. 11 (November 1921): 3–15. *Fanciful Tales* 1, No. 1 (Fall 1936): 5–18. In *CF*$_L$ 1.

"Nyarlathotep." *United Amateur* 20, No. 2 (November 1920): 19–21. *National Amateur* 48, No. 6 (July 1926): 53–54. In *CF*$_L$ 1.

"The Other Gods." *Fantasy Fan* 1, No. 3 (November 1933): 35–38. *WT* 32, No. 4 (October 1938): 489–92. In *CF*$_L$ 1.

"The Outsider." *WT* 7, No. 4 (April 1926): 449–53. *WT* 17, No. 4 (June–July 1931): 566–71. In *CF*$_L$ 1.

"Pickman's Model." *WT* 10, No. 4 (October 1927): 505–14. In *By Daylight Only,* ed. Christine Campbell Thomson. London: Selwyn & Blount, 1929. 37–52. *WT* 28, No. 4 (November 1936): 495–505. In *The "Not at Night" Omnibus,* ed. Christine Campbell Thomson. London: Selwyn & Blount, [1937]. 279–307. In *CF*$_L$ 2.

"The Picture in the House." *National Amateur* 41, No. 6 (July 1919 [*sic*]): 246–49. *WT* 3, No. 1 (January 1924): 40–42. *WT* 29, No. 3 (March 1937): 370–73. In *CF*$_L$ 1.

"Polaris." *Philosopher* 1, No. 1 (December 1920): 3–5. *National Amateur* 48, No. 5 (May 1926): 48–49. *FF* 1, No. 6 (February 1934): 83–85. In *CF*$_L$ 1.

"The Quest of Iranon." *Galleon* 1, No. 5 (July–August 1935): 12–20. In *CF*$_L$ 1.

"The Rats in the Walls." *WT* 3, No. 3 (March 1924): 25–31. *WT* 15, No. 6 (June 1930): 841–53. In *Switch On the Light,* ed. Christine Campbell Thomson. London: Selwyn & Blount, 1931. 141–65. In *CF*$_L$ 1.

"The Shadow out of Time." *Astounding Stories* 17, No. 4 (June 1936): 110–54. In *CF*$_L$ 3.

"The Shadow over Innsmouth." In *CF*$_L$ 3.

"The Shunned House." In *CF*$_L$ 1.

"The Silver Key." *WT* 13, No. 1 (January 1929): 41–49, 144. In *CF*$_L$ 2.

"The Statement of Randolph Carter." *Vagrant* No. 13 (May 1920): 41–48. *WT* 5, No. 2 (February 1925): 149–53. In *CF*$_L$ 1.

"The Strange High House in the Mist." *WT* 18, No. 3 (October 1931): 394–400. In *CF*$_L$ 2.

"The Temple." *WT* 6, No. 3 (September 1925): 329–36, 429–31. *WT* 27, No. 2 (February 1936): 239–44, 246–49. In *CF*$_L$ 1.

"The Terrible Old Man." *Tryout* 7, No. 4 (July 1921): [10–14]. *WT* 8, No. 2 (August 1926): 191–92. In *CF*$_L$ 1.

"The Thing on the Doorstep." *WT* 29, No. 1 (January 1937): 52–70. In *CF*$_L$ 3.

"The Tomb." *Vagrant* No. 14 (March 1922): 50–64. *WT* 7, No. 1 (January 1926): 117–23. In *CF*$_L$ 1.

"The Tree." *Tryout* 7, No. 7 (October 1921): [3–10]. In *CF*$_L$ 1.

"The Unnamable." *WT* 6, No. 1 (July 1925): 78–82. In *CF*$_L$ 1.

"The Very Old Folk." *Scienti-Snaps* 3, No. 3 (Summer 1940): 4–8. In *CF*$_L$ 3. (See Frank Belknap Long, *The Horror from the Hills*.)

"The Whisperer in Darkness." *WT* 18, No. 1 (August 1931): 32–73. In *CF*$_L$ 3.

"The White Ship." *United Amateur* 19, No. 2 (November 1919): 30–33. *WT* 9, No. 3 (March 1927): 386–89. In *CF*$_L$ 1.

Revisions and Collaborations [all in *CF*$_L$ 4, except where noted]

Barlow, R. H. "The Battle That Ended the Century." In *CF*$_L$ 4.

Bishop, Zealia. "The Curse of Yig." *WT* 14, No. 5 (November 1929): 625–36. In *Switch On the Light*, ed. Christine Campbell Thomson. London: Selwyn & Blount, 1931. 9–31. In *The "Not at Night" Omnibus*, ed. Christine Campbell Thomson. London: Selwyn & Blount, [1937]. 13–29.

———. "Medusa's Coil." *WT* 33, No. 1 (January 1939): 26–53 (as by "Z. B. Bishop").

———. "The Mound." *WT* 35, No. 6 (November 1940): 98–120 (abridged; as by "Zealia Brown Bishop").

Crofts, Anna Helen. "Poetry and the Gods." *United Amateur* 20, No. 1 (September 1920): 1–4.

de Castro, Adolphe. "The Electric Executioner." *WT* 16, No. 2 (August 1930): 223–36.

———. "The Last Test." *WT* 12, No. 5 (November 1928): 625–56.

Eddy, C. M. "The Loved Dead." *WT* 4, No. 2 (May–June–July 1924): 54–57. In *The Loved Dead and Other Tales*. Rhode Island: Fenham Publishing, 2008: 1–15.

Heald, Hazel. "The Horror in the Museum." *WT* 22, No. 1 (July 1933): 49–68. In *Terror by Night*, ed. Christine Campbell Thomson. London: Selwyn & Blount, (1934). 111–41. In. *The "Not at Night" Omnibus*, ed. Christine Campbell Thomson. London: Selwyn & Blount, [1937]. 279–307.

———. "The Man of Stone." *Wonder Stories* 4, No. 5 (October 1932): 440–45, 470.

———. "Out of the Aeons." *WT* 25, No. 4 (April 1935): 478–96.

Houdini, Harry. "Under the Pyramids." *WT* 4, No. 2 (May–June–July 1924): 3–12 (as "Imprisoned with the Pharaohs"). In *CF*$_L$ 1.

Jackson, Winifred V. "The Crawling Chaos." *United Co-operative* 1, No. 3 (April 1921): 1–6 (as by "Elizabeth Berkeley and Lewis Theobald, Jun.").

Price, E. Hoffmann. "Through the Gates of the Silver Key." *WT* 24, No. 1 (July 1934): 60–85. In *CF*$_L$ 3.

Poetry [all in *AT*]

"The Ancient Track." *WT* 15, No. 3 (March 1930): 300.

"Astrophobos." *United Amateur* 17, No. 3 (January 1918): 38 (as by "Ward Phillips"). *Fantasmagoria* 1, No. 1 (March 1937): 7–8.

Fungi from Yuggoth.
    I. "The Book." *FF* 2, No. 2 (October 1934): 24.
    II. "Pursuit." *FF* 2, No. 2 (October 1934): 24.
    III. "The Key." *FF* 2, No. 5 (January 1935): 72.
    V. "Homecoming." *FF* 2, No. 5 (January 1935): 72. *Science-Fantasy Correspondent* 1, No. 1 (November–December 1936): 24.
    IX. "The Courtyard." *WT* 16, No. 3 (September 1930): 322.
    X. "The Pigeon-Flyers." *WT* 39, No. 9 (January 1947): 96.
    XI. "The Well." *Providence Journal* (14 May 1930): 15.
    XII. "The Howler." *Driftwind* 7, No. 3 (November 1932): 100.
    XIII. "Hesperia." *WT* 16, No. 4 (October 1930): 464.
    XIV. "Star-Winds." *WT* 16, No. 3 (September 1930): 322.
    XV. "Antarktos." *WT* 16, No. 5 (November 1930): 692.
    XIX. "The Bells." *WT* 16, No. 6 (December 1930): 798.
    XX. "Night-Gaunts." *Providence Journal* (26 March 1930): 15. *Interesting Items* No. 605 (November 1934): [6] (as "Night Gaunts"). *Phantagraph* 4, No. 3 ([June] 1936): 8.
    XXI. "Nyarlathotep." *WT* 17, No. 1 (January 1931): 12.
    XXII. "Azathoth." *WT* 17, No. 1 (January 1931): 12.
    XXIII. "Mirage." *WT* 17, No. 2 (February–March 1931): 1975.
    XXVII. "The Elder Pharos." *WT* 17, No. 2 (February–March 1931): 175.
    XXIX. "Nostalgia." *Providence Journal* (12 March 1930): 15. *Phantagraph* 4, No. 4 (July 1936): 1.
    XXX. "Background." *Providence Journal* (16 April 1930): 13. *Interesting Items* No. 592 (September 1932): [1]. *Galleon* 1, No. 4 (May–June 1935): 8. *The Lovecrafter* 47, No. 1 (20 August 1936): 1 (as "A Sonnet").
    XXXI. "The Dweller." *Providence Journal* (7 May 1930): 15. *Phantagraph* 4, No. 2 (November–December 1935): 1935: [3].
    XXXII. "Alienation." *WT* 17, No. 3 (April–May 1931): 374.
    XXXIII. "Harbour Whistles." *Silver Fern* 1, No. 5 (May 1930): [1]. *L'Alouette* 3, No. 6 (September–October 1930): 161. *Phantagraph* 5, No. 2 (November 1936): 1.
    XXXVI. "Continuity." *Causerie* (February 1936): 1.
"Lines for Poets' Night at the Scribblers' Club." *National Amateur* 46, No. 3 (January 1924): 25. *Pegasus* No. [2] (February 1924): 31–33.
"The Messenger." *WT* 32, No. 1 (July 1938): 52.
"Nemesis." *Vagrant* No. 7 (June 1918): 41–43. *WT* 3, No. 4 (April 1924): 78.
"The Nightmare Lake." *Vagrant* No. 12 (December 1919): 13–14.
"Oceanus." *Tryout* 5, No. 7 (July 1919): [19–20] (as by "Ward Phillips"; as part of "A Cycle of Verse"). *National Enquirer* 7, No. 25 (20 March 1919): 3.
"The Outpost." *Bacon's Essays* 3, No. 1 (Spring 1930): 7. *Fantasy Magazine* 3, No. 3 (May 1934): 24–25. *O-Wash-Ta-Nong* 3, No. 1 (January 1938): 1.

"Psychopompos: A Tale in Rhyme." *Vagrant* No. 10 (October 1919): 13–23. *WT* 30, No. 3 (September 1937): 341–48.

"Recapture." *WT* 15, No. 5 (May 1930): 693. [Later sonnet XXXIV of *Fungi from Yuggoth*.]

"To a Dreamer." *Coyote* No. 16 (January 1921): 4. *WT* 4, No. 3 (November 1924): 54.

"To Clark Ashton Smith, Esq., upon His Fantastic Tales, Verses, Pictures, and Sculptures." *WT* 31, No. 4 (April 1938): 392 (as "To Clark Ashton Smith").

"To Mr. Finlay, upon His Drawing for Mr. Bloch's Tale, 'The Faceless God.'" *Phantagraph* 6, No. 1 (May 1937): 1. (as "To Mr. Finlay").

"Unity." A revision—original author unknown. Also in *Letters to James F. Morton* 280.

"The Unknown." *Conservative* 2, No. 3 (October 1916): [12] (as by "Elizabeth Berkeley"). *Lovecraft Studies* No. 25 (Fall 1991): 36 (includes facsimile of AMS from letter to CAS, 30 July 1923).

Nonfiction

"An Account of a Trip to the Antient Fairbanks House, in Dedham, and to the Red Horse Tavern in Sudbury, in the Province of the Massachusetts-Bay." In *CE* 4.

Antarctic Atlas. Juvenilia, nonextant.

"[Biographical Notice.]" In Edward J. O'Brien, ed. *The Best Short Stories of 1928 and the Yearbook of the American Short Story*. New York: Dodd, Mead, 1928. 324. In *CE* 5.

"The Cancer of Superstition." Synopsis and ch. 1 in *The Dark Brotherhood and Other Pieces* by H. P. Lovecraft and Divers Hands. Sauk City, WI: Arkham House, 1966. 246–61. Synopsis in *CE* 3.

"Commonplace Book." In *CE* 5.

"In Memoriam: Robert Ervin Howard." *Fantasy Magazine* No. 38 (September 1936): 29–31. In *CE* 5.

"Introduction." In Jonathan E. Hoag. *The Poetical Works of Jonathan E. Hoag*. New York: [Privately printed,] 1923. iii–vii. In *CE* 2.

"The *Journal* and the New Deal." In *CE* 5.

"A Layman Looks at the Government." *Lovecraft Studies* No. 44 (2004): 3–22. In *CE* 5.

"Lord Dunsany and His Work." In *CE* 2.

"[Notes to *At the Mountains of Madness*.]" *CE* 5.

"The Poetry of John Ravenor Bullen." *United Amateur* 25, 1 (September 1925): 1–3, 6. In *CE* 2.

"Preface." In John Ravenor Bullen. *White Fire*. Athol, MA: The Recluse Press, 1927 [actually January 1928]. 7–13. In *CE* 2.

"Preface." In Mrs. William B. Symmes. *Old World Footprints*. Athol, MA: W. Paul Cook (The Recluse Press), 1928. [5–6] (as by "Frank Belknap Long, Jr."). In *CE* 5.

"[Review of *Ebony and Crystal* by Clark Ashton Smith.]" *L'Alouette* 1, No. 1 (January 1924): 20–21 (signed "H. P. L."). In *CE* 2.

"Robert Ervin Howard: 1906–1936." *Phantagraph* 4, No. 5 (August 1936): 4–5 (unsigned). In *CE* 5. [Condensed version of "In Memoriam: Robert Ervin Howard."]

"Sleepy Hollow To-day." In Sterling Leonard and Harold Y. Moffett, ed. *Junior Literature: Book Two*. New York: Macmillan, 1930, 1935. 545–46. In *CE* 4. [Extract from "Observations on Several Parts of America" (*CE* 4).]

"Some Current Amateur Verse." *National Amateur* 58, No. 2 (December 1935): 393–95. In *CE* 1.

"Some Notes on a Nonentity." *Beyond the Wall of Sleep*. Sauk City: Arkham House, 1943. xi–xiv (as "Autobiography: Some Notes on a Nonentity"). In *CE* 5.

"Some Notes on Interplanetary Fiction." *Californian* 3, No. 3 (Winter 1935): 39–42. In *CE* 2.

"Some Repetitions on the Times." *Lovecraft Studies* No. 12 (Spring 1986): 13–25. In *CE* 5.

"[Suggestions for a Reading Guide]." In *CE* 2.

"Supernatural Horror in Literature." *Recluse* No. 1 (1927): 23–59. Rev. ed. in *FF* (October 1933–February 1935). In *CE* 2.

"The Weird Work of William Hope Hodgson." *Phantagraph* 5, No. 5 (February 1937): 5–7. [Incorporated into "Supernatural Horror in Literature."]

"The Work of Frank Belknap Long, Jr." *United Amateur* 23, No. 1 (May 1924): 1–4 (unsigned). In *CE* 2.

Letters

"Four Letters to Clark Ashton Smith." *Witchcraft and Sorcery* 1, No. 5 (January–February 1971): 27–28. Fragments of letters dated 16 February 1932 [26 February 1932]; 2 March [1 March] 1932; 4 April 1932; and 18 February 1933.

"A Group of Letters." *Arkham Sampler* 1, No. 2 (Spring 1948): 13–19. 28 January 1932 (15–16); 8 February 1932 (16); 18 February 1932 (16–17); October 1932 (17–18).

"H. P. Lovecraft on Clark Ashton Smith: A Postcard" (late October 1930). *Tolometh* [an amateur journal contributed to the Hyperborean League amateur press association] 1, No. 1 (January 1976): 2. In *CFs* 2.271.

"Last Autumn, Last Winter: Three Episodes." *Science-Fantasy Correspondent* No. 1 (1975): 32–35. [5 February 1937]

"Letter: H. P. Lovecraft to Clark Ashton Smith, June 23, 1930." *Fantasy Crossroads* No. 8 (May 1976): 4.

"A Postcard to Clark Ashton Smith." *Kappa Alpha Tau* 1, No. 1 (15 March 1976): 3.

"A Postcard to Clark Ashton Smith [30 August 1927]." *Xenophile* No. 18 (October 1975): 14.

[Postcard, 5 October 1931.] *Nonconformist* [an amateur journal contributed to the Esoteric Order of Dagon amateur Press association] 1, No. 3 (April 2009): [15].

[Postcards, 19 September 1931 and 1 August 1933.] *Nonconformist* [an amateur journal contributed to the Esoteric Order of Dagon amateur press association] 1, No. 4 (July 2009): [12] and [16].

"Postcards to Jonathan E. Hoag." *Lovecraft Annual* No. 10 (2016): 121–57.

"Dreams and Fancies." Containing extracts of letters to Clark Ashton Smith. In *Dreams and Fancies:* 19 November 1929 (28–29); [early] December 1931 (29); December 1931 [20 November] (30); 24 [27] December 1931 (30–31); 16 January 1932 (31–32); 28 January 1932 (32); 8 February 1932 (32–33); 31 May 1933 (33); 14 June 1933 (34); 29 June 1933 (34–35); 3 October 1933 (35–36); 22 October 1933 (36–37); 29 November 1933 (37–42).

B. Works by Clark Ashton Smith

Books

The Abominations of Yondo. Sauk City, WI: Arkham House. 1960.

The Black Book of Clark Ashton Smith. [Edited by Donald Sidney-Fryer and Rah Hoffman.] Sauk City, WI: Arkham House, 1979. [*BB*]

Collected Fantasies. Edited by Scott Connors and Ron Hilger. San Francisco: Night Shade. [*CFs*]
   1. *The End of the Story.* 2006.
   2. *The Door to Saturn.* 2007.
   3. *A Vintage from Atlantis.* 2007.
   4. *The Maze of the Enchanter.* 2009.
   5. *The Last Hieroglyph.* 2010.

The Complete Poetry and Translations. Edited by S. T. Joshi and David E. Schultz. New York: Hippocampus Press. [*CP*]
   1. *The Abyss Triumphant.* 2008.
   2. *The Wine of Summer.* 2008.
   3. *The Flowers of Evil and Others.* 2007.

The Devil's Notebook: Collected Epigrams and Pensées. Edited by Don Herron. Mercer Island, WA: Starmont House, 1990.

The Double Shadow and Other Fantasies. [Auburn, CA: Clark Ashton Smith, 1933.] [*DS*] (*LL* 880)

Ebony and Crystal: Poems in Verse and Prose. Auburn, CA: Auburn Journal Press, 1922. [*EC*] (*LL* 881)

Genius Loci. Sauk City, WI: Arkham House. 1948.

Incantations. Not published as book. See *Selected Poems.*

The Jasmine Girdle. Not published as book. See *Selected Poems.*

Letters to H. P. Lovecraft. Ed. Steve Behrends. West Warwick, RI: Necronomicon Press, 1987.

Lost Worlds. Sauk City, WI: Arkham House. 1944.

The Miscellaneous Writings of Clark Ashton Smith. Edited by Scott Connors and Ron Hilger. San Francisco: Night Shade, 2011.

Nostalgia of the Unknown: The Complete Prose Poetry of Clark Ashton Smith. Edited by Marc and Susan Michaud, Steve Behrends, and S. T. Joshi. West Warwick, RI: Necronomicon Press, 1988 (rev. ed. 1993).

Odes and Sonnets. San Francisco: Book Club of California, 1918. [*OS*] (*LL* 882)

Other Dimensions. Sauk City, WI: Arkham House. 1970.

Out of Space and Time. Sauk City, WI: Arkham House. 1942.

Planets and Dimensions: Collected Essays of Clark Ashton Smith. Edited by Charles K. Wolfe. Baltimore: Mirage Press, 1973. [*PD*]

Poems in Prose. Sauk City, WI: Arkham House. 1965. [*PP*]

Sandalwood. Auburn, CA: Auburn Journal Press, 1925. [*S*] (*LL* 883)

Selected Letters of Clark Ashton Smith. Edited by David E. Schultz and Scott Connors. Sauk City, WI: Arkham House, 2003.

Selected Poems. Sauk City, WI: Arkham House, 1971. [*SP*]

Strange Shadows: The Uncollected Fiction and Essays of Clark Ashton Smith. Edited by Steve Behrends with Donald Sidney-Fryer and Rah Hoffman. Westport, CT: Greenwood Press, 1989. [*SS*]

The Star-Treader and Other Poems. San Francisco: A. M. Robertson, 1912. [*ST*] (*LL* 884)

The Shadow of the Unattained: The Letters of George Sterling and Clark Ashton Smith. Edited by David E. Schultz and S. T. Joshi. New York: Hippocampus Press, 2005.

Tales of Science and Sorcery. Sauk City, WI: Arkham House. 1964.

The Unexpurgated Clark Ashton Smith. Series editor, Steve Behrends. West Warwick, RI: Necronomicon Press. Comprises: *The Dweller in the Gulf* (1987); *The Monster of the Prophecy* (1988); *Mother of Toads* (1987); *The Vaults of Yoh-Vombis* (1988); *The Witchcraft of Ulua* (1988); *Xeethra* (1988).

The White Sybil [by CAS] *and Men of Avalon* [by David H. Keller]. Everett, PA: Fantasy Publications, 1934.

Fiction

"The Abominations of Yondo." *Overland Monthly* 84, No. 4 (April 1926): 100–101, 114, 126. In *CFs* 1.

"The After-Men" (synopsis). In *SS.*

"An Adventure in Futurity." *Wonder Stories* 2, No. 11 (April 1931): 1230–51, 1328. In *CFs* 2.

"The Amazing Planet." See "A Captivity in Serpens."

"The Beast of Averoigne." *WT* 21, No. 5 (May 1933): 628–35. In *CFs* 4.

"Beyond the Singing Flame." *Wonder Stories* 3, No. 6 (November 1931): 752–61. In *CFs* 3.

"The Black Abbot of Puthuum." *WT* 27, No. 3 (March 1936): 308–22. In *CFs* 5.

"A Captivity in Serpens." *Wonder Stories Quarterly* 2, No. 4 (Summer 1931): 534–51, 569 (as "The Amazing Planet"). In *CFs* 2.

"The Chain of Aforgomon." *WT* 26, No. 6 (December 1935): 695–706. In *CFs* 5.

"The Charnel God." *WT* 23, No. 3 (March 1934): 316–30. In *CFs* 4.

"The City of the Singing Flame." 17.*Wonder Stories* 3, No. 2 (July 1931): 202–13. *Tales of Wonder* No. 10 (Spring 1940): 6–31 (combined with "Beyond the Singing Flame"). In *CFs* 2.

"The Clouds." See "The Primal City."

"The Colossus of Ylourgne." *WT* 23, No. 6 (June 1934): 696–720. In *CFs* 3.

"The Coming of the White Worm."*Stirring Science Stories* 1, No. 2 (April 1941): 105–14. In *CFs* 5.

"The Dark Eidolon." *WT* 25, No. 1 (January 1935): 93–111. In *CFs* 4.

"The Death of Malygris." *WT* 30, No. 3 (April 1934): 488–96. In *CFs* 5.

"The Demon of the Flower." *Astounding Stories* 12, No. 4 (December 1933): 131–38. In *CFs* 3.

"The Devotee of Evil." In *DS, CFs* 1.

"The Dimension of Chance." *Wonder Stories* 4, No. 6 (November 1932): 521–29. In *CFs* 4.

"The Disinterment of Venus." *WT* 24, No. 1 (July 1934): 112–17. In *CFs* 4.

"The Door to Saturn." *Strange Tales of Mystery and Terror* 1, No. 3 (January 1932): 390–403. In *CFs* 2.

"The Double Shadow." In *DS*. *WT* 33, No. 2 (February 1939): 47–55.

"The Dweller in the Gulf." *Wonder Stories* 4, No. 10 (March 1933): 768–75 (as "The Dweller in Martian Depths"). In *CFs* 4.

"The Eggs of Saturn" (synopsis). In *SS*.

"The Eidolon of the Blind." See "The Dweller in the Gulf."

"The Empire of the Necromancers." *WT* 20, No. 3 (September 1932): 338–44. In *CFs* 3.

"The End of the Story." *WT* 15, No. 5 (May 1930): 637–48. In *CFs* 1.

"The Epiphany of Death." *FF* 1, No. 11 (July 1934): 165–68. In *CFs* 1.

"The Eternal World." *Wonder Stories* 3, No. 10 (March 1932): 1130–37. In *CFs* 3.

"The Flower-Women." *WT* 25, No. 5 (May 1935): 624–32. In *CFs* 4.

"The Face by the River." *Lost Worlds* No. 1 (2004): 3–7. In *CFs* 2.

"Genius Loci." *WT* 21, No. 6 (June 1933): 747–58. In *CFs* 4.

"The Ghoul." *FF* 1, No. 5 (January 1934): 69–72. In *CFs* 2.

"The Ghoul from Mercury" (synopsis). In *SS*.

"A Good Embalmer." In *SS, CFs* 2.

"The Gorgon." *WT* 19, No. 4 (April 1932): 551–58. In *CFs* 2.

"Hecate" (synopsis). In *SS*.

"The Holiness of Azédarac." *WT* 22, No. 5 (November 1933): 594–607. In *CF*s 3.

"The House of Haon-Dor" (fragment). *Crypt of Cthulhu* No. 27 (Hallowmas 1984 [special issue: *Untold Tales*]): 12–14. In *SS*.

"The Hunters from Beyond." *Strange Tales of Mystery and Terror* 2, No. 3 (October 1932): 292–303. In *CF*s 2.

"The Ice Demon." *WT* 21, No. 4 (April 1933): 484–94. In *CF*s 4.

"The Immeasurable Horror." *WT* 18, No. 2 (September 1931): 233–42. In *CF*s 1.

"The Immortals of Mercury." New York: Stellar Publishing Corp., 1932. In *CF*s 3.

"In a Hashish-Dream" (fragment). *Crypt of Cthulhu* No. 27 (Hallowmas 1984 [special issue: *Untold Tales*]): 15–16. In *SS*.

"The Infernal Star" (fragment). In *SS*.

"The Invisible City." *Wonder Stories* 4, No. 1 (June 1932): 6–13. In *CF*s 3.

"The Interstellar Changelings." Nonextant, or not written.

"The Isle of the Torturers." *WT* 21, No. 3 (March 1933): 362–72. In Christine Campbell Thomson, ed. *Keep On the Light!* London: Selwyn & Blount, 1933. 237–54. In *CF*s 4.

"Jim Knox and the Giantess." See "The Root of Ampoi."

"The Justice of the Elephant." *Oriental Stories* 1, No. 6 (Autumn 1931): 856, 858, 863–64. In *CF*s 2.

"The Kingdom of the Worm." *FF* 1, No. 2 (October 1933): 17–22. In *CF*s 2.

"The Kiss of Zoraida." *Magic Carpet Magazine* 3, No. 3 (July 1933): 373–76. In *CF*s 2.

"The Last Hieroglyph." *WT* 25, No. 4 (April 1935): 466–77. In *CF*s 5.

"The Last Incantation." *WT* 15, No. 6 (June 1930): 783–86. In *CF*s 1.

"The Letter from Mohaun Los." *Wonder Stories* 4, No. 3 (August 1932): 218–29 (as "Flight into Super-Time"). In *CF*s 2.

"The Light from Beyond." See "The Secret of the Cairn."

"Like Mohammed's Tomb." Lost.

"The Lord of Lunacy" (fragment). In *SS*.

"The Madness of Chronomage" (synopsis). In *BB*.

"The Mandrakes." *WT* 21, No. 2 (February 1933): 254–59. In *CF*s 4.

"The Mahout." *Black Cat* 16, No. 11 (August 1911): 25–30. In *Miscellaneous Writings*.

"The Maker of Gargoyles." *WT* 20, No. 2 (August 1932): 198–207. In *CF*s 3.

"The Manichaean" (synopsis). In *SS*.

"Marooned in Andromeda." *Wonder Stories* 2, No. 5 (October 1930): 390–401, 465. In *CF*s 1.

"The Martian." See "Seedling of Mars."

"The Master of Destruction" (fragment). *Crypt of Cthulhu* No. 27 (Hallowmas 1984 [special issue: *Untold Tales*]): 28–31. In *SS*.

"Master of the Asteroid." *Wonder Stories* 4, No. 5 (October 1932): 435–39, 469. *Tales of Wonder* No. 11 (Summer 1940): 46–55. In *CF$_S$* 3. [Original title: "God of the Asteroid."]

"The Maze of Maal Dweb." See "The Maze of the Enchanter."

"The Maze of the Enchanter." In *DS, CF$_S$* 4.

"Medusa." See "The Gorgon."

"The Metamorphosis of Earth." See "The Metamorphosis of the World."

"The Metamorphosis of the World." *WT* 43, No. 6 (September 1951): 62–79. In *CF$_S$* 1.

"The Monster of the Prophecy." *WT* 19, No. 1 (January 1932): 8–31. In *CF$_S$* 1.

"The Moon-Spectre" (synopsis). In *SS*.

"Murder in the Fourth Dimension." *Amazing Detective Tales* 1, No. 10 (October 1930): 908–37. In *CF$_S$* 1.

"The Nameless Offspring." *Strange Tales of Mystery and Terror* 2, No. 2 (June 1932): 264–76. In *CF$_S$* 3.

"Necromancy in Naat." *WT* 28, No. 1 (July 1936): 2–15. In *CF$_S$* 5.

"The Necromantic Tale." *WT* 17, No. 1 (January 1931): 54–61. In *CF$_S$* 1.

"A Night in Malnéant." In *DS, CF$_S$* 1.

"The Ninth Skeleton." *WT* 12, No. 3 (September 1928): 363–66. In *CF$_S$* 1.

"The Ocean-World of Alioth." *Crypt of Cthulhu* No. 27 (Hallowmas 1984 [special issue: *Untold Tales*]): 32–33. In *SS*.

"An Offering to the Moon." *WT* 45, No. 4 (September 1953): 54–61. In *CF$_S$* 2.

"The Offspring of the Grave" (synopsis). In *BB* and *SS*.

"The Oracle of Sadoqua" (synopsis). In *BB*.

"The Parrot." In *SS; Miscellaneous Writings*.

"The Phantoms of the Fire." *WT* 16, No. 3 (September 1930): 363–66. In *CF$_S$* 1.

"The Planet Entity." See "The Seedling of Mars."

"The Planet of the Dead." *WT* 19, No. 3 (March 1932): 364–72. In *CF$_S$* 1.

"The Plutonian Drug." *Amazing Stories* 9, No. 5 (September 1934): 41–48. In *CF$_S$* 3.

"The Primal City." *FF* 2, No. 3 (November 1934): 41–45; *Comet Stories* 1, No. 1 (December 1940): 102–6. In *CF$_S$* 5.

"Prisoners of the Black Dimension" (synopsis). In *SS*.

"The Raja and the Tiger." *Black Cat* 17, No. 5, (February 1912):12–18. In *Miscellaneous Writings*.

"The Rebirth of the Flame" (synopsis). *Crypt of Cthulhu* No. 27 (Hallowmas 1984 [special issue: *Untold Tales*]): 37. In *SS*.

"The Red World of Polaris." In *CF$_S$* 2.

"A Rendezvous in Averoigne." *WT* 17, No. 3 (April–May 1931): 364–74. In *CF$_S$* 2.

"The Resurrection of the Rattlesnake." *WT* 18, No. 3 (October 1931): 387–90. In *CF$_S$* 1.

"The Return of the Sorcerer." *Strange Tales of Mystery and Terror* 1, No. 1 (September 1931): 99–109. In *CFs* 2.

"The Root of Ampoi." *Arkham Sampler* 2, No. 2 (Spring 1949): 3–16. *Fantastic Stories of Imagination* 10, No. 8 (August 1961): 31–46. In *CFs* 1. [First title: "Jim Knox and the Giantess."]

"Sadastor." *WT* 16, No. 1 (July 1930): 133–35. In *CFs* 1.

"The Satanist." See "The Manichean."

"The Satyr." *La Paree Stories* 2, No. 5 (July 1931): 9–11, 48. In *CFs* 1.

"The Second Interment." *Strange Tales of Mystery and Terror* 3, No. 1 (January 1933): 8–16. In *CFs* 3.

"The Secret of the Cairn." *Wonder Stories* 4, No. 11 (April 1933): 823–29 (as "The Light from Beyond"). In *CFs* 4.

"The Seed from the Sepulchre." *WT* 22, No. 4 (October 1933): 497–505. In *CFs* 3.

"Seedling of Mars." *Wonder Stories Quarterly* 3, No. 1 (Fall 1931): 110–25, 136 (as "The Planet Entity"). In *CFs* 3.

"The Seven Geases." *WT* 24, No. 4 (October 1934): 422–35. In *CFs* 5.

"Slaves of the Black Pillar" (fragment). *Crypt of Cthulhu* No. 27 (Hallowmas 1984 [special issue: *Untold Tales*]): 17–18 (synopsis on p. 19). In *SS*.

"The Sorceress of Averoigne/The Tower of Istarelle" (synopsis). *Crypt of Cthulhu* No. 27 (Hallowmas 1984 [special issue: *Untold Tales*]): 34–36. In *SS*.

"A Star-Change." *Wonder Stories* 4, No. 12 (May 1933): 962–69 (as "The Visitors from Mlok"). *Tales of Wonder and Super-Science* No. 15 (Autumn 1941): 57–67 (as "Escape to Mlok"). In *CFs* 4.

"The Supernumerary Corpse." *WT* 20, No. 5 (November 1932): 693–98. In *CFs* 3.

"The Tale of Satampra Zeiros." *WT* 18, No. 4 (November 1931): 491–99. In *CFs* 1.

"A Tale of Sir John Maundeville." See "The Kingdom of the Worm."

"The Testament of Athammaus." *WT* 20, No. 4 (October 1932): 509–21. In *CFs* 2.

"The Third Episode of Vathek" (with William Beckford). *Leaves* No. 1 (Summer 1937): 1–24. In *CFs* 4.

"The Tomb-Spawn." *WT* 23, No. 5 (May 1934): 634–40. In *CFs* 5.

"The Transformation of Athanor" (synopsis). In *SS*.

"The Treader of the Dust." *WT* 26, No. 2 (August 1935): 241–46. In *CFs* 5.

"The Trilithon" (synopsis). In *SS*.

"Ubbo-Sathla." *WT* 22, No. 1 (July 1933): 112–16. In *CFs* 3.

"The Uncharted Isle." *WT* 16, No. 5 (November 1930): 605–8, 710–14. In *CFs* 1.

"The Vaults of Yoh-Vombis." *WT* 19, No. 5 (May 1932): 599–610. In *CFs* 3.

"The Venus of Azombeii." *WT* 17, No. 4 (June–July 1931): 496–514. In *CFs* 1.

"A Vintage from Atlantis." *WT* 22, No. 3 (September 1933): 394–99.

"The Visitors from Mlok." See "A Star-Change."

"Vizaphmal in Ophiuchus" (synopsis). *Crypt of Cthulhu* No. 27 (Hallowmas 1984 [special issue: *Untold Tales*]): 33–34. In *SS*.

"The Voyage of King Euvoran." In *DS*, *CF*s 4.

"A Voyage to Sfanomoë." *WT* 18, No. 1 (August 1931): 111–15. In *CF*s 1.

"Vulthoom." *WT* 26, No. 3 (September 1935): 336–52. In *CF*s 4.

"The Weaver in the Vault." *WT* 23, No. 1 (January 1934): 85–93. In *CF*s 4.

"The Weird of Avoosl Wuthoqquan." *WT* 19, No. 6 (June 1932): 835–40. In *CF*s 3.

"The White Sybil." In *The White Sybil and Men of Avalon*. In *CF*s 4.

"The Willow Landscape." *Philippine Magazine* 27, No. 12 (May 1931): 728, 752, 756. In *DS*, *CF*s 2.

"The Witchcraft of Ulua." *WT* 23, No. 2 (February 1934): 253–59. In *CF*s 5.

"Xeethra." *WT* 24, No. 6 (December 1934): 726–38. In *CF*s 5.

Poems

"The Absence of the Muse." *Lyric West* 1, No. 6 (October 1921): 14. In *EC*, *SP*, *CP* 1.

"After Armageddon." *Recluse* (1927): 15. In *SP*, *CP* 1.

"Alienage." *Auburn Journal* 23, No. 38 (5 July 1923): 6. *Wanderer* 1, No. 6 (November 1923): 4–5. In *S*, *SP*, *CP* 1.

"Amor Autumnalis." In *CP* 2.

"L'Amour supreme" [in both English and French]. In *CP* 2.

"Apologia." *Auburn Journal* 25, No. 1 (16 October 1924): 6. *Step Ladder* 10, No. 3 (February 1925): 49. *United Amateur* 24, No. 1 (July 1925): [1]. In *S*, *SP*, *CP* 1.

"Au bord du Léthé." In *SP*, *CP* 2.

"Calendar." *Troubadour* 2, No. 6 (February 1930): 11. In *SP*, *CP* 2.

"Canticle." *Troubadour* 3, No. 8 (July 1931): 26. In *SP*, *CP* 2.

"The Cherry-Snows." In *ST*. In LeRoy E. Armstrong, ed. *California State Series: Sixth Year Literature Reader*. Sacramento: Robert L. Telfer, Superintendent State Publishing, 1916 (11th ed. 1928). 86.

"Consolation." In *S*. *Step Ladder* 13, No. 5 (May 1927): 130. In *California Poets: An Anthology of 224 Contemporaries*. New York: Henry Harrison, 1932. 666. In *Today's Literature*, ed. Dudley Chadwick Gordon, Vernon Rupert King, and William Whittingham Lyman. New York: American Book Co., 1935. 449. In *SP*, *CP* 1.

"De Consolation." In *CP* 2.

"Crepuscule." In *EC*, *SP*, *CP* 1.

"Cumuli." *Interludes* 8, No. 1 (Spring 1931): 11. In *SP*, *CP* 2.

"Dissonance." *Thrill Book* 2, No. 6 (15 September 1919): 149. In *EC*, *SP*, *CP* 1.

"The Doom of America." In *CP* 1.

"A Dream of the Abyss." *FF* 1, No. 3 (November 1933): 41. In *SP* 2.

"Duality." *WT* 2, No. 1 (July–August 1923): 69 (as "The Garden of Evil").
   Auburn Journal 24, No. 20 (28 February 1924): 6. In *S, SP, CP* 1.

"Ennui" (Thou art immured in some sad garden sown with dust). *WT* 27,
   No. 5 (May 1936): 547. In *SP, CP* 2.

"The Envoys." *Auburn Journal* 26, No. 13 (7 January 1926): 4. *Overland Monthly*
   84, No. 6 (June 1926): frontispiece. *Overland Monthly* 84, No. 7 (July 1926):
   230 (corrected version). In *SP, CP* 1.

"L'Espoir du néant." In *SP, CP* 2.

"Exotique." In *OS, EC, SP, CP* 1.

"A Fable." *WT* 10, No. 1 (July 1927): 76. In *SP, CP* 2.

"Fantasie d'antan." *WT* 14, No. 6 (December 1929): 724. In *SP, CP* 2.

"Fellowship." *WT* 16, No. 4 (October 1930): 550. In *CP* 2.

"From 'The Song of Xeethra.'" Epigraph to "The Dark Eidolon" (q.v.). In *CP* 2.

The Fugitives. In *CP* 1. Verse drama begun 17 September 1922 but never
   completed. CAS published four "songs" separately, as follows:
      "The Song of Aviol." *Auburn Journal* 23, No. 25 (5 April 1923): 6. *Lyric
      West* 3, No. 11 (March 1924): 28. In *S, SP, SS* (as "Song").
      "Song." Unpublished.
      "The Love-Potion." *Auburn Journal* 23, No. 29 (3 May 1923): 6. In *S. Step
      Ladder* 13, No. 5 (May 1927): 135. In *SP*.
      "The Song of Cartha." *Auburn Journal* 23, No. 29 (3 May 1923): 6. *Wan-
      derer* 2, No. 8 (August 1924): 103. In *S, SP*.

"The Garden of Evil." *See* "Duality."

"The Hashish Eater; or, The Apocalypse of Evil." In *EC, SP, CP* 1.

"Haunting." *Lyric West* 1, No. 10 (February 1922): 6. In *EC, SP, CP* 1.

"The Hill-Top." In *The Laureate's Wreath: An Anthology in Honor of Dr. Henry
   Meade Bland, Poet Laureate of California,* ed. The Edwin Markham Poetry
   Society. San Jose: Edwin Markham Poetry Society, 1934. 108. In *The
   Golden Year: A Calendar of the Poets,* ed. Rufus Rockwell Wilson. New
   York: Wilson-Erickson, 1936. 15. In *SP, CP* 2.

"Idylle païenne" [in both English and French]. In *CP* 2.

"In Saturn." *Sonnet* 2, No. 2 (January–February 1919): 2. In *EC, SP, CP* 1.

"In Lemuria." *Lyric West* 1, No. 4 (July–August 1921): 6. In *EC, SP, CP* 1.

"In Slumber." *WT* 24, No. 2 (August 1934): 253. In *CP* 2.

"The Incubus of Time." In August Derleth, ed. *Fire and Sleet and Candlelight.*
   Sauk City, WI: Arkham House, 1961, pp. 184–85. In *SP, CP* 1.

"Inferno." In *EC, SP, CP* 1.

"The Infinite Quest." *Lyric West* 1, No. 4 (July–August 1921): 6. In *EC, SP, CP* 1.

"Interrogation." In *S. WT* 10, No. 3 (September 1927): 414. In *Principal Poets
   of the World: Volume 1: 1930–1931,* ed. William Kingston Fudge. London:
   Mitre Press, 1932. 182. In *SP, CP* 1.

"Jungle Twilight." *Oriental Stories* 2, No. 3 (Summer 1932): 420 (15 lines only).
   In *SP, CP* 2.

"Lichens." *Wings* 1, No. 2 (Summer 1933): 7. *Berkeley Daily Gazette* (1933?). In *SP, CP* 2.

"Loss." In *S. United Amateur* 25, No. 2 (May 1926): 8. In *SP, CP* 1.

"The Love-Potion." See *The Fugitives*.

"Ludar's Litany to Thasaidon" [I]. Epigraph to "The Death of Ilalotha" (q.v.). In *CP* 2.

"Ludar's Litany to Thasaidon" [II]. Epigraph to "The Garden of Adompha" (q.v.). In *CP* 2.

"A Madrigal." In *SP, CP* 1.

"Un Madrigal." In *CP* 1.

"Medusa." In *ST. FF* 2, No. 3 (November 1934): 46–47. In *SP, CP* 1.

"La Méduse des cieux" (CAS's translation of his "The Medusa of the Skies.") In *CP* 1.

"The Melancholy Pool." In *EC. WT* 3, No. 3 (March 1924): 21. In *SP, CP* 1.

"Memnon at Midnight." In *OS, EC*. In *Songs and Stories*, ed. Edwin Markham. Los Angeles: Powell Publishing Company, 1931; Freeport, NY: Books for Libraries Press, 1974. 425. In *SP, CP* 1.

"Le Miroir des blanches fleurs" [in both English and French]. In *CP* 2.

"Moon-Dawn." *WT* 2, No. 1 (July–August 1923): 48 (as "The Red Moon"). *Auburn Journal* 24, No. 15 (24 January 1924): 6 (as "The Red Moon"). In *S, SP, CP* 1.

"Nero." In *ST*. In *Golden Songs of the Golden State*, ed. Marguerite Wilkinson. Chicago: A. C. McClurg & Co., 1917; rpt. Greak Neck, NY: Granger Book Co., 1979. 116–20. In *OS*. In *The Book of Poetry*, ed. Edwin Markham. New York: William H. Wise & Co., 1926 [3 vols.], 1927 [2 vols.], 1928 [10 vols.]. 749–50 (extracts; as "From Nero"). In *SP, CP* 1.

"The Nereid." *Yale Review* 2, No. 4 (July 1913): 685–86. In *EC*. In *California Poets: An Anthology of 224 Contemporaries*, [ed. Helen Hoyt]. New York: Henry Harrison, 1932. 665. In *SP, CP* 1.

"Nightfall." *Home Brew* 3, No. 2 (March 1923): 23.

"Nightmare." In *EC, SP, CP* 1.

"Nyctalops." *WT* 14, No. 4 (October 1929): 516. In *The Laureate's Wreath: An Anthology in Honor of Dr. Henry Meade Bland, Poet Laureate of California*, ed. The Edwin Markham Poetry Society. San Jose: Edwin Markham Poetry Society, 1934. 109. In *Today's Literature*, ed. Dudley Chadwick Gordon, Vernon Rupert King, and William Whittingham Lyman. New York: American Book Co., 1935. 449. In *SP, CP* 2.

"Ode to the Abyss." In *ST, OS, SP, CP* 1.

"On a Chinese Vase." *Oriental Stories* 2, No. 2 (Spring 1932): 174. In *SP, CP* 2.

"On the Cañon-Side." *Auburn Journal* 23, No. 50 (27 September 1923): 6. In George Sterling, Genevieve Taggard, and James Rorty, ed. *Continent's End: An Anthology of Contemporary California Poets*. San Francisco: Book Club of California, 1925, p. 54. In *SP, CP* 1.

"Ougabalys." *WT* 15, No. 1 (January 1930): 135. [Later revised as "Tolometh." Both in *CP* 2.]

"Palms." *Asia* 20, No. 3 (April 1920): 330. In *EC*. In *Songs and Stories*, ed. Edwin Markham. Los Angeles: Powell Publishing Co., 1931; Freeport, NY: Books for Libraries Press, 1974. 424. In *SP, CP* 1.

"Plum-Flowers." *L'Alouette* 1, No. 2 (March 1924): 44. In *S, CP* 1.

"Psalm." In *EC, CP* 1.

"A Psalm to the Best Beloved." In *EC, SP, CP* 1.

"Query." *Auburn Journal* 25, No. 26 (9 April 1925): 4. In *S. United Amateur* 25, No. 2 (May 1926): 7. *Step Ladder* 13, No. 5 (May 1927): 131. In *SP, CP* 1.

"The Red Moon." See "Moon-Dawn."

"The Refuge of Beauty." In *OS, EC. L'Alouette* 1, No. 3 (May 1924): 66. In *SP, CP* 1.

"Revenant." *Fantasy Fan* 1, No. 7 (March 1934): 106–7. In *The Dark Chateau, SP, CP* 2.

"Rosa Mystica." *Lyric West* 1, No. 8 (December 1921): 7. In *EC, SP, CP* 1.

"The Saturnienne." *WT* 10, No. 6 (December 1927): 728. In *SP, CP* 2.

"The Sea-Gods." *Auburn Journal* 23, No. 36 (21 June 1923): 6. In *CP* 2.

"The Secret." *Auburn Journal* 23, No. 27 (19 April 1923): 6. In *S*. In *Today's Literature*, ed. Dudley Chadwick Gordon, Vernon Rupert King, and William Whittingham Lyman. New York: American Book Co., 1935. 448. In *SP, CP* 1.

"Semblance." *Auburn Journal* 23, No. 26 (12 April 1923): 6. *Auburn Journal* 23, No. 27 (19 April 1923): 6 (with corrections). *Wanderer* 1, No. 2 (July 1923): 7. In *S. Outré* 1, No. 4 (November 1939): 8. [This entire issue was included in and attached to *Golden Atom* 1, No. 7 (April 1940): [25].] In *SP, CP* 1.

"September." In *SP*, and *CP* 2.

"Sepulture." *Smart Set* 57, No. 2 (October 1922): 122. In *EC*. In *California Poets: An Anthology of 224 Contemporaries*, [ed. Helen Hoyt]. New York: Henry Harrison, 1932. 664. In *SP, CP* 1.

"Shadow of Nightmare." In *ST, SP, CP* 1.

"Shadows." *WT* 15, No. 2 (February 1930): 154. In *SP, CP* 2.

"Solution." In *EC. WT* 3, No. 1 (January 1924): 32. In *SP, CP* 1.

"Sonnet" (Empress with eyes more sad and aureate). *WT* 13, No. 4 (April 1929): 542. In *SP, CP* 2.

"The Song of Aviol." See *The Fugitives*.

"The Song of Cartha." See *The Fugitives*.

"Song of the Necromancer." *WT* 29, No. 2 (February 1937): 220. In In *SP, CP* 2.

"Spectral Life" [English version of the French poem "Une Vie spectrale"]. In *CP* 2.

"The Star-Treader." In *ST, SP, CP* 1.

"Symbols." *London Mercury* No. 33 (July 1922): 245 (as by "A. Clark Ashton Smith"). In *EC*. In *California Poets: An Anthology of 224 Contemporaries*, [ed. Helen Hoyt]. New York: Henry Harrison, 1932. 664. In *SP, CP* 1.

"To George Sterling: A Valediction." *Overland Monthly* 85, No. 11 (November 1927): 338. In *SP, CP* 1.

"To Howard Phillips Lovecraft." *WT* 30, No. 1 (July 1937): 48. In H. P. Lovecraft [et al.]. *Marginalia*. Ed. August Derleth and Donald Wandrei. Sauk City, WI: Arkham House, 1944, pp. 370–71. In *SP, CP* 2.

"To The Chimera." *Auburn Journal* 24, No. 25 (3 April 1924): 6. *United Amateur* 23, No. 1 (May 1924): 7. In *SP, CP* 1.

"Triple Aspect." In *EC, SP, CP* 1.

"Une Vie spectrale." In *SP, CP* 2.

"White Death." In *ST, SP, CP* 1.

"Warning." *WT* 12, No. 4 (October 1928): 525. In *Dark of the Moon: Poems of Fantasy and the Macabre*, ed. August Derleth. Sauk City, WI: Arkham House, 1947: 320–21. In *SP, CP* 2.

"The Witch in the Graveyard." In *EC, SP, CP* 1.

Translations [all in *CP* 3]

"The Albatross."

"Au lecteur." In *CP* 3 as "Preface."

"L'Aube Spirituelle." See "The Spiritual Dawn."

"Brumes et Pluies." See "Mists and Rains."

"The Gulf."

"Les Hiboux." See "The Owls."

"The Irremediable." *Auburn Journal* 25, No. 41 (23 July 1925): 3 (as "L'Irrémédiable"). In *S* (as "L'Irrémédiable"; part I only). In *Flowers of Evil*, ed. James Laver. London: Limited Editions Club/Fanfare Press, 1940. 172–74.

"L'Irréparable." *WT* 12, No. 12 (August 1928): 261 (as one of "Three Poems in Prose").

"Mists and Rains." *Auburn Journal* 26, No. 6 (19 November 1925): 5 (as "Brumes et Pluies"). *Recluse* No. 1 (1927): 60. In *SP*.

"Obsession." In *S. Step Ladder* 13, No. 5 (May 1927): 139. In *SP*.

"The Owls." *Auburn Journal* 25, No. 51 (1 October 1925): 4 (as "Les Hiboux"). *Step Ladder* 13, No. 5 (May 1927): 138 (as "Les Hiboux"). *WT* 36, No. 2 (November 1941): 120 (as translated by "Timeus Gaylord"). In *Dark of the Moon: Poems of Fantasy and the Macabre*, ed. August Derleth. Sauk City, WI: Arkham House, 1947. 346–47 (as by [not translated by] "Timeus Gaylord"). In *SP*.

"Rêve Parisien." In *S*. In *CP* 3 as "Parisian Dream."

"Les Sept Vieillards." *WT* 12, No. 2 (August 1928): 261–62 (as one of "Three Poems in Prose").

"Spleen." *WT* 7, No. 2 (February 1926): 254. In *SP*.

"The Spiritual Dawn." *Auburn Journal* 25, No. 53 (15 October 1925): 4 (as "L'Aube Spirituelle"). In *S* (as "L'Aube Spirituelle").

"Une Charogne." *WT* 12, No. 2 (August 1928): 262–63 (as one of "Three Poems in Prose").

"Le Voyage." In *CP* 3 as "The Voyage."

CXXIV. [Untitled.]

Poems in Prose [all in *PP*]

"The Abomination of Desolation." *Fantasmagoria* 1, No. 4 (November 1938): 10.

"The Demon, The Angel, and Beauty." In *EC*.

"The Flower-Devil." In *EC*.

"From the Crypts of Memory." *Bohemia* 2, No. 3 (April 1917): 27. In *EC, CF$_S$* 1.

"The Memnons of the Night." *Bohemia* 2, No. 2 (1 February 1917) (as "Memnons of the Night"). In *EC. Phantagraph* 4, No. 2 (November–December 1935): [9].

"Remoteness." In *EC*.

"The Touchstone."

"The Traveller." In *EC, CF$_S$* 5.

Prose Pastels [all in *PP*]

1. Chinoiserie. *Philippine Magazine* 28, No. 6 (November 1931): 269. *FF* 1, No. 8 (April 1934): 116. *Acolyte* 1, No. 4 (Summer 1943): 3.

2. The Mirror in the Hall of Ebony. *FF* 1, No. 9 (May 1934): 140, 144. *Acolyte* 1, No. 4 (Summer 1943): 3.

3. The Muse of Hyperborea. *FF* 1, No. 10 (June 1934): 154. *Acolyte* 1, No. 4 (Summer 1943): 4.

4. The Lotus and the Moon. *FF* 2, No. 1 (September 1934): 7. *Acolyte* 1, No. 4 (Summer 1943): 4.

5. The Passing of Aphrodite. *FF* 2, No. 4 (December 1934): 59–60. *Acolyte* 1, No. 4 (Summer 1943): 4.

6. To the Daemon. *Acolyte* 2, No. 1 (Fall 1943): 3.

7. The Forbidden Forest. *Acolyte* 2, No. 1 (Fall 1943): 3.

8. The Mithridate. *Acolyte* 2, No. 1 (Fall 1943): 4.

9. Narcissus. *Acolyte* 3, No. 1 (Winter 1945): 3.

10. The Peril That Lurks among Ruins. *Acolyte* 3, No. 1 (Winter 1945): 3.

Epigrams

"Cocktails and Crème de Menthe." *Auburn Journal* (13 columns published between 11 October 1923 and 31 January 1924).

"The Epigrams of Alastor." *Dragon-Fly*, No. 1 (15 October 1935): [10].

Letters

"'Dear Éch-Pi-El': 2 Unpublished Letters to H. P. Lovecraft." *Kadath* No. 1

(1974): 16–19. Contains abridged letters dated "early 1934" [i.e., mid-March 1932] and "June 1934" [late June 1935]. [*Note:* The issue was printed but not officially distributed; the editor provided copies to a few friends.]

"[Fantasy and Human Experience.]" *Amazing Stories* 7, No. 7. (October 1932): 670–71 (under "Discussions"). In *PD.*

"[On the Forbidden Books.]" See "Startling Fact."

"[On Garbage-Mongering.]" *Wonder Stories* 4, No. 3 (August 1932): 281. In *PD.*

"[On H. P. Lovecraft—I.]" Letter in "The Eyrie." *WT* 30, No. 1 (July 1937): 122 (as "From Clark Ashton Smith"). In *PD.*

"[On H. P. Lovecraft—II.]" Letter to Claire Beck. *Science Fiction Critic* 1, No. 9 (May 1937): 1–2 (under "A Note from the Editor"). In *PD.*

"[On the Forbidden Books.]" *FF* 1, No. 3 (November 1933): 38 (in unsigned column, "Startling Fact"). In *PD.*

"Our Readers Say." *FF* 1, No. 2 (October 1933": 14

"[Realism and Fantasy.]" *Wonder Stories* 4, No. 9 (February 1933): 735–36. In *PD.*

"Startling Fact" [within unsigned editorial by Charles Hornig]. *FF* 1, No. 3 (November 1933): 38; rpt. as "On the Forbidden Books," *PD* 29.

"The Tale of Macrocosmic Horror." *Strange Tales of Mystery and Terror* 3, No. 1 (January 1933): 137–38. In *PD.*

Nonfiction

"Checklist: The Carvings of Clark Ashton Smith." *Arkham Sampler* 1, No. 1 (Winter 1948): 43–48.

"Excerpts from *The Black Book.*" *Acolyte* 2, No. 2 (Spring 1944): 15–16. In *BB.*

"The Family Tree of the Gods." *Acolyte* 2, No. 3 (Summer 1944): 9. Without title in *The Shuttered Room and Other Pieces* by H. P. Lovecraft et al., comp. August Derleth. Sauk City: Arkham House, 1959. 274–76. In *PD.* From letter by Smith to R. H. Barlow (16 June 1934).

"George Sterling: An Appreciation." *Overland Monthly* 85, No. 3 (March 1927): 79–80. In *PD.*

"In Memoriam: H. P. Lovecraft." *Tesseract* 2, No. 4 (April 1937): 5. In *PD.*

"On Fantasy." *FF* 2, No. 3 (November 1934): 37, 45. In *PD.*

"The Philosophy of the Weird Tale." *BB* 10–11.

>>"Introduction." *Shadows of Wings* by Susan Myra Gregory. San Diego, 1930: 7. In *SS.*

"The Weird Works of M. R. James." *FF* 1, No. 6 (February 1934): 89–90. In *PD.*

C. Works by Others

Dates in angular brackets indicate first publication.

Allen, Hervey (1889–1949). *Anthony Adverse.* New York: Farrar & Rinehart, 1933.

———. *Israfel: The Life and Times of Edgar Allan Poe.* New York: George H. Doran Co., 1927. 2 vols. (*LL* 27)

Andreyev, Leonid Nikolaevich (1871–1919). *The Seven That Were Hanged.* Introduction by Thomas Seltzer. New York: Boni & Liveright (Modern Library), [1918] or [1925]. [Also contains *The Red Laugh.* (*LL* 40).]

Apuleius, Lucius (123?–180?). *The Golden Asse of Lucius Apuleius.* Tr. William Adlington [1566]. London: Chapman & Dodd, [1898]. (*LL* 48)

The Arabian Nights Entertainments. Selected and Edited by Andrew Lang. New York: Longmans, Green, 1898. (*LL* 49)

Arlen, Michael (1895–1936). *Ghost Stories.* London: Collins, [1927]. (*LL* 52)

Asbury, Herbert (1891–1963), ed. *Not at Night!* New York: Macy-Masius (The Vanguard Press), 1928. (*LL* 54)

Asquith, Cynthia (1887–1960), ed. *The Ghost Book.* London: Hutchinson, 1927. New York: Charles Scribner's Sons, 1927.

———, ed. *Shudders: A Collection of New Nightmare Tales.* London: Hutchinson; New York: Charles Scribner's Sons, 1929.

———, ed. *When Churchyards Yawn: Fifteen New Ghost Stories.* London: Hutchinson, 1931.

Astor, John Jacob (1864–1912). *A Journey in Other Worlds: A Romance of the Future.* New York: D. Appleton & Co., 1894. (*LL* 56)

Austin, F. Britten (1885–1941). *On the Borderland.* Garden City, NY: Doubleday, Page & Co., 1923. (*LL* 61)

Bailey, James Osler (1903–1979). *Pilgrims through Space and Time: Trends and Patterns in Scientific and Utopian Fiction.* New York: Argus Books, 1947.

Barbey d'Aurevilly, Jules (1808–1889). *The Story without a Name.* Tr. Edgar Saltus. New York: Bedford & Co., 1891; *or* New York: Brentano's, 1919. (*LL* 74) [Translation of *Une Histoire sans nom* (1882).]

Baring-Gould, S. (1834–1924). *The Book of Were-Wolves: Being an Account of a Terrible Superstition.* London: Smith, Elder, 1865.

———. *Curious Myths of the Middle Ages.* <1866> (*LL* 75)

Barnette, Jack. "The Vapor Intelligence." *Science Wonder Stories* 1, No. 8 (January 1930): 702–7.

Barlow, R. H. (1918–1951). "R. E. H." *WT* 28, No. 3 (October 1936): 353.

Baudelaire, Charles Pierre (1821–1867). *Baudelaire: His Prose and Poetry.* Ed. T. R. Smith. New York: Boni & Liveright (Modern Library), [1919]. (*LL* 78)

———. *Les Fleurs du mal; Petits poèmes en prose; Les Paradis artificiels.* Tr. Arthur Symons. London: Casanova Society, 1925. New York: Boni & Liveright, 1926 (as *Baudelaire: Prose and Poetry*).

———. *Lettres 1841–1866.* Paris: Société de Mercure de France, 1907. (*LL* 79)

Beckford, William (1759–1844). *The Episodes of Vathek* <1912> Tr. Sir Frank T. Marzials. Boston: Small, Maynard & Co., [1922?] or [1924?]. (*LL* 74)

———. *Vathek.* <1786> Introduction by Ben Ray Redman, illustrated by Mahlon Blaine. New York: John Day Co., 1928. (*LL* 83)

Beddoes, Thomas Lovell (1803–1849). *Death's Jest Book; or, The Fool's Tragedy.* London: William Pickering, 1850.

Benoit, Pierre (1886–1962). *Atlantida.* Tr. Mary C. Tongue and Mary Ross. New York: Duffield, 1920. [Translation of *L'Atlantide* (1920).]

Benson, E. F. (1867–1940). *The Room in the Tower and Other Stories.* <1912> London: Alfred A. Knopf, 1929.

———. *Spook Stories.* London: Hutchinson, 1928.

———. *Visible and Invisible.* New York, George H. Doran, 1923 or 1924. (*LL* 90) [Contains "Negotiam Perambulans."]

———, and Brander Matthews (1852–1929). *Two Masterly Ghost Stories.* Girard, KS: Haldeman-Julius, 1926. (*LL* 91) [Contains "The Man Who Went to Far."]

Béraud, Henri (1885–1958). *Lazarus.* Tr. Eric Sutton. New York: Macmillan, 1925. (*LL* 92) [Translation of *Lazare* (1924).]

Besant, Annie (1847–1933). *The Pedigree of Man.* London: Theosophical Publishing Society, 1904.

Bierce, Ambrose (1842–1914?). *Black Beetles in Amber.* San Francisco: Western Authors Publishing Co., 1892.

———. *Can Such Things Be?* <1893> New York: Boni & Liveright (Modern Library), 1918. (*LL* 98)

———. *In the Midst of Life: Tales of Soldiers and Civilians.* <1891> Introduction by George Sterling. New York: Modern Library, [1927]. (*LL* 99)

———. *The Monk and the Hangman's Daughter; Fantastic Fables;* [etc.]. <1911> New York: A. & C. Boni, 1925. 383 pp. (*LL* 100)

———. *Twenty One Letters of Ambrose Bierce.* Ed. Samuel Loveman. Cleveland: George Kirk, 1922. (*LL* 101)

Birch, A. G. *The Moon Terror.* And Stories by Anthony M. Rud, Vincent Starrett, and Farnsworth Wright. Indianapolis: Popular Fiction Publishing Co., [1927]. (*LL* 104)

Birkhead, Edith (1889–1951). *The Tale of Terror: A Study of the Gothic Romance.* New York: E. P. Dutton, 1921. (*LL* 105)

[Birkin, Charles (1907–1985), ed.] *Creeps: A Collection of Uneasy Tales.* London: Philip Allan, 1932. (*LL* 223)

[———, ed.] *Shudders: A Collection of Uneasy Tales.* London: Philip Allan, 1932. (*LL* 873)

Biss, Gerald (1876–1922). *The Door of the Unreal.* New York: G. P. Putnam's Sons, 1920.

Blackwood, Algernon (1869–1951). *The Centaur.* London: Macmillan, 1911.

———. *The Extra Day.* London: Macmillan, 1915.

———. *The Garden of Survival.* New York: E. P. Dutton, 1918.

———. *Incredible Adventures.* London: Macmillan, 1914. New York: Macmillan, 1914. [Contains "A Descent into Egypt."]

———. *Jimbo: A Fantasy.* New York: Macmillan, 1909. (*LL* 106)

————. *John Silence—Physician Extraordinary.* London: Eveleigh Nash, 1908. Boston: John W. Luce, 1909. London: Macmillan, 1912. New York: Vaughan & Gomme, 1914. (*LL* 97) New York: Knopf, 1917. New York, E. P. Dutton, [1920]. (*LL* 107)

————. *Tongues of Fire and Other Sketches.* London: Herbert Jenkins, 1924. New York:, Dutton, 1925.

————. *The Wave: An Egyptian Aftermath.* London: Cassell, 1916. New York: E. P. Dutton, 1916.

Blakeborough, Richard (1850–1918). *The Hand of Glory and Further Grandfather's Tales and Legends of Highwaymen and Others.* Collected by the Late R. Blakeborough. Edited by J. Fairfax Blakeborough. London: Grant Richards, [1924]. (*LL* 116)

Blavatsky, Madame Helena Petrovana (1831–1891). *The Secret Doctrine.* London: Theosophical Publishing Co., 1888.

Boguet, Henri (d. 1619). *An Examen of Witches.* Tr. E. Allen Ashwin, ed. Montague Summers. [Bungay, UK]: John Rodker, 1929. [Translation of *Discours execrable des sorciers* (1606).]

Bond, Mary Bligh (1895–?). *Avernus.* Oxford: Basil Blackwell, 1924. (*LL* 118)

The Book of the Dead. An English Translation of the Chapters, Hymns, etc. of the Theban Recension, with Introduction, Notes, etc., by Sir E. A. Wallis Budge (1857–1934). 2nd ed., rev. & enl. London: Kegan Paul, Trench, Trübner & Co.; New York: E. P. Dutton, 1923. 3 vols. in 1. (*LL* 121)

Brown, J. Macmillan. Brown (1846–1935). *The Riddle of the Pacific.* London: T. Fisher Unwin, 1924.

Brucker, Johann Jakob (1696–1770). *Historia Critica Philosophiae a Mvndi Incvnabvlis ad Nostram vsqve Aetatem Dedvcta.* 2nd ed. Lipsiae [i.e., Leipzig]: Weidemanni et Reichii, 1766–77. 6 vols. (*LL* 137; HPL had only Vol. 4, parts 1 and 2)

Buchan, John (1875–1940). *The Runagates Club.* Boston: Houghton Mifflin, 1928. (*LL* 141)

Bulfinch, Thomas (1796–1867). *The Age of Fable; or, Beauties of Mythology.* <1855> Ed. J. Loughran Scott. Rev. ed. Philadelphia: D. McKay, [1898]. (*LL* 142)

Bullen, John Ravenor (1886–1927). *White Fire.* Athol, MA: The Recluse Press, 1927 [actually January 1928]. (*LL* 143)

Bulwer-Lytton, Edward (1803–1873). *A Strange Story; The Haunted House [sic]; Zanoni.* <1862; 1859; 1842> Boston: Desmond Publishing Co., [18—?]. (*LL* 145). [The second story is "The Haunted and the Haunters; or, The House and the Brain."]

Burks, Arthur J. (1898–1974). "Guatemozin the Visitant." *Strange Tales of Mystery and Terror* 1, No. 2 (November 1931).

Busson, Paul (1873–1924). *The Man Who Was Born Again.* Tr. Prince Mirski and Thomas Moult. New York: John Day Co., 1927. (*LL* 156) [Translation of *Die Wiedergeburt des Melchior Dronte* (1924).]

Cabell, James Branch (1879–1958). *Jurgen: A Comedy of Justice.* New York: Robert M. McBride & Co., 1919.

———. *The Silver Stallion: A Comedy of Redemption.* New York: Robert M. McBride & Co., 1926.

Cannon, Peter, ed. *Lovecraft Remembered.* Sauk City, WI: Arkham House: 1998.

Chambers, Robert W. (1865–1933). *In Search of the Unknown.* New York: Harper & Brothers, 1904. (*LL* 183)

———. *The King in Yellow.* Chicago: F. Tennyson Neely, 1895. (*LL* 184) [Contains: "The Yellow Sign."]

———. *The Maker of Moons.* New York: D. Appleton & Co., 1896.

———. *The Mask.* Racine, WI: Whitman Publishing, 1929.

———. *The Slayer of Souls.* New York: George H. Doran, 1920.

Chambers's Encyclopædia: A Dictionary of Universal Knowledge. London: W. & R. Chambers, 1860–68. 10 vols. Philadelphia: J. B. Lippincott Co., 1860–69. 10 vols. [Rev. eds. up to 1935.] (*LL* 185)

Chase, Stuart (1888–1885). *The Economy of Abundance.* New York: Macmillan, 1934.

Churchward, James (1852–1936). *The Children of Mu.* New York: Ives Washburn, 1931.

———. *The Lost Continent of Mu, the Motherland of Man.* New York: W. E. Rudge, 1926.

Cline, Leonard (1893–1929). *The Dark Chamber.* New York: Viking Press, 1927. (*LL* 198)

Coblentz, Stanton A. (1896–1982). "The Blue Barbarians." *Amazing Stories Quarterly* 4, No. 3 (Summer 1931): 290–370.

Comte de Lautréamont (pseud. of Isidore Lucien Ducasse, 1846–1870). *Les Chants de Maldoror* (1868). *From the Lay of Maldoror: (Canto I)* tr. John Rodker. Paris: Transition, 1927.

Cowan, Frank (1844–1905). *Revi-Lona: A Romance of Love in a Marvellous Land.* [Greensburg, PA: Tribune Press Publishing Co., 188-?]. (*LL* 217)

Cummings, Ray (1887–1957). "The Girl in the Golden Atom." *All-Story Weekly* (15 March 1919): 1–136.

David-Néel, Alexandra (1868–1969). *Magic and Mystery in Tibet.* New York: Claude Kendall, 1932.

De Casseres, Benjamin (1873–1945). *Chameleon: Being a Book of My Selves.* New York: Lieber & Lewis, 1922.

———. *The Shadow-Eater.* New York: Albert & Charles Boni, 1915. Illustrated ed. New York: American Library Service, 1923.

de Castro, Adolphe [Danziger] (1859–1959). "Ambrose Bierce as He Really Was: An Intimate Account of His Life and Death," *American Parade* (October 1926): 28–44.

———. *Portrait of Ambrose Bierce.* New York; London: Century Co., 1929.

de la Mare, Colin (1906–1983), ed. *They Walk Again: A Collection of Ghost Stories.* New York: E. P. Dutton, 1931.

de la Mare, Walter (1873–1956). *The Connoisseur and Other Stories.* London: Collins, 1926. New York: Alfred A. Knopf, 1926. (*LL* 243) [Contains "All Hallows" and "Mr. Kempe."]

———. *The Riddle and Other Stories.* <1923> New York: Alfred A. Knopf, 1930. [Contains "Seaton's Aunt" and "The Tree."] (*LL* 244)

———. *On the Edge.* London: Faber & Faber, 1930. [Contains "A Recluse."]

De Mille, James (1837–1880). *A Strange Manuscript Found in a Copper Cylinder.* <1888> New York: Harper & Brothers, 1900. (*LL* 245)

Derleth, August (1909–1971). "The Dark Brotherhood" (as by H. P. Lovecraft and August Derleth). In *The Dark Brotherhood and Other Pieces,* by H. P. Lovecraft and Divers Hands. Sauk City, WI: Arkham House, 1966. 3–29.

———. "The Early Years." Unpublished.

———. *Evening in Spring.* New York: Charles Scribner's Sons, 1941.

———. *The Man on All Fours.* New York: Loring & Mussey, 1934.

———. "Nella." *Pagany* 3, No. 1 (Winter 1932): 134–9.

———. "Old Ladies." *Midland* 19, No. 1 (Jan.–Feb. 1932): 5–9. Rewritten and included in *Evening in Spring* as "Take Arms!"

———. "The Return of Hastur." *WT* 33, No. 3 (March 1939): 66–84.

———. *The Sign of Fear.* New York: Loring & Mussey, 1935. (*LL* 251)

———. *Sleep No More: Twenty Masterpieces of Horror for the Connoisseur.* New York: Farrar & Rinehart, 1944. [Contains "The House of Sounds" by M. P. Shiel]

———. "The Thing That Walked on the Wind." *Strange Tales of Mystery and Terror* 3, No. 1 (January 1933): 18–26.

———. *Three Who Died.* New York: Loring & Mussey, 1935. (*LL* 253)

———. "The Weird Tale in English since 1890." <1930> *Ghost* No. 3 (1945): 5–32.

———, and Mark Schorer. "The House in the Magnolias." *Strange Tales of Mystery and Terror* 2, No. 2 (June 1932): 220–31.

———. "In the Left Wing." *WT* 19, No. 6 (June 1932): 772–83.

———. "The Lair of the Star-Spawn." *WT,* 20, No. 2 (August 1932): 184–94.

———. "They Shall Rise." *WT* 27, No. 4 (April 1936): 437–49.

Dial 73, No. 5 (November 1922). [Contains *The Waste Land* by T. S. Eliot, 473–85.] (*LL* 254)

Donnelly, Ignatius (1831–1901). *Atlantis: The Antediluvian World.* New York: Harper & Brothers, 1882.

Doyle, Sir Arthur Conan (1859–1930). *Tales of Twilight and the Unseen.* London: John Murray, 1922. (*LL* 278)

Dunsany, Lord (Edward John Moreton Drax Plunkett, 18th baron, 1878–1957). "At the Time of the Full Moon." *Saturday Evening Post* 201, No. 10 (8 September 1928): 74. *London Mercury* No. 107 (September 1928): 468–69.

Literary Digest 99, No. 3 (20 October 1928): 44.

―――. *The Blessing of Pan.* London: G. P. Putnam's Sons, 1927. (*LL* 287)

―――. *The Book of Wonder* <1912> [and *Time and the Gods* <1906>]. New York: Boni & Liveright (Modern Library), [1918]. (*LL* 288)

―――. *The Charwoman's Shadow.* New York: G. P. Putnam's Sons, 1926.

―――. *The Curse of the Wise Woman.* London: William Heinemann; New York: Longmans, Green, 1933.

―――. *Don Rodriguez: Chronicles of Shadow Valley.* New York: G. P. Putnam's Sons, 1922. (*LL* 289)

―――. *A Dreamer's Tales and Other Stories* [*A Dreamer's Tales* <1910> and *The Sword of Welleran* <1908>]. New York: Boni & Liveright (Modern Library), [1917], [1919], or [1921]. (*LL* 290)

―――. *Fifty Poems.* London & New York: G. P. Putnam's Sons, 1929.

―――. *Five Plays.* <1914> Boston: Little, Brown, 1923. (*LL* 276)

―――. *The Gods of Pegāna.* <1905>. (*LL* 277)

―――. *The King of Elfland's Daughter.* London: G. P. Putnam's Sons, 1924. (*LL* 294)

―――. *The Last Book of Wonder.* Boston: John W. Luce, 1916. (*LL* 295)

―――. *Mr. Jorkens Remembers Africa.* London: William Heinemann, 1934. New York: Longmans, Green, 1934 (as *Jorkens Remembers Africa*).

―――. *Plays of Gods and Men.* Boston: John W. Luce, [1917]. (*LL* 296)

―――. *Plays of Near and Far.* New York: G. P. Putnam's Sons, 1923. (*LL* 297)

―――. "To the Fallen Irish Soldiers." *London Mercury* No. 107 (September 1928): 468. *Literary Digest* 99, No. 3 (20 October 1928): 44.

Dwyer, Bernard Austin. "Ol' Black Sarah." *WT* 12, No. 4 (October 1928).

Eddison, E. R. (1882–1945). *The Worm Ouroboros: A Romance.* Illustrated by Keith Henderson. New York: A. & C. Boni, 1926. (*LL* 309)

The Encyclopaedia Britannica: A Dictionary of Arts, Sciences, and General Literature . . . With . . . Revisions and Additions by W. H. De Puy. 9th Ed. Chicago: Werner Co., 1896. 24 vols. (*LL* 318)

Faig, Kenneth W., Jr. *Lovecraftian Voyages.* New York: Hippocampus Press, 2017.

Ferriar, John (1761–1815). *An Essay towards a Theory of Apparitions.* London: Cadell and Davies, 1813.

Field, John (1520/1530–1587). *Ephemeris anni. 1557. currentis iuxta Copernici et Reinhaldi canones fideliter per Ioannem Feild Anglum, supputata ac examinata ad meredianum Londinensem qui occidentalior esse indicatur a Reinhaldo quam sit Regij Montis, per horam. 1. Scr. 50. Adiecta est etiam breuis quædam epistola Ioannis Dee, qua vulgares istos ephemeridum fictores merito reprehendit. Tabella deniq[ue], pro cœlesti themate erigendo iuxta modum vulgariter rationalem dictum, per eundem Ioannem Feild confecta, Londinensis poli altitundini inseruiens exactissime.* Londini: [In ædibus Thomæ Marshe], M.D. LVI. [1556] Septembris. XII.

Fiske, John (1842–1901). *Myths and Myth-Makers: Old Tales and Superstitions Interpreted by Comparative Mythology.* <1872> Boston: Houghton Mifflin, 1900. (*LL* 338)

Flammarion, Camille (1842–1925). *Haunted Houses.* London: T. Fisher Unwin, [1924]. (*LL* 320) [Translation of *Les Maisons hantées* (1923).]

Flaubert, Gustave (1821–1880). *The Temptation of St. Anthony.* Tr. Lafcadio Hearn <1910>. New York: Boni & Liveright (Modern Library), 1920. (*LL* 322) [Translation of *La Tentation de Saint Antoine* (1874).]

Forbes, Esther (1891–1967). *A Mirror for Witches.* London: William Heinemann, 1928. Boston: Houghton Mifflin, 1928. (*LL* 343)

Fort, Charles (1874–1932). *The Book of the Damned.* New York: Boni & Liveright, 1919.

———. *New Lands.* New York: Boni & Liveright, 1923.

Frank, Waldo (1889–1967). *Chalk Face.* New York: Boni & Liveright, 1924.

French, Joseph Lewis (1858–1936), ed. *The Best Ghost Stories.* New York: Modern Library, 1919.

———, ed. *The Best Psychic Stories.* Introduction by Dorothy Scarborough. New York: Boni & Liveright (Modern Library), 1920. (*LL* 355)

———, ed. *Masterpieces of Mystery.* Garden City, NY: Doubleday, Page & Co., 1920f. 4 vols. (*LL* 356) [HPL owned only three volumes.]

French, Nora May (1881–1907). *Poems.* San Francisco: Strange Company, 1910.

Galpin, Alfred (1901–1983). "Echoes from Beyond Space." *United Amateur* 24, No. 1 (July 1925): 3–4. In Lovecraft, *Letters to Alfred Galpin* 273–75.

———. "Marsh-Mad: A Nightmare." *Philosopher* 1, No. 1 (December 1920): 7–8 (as by "Consul Hasting"). In Lovecraft, *Letters to Alfred Galpin* 236–38.

Garland, Hamlin (1860–1940). *Forty Years of Psychic Research: A Plain Narrative of Fact.* New York: Macmillan, 1936.

Gautier, Théophile (1811–1872). *Clarimonde.* New York: Brentano's, 1899. *or Clarimonde and Other Stories.* London: T. C. & E. C. Jack, 1908. (*LL* 365) [Translation of "Clarimonde" (1836).]

———. "La Morte amoureuse" ("Clarimonde"). In Gautier's *Nouvelles.* Paris: Charpentier, 1845. *Translation:* In Gautier's *One of Cleopatra's Nights and Other Fantastic Romances.* Tr. Lafcadio Hearn. New York: Worthington, 1882. (*LL* 367)

———, and Prosper Mérimée (1803–1870). *Tales Before Supper.* Told in English by Myndart Verelst [i.e., Edgar Saltus] and Delayed with a Poem by Edgar Saltus. New York: Brentano's, 1887. (*LL* 368) [Contains Gautier's "Avatar" and Mérimée's "The Venus of Ille."]

Gessler, Clifford. "Treader of Obscure Stars." *Honolulu Star-Bulletin* (28 July 1928) Part 3 p. 12.

de Givry, Grillot (1870–1929). *Witchcraft, Magic & Alchemy.* Tr. J. Courtenay Locke. London: G. G. Harrap, [1931]. [Translation of *La Musée des sorciers, mages et alchemistes* (1929).]

Gorman, Herbert (1893–1954). *The Place Called Dagon.* New York: George H. Doran, 1927. New York: Hippocampus Press, 2003.

Gourmont, Remy de (1858–1915). *A Virgin Heart: A Novel.* Tr. Aldous Huxley. New York: N. L. Brown, 1921. [Translation of *Un Coeur virginal* (1907).]

Grattan, C. Hartley (1902–1980). *Bitter Bierce: A Mystery of American Letters.* Garden City, NY: Doubleday, Doran & Co., 1929. (*LL* 395)

Green, John Richard (1837–1883). *History of the English People.* New York: Harper & Brothers, [1878]–1903. (*LL* 400)

Greene, Frederick Stuart (1870–1939), ed. *The Grim Thirteen* (New York: Dodd, Mead, 1917).

Gregory, Susan Myra (1884–1939). *Shadows of Wings.* San Diego: Troubadour Press, 1930.

Haggard, H. Rider (1856–1925). *She: A History of Adventure.* <1887> New York: Gorton & Payne, [19—]. (*LL* 411)

———, and Andrew Lang (1844–1912). *The World's Desire.* London: Longmans, Green, 1890.

Haldane, J. B. S. (1892–1964). *Daedalus; or, Science and the Future: A Paper Read to the Heretics, Cambridge, on February 4th, 1923.* London: Kegan Paul, Trench, Trübner & Co., 1924 *or* New York: E. P. Dutton, 1924. (*LL* 413)

———. *The Last Judgment: A Scientist's Vision of the Future of Man.* New York: Harper & Brothers, 1927. (*LL* 414)

Hall, Austin (1885?–1933). *The Spot of Life. Argosy* (13 August–10 September 1932). New York: Ace, 1964.

———, and Homer Eon Flint (1892–1924). *The Blind Spot. Argosy* (14 May–18 June 1921). Philadelphia: Prime, 1953.

Hall, Leland (1883–1957). *Sinister House.* Boston: Houghton Mifflin, 1919. New York: Hippocampus Press, 2008.

Hammett, Dashiell (1894–1961), ed. *Creeps by Night: Chills and Thrills.* New York: John Day Co., 1931. (*LL* 421) [Contains HPL's "The Music of Erich Zann."]

———, ed. *Modern Tales of Horror.* London: Victor Gollancz, 1932. (*LL* 422)

Harper, Vincent (pseud. of Henry Austin Adams, 1849–1909). *The Mortgage on the Brain: Being the Confessions of the Late Ethelbert Croft, M.D.* New York: Doubleday, Page, 1905.

Harré, T. Everett (1884–1948), ed. *Beware After Dark! The World's Most Stupendous Tales of Mystery, Horror, Thrills and Terror,* New York: Macaulay, 1929. (*LL* 425)

Hawthorne, Julian (1846–1934), ed. *The Lock and Key Library: Classic Mystery and Detective Stories.* New York: Review of Reviews Co., 1909. 10 vols. (*LL* 428)

Hawthorne, Nathaniel (1804–1864). *The House of the Seven Gables, and The Snow-Image and Other Twice-Told Tales.* <1851; 1852> Boston: Houghton Mifflin, 1886. (*LL* 430)

Hearn, Lafcadio (1850–1904). *Fantastics and Other Fancies.* Ed. Charles Woodward Hutson. Boston: Houghton Mifflin, 1914.

———. *Kwaidan: Stories and Studies of Strange Things.* <1904> Boston: Houghton Mifflin, 1930. (*LL* 440)

———. *Some Chinese Ghosts.* Boston: Roberts Brothers, 1887.

Hecht, Ben (1894–1964). *Fantazius Mallare: A Mysterious Oath.* Chicago: Covici-McGee, 1922.

———. *The Kingdom of Evil: A Continuation of the Journal of Fantazius Mallare.* Illustrated by Anthony Angarola (1893–1929). Chicago: Pascal Covici, 1924.

Herodotus (fl. 5th c. B.C.E.). *The Ancient History of Herodotus.* Tr. William Beloe. New ed., rev., & cor. New York: Bangs Brothers, 1855. (*LL* 446)

Hersey, Harold Brainerd (1893–1956). *Night.* Illustrated by [William] Elliot Dold, Jr. (1892–1957). New York: Privately printed, 1923. (*LL* 447)

Hodgson, William Hope (1877–1918). *The Boats of the "Glen Carrig."* London: Chapman & Hall, 1907.

———. *Carnacki the Ghost-Finder.* London: Eveleigh Nash, 1913.

———. *The Ghost Pirates.* London: Stanley Paul, 1909.

———. *The House on the Borderland.* London: Chapman & Hall, 1908.

———. *The Night Land.* London: Eveleigh Nash, 1912.

Hoffmann, E. T. A. (1776–1822) *Weird Tales* (New York: Charles Scribner's Sons, 1885; 2 vols.).

Homer. *The Iliad of Homer.* Done into English Prose by Andrew Lang, Walter Leaf, and Ernest Myers. London: Macmillan, 1883.

———. *The Odyssey of Homer.* Done into English Prose by S. H. Butcher and Andrew Lang. London: Macmillan, 1879.

Houdini, Harry (pseud. of Ehrich Weiss, 1874–1926). *A Magician among the Spirits.* New York: Harper & Brothers, 1924. (*LL* 470)

Housman, Clemence (1861–1955). *The Were-Wolf.* London J. Lane at the Bodley Head; Chicago: Way & Williams, 1896.

Howard, Robert E. (1906–1936). *The Hyborian Age.* Los Angeles: LANY Cooperative Publications, 1938.

[Hoyt, Helen (1887–1972), ed.] *California Poets: An Anthology of 224 Contemporaries* New York: Henry Harrison, 1932.

Hugo, Victor (1802–1885). *Hans of Iceland.* <1823> (*LL* 477)

Huysmans, Joris-Karl (1848–1907). *Against the Grain.* Tr. John Howard. New York: A. & C. Boni, 1930. (*LL* 483) [Translation of *A Rebours* (1884).]

Ingram, John H. (1842–1916). *The Haunted Homes and Family Traditions of Great Britain.* London: Gibbings, 1901. (*LL* 489)

Jackson, Charles Loring (1847–1935). *The Gold Point and Other Strange Stories.* Boston: Stratford Co., 1926. (*LL* 497)

Jacobi, Carl. "The Tomb from Beyond." *Wonder Stories* 5, No. 4 (November 1933): 354–65.

James, Henry (1843–1916). *The Two Magics: The Turn of the Screw; Covering End.* <1898> New York: Macmillan, 1911. (*LL* 498)

James, M. R. (1862–1936). *The Collected Ghost Stories of M. R. James*. London: Edward Arnold, 1931.

———. *Ghost-Stories of an Antiquary*. London: Edward Arnold, 1904. (*LL* 499) [Contains "Count Magnus," "The Treasure of Abbot Thomas."]

———. *More Ghost Stories of an Antiquary*. <1911> (*LL* 500)

———. *A Thin Ghost and Others*. <1919> London: Edward Arnold, 1925. (*LL* 501)

———. *A Warning to the Curious*. London: Edward Arnold, 1925. (*LL* 502) [Contains: "A View from a Hill."]

Jenks, William (1778–1866), ed. *The Comprehensive Commentary on the Holy Bible*. Brattleboro, VT: Fessenden & Co., 1835–39; 5 vols. (*LL* 505)

The Jewish Encyclopedia (New York: Funk & Wagnalls Co., 1901–06).

Joshi, S. T. *I Am Providence The Life and Times of H. P. Lovecraft*. New York: Hippocampus Press, 2010. 2 vols.

Joshj, S. T., ed. *A Weird Writer in Our Midst: Early Criticism of H. P. Lovecraft*. New York: Hippocampus Press, 2010.

Joshi, S. T., and Marc A. Michaud, ed. *H. P. Lovecraft in "The Eyrie."* West Warwick, RI: Necronomicon Press, 1979.

Joshi, S. T., David E. Schultz, and Scott Connors. *Clark Ashton Smith: A Comprehensive Bibliography*. New York: Hippocampus Press, 2020.

Joshi, S. T., with David E. Schultz. *Lovecraft's Library: A Catalogue*. 4th ed. New York: Hippocampus Press, 2017.

Jung-Stilling, Johann Heinrich (1740–1817). *Theory of Pneumatology, in Reply to the Question, What Ought to Be Believed or Disbelieved concerning Presentiments, Visions, and Apparitions, According to Nature, Reason, and Scripture*. Tr. Samuel Jackson. London: Longman, Rees, Orme, Brown, Green & Longman, 1834. (*LL* 521) [Translation of *Theorie der Geister-Kunde* (1816).]

King, Basil (1859–1928). *The Spreading Dawn: Stories of the Great Transition*. New York: Harper & Brothers, 1927. (*LL* 530)

Kipling, Rudyard (1865–1936). *The Mark of the Beast, and The Head of the District*. Girard, KS: Haldeman-Julius Co., [19—]. (*LL* 536)

———. *The Phantom 'Rickshaw and Other Tales*. <1888> (*LL* 537)

Kittredge, George Lyman (1860–1941). *Witchcraft in Old and New England*. Cambridge, MA: Harvard University Press, 1929.

Kleiner, Rheinhart (1892–1949). "After a Decade." *Californian* 4, No. 2 (Fall 1936): 44. In *Lovecraft's New York Circle: The Kalem Club, 1924–1927*, ed. Mara Kirk Hart and S. T. Joshi. New York: Hippocampus Press, 2006. 244.

———. "After a Decade and the Kalem Club" *Californian* 4, No. 2 (Fall 1936): 45–47. In *Lovecraft's New York Circle: The Kalem Club, 1924–1927*, ed. Mara Kirk Hart and S. T. Joshi. New York: Hippocampus Press, 2006. 248–51.

Kremer, Heinrich (1430–1505), and Jakob Sprenger (1436?–1495). *Malleus Maleficarum*. Tr. Montague Summers. London: J. Rodker, 1928. [Translation of *Malleus Maleficarum* (1484).]

Krutch, Joseph Wood (1893–1970). *Edgar Allan Poe: A Study in Genius.* New York: Alfred A. Knopf, 1926.

Khun de Prorok, Byron (1896–1954). *Digging for Lost African Gods: The Record of Five Years Archaeological Excavation in North Africa.* With notes and translations by Edgar Fletcher Allen. New York: London: G. P. Putnam's Sons, 1926.

La Motte-Fouqué, Friedrich Heinrich Karl, baron de (1777–1843). *Undine and Sintram.* <1811; 1815> Boston: Estes & Lauriat, [18—]. (*LL* 549)

Le Fanu, J. Sheridan (1814–1873). *The House by the Churchyard.* <1863> London: Macmillan, 1899. (*LL* 559)

Leadbeater, C. W. (1854–1934). *The Inner Life.* Chicago: Rajput Press, 1911–12. 2 vols.

Leblanc, Maurice (1864–1941). *The Three Eyes.* Tr. Alexander Teixeira de Mattos. New York: Macaulay, 1921. New York: A. L. Burt, n.d. [Translation of *Les Trois Yeux* (1919).]

Leith, W. Compton (pseud. of Ormonde Maddock Dalton, 1866–1945). *Sirenica.* <1916> Portland, ME: Thomas Bird Mosher, 1927. (*LL* 560)

Level, Maurice (1875–1926). *Tales of Mystery and Horror.* Tr. Alys Eyre Macklin. New York: Robert M. McBride & Co., 1920. (*LL* 565)

———. *Those Who Return [L'Ombre].* Tr. B. Drillien. New York: Robert M. McBride & Co., 1923. (*LL* 566) [Translation of *L'Ombre* (1921).]

Lewis, Matthew Gregory (1775–1818). *The Monk: A Romance.* <1796> London: Brentano's, [1924]. (*LL* 567)

Liddell, Henry George (1811–1898), and Robert Scott (1811–1887). *A Greek-English Lexicon.* Oxford: Oxford University Press, 1843. (*LL* 569)

London, Jack (1876–1916). *The Star Rover.* <1915> (*LL* 579)

Long, Frank Belknap (1901–1994). "At the Home of Poe." *United Amateur* 21, No. 5 (May 1922): 53–54.

———. "The Beautiful City." *Leaves* No. 1 (Summer 1937): 49.

———. "Cones." *Astounding Stories* 16, No. 6 (February 1936): 122–38.

———. "The Desert Lich." *WT* 4, No. 3 (November 1924): 49–53.

———. "The Dark Beasts." *Marvel Tales* No. 2 (July–August 1934): 1–10.

———. "The Eye Above the Mantel." *United Amateur* 20, No. 4 (March 1921): 53–56.

———. "Flowers of Iniquity." *Home Brew* 1, No. 6 (July 1922).

———. *The Goblin Tower.* Cassia, FL: Dragon-Fly Press, 1935. (*LL* 580)

———. *The Horror from the Hills.* *WT* 17, No. 1 (January 1931): 32–53 ; 17, No. 2 (February/March 1931): 245–71. Sauk City, WI: Arkham House, 1963.

———. "In the Lair of the Space Monsters." *Strange Tales of Mystery and Terror* 2, No. 3 (October 1932): 408–23.

———. "In the Tomb of Semenses." *United Amateur* 21, No. 2 (November 1921): [13]–17.

———. *A Man from Genoa and Other Poems.* Athol, MA: W. Paul Cook, 1926. (*LL* 581)

———. "The Man with a Thousand Legs." *WT* 10, No. 2 (August 1927): 219–33.

———. "The Marriage of Sir John Mandeville." In *A Man from Genoa.*

———. "The Migration of Birds." *United Amateur* 21, No. 4 (March 1922): 41–42.

———. "The Red Fetish." *WT* 15, No. 1 (January 1930): 107–14.

———. "The Thought-Materializer." *Science Wonder Quarterly* (Spring 1930): 414–17.

———. "A Visitor from Egypt." *WT* 16, No. 3 (September 1930): 356–62. In *Creeps by Night: Thrills and Chills,* ed. Dashiell Hammett. New York: John Day Co., 1931. 505–25.

Loveman, Samuel (1887–1976). *The Hermaphrodite: A Poem.* Athol, MA: W. Paul Cook, 1926. (*LL* 593)

———. *The Sphinx: A Conversation.* [North Montpelier, VT: W. Paul Cook, 1944.]

———. *The Hermaphrodite and Other Poems.* Caldwell, ID: Caxton Printers, 1936. (*LL* 594)

———. *Out of the Immortal Night: Selected Works of Samuel Loveman.* Ed. S. T. Joshi and David E. Schultz. New York: Hippocampus Press, 2004.

Lucretius (T. Lucretius Carus, 99–55 B.C.E.). *On the Nature of Things.* Tr. H. A. J. Munro (1819–1885). <1864> London: Routledge, 1907.

Ludlow, Fitz Hugh (1836–1870), *The Hasheesh Eater: Being Passages from the Life of a Pythagorean.* New York: Harper & Brothers, 1857). (*LL* 601)

Lynch, John Gilbert Bohun (1884–1928), ed. *The Best Ghost Stories.* Boston: Small, Maynard & Co., [1924]. (*LL* 602)

MacDonald, George (1824–1905). *Lilith: A Romance.* New York: Dodd, Mead, 1895. (*LL* 611)

Machen, Arthur (1863–1947). *The Green Round.* London: Ernest Benn, 1933. Sauk City, WI: Arkham House, 1968.

———. *The Hill of Dreams.* London: E. Grant Richards, 1907. New York: Alfred A. Knopf, 1923. (*LL* 617)

———. *The House of Souls.* <1906> New York: Alfred A. Knopf, 1923. (*LL* 618) [Contains "The White People" and "The Great God Pan."]

———. Machen, Arthur. *The Secret Glory.* London: M. Secker; New York: A. A. Knopf, 1922. (*LL* 620)

———. *The Shining Pyramid.* London: Martin Secker, 1925. (*LL* 621)

———. *The Three Impostors.* <1895> New York: Alfred A. Knopf, 1930. (*LL* 623)

McKenna, Stephen (1888–1967). *The Oldest God: A Novel.* Boston: Little, Brown, 1926. (*LL* 624)

MacLeish, Archibald (1892–1982). *Conquistador.* Boston: Houghton Mifflin, 1932.

MacPhilpin, John, ed. *The Apparitions and Miracles at Knock: Also the Official Depositions of the Eyewitnesses.* New York: D. & J. Sadlier & Co., 1880. (*L* 626)

McSpadden, J. Walker (1874–1960), ed. *Famous Psychic Stories.* New York: Thomas Y. Crowell Co., 1920. (*LL* 629)

Markham, Edwin (1852–1940). *Our Israfel: In Memory of Edgar Allan Poe.* New York: Eugene R. Trott Company, 1925.

Markham, Virgil (1899–1973). *Death in the Dusk: Being Alfred Bannerlee's Own Revision and Enlargement of His Journal Notes from the Evening of October 2nd, 1925, to the Breaking Off, October 9th; Together with the Conclusion of the Narrative Later Supplied by Him; and the Communication of April 17th, 1926.* New York: Alfred A. Knopf, 1928.

Marryat, Capt. Frederick (1792–1848). *The Phantom Ship.* <1839> (LL 640)

Marsh, Richard (1857–1915). *The Beetle.* London: Skeffington, 1897. (LL 642)

Mather, Cotton (1663–1728). *Magnalia Christi Americana.* London: Printed for T. Parkhurst, 1702. (LL 645)

Maturin, Charles Robert (1782–1824). *Melmoth the Wanderer.* <1820> London: Richard Bentley & Son, 1892. 3 vols. (LL 646)

Maurice, Michael (pseud. of Conrad Arthur Skinner, 1889–1975). *Not in Our Stars.* Philadelphia: J. B. Lippincott Co., 1923. (LL 649)

Mérimée, Prosper. See Gautier, Théophile, and Prosper Mérimée.

Merritt, A[braham] (1882–1943). *Burn, Witch, Burn! Argosy* (22 October–26 November 1932). New York: Liveright, 1933.

———. *The Conquest of the Moon Pool. Argosy* (15 February–22 March 1919). New York: G. P. Putnam's Sons, 1919 (includes a truncated version of "The Moon Pool").

———. *Creep Shadow. Argosy* (8 September–20 October 1934). Garden City, NY: Doubleday, Doran, 1934.

———. "The Drone." *Fantasy Magazine* 4, No. 1 (September 1934): 1–10

———. *The Dwellers in the Mirage. Argosy* (23 January–27 February 1932).

———. *The Face in the Abyss.* New York: Liveright, 1931. [Combination of "The Face in the Abyss" (*Argosy All-Story Weekly*, 8 September 1923) and *The Snake Mother* (*Argosy*, 25 October–6 December 1930).]

———. *The Metal Monster. Argosy All-Story Weekly* (7 August–25 September 1920). New York: Hippocampus Press, 2002. Rev. as *The Metal Emperor. Science and Invention* (October 1927–August 1928).

———. "The Moon Pool." *All-Story Weekly* (22 June 1918). (LL 26) Incorporated into *The Moon Pool.* New York: G. P. Putnam's Sons, 1919.

———. "The People of the Pit." *All-Story Weekly* (5 January 1918). *Amazing Stories* (March 1927).

Meyrink, Gustav (1868–1932). *The Golem.* Tr. Madge Pemberton. London: Gollancz; Boston: Houghton Mifflin, 1928. [Translation of *Der Golem* (1915).]

Miller, P. Schuyler (1912–1974), and John D. Clark. *A Probable Outline of Conan's Career.* Los Angeles: LANY Cooperative Publications, 1938.

Milton, John (1608–1674). *Paradise Lost of Milton.* <1667> With Illustrations, Designed and Engraved by John Martin. London: Septimus Prowett, 1827.

———. *Paradise Lost.* <1667> Illustrated by Gustave Doré <1866>. (LL 657)

The Modern Encyclopedia: A New Library of World Knowledge. Ed. A. H. McDannald. New York: Grosset & Dunlap, 1935. (*LL* 668) First published by W. H. Wise & Co. (New York), 1933.

Moore, Thomas (1779–1852) *The Epicurean: A Tale*. London: Printed for Longman, Rees, Orme, Brown, & Green, 1827. (*LL* 674).

Morrow, W. C. (1854–1923). *The Ape, the Idiot and Other People*. Philadelphia: J. B. Lippincott Co., 1897.

Morse, Richard Ely (1909–1986). "Dark Garden." *Phantagraph* 4, No. 6 (September 1936): [1]. *Californian* 4, No. 2 (Fall 1936): 27.

———. "Mad Dream." *Phantagraph* 5, No. 1 (October 1936): [1]. *Californian* 4, No. 2 (Fall 1936): 39.

Murray, Margaret A. (1863–1963). *The Witch-Cult in Western Europe*. Oxford: Clarendon Press, 1921.

Neale, Athur, ed. *The Great Weird Stories*. New York: Duffield & Co., 1929. (*LL* 690)

Neale, Walter (1873–1933). *Life of Ambrose Bierce*. New York: Walter Neale, 1929.

Nietzsche, Friedrich Wilhelm (1844–1900) *Human, All Too Human: A Book for Free Spirits—Part 1*. Chicago: C.H. Kerr, 1908. Translated by Alexander Harvey from *Menschliches, Allzumenschliches: Ein Buch für freie Geister* (1878).

O'Brien, Edward J. (1890–1941). *The Dance of the Machines: The American Short Story and the Industrial Age*. New York: Macaulay Co., 1929. (*LL* 715)

O'Brien, Fitz-James (1828–1862). "The Diamond-Lens." *Atlantic Monthly* (January 1858): 354–67. *WT* 13, No. 4 (April 1929).

O'Neill, Eugene (1888–1953). *The Emperor Jones, The Straw, and Diff'rent: Three Plays*. London: J. Cape, 1922.

———. *Strange Interlude*. New York: Boni & Liveright, 1928.

Oxenford, John (1812–1877), and C. A. Feiling, ed. & tr. *Tales from the German: Comprising Specimens from the Most Celebrated Authors*. London: Chapman & Hall, 1844. (*LL* 730)

Owen, Frank (pseud. of Roswell Williams, 1893–1968). *The Wind That Tramps the World: Splashes of Chinese Color*. New York: Lantern Press, 1929. (*LL* 731)

Owings, Mark, and Irving Binkin. *A Catalog of Lovecraftiana: The Grill/Binkin Collection*. Baltimore: Mirage Press, 1975.

Pain, Barry (1864–1928). *An Exchange of Souls*. London: Eveleigh Nash, 1911. (*LL* 735); rpt. New York: Hippocampus Press, 2007.

———. *Stories in the Dark*. London: Grant Richards, 1901. [Contains "The Undying Thing."]

Pattee, Fred Lewis (1863–1950). *The House of the Black Ring*. Harrisburg, PA: Mount Pleasant Press, 1916. (*LL* 744)

Perutz, Leo (1884–1957). *The Master of the Day of Judgment*. Tr. Hedwig Singer. London: Elkin Mathews & Marrot, 1929. New York: Charles Boni, 1930. (*LL* 753) [[Translation of *Der Meister des Jüngsten Tages* (1923).]

Petronius (T. Petronius Arbiter) (fl. 1st c. C.E.). *The Satyricon of T. Petronius Arbiter.* [William] Burnaby's Translation, 1694. With an Introduction by Martin Travers. London: Simpkin, Marshall, Hamilton, Kent, [1923]. (*LL* 754)

Pierce, Frederick Clifton (1855–1904). *Field Genealogy.* Chicago: W. B. Conkey Co., 1901.

Pironti, Francesco. *Il Deciframento della lingua etrusca attraverso la traduzione completa, libera e letterale, italiana e latina, dei testi etruschi maggiori. Con esteso commento critico e grammaticale.* Vol. 1Lanciano, 1933-.

Poe, Edgar Allan (1809–1849). *The Narrative of Arthur Gordon Pym of Nantucket.* <1837–38>

———. *Tales of Mystery and Imagination.* Illustrated by Harry Clarke. <1919> New York: Tudor Publishing Co., 1933. (*LL* 768)

———. *The Works of Edgar Allan Poe.* The Raven Edition. New York: P. F. Collier & Son, 1903. 5 vols. (*LL* 769)

Prevot, Francis C. (1887–1967). *Ghosties and Ghoulies.* Chelsea, UK: Chelsea Publishing Co., 1933.

Quiller-Couch, Sir Arthur (1863–1944). *Noughts and Crosses: Stories, Studies, and Sketches.* London: Cassell, 1893. (*LL* 784)

———. *Old Fires and Profitable Ghosts: A Book of Stories.* New York: Charles Scribner's Sons, 1900. (*LL* 785)

———. *Wandering Heath: Stories, Studies, and Sketches.* New York: Charles Scribner's Sons, 1896. (*LL* 786)

Radcliffe, Ann (1764–1823). *The Mysteries of Udolpho.* <1794> London: George Routledge & Sons, [1882]–[192-]. (*LL* 787)

Reeve, Clara (1729–1807). *The Old English Baron: A Gothic Story.* London: Colchester, 1777 (as *The Champion of Virtue*). (*LL* 793)

Rennell, James Rennell Rodd, baron (1858–1941). *Rose Leaf and Apple Leaf.* Philadelphia: J. M. Stoddart & Co., 1882. 102 pp. *or* Portland, ME: Thomas Bird Mosher, 1906. (*LL* 794)

Renshaw, Anne Tillery (1890–c. 1945). *Well Bred Speech: A Brief, Intensive Aid for English Students.* Washington, DC: Standard Press, 1936. (*LL* 796)

Reynolds, George W. M. (1814–1879). *Faust: A Romance of the Secret Tribunals.* London: Vickers, 1847. New York: Hurst, n.d. (as *Faust and the Demon*).

———. *Wagner, the Wehr-Wolf.* London: J. Dicks, 1848, 1857, 1872.

Richardson, Leon Burr (1878–1951). *History of Dartmouth College.* Hanover, NH: Stephen Daye Press, 1932. 2 vols.

Rickard, Dennis. *The Fantastic Art of Clark Ashton Smith.* Baltimore: Mirage Press, 1973.

Rohmer, Sax (pseud. of Arthur Sarsfield Ward, 1883–1959). *Brood of the Witch-Queen.* <1918> New York: A. L. Burt, 1926. (*LL* 811)

Rudwin, Maximilian J. (1885–1946), ed. *Devil Stories: An Anthology.* New York: Alfred A. Knopf, 1921. (*LL* 816)

Russell, W. Clark (1844–1911). *The Flying Dutchman; or, The Death Ship.* <1888> New York: Hurst, n.d. (*LL* 820)

——. *The Frozen Pirate.* London: Sampson, Low & Co., 1887. 2 vols. (*LL* 821)

Saintsbury, George (1843–1933), ed. *Tales of Mystery.* New York: Macmillan, 1891. (*LL* 824) [Contains extracts from Ann Radcliffe, *The Mysteries of Udolpho;* Matthew Gregory Lewis, *The Monk;* and Charles Robert Maturin, *Melmoth the Wanderer.*]

Savile, Frank Mackenzie (1865–1950). *Beyond the Great South Wall: The Secret of the Antarctic.* London: Sampson Low, Marston, 1899. New York: Grosset & Dunlap, 1901. (*LL* 828)

Sayers, Dorothy L. (1893–1957), ed. *The Omnibus of Crime.* <1928> Garden City, NY: Garden City Publishing Co., 1931. (*LL* 830)

——. *The Second Omnibus of Crime: The World's Great Crime Stories.* <1931> New York: Blue Ribbon Books, 1932.

Scott, Sir Walter (1771–1832). *Letters on Demonology and Witchcraft.* <1830> London: George Routledge & Sons, 1884. (*LL* 840)

Scott-Elliot, William (1849–1919). *The Story of Atlantis and The Lost Lemuria.* London: Theosophical Publishing Society, 1925.

Shelley, Mary (1797–1851). *Frankenstein; or, The Modern Prometheus.* <1818> New-York: H. G. Daggers, 1845. (*LL* 864)

Shiel, M. P. (1865–1947). *The Pale Ape and Other Pulses.* London: T. Werner Laurie, 1911. [Contains "The House of Sounds."]

——. *Prince Zaleski.* Boston: Roberts Brothers, 1895. (*LL* 870)

——. *The Purple Cloud.* London: Chatto & Windus, 1901; New York: Vanguard Press, 1930 (*LL* 871); rpt. in *The House of Sounds and Others,* ed. S. T. Joshi. New York: Hippocampus Press, 2005.

——. *Shapes in the Fire.* London: John Lane, 1896.

Sidney-Fryer, Donald. "Klarkash-Ton and Ech-Pi-El: On the Alleged Influence of H. P. Lovecraft on Clark Ashton Smith." *Mirage* 1, No. 6 (Winter 1963–64): 30–33 (as by "Donald S. Fryer").

Sinclair, Upton (1878–1968). *I, Governor of California, and How I Ended Poverty.* Los Angeles: Upton Sinclair, 1933.

Sinnett, A. P. (1840–1921). *Esoteric Buddhism.* Boston: Houghton, Mifflin, 1898.

Sitwell, Sir Osbert (1892–1969). *The Man Who Lost Himself.* London: Duckworth, 1929 *or* New York: Coward-McCann, 1930. (*LL* 876)

Snow, Royall H. (1898–1976). *Thomas Lovell Beddoes, Eccentric & Poet.* New York: Covici, Friede, 1928. (*LL* 897)

Spence, Lewis (1874–1955). *An Encyclopaedia of Occultism: A Compendium of Information on the Occult Sciences, Occult Personalities, Psychic Science, Magic, Demonology, Spiritism and Mysticism.* New York: Dodd, Mead, 1920. (*LL* 898)

——. *The History of Atlantis.* London: Rider & Co., 1926.

———. *The Mysteries of Britain; or, The Secret Rites and Traditions of Ancient Britain Restored.* London: Rider, 1928.

Spencer, R. E. (1896–1956). *The Lady Who Came to Stay.* New York: Book League of America, 1931. New York: Hippocampus Press, 2009.

Spengler, Oswald (1880–1936). *The Decline of the West.* Tr. Charles Francis Atkinson. London: George Allen & Unwin, 1922–26. 2 vols. [Translation of *Der Untergang des Abendlandes* (1918–22).]

Squires, Roy A. (1920–1988). *Arkham House Authors and Some Science Fiction Material in Private Press Editions, and a Few Associational Items. Catalog IV.* Glendale, CA: Roy A. Squires, [April] 1971.

———. *Beyond the Bibliographies: Catalog 7.* Glendale, CA: Roy A. Squires, [1973].

———. *A Bibliographic Catalog of the Largest Collection Ever Offered for Sale of the Works of Clark Ashton Smith & H. P. Lovecraft.* [Catalog 1.] Glendale, CA: Roy A. Squires, June 1968; *Supplement* thereto, January 1969.

———. *Clark Ashton Smith—H. P. Lovecraft—Robert H. Barlow: Catalog II.* Glendale, CA: Roy A. Squires, [1969].

———. *A Fantasy and Science Fiction Panmixia: Catalog 9.* Glendale, CA: Roy A. Squires, [1976].

———. *H. P. Lovecraft: A Basic Collection of 100 Items; Ten Notable Items Offered Separately; A Noble Group of 115 Items . . . and a Smaller Group.* [Catalog 3] Glendale, CA: Roy A. Squires, [1970/71].

———. *H. P. Lovecraft and the Lovecraft Circle—Books & Autographs: Catalog 8.* Glendale, CA: Roy A. Squires, [1974].

———. *Modern Literature: Catalog 6.* Glendale, CA: Roy A. Squires, [1972].

———. *Science Fiction & Modern Fantasy—Scarce Books & Rare Ephemerae: Catalog 5.* Glendale, CA: Roy A. Squires, [1971].

Sterling, George (1869–1926). "A Wine of Wizardry." *Cosmopolitan Magazine* 43, No. 5 (September 1907): [551–56].

Sterling, Kenneth (1920–1995). "The Horror Element in Poe." *Californian,* 5, No. 3 (Winter 1937): 33–45. In *Letters to Robert Bloch and Others* 471–85.

Stevenson, Robert Louis (1850–1894). *Dr. Jekyll and Mr. Hyde and The Merry Men and Other Tales.* <1886; 1887> (LL 922)

Strauch, Carl F. (1908–1989). *Twenty-nine Poems.* Boston: Bruce Humphries, Inc., 1932.

Summers, Montague (1880–1948). *The Geography of Witchcraft.* London: Kegan Paul, Trench, Trübner & Co.; New York, Knopf, 1927.

———. *The History of Witchcraft and Demonology.* London : Routledge & Kegan Paul, 1926.

———. *The Vampire: His Kith and Kin.* London: Kegan Paul, Trench & Trübner, 1928.

Suter, J. Paul (1884–?). "Beyond the Door." *WT* 1, No. 2 (April 1923); rpt. 16, No. 3 (September 1930).

Symons, Arthur (1865–1945). *Charles Baudelaire: A Study.* London: Elkin Mathews, 1920.

Taine, John (pseud. of Eric Temple Bell, 1883–1960). *The Greatest Adventure.* New York: E. P. Dutton, 1929.

———. *The Iron Star.* New York: E. P. Dutton, 1930.

———. "Seeds of Life." *Amazing Stories Quarterly* (Fall 1931): 434–505.

Thompson, Charles John Samuel (1862–1943). *The Mysteries and Secrets of Magic.* London: John Lane/The Bodley Head, 1927.

Thomson, Christine Campbell (1897–1985), ed. *By Daylight Only.* London: Selwyn & Blount, 1929. (*LL* 960)

———, ed. *Gruesome Cargoes.* London: Selwyn & Blount, 1928. (*LL* 962)

———, ed. *Keep On the Light!* London: Selwyn & Blount, 1933.

———, ed. *Not at Night.* London: Selwyn & Blount, 1925. (*LL* 963)

———, ed. *Switch On the Light.* London: Selwyn & Blount, 1931. (*LL* 965)

———, ed. *You'll Need a Night Light.* London: Selwyn & Blount, 1927. *LL* 966)

Thomson, James ("B. V.") (1832–1882). *The City of Dreadful Night and Other Poems.* <1886>

Toksvig, Signe (1891–1983). *The Last Devil.* New York: John Day Co., 1927. (*LL* 973)

Verlaine, Paul (1844–1896). *Poems of Paul Verlaine.* Translated by Gertrude Hall Brownell. Chicago, Stone & Kimball, 1895.

Verne, Jules (1828–1905). *From the Earth to the Moon.* <1865> (*LL* 995)

———. *Off on a Comet. Amazing Stories* 1, No. 1 (April 1926): 4–56; 1, No. 2 (May 1926): 148–92.

Villiers de l'Isle-Adam, Jean-Marie-Mathias-Philippe-Auguste, comte de (1838–1889). *Claire Lenoir.* Tr. Arthur Symons. New York: Albert & Charles Boni, 1925. [Translation of *Claire Lenoir* (1887).]

Virgil (P. Vergilius Maro, 70–19 BCE). *The Æneid of Virgil.* Tr. [verse] John Conington (1825–1869). New York: Armstrong and Son, 1886.

———. *The Aeneid of Virgil.* Tr. [prose] John Conington. With introduction and notes by Edgar S. Shumway. New York: Macmillan, 1910.

Wakefield, H. Russell (1890–1964). *Others Who Returned: Fifteen Disturbing Tales.* New York: D. Appleton, 1929. (*LL* 1003) [Contains "The Cairn."]

———. *They Return at Evening.* New York: D. Appleton, 1928. (*LL* 1004)

Walpole, Horace (1717–1797). *The Castle of Otranto.* London: Thomas Lowndes, 1765 [i.e. 1764]. (*LL* 1007)

Walpole, Hugh (1884–1941). *Portrait of a Man with Red Hair.* London: Macmillan, 1925.

Wandrei, Donald (1908–1987). "The Chuckler." *Fantasy Magazine* 4, No. 1 (September 1934): 26–33.

———. "Colossus." *Astounding Stories* 12, No 5 (January 1934): 40–72.

———. *Dark Odyssey.* St. Paul, MN: Webb Publishing Co., [1931]. (*LL* 1009)

————. *Dead Titans, Waken!/Invisible Sun—Two Novels by Donald Wandrei.* Ed. S. T. Joshi. Lakewood CO: Centipede Press, 2011.

————. "The Door of the Room." See "Nightmare."

————. *Ecstasy and Other Poems.* Athol, MA: Recluse Press, 1928. (*LL* 1010)

————. "The Emperor of Dreams." *Overland Monthly* 84, No. 12 (December 1926): 380–81, 407, 409. *Klarkash-Ton: The Journal of Smith Studies* No. 1 (1988): 3–8, 25.

————. "A Fragment of a Dream." *Recluse* No. 1 (1927): 18–21.

————. "The Lives of Alfred Kramer." *WT* 20, No. 6 (December 1932).

————. "The Messengers." *Minnesota Quarterly* 4, No. 1 (Fall 1926): 58–59.

————. "Nightmare" [formerly "The Door to the Room."] In *Strange Harvest.* Sauk City, WI: Arkham House, 1965.

————. "A Race Through Time." *Astounding Stories* 12, No. 2 (October 1933).

————. "Raiders of the Universes." *Astounding Stories* 11, No. 1 (September 1932): 63–77.

————. *Sanctity and Sin: The Collected Poems and Prose Poems of Donald Wandrei.* New York: Hippocampus Press, 2008.

————. "Spawn of the Sea." *WT* 21, No. 5 (May 1933): 567–76.

————. "The Twilight of Time." *WT* 10, No. 4 (October 1927): 431–36 (as "The Red Brain"). In Hammett, *Creeps by Night* (q.v.). *Leaves* No. 1 (Summer 1937): 71–75.

Webster, J. Provand. *The Oracle of Baal: A Narrative of Some Curious Events in the Life of Professor Horatio Charmichael, M.A.* Philadelphia: J. B. Lippincott Co., 1896. (*LL* 1019)

Webster, Noah (1758–1834). *An American Dictionary of the English Language.* Rev. & enl. by Chauncey A. Goodrich and Noah Porter. Springfield, MA: G. & C. Merriam, 1864. (*LL* 1021)

————, with Chauncey A Goodrich, Noah Porter, and Loomis J Campbell. *Supplement of Additional Words and Definitions.* [Springfield, MA]: [G. & C. Merriam], 1879.

Weigall, Arthur (1880–1934). *Wanderings in Roman Britain.* London: Butterworth, 1926. (*LL* 1025)

Wells, H. G. (1866–1946). "Æpyornis Island." In *Thirty Strange Stories.* New York: Harper & Brothers, 1897.

————. *The First Men in the Moon.* Indianapolis: Bowen-Merrill Co., [1901].

————. *The Island of Dr. Moreau. Amazing Stories* 1, No. 7 (October 1926): 636–55; 1, No. 8 (November 1926): 702–23.

————. *The Time Machine. Amazing Stories* 2, No. 2 (May 1927): 148–79.

————. *The War of the Worlds. Amazing Stories* 2, No. 5 (August 1927): 422–50; 2, No. 6 (September 1927): 598–67.

————, Julian Huxley (1887–1975), and G. P. Wells (1901–1985). *The Science of Life: A Summary of Contemporary Knowledge about Life and Its Possibilities.* London: Amalgamated Press, 1930. 2 vols. New York: Doubleday, 1931. 4 vols.

Werfel, Franz (1890–1945). *Goat Song.* Tr. Ruth Langner. Garden City, NY: Doubleday, Page, 1926. [Translation of *Bocksgesang* (1921).]

White, Edward Lucas (1866–1934). *Lukundoo and Other Stories.* New York: George H. Doran, 1927. (*LL* 1036)

———. *The Song of the Sirens and Other Stories.* New York: E. P. Dutton, 1919. (*LL* 1037)

Whitehead, Henry S. (1882–1932). "The Black Beast." *Adventure* (15 July 1931).

———. "Cassius." *Strange Tales of Mystery and Terror* 1, No. 2 (November 1931).

———. "The Great Circle. *Strange Tales of Mystery and Terror* 2, No. 2 (June 1932).

———. "The Moon Dial." *Strange Tales of Mystery and Terror* 1, No. 3 (January 1932).

Wilde, Oscar (1854–1900). *The Picture of Dorian Gray* <1890> (New York, Boni & Liveright [Modern Library], 1918. (*LL* 1051)

Williams, Blanche Colton (1879–1944), ed. *O. Henry Memorial Prize Stories.*Garden City, NY: Doubleday, 1919–32.

Williams, Charles (1886–1945). *War in Heaven.* Victor Gollancz: London, 1930.

Worrell, Everil (1893–1969). "The Canal." *WT* 10, No. 6 (December 1927).

Young, Francis Brett (1884–1964). *Cold Harbour.* London: Collins, 1924. New York: Hippocampus Press, 2008.

D. Items Published in Weird Tales

Appearances by HPL and CAS and stories they mentioned in their correspondence.

1, No. 4 (June 1923)
The Invisible Terror   Hugh Thomason

2, No. 1 (July–August 1923)
The Garden of Evil [v]   Clark Ashton Smith
The Red Moon [v]   Clark Ashton Smith

2, No. 4 (October 1923)
Dagon   H. P. Lovecraft

2, No. 5 (November 1923)
The Crawling Death   P. A. Connolly

3, No. 1 (January 1924)
The Picture in the House   H. P. Lovecraft
Solution [v]   Clark Ashton Smith

3, No. 2 (February 1924)
The Hound   H. P. Lovecraft

3, No. 3 (March 1924)
The Melancholy Pool [v]   Clark Ashton Smith
The Rats in the Walls   H. P. Lovecraft

3, No. 4 (April 1924)
Nemesis [v]   H. P. Lovecraft
The White Ape   H. P. Lovecraft

4, No. 2 [*sic*] (May–June–July 1924)
Hypnos   H. P. Lovecraft
Imprisoned with the Pharaohs   Harry Houdini [and H. P. Lovecraft]
The Loved Dead   C. M. Eddy, Jr. [and H. P. Lovecraft]

4, No. 3 (November 1924)
The Brain in the Jar   Norman Elwood Hammerstrom and R. F. Searight
The Desert Lich   Frank Belknap Long, Jr.
To a Dreamer [v]   H. P. Lovecraft

4, No. 6 (December 1924)
Death Waters   Frank Belknap Long, Jr.

5, No. 1 (January 1925)
The Festival   H. P. Lovecraft
The Ocean Leech   Frank Belknap Long, Jr.

5, No. 2 (February 1925)
The Statement of Randolph Carter   H. P. Lovecraft

5, No. 5 (May 1925)
Men Who Walk upon the Air   Frank Belknap Long, Jr.
The Music of Erich Zann   H. P. Lovecraft

6, No. 1 (July 1925)
The Unnamable   H. P. Lovecraft

6, No. 2 (August 1925)
Stallions of the Moon [v]   Frank Belknap Long, Jr.

6, No. 3 (September 1925)
The Temple   H. P. Lovecraft

6, No. 6 (December 1925)
The Sea Thing   Frank Belknap Long, Jr.

7, No. 1 (January 1926)
The Tomb   H. P. Lovecraft

7, No. 2 (February 1926)
The Cats of Ulthar · H. P. Lovecraft
Spleen [v] · Charles P. Baudelaire [tr. Clark Ashton Smith]

7, No. 4 (April 1926)
The Outsider · H. P. Lovecraft

7, No. 5 (May 1926)
Horreur Sympahique [v] · Charles P. Baudelaire [tr. Clark Ashton Smith]

7, No. 6 (June 1926)
The Moon-Bog · H. P. Lovecraft

8, No. 2 (August 1926)
The Terrible Old Man · H. P. Lovecraft

8, No. 3 (September 1926)
He · H. P. Lovecraft

8, No. 5 (November 1926)
The City of Spiders · H. Warner Munn

8, No. 6 (December 1926)
Yule Horror [v] · H. P. Lovecraft

9, No. 1 (January 1927)
The Horror at Red Hook · H. P. Lovecraft

9, No. 3 (March 1927)
The White Ship · H. P. Lovecraft

10, No. 1 (July 1927)
A Fable [v] · Clark Ashton Smith

10, No. 2 (August 1927)
The Man with a Thousand Legs · Frank Belknap Long
Two Black Bottles · Wilfred Blanch Talman [and H. P. Lovecraft]

10, No. 3 (September 1927)
Interrogation [v] · Clark Ashton Smith

10, No. 4 (October 1927)
Pickman's Model · H. P. Lovecraft
The Red Brain · Donald Wandrei

10, No. 6 (December 1927)
The Canal   Everil Worrell
The Infidel's Daughter   E. Hoffmann Price
The Saturnienne [v]   Clark Ashton Smith

11, No. 1 (January 1928)
In Amundsen's Tent   John Martin Leahy

11, No. 2 (February 1928)
The Call of Cthulhu   H. P. Lovecraft
Clarimonde [orig. La Morte Amoreuse]   Théophile Gautier

11, No. 3 (March 1928)
Epigraphe Pour un livre Condamne [v]
                    Charles P. Baudelaire [tr. Clark Ashton Smith]

11, No. 4 (April 1928)
The Chain   H. Warner Munn
The Legend of St. Julian the Hospitaller   Gustave Flaubert

11, No. 6 (June 1928)
The Lurking Fear   H. P. Lovecraft

12, No. 1 (July 1928)
The Space-Eaters   Frank Belknap Long, Jr.

12, No. 2 (August 1928)
Three Poems in Prose   Charles P. Baudelaire [tr. Clark Ashton Smith]
   [L'Irreparable; Les Sept Viellards; Une Charogne]

12, No. 3 (September 1928)
The Ninth Skeleton   Clark Ashton Smith

12, No. 4 (October 1928)
Ol' Black Sarah [v]   Bernard A. Dwyer
Warning [v]   Clark Ashton Smith

12, No. 5 (November 1928)
The Flying Death   B. Wallis
The Last Test   Adolphe de Castro [and H. P. Lovecraft]

13, No. 1 (January 1929)
The Chemical Brain   Francis Flagg
The Silver Key   H. P. Lovecraft

13, No. 3 (March1929)
The Hounds of Tindalos   Frank Belknap Long

13, No. 4 (April 1929)
The Diamond Lens — Fitz-James O'Brien
The Dunwich Horror — H. P. Lovecraft
Sonnet [v] — Clark Ashton Smith

13, No. 5 (May 1929)
The Inn in the Wood — C. I. Martin
Le Revenant [v] — Charles P. Baudelaire [tr. Clark Ashton Smith]

14, No. 3 (September 1929)
The Hound — H. P. Lovecraft

14, No. 4 (October 1929)
The Lost Room — Fitz-James O'Brien
Nyctalops [v] — Clark Ashton Smith

14, No. 5 (November 1929)
The Curse of Yig — Zealia Brown Reed [and H. P. Lovecraft]
The Nightmare Tarn [v] — Clark Ashton Smith

14, No. 6 (December 1929)
Fantaisie d'Antan [v] — Clark Ashton Smith

15, No., 1 (January 1930)
Ougabalys [v] — Clark Ashton Smith
The Red Fetish — Frank Belknap Long, Jr.

15, No. 2 (February 1930)
Shadows [v] — Clark Ashton Smith

15, No. 3 (March 1930)
The Ancient Track [v] — H. P. Lovecraft

15, No 4 (April 1930)
On Icy Kinarth [v] — Frank Belknap Long, Jr.

15, No. 5 (May 1930)
The End of the Story — Clark Ashton Smith
The Land of Lur — Earl Leaston Bell
Recapture [v] — H. P. Lovecraft

15, No. 6 (June 1930)
The Last Incantation — Clark Ashton Smith
The Rats in the Walls — H. P. Lovecraft

16, No. 1 (July 1930)
The Black Druid — Frank Belknap Long, Jr.
Sadastor — Clark Ashton Smith

16, No. 2 (August 1930)

The Hills of the Dead	Robert E. Howard
The Last Test	Adolphe de Castro [and H. P. Lovecraft]

16, No. 3 (September 1930)

Beyond the Door	Paul Suter
Black Chant Imperial [v]	Robert E. Howard
Fungi from Yuggoth:	H. P. Lovecraft
1. The Courtyard [v]	
2. Star-Winds [v]	
The Phantoms of the Fire	Clark Ashton Smith
A Visitor from Egypt	Frank Belknap Long, Jr.

16, No. 4 (October 1930)

Fellowship [v]	Clark Ashton Smith
Fungi from Yuggoth: 3. Hesperia [v]	H. P. Lovecraft

16, No. 5 (November 1930)

The Cosmic Cloud	Edmond Hamilton
Fungi from Yuggoth: 4. Antarktos [v]	H. P. Lovecraft
Great Ashtoreth [v]	Frank Belknap Long, Jr.
Kings of the Night	Robert E. Howard
A Message from Mars	Derek Ironside
A Million Years After	Katherine Metcalf Roof
Stealthy Death	Seabury Quinn
Tales of the Werewolf Clan: The Master Strikes	H. Warner Munn
Teotehuacan [v]	Alice I'Anson
The Uncharted Isle	Clark Ashton Smith

16, No. 6 (December 1930)

Fungi from Yuggoth: 5. The Bells [v]	H. P. Lovecraft
Something from Above	Donald Wandrei

17, No. 1 (January 1931)

The Avenging Shadow	Arlton Eadie
Fungi from Yuggoth:	H. P. Lovecraft
6. Nyarlathotep [v]	
7. Azathoth [v]	
The Horror from the Hills [1/2]	Frank Belknap Long, Jr.
The Necromantic Tale	Clark Ashton Smith
Passing of a God	Henry S. Whitehead

17, No. 2 (February–March 1931)

Fungi from Yuggoth:	H. P. Lovecraft
7. Mirage [v]	

8. The Elder Pharos [v]
The Horror from the Hills [2/2]   Frank Belknap Long, Jr.

17, No. 3 (April–May 1931)
The Children of the Night   Robert E. Howard
The Dead-Alive   Nat Schachner and Arthur L. Zagat
The Dust of Death   Hugh Jeffries
Fungi from Yuggoth: 10. Alienation [v]   H. P. Lovecraft
A Rendezvous in Averoigne   Clark Ashton Smith
Ten Million Years Ahead   Edmond Hamilton

17, No. 4 (June–July 1931)
Hill Drums   Henry S. Whitehead
The Outsider   H. P. Lovecraft
The Seeds of Death   David H. Keller
The Venus of Azombeii   Clark Ashton Smith

18, No. 1 (August 1931)
A Voyage to Sfanamoë   Clark Ashton Smith
The Whisperer in Darkness   H. P. Lovecraft

18, No. 2 (September 1931)
The Footfalls Within   Robert E. Howard
The Immeasurable Horror   Clark Ashton Smith
Satan's Stepson   Seabury Quinn

18, No. 3 (October 1931)
Black Terror   Henry S. Whitehead
The Captain Is Afraid   August Derleth
The Gods of Bal-Sagoth   Robert E. Howard
The Resurrection of the Rattlesnake   Clark Ashton Smith
The Strange High House in the Mist   H. P. Lovecraft

18, No. 4 (November 1931)
The Black Stone   Robert E. Howard
The Doom Around the Corner   Wilfred Blanch Talman
Subterranea   W. Elwyn Backus
The Tale of Satampra Zeiros   Clark Ashton Smith

19, No. 1 (January 1932)
Mive   Carl Jacobi
The Monster of the Prophecy   Clark Ashton Smith
Those Who Seek   August W. Derleth

19, No. 3 (March 1932)

The Answer of the Dead	J. Paul Suter
The House of the Living Dead	Harold Ward
The Island of Doom	Bassett Morgan
The Planet of the Dead	Clark Ashton Smith
The Thing in the Cellar	David H. Keller

19, No. 4 (April 1932)

Conjure Bag	Kadra Maysi
The Earth-Brain	Edmond Hamilton
The Gorgon	Clark Ashton Smith
In the Vault	H. P. Lovecraft
Mrs. Lorriquer	Henry S. Whitehead
The Vrykolakas	Robert C. Sandison

19, No. 5 (May 1932)

The Brotherhood of Blood	Hugh B. Cave
The Horror from the Mound	Robert E. Howard
The Last Magician	David H. Keller
The Terror Planet	Edmond Hamilton
The Vaults of Yoh-Vombis	Clark Ashton Smith

19, No. 6 (June 1932)

The Brain-Eaters	Frank Belknap Long, Jr.
The Devil's Pool	Greye La Spina
In the Left Wing	August W. Derleth & Mark Schorer
The Weird of Avoosl Wuthoqquan	Clark Ashton Smith

20, No. 2 (August 1932)

| The Maker of Gargoyles | Clark Ashton Smith |

20, No. 3 (September 1932)

| The Empire of the Necromancers | Clark Ashton Smith |

20, No. 4 (October 1932)

| The Testament of Athammaus | Clark Ashton Smith |

20, No. 5 (November 1932)

| The Supernumerary Corpse | Clark Ashton Smith |

20, No. 6 (December 1932)

| The Lives of Alfred Kramer | Donald Wandrei |

21, No. 2 (February 1933)

| The Cats of Ulthar | H. P. Lovecraft |
| The Chadbourne Episode | Henry S. Whitehead |

The Mandrakes   Clark Ashton Smith
The Vanishing of Simmons   August W. Derleth

21, No. 3 (March 1933)
In Memoriam: Henry St. Clair Whitehead   [H. P. Lovecraft]
The Isle of the Torturers   Clark Ashton Smith
The Tower of the Elephant   Robert E. Howard

21, No. 4 (April 1933)
The Ice-Demon   Clark Ashton Smith

21, No. 5 (May 1933)
The Beast of Averoigne   Clark Ashton Smith
Spawn of the Sea   Donald Wandrei

21, No. 6 (June 1933)
Genius Loci   Clark Ashton Smith

22, No. 1 (July 1933)
The Dreams in the Witch-House   H. P. Lovecraft
The Horror in the Museum   Hazel Heald [and H. P. Lovecraft]
Ubbo-Sathla   Clark Ashton Smith

22, No. 3 (September 1933)
The Horror on the Asteroid   Edmond Hamilton
The Return of Andrew Bentley   August W. Derleth & Mark Schorer
The Slithering Shadow   Robert E. Howard
A Vintage from Atlantis   Clark Ashton Smith
The Watcher in the Green Room   Hugh B. Cave

22, No. 4 (October 1933)
The Black, Dead Thing   Frank Belknap Long, Jr.
The Festival   H. P. Lovecraft
The House of the Worm   Mearle Prout
The Plutonian Terror   Jack Williamson
The Pool of the Black One   Robert E. Howard
The Seed from the Sepulcher   Clark Ashton Smith

22, No. 5 (November 1933)
The Holiness of Azédarac   Clark Ashton Smith
The Rogues in the House   Robert E. Howard
Shambleau   C. L. Moore

22, No. 6 (December 1933)
Abd Dhulma, Lord of Fire   G. G. Pendarves
The Lady in Gray   Donald A. Wandrei
Old Garfield's Heart   Robert E. Howard

22, No. 5 (January 1934)
In the Triangle   Howard Wandrei
Rogues in the House   Robert E. Howard
The Solitary Hunters [1/3]   David H. Keller
The Weaver in the Vault   Clark Ashton Smith
The Woman in the Wood   A. Merritt

23, No. 2 (February 1934)
The Sapphire Goddess   Nictzin Dyalhis
The Solitary Hunters [2/3]   David H. Keller
Tarbis of the Lake   E. Hoffmann Price
The Virus of Hell   William H. Pope
The Witchcraft of Ulua   Clark Ashton Smith

23, No. 3 (March 1934)
The Solitary Hunters [3/3]   David H. Keller
The Charnel God   Clark Ashton Smith
Winged Death   Hazel Heald [and H. P. Lovecraft]

23, No. 4 (April 1934)
Bells of Oceana   Arthur J. Burks
The Death of Malygris   Clark Ashton Smith

23, No. 5 (May 1934)
Queen of the Black Coast   Robert E. Howard
The Satanic Piano   Carl Jacobi
Scarlet Dream   C. L. Moore
The Tomb Spawn   Clark Ashton Smith

23, No. 6 (June 1934)
The Colossus of Ylourgne   Clark Ashton Smith

24, No. 1 (July 1934)
The Disinterment of Venus   Clark Ashton Smith
Through the Gates of the Silver Key   H. P. Lovecraft & E. Hoffmann Price

24, No. 2 (August 1934)
In Slumber [v]   Clark Ashton Smith

24, No. 3 (September 1934)
The Coming of Abel Behenna   Bram Stoker24, No. 4 (October 1934)
The Seven Geases   Clark Ashton Smith

24, No. 5 (November 1934)
The Music of Erich Zann   H. P. Lovecraft

24, No. 6 (December 1934)
Xeethra — Clark Ashton Smith

25, No. 1 (January 1935)
The Dark Eidolon — Clark Ashton Smith
The Feast in the Abbey — Robert Bloch
Rulers of the Future [1/3] — Paul Ernst

25, No. 2 (February 1935)
The Fireplace — Henry S. Whitehead
The Metronome — August W. Derleth
Rulers of the Future [2/3] — Paul Ernst

25, No. 3 (March 1935)
Julhi — C. L. Moore
The Lord of the Lamia [1/3] — Otis Adelbert Kline
Rulers of the Future [3/3] — Paul Ernst
The Sealed Casket — Richard F. Searight
The Judge's House — Bram Stoker

25, No. 4 (April 1935)
The Last Hieroghlyph — Clark Ashton Smith
The Hand of the O'Mecca — Howard Wandrei
The Man Who Was Two Men — Arthur William Bernal
Out of the Eons — Hazel Heald [and H. P. Lovecraft]
Shadows of Blood — Eando Binder

25, No. 5 (May 1935)
Arthur Jermyn — H. P. Lovecraft
The Secret in the Tomb — Robert Bloch

25, No. 6 (June 1935)
Dominion [v] — Clark Ashton Smith

26, No. 2 (August 1935)
The Treader of the Dust — Clark Ashton Smith

26, No. 3 (September 1935)
The Shambler from the Stars — Robert Bloch
Vulthoom — Clark Ashton Smith

26, No. 4 (October 1935)
The Cold Gray God — C. L. Moore
The Mystery of the Last Guest — John Flanders
The Song of Autumn [v] — Charles P. Baudelaire [tr. Clark Ashton Smith]

26, No. 5 (November 1935)

The Hand of Wrath	E. Hoffmann Price
In Thessaly [v]	Clark Ashton Smith
Mr. Berbeck Had a Dream	August W. Derleth
Shadows in Zamboula	Robert E. Howard
The Way Home	Paul Frederick Stern
When the Flame-Flowers Blossomed	Leslie F. Stone

26, No. 6 (December 1935)

The Chain of Aforgomon	Clark Ashton Smith
The Hour of the Dragon [1/5]	Robert E. Howard

27, No. 1 (January 1936)

Dagon	H. P. Lovecraft
The Hour of the Dragon [2/5]	Robert E. Howard

27, No. 2 (February 1936)

The Hour of the Dragon [3/5]	Robert E. Howard
The Temple	H. P. Lovecraft

27, No. 3 (March 1936)

The Black Abbott of Puthuum	Clark Ashton Smith
The Creaking House	Edmond Hamilton
The Crystal Curse	Eando Binder
The Graveyard Rats	Henry Kuttner
The Hour of the Dragon [4/5]	Robert E. Howard

27, No. 4 (April 1936)

The Druidic Doom	Robert Bloch
The Face in the Wind	Carl Jacobi
The Hour of the Dragon [5/5]	Robert E. Howard
The Sick Muse [v]	Charles P. Baudelaire [tr. Clark Ashton Smith]
They Shall Rise	August W. Derleth & Mark Schorer

27, No. 5 (May 1936)

Child of the Winds	Edmond Hamilton
Ennui [v]	Clark Ashton Smith
The Faceless God	Robert Bloch
The Room of Shadows	Arthur J. Burks

27, No. 6 (June 1936)

Black Canaan	Robert E. Howard
The Grinning Ghoul	Robert Bloch
The Harbor of Ghosts	M. J. Bardine
The Telephone in the Library	August W. Derleth

28, No. 1 (July 1936)
Necromancy in Naat   Clark Ashton Smith

28, No. 3 (October 1936)
R.E.H. [v]   R. H. Barlow

28, No. 4 (November 1936)
Black Hound of Death   Robert E. Howard
Brother Lucifer   Chandler H. Whipple
The Crawling Horror   Thorp McClusky
The Dark Demon   Robert Bloch
Pickman's Model   H. P. Lovecraft

28, No. 5 (December 1936)
The Album   Amelia Reynolds Long
The Cyclops of Xoatl   E. Hoffmann Price and Otis Adelbert Kline
The Fire of Asshurbanipal   Robert E. Howard
The Haunter of the Dark   H. P. Lovecraft
It Walks by Night   Henry Kuttner
Mother of Serpents   Robert Bloch
Out of the Sun   Granville S. Hoss
Portrait of a Murderer   John Russell Fearn
The Theater Upstrairs   Manly Wade Wellman
The Woman of Loon Point   August W. Derleth & Mark Schorer

29 No. 1 (January 1937)
The Thing on the Doorstep   H. P. Lovecraft

29, No. 2 (February 1937)
The Song of the Necromancer [v]   Clark Ashton Smith

29, No. 3 (March 1937)
The Picture in the House   H. P. Lovecraft

29, No. 3 (July 1937)
To Howard Phillips Lovecraft [v]   Clark Ashton Smith

31, No. 4 (April 1938)
To Clark Ashton Smith [v]   H. P. Lovecraft

Index

À *Rebours* (Huysmans) 393, 613
"Abominations of Yondo, The" (Smith)
  11, 73, 75, 76, 77, 78, 79, 80, 82, 85,
  126n3, 149, 158, 167, 173, 355
Ackerman, Forrest J 431, 445, 476, 483,
  572, 595, 682–91
Adventure 284, 313, 315
"Adventure in Futurity, An" (Smith)
  289, 298, 300, 307
Aeneid (Virgil) 153
"Æpyornis Island" (Wells) 246
"Affair of the Centaurs, The" (Edkins) 661
"After Armageddon" (Smith) 90n2
Age of Fable, The (Bulfinch) 477
Aiken, Conrad 329
akashic records 412
Alastair 633
Albany, NY 175
"Albatross, The" (Baudelaire [tr. Smith])
  161
"Album, The" (Long) 660
"Alchemist, The" (Lovecraft) 9, 45n2, 57
Alciphron (Berkeley) 376, 431
Alexander, Donald 686, 690
Alhazred, Abdul 9, 15, 149–50, 187, 269,
  277, 284, 302, 493
"Alienage" (Smith) 61
"All Hallows" (de la Mare) 107, 450, 459,
  465, 479, 488, 490, 502
All-Story Weekly 246, 322–23, 324, 504
Allen, Hervey 184, 185
Alma-Tadema, Sir Lawrence 136
"Almanac of the Renaissance, An"
  (Mitchell) 118
Alondine, Prince 87, 89
Alouette, L' 9, 64n6, 71
Alter, Dinsmore 531, 543
"Amazing Planet, The" (Smith). *See*
  "Captivity in Serpens, A"
Amazing Stories 101, 134, 136, 151, 176,
  184, 186, 190, 193, 197, 199, 208, 210,
  218, 233, 239, 252, 257, 290, 313, 316,
  322, 323, 324, 326, 327, 328, 362,
  377–78, 381, 392, 396, 405, 669
Ambrosius, Aurelius 529

American Author 380, 387
American Fiction Guild 377, 631
American Mercury 159
American Museum of Natural History (New
  York) 207, 246, 504, 531, 631, 639
American News Co. 505, 516
American Weekly 512, 523, 558, 590, 612
"Amor Autumnalis" (Smith) 151
"Amour supreme, L'" (Smith) 172
"Anachronism" (Cloukey) 290
Anacreon 138n2
"Ancient Track, The" (Lovecraft) 195,
  197, 199
Andreyev, Leonid 123n2
Andros, Sir Edmund 550
Angarola, Anthony 108
Angell, Sir Norman 627
Anger, William Frederick 600, 605, 608,
  611, 613
Antarctic Atlas (Lovecraft) 184
Antarctica 184, 277, 282, 285, 367, 550,
  630
Anthony Adverse (Allen) 525
"Apologia" (Smith) 64n8, 75n5, 77, 78
Apuleius, Lucius 515
Arabian Nights 9, 252, 269, 275
Archer, Denis (publisher) 417, 419
Argosy 64n2, 239, 274, 367, 513, 572
Argosy Book Store 179
Arkham, MA 15, 127, 142, 150, 163, 171,
  329, 332, 353, 395, 398, 438, 452, 453
Arkham House 19, 22, 27
Arkham House transcripts 20–22,
  23n27, 26
Arkham Sampler 19
Arnold, Benedict 378
Arnold, H. F. 552
Arnold, Matthew 40n2
Arthur, King 529
"Arthur Jermyn" (Lovecraft). *See* "Facts
  concerning the Late Arthur Jermyn
  and His Family"
Artistes d'Aujourd'hui, Les 160
"Asmodeus" (Smith) 625
Asquith, Lady Cynthia 465, 488, 516, 525

"Empire of the Necromancers, The"
(Smith) 341, 343
Encyclopaedia Britannica 84
Encyclopedia of Occultism, An (Spence) 626
"End of the Story, The" (Smith) 181,
183, 184, 212, 213, 216, 232n2, 257
Endless Caverns 163–64, 165, 166
"Ennui" (Smith) 644
"Ennuyé, The" (Smith) 54
"Entity from Algol, The" [carving]
(Smith) 653
"Envoys, The" (Smith) 92, 106, 119
Epicurean, The (Moore) 612
"Epigrams" (Smith) 64n1
"Epiphany of Death, The" (Smith) 201,
203, 206, 207, 417
Episodes of Vathek, The (Beckford) 247,
381, 382, 386, 395, 408, 411
Erlette, Comte d' 611
Ernst, Paul 571, 595, 622, 627
Eshbach, Lloyd Arthur 595
Esoteric Buddhism (Sinnett) 410
"Espoir du Néant, L'" (Smith) 151
Essay towards a Theory of Apparitions, An
(Ferriar) 472, 483
"Eternal World, The" (Smith) 324, 326,
331, 335, 364
Etruscans 549
"Eulalie" (Poe) 471n2
Evening in Spring (Derleth) 268, 279, 324,
436, 441
Evening Standard (London) 397
Ewers, Hanns Heinz 329
"Ex Oblivione" (Lovecraft) 39
Examen of Witches, An (Boguet) 472, 478,
483
"Exotique" (Smith) 36
Extra Day, The (Blackwood) 359
"Eye Above the Mantel, The" (Long) 39
"Eyrie, The" (*Weird Tales*) 11, 59, 111,
153, 212, 223–24, 225, 245, 419, 436,
452, 460, 469, 622, 688

"Fable, A" (Smith) 120, 126
"Face, The" (Benson) 363, 398
"Face by the River, The" (Smith) 257,
262, 267
"Face in the Abyss, The" (Merritt) 323, 388
"Faceless God, The" (Bloch) 644, 66
"Facts concerning the Late Arthur
Jermyn and His Family" (Lovecraft)

64n3, 69–70, 201, 204, 207, 210, 211,
214, 216, 221
"Facts in the Case of M. Valdemar, The"
(Poe) 600
"Fall of the House of Usher, The" (Poe)
299
"Family Tree of the Gods, The" (Smith)
561n1
Famous Psychic Stories (McSpadden) 402
Fanciful Tales 650, 660–61
"Fantasie d'Antan" (Smith) 130
Fantastics (Hearn) 372, 392, 393, 395, 398
Fantasy Fan 423, 425, 430, 435, 442, 448,
464, 476, 477, 480, 483, 510, 522, 526,
547, 552, 556, 572, 586, 595, 596, 613,
623, 688
Fantasy Magazine 514, 516, 522, 526, 572,
595, 619, 627, 630, 649, 665
Far East Adventure Stories 291, 295
Farnese, Harold S. 380
Farrar, John 80–81
Faulkner, William 329
Faust and the Demon (Reynolds) 600
"Fear" (Smith) 146
"Feast in the Abbey, The" (Bloch) 585
"Fellowship" (Smith) 181
Ferriar, John 472, 483
"Festival, The" (Lovecraft) 63, 65, 75,
452, 456, 459
Field, John 643–44
Finlay, Virgil 651, 660, 662
"Five Alone" (Derleth) 397
Flagg, Francis. *See* Weiss, Henry George
Flammarion, Camille 244
Flanders, John 619
"Flash" (Dwyer) 406, 411
Flaubert, Gustave 106
Fleming, Peter 329
Fleurs du mal, Les (Baudelaire) 19, 132n3,
153, 155, 157, 159, 167
"Flight into Super-Time" (Smith). *See*
"Letter from Mohaun Los, A"
Flint, Homer Eon 367
Florida 310–12, 361, 614
Flower, James Howard 195
"Flower-Devil, The" (Smith) 49, 328
"Flower-Women, The" (Smith) 394, 408,
414, 415, 430, 436
"Flowers of Iniquity" (Long) 39
"Flying Death, The" (Wallis) 166

CPSIA information can be obtained
at www.ICGtesting.com
Printed in the USA
BVHW090800171122
652109BV00006B/387

9 781614 982999